201

The Management Process

By the same author

Intelligence in the United States (1957)

The Tomkins-Horn Picture Arrangement Test (PAT) (1957) (with Silvan Tomkins)

PAT Interpretation—Scope and Technique (1959) (with Silvan Tomkins)

Breakdown and Recovery (1959) (with Eli Ginzberg, James K. Anderson, Sol W. Ginsberg, and John L. Herma)

The Management of Ineffective Performance (1963)

Studies in Management Education (1965)

Introduction to Industrial Clinical Psychology (1966)

The School Administrator and Organizational Character (1967)

Personnel and Industrial Relations: A Managerial Approach (1969); Second Edition (1973) (with Mary Green Miner)

Personnel Psychology (1969)

Management Theory (1971)

Personnel and Labor Relations: An Evolutionary Approach (1973) (with Allan Nash)

The Management Process: Cases and Readings (1973) (with Stephen Carroll and Frank Paine)

The Management Process

Theory, Research, and Practice

John B. Miner
Professor of Business Administration and Psychology
University of Maryland

The Macmillan Company, New York
Collier-Macmillan Limited, London

Copyright © 1973, John B. Miner

Printed in the United States of America

All rights reserved. No part of this book may be reproduced or transmitted in any form or by any means, electronic or mechanical, including photocopying, recording, or any information storage and retrieval system, without permission in writing from the Publisher.

The Macmillan Company
866 Third Avenue, New York, New York 10022

Collier-Macmillan Canada, Ltd., Toronto, Ontario

Library of Congress catalog card number: 70-190670

Printing: 2 3 4 5 6 7 8   Year: 3 4 5 6 7 8 9

To Mary

Preface

In writing *The Management Process* I had two primary objectives. One was to achieve an integration of the diverse literature and thought in the management field. The goal was not to present the student and the practicing manager with the classical management view, the behavioral science view, or some other view, but to pull all these approaches together to see what, in total, they have to contribute to solutions in the many problem areas that constitute the management process. The first objective then was to integrate what in large part has heretofore been found in separate and segmented sources.

The second objective was to put major emphasis on findings from scientific research. It seems to me that it is only through extensive and well-controlled research that we are going to achieve anything approaching lasting solutions to the problems that dot the management landscape. This book represents an attempt to report and synthesize as much research relevant to each problem area as possible. A glance at the lists of references at the end of each chapter indicates that a considerable volume of such research has been conducted. While some of the references cited refer the reader to general discussions of particular topics, a high proportion are reports of original investigations.

In years past there was a tendency to draw heavily on the subject matter of other fields of business administration in writing basic management books. I feel it is desirable to avoid this dependency and thus to deal with the management field as a separate and distinct entity concerned primarily with problems related to *human* resources. *The Management Process* largely reflects this viewpoint. The major area of possible overlap in coverage is personnel management and industrial relations, which also is a field concerned with human resources. Such areas as executive personnel management or staffing, organization planning, manpower planning, labor relations, and organization development clearly bridge the two fields.

Preface

Many other topics have been discussed by various writers in the contexts of both general management and personnel management.

This dilemma is accentuated in the present instance because I have also written a basic volume in the personnel field with the title *Personnel and Industrial Relations*. How does *The Management Process* relate to that book? Insofar as possible I have kept the two completely separate. In those instances where topics must be treated in both books in order to achieve comprehensiveness, the approach and emphasis are different. In most cases those topics that are considered in both places are given major treatment in one and much more limited treatment in the other. As a result, the reader will find very little overlap.

A similar question arises with regard to my short volume, *Management Theory*. Here the overlap is considerable. *Management Theory* is in essence Part I of *The Management Process*, although the smaller book does provide an expanded treatment in some areas—most notably in the consideration of integration theory.

The comments of Stephen Kerr of The Ohio State University, Fred Luthans of the University of Nebraska, Daniel J. McCarthy of Northeastern University, and my wife, Mary Green Miner of The Bureau of National Affairs, have proved extremely helpful. It is self-evident that without the further assistance of my two secretaries, Isabel Thompson and Dorothy Vance, and of my editor, John C. Neifert, this book would never have appeared. I thank them all.

J. B. M.

Contents

Introduction 1

Part I *Management Theory*

  1 *A Framework for Viewing Organizations* 9

      Organizational and Corporate Goals 10
      Systems Theory 18
      Role Theory 27
      Integration Theory 34

  2 *Management Functions or Process* 43

      Views of Management Functions 45
      Studies of Managerial Behavior 51
      The Universality of Management Functions 58
      Management Process and the Organizational Model 63

  3 *Management Principles and Scientific Theory* 73

      The Nature of Science 74
      Views of Management Principles 82
      Management Principles as Scientific Theory 94
      From Management Philosophy to the Science of Management 98

Part II *Planning: The Establishment of Role Prescriptions*

  A POLICY PLANNING 109

  4 *The Nature of Policy Planning* 111

      Definitions and Scope 113
      Effectiveness and Importance of Planning 122
      Organizational and Self-established Plans 128

Contents

5 The Development of Plans 139

Formulating Role Prescriptions at the Top Level 141
Specific Policy Formulation and Acceptance 149
Forecasting 158

6 Decision-Making Tools and Processes 169

Economic Man and the Problem of Rationality 170
Tools for Decision Making 178
Decision-Making Processes 189

B ORGANIZATION PLANNING 203

7 Organization Structure: Vertical Aspects 205

Hierarchic Position, Delegation, and Decentralization 207
The Number of Hierarchic Levels and Span of Control 218
The Role of the Board of Directors 226

8 Organization Structure: Horizontal Aspects 235

Division of Labor and Job Enlargement 236
Departmentation 242
The Line-Staff Structure 246
Project Management and Related Forms 251
Committees 256

9 Organizational Growth and Change 265

Resistance to and Facilitation of Change 266
Direct Change Through the Hierarchy 271
Organization Development and Other Participative Procedures 275
The Impact of Technological Change 283
The Impact of Growth 286

Part III Directing: An Input-Improving Mediator

10 Authority and Motivation 297

Authority, Power, and Influence 298
Process Theories of Motivation 308
Content Theories of Motivation 313

11 Leadership and Supervision 327

    Does Leadership Make Any Difference? 328
    Characteristics of Successful Managers 332
    Role Behaviors of Successful Managers 341

12 Communication in Organizations 359

    Interpersonal and Intragroup Communication 361
    Organizational Communication 368
    Management Information Systems 376

Part IV Coordinating and Controlling: Sustaining and Restoring Input Potential Levels

13 Managing Internal Conflict 391

    The Coordination Function Defined 392
    Conditions for Conflict 394
    The Prevention of Conflict 407

14 Control Procedures and Human Resource Utilization 429

    The Control Model 430
    Performance Control 435
    The Auditing Approach 447
    Accounting, Human Resources, and Behavior 452

Part V Secondary Management Functions

15 Staffing: Executive Personnel Management 469

    Management Recruiting 471
    Management Selection 475
    Management Development 482
    Executive Compensation 487
    Management Appraisal 494

16 Representing: Dealing with the External Environment 503

    Public Relations and the Corporate Image 505
    Social Responsibility and Business Ethics 507
    Helping the Culturally Disadvantaged 515
    International Management in Varying Cultural Contexts 524

Conclusion 537

Indexes 543

Introduction

A workshop held at a recent meeting of the Academy of Management had as its theme: *Behavioral Science and Management: Why the Troubled Marriage?* (14). Speaker after speaker noted the isolation, or separatism, existing within the management field between the behavioral and non-behavioral literatures and approaches—between contributions from psychology, sociology, political science, and cultural anthropology on the one hand, and contributions from economics and the various functional fields of business including classical management theory, on the other. Some speakers viewed the relationship as not involving a marriage at all; some considered the term *shotgun marriage* more descriptive; others were willing to settle for the *troubled marriage* terminology. But all viewed division within the field of management broadly conceived as a reality, and a situation to be abhorred.

The conclusions emerging from this particular workshop are in no sense unique. Various writers have noted and in some cases documented that within the field of management there exist parallel literatures which, although concerned with the same subject matter, have developed in almost complete isolation (2, 10, 13).

Several analyses of references cited in management textbooks provide a case in point (8, 12). These analyses indicate that the textbooks tend to be of two types. One group relies heavily on behavioral science journals such as the *American Sociological Review, Journal of Applied Psychology,*

Introduction

American Political Science Review, Human Organization, Administrative Science Quarterly, and *Organizational Behavior and Human Performance*; these books have few citations to the nonbehavioral science literature. The second group emphasizes material derived from journals such as the *Academy of Management Journal, American Economic Review, Harvard Business Review, Business Horizons, Journal of Business,* and *California Management Review*; behavioral science citations are infrequent.

Where textbooks in the field have attempted to encompass both literatures, and there are only a limited number of such instances, the tendency has been to treat them separately, in different chapters (15). One approach involves presenting each major topic area in two sections: the first deals with the subject in nonbehavioral science terms, and the second with behavioral science concepts and research (5). An alternative is to have one part of the book deal with the classical management contributions and a second with behavioral science contributions. To these, a third part dealing with management science or quantitative contributions may be added (3). Such books, although providing a more comprehensive coverage, again serve to emphasize the segmentation, even fragmentation, that characterizes the field.

There have, in fact, been very few attempts to integrate and merge knowledge derived from various sources and disciplines, and to apply this combined knowledge to major problem areas within the management field. What is needed is to break down the barriers created by differing terminologies and values so that investigation, discovery, learning, and finally problem solution become the central focus, irrespective of the source of knowledge. This kind of amalgamation is what the speakers at the Academy of Management workshop advocated (14).

Sources and Consequences of Segmentation

The primary factor accounting for the two literatures noted appears to be the sizable influx into business teaching and research of professors whose original training was in behavioral science disciplines (1). The majority of these individuals come from psychology, but a number are sociologists, and both political science and anthropology are represented as well. Surveys indicate that for the most part these behavioral scientists have been added to the management and organization area alongside the professors already working in that field, although some have gone into personnel management, marketing, and other areas also (9, 11). The extent of this management-organization emphasis among psychologists is evident in Table 1.

The influx of behavioral scientists into the management field has been unusually rapid. During the decade of the sixties there was no time for an integration of the old and the new—for the type of effective cross-fertilization that permits the best aspects of both strains to emerge in a final, superior product. That is apparently why we find the type of segmentation noted typifying that period.

The consequences of this segmentation insofar as practicing managers and most students are concerned has been a monumental confusion. When major segments of a field support diametrically opposed methods of dealing with a great number of practical problems, and when in the process they note almost entirely distinct sources of support for their conclusions, the practitioner is left largely to his own devices. He is unlikely to be interested in whether one group, or the other, is right. What he wants to know is what will work. Presumably as a result of uncertainty on this score, many executives appear to be reading very little of what behavioral scientists consider their best writings (4). In all probability this is true,

Table 1 Areas of Specialization for Psychologists Associated with Schools of Business and Industrial Administration (N = 145)

Areas of Specialization	Percent Indicating Specialization	Percent Indicating Teaching Specialization	Percent Indicating Research or Writing Specialization
Organizational Behavior	78	70	58
Management	47	44	30
Personnel Management	46	45	23
Experimental Design	21	19	6
Labor Relations	14	10	7
Marketing	13	11	10
Statistics	12	11	3
Advertising	5	4	3
Human Engineering	4	2	3
Operations Research	3	2	2

Source: J. B. Miner, "Psychologists in Marketing Education," Journal of Marketing, Vol. 30 (1966), No. 1, 9.

Introduction

although to a somewhat lesser extent, of nonbehavioral writings as well (6).

Thus there appears to be at least as large a gap at the present time between management teachers and scholars on the one hand and management practitioners on the other, as there is between those with and without a behavioral science background. And this is not the end of it. Agreement among practicing managers, even in very successful firms, on the appropriate solutions to particular problems is likely to be far from complete (7).

This, then, is the state of the management field. There appears to be considerable, if still far from sufficient, knowledge and information available. But the problem areas in which anything approximating a consensus has been achieved are few and far between.

Dealing with Segmentation

Against this backdrop, it seems desirable that a book which purports to provide an introduction to the management field do two things:

1. It must utilize a logical framework or model to weave together the diverse strands of management theory, research, and practice.
2. It must bring a value system to bear on its subject matter so as to differentiate between what is significant and important, and what is not.

In this book these imperatives are handled as follows:

1. An input-output model is used to provide a framework for organizing the field. This model is presented in Chapter 1 and elaborated in Chapter 2. It is manifest in the table of contents and is utilized throughout the book.
2. The value system of science is used as a basis for selecting what is to be emphasized. Wherever possible the results of original scientific research are presented, and these results guide the formulation of conclusions. The nature of science and the value system inherent in it are discussed in Chapter 3.

The objective is to achieve sufficient integration of the various approaches and contributions to the study of management by focusing on a general theoretical framework and on the findings of research so that improvements in management practice can in fact be made.

References

1. Bass, B. M. "The Psychologist and the Business School." *The Industrial Psychologist*, Vol. 2 (1965), No. 3, 14–18.
2. Dill, W. R. "Desegregation or Integration? Comments About Contemporary Research on Organizations." In W. W. Cooper, H. J. Leavitt, and M. W. Shelly (eds.), *New Perspectives in Organization Research*. New York: Wiley, 1964, pp. 39–52.
3. Donnelly, J. H., J. L. Gibson, and J. M. Ivancevich. *Fundamentals of Management: Functions, Behavior, Models*. Austin, Texas: Business Publications, 1971.
4. Dunnette, M. D., and Z. M. Brown. "Behavioral Science Research and the Conduct of Business." *Academy of Management Journal*, Vol. 11 (1968), 177–188.
5. Flippo, E. B. *Management: A Behavioral Approach*. Boston: Allyn & Bacon, 1970.
6. Hekimian, J. S. "The Growing Split Between Management Theory and Practice." In W. G. Scott and P. P. LeBreton (eds.), *Academy of Management Proceedings: Annual Meeting 1969*. Academy of Management, 1970, pp. 115–116.
7. Holden, P. E., C. A. Pederson, and G. E. Germane. *Top Management*. New York: McGraw-Hill, 1968.
8. House, R. J., and J. B. Miner. "Merging Management and Behavioral Theory: The Interaction Between Span of Control and Group Size." *Administrative Science Quarterly*, Vol. 14 (1969), 451–464.
9. Miner, J. B. "Psychology and the School of Business Curriculum." *Academy of Management Journal*, Vol. 6 (1963), 284–289.
10. Miner, J. B. "The Psychologist's Impact Upon Collegiate Management Education." In P. J. Gordon (ed.), *Academy of Management Proceedings: Annual Meeting 1963*. Academy of Management, 1964, pp. 62–68.
11. Miner, J. B. "Psychologists in Marketing Education." *Journal of Marketing*, Vol. 30 (1966), No. 1, 7–9.
12. Miner, J. B. *Management Theory*. New York: Macmillan, 1971.
13. Strother, G. B. "Problems in the Development of a Social Science of Organization." In H. J. Leavitt (ed.), *The Social Science of Organizations: Four Perspectives*. Englewood Cliffs, N.J.: Prentice-Hall, 1963, pp. 1–37.
14. Webber, R. A., T. P. Ference, W. M. Fox, R. E. Miles, and L. W. Porter. "Behavioral Science and Management: Why the Troubled Marriage?" In T. J. Atchison and J. V. Ghorpade (eds.), *Academy of Management Proceedings: Annual Meeting 1970*. Academy of Management, 1971, pp. 377–395.
15. Wortman, M. S. "Shifts in the Conceptual Approaches Which Underlie Principles of Management." *Academy of Management Journal*, Vol. 13 (1970), 439–448.

Part I
Management Theory

1 A Framework for Viewing Organizations

I. Organizational and Corporate Goals
  1. Defining Organizations
  2. The Nature of Goals
     a. Official Goals
     b. Operative Goals
  3. Task and Maintenance Goals
  4. Constraining and Facilitating Factors
     a. Capitalism as a Goal-Setting Process
     b. The Societal Environment
     c. Resource Availability
     d. Internal Constraints and Facilitators

II. Systems Theory
  1. Inputs and Outputs
     a. Inputs as Resources
     b. The Mix of Outputs
  2. Input and Output Processes
     a. Monetary Resources
     b. Material Resources
     c. Human Resources
  3. Input-Output Mediators
     a. Control Mediators
     b. Input-Improving Mediators
     c. Input-Sustaining Mediators

III. Role Theory
  1. Role Prescriptions
     a. Formal and Informal Role Prescriptions
     b. Organizational and Self-established Role Prescriptions
     c. Role Conflict
     d. Role Ambiguity
  2. Role Behavior
     a. Role Perceptions, Motivation, and Capabilities
     b. Role Sanctions and the Zone of Indifference
  3. Organizational Goals and Role Phenomena

IV. Integration Theory
  1. Integration Within the Value Structure
  2. Integration Within the Reward Structure
  3. Integration of Value and Reward Structures

A basic framework, or theoretical model, may be used to systematize our knowledge of organizations and management process. The need for such a device is evident from the Introduction.

Models are constructed for the purpose of identifying essential elements. Models are not intended to be exact replicas of a larger whole; nor are they intended to be all-inclusive. They are deliberate simplifications, designed to make it easier to understand a much more complex subject (37). Thus, an architect's scale model of a building includes very little detail; only major aspects of proportion and construction. Yet such a model is very useful in designing the much more complex, total building. Similarly development engineers and scientists often construct a pilot operation or model as an intermediate step between new ideas generated from research, and a revised manufacturing procedure. The pilot operation does not include all elements of the new production process, but it does help in eliminating "bugs," in gaining understanding, and in designing equipment for subsequent use in the plant.

This, then, is the intent of this chapter: to develop a simplified model that can be used to provide order and understanding within the complex subject matter of the management field. The model uses as its building blocks a number of concepts that may be new to the reader—organizational goals, constraints, role prescriptions, inputs and outputs, reward and value structures, and mediators, to name a few. It draws heavily on systems theory (21, 23), role theory (7), and integration theory (30, 32). These concepts are described and discussed in the following pages.

Potentially the framework used here could be extended in a mathematical sense. Models often use mathematical terms and relationships, and in fact theories of organizational functioning of this kind have been constructed (11). However, for current purposes such an approach is not warranted. To attempt to amplify the model in mathematical terms might well only add to the complexity of explanation.

Organizational and Corporate Goals

Managing implies the existence of something to be managed. This "something" is an organization—in the business world a corporation or possibly a partnership. In order to understand the process of managing we must begin with some view of what an organization is.

Defining Organizations

Although statements regarding the defining characteristics of organizations vary somewhat in specific detail, there remains considerable agreement (14, 38). Thus definitions consistently refer to a combining of individual efforts in pursuit of certain common purposes or *organizational goals*.

Second, organizations are characterized by some type of *division of labor*. The tasks carried out by different members vary; the functions that need to be performed are divided in a way that appears to be meaningfully related to goal attainment.

Third, there exist within all organizations one or more *power centers* that serve to direct the efforts of members toward goals. This concept of power center usually is translated in terms of a hierarchy of authority, with individuals at higher levels guiding, limiting, or controlling the activities of members at lower levels. It is through this requirement of power centers, or hierarchy, that managing becomes an essential aspect of organizational functioning.

The Nature of Goals

Among the defining characteristics of organizations our major concern at present is with the matter of goals. In economics there are two classic formulations regarding the goals of business organizations (11). One of these posits an entrepreneur at the head of his firm. This entrepreneur, or in some cases the ownership group (stockholders), establishes the objectives of the organization. Second, there is the view that a company's goals represent a consensus of its members. An implicit agreement is reached regarding those specific objectives the organization shall seek.

Although formulations of this kind may be useful as postulates underlying economic theory (10), they are not very useful for our purposes, primarily because they are too incomplete. A more appropriate approach is to start with the distinction between official and operative goals (33, 34). Official goals are those expressed in charters, annual reports, statements by top executives, and public relations releases. They are likely to coincide very closely with what the public generally expects of the organization. They are strongly influenced by existing ideologies (5). Operative goals, on the other hand, are identified by observing "what really happens." They are the objectives sought by the policies that actually guide decisions within a firm. These two types of goals may be identical, but more often than not they differ.

Official Goals. What we have called the official goals represent expectations that the larger society has for its constituent organizations. Thus manufacturing firms are expected to make certain products available to the members of society (consumers); educational organizations are expected to transmit knowledge; hospitals are expected to promote health. Characteristically, these are maximizing expectations in that the organization is supposed to contribute as much output as possible. This output may be in the form of profit, products, and/or services.

In essence, then, official goals (a) derive from the larger society, (b) apply equally to all organizations within a sector of that society (economic, educational, medical, military, etc.), and (c) require an effort to maximize output. Goals of this kind are, in fact, *role prescriptions* established by society. These prescriptions foster a division of labor within society and are established with a view to achieving society's own goals for its members.

Operative Goals. It is not true, however, that because an organization is expected to seek certain objectives it will actually do so. Operative goals may deviate from official goals because understanding of what is expected is deficient, because the knowledge required to make official goals operational is lacking, or because there is no desire to attain them. Much has been written in the literature of management and economics about *satisficing*, whereby companies settle for considerably less than maximization. The goal becomes some normal or acceptable level of profits, rather than the highest level of profits possible. There is good reason to believe that satisficing does occur in many cases (1, 40). In other words the policies that guide a company's actions may be, and often are, somewhat different from what society may expect them to be.

What appears to happen is that official and operative goals characteristically tend in the same direction; they are positively correlated, usually to a high degree. As a result they are often confused, and people will speak of company goals in a way that assumes an identity. However, a clear differentiation is important, if only to permit greater understanding of decisions and actions in those organizations that do not exhibit a close match with official expectations.

Task and Maintenance Goals

In the literature of management it is increasingly common to separate maintenance considerations from task considerations (24, 44). The concept of task refers to the profits, products, and services produced by an organization, and task goals relate to these matters. Maintenance, on the other hand, has reference to the survival of the organization as an ongoing entity. Maintenance goals are those that relate to the protection of the organization against internal and external stresses.

These concepts will be more meaningful, perhaps, if we use specific examples. Table 1-1 contains information derived from a study of 75 independently owned and managed life insurance agencies (39). Each had from 10 to 60 salesmen plus a supporting staff. Firm records extending over an 11-year period were analyzed for information on 76 measures assumed to be associated with the success of the agencies.

Table 1-1 Performance Factors: Insurance Agency Organizations

Factor Number	Goal Measures Involved
I	Number of policies in force, year end New insurance sold, dollar volume Renewal premiums collected, dollars Number of lives insured, year end Agency manpower, number of agents
II	Production cost per new policy Production cost per $1,000 of insurance Production cost per $100 of premium
III	Average productivity per new agent Ratio of new agent vs. old agent productivity
IV	Ratio of younger to total membership Ratio of productivity of younger members to agency total
V	Average premium per $1,000 Percent of new policies with quarterly payments Percent of business in employee trust
VI	Net change in manpower during year Ratio of net change to initial manpower
VII	Manager's personal commissions
VIII	Maintenance cost per collection Maintenance cost per $100 premium collected
IX	Average new business volume per agent
X	Insurance in force per capita Number of lives covered per 1,000 insurables

Source: S. E. Seashore and E. Yuchtman, "The Elements of Organizational Performance," in Bernard P. Indik and F. Kenneth Berrien (eds.), *People, Groups, and Organizations.* (New York: Teachers College Press, 1968), p. 176. Copyright 1968 by Teachers College, Columbia University. Reprinted by permission of the publisher.

These measures were then subjected to a mathematical procedure known as factor analysis, which achieves a grouping or clustering, such that those indexes which are most alike may be grouped together. In this study 10 such clusters, or factors as they are called, were found. The measures of organizational success which were particularly characteristic of each factor are noted in Table 1–1.

Some of the factors, such as I, appear to relate primarily to product (policy) sales. Others, such as II, relate to costs and thus ultimately to profits. In several instances the emphasis is on growth, which is presumably a source of increased productivity. In any event the goal measures included in Table 1–1 are typical indexes of what we have called task goals. Also, because of their source in firm records, they are related more directly to operative goals than to official.

A second study extends beyond task considerations to maintenance (13). A group of 1,072 managers, almost all of whom were either officers of their various companies or reported to the vice-presidential level, were asked to rate certain corporate goals both as to their importance and as to their significance for company success. Although this kind of approach does not permit a clear distinction between official and operative goals, it seems likely that the "importance" ratings were influenced more by official considerations and the "success" ratings by operative. The results are given in Table 1–2.

Table 1–2 Evaluation of Corporate Goals by 1,072 Business Managers

Type of Goal	Percent Rating as Highly Important	Percent Indicating Significant for Corporate Success
Organizational Efficiency	81	71
High Productivity	80	70
Profit Maximization	72	70
Organizational Growth	60	72
Industrial Leadership	58	64
Organizational Stability	58	54
Employee Welfare	65	20
Social Welfare	16	8

Source: G. W. England, "Organizational Goals and Expected Behavior of American Managers," Academy of Management Journal, Vol. 10 (1967), 108.

The first three goals clearly relate to task achievement; they would appear to have both official status and to be viewed as operative goals in many companies. Organizational growth is not an official goal to the same extent, but it does appear to be an operative goal. Although growth certainly has task implications in that increased size implies increased output, there is a strong maintenance implication as well. If continuing growth can be ensured, survival seems more likely.

Industrial leadership is a rather nebulous term, and this goal may have been interpreted somewhat differently by different managers. Many no doubt had in mind such things as prestige and invulnerability to attack. To the extent this is true, a maintenance goal is involved, since such a firm would be more resistant to external stress and thus more capable of survival. Organizational stability is essentially a maintenance goal.

Employee welfare has official status, and presumably companies recognize this as something society expects, but it is much less likely to be a significant operative goal. Social welfare does not appear here to be either an official or an operative goal of any significance.

Overall, the study suggests that task goals are preeminent, but that maintenance goals also are significant. Companies are supposed to—and to a large extent do—seek both high levels of output in the form of profits, goods, and services and continued existence as stable ongoing organizations.

Constraining and Facilitating Factors

Some writers view goals, such as profit, as a type of constraint on decision making and action (41). This is consistent with what has been said regarding official goals. These goals are role prescriptions established by the larger society. As such they limit and direct decisions and actions within organizations in various sectors of society. Thus, universities are focused on teaching and research. They would face many difficulties were they to devote major efforts to making products at a profit. In this sense, then, the teaching and research goals serve as constraining forces insofar as other types of activities are concerned.

Capitalism as a Goal-Setting Process. Under a capitalistic system economic organizations are expected to compete for profits. This means that a company is not supposed to devote its primary efforts to social welfare, higher education, military activities, and so on. These are the responsibilities of other sectors of society. Thus the existence of a capitalistic economic system not only establishes certain goals which companies are supposed to seek, but it very clearly constrains them from seeking other types of goals.

It is important to remember, however, that capitalism is only one of many possible societal approaches to establishing role prescriptions, goals, and constraints within the economic sector. For many societies it appears to be a very effective approach in stimulating the production of needed goods and services, yet in a historical sense it is relatively rare (17). Only in the modern world has it achieved anything approaching widespread use.

Furthermore, it seems apparent that the intense stimulation of competitive motives produced by the capitalistic system can pose a major threat to societal maintenance. There is always the real possibility that competition for profits could run out of control and break the society apart. The task objective may be achieved, and goods and services produced in abundance, only to have the society fail to survive as a separate unit. This is why capitalism seems to work most effectively in the economic sector when coupled with democracy in government. The voice of society can then be heard. As we shall see, the maintenance goal is very effectively served by shared decision-making processes of the kind provided for in a democratic system.

The Societal Environment. Practical considerations require that the profit goal of capitalism be set in a context of limiting and facilitating factors. Pure, unfettered competition, as discussed in economic theory, is a rarity. Rather profit seeking is channeled and directed by a host of laws and pressures. The economic competitor, like the athletic competitor, is expected to abide by a great number of "rules of the game." Some of these rules, such as the tariff barriers that lessen competition from foreign producers, make competition within a national market easier. Other rules clearly limit competition and make it more difficult to achieve profits.

In the latter category are the antitrust laws which serve to prevent a single company from gaining so large a share of a given market that it can dominate that market and set prices at will. In a sense these laws ensure that there always will be two teams on the field to compete; that no one will be in a position to win continually by default, because there are no teams left to play against. Laws of this kind have, for instance, prevented many of the largest and more successful corporations from expanding product lines through acquisition and merger. As a result they have been forced to seek growth through internal efforts. The societal constraints have accordingly been a major factor in decisions to invest heavily in research and development (18).

Resource Availability. In order to achieve productivity goals, organizations need to draw on resources in the world around them. The quantity and quality of available resources can exert a considerable influence on decisions made in the pursuit of goals.

One type of resource that exerts such an influence is people. Human beings vary tremendously in personality characteristics, abilities, knowledge, skills, and so on. Companies invariably require different mixes of these characteristics, that is, different kinds of people, to achieve their various task goals. In some instances the type of human resources needed will be readily available, thus facilitating goal achievement. In other cases the type of people a particular firm requires will be in short supply, as computer programmers were in the 1950s, and the result will be a major constraint on the decision alternatives that can realistically be selected.

Second, material resources that are needed may vary in availability. A petroleum refiner may have difficulty obtaining the particular kind of crude oil required to operate a given refinery. A manufacturer may not be able to obtain plant equipment meeting his technological and time requirements. Land may not be available to build a department store within a retail area known to have a high sales potential. Or all of these material resources may be obtained easily. In any event the availability of material resources can exert a major influence on company decisions.

Finally, monetary resources may vary in their availability. Money is essential, not only to start a company, but to operate it and to finance growth. It may be possible to meet monetary needs from existing profits, or it may not be. Borrowing may be easy or difficult. A stock issue may be a realistic approach to financing, or it may be out of the question. Clearly the extent to which money can be obtained represents a major influence on company decisions. This is true not only for business firms but for governments, hospitals, universities, and many other types of organizations as well.

Internal Constraints and Facilitators. In addition to official goals and other forces generated by society, and the availability of resources, organizational decisions in pursuit of goals are influenced by many internal factors. Among these are the type and quality of the existing work force, land and equipment owned, inventories of raw materials and products, cash reserves and assets that can readily be converted to cash. In a particular location at a particular point in time the level of any of these internal resources can exert a great deal of influence on decisions. This does not mean, of course, that any limitations thus imposed might not be overcome eventually. A lack of engineering personnel for a new facility might, for instance, be overcome by transfers from other locations, through hiring from the outside, or perhaps even through training of existing employees. But in any event the lack of engineers would exert a strong influence on decisions regarding a start-up date for the new facility.

A second type of constraint or facilitator has no direct relationship to the availability of internalized resources. In this category are policies, rules, plans, existing organization structures, assigned job duties, contracts with employees, and the like. These are the role prescriptions the organization develops for its employees. Many of these can be changed in time, but this is often not immediately possible. As we shall see, these role prescriptions can facilitate goal attainment in many ways, but once established they tend to foster certain types of decisions and to constrain others.

Systems Theory

In constructing models of total organizations and of major units or functions within organizations, theorists frequently use some version of the input-output system. The first detailed applications of systems theory specifically to organizational functioning appear to have been made in the late 1950s (42), although some applications at the level of total societies had occurred earlier. During the decade of the 1960s, however, the approach achieved widespread acceptance within the management field, and a number of comprehensive theoretical statements utilizing systems concepts have appeared (24, 27, 45, 47).

In addition, systems theory has proved increasingly useful in gaining an understanding of various functions *within* a total corporate entity. In view of its origins in engineering, it is not surprising that the theory saw its first major applications in the area of manufacturing (21). However, its horizons have expanded considerably in recent years. Textbooks with the systems concept as their major theme have been published in both marketing (15) and personnel and industrial relations (31).

Inputs and Outputs

For our purposes it is sufficient to differentiate three categories of inputs to an organization; and three related outputs. These are identified in Figure 1–1.

Figure 1-1 Input-Output Relationships

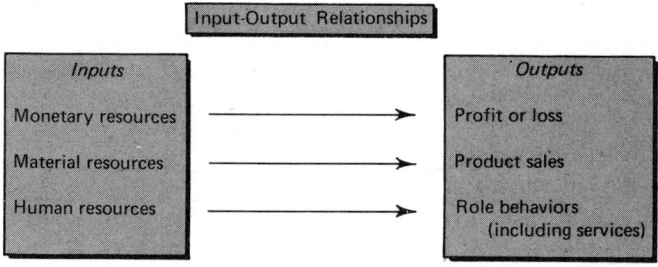

Inputs as Resources. The classification scheme in Figure 1-1 has the advantages of simplicity and clear relationship to goals. Several other writers have used considerably different patterns of inputs. Some of these alternative approaches are presented in Table 1-3. The various categories

Table 1-3 Input Categories Used by Various Writers

Writers	Inputs
Johnson, Kast, and Rosenzweig (21)	Information Energy Materials
Voich and Wren (47)	Money Resources Fixed-Use Resources Current-Use Resources Human Resources Data Resources
Triandis (46)	Environment Organizational History Resources Technology

noted have proved useful for the particular purposes these writers had in mind. They appear to facilitate understanding within the specified problem areas, and thus have contributed in the way models are supposed to contribute. It seems evident, therefore, that the particular classification procedure one uses depends in large part on what one wishes to accomplish. For our purposes the breakdown into monetary, material, and human resources seems most useful. When the concept of constraints and facilitators is added, our model seems capable of handling all the factors noted in Table 1-3.

Perhaps most important is the view of inputs as resources that may be used in achieving organizational goals. Although management is itself a human resource, it also assumes the role of attracting, selecting, and allocating other resources. The necessary decisions are made in a context of external and internal factors which serve to facilitate and constrain various alternatives. *In this view managing becomes a process of guiding a complex organizational system—made up of interacting parts and forces, through an environment that provides resources, assistance, and restrictions— to a set of goals that may on occasion be very difficult to reconcile.*

The Mix of Outputs. Within the economic sector of a capitalistic society profits are an output of major significance. But this is not true of all organizations. Schools, governments, hospitals, churches, and the like are not usually profit-making organizations, although in each instance certain exceptions may occur. Similarly some organizations produce products that are sold, but some produce products that are given away (various welfare agencies) and some produce only services.

It is evident, then, that Figure 1–1 in its entirety is applicable primarily to certain kinds of business organizations, particularly those engaged in manufacturing. Certainly the output mix will vary depending upon the operative goals of the particular organization.

A word should be added regarding the *role behavior output*, since this term is used prior to the discussion of role theory later in this chapter. Basically role behavior is what an individual does which is related to his job. Thus, outputs in the form of legal services, medical services, repair services, and the like are clearly role behaviors. However, many people work at jobs that do not directly involve services to clients or customers. These people are engaging in role behaviors just as much as those who do provide services.

Accordingly, we will treat all role behaviors as outputs. These role behaviors represent the individual, human contribution to organizational goal attainment, just as material resources contribute through product sales. It does not matter whether the role behavior occurs in relation to selecting inputs, as in purchasing real estate for the company, or in relation to disposing of outputs, as in selling a product to a customer. In all instances the role behavior is the individual organization member's contribution to goal attainment; it is thus as close as he can get to the organization's goals.

Management Theory

Input processes for securing them include purchase, leasing, or, especially outside the business world, expropriation or condemnation. In some cases resources of this kind are extremely difficult to locate; in other cases it is necessary to select among various readily available alternative sources. In mining and the extractive industries, extensive organizational components are devoted to exploration and prospecting for raw materials.

As with money, output processes related to material resources are characteristically introduced for purposes of evaluation. Are materials being used effectively to create a salable product? Sales analyses may be carried out based on product, customer class, order size, or geographical groupings. Sales are then compared against standards provided by the industry (share of market), performance in prior years, or established quotas. The objective of all such output processes is to determine whether material resources have been used to produce a satisfactory or maximum volume of sales.

Human Resources. We have noted that monetary resources must be located, and then selection decisions made among alternatives, if alternatives exist. Material resources also must be found, and then purchasing or other choices made. This same search-decision dichotomy exists with regard to human resources. Here the input processes are called recruiting and selection. A number of individuals who might fill a given position are located and then a selection decision is made using interviews, application blank data, psychological tests, and other techniques.

On the output side, the processes related to human resources also have much in common with those discussed for monetary and material resources. Again the major requirement is to evaluate performance against some type of standard or expectation. What the individual does, and on occasion how he feels, are compared with what he is expected to do and feel. For this purpose individual productivity measures are obtained, ratings are made, and attitude surveys are conducted.

Throughout this book our major concern will be with input and output processes related to human resources, rather than with monetary and material resource processes. A comprehensive treatment of the *business* field as a whole would of course deal with all inputs and outputs at length. But within institutions devoted to educating men and women for business careers there has been a division of labor. Basic courses in finance and accounting consider monetary inputs and outputs; courses in purchasing, production management, and marketing deal with material inputs and

Input and Output Processes

Organizations carry out certain processes on both the input output sides calculated to contribute to goal achievement. Certain processes as they relate to business firms are noted in Figure 1-2.

Figure 1-2 Input and Output Processes

Input Processes	Output Processes
Monetary Resources	
Financing	Profit and Loss Accounting
Stock issues	Income statement
Reinvested profits	Return on investment
Borrowing (debt)	
Material Resources	
Purchasing	Sales Analysis
Exploration and Prospecting	Market share
Real Estate Acquisition	Sales volume
Human Resources	
Recruiting	Management Appraisal
Selection	Employee Evaluation

Monetary Resources. In business, monetary resources come eit equity sources, such as stock issues and reinvested profit, or fr sources, through long- or short-term loans. Other types of orga use other means. Governments and government-supported orga such as public schools rely heavily on taxation and bond issues. (tend to rely on gifts, as do private universities.

On the output side the relevant processes related to money calculating the efficiency with which resources have been used (8 or losses are established for cost centers within the organization fo products, for marketing areas, and on other bases. The variou processes related to money indicate how much value has been a manufacturing and/or marketing and compare these results witl standards—return on investment in the same industry generally pated return from alternative uses of the same money, or profit mance in prior years.

Material Resources. Material resources cover a whole host of raw materials, supplies, land, machinery, plant, office space, an(

outputs. Thus it is appropriate that an introductory consideration of the *management* field limit its treatment of input and output processes to those related to human resources.

Input–Output Mediators

The second major aspect of our systems model operates between the input and output processes just discussed to enhance the value of monetary, material, and human inputs. Processes of this kind are known as *mediators*.

To clarify how mediators work, let us start with an example—a typical integrated oil company. Such companies are termed integrated when they perform all functions from locating crude oil in the ground through to selling petroleum products at retail to the consumer. The sequence of processes follows. Subsidiary activities or groups are noted in parentheses.

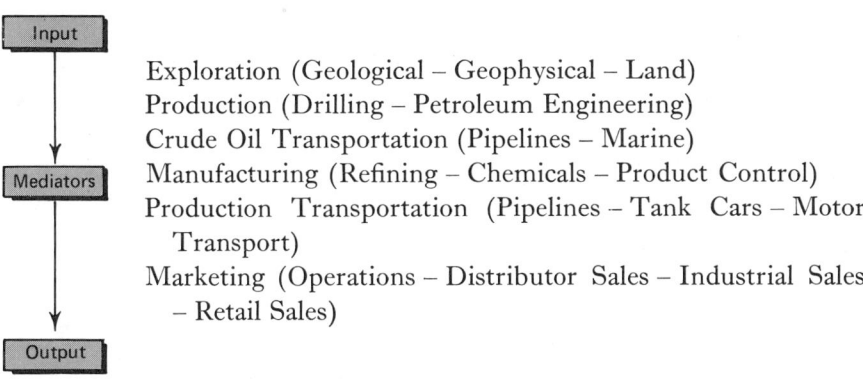

Exploration (Geological – Geophysical – Land)
Production (Drilling – Petroleum Engineering)
Crude Oil Transportation (Pipelines – Marine)
Manufacturing (Refining – Chemicals – Product Control)
Production Transportation (Pipelines – Tank Cars – Motor Transport)
Marketing (Operations – Distributor Sales – Industrial Sales – Retail Sales)

In this instance the mediating processes transform a raw material resource located in the earth, perhaps below a lake in Venezuela, into a petroleum product such as the gasoline sold in a service station. The mediators are the processes associated with production, crude oil transportation, manufacturing, product transportation, and certain initial phases of marketing.

It is also true that there are many firms in the oil industry that are not fully integrated. For them the inputs and outputs occur at different points in the chain. There are companies limited to exploration and production. For them the material output is a barrel of crude oil. Other firms are marketers whose input is the product of a refinery. Our integrated oil company may even be viewed as a series of stages with each stage using as its input the product or output of the previous stage and yielding inputs for the next stage (45). Clearly the nature of the material resource chain will vary considerably from company to company, and as it varies so too will the specific mediator processes in the chain. Extractive, manufacturing, and merchandising organizations, for instance, may be expected to have markedly different mediator processes insofar as material resources are concerned.

On the other hand, the input-mediator-output chains associated with monetary and human resources tend to be quite similar from company to company. In relation to monetary resources it is typical for companies to have such mediators as auditing, credit, tax, budget, accounts receivable, cash management, and cost accounting for various activities or divisions. These groups and processes are designed to keep costs down and income up. In this way they contribute to earnings on investment, and thus to monetary output.

In the human resource area companies provide such mediator processes as training, wage and salary administration, safety, labor relations, job analysis, employee communications and, of course, the comprehensive managing or supervising of the company's human resources. Again, as with input and output processes, we will be concerned more in this book with these mediators related to human resources than with those in the money and material resource chains. Activities of the latter kinds are treated in basic courses in finance, accounting, economics, business law, production, and marketing. Yet we will consider at length the various mediator processes that cut across resource types, and are, therefore, of central concern to those at the highest levels of management. In this category are such activities as planning, policy formulation, research, controlling, and the creation of man-machine systems.

Control Mediators. One way of viewing the action of mediators is in terms of the control concept. As it has been used in the management literature this concept implies a three-step process:

1. Establishing a set of standards.
2. Measuring actual performance against these standards.
3. Correcting all negative deviations from standard.

To this listing an additional step might be added between 2 and 3 providing for a process of diagnosis, so that the specific types of corrective actions instituted would be appropriate to the particular causes of the negative deviations from standard.

Mediators of this kind are widely used in business and in other kinds of organizations. The intent is to create a self-sustaining system such that an undesirable deviation from standard immediately triggers a feedback process which serves to correct the deviation. Governors that control automobile engine speeds, and thermostats that control room temperatures are engineering examples.

Budgeting activities provide an example of a control mediator process related to monetary resources. Production control or quality control operates in a similar manner with regard to material resources; so too does inventory control. In the human resources area any technique that identifies individuals whose performance is below standard and that subsequently serves to initiate corrective action operates as a control mediator. In this category are medical diagnosis and treatment, much employee counseling, and formal disciplinary actions.

Although some writers have considered the control concept adequate to the task of understanding all mediators used in managing, it now seems apparent that this is not true. For one thing, open systems of the type represented by human organizations are subject to a great variety of continuing influences from their environments. Thus the causes of deviations from standard are often difficult to establish and feedback corrections may over- or under-compensate (9). In many instances, especially those close to the input and output sectors of the organization, control mediators are far from satisfactory.

Second, the standards used in control tend to be set at the minimum acceptable. Corrective feedback is introduced only when there is a negative deviation from this relatively low level. But in many instances the objective is to achieve performance well above the merely acceptable (2). Thus there are mediator processes that clearly seem calculated to go well beyond what can be achieved on a control basis.

Input-Improving Mediators. Many mediators used with human resources are introduced with a view to improving on the initial input to the greatest degree possible. The processes applied seek only to improve role behavior, without reference to any particular minimum acceptable standard. In this category are such activities as training, organization planning, and payment programs. In these cases the mediators are calculated to improve either the knowledge or the motivation of the individual, so that he is now capable of levels of performance that he could not attain when hired.

Similar mediators are used in dealing with material resources. Research and development efforts are introduced to improve the productivity of machinery and to increase the variety of useful products that may be derived from raw materials. In the wood products and petroleum industries major research investments have been made over a considerable period of time with a view to finding products that may be made from mill and refinery wastes. Clearly the objective of such efforts is to improve the quantity and quality of outputs obtainable from existing inputs.

Advertising, sales promotion, market research, and packaging have this same input-improving characteristic. They are mediators introduced to achieve the greatest possible sales of existing or potential products.

With regard to monetary resources, pricing serves essentially the same purpose. Prices are set as high as possible to increase profits per item without in fact reducing total profits by decreasing sales. Cost improvement efforts have a similar objective: to reduce internal costs so that an eventual improvement in earnings occurs.

Input-Sustaining Mediators. There are other mediator processes that attempt only to maintain the potential inherent in the input. These are essentially preventive in nature. They do not attempt to maximize performance, nor to control negatively deviant cases. The objective is merely to head off possible future difficulties.

In the human resources area preventive medicine, safety management, labor relations, employee benefits, and internal communications are largely of this kind. Most mediators aimed at organizational maintenance, rather than task goals, are input-sustaining. Preventive maintenance is an input-sustaining mediator related to material resources. So too are plant protection efforts aimed at preventing the theft of company materials. When these efforts extend to auditing, bonding, and other accounting practices that may serve to prevent the theft of money, we are dealing with input-sustaining mediators in the monetary resource area.

Thus the view of mediators as essentially controlling must be extended to include input-improving and input-sustaining types. In each instance these mediators may relate primarily to human resources, material resources, or monetary resources. And the mediator may serve primarily task or maintenance goals.

Role Theory

We already have considered several aspects of role theory in the preceding discussions. The concept of *role prescription* was introduced initially in connection with official goals. It was reintroduced in the discussion of capitalism as a goal-setting process, and again when internal constraints and facilitators were described. The concept of *role behavior* was given an important position in our input-output model as the human resource output of organizations.

Antecedents of role theory can be traced back into the last century, but a specific set of concepts did not appear until the 1930s. It was in this period, just prior to World War II, that a language of role concepts emerged and systematic research dealing with role prescriptions and role behavior was undertaken (7).

Since then, this role language has grown in size and taken on increased precision, to the point where it now approximates a universal theoretical language within sociology and social psychology. It is of value to us, however, not so much because of its widespread acceptance, as because of its usefulness in filling certain gaps in our theoretical framework—gaps which systems theory alone is inadequate to handle.

Role Prescriptions

Role prescriptions specify that certain behaviors should be engaged in. They serve as guides or standards for action. Within an organization they become attached to a position and indicate what the incumbent is expected to do. These expectations may, of course, vary from person to person and, as we shall see, this in itself represents a special problem. Role prescriptions of one kind or another may be established for a line manager, for instance, by his subordinates, other managers at much the same level, various staff specialists, and even union stewards. All of these people may have quite definite views regarding what the manager is expected to do.

Research evidence indicates, however, that role prescriptions or requirements stemming from certain specific types of sources are most important and exert the greatest influence (22). These sources are:

1. People in the same department.
2. People who are superiors in the hierarchy.

3. People who care about what the man does on the job, without being so dependent on him that they do not feel free to express demands.

In general individuals at the same level (peers), especially those in other departments, have little influence in establishing role prescriptions. It is apparent that the most important role prescriptions are those transmitted through one's superiors in the hierarchy.

Formal and Informal Role Prescriptions. Almost without exception organizations establish a great variety of formal role prescriptions. These may apply to all members, to particular types such as managers in general, or to incumbents of specific positions. Examples are rules, policies, job descriptions, organization plans, top management decisions that must be implemented at lower levels, plans for attracting and utilizing various resources, and the terms of union contracts—the same type of thing discussed previously as internal constraints and facilitators. One writer has described these formal role prescriptions as resembling a huge computer program that determines courses of action to be taken over the range of circumstances that may arise (41).

But not all role prescriptions are formal. There are a variety of expectations that permeate an organization, specifying desirable personality characteristics, beliefs, and behaviors. These requirements are rarely if ever written down. Frequently organization members are not even consciously aware of them. Yet they serve as role prescriptions no less effectively than the formal requirements (4, 30). Insofar as management is concerned, they tend, among other things, to specify patterns of competitive behavior, attitudes toward superiors, methods of dealing with subordinates individually and in groups, permissible degrees of assertiveness, and expected modes of communication and decision making (28). Informal role prescriptions of this kind may apply to large segments of an organization, as, for instance, the total management component of a corporation, or to small units (48).

Organizational and Self-established Role Prescriptions. In considering formal and informal role prescriptions, we have dealt with requirements established either consciously or unconsciously by other members of the organization. Usually these people are superiors, and they may well be policy makers at very high levels.

But it is also true that there are cases where a manager "writes his own job description." And we hear often of "the man making the job." Certainly there are managers in every company who are able to assume power and a breadth of influence quite incommensurate with their level in the hierarchy. In addition, there are many who believe that insofar as possible individuals should establish their own role prescriptions; that having done so a man will be more strongly motivated to achieve on the job. Out of these considerations have come a number of instances where the man does write his own job description. Usually an individual will establish role prescriptions in certain areas, while the organization sets the requirements in others. Self-established role prescriptions become more common as one goes up the hierarchy, but they also appear with some frequency in sales and professional jobs.

When the individual takes his employing organization as a reference group (20), and thus incorporates the operative goals of the company in his self-established role prescriptions, difficulties are likely to be at a minimum. Under these conditions the requirements for different jobs can be adequately coordinated, and motivation to meet these self-determined requirements is likely to be enhanced. But should an individual select as his point of reference some group whose goals are antithetical to those of the company, permitting a man to establish his own role prescriptions can become self-defeating.

Role Conflict. There are two major problems associated with the creation of role prescriptions: role conflict and role ambiguity. Both can be a source of tension on the job and of dissatisfaction (22, 36). Both may also be inevitable (19).

Role conflict is best described with an example. There is a type of management training known as Laboratory Training which has as its objective teaching managers to express their feelings freely, to collaborate on a democratic basis, to provide freedom for individual choice to their subordinates, and to be authentic in relations with others (6). Training of this kind may be given by company representatives who are presumably reflecting the views of at least a major portion of the company's higher management. At the same time, however, a manager participating in the training may be working for an authoritarian superior who tells those who report to him exactly what to do, who tolerates no back talk, and who expects his subordinates to exercise control in the same way he does. Obviously very different and at times opposite role prescriptions are emanating from the two sources—the training and the actual job situation. The result is role conflict.

This is an extreme case, but conflicts of a similar kind are common. Role conflict is particularly prevalent at the upper-middle levels of management. It is somewhat less frequent at the very top and at the lowest levels of supervision (22).

Role Ambiguity. Role conflict occurs when two different and contradictory but nevertheless perfectly clear role prescriptions are applied to the same individual. In the case of role ambiguity clarity is lacking. The manager simply does not know what he is supposed to do. The role prescriptions are vague and uncertain. This can happen when written job descriptions and organization charts do not exist and when policies are not explicitly formulated.

It is an extremely frustrating experience to know that somewhere there is a rule regarding an action that one is considering, but to have no idea what the rule is. Widespread ambiguity in role prescriptions can result in a lack of understanding regarding areas of responsibility. As a result things that need to be done may be left undone, while in other cases conflict may arise because two managers attempt to assume responsibility in the same area. The consequence of role ambiguity may thus be a threat to both task and maintenance goals.

Role Behavior

For our purposes role behavior is defined as what an organization member does which is system- or organization-relevant. The behavior may or may not be congruent with existing role prescriptions, but it is nevertheless related to them. Almost without exception there will be organizational forces that exert pressure so that role behavior will come as close to role prescriptions as possible.

Role Perceptions, Motivation, and Capabilities. Assuming that problems related to role conflict and ambiguity have been minimized, it still does not necessarily follow that the role behavior of individuals will be consistent with role prescriptions. There are three types of factors that may account for disparities of this kind:

1. The individual may not perceive his job in the same way that the role prescriptions specify.
2. The individual may not want to behave in the way the role prescriptions specify.
3. The individual may not have the knowledge, mental ability, or physical skills needed to behave in the way the role prescriptions specify.

The second and third points are obvious. If a man does not want to do what his boss tells him, there is a good chance that he will find some way not to do it, or he may do it halfheartedly and ineffectively. Similarly, if a man cannot do what he is told because he does not know how or is not physically capable of doing it, his behavior will fall short of expectations.

The first point, on the other hand, refers to the degree to which role prescriptions are understood and incorporated by the individual. In part, of course, this is a matter of role ambiguity. The role prescriptions themselves may be unclear. But the individual may also misunderstand and distort what is clear to others. Thus, at the beginning of a semester a professor may give out an assignment sheet indicating material to be read and examination dates. This is a set of role prescriptions for his students. Yet a student may misplace his assignment sheet or misread it, and as a result show up for class having read the wrong material or even without knowledge that an examination was scheduled. The potential impact on the role behavior of such a student is obvious. In the same way incorrect or deficient role preceptions may have a sizable impact on job behavior in the business setting (35).

Where role behavior deviates from role prescriptions because of faulty role perceptions or insufficient role capability, the usual solution is either to provide more information or to alter the individual's role prescriptions so that he can meet them. Where motivation is lacking or inappropriate, it is typical to manipulate sanctions with a view to inducing a greater desire to act in accord with role requirements.

Role Sanctions and the Zone of Indifference. Organizations use a variety of sanctions, both positive and negative, to get members to contribute. In the business world these sanctions typically take such forms as salary and wage payments, changes in hierarchic level, and threats of dismissal. The individual is given something he wants as an inducement to behave in accord with role prescriptions. Or he is faced with the prospect of losing something he wants if he does not act to meet requirements. Where adequate rewards and censures are lacking or discontinued, it is evident that role behavior can disintegrate to the point where it is almost totally divorced from role prescriptions (16).

This brings us to the *zone of indifference*, a concept developed by Chester Barnard (4). Although not normally considered a part of role theory, this concept is, in fact, closely related to it. The zone of indifference is the range of role behaviors that an individual is willing to make available to his employing organization. Within this zone he does not care what specifically he is asked to do, that is, what the role prescriptions are. Outside the zone are behaviors which for one reason or another he finds unacceptable. Thus an employee of a consulting firm may expect to be away from home overnight during the regular work week, and it may be a matter of indifference to him whether he has to spend his nights in Los Angeles, Chicago, or Houston. But he may absolutely refuse to spend weekends away from home.

The width of this zone of indifference is influenced markedly by role sanctions. Our consultant did not include weekends away from home in his zone, but he might well do so if the reward for including them were great enough. Many companies offer inducements for overseas assignments which are so attractive that it seems almost impossible to say No. At the same time role sanctions of a negative nature may be introduced also to widen the zone of indifference. Weekends away from home and overseas assignments may well become acceptable if refusal is coupled with the prospect of reduced promotional opportunity or even discharge. Where role sanctions are minimal, on the other hand, the zone of indifference can become exceedingly narrow. There may be very little that an individual is willing to do in connection with his job. He may, for instance, refuse all overtime work if overtime is not compensated and his refusal will go unpunished.

Organizational Goals and Role Phenomena

The concepts and relationships we have been discussing are outlined in Figure 1-3. This figure presents in detail what is defined as the role behavior output of Figure 1-1.

Thus, our basic input-output system has now been expanded to include not only various types of mediators, but also a specific set of role concepts. To tie the contributions to our model stemming from role theory more

Figure 1-3 Role Concepts and Their Relationships

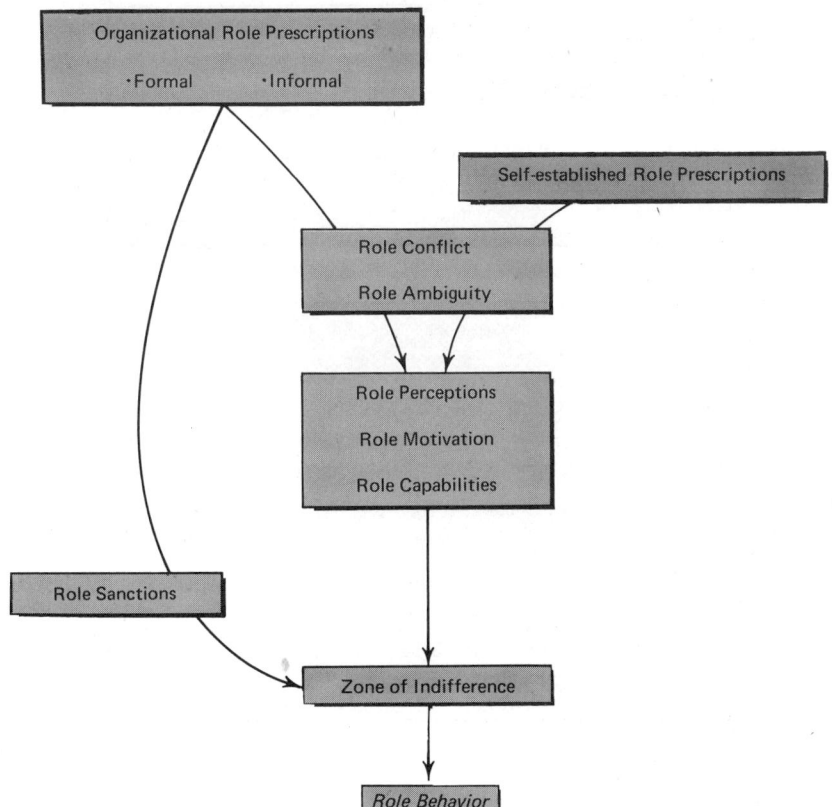

closely to those from systems theory, it is necessary to point out that role prescriptions are at one and the same time both internal constraints and facilitators, and also input-improving mediators. Output processes such as management and employee appraisal are methods of evaluating the relationship between role prescriptions and role behavior. When there is a close match between the two, the man is considered effective. If the deviation is large, he is not.

The relationship between organizational goals and role behavior is outlined in Figure 1–4. Just as operative goals are approximations to official goals, so role prescriptions are approximations to operative goals, and role behaviors are approximations to role prescriptions. Insofar as

Management Theory

Figure 1-4 *The Nature of Goal-Behavior Relationships*

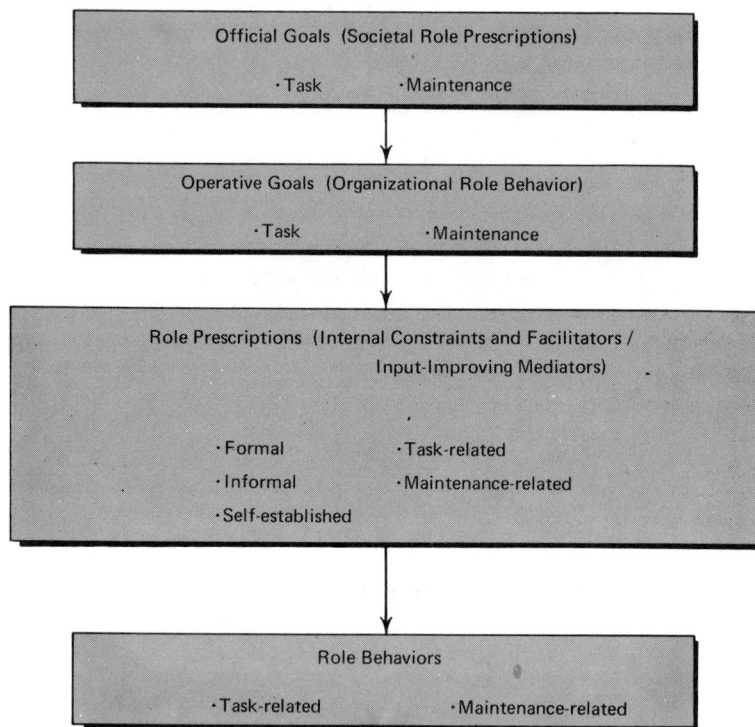

possible, role prescriptions, such as plans and policies, are formulated to support operative goals. They then serve to channel individual efforts in a manner calculated to foster both task achievement and the survival of the organization.

Integration Theory

While the variations of viewpoint and emphasis among systems theorists and among role theorists are often sizable, this tendency is even more pronounced within integration theory. In fact one could easily argue that there is no single integration theory at all, but only a number of separate theories having some view regarding organizational integration as a common element.

When Argyris (3) speaks of integration, he is concerned with the relation between the motives or desires of members and the operative goals of the company—the integration of individual and organization. When Lawrence and Lorsch (26) speak of integration, they mean collaboration among departments within a company to achieve a unity of effort in dealing with the environment. When Stogdill (43) speaks of integration, he is referring to the maintenance of structure and functions within an organization when it is exposed to either internal or external stress. Thus, he has in mind a general cohesiveness which is closely associated with organizational maintenance.

What all of these theories have in common is an emphasis on some kind of integration of effort behind company goals. All would argue that integration is necessary either for task effectiveness or survival, or both. None would contend that integration of effort is the only factor making for organizational success.

Our use of integration theory has these same qualities (32). In completing our organization model we will introduce yet another view of integration. But integration of effort behind goals and a recognition that many other factors are important for company success remain as central concepts.

Integration Within the Value Structure

The value structure of an organization or of a unit within an organization is a set of informal role prescriptions. It indicates what behaviors, and often what attitudes and characteristics behind behaviors, are considered good and bad. The presence of a particular value structure does not necessarily mean that those who hold it are fully aware of its nature. They may or may not be.

Thus in one company, youth, nonconformity, self-confidence, hard work, and problem solving were found to be elements of the value structure (30). Most of these are generally considered desirable characteristics and thus one would expect that many of the managers involved would be aware of their importance in the company. On the other hand, a particular school district was found to value spending as much time as possible with superiors, devoting little effort to work, and a minimum of emotional control (29). It seems unlikely that the administrators in this district would have consciously selected a value structure so far removed from official task goals, or that they were fully aware of the nature of their informal role prescriptions.

Integration within a value structure means simply that agreement is present in this area. Thus, a truly integrated structure exists where organization members have similar feelings regarding what is good and bad role behavior, and where a man is typically judged to be a good or bad performer in all respects. Ideally there would be agreement, not only among various superiors, but among superiors, peers, subordinates, and the man himself (25). This is another way of saying that role conflict is at a minimum. When there is integration around a value structure in this manner, and the value structure is of a kind that will contribute to goal attainment, a company possesses an attribute that can be a tremendous potential contributor to success (4).

Integration Within the Reward Structure

The term *reward structure* refers to the role sanctions used by an organization and the role behaviors to which they are attached. The most commonly used role sanctions are the level of one's position in the hierarchy and the amount of one's pay. Typically rewards in terms of promotion and pay increases are given to people who behave in certain ways and who have certain characteristics. As with value structures the members of an organization may or may not be fully aware of what characteristics are being rewarded.

In one company the rewarded personality characteristics proved to be of both a positive and negative nature—considerable independence and self-control coupled with a pervasive anxiety that served to limit social contacts, assertiveness, and even work effort (30). In another instance rewards typically went to men who were Masonic Order members, who were either Anglo-Saxon or German in ethnic background, and who were members of a particular yacht club (12).

An integrated reward structure is one where all role sanctions consistently support the same role behaviors. Thus, the greatest monetary and status rewards must go to the same people and must be attached to the same characteristics and behaviors. Given this kind of integration and a set of role behaviors that contribute to goal attainment, the reward structure can be a potent force contributing to a company's success.

Integration of Value and Reward Structures

Finally, our model implies that reward structures should support value structures; that role sanctions should be varied so as to elicit role behavior which matches role prescriptions (see Figure 1-3). This implies two things:

1. That rewards be given to people who are considered effective performers, who are valued by the organization.
2. That behaviors and characteristics which are rewarded be the same as those which are valued.

Thus, an organization to pursue its goals effectively should achieve not only integration within value and reward structures, but integration between the two as well. Information on the extent to which the latter was achieved in one company is provided in Figure 1-5. The appraisals of overall effectiveness and potential for advancement (the value measures) represent the pooled judgments of several superiors who were familiar with each man's work. The periods subsequent to these appraisals over which promotions (reward measures) were obtained varied from division to division; so too did the number of openings which developed during this follow-up period (30).

Divisions such as A clearly are fostering integration. Here promotions typically go to men who are rated high; very few who are rated low have moved up. In Division C, on the other hand, promotions are actually more often given to managers rated low in overall effectiveness than to those rated high, and a number of apparently good men remain unpromoted. It is clear from this and other evidence that reward and value structures often are not integrated (29, 35). Where integration of rewards and values is lacking, movement toward operative goals is likely to be hesitant and uncertain.

We will return to this organization model, developed from systems theory, role theory, and integration theory, on numerous occasions in the pages that follow. It provides a means of sorting and understanding the often-conflicting data that are available in the management field. In Chapter 2 we will use the model to facilitate our understanding of the management job and the functions of the manager.

Management Theory

Figure 1-5 *Management Appraisals Compared with Subsequent Promotions*

	Division A (60 men)	Division B (100 men)	Division C (76 men)	Division D (157 men)	Division E (90 men)

Overall effectiveness

- Division A: Promoted within 3 years — 48%, 40%; Not promoted 52% — 8%, 19%, 33%
- Division B: Promoted within 3 years — 39%, 27%, 12%; Not promoted 61% — 18%, 43%
- Division C: Promoted within 4 years — 25%, 11%, 14%; Not promoted 75% — 37%, 38%
- Division D: Promoted within 3 years — 24%, 15%, 9%; Not promoted 76% — 33%, 43%
- Division E: Promoted within 18 months — 17%, 13%, 4%; Not promoted 83% — 30%, 53%

Potential for advancement

- Division A: Promoted within 3 years — 48%, 43%, 5%; Not promoted 52% — 14%, 38%
- Division B: Promoted within 3 years — 39%, 19%, 20%; Not promoted 61% — 9%, 52%
- Division C: Promoted within 4 years — 25%, 16%, 9%; Not promoted 75% — 22%, 53%
- Division D: Promoted within 3 years — 24%, 14%, 10%; Not promoted 76% — 22%, 54%
- Division E: Promoted within 18 months — 17%, 11%, 6%; Not promoted 83% — 19%, 64%

Key: ☐ Rated high   ▨ Rated low

Source: J. B. Miner, "Bridging the Gulf in Organizational Performance," *Harvard Business Review*, Vol. 46, (1968), No. 4, 106.

Questions

1. Define the following terms and indicate how each is important to an understanding of organizations and their management:
   a. Zone of indifference
   b. Role ambiguity
   c. Satisficing
   d. Input-improving mediators
   e. Value structures
   f. Maintenance goal
   g. Self-established role prescriptions
2. What are some of the reasons that might cause a company to develop value and reward structures that lack integration with each other? What can a company do to improve such a situation?
3. In what sense can the capitalistic system be viewed as a constraint on organizational decision making? In what sense as providing role prescriptions for companies?
4. What types of inputs and outputs characterize the following?
   a. A hospital
   b. A manufacturing firm
   c. A university
   d. A professional football team
5. How does role theory serve to define effective and ineffective performance in an organization?

References

1. Anthony, R. N. "The Trouble with Profit Maximization." *Harvard Business Review*, Vol. 38 (1960), No. 6, 126–134.
2. Anthony, R. N. *Planning and Control Systems: A Framework for Analysis.* Boston: Division of Research, Harvard Business School, 1965.
3. Argyris, C. *Integrating the Individual and the Organization.* New York: Wiley, 1964.
4. Barnard, C. I. *The Functions of the Executive.* Cambridge, Mass.: Harvard University Press, 1938.
5. Bendix, R. "Industrialization, Ideologies, and Social Structure." *American Sociological Review*, Vol. 24 (1959), 614–623.
6. Bennis, W. G. *Changing Organizations.* New York: McGraw-Hill, 1966.
7. Biddle, B. J., and E. J. Thomas. *Role Theory: Concepts and Research.* New York: Wiley, 1966.
8. Bierman, H., and A. R. Drebin. *Managerial Accounting: An Introduction.* New York: Macmillan, 1972.

9. Brown, W. B. "Systems, Boundaries, and Information Flow." *Academy of Management Journal*, Vol. 9 (1966), 318–327.
10. Cohan, A. B. "The Theory of the Firm: A View on Methodology." *Journal of Business*, Vol. 36 (1963), 316–324.
11. Cyert, R. M., and J. G. March. *A Behavioral Theory of the Firm*. Englewood Cliffs, N.J.: Prentice-Hall, 1963.
12. Dalton, M. "Informal Factors in Career Achievement." *American Journal of Sociology*, Vol. 56 (1951), 407–415.
13. England, G. W. "Organizational Goals and Expected Behavior of American Managers." *Academy of Management Journal*, Vol. 10 (1967), 107–117.
14. Etzioni, A. *Modern Organizations*. Englewood Cliffs, N.J.: Prentice-Hall, 1964.
15. Fisk, G. *Marketing Systems: An Introductory Analysis*. New York: Harper & Row, 1967.
16. Goode, W. J. "Norm Commitment and Conformity to Role-Status Obligations." *American Journal of Sociology*, Vol. 66 (1960), 246–258.
17. Herskovitz, M. J. *Economic Anthropology*. New York: Knopf, 1952.
18. Holden, P. E., C. A. Pederson, and G. E. Germane. *Top Management*. New York: McGraw-Hill, 1968.
19. House, R. J. "Role Conflict and Multiple Authority in Complex Organizations." *California Management Review*, Vol. 12 (1970), No. 4, 53–60.
20. Hyman, H. H., and E. Singer. *Readings in Reference Group Theory and Research*. New York: Free Press, 1968.
21. Johnson, R. A., F. E. Kast, and J. E. Rosenzweig. *The Theory and Management of Systems*. New York: McGraw-Hill, 1967.
22. Kahn, R. L., D. M. Wolfe, R. P. Quinn, J. D. Snoek, and R. A. Rosenthal. *Organizational Stress: Studies in Role Conflict and Ambiguity*. New York: Wiley, 1964.
23. Kast, F. E., and J. E. Rosenzweig. *Organization and Management: A Systems Approach*. New York: McGraw-Hill, 1970.
24. Katz, D., and R. L. Kahn. *The Social Psychology of Organizations*. New York: Wiley, 1966.
25. Lawler, E. E. "The Multitrait-Multirater Approach to Measuring Managerial Job Performance." *Journal of Applied Psychology*, Vol. 51 (1967), 369–381.
26. Lawrence, P. R., and J. W. Lorsch. *Organization and Environment: Managing Differentiation and Integration*. Boston: Division of Research, Harvard Business School, 1967.
27. Miller, E. J., and A. K. Rice. *Systems of Organization: The Control of Task and Sentient Boundaries*. London: Tavistock Publications, 1967.
28. Miner, J. B. *Studies in Management Education*. New York: Springer, 1965.

29. Miner, J. B. *The School Administrator and Organizational Character.* Eugene: Center for the Advanced Study of Educational Administration, University of Oregon, 1967.
30. Miner, J. B. "Bridging the Gulf in Organizational Performance." *Harvard Business Review,* Vol. 46 (1968), No. 4, 102–110.
31. Miner, J. B. *Personnel and Industrial Relations: A Managerial Approach.* New York: Macmillan, 1969.
32. Miner, J. B. *Management Theory.* New York: Macmillan, 1971.
33. Perrow, C. "The Analysis of Goals in Complex Organization." *American Sociological Review,* Vol. 26 (1961), 854–866.
34. Perrow, C. *Organizational Analysis: A Sociological View.* Belmont, Calif.: Wadsworth, 1970.
35. Porter, L. W., and E. E. Lawler. *Managerial Attitudes and Performance.* Homewood, Ill.: Irwin, 1968.
36. Rizzo, J. R., R. J. House, and S. I. Lirtzman. "Role Conflict and Ambiguity in Complex Organizations." *Administrative Science Quarterly,* Vol. 15 (1970), 150–163.
37. Rubenstein, A. H., and C. J. Haberstroh. *Some Theories of Organization.* Homewood, Ill.: Irwin, 1966.
38. Schein, E. H. *Organizational Psychology.* Englewood Cliffs, N.J.: Prentice-Hall, 1965.
39. Seashore, S. E., and E. Yuchtman. "The Elements of Organizational Performance." In B. P. Indik and F. K. Berrien (eds.), *People, Groups, and Organizations.* New York: Teachers College Press, 1968, pp. 172–188.
40. Simon, H. A. "Theories of Decision-Making in Economics and Behavioral Science." *American Economic Review,* Vol. 49 (1959), 253–283.
41. Simon, H. A. "On the Concept of Organizational Goal." *Administrative Science Quarterly,* Vol. 9 (1964), 1–21.
42. Stogdill, R. M. *Individual Behavior and Group Achievement.* New York: Oxford University Press, 1959.
43. Stogdill, R. M. "Dimensions of Organization Theory." In J. D. Thompson (ed.), *Approaches to Organizational Design.* Pittsburgh: University of Pittsburgh Press, 1966, pp. 1–56.
44. Suojanen, W. W. *The Dynamics of Management.* New York: Holt, Rinehart and Winston, 1966.
45. Thompson, J. D. *Organizations in Action.* New York: McGraw-Hill, 1967.
46. Triandis, H. C. "Notes on the Design of Organizations." In J. D. Thompson (ed.), *Approaches to Organizational Design.* Pittsburgh: University of Pittsburgh Press, 1966, pp. 57–102.
47. Voich, D., and D. A. Wren. *Principles of Management—Resources and Systems.* New York: Ronald, 1968.
48. Whyte, W. F. *Money and Motivation.* New York: Harper, 1955.

2 Management Functions or Process

I. Views of Management Functions
1. Henri Fayol
2. Lyndall Urwick, Ralph Currier Davis, Chester Barnard
3. Recent Views
4. Evaluations of the Functional Approach

II. Studies of Managerial Behavior
1. Comprehensive Research
   a. University of Minnesota Studies
   b. Hemphill's Research
   c. Single-Function Studies
2. Single-Company Studies

III. The Universality of Management Functions
1. Research Evidence
2. Professional vs. Administrative Organizations
   a. Studies of Professional Organizations
   b. Power Distribution in Professional Organizations

IV. Management Process and the Organizational Model
1. Primary Management Functions
   a. Planning *as Establishing Role Prescriptions*
   b. Directing *as an Input-Improving Mediator*
   c. Coordinating *as an Input-Sustaining Mediator*
   d. Controlling *as a Mediator*
2. Secondary Management Functions
   a. Staffing *as Executive Personnel Management*
   b. Representing *as Influencing External Constraints and Facilitators*

Two major threads run through management thought as it has developed in this century. One is the concept of a set of established principles, or role prescriptions, to guide managerial actions toward organizational goal attainment. This will concern us in Chapter 3. The second thread is the concept of management functions or process—the subject of this chapter.

In earlier days the distinction between a management principle and a management function was not always established clearly. Increasingly, however, the two have been differentiated. Now the terms *function* and *process* are used with the same meaning in the management context, and in this context refer to areas of activity—things the manager does. In contrast to principles, they do not specify how he should carry out these activities.

The sum total of all management functions (or processes) is *the* management process. A distinction should be maintained between *management functions* (planning, organizing, controlling, and the like) and *organizational* functions (marketing, manufacturing, accounting, personnel). Unfortunately the same term is used in both contexts; although, of course, a reference to areas of activity is inherent in both usages.

Lists of managerial functions, and descriptions of them, generally have been derived from individual experiences rather than from systematic observation. In the course of other duties, a writer developed a particular conceptual grouping of managerial activities. Such a formulation is likely to be a consequence of this individual's relationship to his organization, and to the managers whose work he is in a position to observe. Because many of the early contributions in this field come from chief executives and consultants to top management, it is not surprising that the lists and descriptions have what may be described as a *top management aura*. Yet it is nevertheless true that the lists of functions have come to be regarded as descriptive of all managerial jobs from foreman to chief executive in all organizations.

In recent years, however, a number of systematic studies have been conducted to determine what managers actually do. Samples of managers are selected specifically for purposes of study, rather than as they happen to become available. Furthermore, efforts are made to obtain as comprehensive a picture of managerial activities as possible. Thus, research is available which may be used to test the generalizations and theories derived from experience.

In many respects the various viewpoints regarding managerial activities have come to represent a distinct theory, or closely related group of theories, within the management field. This theory of managerial process need not, however, and probably should not, remain isolated from a more comprehensive theory of organizational processes. Initial efforts to integrate these theories have in fact been made using the systems concept as a base (12, 30). A further extension of this approach, using the organizational model described in Chapter 1, appears later in this chapter.

Views of Management Functions

The initial formulations regarding management functions came from Henri Fayol during the second decade of this century. A number of distinguished management theorists revised and extended these formulations over the ensuing years, writing primarily in books intended for practitioners and scholars. In recent years, however, the major contributions to management process theory have appeared in textbooks directed to a student audience.

Henri Fayol

Fayol's views on management process were first published in 1916 under the title *Administration industrielle et générale*. This book, which is his major work, has since been translated into English (10). Originally Fayol intended that his presentation would be divided into four parts:

Necessity and possibility of teaching management.
Principles and elements of management.
Personal observations and experience.
Lessons of the war.

Only the first two parts were ever published, however.
Trained as a mining engineer, Fayol spent his entire career with a single French coal and steel company. For 30 years he was managing director of the firm. His early experience was as an engineer and subsequently as a manager of coal mines. He wrote about what he was doing: first a series of geological monographs on the depletion of coal deposits and then, after many years as a chief executive, on his views of management process.
Fayol's first managerial function was *planning*. He spoke of establishing forecasts, drawing up a plan of action, and planning at the national level.

Second was *organizing*. Here his observations ranged widely, considering the structure and composition of the corporation, Frederick W. Taylor's views on organization, the evaluation of managers, organization charts, selection, and the education of managers. The third function was *command*, which he viewed as setting the organization in motion. The stated objective was to get the optimum return from employees. Fourth was *coordination*, defined as a harmonizing process pulling the various parts of the corporation together. According to Fayol, this could be accomplished by such methods as conferences between department heads and the use of liaison officers. Finally, there was *control*, the process of verifying whether things occurred in accordance with the original plan.

In Fayol's view these were the five essential functions of management. They remain widely accepted today.

Lyndall Urwick, Ralph Currier Davis, Chester Barnard

In the late 1930s and early 1940s the functions of management were given a central position in the formulations of several writers. Among these, the most significant were Lyndall Urwick, R. C. Davis, and Chester Barnard. Like Fayol, Urwick and Barnard had had considerable experience with the top levels of management prior to developing their views. Urwick served for many years as managing director of a British consulting firm that still bears his name. Barnard spent almost his entire career with the American Telegraph and Telephone Company, rising to the presidency of the New Jersey Bell Telephone Company. Although Davis was a university professor (Ohio State University) and had less firsthand managerial experience, he did maintain a consulting practice in the field of industrial management.

Of the three, Urwick's formulations are clearly in the Fayol tradition. In his early writings (42), he accepts the processes of organizing, command, coordination, and control without modification. However, he emphasizes the forecasting function by separating it from planning, to create six functions. In addition, he discusses the process of *investigation*, which underlies the whole of management, in terms which suggest that it, too, might be considered an important function. Investigation is given a meaning essentially synonymous with research.

In later years, Urwick has on occasion treated *communicating* as a seventh aspect of management (43). At other times, however, he has essentially reasserted his earlier position, while continuing to emphasize the importance of investigation (44).

R. C. Davis, whose writings on the subject extend back to 1934, argues for a telescoping rather than an expansion of the Fayol functions (7). In his view the basic and essential (organic) management functions are planning, organizing, and controlling. Commanding and coordinating are merely phases within the control process. Especially in the case of coordination, this simplification has met with considerable resistance. Urwick argues at some length that coordination should be retained in a primary position because of the time and effort executives typically devote to it (45). Mary Parker Follett supports this view and in fact makes coordination the cornerstone of her theory of management process (11).

In contrast to Urwick and Davis, who based their formulations directly on Fayol's thinking, Barnard attempts to provide an alternative approach (1). He clearly did not interpret his own experience as a chief executive in the same manner as Fayol did. Thus, he rejects previous descriptions of management functions and seeks to elaborate a new viewpoint based on his observations of those managers to whom he was exposed in the course of his work. For Barnard the essential functions are:

1. Providing a system of communication.
2. Securing essential efforts.
3. Formulating and defining purpose.

The elements of the *communication* system are the selection of people to fill management positions and the establishment of these positions—executive personnel and executive positions. Barnard discusses organizational structure, executive characteristics, and informal organization in this context. *Securing efforts* is in part a matter of recruiting; in part a matter of eliciting desired role behavior through the use of inducements and incentives. *Formulating purpose* is in essence the specification of what work is to be done. Put somewhat differently, it is the planning and formulating of role prescriptions.

There is, of course, considerable overlap between these functions and those proposed by Fayol, Urwick, and Davis. Yet Barnard does provide a different emphasis. He moves communication into the foreground; he is aware of the need to motivate work effort, going beyond the mere specification of command and control; he is concerned about the difficulties of securing *cooperative* effort.

Management Theory

Recent Views

A list of more recent, alternative proposals is contained in Table 2–1.

Table 2–1 Lists of Management Functions

Dale (6)
- Planning
- Organizing
- Staffing
- Direction
- Control
- Innovation
- Representation

Greenwood (14)
- Planning
- Decision Making
- Organizing
- Staffing
- Direction and Leadership
- Controlling

Gross (15)
- Decision Making
- Communicating
- Planning
- Activating
- Evaluating

Johnson, Kast, and Rosenzweig (19)
- Planning
- Organizing
- Control
- Communication

Koontz and O'Donnell (22)
- Planning
- Organizing
- Staffing
- Directing
- Controlling

Longenecker (23)
- Planning
- Organizing
- Directing and Motivating
- Controlling

Massie (27)
- Decision Making
- Organizing
- Staffing
- Planning
- Controlling
- Communicating
- Directing

Newman, Summer, and Warren (34)
- Organizing
- Planning
- Leading
- Controlling

Voich and Wren (46)
- Planning
- Organizing
- Controlling
- Administering

Most are drawn from textbooks, but an attempt has been made to include diverse orientations. It is clear that even after 50 years of effort, generalization from the experiences of knowledgeable individuals has not produced a real consensus. However, it is evident that the three functions of R. C.

Davis—planning, organizing, and controlling—have achieved widespread acceptance.

Several items in Table 2-1 require further explanation. Dale and a number of others introduce *staffing* as a separate, distinct function. Staffing includes not only selection and placement but performance appraisal and training as well. Dale also introduces *innovation* and *representation*. The former is essentially a process of replanning, reorganizing, and then implementing the changed procedures. Representing involves representing the company to the outside world, in the sense of public relations broadly defined. Some writers argue that this is not an exclusively managerial activity, or that in any event it is merely a special variant of communicating.

Gross fails to mention organizing and control as such—the only writer noted in Table 2-1 to thus break with tradition. In this approach, organizing is viewed as an object of planning, activating, and evaluating. Control is a combination of evaluating and activating. The *activating* process seems analogous to Barnard's securing efforts in a number of respects. What Gross says is that such concepts as command and direction are too narrow. They do not cover all that is involved in inducing contributions to organizational goals. Under activating he places persuasion, pressuring, promoting self-activation, and campaign leadership.

Note that none of these more recent writers include the process of coordination, which is so strongly emphasized by Fayol, Urwick, and Mary Parker Follett. Even the longer lists of Dale and Massie do not include it. Perhaps a clue is provided by Massie. He feels that coordination (and leading, evaluating, and integrating, also) is too general and vague to be truly useful. In this view, coordination is best considered as a resultant of the interplay of the seven functions noted. These and other comments suggest that the coordination function may have fallen into disrepute largely because of uncertainty as to what was really meant by the term.

The Voich and Wren list includes the familiar three—planning, organizing, and controlling—plus a new function: *administering*. This is defined as a composite process designed to achieve integration of subsystems within the organization. It involves coordinating, as well as leading and motivating.

The various functions noted by all the writers we have been discussing have been combined in Table 2-2. No attempt has been made to eliminate overlapping concepts or to equate terms, other than in the case of directing, leading, and motivating, where authors have already done so (see Table 2-1).

Table 2–2 Combined List of Management Functions

Planning	Staffing
Organizing	Directing, Leading, Motivating
Commanding	Innovating
Coordinating	Representing
Controlling	Decision Making
Investigating	Activating
Communicating	Evaluating
Securing Efforts	Administering
Formulating Purpose	

Evaluations of the Functional Approach

Lists of managerial functions, whether they contain three items or seven, have proved useful as a framework for discussing managerial work. Yet there have been a number of criticisms of the approach we have been considering—the approach which had its genesis in the work of Fayol.

One difficulty is that there is not complete agreement on what functions should be included. Logical analysis from individual experience in observing managers at work has been successful to a degree. But there is considerable feeling that it has not gone as far as is needed. New and different types of information must be integrated with the functional approach as it has operated in the past if we are to achieve true agreement on the tasks of management.

A second, related criticism also is evident from our review of varying views of management process. Terms, or functions, have not been defined with a sufficient degree of precision. It is often difficult to know what a writer really means by a given concept. If a manager is observed doing a certain thing, would several different observers all put it in the same category—or might not one consider it controlling, another directing, and a third organizing? There is a certain ambiguity, a lack of clearly defined and mutually exclusive concepts, in the functional approach as it has developed, which leaves it open to criticism. It is difficult for a manager to judge whether he is controlling poorly or well, when he is not sure whether he is controlling or doing something else.

These and other criticisms have led a number of writers, especially certain of the behavioral scientists, to reject the functional approach as mere "armchair philosophizing." These writers have contended that functional theory represents a prime example of poorly constructed, ambiguous conceptualization, unsupported by systematic research (28).

This suggests that research is needed. What systematic studies of the managerial job have been conducted that might serve as a test of functional theory? Has the theory in fact generated such studies? What do we really know about managerial work from research?

Studies of Managerial Behavior

A number of articles have been published by *Fortune* and other magazines which report on surveys of executive views regarding the functions of management. Although information of this kind is often interesting, it is not really adequate for our purposes. In general the surveys tend to support functional theory (24), but typically the respondents were aware of the theory, and this knowledge may well have colored their responses. Furthermore, there is reason to question whether such self-reports regarding job activities, based on random memories as they are, correspond closely with actual observations (39).

It seems best to rely on observations made by others or on those systematically recorded by the manager himself as he actually performs in his role (4). When questionnaires are used, they should focus on specific acts. Does the manager do this or that? Or has he? This allows less room for ambiguous definitions and preconceived views to distort the results. In addition, there should be evidence that the questionnaires are producing results comparable to what direct observation would provide.

Comprehensive Research

Research on managerial behavior may be either comprehensive, in that it utilizes managers drawn from a number of firms, or it may be restricted to a single firm. In either case, it may deal only with the upper ranks or it may cover much lower levels of managerial work as well.

University of Minnesota Studies. One of the most extensive research programs is that conducted by the University of Minnesota Industrial Relations Center (25, 26). A total of 452 managers at all levels in 13 companies reported on their own day-to-day performance, noting the average

Management Theory

amount of time devoted to various activities. Eight functions were studied:

Planning
Investigating
Coordinating
Evaluating
Supervising
Staffing
Negotiating
Representing

In each instance the activities to be included were spelled out in specific detail. The authors note that organizing was not included as a separate function because of overlapping with planning and staffing. Separate studies suggest that in this instance the reported time estimates were closely allied to actual behavior.

As indicated in Table 2–3, supervising (directing, leading) absorbed

Table 2–3 *Percentage of Workday Spent on Various Managerial Functions*

Function	Percent
Planning	19.5
Investigating	12.6
Coordinating	15.0
Evaluating	12.7
Supervising	28.4
Staffing	4.1
Negotiating	6.0
Representing	1.8

Source: T. A. Mahoney, T. H. Jerdee, and S. J. Carroll, "The Job(s) of Management," *Industrial Relations*, Vol. 4 (1965) No. 2, 103.

the most time; staffing, negotiating, and representing were not major functions. However, these overall data are misleading. Certain managers devoted a high proportion of their time to activities which others spent practically no time in at all.

In order to study this phenomenon, the managers were classified in terms of functions which required a disproportionate amount of their time:

Planners
Investigators
Coordinators
Evaluators
Supervisors
Negotiators
Generalists
Multispecialists

The generalists were those who performed numerous functions, but none to a marked degree. The multispecialists tended to concentrate their efforts in two functions.

The proportion of the managers studied at each hierarchic level who performed each type of job is indicated in Figure 2–1. Planners, supervisors, and generalists predominate at all levels, but the balance among them shifts drastically. Not surprisingly, planners and generalists, as well as evaluators, increase as one moves up the hierarchy.

Overall, the Minnesota research supports a view of management process that would stress planning, investigating, coordinating, evaluating, and supervising, and add negotiating as a significant function in certain jobs. Among the activities included in this study, staffing and representing receive little support.

Hemphill's Research. A second major study, conducted by Hemphill, took a considerably broader approach, incorporating aspects of the managerial job, such as concerns, responsibilities, demands, and restrictions, that go well beyond work performance per se (18). Nevertheless, the 575 questionnaire items used did include a large number dealing with quite specific managerial activities. Thus the study is relevant to functional theory.

The lengthy questionnaire was administered to 93 managers in five large corporations—all much larger than any in the Minnesota study. Those studied ranged from vice-presidents down to the lowest level of manager who still had managers as subordinates. The completed questionnaires were analyzed using factor analysis to separate groups of items that clustered together. In this way a number of significant components or

Management Theory

Figure 2-1 Percent of Managers Studied at Each Level Assigned to Jobs of Each Type*

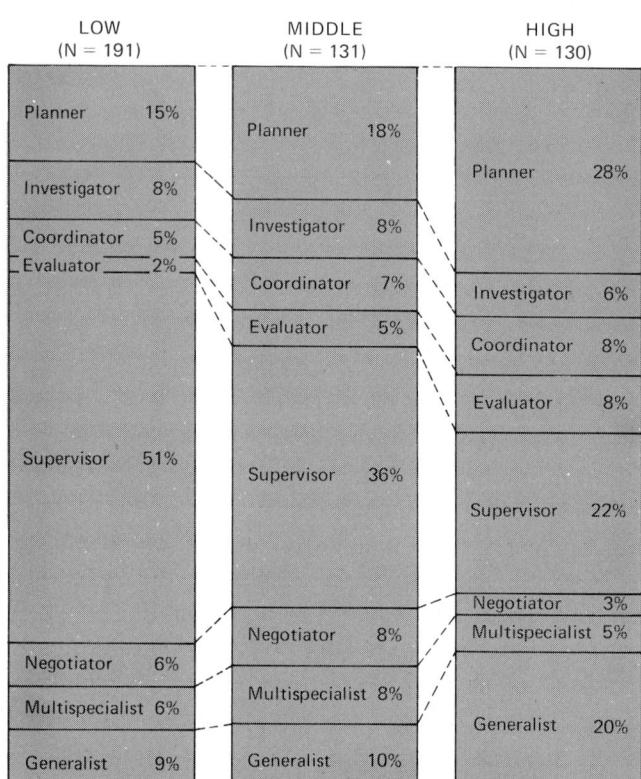

* Totals do not add up to 100 per cent because of rounding.
Source: T. A. Mahoney, T. H. Jerdee, and S. J. Carroll, "The Job(s) of Management," *Industrial Relations,* Vol. 4 (1965) No. 2, 109.

dimensions of the managerial job were identified. These are described as follows (characteristic jobs of each type are indicated in parentheses):

1. Providing a staff service in a nonoperational area (assistant treasurer, director of personnel services)
2. Supervision of work (manager of manufacturing, section supervisor)
3. Business control (budget administrator, plant manager)
4. Technical concern with products and markets (sales vice-president, engineering section manager)

5. Human, community, and social affairs (regional manager, employment supervisor)
6. Long-range planning (retail sales manager, research supervisor)
7. Exercise of broad power and authority (general manager, vice-president for manufacturing)
8. Business reputation (employment manager, purchasing vice-president)
9. Personal demands (controller, division works manager)
10. Preservation of assets (timberland manager, assistant treasurer)

Any study of this kind can identify only functions that are represented in the original questionnaire. Thus, the absence of a function in the list of 10 factors has no particular meaning; its presence does. Planning is supported (#6) as are controlling (#3) and directing (#2 and #7). In addition representing seems to emerge in #5 and particularly in #8. Information provided by the author indicates that staffing also is inherent in #5, and in #1. In contrast to the findings from the Minnesota research, staffing and representing do appear to be significant functions here—in these larger companies.

Single-Function Studies. Several smaller-scale, but still multicompany, studies have been conducted. These generally document a particular function. Thus, Carlson's study of nine chief executives in Sweden deals primarily with communicating in its many variations (5). Data were collected through logs kept by the manager himself, and from people in his immediate work environment. These show that visits, conferences, telephone conversations, and other types of communication absorbed the great majority of the managers' time. Clearly this function cuts across and intermeshes with other management functions.

Another study dealt with 97 small businesses having only one level of management (13). Questionnaire data were obtained from the managers, customers, suppliers, creditors, and employees. The study emphasizes the difficulties of satisfying demands from these various sources. In spite of considerable time and effort devoted to the problem, very few managers are able to fulfill the needs of all groups simultaneously. Yet it is clear that the managerial job entails a continuing effort to *coordinate* functions within the organization, and to relate these to the societal environment.

Finally, the conclusions from two major reviews of scattered research related to management process should be noted (8, 36). Certain of the

Management Theory

conclusions from these reviews bear directly on the importance of particular functions. Both reviews agree with Carlson that obtaining information and communicating it are major management functions. Decision making and giving orders, on the other hand, appear to require a somewhat smaller proportion of the managers' time than a number of writers have hypothesized.

Single-Company Studies

A study resembling in a number of respects the comprehensive Minnesota research was conducted with 355 officers of a large, metropolitan bank (16). The questionnaire used included very explicit definitions. However, information is not available regarding the match between these self-reports and actual behavior. The managers were asked to estimate time spent in the six functions shown in Table 2–4.

Table 2–4 Percentage of Workday Spent on Various Managerial Functions (Bank Officers)

Function	Percent
Negotiating	24.2
Supervising	20.7
Evaluating	13.2
Coordinating	13.1
Investigating	12.8
Planning	12.2

Source: J. A. Haas, A. M. Porat, and J. A. Vaughan, "Actual vs. Ideal Time Allocations Reported by Managers: A Study of Managerial Behavior," *Personnel Psychology*, Vol. 22 (1969), 66.

It is evident that negotiating and supervising were the major functions reported, although the other four require sufficient time to be considered significant aspects of the job. Although the questionnaire requested the addition of other functions should a manager view them as important, only 3.9 percent of the work was considered to fall outside the six areas designated. This says little about the true significance of other functions. Had these been explicitly noted in the questionnaire, they might well have been given greater weight. In any event, we do have evidence supporting six functions.

Perhaps most striking is the central position of negotiating. In the Minnesota study this took 6 percent of the time (Table 2–3); in the bank, it takes over 24 percent. Evidently bank management requires a degree of activity in this area, presumably related to making loans, that other businesses do not. The negotiating function is particularly pronounced at the middle management level. As in the Minnesota study, planning, coordinating, and evaluating receive the greatest emphasis within top management.

A second study was conducted with 96 managers at the vice-presidential level and below in a firm manufacturing business forms (3). Data were obtained from the manager himself, his superior, and his subordinates. Comparison of those at the plant manager level and above with lower-level managers emphasized such activities as the following:

Selecting people for jobs
Coordinating work
Pushing innovations in work
Giving praise
Evaluating performance
Developing subordinates
Planning time
Participating in community affairs
Delegating

In contrast, the lower-level superintendents and department heads spent more time on:

Getting the work done
Deciding on work schedules
Motivating subordinates
Controlling production

Overall the study provides support for a number of functions:

Staffing
Coordinating
Innovating
Communicating
Evaluating
Directing, leading, motivating
Planning
Representing
Controlling

A final investigation dealt only with nine manufacturing foremen, but it did utilize direct observation techniques (39). The foremen were observed at intervals until 3,295 observations were obtained. These men spent almost three-quarters of their time in controlling and coordinating. Planning and organizing activities were minimal, accounting for only 10 percent of the time. These matters were handled by a special group established to plan production. Also, rather surprisingly, supervision or giving orders (actual directing) was low (7 percent). Policy and work orders, both emanating from other parts of the firm, served largely to guide work performance. Subordinates spent very little time in direct contact with their foreman. Again, as with a number of the other studies, one gets the impression that managing at one level may not be much like managing at another.

The Universality of Management Functions

An additional question relates to the matter of the generality of functions. Is the managerial job as it exists in one organization, department, and hierarchic level essentially the same as in another organization, department, and hierarchic level? And, accordingly, does sufficient transferability exist so that managers can move successfully not only upward, but laterally from, say, marketing to manufacturing, or from one firm to another, or even from one type of organization to another, that is, government to business?

There has been and still is considerable controversy on this point (21, 38). The answer is not obtained by observing that many managers have made successful transitions. The fact that successful business and university administrators serve very effectively at policy levels in government says nothing about whether the management process is the same in these instances. It may be merely that these are very talented and flexible individuals who have no difficulty in shifting from one particular set of activities to another.

Research Evidence

The answer regarding the universality of functions must come from research on different managerial jobs. Some of this research was reviewed in the preceding section. It leaves little doubt that major differences do exist. The Minnesota studies indicate clear differences in the significance of certain managerial functions between jobs at various levels. Several other studies support this finding.

Even more pronounced were the differences between job types (25, 26). Those whose positions involved considerable negotiating spent an average of 45 percent of their time in this activity. But planners spent only an insignificant 4 percent of their time in negotiating. Investigators devoted 44 percent of the workday to investigating, but evaluators and supervisors devoted only 8 percent to it.

These data may be supplemented from an additional study (29). Questionnaires requesting estimates of the importance of some 65 skill and knowledge requirements were obtained from 520 managers above the first level in 32 manufacturing firms. Each manager was to describe his own job. The data indicate some agreement. There are a number of skills that seem to be important across both the functional areas of the business and the various levels of management. But uniqueness is evident, too. Many skills were extremely important in certain types of jobs, but of negligible importance in others. This argues against the certain transferability of skills from one management position to another and casts additional doubt on the universality of management functions.

Professional vs. Administrative Organizations

The research reviewed to this point bears primarily on differences in management functions existing between various types of positions *within* firms. Little attention has been given to differences between managing in one organization and managing in another.

In recent years a number of writers from diverse disciplinary backgrounds have stressed what they believe to be major differences in the managerial aspects of professional and administrative organizations (9, 20, 40). Professional organizations operating extensively in the economic sector include accounting firms, law firms, consulting firms, research organizations and laboratories, architectural firms, and advertising agencies. Hospitals and clinics, universities, social work agencies, and many other similar organizations are also basically of the professional type, although in the case of very large educational institutions much of the professional quality may be lost (33, 37). These organizations are contrasted with the administrative type, where the range of skills is typically much greater, and where a single profession does not predominate. Corporations in manufacturing, retailing, insurance, transportation, and so on, are administrative in nature. Professional groups of various kinds may, of course, exist as components within these companies.

The clear definition of professional organizations is made difficult by disagreements regarding the defining characteristics of a profession, and by the fact that a number of occupations are currently aspiring to or moving toward professional status (47). In general, however, definitions of professional practice include the following:

1. The acquisition of a set of specialized techniques, supported by a body of theory.
2. The development of a career, supported and influenced by an association of colleagues (the professional association or society).
3. The establishment of a consensus within society that recognizes professional status.

Studies of Professional Organizations. The studies we have considered to this point all have dealt with management functions as they are performed in administrative organizations. There are, in addition, a number of studies that carry clear implications for management process in professional organizations.

In one study information was obtained from the professionals in 23 organizations (17). Nine of these were professional organizations (law, medicine, accounting, advertising); the remainder were administrative in varying degrees. The administrative organizations have a more pronounced hierarchy of authority, a greater division of labor, place more emphasis on rules, utilize organizationally defined procedures more, and are more impersonal. In general this means they are more bureaucratic. In contrast, the professional organizations show little evidence of this type of bureaucracy. On the other hand, the professional organizations were characterized by a stronger emphasis on technical competence in hiring and promotion.

The implication of this study appears to be that in professional organizations power and authority tend to shift from the managerial job to the nonmanaging professionals. A second study supports this conclusion (2). In this instance employees working in a hospital were questioned about their work to determine how much freedom they had to make their own decisions; a discretion score was calculated from their answers. These discretion scores for all occupations represented are contained in Table 2–5.

Table 2-5 Average Discretion Scores for Different Occupational Groups in a Hospital

Occupation	Discretion Score
Administrators	5.7
Doctors	5.6
Department Head	5.3
Assistant Department Head	4.9
Nurses	4.5
Dietary Supervisors	3.7
Plumbers and Carpenters	3.2
Secretaries	3.1
Pharmacists	3.0
Laboratory Technicians	3.0
Orderlies	3.0
X-ray Technicians	2.3
Nurses' Aides	2.2
Cooks	2.0
Dietary Helpers	1.4
Housekeepers	1.3

Source: G. D. Bell, "Predictability of Work Demands and Professionalization as Determinants of Workers' Discretion," *Academy of Management Journal*, Vol. 9 (1966), 23.

In an administrative organization one would anticipate that management would have the highest scores, followed by the nonmanagement occupations. The order would be approximately as follows:

Administrators
Department head
Assistant department head
Dietary supervisors
All others (in some order)

But actually the dominant professional group, the doctors, have as much discretion as the top administrators. And even the second professional group, the nurses, have more freedom to make decisions than certain managers, the dietary supervisors. One can assume that when decision-making authority is dispersed in this way, some very sizable changes in managerial functions must occur, relative to administrative organizations. In the hospital there was a definite tendency for discretion to increase with the degree of professionalization of the job; not just with managerial level.

Another study dealt with the degree to which professionals were encouraged or expected to sell their own research ideas, that is, the degree of individual entrepreneurship within the organizational setting—another type of professional freedom (47). The order, in terms of decreasing entrepreneurship within the five organizations studied, was:

1. A research laboratory attached administratively to the department of electrical engineering of a university.
2. A diversified, independent research organization.
3. A research division of an aerospace company.
4. A research division of a company in the atomic equipment industry.
5. A government laboratory in the defense electronics area.

The first two are professional organizations; the last three are components of administrative organizations. Again the freedom to make one's own decisions and to implement one's own ideas among professionals who are not managers seems to be much greater in the professional organizations.

Finally, a major review of other related studies indicates that within professional organizations, shifting decisions downward in the hierarchy to the nonmanagerial professionals produces a more effective organization (35). If this is not done, task and organizational maintenance goals will suffer—at least to the degree they are influenced by professional considerations.

Power Distribution in Professional Organizations. What does this mean in terms of managerial functions in professional organizations? It would appear that in many professional organizations, particularly in the more effective ones, the services provided by prestigious professionals are so crucial that the threat of their withdrawal results in a sharing of managerial functions by the administrative group. It is not pure chance that outstanding professors exert influence on universities entirely incommensurate with their hierarchic positions and that consultants with important clients do the same in consulting firms. In such instances the existing professional group may be replaceable, but only at considerable cost to organizational goal attainment. The more popular alternative appears to be an increase in the decision-making power and influence of the professionals, as individuals and as a group. This is particularly true of matters closely associated with the profession and professional role behavior.

Thus, self-established role prescriptions are more characteristic for professionals in professional organizations. Role prescriptions in general are strongly influenced by forces outside the organizations—statements by professional bodies and associations, professional ethics and values, professional licensing and certification laws. Accordingly many activities that fall into such categories as planning, organizing, and decision making no longer serve as managerial functions but as professional ones.

Other similar shifts can be noted. Staffing, including input processes such as recruiting and selection as well as promotional decisions, becomes primarily a concern of professionals rather than of managers. Innovating, representing, investigating, communicating, coordinating, evaluating, and the like are frequently carried out by professionals, either as individuals or through committees. Even the very large universities do not operate entirely like corporations (41). Curriculum changes typically come from the faculty, for instance. In a consulting firm performance evaluations are made by senior professional staff members whether or not they hold managerial appointments.

Our analysis of professional versus administrative organizations once again leads to the conclusion that managerial functions are not universal. Not only do managerial jobs differ in their mix of functions depending on their level and the particular department involved, but they also differ from organization to organization. This interorganizational difference is particularly noticeable when administrative and professional types are compared.

Management Process and the Organizational Model

We have now established a list of proposed or hypothesized management functions (Table 2-2) and reviewed a number of studies that provide some test of these hypotheses. We have also established that management jobs differ in a number of respects and that accordingly the mix and relative importance of functions cannot be expected to be the same from job to job, and from organization to organization.

Despite this diversity, it is still possible to ask whether there are any management functions that emerge consistently from the various studies as being, at least on the average, of considerable importance across a variety of management positions. We can also ask whether there are any additional functions that appear as important in some studies, but not in others.

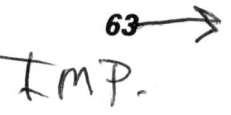

Primary Management Functions

Four functions that the research consistently identifies as important are planning, directing, coordinating, and controlling. All of these are meaningfully related to our theoretical model. Thus we can define management process within the organizational framework developed in Chapter 1. In doing so we will focus on that aspect of each management function which is most salient and at the highest level in terms of relationship to organizational goal attainment (32).

Planning as Establishing Role Prescriptions. Planning was identified as an important function in four of the five studies which dealt with it (3, 16, 18, 25). In the one instance where it was not important the analyses were restricted to the foreman level (39). This and other data indicate that planning is frequently done above the very lowest level of management in administrative organizations.

In connection with the research, planning is characteristically defined rather broadly to include a number of other functions noted in Table 2–2. These are:

Organizing (or organization planning)
Formulating purpose
Innovating
Decision making

In the theoretical literature organizing is almost universally viewed as a separate and distinct function; in the research literature it is not. Planning and organizing both are procedures for establishing role prescriptions, and thus both operate as input-improving mediators within the framework of our organizational model. There seems little reason to make a basic distinction between them here, since they contribute to organizational goal attainment in essentially the same manner.

Formulating purpose as used by Barnard is defined to include the development of the organization's operative goals, but is primarily a matter of planning role prescriptions. Innovating means replanning and reorganizing. Decision making, of course, is inherent in all functions. In this respect it is similar to communicating. But it is particularly manifest in the planning area. For this reason it has become common practice to deal with the subject within the planning context while recognizing its contribution to other management processes as well. In the research literature the two concepts are typically used interchangeably—in studies where planning is considered, decision making is not, and vice versa.

Although much of planning results in policy statements and organization charts, it is not limited to these formal aspects. Barnard emphasizes informal organization, especially at the executive level (1). The result is the emergence of informal, in addition to formal, role prescriptions—what we have called the value structure. Ideally this value structure is a product of conscious planning. Not infrequently, however, it is in fact a consequence of far more subtle forces, which yield role prescriptions lacking integration with organizational goals.

Directing as an Input-Improving Mediator. Directing—or to be more exact, supervising—is emphasized in four of the studies (3, 16, 18, 25). There is some evidence that "giving orders" alone may not be an important function (8, 39), but this is a very narrow concept in comparison with what is usually meant by supervising, or directing. Actually the more inherently comprehensive terms are motivating, activating, and securing efforts. These concepts appear to encompass the totality of activities included in the research definitions. However, we will use the more common word *directing*, with this broad definition in mind, primarily because this is the traditional practice in the management literature. Such terms as *commanding*, *leading*, and *administering* have much the same connotation.

In addition, we will deal with the concept of communicating within the framework of directing. Like decision making, communicating permeates all functions, but in the management literature it has often been considered as primarily an aspect of directing and leadership. Furthermore, a number of the studies that have emphasized its importance seem to have considered it as an alternative to, or aspect of, directing (5, 8, 36).

Directing, as defined, appears to be essentially a means for getting the best performance out of organization members once they are hired. It is thus a means for motivating their role behavior—an input-improving mediator. Supervision attempts to obtain the closest match possible between role prescriptions and role behavior by inducing a maximal contribution.

Coordinating as an Input-Sustaining Mediator. There are five studies that indicate coordinating is a very significant management function (3, 13, 16, 25, 39); only one major study does not, and that apparently does not consider the subject at all (18). This is very strong support. In addition, the early writers including Fayol, Urwick, and Follett emphasized coordinating as a major function; yet none of the more recent writers (Table 2-1) seems to consider it important.

Why coordinating has fallen into such disfavor is an open question. Whatever the reason, it is not supported by the research literature; quite the contrary. As a management process, coordinating protects against any diminution of the potential inherent in the input. It is a preventive to conflict and misunderstanding. As such it contributes to role behavior as an input-sustaining mediator. Coordination attempts to keep intergroup and interindividual difficulties from arising and increasing the gap between role prescriptions and role behavior beyond what could be anticipated without the organizational or social context. In this sense it contributes to integration of effort.

Controlling as a Mediator. In actual fact, controlling emerges as an important function in only three of the studies (3, 18, 39). But none of the other investigations deal with it directly. On the other hand there are two additional studies which use both evaluating and investigating in ways that suggest they may be viewed as components of the control process (3, 25). In both these instances, where controlling is lacking as an alternative, evaluating and investigating are established as important management functions. In view of their nature it seems likely that they would not have emerged had controlling been considered. Thus the sum of the evidence seems to strongly support controlling as a significant management function. It is, of course, an input-output mediator in terms of our model and hence a means to moving role behavior toward role prescriptions. It is the essence of the control mediator and is therefore always "after the fact" rather than "before the fact" as are input-sustaining mediators.

Secondary Management Functions

In addition to the four major functions, several others receive considerable support in certain studies, but not in others. These are staffing, representing, and negotiating—the latter a function not noted by any of the theoretical writers considered in our discussion of various views on management process.

Staffing as Executive Personnel Management. Staffing is emphasized as an important function in two studies (3, 18). In one additional study it is not important (25), and otherwise it is not really considered. One can only conclude that in some jobs and in some companies it is important, but that many managers spend very little time at it.

The concept of staffing is in fact considerably broader than the name implies. As used in the literature it includes:

Management recruiting
Management selection
Management development
Executive compensation
Management appraisal

Thus for all practical purposes, staffing is executive personnel management. As such it does not fall neatly into any one category of our model. Management recruiting and selection are input processes; management appraisal is an output process; management development and executive compensation are input-improving mediators. At the same time procedures for selecting managers for particular positions, whether from within the firm or from without, combine with executive compensation to establish the reward structure. Thus staffing, defined as executive personnel management, like personnel management in general (31), bridges the whole range of our conceptual model.

Representing as Influencing External Constraints and Facilitators. Like staffing, representing receives support in two studies (3, 18), but not in a third (25). Certainly the evidence does not permit a conclusion that it is a highly significant management function in terms of time devoted to it, but there are a number of management jobs that do require this type of activity.

In the management literature, representing has only rarely been considered as a separate function. Staffing is mentioned much more frequently (Table 2–1). Yet there is a certain logic to including aspects of public relations if one is to include aspects of employee relations (personnel management). And the research literature appears to support both to approximately the same degree.

In terms of our model, representing may be viewed as a mediator that achieves its ends not by establishing role prescriptions, or influencing inputs

Management Theory

directly, but by influencing the world external to the firm. It thus makes possible the more effective operation of input processes, other mediators, and output processes. More specifically, representing attempts to influence external constraints and facilitators such as laws, societal values and ethics, resource availability, and the attitudes of potential customers or clients.

Negotiating presents something of a dilemma in relation to representing. In one study, where it emerged as very important, it was defined in such a way as to overlap to a marked degree with representing; representing was not considered as a separate function (16). In the second study, where it was emphasized, the two functions were studied separately (25). However, negotiating was found to be important only in certain types of management jobs, and these were limited in number; otherwise it was of minimal significance. In view of the nature of the research findings, and the consistent failure to emphasize negotiating in the management literature generally, it seems most appropriate not to consider negotiating apart from representing as a primary or secondary function. Subsequent research may, however, require a revision of this conclusion.

The relationships of the various functions we have been discussing to the theoretical model outlined in Chapter 1 are presented in Figure 2-2.

Figure 2-2 *The Nature of Management Process*

Input Processes	Mediating Processes	Output Processes
Staffing (Recruiting)	· Establishing Role Prescriptions	Staffing (Appraising)
Staffing (Selecting)	Planning	
	Organizing	
	· Dealing with Inputs	
	Input-Improving	
	Directing	
	Staffing (Developing)	
	Staffing (Compensating)	
	Input-Sustaining	
	Coordinating	
	Input-Controlling	
	Controlling	
	· Dealing with External Constraints and Facilitators	
	Representing	

Questions

1. Assume that you have been hired as a consultant to conduct a research study for a particular company to determine what activities take up the greatest part of management's time. How would you conduct the study?
2. Why are planning, directing, coordinating, and controlling considered the primary management functions in this book?
3. Trace the history of the coordinating function. How might the marked fluctuations in its popularity be accounted for?
4. How does the distinction between professional and administrative organizations relate to the question of the universality of management functions? Can you think of any other types of differences between organizations that might also bear on the universality question?
5. How do you account for the fact that two chief executives such as Fayol and Barnard came up with such widely differing lists of management functions?

References

1. Barnard, C. I. *The Functions of the Executive.* Cambridge, Mass.: Harvard University Press, 1968.
2. Bell, G. D. "Predictability of Work Demands and Professionalization as Determinants of Workers' Discretion." *Academy of Management Journal,* Vol. 9 (1966), 20–28.
3. Brooks, E. "What Successful Executives Do." *Personnel,* Vol. 32 (1955), 210–225.
4. Campbell, J. P., M. D. Dunnette, E. E. Lawler, and K. E. Weick. *Managerial Behavior, Performance, and Effectiveness.* New York: McGraw-Hill, 1970.
5. Carlson, S. *Executive Behavior.* Stockholm: Strombergs, 1951.
6. Dale, E. *Management: Theory and Practice.* New York: McGraw-Hill, 1969.
7. Davis, R. C. *The Fundamentals of Top Management.* New York: Harper, 1951.
8. Dubin, R. "Business Behavior Behaviorally Viewed." In G. B. Strother (ed.), *Social Science Approaches to Business Behavior.* Homewood, Ill.: Irwin, 1962, pp. 11–55.
9. Etzioni, A. *Modern Organizations.* Englewood Cliffs, N.J.: Prentice-Hall, 1964.
10. Fayol, H. *General and Industrial Management.* London, Pitman, 1949.

Management Theory

11. Follett, M. P. *Freedom and Co-ordination: Lectures in Business Organization by Mary Parker Follett*, ed. L. Urwick. London: Pitman, 1949.
12. French, W. "Processes Vis-à-Vis Systems: Toward a Model of the Enterprise and Administration." *Academy of Management Journal*, Vol. 6 (1963), 46–57.
13. Friedlander, F., and H. Pickle. "Components of Effectiveness in Small Organizations." *Administrative Science Quarterly*, Vol. 13 (1968), 289–304.
14. Greenwood, W. T. *Management and Organizational Behavior Theories: An Interdisciplinary Approach*. Cincinnati: South-Western, 1965.
15. Gross, B. M. *Organizations and Their Managing*. New York: Free Press, 1968.
16. Haas, J. A., A. M. Porat, and J. A. Vaughan. "Actual vs. Ideal Time Allocations Reported by Managers: A Study of Managerial Behavior." *Personnel Psychology*, Vol. 22 (1969), 61–75.
17. Hall, R. H. "Some Organizational Considerations in the Professional-Organizational Relationship." *Administrative Science Quarterly*, Vol. 12 (1967), 461–478.
18. Hemphill, J. K. *Dimensions of Executive Positions*. Research Monograph No. 98. Columbus: Bureau of Business Research, Ohio State University, 1960.
19. Johnson, R. A., F. E. Kast, and J. E. Rosenzweig. *The Theory and Management of Systems*. New York: McGraw-Hill, 1967.
20. Katz, D., and R. L. Kahn. *The Social Psychology of Organizations*. New York: Wiley, 1966.
21. Koontz, H. "A Model for Analyzing the Universality and Transferability of Management." *Academy of Management Journal*, Vol. 12 (1969), 415–429.
22. Koontz, H., and C. O'Donnell. *Principles of Management: An Analysis of Managerial Functions*. New York: McGraw Hill, 1968.
23. Longenecker, J. G. *Principles of Management and Organizational Behavior*. Columbus, Ohio: Merrill, 1964.
24. Mahoney, T. A. *Building the Executive Team*. Englewood Cliffs, N.J.: Prentice-Hall, 1961.
25. Mahoney, T. A., T. H. Jerdee, and S. J. Carroll. *Development of Managerial Performance . . . A Research Approach*. Monograph C–9. Cincinnati: South-Western, 1963.
26. Mahoney, T. A., T. H. Jerdee, and S. J. Carroll. "The Job(s) of Management." *Industrial Relations*, Vol. 4 (1965), No. 2, 97–110.
27. Massie, J. L. *Essentials of Management*. Englewood Cliffs, N.J.: Prentice-Hall, 1964.
28. McFarland, D. E. *Management: Principles and Practices*. New York: Macmillan, 1970.
29. McLennan, K. "The Manager and His Job Skills." *Academy of Management Journal*, Vol. 10 (1967), 235–245.

30. Millman, R. W. "A General Systems Approach to the Analysis of Managerial Functions." In D. E. McFarland (ed.), *Academy of Management Proceedings: Annual Meeting, 1962*. Academy of Management, 1963, pp. 133–138.
31. Miner, J. B. *Personnel and Industrial Relations: A Managerial Approach*. New York: Macmillan, 1969.
32. Miner, J. B. *Management Theory*. New York: Macmillan, 1971.
33. Miner, J. B. "Changes in Student Attitudes Toward Bureaucratic Role Prescriptions During the 1960s." *Administrative Science Quarterly*, Vol. 16 (1971), 351–364.
34. Newman, W. H., C. E. Summer, and E. K. Warren. *The Process of Management*. Englewood Cliffs, N.J.: Prentice-Hall, 1967.
35. Price, J. L. *Organizational Effectiveness: An Inventory of Propositions*. Homewood, Ill.: Irwin, 1968.
36. Sayles, L. R. *Managerial Behavior*. New York: McGraw-Hill, 1964.
37. Scott, J. W., and M. El-Assal. "Multiversity, University Size, University Quality and Student Protest: An Empirical Study." *American Sociological Review*, Vol. 34 (1969), 702–709.
38. Shetty, Y. K. "A Model for Analyzing the Universality and Transferability of Management: Comment." *Academy of Management Journal*, Vol. 13 (1970), 220–224.
39. Skeaff, L. J. M. "What Do Managers Do?" *Personnel Journal*, Vol. 46 (1967), 630–637.
40. Suojanen, W. W. *The Dynamics of Management*. New York: Holt, Rinehart and Winston, 1966.
41. Surface, J. R. "Universities Aren't Corporations." *Business Horizons*, Vol. 14 (1971), No. 3, 75–80.
42. Urwick, L. F. *The Elements of Administration*. New York: Harper, 1943.
43. Urwick, L. F. *Notes on the Theory of Organization*. New York: American Management Association, 1952.
44. Urwick, L. F. *The Pattern of Management*. Minneapolis: University of Minnesota Press, 1956.
45. Urwick, L. F. "Management and Human Relations." In R. Tannenbaum, I. R. Weschler, and F. Massarik (eds.), *Leadership and Organization: A Behavioral Science Approach*. New York: McGraw-Hill, 1961, pp. 416–428.
46. Voich, D., and D. A. Wren. *Principles of Management: Resources and Systems*. New York: Ronald, 1968.
47. Vollmer, H. M., and D. L. Mills. *Professionalization*. Englewood Cliffs, N.J.: Prentice-Hall, 1966.

3 Management Principles and Scientific Theory

I. The Nature of Science
  1. Scientific Method
     a. Assumptions of Science
     b. Rules of Science
  2. Scientific Theory
     a. The Characteristics of Good Theory
     b. Principles and Theory
  3. Scientific and Managerial Decisions

II. Views of Management Principles
  1. Classical Concepts
     a. Scientific Management
     b. Fayol
     c. Mooney and Reiley
     d. Synthesis and Expansion
  2. Behavioral Science Concepts
     a. Max Weber
     b. March and Simon
     c. Inventories of Propositions

III. Management Principles as Scientific Theory
  1. Philosophy or Science?
  2. Universality or Contingency?

IV. From Management Philosophy to the Science of Management
  1. History of Science
  2. Schools of Management Thought
     a. Classical
     b. Human Relations
     c. Structuralist
     d. Behavioral Humanist
     e. Decision Making
  3. Value Resolution

As noted in the Introduction, there are two essential requirements for a comprehensive book in the management field: it must utilize a logical framework or model to weave together the diverse strands, and it must bring some value system to bear to differentiate the important from the unimportant. Chapters 1 and 2 dealt with the organizational model and the position of management process within this model. This chapter sets forth the value system—the value system of science.

There is an additional aspect to this chapter. In Chapter 2 we noted that there are two major threads running through the management literature. The first of these, the idea of management functions, has already been discussed. The second, the idea of management principles, remains to be considered. It is not enough to identify the various areas of activity or functions within managerial work; one must also establish how managers should behave to be effective. This is the matter of principles or role prescriptions. What should managers do in order to contribute to the achievement of operative goals?

The matter of normative precepts is closely allied to the scientific value system, and to the development of scientific theory. In fact it is the value system of science that establishes which "principles" are to be taken seriously, and which are to be discarded or given a tentative status—to be considered as hypotheses for future investigation. We will first consider the nature of science—its method and its theory—and then relate management principles to this value system. In the process we will attempt to pinpoint the current status of the management discipline in its gradual movement out of philosophy into the realm of science.

The Nature of Science

Science may be viewed in terms of its structure, its goals, and its methods (45). In terms of its structure it is a number of scientific disciplines: physics, biology, psychology, economics, management, and many others. Each of these sciences attempts to provide a set of internally consistent hypotheses, principles, laws, and theories dealing with an aspect of our total knowledge. To the extent a science is mature such internal consistency may be attained; but there are many younger sciences, like management, that only approximate this state.

The ultimate goal of science is *understanding*—to discover the truth regarding events in nature, to solve the problems imbedded in our world and in our universe. Inherent in the idea of understanding is the concept of *prediction*. If one truly understands, one can predict the subsequent course of events. This means that expectations can be established that are not only logically consistent with all else that is known but that ultimately meet the test of empirical confirmation. If such expectations or predictions are not confirmed, then understanding obviously is incomplete. On the other hand, it is possible for prediction to occur in instances where there is something short of full understanding (11).

In addition scientific understanding permits us to *influence*, or control, the future. Thus, understanding involves not only prediction of subsequent events but a degree of influence over them as well. To the degree we truly understand nature, we can manipulate it to achieve our ends. This is in one sense the challenge of science, but it is also a terrifying responsibility. To know and understand fully is to be able to predict the future and then to influence it to a predetermined end point. This is the goal of science. It is the very essence of an applied science such as management. Ultimately we want to know how to run organizations so as to make them maximally effective in their goal attainment—and we want actually to influence them to this end.

Scientific Method

Scientific method may be viewed as a process fabricated out of symbolizing, description, explanation, and theorizing (6).

Symbolizing provides a method of retaining experience. Symbols are used to indicate particular aspects of events that are of concern to science. The symbolic signs may derive from language, mathematics, or symbolic logic. Regardless of the system of signs used, once the transformation from event to symbol has been made, a permanent record of experience exists. The symbols (words or numbers) may then be mentally manipulated and relationships established.

Description is a matter of ordering symbols so as to make them correspond most closely to the events themselves. Descriptions involve a very low order of abstraction. They are closely tied to observation and sensory experience. At most, description involves classifying, ordering, and correlating events in symbolic form.

Explanation operates at a higher level of abstraction. It establishes the meanings behind events, the causal relationships involved. As such it gradually shades over into *theorizing*. When explanation moves to the point of producing a pattern of logical constructs into which all facts relevant to a phenomenon may be fitted, we speak of a theory. A theory is thus a framework of interrelated symbolic concepts. It provides a systematic view of some area by specifying the relationships inherent in it. In doing so it permits understanding, prediction, and the exercise of influence (29).

In order for this scientific method composed of symbolization, description, explanation, and theorizing to operate effectively as a means to understanding, certain assumptions must be made and certain rules followed.

Assumptions of Science. There are several assumptions or postulates underlying science which must be accepted if one is to apply scientific method. With these assumptions, one can conduct research into any problem in nature. It may not be possible to solve the problem, but at least the method of science may be brought to bear. Without these assumptions, scientific investigation would be pointless. This is not to say, however, that all scientists are consistently aware of these assumptions as they go about their work; only that if these assumptions were not held, at least implicitly, there could be no science as we know it (6). The assumptions have been named as follows:

The postulate of natural kinds
The postulate of permanence
The postulate of determinism
The postulate of reliability of perceiving, remembering, and reasoning

We assume, first, that resemblances are in fact widespread in nature; that natural groupings, or kinds, exist which permit the classification of events and objects into categories. Without this assumption generalization would be meaningless. Each event would be separate and distinct from all others, and to understand it would tell us nothing about other events. Science could not predict and influence if such a state of affairs existed in nature.

Second, a degree of permanence or stability over time must be assumed in nature. This stability need not be absolute—only relative. But just as objects and events must resemble other objects and events in some respect, so too an object or event at T_1 must resemble that object or event at T_2. Without some degree of constancy in nature, prediction and influence become impossible.

Third, all phenomena in nature are assumed to be determined, to have one or more causes. This is what explanation and theorizing attempt to achieve—a statement of causality. If stable processes were not assumed to operate behind events, efforts at understanding would be pointless. It is the postulate of determinism that constantly leads scientists to investigate new fields—to look for scientific answers where none have existed before.

Finally, we must accept the human processes of perceiving, remembering, and reasoning as basically trustworthy. If these processes cannot be relied upon, then efforts at symbolizing, description, explanation, and theorizing are pointless. This is not to say that these human processes cannot be in error; quite obviously they can be. But they must produce some reliable data for science to exist. To the extent that reliability of perceiving, remembering, and reasoning can be fostered, science will be more effective in achieving its goals. The rules of science exist to foster this reliability.

Rules of Science. One of the most important rules of science is that concepts be defined clearly in terms of the procedures involved in their measurement. We have to know exactly what we are talking about when we use a given term. Meanings have to be clear and unambiguous to avoid confusion and erroneous classification. Furthermore, statements must be made in a manner that will permit generalization beyond a specific experience or event to a class or grouping having a particular resemblance in common.

In science, observations must be controlled so that causation may be imputed correctly. The most common method of eliminating a given factor as a possible cause of an event is to hold it constant—to keep it from varying so that it cannot operate as a source of change. Controlled observation which removes any possible effects of factors not under study is essential. This is a difficult rule to follow, especially in studying organizational phenomena (14). Recent research indicates, for instance, that the results of laboratory experiments in psychology may vary depending on which psychologist conducts the study (19). A variable that was thought to be irrelevant was thus found to exert a causal influence and to require control. The effort to identify factors that must be controlled and to develop procedures to accomplish this is a continuing one. To the extent that this effort is successful, reliability of perception and reasoning, and hence valid explanation, are possible.

Another rule requires that generalizations to groups or classes of objects and events be made only from repeated observations of an adequate sample drawn from the total group. In studying managers, for example, it is not sufficient to observe only one or two managers. One must observe an adequate sample to permit generalization.

Finally, explanation including theorizing must be in terms that permit empirical confirmation. Scientific statements must be testable and the tests must be capable of repetition with the same result. Furthermore, explanatory statements must be logically consistent with other explanatory statements that have been frequently confirmed. The rationality of the total scientific system must be maintained.

In summary, the rules of science require that scientists know what they are talking about, that their statements not be limited to single instances, that explanations be justified in terms of adequately controlled observations, that statements be applied to the appropriate group of objects or events, and that explanations meet the requirements of empirical testability and logical consistency (1).

There is much in the scientific method as related to description and explanation that parallels the legal process. The rules of evidence attempt to achieve understanding and truth in much the same manner as the rules of science do. Methods of this kind should be contrasted with other methods of knowing—the appeal to authority, tradition, and accepted practice, spiritual revelation, intuitive knowledge. In this book we reject these methods in favor of the method of science. What is considered important here is what we know as a result of adequate scientific research. In contrast, other methods tend to be unreliable and to produce imperfect understanding. They are not in fact a means for maximizing prediction and influence.

Scientific Theory

Theory pulls together existing knowledge, explains events or relationships, and in the end predicts what has not yet been observed. Scientific theories of this kind are inevitably tentative or provisional, even when they have received widespread confirmation (25, 52). They represent the state of our knowledge at a given point in time. Historically, what is the accepted theory of today tends to become the outmoded theory of tomorrow. New facts and new formulations invariably force changes. A number of writers have emphasized the distinction between theory which is constructed on an *inductive* basis and that which is *deductive* (24). In inductive theory, generalizations are developed from observation—from experiments, case studies, or personal experiences; in deductive theory, a set of premises serves as the starting point. From these, certain subsidiary concepts are then deduced on a logical basis. In actual practice, at least within the field of management, both processes usually are at work in the development of scientific theory.

Thus the process of scientific theory construction and confirmation can be viewed as involving the following steps:

1. The formulation of a problem or complex of problems based on observation.
2. The construction of a theory to provide answers to the problem or problems based on inductions from observation.
3. The deduction of specific hypotheses from the theory.
4. The recasting of hypotheses in terms of specific measures and the operations required to test the hypotheses (this may be referred to as the theorem-formulation step).
5. The devising of factual situations to test the theorem.
6. The actual testing in which confirmation does or does not occur.

The Characteristics of Good Theory. A theory is good to the extent it contributes to the goals of science. This means that better theories are more comprehensive in that they reduce a large number of diverse observations to a much lesser number of underlying statements. The more the theory can explain, the more useful it is.

Second, good theories include explicit statements regarding the limits of their application. Of course, the broader these limits, the more comprehensive the scope of generalization, the better. But it is important that these limiting conditions be specified so that the theory is not applied to phenomena for which it was never intended and has no relevance.

Third, theory should be helpful in focusing research. It should tell us what facts are important and ought to be gathered. It should tell us what questions need to be asked of nature. In this sense it is much more economical than trial-and-error groping. Rather than testing one random hypothesis after another until we finally hit on something worthwhile, good theory permits us to restrict our search to those areas where there is a high probability of obtaining meaningful results.

Fourth is the closely related point that good theory should serve to increase the usefulness of any results that are obtained from research. The findings from a given study may be extended through their relationship to a body of theory. This, too, is a very practical consideration. In a sense more is obtained from a given piece of research than is put into it. One may obtain not merely an isolated fact, but the whole explanatory and predictive power of a related theory. Thus, once research establishes that a particular company consistently operates in ways that are congruent with a given theory, the whole theory becomes available as a basis for understanding.

Fifth, good theory should be logically consistent, both internally and externally. Previous statements have implied that a theory should fit the facts—when subjected to test it should be consistent with what is known of the real world. But it should also be internally consistent. One proposition should not be logically inconsistent with, or contradict, another.

Sixth, to be of value theory must be subject to test. It must be formulated so that confirmation through research is possible. This point has already been noted in connection with our discussion of the rules of science. It means that good scientific theory is stated unambiguously and is reducible to empirical operations.

Seventh, the best theory, all other things being equal, is the one that is most parsimonious. Simplicity of statement is a scientific value. This is why mathematical statements are often preferable to laborious verbal formulations. On the other hand, parsimony should not be sought at the expense of explanation and understanding. In the management field there are many areas where theory of any meaningful kind is virtually nonexistent. In such cases attempts to move to the simplicity and precision of mathematics without first identifying the relevant variables in more general terms is unlikely to prove fruitful.

Principles and Theory. For many scientists a principle is the same as a law. It is a theoretical proposition that has received the support of extensive confirmation. Such a principle is widely accepted by those who are most knowledgeable in the area. It has the backing of consensus, at least at a point in time. Thus, we speak of "principles of economics," "principles of learning," and "principles of management," as theoretical statements about which we have a considerable feeling of certainty. This is more than theory; it is "proven" theory or fact (remembering always the tentative nature of any theory).

Another position is that principles and laws differ in that the former are distinguished by their usefulness, their essentially applied orientation (45). In this view, laws are of relevance primarily for pure or basic science; principles are relevant primarily for practitioners. Both laws and principles require extensive confirmation and the support of expert scientific consensus.

Scientific and Managerial Decisions

In science it is characteristic to be extremely cautious and skeptical. A scientist remains neutral until a convincing body of evidence is accumulated. This is a major aspect of scientific objectivity. Hunch and bias provide no basis for decisions; only controlled research and substantiated theory will do. "I don't know" thus becomes not only an acceptable answer to a question, but in many cases a highly valued one (42). By admitting that adequate knowledge to solve a problem or to make a decision is lacking, science opens the matter to research. From a scientific viewpoint the greatest error is that which occurs when inadequate or insufficient data are overinterpreted or overgeneralized, so that an unsolved problem is accepted as solved. Errors of this kind serve to block scientific progress because problem-identification is made extremely difficult.

Managers, on the other hand, most often make decisions with insufficient or inadequate data. Unlike the scientist, the manager is frequently faced with problems that cannot be answered with "I don't know." Often he must accumulate as much information as possible in the time available and then act. Such decisions may have a large element of risk, but when judgment cannot be deferred there is no alternative.

The difference between these two decision-making processes is substantial, and has resulted in considerable misunderstanding and mutual criticism. The role of the scientist requires that he recognize what is and is not known in order to state problems for research. He must take every precaution to ensure that his findings once obtained are not in error. In contrast, the managerial role does not require the advancement of knowledge but rather the achievement of organizational task and maintenance goals. Time is often a crucial factor in decision making. Risk and uncertainty are everywhere; although they should be recognized and not made an excuse for sloppy thinking, they cannot be avoided. In many cases the process of extended study, which is so essential to the scientist, and at the same time frequently so irritating to the manager when he seeks scientific assistance, simply is not possible.

This does not mean that practical problems cannot be solved in many cases with the aid of scientific theory and research. Although medical decisions were made in earlier times quite independently of an adequate scientific underpinning, this is no longer the case. Similarly practical managerial decisions can increasingly be based on a scientific substratum (9).

Science may contribute to managerial decision making in two ways:

1. Existing research and confirmed theory relevant to the problem may be brought to bear in its solution.
2. Where sufficient time is available research may be conducted to provide information not previously available and to guide solutions accordingly.

As the body of scientific knowledge bearing on management process increases, the first approach will receive wider and wider application, just as it has in medicine. The second approach will of necessity continue to have somewhat limited application because of the widespread time pressures on decision making, but there still are numerous cases where it can be applied. In any event managers should be fully aware when they are making decisions that have a high degree of risk in them. Only then can new scientific knowledge and methods be brought to bear to reduce the risk. To believe final solutions exist where they actually do not can, in the long run, be as detrimental to the manager as to the scientist.

Views of Management Principles

Within the management literature the term *principle* does not always imply substantiation in research. In some instances, there is widespread consensus as to the validity of a principle. In other cases, the "principle" label may be applied by the person who devised the proposition long before there is any opportunity for support for his idea to develop. Thus the term has been used very loosely in the management literature, and does not always carry the implication of scientific law or substantiated theory.

Statements of management principles come in many forms. In some instances they merely imply that a manager ought to behave in a certain manner—a causal relationship is not indicated. It seems safe to conclude, however, that where the causal link is not explicitly stated, it nevertheless is implicitly assumed by the writer (32). Thus, what is really being said is that if a manager wants to contribute to the achievement of official goals, he should do such and such (and by implication that he ought to want to contribute to official goals).

In terms of the model outlined in Chapter 1 a management principle may be viewed as a role prescription—a role prescription that indicates how a manager should behave to be most effective in carrying out the management functions of planning, directing, coordinating, controlling, staffing, and representing.

Classical Concepts

Management theory in some form has been traced back to 5000 B.C., although it took several thousands of years before anything approaching a continuing, logically consistent set of propositions was established (20). In the 1700s, and even more in the 1800s, various economists and operating managers began to develop systematic statements regarding how management should occur. Names such as Robert Owen, Charles Babbage, Adam Smith, W. S. Jevons, Henry Poor, Daniel McCallum, Henry Towne, and Henry Metcalfe are often mentioned in discussing this period. Because our concern is not so much with a detailed analysis of historical origins as with understanding current management thought, we will move directly to one of the major viewpoints underlying present thinking. This is scientific management as developed by Frederick W. Taylor around the turn of the century and further expanded until his death in 1915.

Scientific Management. Taylor was concerned primarily with factory management, and within that context his emphasis was mostly on the management of production workers. In this respect his frame of reference differs sharply from that of Fayol who, as indicated in Chapter 2, developed his ideas from a top management perspective. It is not surprising that the two men, the engineer and the corporation president, created principles of management which were frequently unrelated and on occasion actually contradictory.

Taylor's ideas are set forth in two major works: *Shop Management* (56) and *The Principles of Scientific Management* (57). Although he is often

Management Theory

credited with only four basic principles of management, his writings abound with prescriptive statements indicating in moralistic terms what a manager should do to improve his effectiveness (16). Thus, there are in fact a rather large number of principles. The basic four, most often quoted, state the following:

1. Develop a science for each man's work—a one best way.
2. Scientifically select the best man for the job and train him in the procedures he is expected to follow.
3. Cooperate with the men to insure that the work is in fact done in the way prescribed. This should include, but not be limited to, providing for increased earnings by those who follow the prescribed way most closely.
4. Divide the work so that activities such as planning, organizing and controlling are the prime responsibility of management rather than the individual worker.

It is evident that Taylor was urging the creation of unambiguous role prescriptions known to be closely related to organizational goal achievement. He was also urging that every effort be made to move role behavior as close to these role prescriptions as possible.

In accordance with these views he advocated that the planning of role prescriptions be separated from the work and carried out by a centralized planning group; also that specialized or functional foremanship be introduced. According to this latter concept a production worker would report to different foremen depending on what aspect of his work was involved. Thus, a man might have many bosses, but each would operate within a narrow, strictly delimited zone of influence and expertise.

Taylor placed strong emphasis on the *exception principle*. Output standards and routine procedures were to be established through the use of precise measurement; management should then give its attention only to those cases where standards were not met or exceeded to a marked degree, and where established procedures were not or could not be followed. As the exception principle implies, Taylor generally advocated dealing with one individual at a time, but he was not unaware of the ways in which group influences might operate to produce a restriction of output. The discovery of these restrictive practices is widely attributed to the human relations researchers who followed him by some 15 or 20 years.

Yet Taylor's writings are sprinkled with references to group pressures and their impact on production (4).

It should be emphasized that the use of the adjective "scientific" to describe Taylor's views is by no means a misnomer (28). He was an advocate of research and experimentation in management and he conducted studies to determine how various jobs might best be performed. He developed a number of techniques for controlled observation and the measurement of behavior.

Taylor's principles appear to have had an almost immediate polarizing effect on the environment. There were many who quickly accepted scientific management—who publicized it, expanded it, conducted studies related to various aspects of it, and applied it. Among these contributors are Henry Gantt, Frank and Lillian Gilbreth, Harrington Emerson, Harlow Person, and Morris Cooke. Scientific management had a strong influence on a number of the early business schools including those established at the University of Pennsylvania, Harvard, and Dartmouth.

Attacks on Taylor's work came almost as quickly as the support. An extensive investigation of scientific management in practice by Robert Hoxie (27), although laudatory on some points, was critical in relationship to incentive payment plans and labor relations. In general, Hoxie's views were closely allied to those of the labor movement as a whole. Other critics were less concerned with the ethical and value aspects of Taylor's system than with its lack of theoretical elegance (8). His principles were considered not to be principles at all, and the theory of management proposed was attacked as lacking in internal consistency.

Fayol. In addition to his managerial functions, outlined in Chapter 2, Fayol proposed 14 principles of management, many of which remain significant today. Although described as principles, these statements were not advanced in any sense as absolutes (15). Thus, Fayol was in fact misusing the term *principle* as it has been defined in science. He did not advance any research evidence in favor of his formulations, although such evidence has accumulated since (17).

The principles were stated originally as single words followed by a discussion. They are restated in terms of role prescriptions as follows:

1. There should be a division of labor such that different activities are carried out by different people; the division should not carry specialization beyond certain limits, however.

Management Theory

2. There should be a measure of authority inherent in managerial positions, and responsibility should be directly related to this authority.
3. There should be discipline throughout the organization maintained by good leadership, clear and fair agreements, and judicious penalities.
4. There should be a unity of command such that only one person exercises authority over the same man. (This is in direct opposition to Taylor's functional foremanship.)
5. There should be one person in charge of a group of activities having the same objective, and at the same time only one plan should exist where the objective is the same.
6. There should be continuing subordination of individual interests to those of the organization as a whole. This should be achieved by firmness and good example from superiors, fair agreements and constant supervision.
7. There should be a system of remuneration which is fair, which rewards well-directed effort, and which does not produce over-payments beyond reasonable limits.
8. There should be a degree of centralization or decentralization of authority which is appropriate to existing circumstances.
9. There should be a scalar chain of authority and communication ranging from the highest to the lowest positions except that horizontal communication should be encouraged where it is beneficial to the organization and where it is authorized by immediate superiors. These concepts are diagrammed in Figure 3-1.

Figure 3-1 *The Scalar Chain*

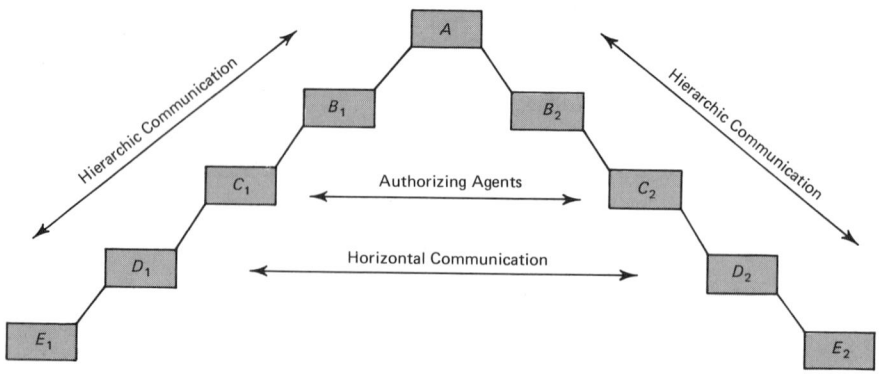

10. There should be material order such that each thing is in its appointed place, and social order such that each individual is in his appointed place. This latter implies that suitable positions be established and that the right person be selected for each position.
11. There should be equity in the treatment of individuals throughout the organization.
12. There should be, insofar as possible, stability of employment both ·in a given position and in the organization as a whole.
13. There should be every opportunity to exercise initiative at all levels in the organization. Initiative is both a means to satisfaction and a stimulant for motivation. As such it is a great source of organizational strength in difficult times.
14. There should be constant encouragement of *esprit de corps* and harmony within the organization rather than conflicts and dissension.

Mooney and Reiley. Another major contribution to the classical management principles literature came from two operating executives at General Motors. Mooney, the major contributor, was vice-president in charge of export and overseas operations and a director of the firm. Their initial publication in 1931 was titled *Onward Industry.* Subsequent editions were published with the title *The Principles of Organization,* first by both authors and then by James Mooney alone (44).

The book sets forth what amounts to four basic principles of management and then develops the significance of these principles through historical analyses of governments, the Catholic Church, the military, and industry. The result is an affirmation of the universality of the principles cited. Based on their interpretation of history, Mooney and Reiley conclude that organizations are in fact successful in attaining their goals to the extent that they follow sound principles of management.

The four principles set forth have much in common with Fayol:

1. The coordinative principle.
2. The scalar principle.
3. The functional principle.
4. The staff phase of the functional principle.

In role prescription terms these may be stated as follows:

1. There should be unity of action in pursuit of a common purpose

which is maintained by authority, community of interest, doctrine, and discipline.
2. There should be a scalar hierarchy of authority with delegation of activities to each successive level of the organization.
3. There should be a specialized division of labor in terms of functions or kinds of duties.
4. Functional specialization should include the creation of staff units to provide information and advice to those in the primary scalar chain.

Synthesis and Expansion. Taylor, Fayol, and Mooney appear to have had a major influence on management theory insofar as classical principles are concerned. But there have been a number of other contributors. Among these are Lyndall Urwick and Ralph Davis, whose work was mentioned in the previous chapter.

Urwick was concerned primarily with integrating the views of others to provide logical consistency of the kind required by a truly comprehensive theory of management. Having achieved a logically coherent classification scheme encompassing principles proposed by Fayol, Mooney, Taylor, Follett, and himself, Urwick took a stronger stand regarding the validity of his principles than had Fayol (59). Thus, in his own view at least he was stating a set of principles which were in fact principles in the scientific sense. In asserting that his was a substantiated and widely applicable theory, he appealed to the concepts of consensus and logical consistency. He makes no reference to experimentation and research. His position remains essentially unchanged today (60).

While Urwick was essentially a synthesizer of principles proposed by others, R. C. Davis moved in the direction of expansion. He attempted to achieve greater precision in his statements than had earlier writers. The result is a strong emphasis on definitions and classification, and the explicit statement of well over 100 principles of management. The flavor of these may be gained from the following list (10):

Principle of limiting factors
Principle of multiple hypotheses
Principles of the objective
Law of the situation
Principles of executive leadership
Principle of participation
Law of functional growth

Principles of delegation
Principles of decentralization
Principle of uniform incentive value
Principle of functional emergence
Principle of staff independence
Principle of the limitation of staff economy
Principles of indoctrination
Principle of focal points
Principle of simulation

It is apparent that Davis viewed these principles as resultants derived from previous thinking, both his own and that of others. He was discussing basic guides for managerial action, not hypotheses for subsequent research.

A more recent comprehensive review of management theory by Massie provides a list of some of the more important principles which are widely stated in the current classical literature (40):

The scalar principle
Unity of command
Organizational specialization
The exception principle
Span of control
The profit center concept

The first three are in Fayol's list of 14 principles; the third and fourth were emphasized by Taylor. The principle of span of control is often credited to V. A. Graicunas (22), although Fayol does consider the matter. It states that there should be a limited number of subordinates reporting to a superior. Various restatements of the principle have considered varying conditions of work and produced different conclusions regarding the number of subordinates (26).

The profit center concept is applicable primarily to large corporations. It states that divisions should be established within the total company which are held responsible for their own profits and losses and which have considerable authority in the decision-making process. This is a relatively recent addition to lists of management principles, although the idea itself appears to have originated in the General Motors and duPont organizations of the 1920s (55).

Behavioral Science Concepts

When principles of management are mentioned, a reference to the classical concepts we have been considering is normally implied. However, there has been a parallel conceptual development in the behavioral sciences. Here the term *principle* is used much less frequently; references are typically to propositions or hypotheses. This tendency to use a more tentative terminology appears to stem in part from the somewhat greater scientific training of the behavioral writers. They generally are more aware than the classical writers of the degree of research support required before the terms *principle* and *law* are fully justified. It is also true that in many cases the behavioral scientists have been at great pains to differentiate their statements from those of men such as Taylor and Fayol. To dissociate themselves from the classical concepts, they have tended to avoid the "principles" terminology.

However, the term principle is used on occasion even by those behavioral scientists who have been most critical of the classical viewpoint. For example, Rensis Likert of the University of Michigan has frequently discussed his *principle of supportive relationships* (36, 37), which states that

> There should be a maximum probability that in all interactions and in all relationships within the organization, each member ... will view the experience as supportive and one which builds and maintains his sense of personal worth and importance.

Max Weber. Viewed by many as the founder of modern sociology, Max Weber wrote on a variety of topics in the social sciences. Most important for our purposes is his formulation of the concept of bureaucracy and of the procedures that permit this type of organization to pursue its goals rationally and effectively (62). Weber's role prescriptions have much in common with those of the classical writers. He was a contemporary of Taylor and Fayol. Yet it seems clear that Weber's ideas were developed independently, and he in turn had practically no influence on the classical management writers; not only those of his own time, but those of the ensuing decades as well.

Some of the role prescriptions that Weber specified for the "corporate group" are stated below:

1. There should be a continuing body of rules which govern expected behavior.

2. There should be a division of labor with the resulting jurisdictions, obligations, and powers clearly specified.
3. There should be a hierarchy of positions, each reporting to a higher level of authority.
4. There should be comprehensive training in the rules and requirements of positions (the role prescriptions).
5. There should be freedom to assign people to positions in accordance with the needs of the organization; no position should be monopolized by an incumbent.
6. There should be extensive use of written communications, and these should be maintained in files so that continuity of decisions and rules can be ensured.

March and Simon. A more recent set of managerial propositions is presented by James March and Herbert Simon in their book *Organizations* (39), published in 1958. Both authors were originally trained as political scientists, and both spent a number of years together on the faculty of the Graduate School of Industrial Administration at Carnegie Institute of Technology. Their propositions are derived, not from personal experience in managerial work, but from an extensive review of the theoretical and research literature dealing with organizations and their functioning. The statements that result represent the first comprehensive set of alternatives to the classical principles of management.

The March and Simon propositions are formulated as hypotheses, and many deal with organizational relationships other than those involving effectiveness or goal-attainment. The objective is to create a scientific theory of organization, rather than to provide specific guides for managerial action. Yet the implications for action are there, as the following examples indicate:

> There will be more conflict between units within a company sharing a common service unit than between those that do not.
> Innovation is most likely where incentives are tied directly to innovation; next most likely with companywide incentives and least likely with incentives for individual productivity.
> The more subordinates participate in policy decisions, the greater their sense of identification with the organization will be.

If conflict reduction, innovation, and organizational identification are desired, these propositions provide role prescriptions to guide behavior.

On the other hand, a number of the March and Simon statements are considerably more abstruse; here, guides for managerial role behavior are much more difficult to identify.

Inventories of Propositions. Since the publication of the March and Simon book, several similar efforts have been made. For the most part these have been undertaken by sociologists or social psychologists whose primary identification has been with the academic world. Following the March and Simon model, they have developed conceptual or propositional inventories drawing in varying degrees on the accumulated research-based knowledge of the social sciences.

By far the most ambitious of these inventories is that of Berelson and Steiner (3). Their work is in essence a synthesis of existing knowledge in the social sciences. The statements are the authors' views of what we really know from scientific study. Thus, a legitimate claim can be made for using terms such as *principle* or *law* to describe them. In each instance they represent findings or generalizations for which there is "some good amount of scientific evidence."

These principles cover a great variety of topics: the individual, the family, small groups, organizations, institutions, social strata, publics, the society, culture. Our concern is primarily in the area of organizations. Here the principles tend to relate to the achievement of either task or maintenance goals. In the former category are statements such as the following:

> The more friendly and helpful the manager the greater the productivity of his unit, provided productivity is in fact an operative goal of the organization and the unit.

This might be restated in role prescription form to read, "There should be friendly and helpful supervision." The same type of restatement is possible with maintenance-oriented principles such as:

> The closer the basic requirements for being hired by an organization are to a man's training the better he likes the organization and the more likely he is to stay.

A major expansion of the Berelson and Steiner work in the organization area has been carried out by Price (47). Basing his analysis on the results of 50 studies, Price developed 31 propositions relating certain organizational mechanisms to effectiveness. A great many of these are statements of what

Management Principles and Scientific Theory

managers must do to achieve an effective organization. A condensed, schematic presentation of Price's propositions is provided in Figure 3-2.

A somewhat different type of inventory has been developed by Thompson (58). Although research is cited in many instances to support propositions, this effort involves a much greater deductive component than those

Figure 3-2 *Schematic Presentation of Price's Propositions Regarding Determinants of Organizational Effectiveness*

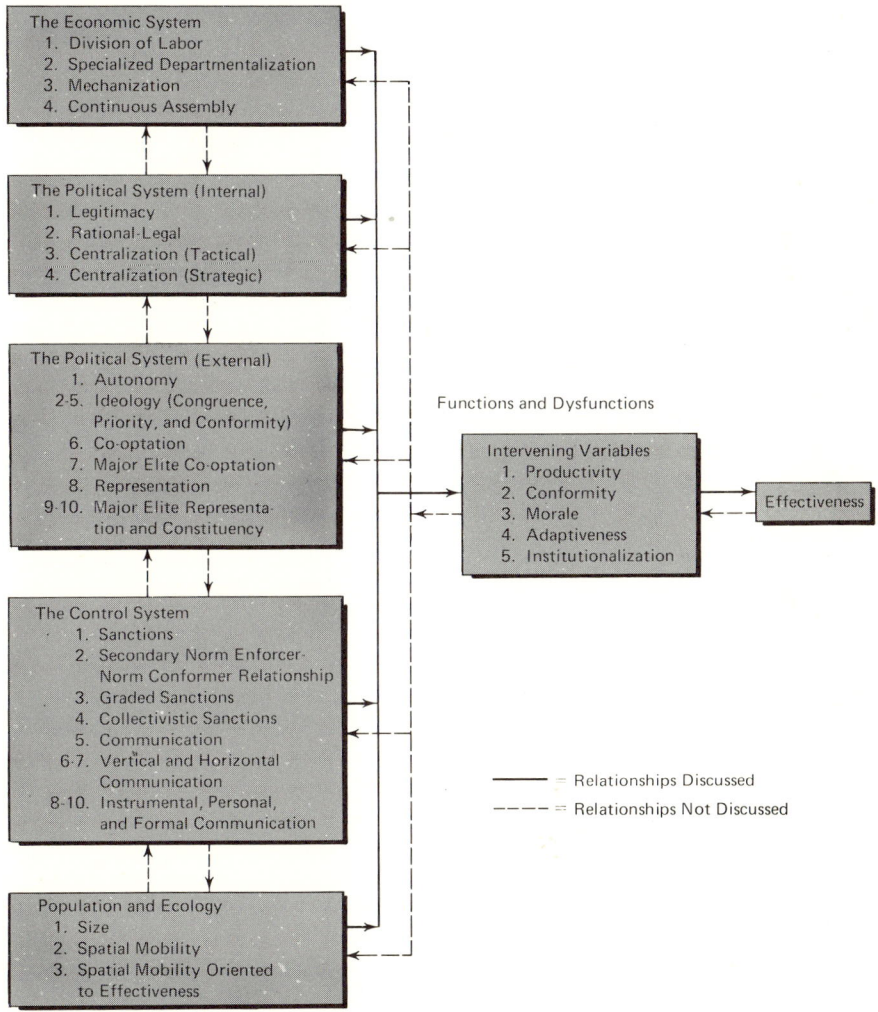

Source: J. L. Price, *Organizational Effectiveness: An Inventory of Propositions.* (Homewood, Ill.: Irwin 1968), 205. Reproduced by permission.

we have been considering. Basically Thompson is concerned with the construction of a logically consistent theory of organizational functioning. Yet like the statements of March and Simon and the others who have produced inventories, a number of his propositions are amenable to restatement in role prescriptions terms.

Management Principles as Scientific Theory

Classical views on management principles have been widely criticized. Behavioral science principles, on the other hand, have been criticized less frequently. This relative freedom from attack appears to result in part from the tendency to emphasize the tentativeness of statements as hypotheses for future research, and in part from the fact that the statements are often made in ways that do not provide explicit guides for managerial practice. Thus, practitioners frequently view many of the behavioral science concepts as irrelevant and ignore them, rather than critiquing them.

One line of attack on the classical views of management principles has been developed by a group of behavioral scientists writing essentially as philosophers. Typical of this approach are several books emanating from the School of Industrial Management at Massachusetts Institute of Technology such as McGregor's *The Human Side of Enterprise* (41) and Bennis' *Changing Organizations* (2). These critics argue that the classical principles create excessive and unhealthy dependence on superiors, are inconsistent with the dignity of the individual, and inhibit personal growth and development (17). Their arguments suggest that they are generally more concerned with certain philosophies of "the good society" than with organizational goal attainment per se.

A second line of criticism, which may be traced to Simon (54), subjects the classical principles to the value system of science rather than to a humanistic value system emphasizing personal freedom, human dignity, and individual worth.

Philosophy or Science?

Simon's original arguments against the classical concepts involved certain of the rules of science and the requirements of good scientific theory. He was especially critical on the grounds of ambiguity of definitions and statement, and logical inconsistency (54). Certainly there has been a great deal of misunderstanding about what various principles mean and considerable difficulty in their application (31). In addition, Simon was critical of the lack of empirical support for the classical principles.

In a later work March and Simon (39) reiterated the pleas for unambiguous definitions, which would permit the formulation of testable statements, and for empirical verification. But they also criticized the classical principles on an additional ground, that of incompleteness. In particular the motivational assumptions, and the limitations imposed by human abilities and capacities were viewed as insufficiently treated. Thus they view classical theory as inadequate to provide comprehensive understanding and prediction within the management realm.

Along these lines, it can also be argued that the supporting evidence for the classical concepts is not based on either controlled observation or adequate sampling. Furthermore, there is no clear view of the domain of application. Fayol implies that his principles do have limits, but does not attempt to specify them. Urwick, Mooney, and other writers have argued for universality of application to all organizational forms. The classical principles were extremely slow in generating research, and thus did not provide for the kind of focusing on crucial problems that one desires of a scientific theory.

Perhaps the most difficult criticism is the contention that by ascribing the status of fact to their principles many classical writers actually discouraged research. By stating that problems were solved when they really were not, they eliminated the "I don't know" so essential to scientific investigation.

One reason the classical theorists may have missed the rules of science and the requirements of good theory by so much is that they were not even trying to achieve them. Men such as Fayol, Mooney, R. C. Davis, Urwick, and even to a degree, Taylor, were essentially philosophers and practitioners, not scientists. They were writing about good and bad, not fact and fiction. They developed philosophies of organization and management and then attempted to argue as convincingly as they could for the adoption of their views. Typically they were not researchers and knew little about research. Their criteria of success were the logic they could marshal and the number of people they could convince, rather than the amount of objective research supporting their conclusions.

Much the same may be said for behavioral humanists such as McGregor, Bennis, Likert, and Argyris. Although trained as behavioral scientists these men have not always written in the realm of science—most have written both as scientists and as philosophers. On the other hand, the formulations of March and Simon, Berelson and Steiner, Price, and Thompson were written as scientific theory with the scientific value system clearly in mind. It is not surprising that they approximate it more closely. A principle is not established until the weight of evidence is overwhelming; most statements are labeled as hypotheses.

In contrast the term *principle* was used by the early classical writers in a way that had no clear relation to science at all. They were merely attempting to convince as many people as possible that their school of thought was the correct one.

Universality or Contingency?

This is not to say that the classical concepts cannot be restated in testable terms and subjected to systematic scientific investigation. As originally formulated and presented they were much closer to philosophy than science, but this does not necessarily mean that they cannot contribute to a useful set of scientific hypotheses. And it does not mean that these hypotheses must prove wrong when subjected to the test of research. To discard the classical principles entirely because they were not good science would be just as inappropriate as refusing to consider any of the newer behavioral science principles because "all the answers are in already."

On one score, however, serious doubt may be raised regarding the classical principles. This is the matter of universality of application. We have seen that management functions are not the same in all jobs and organizations. It would seem to follow that the role prescriptions that will most effectively guide behavior are not the same either. In short, limits must be established within which statements might be expected to apply and outside which the theory cannot be expected to operate. Some progress has been made along these lines.

There is a large body of evidence indicating that for maximum goal attainment to occur, managerial role prescriptions must vary in response to the nature of the task to be performed and environmental constraints (34, 35). In general the classical principles seem most appropriate in stable manufacturing and production situations where labor unions are weak or nonexistent, and perhaps also in areas where unemployment is at a rather high level. As one moves to professional departments such as Research and

Development and to professional organizations per se, the classical principles require considerable modification if not outright rejection in favor of alternative approaches. This idea of contingency according to the requirements of the situation has been built into the behavioral science propositions developed by Price (47) and Thompson (58).

It is perhaps not too surprising that the classical concepts seem most applicable in manufacturing, with relatively weak unions and considerable unemployment. These were the conditions with which men such as Taylor, Fayol, Mooney, and Urwick had the most experience. They developed ideas to deal with what they knew. That these ideas now appear to lack universal application should not be totally unexpected.

Table 3–1 Management Practices Positively Related to Success of Social Fraternities

Practices Concerning Planning (and organizing)
    Extent to which short-range goals of a definite nature existed
    Length of advance planning period for social events
    Existence of a definite social calendar
    Utilization of the position of assistant rush chairman
    Utilization of the position of assistant pledge trainer
    Presence of a formal program for orientation and assistance of new officers

Practices Concerning Directing
    Presence of an active alumni association among graduates of the chapter
    Years of experience possessed by Chapter Advisor
    Chapter rating of the Advisor's effectiveness
    Presence of an individual award for scholastic improvement
    Existence of other individual awards
    Publication of a regular chapter newsletter
    Extent to which committee members were chosen by the committee chairman

Practices Concerning Coordinating
    Extent to which a "group" feeling existed in the organization
    Degree to which members were willing to subordinate personal goals to organizational goals
    Frequency of chapter officer's meetings
    Degree of cooperation among undergraduate chapter officers as perceived by the president

Practices Concerning Controlling
    Existence of a social budget
    Presence of a regular financial budget
    Frequency and extent of financial reports given to chapter by treasurer
    Degree to which actual expenditures were compared with budgeted amounts
    Existence of a formal system for the evaluation of chapter activities and overall progress

Source: W. V. Muse, "The Universality of Management," *Academy of Management Journal*, Vol. 10 (1967), 181–183.

It is also evident that the limits of applicability for the classical concepts have not been established with finality. A recent study of 72 chapters of 11 social fraternities at 60 different colleges provides considerable support for the application of certain principles in the fraternity context (46). A list of various management practices found to be associated to a statistically significant degree with greater success as a chapter is presented in Table 3–1.

Although some of these practices seem unrelated to classical theory, others clearly are related to such concepts as the scalar chain, division of labor, subordination of individual interests, unity of action, and the exception principle. It seems evident that while contingency must be accepted over universality, we still have much to learn regarding the specific types of situations where various managerial role prescriptions are most appropriate. The organizational world is without doubt much more complex than Taylor or Fayol, or even Weber, perceived it to be.

From Management Philosophy to the Science of Management

The field of management is now going through a metamorphosis which is parallel to that occurring in the development of all sciences. Gradually a field of knowledge breaks away from its origins in philosophy, adopts the value system of science, and finally stands as a full-fledged science in its own right. Management appears to be somewhere in the transitional process between philosophy and science. An understanding of this transitional process seems essential if one is to comprehend the management field at the present time.

History of Science

Philosophy may be viewed as an effort to discover the ultimate nature of things through a process of systematic reflection. The term is also used to refer to a set of speculative beliefs or convictions. In either sense it departs from science in that it does not emphasize controlled research.

Management philosophy has been used to refer to such a wide variety of ideas that considerable confusion has resulted. Often the term has carried the implication of a pragmatic, action-oriented approach which is in many respects antithetical to the view of philosophy as systematic reflection and speculation (38). For our purposes we will view management philosophy as the attempt to discover the essential elements of managing organizations through systematic reflection.

Similar efforts characterized early work in the physical and biological sciences. Man had many conceptions regarding the nature of the universe and the world around him before physics, chemistry, astronomy, and biology assumed major roles in this regard. In each instance the desire for something more definite, for more valid understanding and prediction, led to the gradual development of a science where only an aspect of philosophy had been before.

At least in the social sciences it has been typical for the interval between the development within philosophy and emergence as a science completely divorced from philosophical origins to be marked by a great deal of conflict between various schools of thought (61). This is the time when true theory begins to emerge, but evidence to discriminate between conflicting theories is lacking. Because the needed research has not yet been completed, diatribe and invective often replace it. This is a phase; it tends to disappear when theories and hypotheses are adequately tested, when there is enough research evidence so that sophisticated rationalization is no longer of any avail.

Among the social sciences, psychology provides a good example of this historical process. Psychology traces its philosophical origins to the writings of such men as Descartes, Leibniz, Locke, Berkeley, Hume, Hartley, the Mills, Bain, Kant and Herbart (5). They dealt with topics which later became the subject of psychological theory and research. It was not until the 1870s that psychology as a science showed clear signs of emergence.

In the ensuing decades a variety of schools began to appear. By 1933 Heidbreder was able to describe *Seven Psychologies*; her chapter titles are descriptive (23).

> Titchener and Structuralism
> The Psychology of William James
> Functionalism and the University of Chicago
> Behaviorism
> Dynamic Psychology and Columbia University
> Gestalt Psychology
> Freud and the Psychoanalytic Movement

These schools, like those within management, tend to be identified with specific individuals and/or universities. With the deaths of founding fathers and changes in university faculties, the schools of psychological thought have gradually faded. It is not that they have disappeared; nor have they been replaced by other schools. Each has contributed in important ways to present knowledge. Yet no grand superschool or synthesis of conflicting views has appeared. It is simply that the outpouring of psychological research since World War II has caught up with the schools. As a result we know considerably more about which of the pronouncements from each school are correct, which are wrong, and which are unimportant.

Currently there is considerable development of theory in psychology, although many scholars would argue for more. However, a theory does not now typically accelerate into a school with polemics and counterpolemics. Rather, new theories are quickly subjected to the criterion of scientific research by which they stand or fall.

Schools of Management Thought

Management theory at the present time is clearly in the "schools" phase. There are a number of often-conflicting viewpoints and theories. As yet there is insufficient research to move the field entirely into science, completely divorced from philosophy. However, the amount of research is increasing, as is the degree of commitment to the scientific value system (12, 18). Given these trends, it may not be too long before such residuals of the schools as the bimodality between the behavioral sciences and other management views have completely disappeared.

For the moment, however, schools of management thought are very much a reality, and the management student who approaches the field without at least a minimal understanding of them does so at some risk. The major division is between the classical group and various behavioral science groups. Although the behavioral science schools have tended to attack the classical concepts, there has been an equal degree of conflict among certain of the behavioral groups.

Even the labels "behavioral" and "classical" are misleading (43). So-called behavioral scientists within the management context are not usually proponents of behaviorism within psychology. Many are sociologists, anthropologists, or political scientists and have little concern with psychology at all. Even among the psychologists a number are concerned with drawing inferences about human experience and thought (consciousness), not just behavior. Similarly the classical label does not necessarily identify a group whose views are static and time-bound. Many classical writers would be the last to claim unalterable allegiance to historic principles, and are deeply immersed in restating the classic concepts as scientific hypotheses and subjecting them to the test of research.

There have been many lists of the existing schools within management (2, 13, 21, 30, 33, 48, 50, 63). Some of these are deliberately partisan, attempting to bias the categorization in favor of a given school; others are attempts at descriptive objectivity. The listing which follows and the very brief descriptions are reasonably typical.

Classical. In general, schools are best described in terms of the views of their founders and major proponents. We have already considered a number of these in the classical area: Fayol, Urwick, R. C. Davis, Taylor, Mooney, and others. As these writings indicate, the classical school has primarily concerned itself with management functions and principles of management. It has allied itself closely with practicing managers.

The school thus has focused on input-output mediators, has given less attention to input and output processes, and practically no attention to constraining and facilitating factors in the external environment. Although the classical concepts are not characteristically stated in terms of role theory, they are easily translated as role prescriptions, role behavior, role ambiguity, and so on. Yet rather surprisingly, the writers of this school have dealt with human motivation in only a most rudimentary manner.

Human Relations. Because of its almost total lack of concern with management principles and functions, this school has received little attention in our discussions to date. The human relations school had its origins in the widely known studies conducted at the Western Electric Company's Hawthorne Works in Chicago from 1927 to 1932. Elton Mayo, a psychiatrist, is generally considered to be the founder of the school, and the most comprehensive report on the Hawthorne research is contained in Roethlisberger and Dickson's *Management and the Worker* (49). The academic base for the school was for many years Harvard University. Of the writings discussed in this and previous chapters, those of Chester Barnard come closest to the human relations viewpoint, although Barnard has also been claimed by both the classical and decision-making schools. Many of the human relations proponents identify themselves either as sociologists or as cultural anthropologists.

The focus of much of the writing is on production groups and first-line supervision, the same focus as that of Taylor. In fact, the human relations school appears to have arisen in reaction against scientific management. But there is a shift of emphasis to the natural group, norms of productivity, noneconomic rewards, and the effects of informal leadership. Self- and group-defined role prescriptions, which are at variance with those of the formal organization, are documented at length. The value structure is given considerable attention, and human relations training for supervisors is advocated as a means to improved communication and increased integration within the value structure, as well as between value and reward structures. The school has been very effective in drawing attention to motivational factors that the classical writers ignored or treated in a peripheral manner, but in other respects as a management theory, its coverage is decidedly limited. In addition there has been much controversy over the correct interpretation of the Hawthorne research (7, 53).

Structuralist. The structuralists trace their origins to Max Weber. This has probably been the predominant school within sociological organization theory. There has in fact been a lengthy warfare within sociology between the structuralists and the human relationists. In contrast to human relations, however, the structural school has had only limited criticism for the classical writings (13).

Historically the major concern of the structuralists has been with methods and approaches to the establishment of role prescriptions and concommitantly with aspects of the reward structure. As with the classical group there was little emphasis on input and output processes and environmental constraints. Since Weber, however, there has been considerable extension and broadening of the theory, so that now it includes many human relations concepts (13). In this form the structuralist school has to a large extent lost its separate identity.

Behavioral Humanist. The behavioral humanists were mentioned previously in connection with our discussion of criticisms of the classical principles. The school is strongly identified with two universities—Massachusetts Institute of Technology and the University of Michigan—both of which have at various times housed the Research Center for Group Dynamics. We have already discussed some of the contributions by Argyris, Likert, McGregor, and Bennis.

Although this school is closely related to human relations both conceptually and in terms of values, it is important to differentiate the two

(51). The behavioral humanists are primarily social psychologists, not sociologists. They look upon Kurt Lewin, not Elton Mayo, as the founder of their school. They, not the human relationists, introduced T-group or sensitivity training as a method of managerial improvement and organizational change. Furthermore, the school has come to take a much broader perspective on managing and the organization. It is concerned with input and output processes, with the external environment, as well as with mediator processes. It has tended to emphasize above all else the introduction of democracy in organizations—this is its identifying characteristic. The end desired is that people at lower levels have considerable influence on their own role prescriptions. At times the behavioral humanists have appeared to advocate abolishing hierarchy altogether.

Decision Making. Our final school is associated with the Carnegie Institute of Technology (now Carnegie-Mellon University) and includes such scholars as Herbert Simon, James March, and Richard Cyert. It owes much to Chester Barnard.

As the name implies, the primary focus is on managerial decision making, and also on quantative analysis. Information processing, the search for alternatives, coping with environmental constraints, and organizational learning are important concepts. The propositions developed by James Thompson are an extension of this viewpoint. Others have been concerned with developing mathematical models of and for decision making. At least in its more recent formulations the school has achieved a breadth of scope equal to that of the behavioral humanists.

Value Resolution

These schools present an extremely varied mix. In addition there are many writers concerned with management and organization theory who cannot appropriately be identified with any school. Among these are individuals whose contributions have been at least the equal of those made by the men we have been considering.

The choice of a school or writer to follow presents a serious dilemma. Managers need to make decisions now and they need guidelines. Scientists, however, are in a quite different position, and they should not make a choice as yet. "I don't know" remains the appropriate answer. When sufficient research has been compiled, the schools will fade of their own accord. That they have not faded is good evidence that the quantity and quality of our research to date is insufficient to render judgment.

There is some research, however. In the chapters that follow we will discuss this research in detail; we will consider existing knowledge in the management field in terms of the scientific value system. Inevitably the result will provide guidelines for managerial action. A number of these guidelines may subsequently prove erroneous, but when taken as a whole, there is no doubt they contribute to managerial decisions. We do know something from scientific research in the management field, and what we know can help to reduce uncertainty and risk even if it cannot eliminate them.

How far we have moved in the direction of scientific principles and laws is another matter. No amount of argument between conflicting schools—classical, human relations, structuralist, behavioral humanist, and decision making—is likely to achieve either consensus or truth. The ultimate value resolution in fields such as management has historically come only from scientific research.

Questions

1. If our value resolution proves correct and scientific research is the final arbiter, which among the schools of management thought are likely to see many of their views survive? Which very few? Why?
2. How do we differentiate among the structure, goals, method, assumptions, and rules of science?
3. Evaluate Fayol's principles of management in terms of the seven characteristics of good theory. What are your conclusions? Is this a fair evaluation?
4. How do the five schools of management thought discussed fall in terms of the distinction between behavioral science and nonbehavioral science approaches discussed in the Introduction? What factors associated with the development of these schools might account for the particular type of segmentation noted in the Introduction?
5. How do scientific and managerial decisions differ? Can you offer any evidence that a failure to understand these differences may have contributed to the confusion and conflict surrounding the principles of management?

References

1. Anderson, B. F. *The Psychology Experiment: An Introduction to the Scientific Method.* Belmont, Calif.: Wadsworth, 1966.
2. Bennis, W. G. *Changing Organizations.* New York: McGraw-Hill, 1966.

3. Berelson, B., and G. A. Steiner. *Human Behavior: An Inventory of Scientific Findings.* New York: Harcourt Brace & World, 1964.
4. Boddewyn, J. "Frederick Winslow Taylor Revisited." *Academy of Management Journal*, Vol. 4 (1961), 100–107.
5. Boring, E. G. *A History of Experimental Psychology.* New York: Appleton-Century-Crofts, 1950.
6. Brown, C. W., and E. E. Ghiselli. *Scientific Method in Psychology.* New York: McGraw-Hill, 1955.
7. Carey, A. "The Hawthorne Studies: A Radical Criticism." *American Sociological Review*, Vol. 32 (1967), 403–416.
8. Church, A. H., and L. P. Alford. "The Principles of Management." *American Machinist*, Vol. 36 (1912), 857–861.
9. Cummings, L. L., and D. L. Harnett. "Managerial Problems and the Experimental Method." *Business Horizons*, Vol. 11 (1968), 41–48.
10. Davis, R. C. *The Fundamentals of Top Management.* New York: Harper, 1951.
11. Dubin, R. *Theory Building.* New York: Free Press, 1969.
12. Duncan, W. J. "Methodological Orientations and Management Theory: An Analysis of Academic Opinion." *Academy of Management Journal*, Vol. 13 (1970), 337–348.
13. Etzioni, A. *Modern Organizations.* Englewood Cliffs, N.J.: Prentice-Hall, 1964.
14. Evan, W. M. *Organizational Experiments: Laboratory and Field Research.* New York: Harper & Row, 1971.
15. Fayol, H. *General and Industrial Management.* London: Pitman, 1949.
16. Filipetti, G. *Industrial Management in Transition.* Homewood, Ill.: Irwin, 1953.
17. Filley, A. C., and R. J. House. *Managerial Process and Organizational Behavior.* Glenview, Ill.: Scott, Foresman, 1969.
18. Filley, A. C., and R. J. House. "Management and the Future." *Business Horizons*, Vol. 13 (1970), No. 2, 7–20.
19. Friedman, N. *The Social Nature of Psychological Research.* New York: Basic Books, 1967.
20. George, C. S. *The History of Management Thought.* Englewood Cliffs, N.J.: Prentice-Hall, 1968.
21. Gordon, P. J. "Transcend the Current Debate on Administrative Theory." *Academy of Management Journal*, Vol. 6 (1963), 290–302.
22. Graicunas, V. A. "Relationship in Organization." In L. Gulick and L. Urwick (eds.), *Papers on the Science of Administration.* New York: Institute of Public Administration, 1937.
23. Heidbreder, E. *Seven Psychologies.* New York: Appleton-Century-Crofts, 1933.

24. Hicks, H. G., and F. Goronzy. "On Methodology in the Study of Management and Organization." *Academy of Management Journal*, Vol. 10 (1967), 371–384.
25. Hough, L. *Modern Research for Administrative Decisions*. Englewood Cliffs, N.J.: Prentice-Hall, 1970.
26. House, R. J., and J. B. Miner. "Merging Management and Behavioral Theory: The Interaction Between Span of Control and Group Size." *Administrative Science Quarterly*, Vol. 14 (1969), 451–464.
27. Hoxie, R. F. *Scientific Management and Labor*. New York: Appleton-Century-Crofts, 1915.
28. Kakar, S. *Frederick Taylor: A Study in Personality and Innovation*. Cambridge, Mass.: The M.I.T. Press, 1970.
29. Kerlinger, F. N. *Foundations of Behavioral Research*. New York: Holt, Rinehart and Winston, 1964.
30. Koontz, H. "The Management Theory Jungle." *Academy of Management Journal*, Vol. 4 (1961), 174–188.
31. Koontz, H. *Toward a Unified Theory of Management*. New York: McGraw-Hill, 1964.
32. Koontz, H., and C. O'Donnell. *Principles of Management*. New York: McGraw-Hill, 1968.
33. Krupp, S. *Pattern in Organization Analysis: A Critical Examination*. Philadelphia: Chilton, 1961.
34. Lawrence, P. R., and J. W. Lorsch. *Organization and Environment: Managing Differentiation and Integration*. Boston: Division of Research, Harvard Business School, 1967.
35. Leavitt, H. J. "Management According to Task: Organizational Differentiation." *Management International*, No. 1 (1962), 13–22.
36. Likert, R. *New Patterns of Management*. New York: McGraw-Hill, 1961.
37. Likert, R. *The Human Organization*. New York: McGraw-Hill, 1967.
38. Litzinger, W. D., and T. E. Schaefer. "Perspective: Management Philosophy Enigma." *Academy of Management Journal*, Vol. 9 (1966), 337–343.
39. March, J. G., and H. A. Simon. *Organizations*. New York: Wiley, 1958.
40. Massie, J. L. "Management Theory." In J. G. March (ed.), *Handbook of Organizations*. Chicago: Rand McNally, 1965, pp. 387–422.
41. McGregor, D. *The Human Side of Enterprise*. New York: McGraw-Hill, 1960.
42. Miner, J. B. *The Management of Ineffective Performance*. New York: McGraw-Hill, 1963.
43. Miner, J. B. "The Psychologist's Impact Upon Collegiate Management Education." In P. J. Gordon (ed.), *Academy of Management Proceedings: Annual Meeting, 1963*. Academy of Management, 1964, pp. 62–68.
44. Mooney, J. D. *The Principles of Organization*. New York: Harper, 1947.

45. Murdick, R. G. *Business Research: Concept and Practice*. Scranton, Pa.: International Textbook, 1969.
46. Muse, W. V. "The Universality of Management." *Academy of Management Journal*, Vol. 10 (1967), 179–184.
47. Price, J. L. *Organizational Effectiveness: An Inventory of Propositions*. Homewood, Ill.: Irwin, 1968.
48. Pugh, D. S. "Modern Organization Theory: A Psychological and Sociological Study." *Psychological Bulletin*, Vol. 66 (1966), 235–251.
49. Roethlisberger, F. J., and W. J. Dickson. *Management and the Worker*. New York: Wiley, 1964.
50. Scott, W. G. "Technology and Organization Government: A Speculative Inquiry into the Functionality of Management Creeds." *Academy of Management Journal*, Vol. 11 (1968), 301–313.
51. Scott, W. G., and D. K. Hart. "The Moral Nature of Man in Organizations: A Comparative Analysis." *Academy of Management Journal*, Vol. 14 (1971), 241–255.
52. Selltiz, C., M. Jahoda, M. Deutsch, and S. W. Cook. *Research Methods in Social Relations*. New York: Holt, Rinehart and Winston, 1959.
53. Shepard, J. M. "On Alex Carey's Radical Criticism of the Hawthorne Studies." *Academy of Management Journal*, Vol. 14 (1971), 23–32.
54. Simon, H. A. *Administrative Behavior*. New York: Free Press, 1957.
55. Sloan, A. P. *My Years with General Motors*. Garden City, N.Y.: Doubleday, 1963.
56. Taylor, F. W. *Shop Management*. New York: Harper, 1911.
57. Taylor, F. W. *The Principles of Scientific Management*. New York: Harper, 1911.
58. Thompson, J. D. *Organizations in Action*. New York: McGraw-Hill, 1967.
59. Urwick, L. *The Elements of Administration*. New York: Harper, 1943.
60. Urwick, L. F. "Papers in the Science of Administration." *Academy of Management Journal*, Vol. 13 (1970), 361–371.
61. Wadia, M. S. *Management and the Behavioral Sciences*. Boston: Allyn & Bacon, 1968.
62. Weber, M. *The Theory of Social and Economic Organization*. Trans. A. M. Henderson and T. Parsons. Oxford: Oxford University Press, 1947.
63. Woolf, D. A. "The Management Theory Jungle Revisited." *Advanced Management Journal*, Vol. 30 (1965), No. 4, 6–15.

Part II
Planning: The Establishment of Role Prescriptions

A
Policy Planning

4 The Nature of Policy Planning

I. Definitions and Scope
 1. Planning as Role Formation
 2. History and Growth of Planning
 3. Place of Planning in the Organization Structure
 4. The Time Span of Planning

II. Effectiveness and Importance of Planning
 1. Research Evidence
  a. Studies of Top Management Planning
  b. Planning Below the Top Level
  c. Laboratory Research
 2. Factors in the Importance of Planning
 3. The Limits of Planning

III. Organizational and Self-established Plans
 1. Motivation to Implement Plans
 2. Management by Objectives
  a. The Nature of MBO
  b. Research Evidence
  c. Strengths and Weaknesses

The planning function is a major aspect of most managerial jobs, especially those at higher levels; consequently it has been the object of considerable discussion, both written and spoken. To a lesser degree, it has been an object for research as well. When the planning concept is widened to include organizing, as it has been in the research on management process, the volume of literature on the subject becomes very sizable indeed.

In order to synthesize this extensive material in a meaningful way, planning will be considered in its two aspects separately. Part II A deals with policy planning; Part II B with organization planning. This approach still maintains the essential unity of the planning function (1). Whether related to policies or to organization structure, all planning ultimately comes down to what an individual person is expected to do in the performance of his or her job. Thus it serves to provide role prescriptions, which will guide the role behavior of individuals.

Insofar as organizing, or organization planning, is concerned, planning becomes a matter of specifying what an individual is supposed to do in his particular position, as distinct from other positions. Within management this planning function is reflected in organization charts and similar statements of the jurisdictions, duties, and relationships of various managers. At lower levels organization planning is often supplemented by job analysis, which is typically a more detailed procedure for determining what an individual is expected to do in his job. Both organization planning and job analysis relate to the role prescriptions associated with particular positions in an organization (29).

In contrast, the role prescriptions that emanate from policy planning are not tied to specific positions. Typically they apply to large groups of individuals and positions; thus one speaks of marketing policies, manufacturing policies, and the like. Many such role prescriptions apply to all members of the organization, as with certain personnel policies. This distinction within the planning function between organization planning on the one hand and policy planning on the other is reflected in the fact that most companies have separate organizational units devoted to the two activities; hence it is an appropriate basis for organizing the discussion in this book.

Definitions and Scope

It has been common practice in considering planning to differentiate a number of types of plans. Thus distinctions are frequently made between objectives, policies, procedures, rules, programs, budgets, and strategies (17). These are said to differ in complexity, in level of abstraction, and in certain other respects. However, in practice it is often difficult to separate one from the other, and as a result a number of these terms have come to be used interchangeably.

The most significant feature of the different types of plans is that they represent role prescriptions which are formed to guide organization members in their work. All types have this in common. For present purposes there seems little point in differentiating further among them. Thus, the policy planning rubric will be used to encompass not only policies but what is normally meant by such terms as *objectives*, *procedures*, *rules*, and the like, as well. Frequently, the term *planning* will be used alone to refer to policy planning. This is in line with common usage.

Planning as Role Formation

There are a number of aspects of planning that derive directly from its definition as a role formation process within the theoretical framework described in Chapter 1. For one thing such role prescriptions are formulated to support operative goals insofar as possible. They are means to the end of goal attainment. Thus, in many of its applications the planning process starts with a definition of corporate task and maintenance goals. Plans for units within the organization are then developed with these more comprehensive goals in mind.

Second, like all role prescriptions, plans are statements of expectations. They indicate what people *should* do—not what they are doing or will in fact do. Role behavior does not necessarily equal role prescriptions, although it does tend to approximate expectations in varying degrees. Thus, planning is carried out to provide an indication of intent, to specify what kinds of things people should and should not do at different points in time.

Third, it is not appropriate to equate planning with change alone, as some writers have done (8). Frequently planning does involve a process of developing new role prescriptions which will be appropriate to the demands

Planning: The Establishment of Role Prescriptions

of a changing environment, or which will more effectively contribute to goal attainment under existing conditions. But there are other instances when, after all the evidence is collected and evaluated, a decision is made to stay with existing policies. In such cases planning is no less involved than when new role prescriptions are introduced.

Finally, it follows from the definition of planning as role formation that when reduced to the point of actual practice it is always a guide to individual behavior. Planning operates as an input-improving mediator. It attempts to elicit maximum motivation to contribute to goal achievement from an individual organization member. This point is important to stress because financial and technological planners have on occasion lost sight of it in their concern for matters associated with monetary and material resources (10). As a result of insufficient attention to motivational considerations (to formulating specific role prescriptions), people may not do what is expected of them, and extensive plans are never implemented.

Given these derivations from role theory, planning is probably best understood in terms of the structure and processes included in it. One model that has been developed to describe the scope of planning is presented in Figure 4–1 (38). Many of the elements of this model will be considered in this and the following chapters.

History and Growth of Planning

Prior to World War II formal planning was rarely attempted on anything but a short-range basis. There is no question that top-level managers often did give thought to the future of the company, but what we now consider formal planning was not characteristic. That is, plans were not prepared on a regular time cycle, with systematic procedures, using comprehensive data, by a group of people working together, and recorded in writing. Such formal planning as there was, was concerned with short-term market activities and related production schedules.

Since World War II there has been a continuing, and in many respects dramatic, expansion of planning efforts. Increasing numbers of companies have initiated activities in this area, and once initiated the proclivity for growth has been remarkable. The number of people involved in the planning process tends to increase, the amount of information utilized expands, and the time span of planning is extended further into the future.

It is not possible to pinpoint any one cause of this rather sudden blossoming of formal, long-range corporate planning. There have been marked

Figure 4-1 Structure and Process of Business Planning

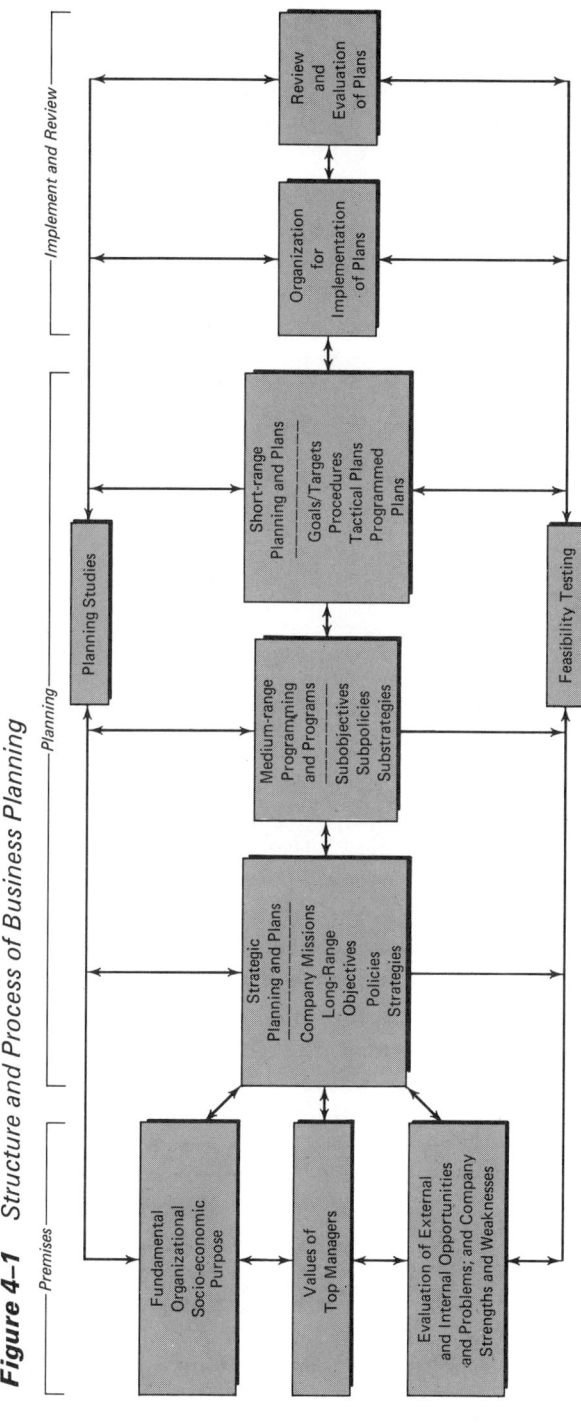

Source: G. A. Steiner, *Top Management Planning* (New York: Macmillan, 1969), p. 33.

advances in decision making and information-gathering procedures and technologies with the result that both the accuracy of forecasts and the effectiveness of plans based on them have increased. There has been an increasing feeling on the part of economists and managers that the economy can be controlled so that individual companies are not at the complete mercy of the business cycle. Thus, this major source of uncertainty is no longer considered so preeminent that long-term planning is pointless. At the same time other sources of uncertainty have been introduced with rapidly changing technologies and market environments. Increasingly managers have come to believe that these sources of uncertainty can be predicted with some accuracy and in fact that some effort to plan for a changing future may be absolutely essential to company survival and growth. Thus, ultimately, the boom in formal planning which has been particularly pronounced over the past 20 to 30 years seems to be best explained on the simple basis that managers have finally come to believe it will work (39).

It should not be assumed that all companies engage in planning of an equal scope. Table 4-1 presents data on the varying levels of planning sophistication among 35 firms in the paint and varnish industry (20). Only 23 percent of the companies had highly developed plans in every respect. These tended to be larger organizations in terms of number of employees and those that were strongly oriented toward research rather than market penetration and development alone as a basis for growth. Many of the companies failed to develop formalized written procedures to implement plans; that is, they did not establish definite role prescriptions as a basis for action. Furthermore, there was a tendency to limit planning to certain functional areas of the business, almost invariably marketing and finance. The data suggest that roughly 37 percent of these companies had not carried planning much beyond what was described as the typical state of the planning process prior to World War II. However, in much larger corporations than those represented in the paint and varnish industry, planning—much of it at a very sophisticated level—has become almost universal (11).

Place of Planning in the Organization Structure

Planning may be carried out by managers as one among the various functions they perform and/or it may be specialized in groups which devote

Table 4-1 Extent of Variations in Sophistication of Operational Plans in Relation to Strategy Emphasis and Company Size

Level of Sophistication of Operational Plans	Strategy Emphasis		Number of Employees		
	Marketing	Research	1–49	50–249	250+
V. Formal short-range plans were established Formal long-range plans were composed of programs in more than two areas of functional specialization Formal procedures were established to implement programs	1	7	1	1	6
IV. Formal short-range plans were established Formal long-range plans were composed of programs in more than two areas of functional specialization No formal procedures were established to implement programs	1	6	4	2	1
III. Formal short-range plans were established Formal long-range plans were composed of programs in only one or two areas of functional specialization No formal procedures were established to implement programs	7	0	2	1	4
II. Formal short-range plans were established Informal long-range plans were composed of programs in only one or two areas of functional specialization No formal procedures were established to implement programs	8	0	2	5	1
I. Informal short-range plans were established Informal long-range plans were composed of programs in only one or two areas of functional specialization No formal procedures were established to implement programs	4	1	4	1	0

Source: Adapted from R. J. Litschert, "Some Characteristics of Long-Range Planning: An Industry Study," *Academy of Management Journal*, Vol. 11 (1968), 321, 322, 327.

almost all of their time to planning activities. The organizational structures used to accomplish planning are extremely varied (37). Examples of four common alternatives are given in Figure 4–2. These can be viewed as stages in the development of a planning operation from relatively low to high levels of sophistication and complexity (25). However, many companies stabilize their planning organizations at various points short of introducing planning committees and groups at both the corporate and divisional levels.

Planning: The Establishment of Role Prescriptions

As indicated in Chapter 2, planning is a function that appears to require a greater amount of a manager's time the higher the level of his position. Certainly, short-range planning is inherent in most managerial jobs on either an informal or formal basis. But long-range planning tends to emerge primarily at the top of the organization. It is a major concern of most chief executives and many at the vice-presidential level.

Typically a chief executive is involved in planning activities in conjunction with a corporate planning committee whose members are also

Figure 4-2 *Planning Organizations of Varying Degrees of Complexity*

Figure 4-2 *(Cont.)*

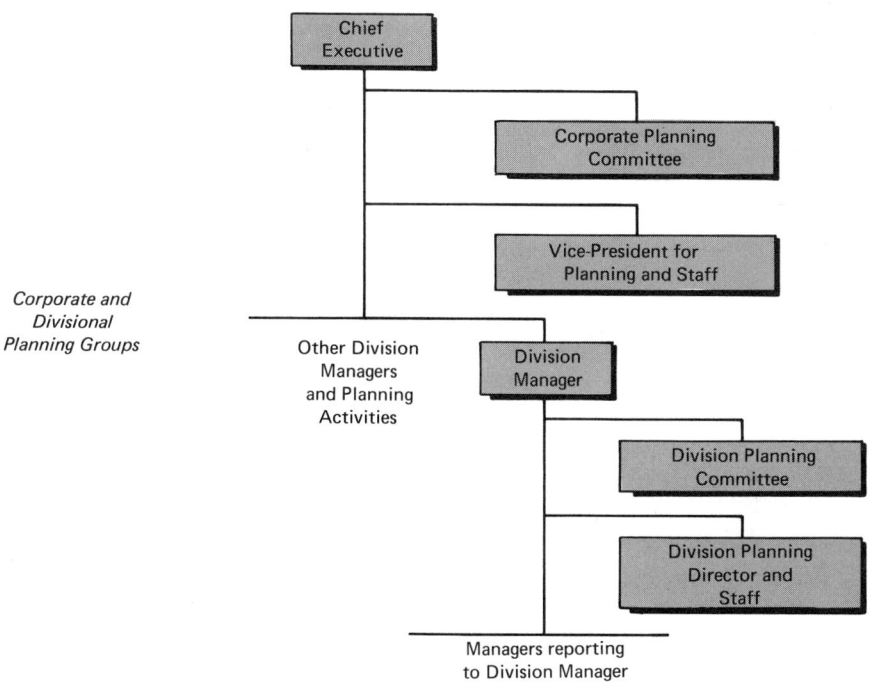

senior executives of the company. Chief executives and other members of top management may spend over 50 percent of their time in planning, although the average would appear to be well below that figure—perhaps as low as 25 percent (38). In general the chief executive is most heavily involved in planning activities toward the beginning and at the end of a particular planning effort (11). His initial concern tends to be with overall corporate objectives and general guidelines for planning; his later concern is with review and approval of specific plans.

Where planning groups exist they may report to a planning committee or now more frequently to a single executive at either the corporate or divisional level (21) (as in Figure 4–2). Usually planning groups operate in an advisory capacity and as a source of information, with decision-making authority residing with senior executives. On occasion, however, such groups actually "make" plans. The group may consist only of the director and his secretary or it may be a rather large unit containing a variety of specialists. In the latter case the scope of activities carried out can be quite large, as indicated by the following list:

Study ways of entering new markets and expanding into new product lines.
Recommend regarding product planning, pricing, and promotion.
Collect information on business and economic conditions as they affect the firm.
Forecast future market volume.
Study distribution trends.
Define the firm's existing markets both by size and by characteristics.
Appraise and implement acquisitions.
Recommend regarding staffing needs.
Survey changing customer actions, attitudes toward the company, and views of its products.
Collect information on new developments in science and engineering of possible relevance for the firm.
Maintain up-to-date information on the activities of present and prospective competitors.
Study legal and political trends that may influence the company.

As might be expected, the members of planning groups tend to have varied backgrounds. However, there is a tendency to stress advanced degrees and educational specialization which is directly relevant to the technology employed in making the company's products (19). It is not uncommon for senior members of planning groups to have M.B.A. degrees or doctorates; backgrounds in economics, market research, and research and development are frequent.

The Time Span of Planning

To this point the discussion has often touched on short- and long-range planning without being very specific on these matters. What is the time span over which companies may plan?

The answer appears to be that there are sizable variations among companies and between different aspects of a single company's operations. The average period over which planning occurs now appears to be approximately five years (38), although this period is lengthening and may well reach ten years in the not far distant future (11).

There are a number of considerations that influence the length of the planning period for a given firm or in a particular aspect of its operation. Most obvious is the degree of uncertainty in forecasts and predictions. If beyond a certain period of time in the future predictive efficiency drops to a level little better than guesswork, there is nothing to be gained in evolving a complex set of plans for the unpredictable period. Thus it is not uncommon to restrict planning related to consumer markets to three years simply because for many products these markets may become nearly unpredictable beyond that point. Almost without exception predictive efficiency falls off over time; sometimes it decreases sharply.

The time span of planning is also influenced by need. In product planning the time required to get a new product established in a market becomes a crucial factor in the length of planning periods. One of the major values of planning is that it indicates what role prescriptions must be established today if a certain event, such as the introduction of a new product, is to occur at a particular time in the future. Thus planning periods are strongly influenced by considerations related to inventing, engineering, producing, and marketing new products. When one is concerned with developing a new type of aircraft, for example, this factor may force a rather long planning period, if the effort is ever to get under way at all.

Finally, factors that are absolutely crucial to a company's survival and growth may well elicit more extended planning than other factors. Thus, wood products firms often tend to plan with regard to timber resources for periods extending over 50 years into the future. Similar long-range planning is frequent in other firms that are dependent on a particular type of natural resource which might be in short supply. The prospect that some new technology or product might replace one currently in use—as petroleum products have increasingly supplanted coal and the airlines have supplanted long-distance railroad travel—also tends to call for planning over an extended time period.

On occasion one finds extensive use of contingencies in planning. Thus many companies have developed detailed strike plans to apply only if a strike occurs. Such plans may vary further depending on whether members of nonstriking unions or nonunion employees do or do not cross the picket lines of the union calling the strike. Flexibility of this kind can be a major advantage in that it protects against the possibility of being faced with a totally unexpected situation and having to formulate role prescriptions on the spot without adequate time for information gathering and consideration.

Furthermore planning is frequently carried out on a continuing basis with constant recycling and reevaluation. Under this procedure the plan in effect at any given time is the best possible plan for the future that can be devised based on the latest available forecasts of events to come. This approach points up the fact that it is usually desirable to withold the formalization of plans until it is necessary to do so. Initiating plans before any advantage can be gained from them serves to reduce flexibility, and thus makes it harder to adjust to changed circumstances not covered by prior forecasts.

That some companies do little contingency planning or continuous recycling reflects the very sizable costs associated with flexibility. The cost of the human resources required to build planning staffs can be sizable. Flexibility may also be obtained by "covering one's bets," as for instance when land for a manufacturing plant is acquired in two locations because of uncertainty as to where a major market expansion will occur. Here, too, flexibility may well be costly.

Effectiveness and Importance of Planning

In the preceding section the discussion was largely descriptive. On all dimensions considered significant, variations in planning efforts have been noted. The question remains what type of planning is most effective in achieving organizational goals. One may even ask whether planning is of any demonstrated value at all.

A frequent theme in the management literature and in many speeches has been the need to engage in some kind of formal planning (49). Again and again in articles, books, and lectures, advocates have extolled the virtues of planning and argued for major investments of money, time, and effort to this end. As we have seen, the result has been a steady expansion in planning activities in recent years.

To a degree at least this growth has been based on faith. It makes sense that planning should aid a company, and logical derivations from role theory and integration theory tend to support it, but only a limited amount of systematic research has been done on the topic and most of that is of recent origin. Clearly many companies have committed themselves heavily to formal planning without benefit of definite knowledge of its effectiveness.

Research Evidence

Several studies bear primarily on the question of whether doing more planning rather than less (or none) contributes to managerial effectiveness and to increased organizational goal attainment. In a few instances implications regarding the relative effectiveness of different approaches in planning are present in the research as well.

Studies of Top Management Planning. One important study involved the administration of a questionnaire to 217 vice-presidents from 109 of the largest American corporations (36). Of the questions asked, four appear to relate to formal planning; the others relate to corporate decision making more broadly conceived. The answers to the four planning questions were compared for vice-presidents in the more successful firms and in the less successful. Success was measured separately in terms of profit as a percent of sales, profit as a percent of invested capital, and size (as a reflection of growth). The results, as indicated in Table 4–2, consistently support the view that formal, shared planning at the top levels does contribute to corporate success. All four planning questions are strongly related to one or more of the success indexes.

Table 4–2 *Statistically Significant Relationships Between Questions Related to Planning and Indexes of Corporate Success*

Question	Success Index		
	Profit as Percent of Sales	Profit as Percent of Capital	Size
2. Concern over formal steps in decision making at top level (regular meetings, written records, etc.). (Much attention to formal routines)	X		
3. Estimates of cost and anticipated profit to result from a decision. (Always carefully computed)	X		X
4. Discussion among all top executives. (Yes)	X		
5. Use of top-level policy committee. (Yes, active)		X	X

Source: Adapted from R. Stagner, "Corporate Decision Making: An Empirical Study," *Journal of Applied Psychology,* Vol. 53 (1969), 10–11. Copyright 1969 by the American Psychological Association. Reproduced by permission.

A second study compared the goal attainments of companies with and without formal planning programs within six industries: metalworking, pharmaceutical, chemicals, food, steel, and oil (41). Within each industry companies were selected so as to be similar in sales volume and products sold. In all, 36 companies were studied in the six industries. Planning activity was determined by questionnaire. In the metalworking, pharmaceutical, and chemical industries the companies doing formal planning were found to be consistently more successful. In the food industry earnings per share of common stock and increases in stock prices were strongly associated with formal planning, but other profit and growth indexes were less so. In oil and steel there was nothing to suggest a relationship between formal planning and performance. Overall the study indicates that at least for many companies, planning can be of considerable value. In a number of instances a shift from informal planning to formal was followed by a marked improvement in industry position.

Planning Below the Top Level. Below the highest levels of management the most widely known studies bearing on the relationship between planning and success are the classic investigations by the personnel of the University of Michigan's Survey Research Center (15). One finding was that foremen of railroad section gangs who had better production records devoted more time to planning than those with poorer production records. This was true both for the foremen's own perception of time allocations and for the perception of their subordinates. Also, both foremen and production workers in a company making heavy agricultural and construction equipment perceived the level of the planning effort as being higher in the more effective work groups. These results are interpreted as indicating that attention given to planning yields a greater degree of coordination and ordering of work effort and thus a higher output level.

An extended review of the literature since the time the University of Michigan studies were carried out has yielded similar results (6). The studies noted are consistently positive in that they indicate a tendency for greater planning to be associated both with greater satisfaction with aspects of the work and with greater productivity. These researches used school principals and industrial supervisors as subjects.

The research findings, however, are not all positive. One study of civilian, middle managers employed by the United States Army produced no relationship between the extent to which the subjects perceived planning as "a part of their position" and ratings of performance effectiveness by superiors (16). The reasons for this finding are not clear. Perhaps there was a confusion between role prescriptions and role behavior; perhaps military organizations are unique. In any event it appears that there may be circumstances under which planning is not a complete blessing.

Laboratory Research. In addition to studies of managerial planning in its natural context, some research has been done in laboratory settings, using simulated conditions. In one instance comparisons were made between the productive efficiency of three groups: one group did no planning, one planned while they worked, and one preplanned their activities along the lines implied by policy planning in business (35). The results supported the view that planning is a positive force in work effectiveness. Those who did not plan performed poorly; those who preplanned did very well.

The fact that planning and doing resided in the same people in this study emerges as an important variable. In a later study, evidence was obtained indicating that planning of one's own work, at least where the task is complex, may be much superior to separation of planning and doing (2). In the business world it has been the usual practice to separate planners from implementers to some degree; although, as we shall see shortly, certain recent developments have run counter to this tendency. It now appears likely from the results of laboratory studies and from other evidence that at least with certain types of people, planning makes a greater contribution when it is done by those who are to carry out the planning—when individuals develop their own role prescriptions. This appears to be particularly true when the work requires a group or team effort (24).

Factors in the Importance of Planning

The research data indicate that under most circumstances planning is a positive force for organizational goal attainment. It is also true that a great many chief executives of large corporations view it as important. In one study, information was obtained from 280 chief executives distributed throughout the world on the relative *perceived* importance of external relations, meetings, planning, inspection and control, people, personal development, and any other activities (40). Over 65 percent ranked planning first, although they indicated that they were not able to spend as much time in planning as they felt its importance warranted. In general,

Planning: The Establishment of Role Prescriptions

United States executives stressed planning somewhat more than those from other countries. Given these findings, it remains to identify those specific forces that may make planning effective. At least six such factors may be identified.

1. Effectively done, planning can contribute to reduced role ambiguity and role conflict (see Chapter 1). When policy planning has been carried out, and clear role prescriptions have resulted, individuals are more likely to know what they are supposed to do and the probability that conflicting forces will push them in two directions at once is considerably reduced. For example, a policy of promotion from within means that a manager who is charged with making a promotion decision should not be uncertain whether to look for candidates within the ranks of the presently employed or outside the company, and he should not be subjected to conflicting pressures from two superiors, one of whom prefers an outside candidate and one of whom favors a present employee.
2. Closely allied to the first point, effective planning tends to limit arbitrary actions by individual superiors. Because plans typically are thought out rationally and are given considerable visibility, they are much more likely to be fair and equitable than individual decisions. If existing procedures call for a review of all compensation changes by a salary committee, the probability that a particular manager will be able to give his secretary an exorbitant and totally undeserved raise is considerably reduced.
3. Because role prescriptions are the ultimate result, planning leads to a reduction of uncertainty within the organization. Assuming that role behavior tends to follow role prescriptions to some degree, and it does, planning introduces a degree of predictability into a company. Individuals know what other people are likely to do under a given set of circumstances. If preliminary decisions have been made on which days are holidays and these decisions have been publicized, then a salesman is in a much better position to predict whether his boss will be available in his office on February 22 than would otherwise be the case.
4. Planning produces a greater capacity to deal with uncertainty in the environment external to a company, as well as internal uncertainty. Effective planning makes it much less likely that a company will be caught off guard and suffer accordingly. Thus positive adjustment to

a sudden shift in market demand is much more likely if such a shift has been forecast and new role prescriptions established for dealing with this contingency. Even if uncertainty remains high, in that no valid forecast is available, the existence of a plan that can be mobilized on short notice seems far superior to having to create a plan on the spot when the change first appears.
5. The very process of planning tends to lead to decision making that deals with more factors and takes more considerations into account. Systematic planning requires a look at a long list of variables which might influence events. Without such a systematic consideration of influences and alternatives, the likelihood that something of importance will be overlooked is very high. Thus planning by its very nature tends to force a manager to take into account factors that might not otherwise be considered, and to tie plans more closely to operative goals, both task and maintenance.
6. Planning is important in that it contributes to the performance of other management functions. Typically the tie between planning and control has been emphasized (5). Much has been written about the use of feedback mechanisms to achieve control of the plan, and there has been a tendency to list the close relationship between the two functions as one of the reasons that planning is important. Yet in terms of the model developed in Part I, there is no particular reason to emphasize controlling mediators any more than input-improving and input-sustaining mediators in relation to planning. Planning is certainly just as important for directing and coordinating as for controlling, and it has considerable importance for staffing and representing as well. Without role prescriptions to serve as a referent all management functions would be of limited value in that it would be very difficult to channel their effects toward goal attainment.

The Limits of Planning

Both the research evidence and logical arguments present a strong case for a sizable commitment to planning. What factors are there which might limit the extent of this commitment?

The first and most obvious limitation is inherent in the forecasting process. There is little to be gained from establishing an extensive framework of premises, plans, and policies based on forecasts that have little likelihood of coming true or staying true for any extended period of time.

If implementing a plan is dependent on a certain set of circumstances arising in the future and these circumstances never occur, then the planning effort becomes largely worthless. Contingency planning may cover a greater number of exigencies, but it is possible for even such broad-band planning to miss the true course of events. And when forecasting does fail completely a company *can* be worse off than if it had not planned at all—because it may be less likely to be ready to mobilize for sudden change.

Similarly, change may be so rapid that even correct forecasts do not stay true long enough to give the plans based on them a chance to operate at more than marginal levels of effectiveness. At the extreme a company's environment may change so drastically and frequently that most long-term planning is useless. A strategy of rapid adaptation is more to the point. This state of affairs has existed for varying periods of time during the last three decades in such industries as electronics, defense, and aerospace.

Planning is limited further in its effectiveness by the degree of implementation. Planning that produces role prescriptions that are not even approximated in behavior is of very little use. For planning to be of real value, planning and implementation must operate in close parallel, hand in glove (18). It is evident that this may not be the case, that resistances may develop, and that the effort devoted to planning may be vitiated. This matter of implementation will be considered at greater length in the next section and also in connection with organization planning. The conflict that may result from resistance will concern us in connection with the discussion of coordination.

Finally, planning is expensive in terms of time, money, and effort. It simply may not be possible to mobilize time, financial resources, and human work in the right combination to plan with maximum effectiveness. Planning may have to be curtailed, or it may be done poorly, because there are not enough people available with the time and skills needed, nor enough money to acquire such people. There are real limitations on the performance of all management functions. They operate with no less force on the process of policy planning.

Organizational and Self-established Plans

At several points in this chapter we have touched upon the fact that planning may be carried out in large part by the individual who is to do the implementing or it may be almost entirely divorced from implementation.

In the latter instance top management, a planning committee, and/or a planning group do most of the planning. In the terms of the model developed in Part I, this is the distinction between organizational role prescriptions and role prescriptions of a self-established nature, with the added understanding that only in rare instances will there be a pure case of one or the other.

Motivation to Implement Plans

The major argument for a heavy involvement of the implementer in the planning process is that motivation to implement will be increased. That the problem of failure to implement can be an important one is illustrated by an analysis of the fate of 95 industrial projects devised by national planners for a developing nation in Africa (27). Only 37 percent of the planned projects were actually initiated within the five-year planning period. Yet in this same period 37 projects which were not part of national planning were undertaken—a number approximately the same as the number of planned projects started. Clearly divorcing planning from implementing was associated frequently with no action; planning at the level of doing produced many projects that did come to fruition.

This tendency for participation in the decision-making or planning process to facilitate goal attainment has been noted frequently in the literature and there is a considerable amount of research dealing with the topic. It seems quite apparent from the data available that organizational maintenance is fostered (47). Participation in the planning phase leads to greater job satisfaction and greater acceptance of conclusions in many instances. Task accomplishment may be facilitated as well, but here the evidence is less consistent. It is not always true that participation produces greater productivity (30, 33). One study indicated that combining planning and implementation in the same person may be particularly important for more independent and less authoritarian people (46), but this too has not always been found to be true (42).

Irrespective of one's conclusions regarding participation, it does seem clear that when people have specific goals, of the kind planning can provide, they tend to perform more effectively than when they merely attempt to do their best (3). Individuals with low motivation for a job can improve their performance to equal those with much higher motivation, when they have specific, difficult goals to achieve. Furthermore, establishing goals tends to increase interest on boring tasks (22). The more difficult the goals are, the higher the intended level of achievement, the better the performance. One of the reasons participation does not consistently result in high performance is that the self-established goals often are not very difficult (23).

In a study of 51 entrepreneurs who had started small technically based companies in the Boston area, a definite relationship between high aspirations and success was established (48). Those with a strong need to achieve, the kind of people who establish difficult goals for themselves, typically headed firms that had experienced a well above average rate of sales growth. Growth rates for the firms of entrepreneurs who had moderate or low achievement motivation were considerably lower. This particular study is concerned with self-established goals, but the evidence from other research indicates that this is not a necessary condition. Goals set by others clearly can have positive effects (3).

Management by Objectives

The management by objectives (MBO) procedure was developed to foster the implementation of planning through an impact on individual motivation. It has tended to emphasize self-established role prescriptions almost from its beginning (26), although this does not appear to be an absolute requirement for successful application of the approach. The setting of specific planning goals in some manner is, however, inherent in the very nature of management by objectives (45).

The Nature of MBO. Although different companies utilize management by objectives in different ways, the following description is fairly typical (31):

1. The common goals for a given organizational unit are established by its manager in conjunction with his superior. A time span within which these goals are to be attained is set.
2. The unit manager then works out a set of objectives individually with each of his subordinate managers. These objectives are to govern their role behavior over the period.
3. All managers undertake the achievement of the planned goals.
4. Toward the end of the time period the actual performance of the individuals involved is measured against their individual goals.

Accomplishments and variances are discussed between subordinate and superior.

5. The cycle is repeated for each ensuing time period.

Figure 4–3 illustrates the total process in somewhat greater detail.

Figure 4–3 The Cycle of Management by Objectives

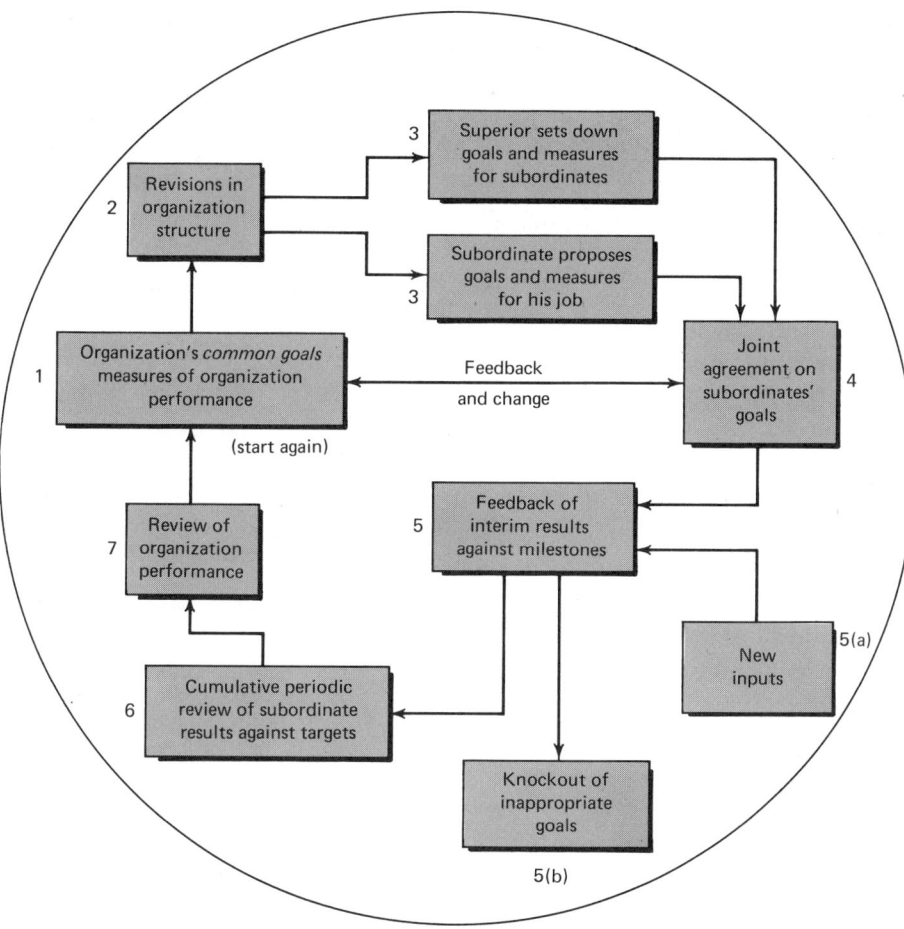

Source: G. S. Odiorne, *Management by Objectives* (New York: Pitman, 1965), p. 78.

Usually the goal setting starts at the top of the organization and moves downward to the lowest managerial levels. On occasion certain professional employees are included as well. At the top the major concern is with specific objectives (amount of profit, share of market, growth in assets, and the like). However, maintenance considerations are also reflected in goals related to employee attitudes and turnover, public relations, and so on.

In setting objectives every effort is made to make them as precise, specific, and concrete as possible. Within the personnel area the objectives of the top manager might be continuous operation (for labor relations), improvement in employee performance (for training), equity and competitiveness (for wage and salary administration), and so on. But at lower levels of management these broad objectives can become quite specific. They are often expressed in numerical terms and in relation to budget items. The goals typically relate to routine job performance, emergency situations, innovation and change, and personal development (31).

The actual goal setting for an individual manager may be done largely by the man himself or by his superior. There is tremendous variation on this point. At Honeywell, Inc., each manager establishes his own goals and in large part these goals taken together come to represent the goals of the unit, although they must fit within a framework established at the top of the company. At General Mills the process of goal setting is much more structured, with individuals being free to develop their own role prescriptions only within very specific responsibilities and accountabilities prepared at higher levels (50). In any case, irrespective of the degree of participation, there must be agreement and acceptance of the specific objectives by both the individual and his superior. Without this, the impact of goal setting on implementation is likely to be lost. The result would be considerable role conflict.

Management by objectives is not merely a method of planning (13). It is often used in connection with management appraisal programs, since objectives and role behavior are compared at the end of the time period. Compensation levels may be tied to the degree of goal-performnace discrepancy. The discussions between manager and subordinate may provide an ideal coaching opportunity and thus contribute to management development and training (32). However, for the present purposes it is the planning-implementation aspect of MBO that is of particular interest.

Research Evidence. An increasing amount of research is being conducted to determine how effective MBO is in achieving effective planning and implementation, and what are the relative values associated with different types of approaches.

The first major research effort in this area was conducted at General Electric, where comparisons were made between managers who operated under management by objectives and others who did not (7, 28). The results consistently indicated the desirability of goal setting as a planning process. They also provided some support for the use of a participative approach.

Yet it seems apparent that the degree to which a manager is likely to exert influence on his own role prescriptions is closely related to his position in the organization. Comparisons have been made between groups of managers on the extent to which role prescriptions are self-established (44). As indicated in Table 4–3 marketing and financial executives appear

Table 4–3 Extent of Subordinate Participation in Goal Setting in Different Functional Areas and at Different Managerial Levels

Managerial Groups	N	Mean Participation Score
Functional Area		
Marketing	19	2.15
Finance	5	2.00
Production	9	1.77
Development Engineering	9	1.55
Managerial Level		
Vice-President	3	3.00
Reporting to Vice-President	11	2.27
Middle Management	17	1.59
Lower Management	12	1.65

Source: H. L. Tosi, and S. J. Carroll, "Some Structural Factors Related to Goal Influence in the Management by Objectives Process," *MSU Business Topics*, Vol. 17 (1969), No. 2, 47–48. Reprinted by permission of the publisher, Division of Research, Graduate School of Business Administration, Michigan State University.

to be relatively free in this regard; those in production, and particularly development engineering, considerably less so. Even more striking is the variation with hierarchic level. Self-established role prescriptions are characteristic at the top, but lower down in management participation in setting objectives appears to become more difficult. This difficulty is in evidence even at the middle management level.

A more extensive analysis of the management by objectives program in this same company provides further information (4, 43). Questionnaires completed by 129 managers were used. The results deal with aspects of MBO which extend beyond planning, but only the latter aspect will concern us here. The most striking result is the emphasis on the need for goal clarity (low role conflict and ambiguity) if management by objectives is to be an effective planning procedure. The more mature and decisive individuals in particular benefited from clear-cut role prescriptions. Very difficult goals had positive consequences among those who were self-assured and mature, but not among those lacking in these characteristics. Participation in setting goals was important for the self-assured managers, but not for others.

Overall, the data of this study indicate that management by objectives will achieve its best results when tailored to the needs of specific individuals and groups. Every effort should be made to achieve clear and precise goals. How difficult these goals should be depends on the individual; so does the amount of participation in setting the goals. Only when thus adjusted to the person involved does MBO appear to achieve its full potential in fostering the implementation of plans. Yet there is also some evidence from this study that the positive motivational impact may be limited to the period when MBO is first introduced. There seems to be some fall off in effect as time goes on. This tendency toward reduced levels of effectiveness beyond the first year or so has also been noted in another study (34), but research to date has not clearly established its cause.

Strengths and Weaknesses. Based on the research evidence and the reports of users of the management by objectives technique, it is now possible to construct a reasonably comprehensive view of its strengths and weaknesses as a planning procedure and as a means to achieving effective implementation of plans.

The distinct strength of the approach is that it does appear to foster implementation—primarily because of the goal-setting aspect, but with many individuals as a result of participation as well. For the independent, self-assured person self-establishment of role prescriptions can be a strong source of motivation to contribute to an organization. It can also be a major factor in job satisfaction (14), and thus might be expected to reduce dissension and turnover.

The difficulties are less apparent but no less real. The major problems are inherent in the use of participation to maximize the motivational return on the investment in MBO. The self-established role prescriptions may not fit well with each other or with the task and maintenance goals of the

The Nature of Policy Planning

organization (9, 12). Organizational plans can be easily adjusted so that integration of effort toward goals is fostered. Policies and job requirements can be established in a way which will minimize conflict among individuals who might all desire to do the same tasks, and duplication of work effort can be held to reasonable levels. With the introduction of participation, adjusting the work of one manager to that of another becomes more difficult. In addition managers can become highly motivated to implement plans which, although of interest to them, may have little relationship to organizational goal achievement. As noted in Chapter 1 there are conditions under which permitting a man to establish his own role prescriptions can be a mixed blessing at best.

Having considered the definition of planning, its value, and the planning-implementation interaction, the discussion now turns to the actual development of plans. How, in fact, do companies go about planning—in addition to using management by objectives?

Questions

1. What is the relationship between self-established role prescriptions and management by objectives? What problems are associated with the use of self-established role prescriptions?
2. How do you account for the rapid growth of planning efforts, to the point where it is now generally agreed that planning has "arrived"? Is this true for all types of firms?
3. A steel company is considering instituting a major planning effort where it has previously done no formal planning at all. You are asked to advise on the matter. What evidence and arguments could you bring to bear in favor of the effort? What against it?
4. In what sense is planning a matter of establishing role prescriptions? What implications for the planning process follow from this type of definition? Distinguish between policy planning and organization planning in this regard.
5. What purposes may management by objectives serve in addition to planning?

References

1. Ackoff, R. L. *A Concept of Corporate Planning.* New York: Wiley, 1970.
2. Bass, B. M., and H. J. Leavitt. "Some Experiments in Planning and Operating." *Management Science,* Vol. 9 (1963), 574–585.

Planning: The Establishment of Role Prescriptions

3. Bryan, J. F., and E. A. Locke. "Goal Setting as a Means of Increasing Motivation." *Journal of Applied Psychology*, Vol. 51 (1967), 274–277.
4. Carroll, S. J., and H. L. Tosi. "Goal Characteristics and Personality Factors in a Management by Objectives Program." *Administrative Science Quarterly*, Vol. 15 (1970), 295–305.
5. Emery, J. C. *Organizational Planning and Control Systems—Theory and Technology*. New York: Macmillan, 1969.
6. Filley, A. C., and R. J. House. *Managerial Process and Organizational Behavior*. Glenview, Ill.: Scott, Foresman, 1969.
7. French, J. R. P., E. Kay, and H. H. Meyer. "Participation and the Appraisal System." *Human Relations*, Vol. 19 (1966), 3–20.
8. Friedman, J. "A Conceptual Model for the Analysis of Planning Behavior." *Administrative Science Quarterly*, Vol. 12 (1967), 225–252.
9. Glasner, D. M. "Patterns of Management by Results." *Business Horizons*, Vol. 12 (1969), No. 1, 37–40.
10. Gross, B. M. "What Are Your Organization's Objectives? A General Systems Approach to Planning." *Human Relations*, Vol. 18 (1965), 195–216.
11. Holden, P. E., C. A. Pederson, and G. E. Germane. *Top Management*. New York: McGraw-Hill, 1968.
12. Hughes, C. L. *Goal Setting*. New York: American Management Association, 1965.
13. Humble, J. W. *Management by Objectives in Action*. New York: McGraw-Hill, 1970.
14. Ivancevich, J. M., J. H. Donnelly, and H. L. Lyon. "A Study of the Impact of Management by Objectives on Perceived Need Satisfaction." *Personnel Psychology*, Vol. 23 (1970), 139–151.
15. Kahn, R. L., and D. Katz. "Leadership Practices in Relation to Productivity and Morale." In D. Cartwright and A. Zander (eds.), *Group Dynamics—Research and Theory*. 2nd ed. New York: Harper & Row, 1960, pp. 554–570.
16. Katzell, R. A., R. S. Barrett, D. H. Vann, and J. M. Hogan. "Organizational Correlates of Executive Roles." *Journal of Applied Psychology*, Vol. 52 (1968), 22–28.
17. Koontz, H., and C. O'Donnell. *Principles of Management—An Analysis of Managerial Functions*. New York: McGraw-Hill, 1968.
18. LeBreton, P. P. *General Administration: Planning and Implementation*. New York: Holt, Rinehart and Winston, 1965.
19. Litschert, R. J. "Some Characteristics of Organization for Long-Range Planning." *Academy of Management Journal*, Vol. 10 (1967), 247–256.
20. Litschert, R. J. "Some Characteristics of Long-Range Planning: An Industry Study." *Academy of Management Journal*, Vol. 11 (1968), 315–328.
21. Litschert, R. J. "The Structure of Long-Range Planning Groups." *Academy of Management Journal*, Vol. 14 (1971), 33–43.

22. Locke, E. A., and J. F. Bryan. "Performance Goals as Determinants of Level of Performance and Boredom." *Journal of Applied Psychology*, Vol. 51 (1967), 120–130.
23. Locke, E. A., J. F. Bryan, and L. M. Kendall, "Goals and Intentions as Mediators of the Effects of Monetary Incentives on Behavior." *Journal of Applied Psychology*, Vol. 52 (1968), 104–121.
24. Lundberg, C. C. "An Experiment Relating Form of Planning to the Nature of Task." In M. W. Frey (ed.), *Management Research and Practice, Proceedings of the Annual Conference*. Eastern Academy of Management, 1970, pp. 141–149.
25. Mason, R. H. "Developing a Planning Organization." *Business Horizons*, Vol. 12, (1969), No. 4, 61–69.
26. McGregor, D. "An Uneasy Look at Performance Appraisal." *Harvard Business Review*, Vol. 35 (1957), No. 3, 89–94.
27. McClelland, D. C., and D. G. Winter. *Motivating Economic Achievement*. New York: Free Press, 1969.
28. Meyer, H. H., E. Kay, and J. R. P. French. "Split Roles in Performance Appraisal." *Harvard Business Review*, Vol. 43 (1965), No. 1, 123–129.
29. Miner, J. B. *Personnel and Industrial Relations—A Managerial Approach*. New York: Macmillan, 1969.
30. Morse, N., and E. Reimer. "The Experimental Change of a Major Organizational Variable." *Journal of Abnormal and Social Psychology*, Vol. 52 (1956), 120–129.
31. Odiorne, G. S. *Management by Objectives*. New York: Pitman, 1965.
32. Odiorne, G. S. *Training by Objectives*. New York: Macmillan, 1970.
33. Powell, R. M., and J. L. Schlacter, "Participative Management—A Panacea?" *Academy of Management Journal*, Vol. 14 (1971), 165–173.
34. Raia, A. P. "A Second Look at Goals and Controls." *California Management Review*, Vol. 8 (1966), No. 4, 49–58.
35. Shure, G. H., M. S. Rogers, I. M. Larsen, and J. Tassone. "Group Planning and Task Effectiveness." *Sociometry*, Vol. 25 (1962), 263–282.
36. Stagner, R. "Corporate Decision Making: An Empirical Study." *Journal of Applied Psychology*, Vol. 53 (1969), 1–13.
37. Steiner, G. A. *Managerial Long-Range Planning*. New York: McGraw-Hill, 1963.
38. Steiner, G. A. *Top Management Planning*. New York: Macmillan, 1969.
39. Steiner, G. A. "Rise of the Corporate Planner." *Harvard Business Review*, Vol. 48 (1970), No. 5, 133–139.
40. Stieglitz, H. *The Chief Executive—And His Job*. Personnel Policy Study No. 214. New York: National Industrial Conference Board, 1969.
41. Thune, S. S., and R. J. House. "Where Long-Range Planning Pays Off." *Business Horizons*, Vol. 13 (1970), No. 4, 81–87.

42. Tosi, H. L. "A Reexamination of Personality as a Determinant of the Effects of Participation." *Personnel Psychology*, Vol. 23 (1970), 91–99.
43. Tosi, H. L., and S. J. Carroll. "Managerial Reaction to Management by Objectives." *Academy of Management Journal*, Vol. 11 (1968), 415–426.
44. Tosi, H. L., and S. J. Carroll. "Some Structural Factors Related to Goal Influence in the Management by Objectives Process." *MSU Business Topics*, Vol. 17 (1969), No. 2, 45–50.
45. Tosi, H. L., J. R. Rizzo, and S. J. Carroll. "Setting Goals in Management by Objectives." *California Management Review*, Vol. 12 (1970), No. 4, 70–78.
46. Vroom, V. H. *Some Personality Determinants of the Effects of Participation.* Englewood Cliffs, N.J.: Prentice-Hall, 1960.
47. Vroom, V. H. *Work and Motivation.* New York: Wiley, 1964.
48. Wainer, H. A., and I. M. Rubin. "Motivation of Research and Development Entrepreneurs: Determinants of Company Success." *Journal of Applied Psychology*, Vol. 53 (1969), 178–184.
49. Warren, E. K. *Long-Range Planning: The Executive Viewpoint.* Englewood Cliffs, N.J.: Prentice-Hall, 1966.
50. Wikstrom, W. S. *Managing By—And With—Objectives.* Personnel Policy Study No. 212. New York: National Industrial Conference Board, 1968.

5 The Development of Plans

I. Formulating Role Prescriptions at the Top Level
1. Specific Goals, Objectives, and Strategies
2. Methods of Approach
   a. How Strategies Are Formed
   b. Strategic Factors
   c. Types of Strategies

II. Specific Policy Formulation and Acceptance
1. Making Specific Policies
   a. Influentials in Policy Formulation
   b. Policy Review
2. Budgeting
3. Acceptance of Policies

III. Forecasting
1. External and Internal Premises
2. Economic and Sales Forecasting
   a. Jury of Executive Opinion
   b. Sales Force Composite
   c. Users' Expectations
   d. Mathematical Analyses
3. Forecasting Innovations

It is often a long way from the top-level operative goals of an organization to the specific role prescriptions influencing the work behavior of a particular, lower-level employee. Ideally all role prescriptions consistently support goals; in practice this may well not occur. The more an individual's work deals with only a small fraction of the total effort, the more remote it is from the task and maintenance goals of the firm and the greater the possibility that the existing role prescriptions may, in fact, have no logical relationship to operative goals at all. They may even be antithetical to these goals, with the consequence that integration of effort is seriously compromised.

This chapter will consider the development of policy plans in two steps. The initial emphasis will be on planning at the very highest levels. Such planning is very close to the operative goals of the company. It tends to establish many of the role prescriptions for company officers directly. It deals with overall corporate objectives and strategies. In most organizations top management is heavily involved in this type of planning.

These broad plans are subsequently broken up into specific policies on their way down through the organization to become role prescriptions for individuals at the lower levels. Top management involvement tends to steadily decrease, and the problems associated with acceptance and implementation may well increase. Thus, because the problems are different and the individuals involved often are different too, the development of specific policies will be considered separately from the formulation of role prescriptions at the top levels of the organization.

In Chapter 2, in connection with the discussion of managerial functions, it was noted that Fayol included forecasting as an aspect of planning (9) and that later Urwick separated the two to treat them as coequal aspects of the managerial process (38). Here forecasting will be considered as a component of the planning function. Yet it is important to understand the differences involved. Forecasting is concerned with *predicting* what will happen in the future; planning is concerned with establishing role prescriptions which may be mobilized to deal with these predicted events. This process of forecasting as it relates to developing plans will be an additional matter of concern in this chapter.

Formulating Role Prescriptions at the Top Level

The discussion of goals—official and operative, task and maintenance—in Part I dealt largely with abstractions. But real companies operate in specific industries, producing and selling specific products and/or services. They deal with particular sets of environmental constraints and facilitators. They are to some degree limited by decisions that have been made in the past. Contrary to the assumptions of classical economic theory, most firms cannot now quickly rearrange their resources so as to produce a new product for which there is considerable customer demand when existing products fall out of favor. They are heavily committed to certain existing tasks.

Specific Goals, Objectives, and Strategies

Planning as it relates directly to specific company goals, external environments, and existing internal circumstances is the central focus of this section. Such planning is typically a top management concern.

The specific task goals of a company relate to the products and services it chooses to offer for sale to its customers or clients. The way in which these goals are conceptualized is important. It makes a difference, for example, whether a steamship company considers itself as engaged in the business of transporting passengers from place to place or as a factor in the resort and recreation industry. In our changing world, planning regarding lines of business requires a large share of the time of many top-level executives.

The operative task goals may not be identical with those of an official nature. A firm may contend it is doing one thing and actually be doing another. Thus, many employment agencies list themselves in telephone directories and elsewhere as management consulting firms. Yet for various reasons they do practically no management consulting in the usual sense, while devoting most of their energies to matching job applicants with suitable positions. Here the stated purpose of the business is not the actual one. Such deviations typically occur because the existing value structure, the personal values of top managers, and/or the capabilities within the organization do not support the official goals.

Planning: The Establishment of Role Prescriptions

A number of companies have devoted considerable time and effort to developing and publicizing statements of company creeds or philosophies. These indicate the business the firm views itself as being in, as well as its responsibilities to various groups. They thus have task and maintenance aspects. Yet it would be a mistake to believe that these statements are universally indicative of the specific, operative goals of the firm. In many cases what top management planning is actually directed toward diverges sharply from what the official creed implies.

In general, planning related to task goals involves some statement as to the point in future time when a desired state of affairs is to be achieved—when a certain share of the market for a given product will be attained, when the product should achieve a certain level of profitability. Typically definite objectives are set, in many cases along the lines of the management by objectives approach. These objectives may relate to profitability, sales, product introduction, financial matters, stabilizing the business, personnel development, organization structure, responsiveness to environmental changes, or research and development efforts (33). Examples would be:

Increase commercial sales so that five years hence they will equal sales to government.
Undertake a study to be completed in 18 months that will determine the market for petrochemicals in South America.
Initiate a research and development effort such that in five years an automobile engine outperforming those currently available will be marketable.

Although some writers take the view that such objective-setting is in fact part of the total strategy formulation process (19, 37), the position taken here is that strategies are methods developed to achieve specific objectives. They are means to the desired ends. Even within a given industry these strategies may differ significantly, and it is not always true that only one effective strategy exists to achieve the same objective. The two cosmetics firms, Avon Products and Revlon, both achieved impressive records by whatever criterion—return on investment, sales volume, growth—using very different strategies (7). Avon utilized an extensive network of saleswomen who sold in the home. Revlon stressed advertising and distribution along more conventional lines, but was able to achieve distinct product and brand images. Similarly the objective of developing a high-quality sales force, or some other employee component may be achieved by a strategy that emphasizes recruiting and selection. But given the appropriate circumstances a strategy that stresses investment in the training and development of existing personnel might give equally satisfactory results (23).

Methods of Approach

How do companies go about formulating strategies to achieve their objectives and foster goal accomplishment? Are there certain kinds of factors that appear to require particular attention in devising strategies? What are some of the more frequently used types of corporate strategies?

How Strategies Are Formed. Probably the most common approach to developing strategies is for a planning expert or top-level manager to apply his intuition and experience directly. In such cases the planner immerses himself in the problem and in the available information bearing on it, but does little to structure his efforts. Assumptions and personal values tend to exert a strong influence on the outcome, but little is done to make them explicit. This approach is inherent in many of the courses in business policy which place strong emphasis on the case method.

In contrast to this more intuitive procedure, another alternative used by some companies involves direct criticism of the planner's ideas. A presentation is made, to the planning committee or to some other top-level group, which attempts to argue for a particular strategy. Then the committee members seek to logically demolish the proposed approach. The assumption is that if the strategy holds up well under attack, it is worth accepting; if not, it should not be undertaken. Here underlying assumptions do tend to be revealed.

These approaches have been criticized on the one hand as overly responsive to incorrect assumptions and on the other hand as incapable of generating new assumptions once old ones are exposed and demolished. Instead a dialectical approach is proposed which utilizes a structured debate (21). A plan and a counterplan are established with advocates of each. Then the underlying assumptions of the two plans as they relate to the industry, product-market relationships, competitors, technologies, consumer reactions, and the like are explored. As each item of relevant information is introduced, it is interpreted by both opposing advocates as supporting evidence for their views. The result is not only a detailed look at the assumptions underlying a given strategy but in most cases either clear support for one alternative or a new composite approach that is superior to either one plan or the other.

Another approach to strategy formulation is also an attempt to overcome some of the difficulties inherent in the more intuitive procedures (2). A set of objectives is formulated and then the current position of the company on each is determined. Every effort is made to develop strategies that will serve to reduce the disparity between objective and existing reality. Prospective strategies are compared against this gap. If strategies have the capacity to eliminate the gap, they are accepted. If they appear to reduce it, they are provisionally accepted and additional strategies that will reduce it further are sought. If they have little impact on the gap or may actually increase it, they are discarded. Throughout this search for strategies assessments of both objectives and current position may be modified if new data suggest this should be done.

In all of these approaches the most difficult problem is ensuring that a clear choice finally be made. All too often only a collection of alternatives emerge from the strategic planning process (7). It is assumed that at some future date a resolution will occur. Often it does not. The result is that role ambiguity and role conflict remain high and integration of effort behind corporate operative goals does not occur.

Ideally this discussion of various approaches to strategy formulation would be supplemented by research data on which approaches are most effective, under what conditions and with what kinds of planners. In fact some research of this type has been initiated (41). However, it is still too early to reach definite conclusions based on scientific evidence.

Strategic Factors. In the course of developing corporate plans it is common practice to use checklists of the various factors that should be considered—those for which objectives should be set and strategies formulated. Such checklists focus on factors considered particularly strategic in the sense that they are of critical importance in the success or failure of the business. Actions, elements, or conditions of this kind may be outside the firm as well as within.

A survey of opinion among 259 executives holding responsible positions in 202 companies provides some interesting data on those factors considered particularly strategic for these firms (34). The executives were given a list of 71 factors which could be grouped into the categories of general managerial, financial, marketing, engineering and production, products, personnel, and materials. They were asked to rate each factor on a 6-point scale to indicate its importance for the success of their company over the next five years. This rating gave a measure of how strategic the factor was considered to be. In addition the executives carried out a similar rating process to indicate their opinions of the current performance of their company on each factor. Thus it was possible to compare the extent to which a factor was considered strategic with the degree of satisfaction with current performance in that area.

Figure 5–1 contains this comparative data for the ten factors that

Figure 5–1 *Mean Importance for 10 Strategic Factors Rated as of Greatest Future Importance Compared with Mean Satisfaction Ratings for Same Factors*

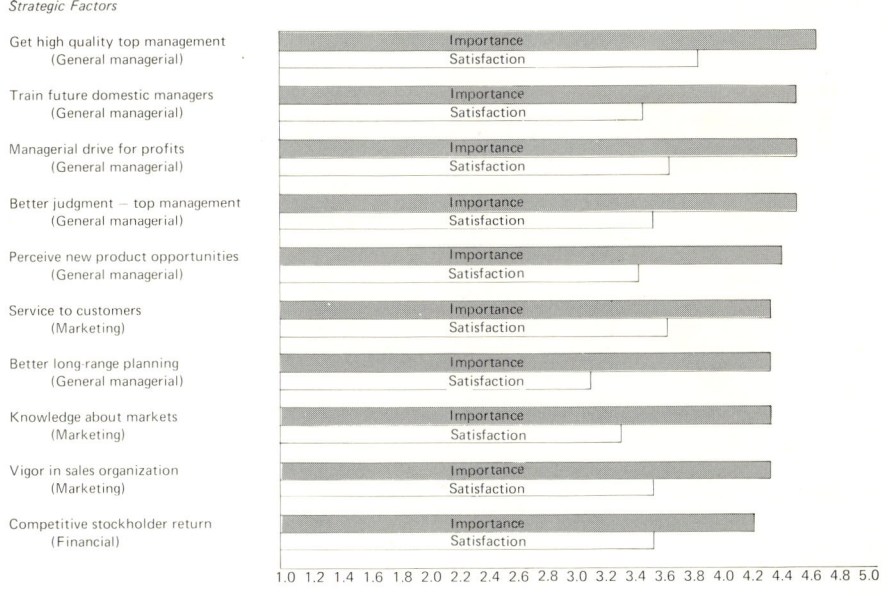

Source: Adapted from G. A. Steiner, *Strategic Factors in Business Success* (New York: Financial Executives Research Foundation, 1969), pp. 58–59.

received the highest mean importance ratings in the total group surveyed. It is clearly evident that factors in the general managerial category are most likely to be considered strategic and that marketing factors come next. There is a consistent pattern of higher ratings for importance than for satisfaction. On those factors considered to be most strategic these executives do not view their firms as currently doing an outstanding job.

Planning: The Establishment of Role Prescriptions

Figure 5–2 lists the ten factors that elicited the highest satisfaction ratings, those on which the companies were viewed as doing the best job. Only one factor (get high-quality top management) appears in both figures, and even here the importance ratings far outstrip those for satisfaction. The high satisfaction items are much more widely spread than the high importance items. However, there is some indication that current performance is viewed as particularly good in the financial area, and perhaps also in engineering and production.

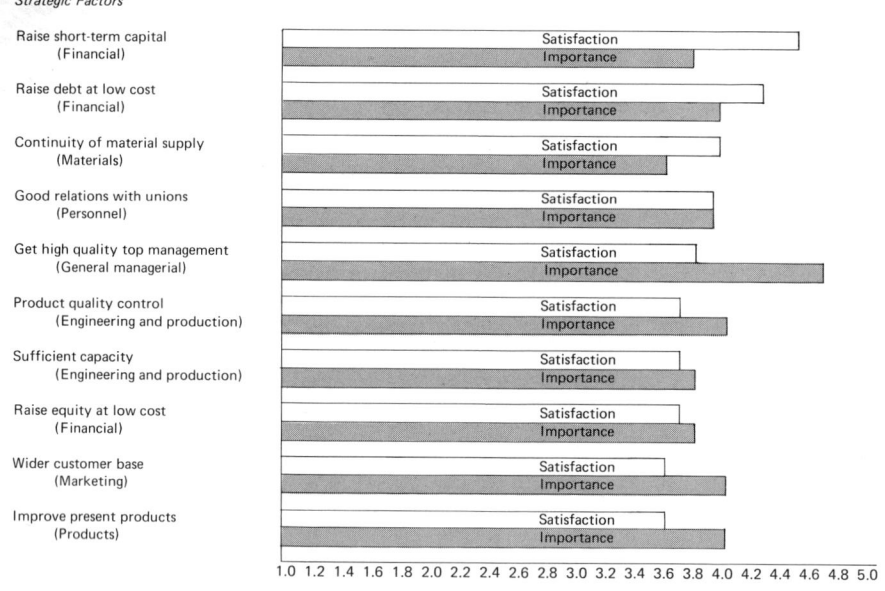

Figure 5–2 *Mean Satisfaction with Current Performance for 10 Strategic Factors Producing Highest Satisfaction Compared with Mean Importance Ratings for Same Factors*

Source: Adapted from G. A. Steiner, *Strategic Factors in Business Success* (New York: Financial Executives Research Foundation, 1969), pp. 58–59.

The data of Figures 5–1 and 5–2 are of course composite ratings by managers from many industries and from many functional specialties. They do not necessarily reflect the situation of a given manager in a particular company. Treasurers and controllers, for example, considered "Better overall control" more strategic than executives in corporate planning jobs did. Even more pronounced differences emerged between industries. Thus, "Better long-range planning" was viewed as very important in chemicals, electronics, and utilities; less so in financial institutions and pharmaceuticals. By contrast the differences between managers in various functional specialties were small.

Types of Strategies. A number of strategies are widely used to increase profits, but the one that occurs to most managers first is some type of growth (35). Growth may be achieved by further penetrating or saturating existing markets with products already being sold. In one investigation dealing with 53 companies that had exhibited rapid growth both in profits and sales, this approach was used by 98 percent of the companies studied (15). A second growth strategy involves selling new products in these same existing markets. This also proves to be a common route, with 80 percent of the firms studied utilizing it. Usually this type of growth is achieved through the generation of new products out of internal research, but acquisitions of other companies can be used for this purpose also.

In contrast to these "existing market" strategies the study of the 53 growth companies revealed considerably less use of "new market" strategies. Only 40 percent had employed an approach involving the introduction of new products in new markets. Such a strategy is often closely tied to a heavy investment in research and development that continually yields new and original products for which an appropriate market must be found. This is the strategy the duPont Company has followed for many years. However, the so-called conglomerates have also followed a new products in new markets strategy and done so almost entirely by acquisition.

Growth may also occur by expanding into new markets with existing products. In the study noted only 6 percent of the firms utilized this route to increase profits. Yet for certain types of businesses it may be the most common approach. Among management consultants, for instance, the major source of growth in recent years has been expansion into foreign markets, especially in Europe (16). McKinsey and Company, one of the more prestigious such firms, which for years had offices only in the United States, has increased its billings to clients dramatically in recent years by opening offices in England, France, Germany, Holland, Switzerland, Italy, Canada, Australia, Japan, and Mexico.

Although growth is widely employed as a means to profit, it does not necessarily have that result and, in fact, profits may be increased by selective contraction. Success can be achieved with a strategy that focuses on eliminating products where declining demand, increasing costs, or technological obsolescence are present (7). Such strategies appear to be used less frequently than they might. They are most common where a company is in serious financial trouble and needs to achieve a rapid turnaround. Other nongrowth strategies aimed at an increased profitability objective include cost reduction efforts, improvements in products, improvements in manufacturing processes, and changes in organizational structure or personnel.

Certain other types of strategies, which may or may not involve growth, should be noted. For instance, there are a number of companies that have adopted a strategy of minimal investment in research. Their intention is to move as rapidly as possible into new product areas and compete on price, but only *after* some other firm has developed and introduced the new product. Their strategy is to follow rather than to innovate (3).

Another approach emphasizes getting as much out of material resources as possible. Many firms are now marketing a large range of products primarily because their research efforts concentrated on using as much of a raw material as possible. Thus, in the petroleum industry refining is now carried out in such a way as to leave very little of the basic crude oil unused. Many petrochemicals are a result of this effort to extract the maximum in products from raw materials that already have been paid for. In the same way, existing markets, manufacturing facilities, computer facilities, cash reserves, and the like may be utilized to the maximum.

The conglomerate approach is also a strategy. Companies diversify by multiple acquisitions for many reasons:

To compensate for a decline in the existing business.
To find concerns with tax losses to offset high profit margins.
To invest excess cash reserves.
To expand in another industry when expansion in one's own industry is blocked by antitrust considerations.
To protect against possible future vulnerability in a limited market or product line.

As expressed these strategies do not appear to involve much conflict. But when they are reduced to specific long-range objectives and detailed role prescriptions, inconsistencies may emerge. If, for example, an objective is expressed in terms of return on investment, short-range profits may be taken at the expense of a long-term goal. Heavy investment in research

The Development of Plans

and development may severely limit a short-range profit objective. Customer service and satisfaction may require a sizeable inventory, which is antithetical to profitability considerations. Conflicts inevitably emerge as one moves to specific policy formulation.

Specific Policy Formulation and Acceptance

As policy formulation moves closer to the actual work roles of individuals throughout the organization, it takes on a number of characteristics which are not present in top-level strategic planning. Yet it is important to keep in mind that whatever the level of generality, policy planning remains a matter of establishing multiple role prescriptions (17). These multiple role prescriptions may be expressed as broad policies, as minor policies, as procedures, as standard operating plans, as rules, or in the form of budgets (33). Such terms differ primarily in the degree of specificity implied, although budgets have a sufficient number of unique characteristics to warrant separate treatment. As one moves to lower levels in the organization and more detailed role prescriptions, acceptance of policies by those to whom they will apply is likely to become an increasing problem.

Making Specific Policies

Numerous classifications of business policy areas have been developed—in some instances to provide an outline structure for policy guides, in other cases as a framework for textbooks on the subject. An example of the latter follows (26); a much more comprehensive listing is contained in Table 5–1.

Marketing policy
   a. Product line and customers
   b. Pricing
   c. Marketing mix policy
Research and development policy
Production policy
Procurement policy
Personnel and industrial relations policy
Financial policy
   a. Allocating capital
   b. Sources of capital
Mergers and acquisitions

Planning: The Establishment of Role Prescriptions

Table 5-1 *A Classification of Business Policy Areas*

I. General Management
  A. Divisions and functional staffs
    1. Authority and responsibility of Divisions concerning pricing, capital authorization, interdivisional transfers, product areas, and authority retained in central headquarters
    2. Functional staff relationships at headquarters and authority in divisions
  B. Growth
    1. Sales rate
    2. Profit rate
    3. Acquisitions
  C. Planning
    1. Budgets
    2. Company basic lines of business
    3. Comprehensive planning
    4. Organization
  D. Policy authority and statements
  E. Miscellaneous
    1. Acceptance of gifts or services by employees
    2. Answering correspondence
    3. Computer procurement
    4. Disaster control
    5. Employment of consultants
    6. Gifts and gratuities to government and company personnel
    7. Internal auditor reports
    8. Political activities of managers
    9. Records management

II. Marketing
  A. Products and services sold
    1. Types
    2. Inventory of parts
    3. Licensing
    4. Modification
    5. Quality
    6. Warranty
  B. Customers
    1. Contract clearance
    2. Export sales
    3. Interdivisional transfers
    4. Market areas
    5. Market channels
    6. Relations with customers, including dealers and distributors
    7. Service for customers
    8. Size of customers
  C. Pricing
    1. Authority to price
    2. Compliance with antitrust laws

Table 5-1 *(Continued)*

        3. Discounting
        4. Resale price maintenance
        5. Timing of price change
    D. Sales promotion
        1. Advertising media
        2. Product publicity

III. Production
    A. Assignments of products to divisions
    B. Contracting
    C. Manufacturing methods
    D. Production control
    E. Production planning
    F. Quality control
    G. Safety
    H. Shipping
    I. Size of production runs
    J. Stabilization of production
    K. Tooling

IV. Procurement
    A. Make-or-buy decisions
    B. Minimum procurement quantities
    C. Purchasing channels
    D. Relations with suppliers
    E. Types of vendors

V. Research
    A. Allocating funds
    B. Basic research
    C. Evaluating results
    D. Inventions
    E. Patents
    F. Research areas
    G. Research records
    H. Trademarks

VI. Finance
    A. Audit
    B. Budget
        1. Developing
        2. Controlling
    C. Credit
        1. Customers
        2. Employees
    D. Dividend policy
        1. Size relative to profit
        2. Stabilizing
    E. Expenditures
        1. Authority to spend company money
        2. Contributions and donations

Table 5-1 *(Continued)*

    F. Protecting capital
       1. Insurance
       2. Reserves
    G. Structure
       1. Debt ratios
       2. Long-term financing
       3. Short-term financing

VII. Facilities
    A. Decision-making process for expenditure
    B. Location
    C. Maintenance
    D. Replacement

VIII. Personnel
    A. Collective bargaining and union relations
    B. Communications systems
    C. Employment and recruiting
    D. Equal opportunities
    E. Hours of work
    F. Incentive and bonuses
    G. Pensions
    H. Selection
    I. Services
       1. Food service
       2. Health and safety
       3. Insurance
       4. Recreational and educational activities
       5. Retirement
       6. Sick leave
       7. Transportation and parking
    J. Training and education
    K. Wages and salaries
    L. Working conditions

IX. Public Relations
    A. Community
    B. Conflict of interests
    C. Contributions
    D. Determining contents of communications
    E. Extent of function
    F. Role of executives
    G. Selecting media for communications

X. Legal
    A. Clearance of contracts
    B. Compliance with law
    C. Patents for employee inventors
    D. Protection of property rights
    E. Reservation of rights and interests
    F. Real property leases

Source: G. A. Steiner, *Top Management Planning* (New York: Macmillan, 1969), pp. 272–273.

The Development of Plans

Specific policies need not be formulated in all areas noted, and in fact it would probably be undesirable to attempt to do so (33). Written policies in these various areas are often contained in policy guides or manuals, but certain policies may be stated in annual reports, the company charter, budgets, planning documents, employee handbooks, and union contracts. On occasion written statements do not exist at all. It is then that role ambiguity tends to be greatest.

Influentials in Policy Formulation. Where policies have companywide impact it is typical for the chief executive to assume responsibility for the ultimate decision, although various committees, top-level executives, and experts may exert considerable influence. When the policy is more restricted in scope, a wide variety of individuals extending far down in the organization may be involved. Thus, in contrast with the formulation of corporate objectives and strategies, specific policy making tends to draw upon a much larger group of people.

In addition to specific policy formulation at the top level to serve top-level purposes, policies may also result from an appeal upward by a manager who does not know what action to take in a given instance. A policy is then developed to deal with such cases. On occasion policies appear to emerge out of a long history of consistent actions. There is no real policy formulation in a conscious sense, but the course of previous events creates a set of role prescriptions, nevertheless. There are certain policies, which if not a direct consequence of external constraints and facilitators, at least appear to be almost inevitable in view of them.

Given the wide participation by many interested individuals and the significant role of special knowledge, it seems best to view specific policy formulation as an outcome of negotiation or bargaining with various influentials or opinion leaders playing a key role (4). On any given policy issue there are likely to be certain influential individuals who can exert leverage on the negotiations. Which particular individuals these are tends to depend on the specific issue (18). For example, the man with the greatest leverage as regards personnel policies is typically not able to exert the same leverage on financial policies.

Identifying the influentials in various policy areas within a company is not always an easy task. To some degree the job titles attached to management positions will serve as a guide, but this is not an entirely reliable approach. Often it is more meaningful to sample the opinions of a number of managers regarding who is really knowledgeable on various subjects, or if possible observe the influence process as it actually operates. Generally, where an integrated value structure exists in an organization, it can be assumed that the type of person who is valued is more likely to exert influence on negotiated policy.

Policy Review. It is difficult to know whether a policy, once established, is the right one—whether it will contribute the most to operative goals. There is even the possibility that in many cases there is no reason to prefer one alternative over another. Both may be equally good.

Policies rarely seem to be perfect. Almost without exception even the best policies have negative implications for the work performance of certain individuals under certain circumstances (13, 22). Thus a policy of promotion from within may serve to motivate existing personnel and assist in the retention of the better people. But on occasion such a policy will produce a situation where a man who is the only possible candidate from within the company must be advanced, even though the promotion places him in a position where he is "over his head" in either an intellectual or emotional sense.

Policy failures of this kind are to some degree inevitable. On occasion they can be avoided by a judicious use of exceptions. But when the number of failures accelerates to sizable proportions, changes may well be in order. However, there is a strong tendency for policies to become traditionalized and rigid to the point where revision is extremely difficult. It is often not the initial policy formulation that is the problem, but rather the continued existence of the policy in the face of changing circumstances (1). Once a policy has been in effect for some time and has demonstrated its value initially there is a tendency to accept it as good in its own right, without reference to the factors which led to its acceptance originally.

The solution generally proposed in such cases is the institution of some kind of continuing or periodic policy review, perhaps in conjunction with the planning cycle. Ideally policy reviews would be conducted as a regular part of the total policy-planning process; in practical reality this tends not to be the case. Such resistance to change was noted in Chapter 4, both in its relationship to policy planning and in relation to organization planning. It is a major factor in the way organizations are managed, and will concern us at numerous points throughout this book.

Budgeting

Although before 1920 budgets were practically unheard of in American industry, they are now in almost universal use (31). A budget is a financial plan, a set of role prescriptions dealing with the future utilization and expenditure of financial resources. As such it may incorporate and even be a formal expression of many other specific goals and policies. A schematic representation of a comprehensive budgeting system, indicating the relationship to the planning process, is given in Figure 5–3. Such a system may be used to develop budgets for longer periods, but the one-year time span is characteristic (31, 40).

Like other specific policies, budgets can establish a standard against which role behavior may be measured. Usually, however, some method of introducing flexibility is provided so that the budgetary role prescriptions may be adjusted over time to keep them as consistent with operative goals as possible. One such approach is to permit supplemental budget requests if the original amount allocated to an organizational unit later appears to have been too low. Or alternative budgets may be prepared initially, the one used being dependent on the actual constraints imposed by external economic factors. Some firms do not use budgets for control purposes at all, but rather as suggested guidelines to be adhered to only to the extent subsequent events warrant. Finally, variable expense budgeting may be used such that expected costs of production are automatically adjusted as changes occur in sales and output.

Laboratory research suggests that the budgeting process is not free of political considerations (28). High-profit managers tend to receive the largest budget allocations, as might be expected. But all else being equal, those managers who attempt the greatest influence on the budget officer receive the most sizable amounts, and those who make the most accurate estimates also benefit. When all factors are combined the data indicate that managers whose projects are very profitable do best, in a budgetary sense, when they estimate costs and profits with accuracy and keep efforts to pressure budget officers for large allocations to a minimum. On the other hand, managers with unprofitable projects achieve larger budgets when they provide estimates biased in their own favor and when they plead strongly for large budgets. Under conditions where profitability is difficult to establish, as in universities and government, it seems likely that the second strategy would be most appropriate to the attainment of large budgetary consignments. From the point of view of organizational goal attainment,

Planning: The Establishment of Role Prescriptions

Figure 5–3 Development and Structure of a Budgeting System

Source: G. A. Welsch, *Budgeting: Profit Planning and Control* (Englewood Cliffs, N.J.: Prentice-Hall, 1964), p. 50.

however, a strong monetary commitment to units with managers who bias estimates and make strong influence attempts can be questioned. Other factors may, in fact, be more relevant.

Acceptance of Policies

In policy formulation generally there is a tendency for wide involvement to be typical. This is true in budgeting, where initial figures nearly always originate with the particular unit to which a budget will apply. It is true of other specific policies, procedures, rules, and so forth, as well. The assumption is that such participation in establishing role prescriptions will increase acceptance of policies and facilitate implementation, especially at lower levels of the organization where sizable gaps between role prescriptions and role behavior are most likely to emerge. It is also true, however, that widespread participation may lead to a greater diversity of viewpoints and knowledge being brought to bear, and thus to the development of better policies. Research on this point will be considered in Chapter 6.

The evidence that participation in developing policies aids in their acceptance is generally positive, although as noted in Chapter 4 there are numerous exceptions to the extreme view that considers participation a panacea for all ills under all circumstances (10). There is reason to believe that participation in specific policy formulation is most effective in the personnel area; less so in developing production policies (36).

Support for the use of participation in personnel policy formulation derives from a study conducted in the 1940s (20). The long-standing policy in a factory where pajamas were manufactured had been to refuse to employ women over the age of 30. A tightening of the labor market made it increasingly desirable to modify this policy. Yet initial efforts to accomplish this met considerable resistance. Older women were said to be slow workers, frequently absent, difficult to teach, and poor long-term employment risks. Exceptions among existing employees who had originally been hired under the age of 30 were attributed to long experience with the company.

Nevertheless, in spite of this widespread resistance, a policy change was eventually achieved and implementation did occur. The medium of change was to involve a number of managers in a research project they designed and carried out themselves comparing the effectiveness of younger and older female employees. The results indicated that the women over 30 were, if anything, superior in performance to those who were younger.

This participative research convinced the managers involved. A policy of no restrictions on the employment of women aged 30 and over was introduced and employment agencies were notified accordingly. At the same time a series of group discussions were conducted at the lowest levels of management. These eventually resulted in group decisions to support the policy change and to conduct additional research on the training of older workers. Thus widespread acceptance was achieved and implementation of the new policy fostered.

In studies such as this it is not always possible to be sure that participation in policy formulation is the crucial factor making for acceptance, although the likelihood that it is important remains high. Those who participate in developing a policy are more likely to understand it and know the reason for its existence. This increase in relevant knowledge may be an important element in the eventual acceptance of a policy. Furthermore, policies such as the one to hire older women, even though developed on a participative basis, are not likely to be introduced without top management support. This support in itself may remain a major factor in ultimate acceptance. Experience in the field of planning has consistently indicated that role prescriptions accepted at the highest levels and promulgated with the implication that sanctions will be mobilized behind them gain much wider acceptance than role prescriptions lacking this type of high-level support (5).

Forecasting

A major factor in the increased use of planning throughout industry in the past few decades has been the marked increase in the effectiveness of forecasting procedures. This improvement has been most pronounced in the two areas where it is most needed—in the prediction of broad economic trends and of product sales by individual companies. There has also developed a whole new area of forecasting concerned with the prediction of technological and other types of innovations.

External and Internal Premises

The term *premise* is used to refer to that which goes before or underlies the actual development of role prescriptions. Premises are the assumptions on which plans are predicated. A major source of premises is forecasting. Forecasts indicate what is to be expected in the future and thus provide a framework on which plans are built. But not all premises are forecasts. Thus a rule indicating how the planning process is to be carried out (a role prescription associated with a planning position) constitutes a planning premise to the same extent as a forecast of future changes in the economy.

Premises external to the firm relate to external constraints and facilitators. Which of these external premises will have particular significance for a specific company depends on the circumstances surrounding that business. Basic trends in the economy and governmental controls or regulations applied to business as a whole are important external premises for practically all firms. However, shifts in population between areas of the country, as, for instance, the outmigration from rural areas into the cities and the rapid rise in the number of residents in the state of California, may or may not be relevant. For the nation's telephone system these population shifts are crucial, since they signify the need for new exchanges and other facilities. For an exporter who markets in Europe they do not constitute significant external premises at all. Similarly the future availability of crude oil in various locations throughout the world would be a major premise for an oil company, but would clearly have no relevance for a great many other kinds of businesses.

External premises relate to events in the environment outside the firm such as changes in society's values and laws, in the economy, in resource availability, and in the marketplace. Internal premises relate to events occurring within the firm—the policies and organizational structures established, the capital investments made, and the like. Internal premises of this kind are associated with internal constraints and facilitators of the type considered in Chapter 1.

In many instances one set of plans will provide an internal premise for another set. Thus a company may intend to continue a policy of promotion from within in the foreseeable future. The resulting policy forecast provides a premise for recruiting plans. These plans will typically de-emphasize executive recruiting at the higher levels and concentrate on attracting individuals with considerable potential for advancement into lower-level, entry positions. Many internal premises are of this kind. They are forecasts of future role prescriptions.

Economic and Sales Forecasting

Although forecasting may relate to any aspect of a business, economic forecasts including sales appear to be both the most important and the most prevalent. In most large companies the job of developing forecasts is assigned to an individual or a group of individuals with considerable background in the field of economics.

In large corporations detailed sales forecasts are almost universal, and these forecasts are frequently developed with reference to predictions regarding both the economy as a whole and the particular industry. In smaller companies formal sales forecasting is much less prevalent and considerations related to the general economy are less likely to be taken into account (29).

General economic forecasting begins with estimates of the Gross National Product for various future years (6). The usual procedure is to project individual components (personal consumption expenditures, gross private domestic investment, net export of goods and services, government purchases of goods and services) and then combine the individual elements. Projections of this type are frequently reported in trade publications, business magazines, government publications, and university research bureau publications. Many larger companies, however, make their own general economic forecasts. Industry forecasts may be derived using the more general expectations for the economy as a base.

Sales forecasts move the level of analysis down one more step to the individual company. They are projections of anticipated sales of various products at various price levels. Techniques used include a jury of executive opinion, the sales force composite, the expectations of users, and a number of mathematical approaches (25). Some of these procedures are applicable to developing industry estimates as well as to individual company sales forecasts.

Jury of Executive Opinion. The procedure using a jury of executive opinion involves assembling the predictions of a number of top-level executives. The method by which these views are then combined varies. Simple averaging may be used to obtain the final forecasts; more frequently weighted averages giving greater emphasis to the views of the chief executive are employed. Information on sales, costs, profits, and the like is usually supplied to the members of the executive jury.

This approach tends to be highly subjective and forecasts obtained from it may be no more than guesswork. Yet where adequate data are obtained as a background for the estimates and averaging is used, there are advantages. The views of individuals who perceive the future from different vantage points and with different types of expertise are taken into account.

The averaging process minimizes the overall effects of extreme positions, which are particularly likely to be erroneous.

Ideally an approach such as this would rely most heavily on those individuals who were known to be the best forecasters. The jury would be selected to include those individuals who had particularly good foresight. Thus individual differences in forecasting ability would be taken into account. Unfortunately, however, the research necessary to identify such individuals has not been carried out. The management literature, although rich in discussions of types of plans and methods of planning, is rarely concerned with the matter of who plans best. The literature of individual psychology, where one might expect to find differences in ability to forecast considered, contains practically no treatment of planning at all (32).

Sales Force Composite. In the sales force composite method the basic data for sales forecasts are obtained from individual salesmen who fill out standard forms dealing with their own territories. These grass-roots estimates are reviewed, modified if necessary, and combined at successively higher levels of the organization. When coordinated with projections of advertising expenditures, product life-spans, and other data available at the corporate level, the salesmen's estimates can provide a useful forecast of the sales to be anticipated.

The most important determinant of the effectiveness of the method is the salesman himself. To the extent salesmen have the ability, motivation, and time to make valid forecasts for their own territories and products this method will succeed. Unfortunately very little is known regarding the relative effectiveness of salesmen and top executives in this type of forecasting. Thus adequate comparison of the sales force composite and executive jury approaches is not possible. On the surface, however, it would appear that combining the two methods might be superior to one alone, since each stresses somewhat different information and information sources.

Users' Expectations. A variation of the sales force composite involves going to customers for their estimates of future purchases, rather than relying on salesmen's assumptions in this regard. These customer expectations are not, of course, commitments to buy, and subsequent events may alter them drastically. The approach becomes cumbersome and expensive where the market is highly fragmented, and this is primarily applicable to industrial products. Under appropriate circumstances users' expectations probably provide better forecasts than salesmen's estimates, but the latter approach has much wider applicability.

Mathematical Analyses. The use of one or more mathematical forecasting methods does not preclude the use of other methods as well. In fact salesmen's estimates, users' expectations, and executive assumptions regarding the probabilities associated with various events may well be utilized as components in a mathematical analysis. As a rule the mathematical approaches are most appropriate for companies of larger size (12).

Time-series analysis is a mathematical approach which separates long-term growth trends, cyclical business fluctuations, and seasonal fluctuations. It shows the interaction between these three factors in the past and uses this information to develop projections for the future. Using this approach the forecasts obtained are firmly rooted in history. Unfortunately for forecasters, however, the future, especially the short-term future, is often far from a recapitulation of prior events. The time-series approach is unresponsive to the impact of new and changing circumstances.

Correlation analysis in its various forms attempts to establish relationships between product sales and other indicators. Where these other indicators can be estimated with some precision for various periods in the future, product sales can also be forecast, with knowledge of the underlying correlations (27). The American Radiator Company finds a close relationship between sales of many of its products and the issuance of new building permits. The Eli Lilly Company has established that there is a high correlation between industry drug sales and disposable personal income. A number of firms have been able to relate their own sales very closely to Gross National Product. Where the relationships established have logical meaning and have held over a considerable period of time, correlational analyses can provide very useful information; otherwise their value must be questioned.

Simulation models programmed for computers are finding increasing use in forecasting. The approach is basically econometric. It seeks to identify those factors that will affect sales and then by projecting these factors make a prediction of future events. In some cases, these models take the uncertainties of the future environment into account; in other cases, these uncertainties are ignored (24). Such methods often begin with masses of data related to a large number of factors and as a result a great many alternatives can be explored. It is essential that the forecasts emanating from such models be checked against reality for a period of time before being used. Like any theory those generated from mathematical models need to be tested before they can be assumed to be true.

Irrespective of the sales forecasting method employed—executive jury, sales force composite, users' expectations, or mathematical—experience has indicated something of the level of efficiency that can be anticipated (33). Short-term forecasts extending up to a calendar quarter should be accurate within a 2 percent margin. For periods up to a year, 5 percent variations are acceptable. Longer-range forecasts extending to five years can reasonably be expected to err in the 10 to 15 percent range for a company's products taken as a whole. Unfortunately for the planning process individual products may vary as much as 25 percent from their long-range forecasts. The general tendency is to underestimate sizable increases and thus to be excessively conservative (39).

Forecasting Innovations

In addition to its widespread use in predicting economic conditions and product sales, forecasting has also been used to develop planning premises in a number of other areas. Among these one of the most interesting is the area of technological and social innovation (30). What new inventions will be created and applied in the future and when will these events occur?

All of the methods discussed for sales forecasting have been applied in the field of technological and other innovations as well. In addition considerable use has been made of the informed judgments of panels of experts. This approach is not unlike the jury of executive opinion method described previously. It appears to be the most effective procedure yet devised for predicting future states of technological knowledge (33).

The name Delphi Method has been applied to one procedure for utilizing expert judgments which has proved particularly useful (8, 11). This method involves the repeated questioning of a group of experts either by interviewers or through questionnaires. It is designed to bring out the reasoning behind predictions. Often information, which is either asked for or implied as relevant by an expert, is provided between rounds of questions. An essential aspect of the approach is that the experts do not confront each other face-to-face. As a result the kind of closed minds that arguing often produces are avoided, and movement toward a common consensus tends to occur. In addition a single strong personality cannot dominate the forecasts.

Planning: The Establishment of Role Prescriptions

Some of the results of an application of the Delphi Method to forecasting employee benefits are presented in Table 5-2. Each of 22 experts received a series of three questionnaires (14). The first asked for graphical extrapolations of historical information dealing with the economy and for lists of the key developments viewed as having an impact on these extrapolations. The second questionnaire fed back all the data of the first and asked for reappraisals of the extrapolations. It also asked for assessments of the probability that the key developments would occur and of their impact on employee benefits. The final questionnaire contained the results of the second; also questions dealing specifically with predicted changes in existing benefits and the creation of new benefits by 1985. Information of this

Table 5-2 *Forecasts of Possible New Benefits by 1985 (Made in 1969)*

Benefit	Year of Earliest Occurrence	Years to General Use
Jobs guaranteed for everyone, with the government the employer of the last resort	1976	6
Maternity benefits for unwed mothers	1974	8
Optional retirement at age 55 with full benefits for all employees	Prior to 1976	6
Pension plans extended to include benefits for retirees such as recreation, education, residential costs, legal services	1972	10
Subsidized housing for employees	1972	10
More generous time off provisions (25 % increase) for civic and political activities	1972	10
More generous time off provisions (25 % increase) for personal reasons	1976	6
Shortening of workday through employer's permitting increased travel time to get to and from work	1972	4
Educational-leave pay available to employees whenever they choose to take such leave	1972	7–10 depending on course length
Several shorter workweeks during the year permitting, say, half a dozen mini-vacation weekends	1972	4
Selection of hours worked during the day and days worked during the week	Prior to 1982	
Credit assistance to all employees through "employer credit card" or cosigning of credit notes	Prior to 1982	
Closer attention to husband-wife vacations when both work	Prior to 1982	

Source: T. J. Gordon and R. E. LeBleu, "Employee Benefits, 1970–1985," *Harvard Business Review,* Vol. 48 (1970), No. 1, 99–101.

kind can be extremely useful in developing plans related to expenditures, facilities, and labor force requirements.

The matter of forecasting melds easily into the topic of decision making which will be of a concern in the next chapter. Both have come to be influenced increasingly by developments of a mathematical nature.

Questions

1. What is meant by the term *strategic factor* in planning? What types of factors are particularly likely to be strategic? List some of the strategic factors for an organization with which you are familiar.
2. Distinguish between external premises, internal premises, and forecasts. How does the concept of premise relate to the organizational model developed in Chapter 1?
3. The idea of influentials or opinion leaders was originally conceived to explain trends in consumer buying behavior. How can such a concept help in understanding policy formulation? Do you see any conflict between this approach and the use of policy review?
4. Select three methods of forecasting, describe each, and then list all advantages and disadvantages associated with the use of each. Would you want to modify these lists to any significant degree depending on the size of the company?
5. What advantages and disadvantages do you see associated with the widespread use of participation in budgeting and in policy making generally? Do the same advantages and disadvantages hold for the use of participation in forecasting?

References

1. Anshen, M. "Price Tags for Business Policies." *Harvard Business Review*, Vol. 38 (1960), No. 1, 71–78.
2. Ansoff, H. I. "A Quasi-Analytic Approach to the Business Strategy Problem." *Management Technology*, Vol. 4 (1964), No. 1, 67–77.
3. Ansoff, H. I., and J. M. Stewart. "Strategies for a Technology-Based Business." In R. Mann (ed.), *The Arts of Top Management*. New York: McGraw-Hill, 1971, pp. 290–307.
4. Bauer, R. A., and K. J. Gergen. *The Study of Policy Formation*. New York: Free Press, 1968.
5. Bell, E. C. "Practical Long-Range Planning." *Business Horizons*, Vol. 11 (1968), No. 6, 45–49.

6. Butler, W. F., and R. A. Kavesh. *How Business Economists Forecast.* Englewood Cliffs, N.J.: Prentice Hall, 1966.
7. Cannon, J. T. *Business Strategy and Policy.* New York: Harcourt, Brace & World, 1968.
8. Dalkey, N., and O. Helmer. "An Experimental Application of the Delphi Method to the Use of Experts." *Management Science*, Vol. 9 (1963), 458–467.
9. Fayol, H. *General and Industrial Management.* London: Pitman, 1949.
10. Filley, A. C., and R. J. House. *Managerial Process and Organizational Behavior.* Glenview, Ill.: Scott, Foresman, 1969.
11. Fusfeld, A. R., and R. N. Foster. "The Delphi Technique: Survey and Comment." *Business Horizons*, Vol. 14, (1971), No. 3, 63–74.
12. Gilmore, F. F. "Formulating Strategy in Smaller Companies." *Harvard Business Review*, Vol. 49 (1971), No. 3, 71–81.
13. Ginzberg, E., J. B. Miner, J. K. Anderson, S. W. Ginsburg, and J. L. Herma. *Breakdown and Recovery.* New York: Columbia University Press, 1959.
14. Gordon, T. J., and R. E. LeBleu. "Employee Benefits, 1970–1985." *Harvard Business Review*, Vol. 48 (1970), No. 1, 93–107.
15. Gutman, P. M. "Strategies for Growth." *California Management Review*, Vol. 6 (1964), No. 4.
16. Higdon, H. *The Business Healers.* New York: Random House, 1969.
17. Katz, D., and R. L. Kahn. *The Social Psychology of Organizations.* New York: Wiley, 1966.
18. Katz, E., and P. F. Lazarsfeld. *Personal Influence.* New York: Free Press, 1955.
19. Learned, E. P., C. R. Christensen, K. R. Andrews, and W. D. Guth. *Business Policy.* Homewood, Ill.: Irwin, 1969.
20. Marrow, A. J., and J. R. P. French. "Changing a Stereotype in Industry." *Journal of Social Issues*, Vol. 1 (1945), No. 3, 33–37.
21. Mason, R. O. "A Dialectical Approach to Strategic Planning." *Management Science*, Vol. 15 (1969), B403–414.
22. Miner, J. B. *The Management of Ineffective Performance.* New York: McGraw-Hill, 1963.
23. Miner, J. B. "An Input-Output Model for Personnel Strategies." *Business Horizons*, Vol. 12 (1969), No. 3, 71–78.
24. Muth, J. F. "Forecasting Models: Their Development and Implications for Decision Making." In M. P. Hottenstein and R. W. Millman (eds.), *Research Toward the Development of Management Thought. Proceedings of the 1966 Annual Meeting.* Academy of Management, 1967, pp. 108–114.
25. National Industrial Conference Board. *Forecasting Sales.* Studies in Business Policy No. 106. New York: the Board, 1963.
26. Newman, W. H., and J. P. Logan. *Strategy, Policy, and Central Management.* Cincinnati: South-Western, 1971.

27. Parker, G. G. C., and E. L. Segura. "How to Get a Better Forecast." *Harvard Business Review*, Vol. 49 (1971), No. 2, 99–109.
28. Pondy, L. R., and J. G. Birnberg. "An Experimental Study of the Allocation of Financial Resources Within Small, Hierarchical Task Groups." *Administrative Science Quarterly*, Vol. 14 (1969), 192–201.
29. Reichard, R. S. *Practical Techniques of Sales Forecasting*. New York: McGraw-Hill, 1966.
30. Roman, D. D. "Technological Forecasting in the Decision Process." *Academy of Management Journal*, Vol. 13 (1970), 127–138.
31. Sord, B. H., and G. A. Welsch. *Business Budgeting, A Survey of Management Planning and Control Practices*. New York: Controllership Foundation, 1958.
32. Stark, S. "Executive Foresight: Definitions, Illustrations, Importance." *Journal of Business*, Vol. 34 (1961), 31–44.
33. Steiner, G. A. *Top Management Planning*. New York: Macmillan, 1969.
34. Steiner, G. A. *Strategic Factors in Business Success*. New York: Financial Executives Research Foundation, 1969.
35. Stemp, I. *Corporate Growth Strategies*. New York: American Management Association, 1970.
36. Strauss, G., and E. Rosenstein. "Workers Participation: A Critical View." *Industrial Relations*, Vol. 9 (1970), 197–214.
37. Tilles, S. "How to Evaluate Corporate Strategy." *Harvard Business Review*, Vol. 41 (1963), No. 4, 111–121.
38. Urwick, L. *The Elements of Administration*. New York: Harper, 1943.
39. Vancil, R. F. "The Accuracy of Long-Range Planning." *Harvard Business Review*, Vol. 48 (1970), No. 5, 98–101.
40. Welsch, G. A. *Budgeting: Profit Planning and Control*. Englewood Cliffs, N.J.: Prentice-Hall, 1964.
41. Wheelwright, S. S. "Strategic Planning in the Small Business." *Business Horizons*, Vol. 14 (1971), No. 4, 51–58.

6 Decision-Making Tools and Processes

I. Economic Man and the Problem of Rationality
 1. Economic Man
 2. Administrative Man
 3. Relevant Research
    a. Evidence from Studies of Decisions
    b. Values and Decisions

II. Tools for Decision Making
 1. Research Design
 2. Marginal Analysis
 3. Return on Investment
 4. Systems Analysis
 5. Statistical Decision Theory
    a. Payoff Matrices
    b. Decision Trees
 6. Simulation
 7. Linear Programming
 8. Program Evaluation and Review Technique (PERT)

III. Decision-Making Processes
 1. Creativity
    a. Characteristics of Creative People
    b. Creative Climates and Performance
    c. Developing Creativity
 2. Group and Individual Decisions
    a. Groups and Individuals Compared
    b. Differences Between Groups
    c. Differences Between Individuals

In Chapter 2 the close proximity between planning and decision making was noted. Both theorists and researchers use the terms interchangeably in a number of instances. Furthermore, it has become widespread practice to treat decision making in conjunction with planning in textbooks and other publications in the management literature.

Despite these considerations, and the obvious fact that we are following convention by taking up the subject of decision making at this point, a clear distinction should be made between planning, whether policy or organizational, and decision making. In terms of the organization model, planning is essentially an input-improving mediator that serves to establish role prescriptions. It is a major management function. In contrast, decision making appears to be not so much a separate function as an aspect of all functions. Like communicating it permeates all the important components of the management process—planning, directing, coordinating, and controlling—as well as the secondary management functions of staffing and representing. It is hard to conceive of anything a manager might do which does not have a relationship to some decision made somewhere.

Economic Man and the Problem of Rationality

Although there is considerable agreement on the desirability of rationality in decision making, there is much less agreement on what rationality really means (58). The topic has been a source of much controversy. In the following discussion, it is recognized, as does Simon (53), that there are a variety of types of rationality. The major concern in a treatment of management functions, however, is the relationship to organizational goal attainment. Thus, primary consideration will be given to the organizational rationality of decisions defined in terms of the degree of contribution to achieving the organizations' goals, task and maintenance.

There is evidence from a study of 34 production organizations in nonindustrial societies that rationality of this kind tends to be most pronounced in organizations where the members are free to make their own decisions regarding employment (62). The findings are given in detail in Table 6–1. Since most business firms in the United States would fall in the "voluntarily out of own self-interest" category, the considerable concern with achieving rationality which has permeated research and development related to decision-making tools and processes here is consistent with expectations from this study.

Table 6-1 *Relationship Between Degree of Organizational Rationality and Basis for Participation*

Basis on Which Members Participate	Degree of Organizational Rationality		
	Low	Medium	High
Voluntarily out of own self-interest	0	0	8
Voluntarily but with a sense of community obligation	0	9	0
Compulsion	16	1	0

Source: S. H. Udy, "Administrative Rationality, Social Setting, and Organization Development," in W. W. Cooper, H. J. Leavitt, and M. W. Shelly (eds.), *New Perspectives in Organization Research* (New York: Wiley, 1964), p. 186.

Economic Man

Decision making may occur under varying conditions. One possibility is that *certainty* is present in that all alternatives are known and each is invariably linked to a particular outcome. Under conditions of *risk*, on the other hand, the alternatives are again known but each alternative is linked to a set of outcomes each of which has a known probability of occurring. Under *uncertainty* the probabilities associated with various outcomes are not known at all (35).

The classic approach to decision making in economics has used the economic man model and is essentially a theory of decisions under conditions of certainty (60). Economic man is completely informed in that he has identified all alternative choices and knows the outcome associated with each. In addition, much of the early work on decision making in economics assumed that alternatives can be stated in terms of measures which are continuous and infinitely devisable, and that economic man as a decision maker is infinitely sensitive to small differences in degree. More recently these latter assumptions have come to be regarded as unnecessary to the theory (24).

Economic man is also rational in that he can order his various preferences according to his hierarchy of values and then actually make his choice so as to maximize some desired value. Normally this desired value would be equivalent to organizational goal attainment and the task goal of profit in particular. Thus economic man theory is closely tied to a concept of organizational rationality. It is a *normative* theory rather than a descriptive theory because it is concerned with what a decision maker *should* do (he should maximize; he should seek official goals), rather than with what he actually does do in reaching his conclusion.

Administrative Man

An alternative approach has been developed primarily by a group of organization theorists at Carnegie-Mellon University following upon concepts developed by Barnard (2). The major proponent of this viewpoint, which considers decision making in its descriptive rather than normative context, has been Herbert Simon (53, 54, 55). Economic man theory is rejected as not being sufficiently congruent with what decision makers actually do, and in its place is substituted the concept of administrative man. The assumption is that because it incorporates the elements of actual decision making in the real world, administrative man theory will provide a more valid prediction of the outcome to be expected from a particular manager's efforts to decide upon a course of action.

Simon argues convincingly that a decision situation rarely, if ever, arises which truly meets the conditions of certainty. Decision makers simply do not have full knowledge of all alternatives and their consequences. Administrative man theory posits that the typical approach taken by a manager is to construct a simplified model of the real situation. Thus complexity is reduced to the point where a human being can handle the decision within the limitations imposed by his thinking capabilities and knowledge. Decisions are made in terms of personal abstractions from the real world rather than its totality. The forms these abstractions take are strongly influenced by the values and personality characteristics of various decision makers. Thus a manager in reaching a decision typically considers only a selected sample of the possible alternatives.

Simon argues further that decisions are rarely made in a manner that is fully consistent with the demands of rationality. Administrative man faced with the need for a decision begins by searching for possible courses of action. He continues to search until he finds an alternative that meets some personally determined minimum acceptable level. He does not continue his search for alternatives and his information gathering beyond this point to find an even better alternative. Thus, instead of maximizing, as full rationality would require, he satisfices. Search for alternatives continues only as long as a manager is dissatisfied. There is no attempt to find all alternatives and then order them according to a hierarchy of value as economic man theory would require.

It is important to recognize that the two theories are not necessarily in complete contradiction. Economic man theory is normative in that it indicates what a manager should do in reaching a decision. Thus it establishes role prescriptions for the decision-making process. Administrative man theory, on the other hand, is descriptive. It attempts to provide an understanding and predictions of actual role behavior. To the extent role prescriptions and role behavior deviate from each other—and in most cases they do deviate to some extent—the two theories produce different results; but since they intend to accomplish different objectives, this does not necessarily invalidate either theory for its own unique purposes. On the other hand, either theory might still be rejected on the grounds of insufficient or contrary evidence, or because it deviates too markedly from the characteristics of good theory as discussed in Chapter 3.

It has also been suggested that the two theories might be reconciled by including the costs of the search for alternatives and of gathering information in the economic man model (68). Search occurs at a cost, and it may be that after a satisficing alternative has been found, searching further for a maximizing decision would not be worth the additional money. This proposal restores full rationality to the satisficing concept. But it remains to be shown that search consistently does stop at exactly the point rationality requires that it should stop. A complete synthesis of normative and descriptive work is an extremely difficult task, and it seems unlikely to be achieved for some time (6).

Relevant Research

There has been considerable argument between proponents of the economic and administrative man theories. Others have felt that both theories suffer from major defects. In such a context of theoretical controversy solutions can only be achieved by resort to research that will yield factual information. What do we know from scientific research that is relevant to these two approaches to decision making?

Evidence from Studies of Decisions. The primary line of evidence advanced by proponents of the administrative man theory has been based on computer simulation (18). Decisions of a kind that occur repeatedly in organizations, such as those on pricing, inventory, and stock purchases, have been simulated with considerable success using computer models based on the satisficing concept. In one of the most interesting studies the stock portfolio selection decisions of a bank trust investment manager were predicted by a computer six months after the manager's decision-making rules were elicited in an interview (13). Data are given in Table 6-2. Thus in cases where there are clear decision rules that actually apply to the situation, where the alternative choices are known at the outset, where some probabilities can be attached to outcomes, and where an ideal solution can be specified, decision models based on administrative man theory have proved reasonably valid. In actuality these decisions do not appear to be characteristically made according to the dictates of the economic man approach.

But as one moves to decision making under a greater degree of uncertainty, to what have been called unprogrammed decisions, both theories appear to fall short, at least in a descriptive sense. The most valuable studies on this point deal with job decisions made by business students completing work on graduate degrees at the Massachusetts Institute of Technology (56). Intensive analyses of these decisions over a period of time using both interviews and questionnaires revealed much that was inconsistent with any existing theory. Clear ordering of alternative jobs in a hierarchy of value was not in evidence. Search for alternatives and information often continued for some time after a satisfactory alternative had been found. Perhaps most striking of all was the finding that an implicit favorite alternative was established rather early in the decision-making process, long before a formal decision was announced, and that search then continued not to find a better solution, but to rationalize and support the favored alternative. A similar resort to early conclusions based on subjective or intuitive factors and with minimal information has been noted in studies of the decision processes of employment interviewers (66).

Yet there is evidence indicating that better, more rational decisions can be achieved under certain circumstances. Although satisficing and the selection of a favored alternative based on intuitive factors seem to be the usual pattern, it is possible to shift decisions closer to the maximizing role prescriptions of economic man theory.

In Table 6-3 the various percentages of high-quality decisions for a human relations problem under various conditions of training are given. Both decisions were made by 361 people—194 with nothing but written instructions to go on; 88 with leaders who had the instructions plus a brief training session in decision making; and 79 with leaders who had a more extended management course in the subject in addition to the instructions and demonstrations (38). It is clear that the increases in relevant training did produce a greater number of higher-quality, maximizing decisions. A similar result is apparent in Table 6-4. In this instance merely

Table 6-2 *Comparison of Portfolios Selected by Computer Program and a Trust Officer*

Simulation of Account 1 (1/8/60)
Growth Account
Funds available for investment: $22,000

The *program* selected the following portfolio	The portfolio selected by the *trust officer* was
60 General American Transportation	30 Corning Glass
50 Dow Chemical	50 Dow Chemical
10 I.B.M.	10 I.B.M.
60 Merck and Company	50 Merck and Company
45 Owens Corning Fiberglas	50 Owens Corning Fiberglas

Simulation of Account 2 (6/10/60)
Income and Growth Account
Funds available for investment: $37,500

The *program* selected	The *trust officer* selected
100 American Can	100 American Can
100 Continental Insurance	100 Continental Insurance
100 Equitable Gas	100 Equitable Gas
100 Duquesne Light	100 General Public Utilities
100 Libbey Owens Ford	100 Libbey Owens Ford
100 International Harvester	50 National Lead
100 Philadelphia Electric	100 Philadelphia Electric
100 Phillips Petroleum	100 Phillips Petroleum
100 Socony Mobil	100 Socony Mobil

Simulation of Account 3 (7/8/60)
Income and Growth Account
Funds available for investment: $31,000

The *program* selected	The *trust officer* selected
100 American Can	100 American Can
100 Continental Insurance	100 Continental Insurance
100 Duquesne Light	100 Duquesne Light
100 Equitable Gas	100 Equitable Gas
100 Pennsylvania Power and Light	100 General Public Utilities
100 International Harvester	100 International Harvester
100 Libbey Owens Ford	100 Libbey Owens Ford
100 Socony Mobil	100 Socony Mobil

Simulation of Account 4 (8/26/60)
Growth Account
Funds available for investment: $28,000

The *program* selected	The *trust officer* selected
100 American Can	100 American Can
100 Continental Insurance	100 Continental Insurance
100 Duquesne Light	100 Duquesne Light
100 Equitable Gas	100 Equitable Gas
100 Pennsylvania Power and Light	100 General Public Utilities
100 International Harvester	100 International Harvester
100 Phillips Petroleum	100 Phillips Petroleum

Source: G. P. E. Clarkson, "A Model of Trust Investment Behavior," in R. M. Cyert and J. G. March, *A Behavioral Theory of the Firm* (Englewood Cliffs, N.J.: Prentice-Hall, 1963), pp. 265–266.

Planning: The Establishment of Role Prescriptions

Table 6–3 Percentage of High-Quality Decisions Under Different Conditions of Training

	Type of Training		
Decision	Instructions Only	Instructions and Demonstration	Instructions, Demonstration, and Management Course
What is best from the company's viewpoint?	39.7%	61.4%	74.7%
What is best from the employee's viewpoint?	39.7%	55.7%	73.4%

Source: N. R. F. Maier and L. R. Hoffman, "Using Trained Developmental Discussion Leaders to Improve Further the Quality of Group Decisions," *Journal of Applied Psychology*, Vol. 44 (1960), 249. Copyright 1960 by the American Psychological Association. Reproduced by permission.

asking people to try again after a first decision was reached served to produce a shift to higher-quality decisions (39). Other evidence also supports the view that extended effort and longer search will yield more effective decisions (44). The tendency to extend decision time and effort in this manner is closely tied to differences in personality (47).

Table 6–4 Percentage of High-Quality Decisions Initially and After a Second Try for Student and Nurse Subjects

	Category of Decisions	
Students	Low Quality	High Quality
First Decisions	84%	16%
Second Decisions	48%	52%
Nurses		
First Decisions	93%	7%
Second Decisions	65%	35%

Source: N. R. F. Maier and L. R. Hoffman, "Quality of First and Second Solutions in Group Problem Solving," *Journal of Applied Psychology*, Vol. 44 (1960), 280. Copyright 1960 by the American Psychological Association. Reproduced by permission.

Values and Decisions. A major factor in the resort to intuition to select a favorite alternative which is then rationalized on the basis of further search appears to be the value system of the individual. Research evidence indicating that values influence perception has been available for some time. Coins tend to be viewed as larger than identical-sized cardboard discs. Poor children perceive coins as larger than do rich children (8). But it is not only the perception of a problem that is influenced by psychological forces within the individual; actual decisions are influenced as well.

Numerous examples of executive decisions based on considerations of which the decision maker could not have been fully aware have been reported. An analysis of such instances has led one writer to suggest that at some time in the distant future stock market quotations on a company may show a factor for the proportion of major decisions made by top management on a largely unconscious basis (26). Clearly we are far from having the measurement capability needed to develop such an irrationality factor at the present time.

One research effort dealing with the influence of values on decisions used freshmen students at the University of Colorado as its subjects (52). A questionnaire measuring a variety of personal values was developed and administered to a large group of students. Then the values of those who made a decision to join a fraternity or sorority were contrasted with the values of those who did not join. The results are presented in Table 6–5.

Table 6–5 Mean Value Scores for Pledging and Nonpledging Freshman

	Males		Females	
Value	Pledging ($N = 187$)	Nonpledging ($N = 103$)	Pledging ($N = 163$)	Nonpledging ($N = 79$)
Intellectualism	−.59	−.39	−.16	−.11
Kindness	−.16	−.20	.17	.54
Social Skills	−.13	−.32	.36	−.02
Loyalty	.79	.27	.78	.10
Academic Achievement	.30	.20	.20	−.02
Physical Development	.04	.06	.18	.08
Status	.22	−.01	.02	−.22
Honesty	.18	.35	.25	.40
Religiousness	.14	.10	.44	.37
Self-control	−.13	−.05	.18	.30
Creativity	−.63	−.26	−.15	−.24
Independence	−.25	.02	−.53	−.18

Source: W. A. Scott, *Values and Organizations* (Chicago: Rand McNally, 1965), pp. 138–139.

For both males and females the decision to pledge occurred in individuals who placed greater value on social skills and loyalty, and less value on independence. Among the males who pledged, it is also true that intellectualism and creativity were relatively undervalued. Among the females who decided to join sororities there was evidence of valuing academic achievement and status more and kindness less. From these results it

Planning: The Establishment of Role Prescriptions

seems clear that the decision to join a fraternity or sorority is closely allied to strong positive values with regard to social and group relationships.

Within the business community there appears to be considerable homogeneity of values as one might expect. Evidence on this point is given in Table 6-6. In all three groups studied, theoretical, economic, and political

Table 6-6 Mean Value Scores in Various Business Samples

	Groups Studied		
Value	Research Managers ($N = 178$)	Scientists Below the Managerial Level ($N = 157$)	Varied Executives ($N = 653$)
Theoretical	49	51	44
Economic	44	41	45
Political	42	41	44
Aesthetic	37	38	35
Religious	36	35	39
Social	32	34	33

Source: W. D. Guth and R. Tagiuri, "Personal Values and Corporate Strategy," *Harvard Business Review*, Vol. 43 (1965), No. 5, 130.

value scores were found to be high and aesthetic, religious, and social value scores low. Yet such evidence of homogeneity should not be overgeneralized. There were businessmen with very strong aesthetic, religious, and social values (29).

Tools for Decision Making

One of the most striking changes in the management field has been the steady increase in the number and diversity of quantitative or quantitatively based decision-making tools. A book such as this cannot hope to cover all of these techniques in any detail; in fact, there is no need to do so. This is typically done in courses in operations research, production management, and management science. Yet a brief survey, primarily nonmathematical, is provided. Some understanding of these techniques is essential to the development of a comprehensive view of the work being done in the field of managerial decision making.

At the outset it is important to recognize that a considerable gap exists between our knowledge in the area of quantitative tools for decision making

Decision-Making Tools and Processes

on the one hand and utilization or implementation on the other (41). A great deal more is known about such tools than is actually applied (7). In one instance authors of cases reported in the journal *Operations Research* over a six-year period were contacted subsequently to determine whether the decisions recommended on the basis of quantitative analyses were actually implemented in the companies (12). The rather pessimistic conclusion was that acceptance of recommendations in their entirety practically never occurred. This is consistent with the writer's own experience in working primarily with various research designs.

The major problem is that the decision-making tools tend to be intensely rational. They seem to compel a particular decision, whether a manager prefers it or not. Thus they often conflict with favored alternatives, intuition, and personal values. In the end many managers are able to retain control over the decision-making process and to continue the use of their preferred decision modes, but this is typically accomplished at the expense of a partial or complete rejection of conclusions emerging from quantitative analyses. The problem of how to *implement* rational decisions even when we know how to make them has not yet been solved in anything like a satisfactory manner.

Research Design

In Chapter 3 it was noted that science may influence managerial decision making either through the use of existing research and confirmed theory, or through the actual conduct of original research. The latter approach is of concern here. Such research is most frequently carried out by marketing and personnel research groups or organizations, but decisions in other functional areas may be influenced as well. Typically research designs are utilized with samples of subjects, and the data collected are analyzed using statistical procedures. Thus the outcome is a statement in probability terms as to whether some hypothesis is likely to be true. Experimental designs and the statistical analyses which go with them can be quite complex, especially if a number of factors are to be considered within the confines of a single study (23).

For our purposes, however, it is sufficient to illustrate the logic of this approach to decision making using the relatively simple procedure that has come to be viewed as the classical or basic design for the conduct of research (33). This is called the *before* and *after* control group design, and it is used to establish whether a predetermined change effort will in fact

Planning: The Establishment of Role Prescriptions

yield a desired result. It can be used to evaluate the effects of changes in organization structures, in payment programs, in training procedures, and for many other purposes (43).

First a group of subjects is selected, ideally at random, and a measure of whatever one wishes to change, say, performance effectiveness, is taken. Then the new payment plan or training procedure or whatever it is that is being evaluated is introduced. Finally a second measurement is taken on the change variable–performance effectiveness. In the language of research design this sequence may be stated as follows:

Pretest on the dependent variable (Before) ⟶ Introduction of the experimental variable ⟶ Posttest on the dependent variable (After)

If there is a definite change from pretest to posttest, then a possibility exists that the experimental variable has been the cause. But it is only a possibility because something else may have happened to produce the change. This is where the notion of control comes in. If another group that is identical to the first can be established and exposed to all the same circumstances as the first group, except that the experimental factor is not introduced, then the two groups differ only in this one respect. Under such circumstances any clear differences between the groups at posttest must be due to the experimental variable; it is the only thing that differs. The sequence for this second, control group is as follows:

Pretest on the dependent variable (Before) ⟶ *No* introduction of the experimental variable ⟶ Posttest on the dependent variable (After)

The use of research designs of this kind to generate decisions on whether or not to use certain approaches, techniques, and procedures may be time consuming and costly. On the other hand, this may be the only way of determining whether a contemplated decision can in fact contribute to organizational goal attainment.

Marginal Analysis

Marginal analysis is by no means a new technique. It is concerned with the next decision, as, for instance, with profit on the next item sold, rather than with averages. As such it is a particularly important tool in ongoing decision situations where certain basic decisions have been made already and flexibility is needed. It is frequently used, for example, to determine whether to produce additional units of a product or not. Will the costs of further production generate enough income to increase profits or will the net result be a reduction in profits?

As an example, Continental Air Lines found that even though it was filling about 15 percent fewer seats on its flights than were other airlines and could have moved up to the national average merely by eliminating 5 percent of its flights, this was not the appropriate decision from a profit viewpoint (9). There were a number of flights which, owing to hangar rental costs, cargo revenue, and other considerations, were profitable irrespective of passenger load. Marginal analyses indicated that a decision to eliminate these flights would in fact have sharply increased the proportion of seats filled per flight, but profits would have been reduced, given decisions regarding investment in equipment and the like which had already been made.

It is evident that marginal decision making requires a great deal of information regarding the costs and revenues associated with alternatives, information which many accounting systems are in no position to provide. Average rather than incremental data are much more likely to be available. Yet where adequate information can be obtained the potential contribution to rational decision processes is considerable.

Return on Investment

As compared with marginal analysis, return on investment is much more widely used (58). It is simply a calculation of the relationship between income and investment cost. Such a calculation might take the form:

$$\frac{\text{Annual Income}}{\text{Original Investment}} \times 100 = \text{Annual Return on Investment}$$

There is no set practice for establishing the value in the denominator. In the instance above, original investment has been used, but it is not uncommon to use book value or replacement cost. Although the wide variation in procedures for computing return on investment makes comparison across companies difficult, all that matters insofar as decision making within a particular company is concerned is that there be a standard procedure for that company. With such a standardized procedure it is possible to make rational comparisons between alternative investment strategies.

In addition to this use in connection with planning, return on investment is also used to measure managerial performance. How efficiently is a manager using the capital entrusted to him? In this capacity it has both advantages and disadvantages. It fits well into the management by objectives approach in that it facilitates the setting of clear and unambiguous goals in quantitative terms. It diverts management from an excessive concern with sales volume alone. But there is a tendency for return on investment measures to overemphasize short-term considerations. Thus a manager can make himself look good by not replacing outdated machinery, failing to invest in research, cutting back on training, and the like. His immediate return on investment will be impressive. By the time his decisions begin to have a negative influence on earnings the manager may well have been promoted, and thus no longer considered accountable. Clearly return on investment alone is an inadequate index of managerial performance.

Systems Analysis

Although the term *systems analysis* has been applied to nearly all techniques that involve systematic comparisons of alternatives, and thus could be used to cover all the decision-making tools considered here, a somewhat narrower definition seems preferable (14). Certainly one aspect of systems analysis is the comparison of alternative means to goal attainment, but in addition the approach typically involves the comparison of alternatives on the basis of resource costs and the benefits to be derived. Thus some type of cost-benefit analysis is essential. Furthermore, systems analysis deals explicitly with uncertainty.

Within this context systems analyses tend to be wide-ranging in their investigation of alternatives. Many are conducted by interdisciplinary teams. The primary intent is to construct some kind of model, usually mathematical, to provide a simplified, workable version of the real world situation. These models have usually been of a general economic nature involving mixes of resources. This is not surprising in view of the fact that systems analysis was originally developed by economists working in the United States Department of Defense. It is no accident that systems analysis and the planning-programming-budgeting system introduced in the federal government have much in common. Both have similar origins and objectives (14). Many of the models that have been developed continue to deal with problems of a governmental nature—the war on poverty, federally assisted housing programs, governmental transportation investments, the operations of federal departments (15).

In part because it attempts to provide such a comprehensive evaluation of alternatives in terms of expected net benefits, systems analyses often may fall short of what is desired. Constraints and facilitators in the future external environment of the organization may not be clearly identifiable, and thus their impacts may not be adequately considered in the model. Also it is often difficult to deal with benefits in truly commensurate terms. This has been a particular problem in governmental decision making where benefits associated with military expenditures frequently have to be considered in relation to benefits from social welfare expenditures. How can these two be viewed on a single benefit dimension so that choices may be made? In business, on the other hand, this problem is somewhat less acute due to the availability of profit-related indexes of effectiveness.

Statistical Decision Theory

Statistical decision theory is a component of statistics. It is concerned with the evaluation of potential outcomes from various decision alternatives. An important factor in the evaluation process is the assignment of probabilities to various occurrences. Two approaches within the broad framework of statistical decision theory and probability theory will be considered: payoff matrices and decision trees.

Payoff Matrices. The general model for a payoff matrix is given in Figure 6–1. N_1, N_2, and N_3 are so-called states of nature. They refer to things that might happen in the future such as decline, stability, and increase

Figure 6–1 The General Model for a Payoff Matrix

Strategies	States of Nature		
	N_1	N_2	N_3
S_1	P_{11}	P_{12}	P_{13}
S_2	P_{21}	P_{22}	P_{23}
S_3	P_{31}	P_{32}	P_{33}

in the total market for a given product. To each of these some probability of occurrence must be assigned either on the basis of sure knowledge or subjective estimate. The degree of certainty behind these probabilities will vary, of course, with the information available.

S_1, S_2, and S_3 are various strategies that a manager might follow. Thus he might decide to concentrate on advertising, to increase the size of his direct sales force, or to improve the quality of his product as a means to increasing his share of the market. P_1, P_2, and P_3 are the payoffs (net benefits) which will accrue from the various strategies under the various states of nature. Thus P_{11} might be the payoff from investment in advertising in a declining market; P_{33} the payoff from product improvement in an increasing market.

Once probabilities are assigned to the various states of nature and values are assigned to the various outcomes in the matrix (there are nine such outcomes in Figure 6–1), it is possible to compute the expected value of the various strategies. If we assume probabilities of .1, .3, and .6 for N_1, N_2, and N_3 respectively and values of 0, 2, and 5 for P_{11}, P_{12}, and P_{13}, then the expected value of strategy one (S_1) would be 3.6, calculated as follows: $(0 \times .1) + (2 \times .3) + (5 \times .6)$. Similar expected values would be computed for the other strategies and the one with the largest expected value selected. Usually the values assigned to the outcomes in the matrix are expressed in monetary terms.

Decision Trees. Like payoff matrices, decision trees utilize the product of the value of an outcome and its probability of occurrence to determine expected value. In fact a single-step problem such as that illustrated in Figure 6–2 is conceptually very similar to a payoff matrix. The technique has added advantages, however, as more decisions are linked together. Decision trees are very useful in evaluating sequences of decisions over a period of time in their relationships to various events and outcomes.

The basic approach may be illustrated with reference to Figure 6–2. A decision must be made in the face of a 60 percent probability of a major sales increase in the next year (and a 40 percent probability of a decrease) whether to purchase new equipment or rely on overtime work should the prospective sales increase occur. The sales increase projected is 20 percent and the decrease 10 percent over the current $100,000 volume. These figures are noted in the first column. Costs are given in the second column, with the new equipment being more expensive, as might be expected, and the cost of overtime dropping to zero where there is no sales increase.

Figure 6–2 A Simple Decision Tree

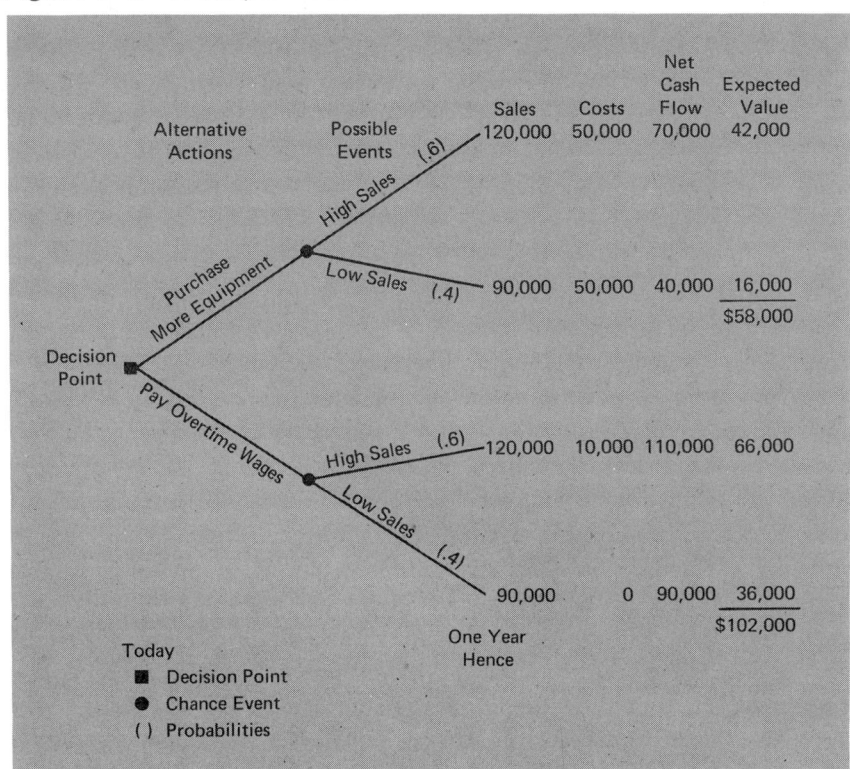

Source: G. A. Steiner, *Top Management Planning* (New York: Macmillan, 1969), p. 430.

Net cash flow is obtained by subtracting costs (column 2) from sales (column 1). Expected value is net cash flow multiplied by the probabilities of occurrence (.6 and .4). When expected values are totaled for the two strategies, the overtime approach emerges as a clear winner—with the proviso, of course, that extending the decision tree into future years might drastically alter this picture.

The major difficulty in the use of decision trees, as with payoff matrices, is in establishing probabilities (25). Where possible, the preferred procedure is to use historical or experimental samples so that the probabilities have a clear basis in fact. Where uncertainty prevails, pooled judgments made by people who are in a position to know must be used. In instances where probabilities have been adequately established, decision theory does provide predictions that are superior to those derived from other more traditional approaches (30).

Planning: The Establishment of Role Prescriptions

Simulation

The technique of computer simulation has already been considered, at least in one of its aspects, in the discussion of research evidence bearing on the economic man-administrative man controversy. There it was noted that so-called programmed decisions, such as those on stock portfolio selection made by a trust investment manager, could be simulated quite effectively. Furthermore simulation models may well be used as one approach in the conduct of a systems analysis, although the two techniques are by no means synonymous, since systems analysis encompasses a much broader range of procedures.

Simulation models have three characteristics that tend to distinguish them from other types of decision-making tools (48). First, they typically cannot be manipulated to produce a best or ideal solution. Thus simulation tends to be applied in situations where procedures for determining an optimal decision are not known or where the cost of developing such procedures would be prohibitive. Second, simulation involves experimenting with a number of alternatives, states of nature, and competitive strategies of other firms, all linked together by mathematical equations. Alternative strategies are tested under varying conditions of external constraints and facilitators via a series of computer runs, with a choice then being made based on the total information generated. Third, the use of this approach typically involves a number of trials. Not only must a variety of strategies be tested under different conditions, but often they must be tested in different time periods and with a sizable sample of computer runs.

Simulation procedures of this kind have been applied to a whole host of decisions including job shop scheduling at General Electric, refinery operation at Standard Oil of California, delinquent loans at Bank of America, customer service at United Airlines, and tanker scheduling at Humble Oil (50). Increasingly simulation procedures such as Monte Carlo methods and the comprehensive analytic approaches of Industrial Dynamics are being applied to large segments of a company's operations rather than to a limited functional area (48).

Linear Programming

In contrast to simulation, linear programming does permit direct identification of the best solution within the framework of existing constraints. It is an optimizing technique concerned with determining the best set of decisions given scarce resources—monetary, material, or human. It provides a basis for maximizing profits or minimizing costs. In its business applications linear programming is a relatively new procedure because in many cases its effective use requires that considerable computer capacity be available.

There are three general types of problems which have proved particularly amenable to solution by linear programming, all involving a set of resource allocation decisions (25). One is the determination of the ideal blend or mix of ingredients in a product which will yield the greatest profit at a point in time. The blending of gasoline stocks or the mixing of chemical fertilizers would be examples. A second application is in connection with planning and scheduling. When applied to production operations, linear programming can be useful in establishing the best pattern of machine use or the preferred product mix. It may also be used to schedule transportation equipment—airline flights, tanker trips, and the like. The third major area of use has been that of distribution cost minimization. Such an analysis may be extended beyond the matter of distribution alternatives alone to take into account warehousing costs and even production costs. These three categories certainly do not exhaust the possibilities, but the great majority of applications have been in these areas.

It is important to recognize that only certain types of problems are appropriate for linear programming. There are limiting assumptions in the mathematics involved, and the mathematical equations required to solve a complex problem correctly are not easily formulated. A given practical problem may simply be more than the linear programming technique or the available computers can handle. Furthermore, the objective desired (maximum profit for instance) must be quantitatively definable, resources must in fact be scarce, and resource alternatives must be comparable in their measurement. Given the requisite conditions, however, the approach can be an extremely powerful aid to management decision making.

Program Evaluation and Review Technique (PERT)

PERT was originally developed in the late 1950s as a planning and scheduling technique to be used in connection with the construction of the Polaris submarine weapons system. The procedure starts with a clear statement of the objective of the project. Then a list of all activities or events required to complete the project is compiled. Examples of such statements selected at random from the PERT network used to install a job evaluation plan to provide data for a wage and salary system are as follows (64):

Job-summary questionnaires are distributed to all employees, along with a cover letter of instructions.

Evaluations are completed on all jobs in Division I that are assigned to the clerical job family.

Job-evaluation manual for the sales and marketing job family is ready for use.

Review progress and plan strategy for presenting results to Division I top management.

A sequencing of these activities is established which includes the specification of lags and leads in the interrelationships. Then specific estimates are made of the elapsed time for completion of each activity. In PERT three such estimates are developed for each activity to permit adequate handling of uncertainty. These are an optimistic estimate of time required, the most likely duration, and a pessimistic estimate. In the so-called Critical Path Method (CPM) uncertainty is not provided for, and only the second value is employed. This is the principal difference between these two techniques (25).

A network diagram of activities and required times (and under certain applications, costs as well) is constructed. This is subjected to mathematical analyses that identify those particular activities that represent the bottlenecks in the system. What critical activities, if delayed, would surely impose an equal delay on the completion of the project? Once this path has been identified, efforts can be made to shorten the time to complete the project by substituting for activities or reducing the duration of activities which are on it. Only when this can be done can the total time to completion be reduced. Thus PERT is essentially a method of planning a project so as to keep the time and money spent to a minimum, although it has other implications in the area of control as well. The technique may also be used to contrast alternative plans. It is not, however, an optimizing procedure in the sense that it will identify the best possible approach.

In one survey of PERT applications it was found to be in use in some form by 44 percent of the companies contacted. This figure has clearly increased in the years since the study (51). The larger companies, in particular, tended to use it. As Table 6–7 shows, PERT is most widely used with construction projects, but its areas of application are diverse.

Table 6–7 Areas of PERT Application in 81 Major Companies

Areas	Percent Noting
Construction	59.3
Research and Development	48.1
Product Planning	37.0
Maintenance	29.6
Other (procurement, personnel, etc.)	29.6
Computer Installation	25.9
Marketing	7.4

Source: P. P. Schoderbek, "A Study of the Applications of PERT," *Academy of Management Journal,* Vol. 8 (1965), 205.

Although PERT has proved itself a useful addition to the list of decision-making tools, the results obtained are highly dependent on a careful statement of activities and on the validity of time estimates. These time estimates, like the probabilities attached to alternatives in other techniques, can be subject to considerable human error. Too much error, and the whole PERT procedure becomes worthless.

Decision-Making Processes

The tools considered in the previous section rely heavily on mathematical calculations and computers for their results. But what about the manager as decision maker? What do we know about him from research into human problem solving? Certain aspects of these decision-making processes were considered in connection with the discussion of the controversy surrounding the economic-man and administrative-man theories. There is, however, considerably more that is known. In particular, research has dealt with creativity in the decision-making process, and with the relative effectiveness of decision making under different circumstances and by different individuals (37).

Creativity

It is generally accepted that to be creative an idea must be original; it must embody something new. Yet this in itself is not sufficient to define creativity. Many original ideas are merely eccentric; some are outright delusions. Thus the originality must be supplemented with some correspondence to reality. To be truly creative an idea must have some redeeming value.

Characteristics of Creative People. The available evidence suggests that in a very general sense people who have more creative ideas tend to be of somewhat higher intelligence (61). Yet the relationship is not a very close one. A number of creative scientists have intelligence test scores that are rather low for scientists in general.

There is also reason to believe that creativity, like intelligence, is influenced in part by hereditary factors. Studies comparing identical twins having exactly the same heredity with fraternal twins having somewhat different heredities indicate that the identical twins are clearly more alike in their manifestations of creativity (3). Thus where hereditary similarity is greatest, creative similarity tends to be greatest also.

Studies of the personality characteristics of creative people, especially creative scientists, abound. There has been a frequent finding that such people exhibit many signs consistent with a diagnosis of emotional disorder. But—and this is an extremely important *but*—they also manifest a great deal of ego strength (3). They have an unusual capacity to keep pathological impulses and anxieties under control, so that their behavior is not seriously distorted. Thus, although creative individuals face a great deal of internal tension, they have the resources to handle it effectively and emerge as quite emotionally stable.

Other evidence from studies of creative individuals has consistently pointed to autonomy, independence, and self-sufficiency as characteristic. Creative people also appear to be more dominant, more resourceful, and more self-controlled (59). Many seem to have a strong need to take risks, as long as they can win out through their own efforts, and to face disorder and even chaos merely for the satisfaction of finding or imposing a new order on things. There is in all this an apparent concern with proving one's own adequacy which far exceeds what is typical of less creative people (3).

Creative Climates and Performance. It does not follow from what has been said that the kind of people under consideration will invariably produce creative decisions; nor that they will necessarily be viewed as effective performers. This depends a great deal on the characteristics of the work environment and on existing role prescriptions and role sanctions.

There is considerable reason to believe that creative decisions occur more frequently in professional than in administrative organizations (17, 57) (see Chapter 2). We know that the emotional state of a person influences his creativity (31). It is clear that to the extent a person feels frustrated, inhibited, and generally under stress he is less likely to actually be creative. Furthermore certain kinds of supervisory behaviors and styles seem to yield greater creativity. Groups managed by superiors who are very sensitive to differences in their environments (the kind of people who are often creative themselves) tend to produce more creative ideas (28). In a study of industrial chemists almost all new research proposals and contracts came from people identified as creative in groups directed by individuals who clearly differentiated their environments, who for instance saw sizable differences between various subordinates rather than viewing them as all the same. Equally creative researchers in other supervisory climates were not productive at all. Similarly the evidence indicates that superiors who make procedural suggestions, who encourage or reject the ideas of their subordinates, but who do not contribute any ideas of their own obtain more creative decisions from those working for them than superiors who actually participate in the creation of ideas, who state what *they* believe (1). It is clear that people with really good ideas must feel free to express their creativity and expect recognition, or nothing worthwhile will emerge (34). This seems most likely in professional organizations, but exceptions may occur even there.

It is not only supervisory climate that determines whether creative ability will emerge and yield superior performance. In a major study of research scientists it was found that creativity was most useful among relative newcomers to a project or an area of research. Longer exposure to the same problem area typically produced fewer creative results (46). This same study again indicated that creative ability had little payoff, perhaps even negative consequences, in a highly restrictive situation. All in all the evidence is very strong that creative people do not necessarily perform in a creative manner, and even if they do, it does not necessarily follow that their ideas will be valued. Creativity expressed, recognized, and valued is very much a function of the existing situation and value structure. It is not surprising that it appears to be rather rare (28).

Developing Creativity. It might appear from the evidence regarding a hereditary basis for creativity that training and developmental efforts would have little impact in producing more creative decisions. This does not appear to be the case (3, 59). There is ample evidence that various kinds of educational approaches can stimulate creativity in decision making.

The results obtained from one such course which emphasizes *brainstorming* techniques, learning to express ideas freely in a group setting, are given in Table 6–8. In this instance individuals who had completed the course some time before were compared with two groups of individuals who had not been exposed to the course. The three groups appear to have been

Table 6–8 Mean Scores on Creativity Measures for Students With and Without a Course in Creative Problem Solving

Creativity Measure	Group With Course ($N = 24$)	Groups Without Course	
		A ($N = 24$)	B ($N = 24$)
AC Test of Creative Ability			
Quantity score	15.6	9.6	8.7
Quality score	7.5	3.7	2.5
Guilford Apparatus Test	22.3	18.7	16.8
Guilford Plot Titles Test			
High score	8.8	5.6	4.2
Low score	21.9	14.6	14.5
Guilford Unusual Uses Tests	18.1	16.3	13.7

Source: S. J. Parnes and A. Meadow, "Evaluation of Persistence of Effects Produced by a Creative Problem-Solving Course," *Psychological Reports*, Vol. 7 (1960), 357–361. Reprinted with permission of author and publisher.

of equal creative ability and intelligence prior to the creativity training (45). Yet on all six measures obtained from the four creativity tests those with the course scored markedly higher than those without it at the time of the postcourse follow-up. This is strong evidence that the training did increase creativity and that the increase was maintained for substantial periods of time afterward.

Group and Individual Decisions

One of the major concerns of research has been to learn more about the conditions for effective decision making. What kinds of people make the best decisions? Do groups or individuals perform best in decision making? Under what conditions are groups most likely to come up with an optimum decision? The answers to these questions carry strong implications for the selection of individuals to fill managerial positions and for the organization of managerial work. Evidence already reviewed, for instance, suggests that widespread participation in policy making can be an aid to the implementation of policy. But what about the quality of the decisions that emerge from, say, the extended discussion of a personnel policy committee? Is implementation achieved at a cost in other respects?

Groups and Individuals Compared. Research indicates that more and better ideas emerge when a number of individuals work on a problem alone than when these same individuals work on the problem together in a face-to-face group (63). This finding has been obtained not only with student groups (5, 49) but with research scientists and advertising men (22) and with managers who are used to working together (10). Thus it is clearly applicable to the ongoing decision-making processes of an organization. The evidence seems to indicate that working together in a group has an inhibitory effect on the production of ideas which is not present when people work alone.

This should not be interpreted to mean that decisions are at their best when made by a single, all-powerful manager who relies only on his own judgment. The inclusion of a number of informed people in the decision-making process brings new knowledge, viewpoints, and insights to bear. There is good reason to believe that even face-to-face groups can do better than most single individuals (40), although groups frequently take longer to reach a decision. The ideal seems to be to have a number of individuals develop their own solutions, decisions, and policies entirely independently and then combine these into an ultimate conclusion. This may be costly in terms of man-hours devoted to the decision, but no more so than with a group or committee decision process.

A further focus of research comparing individuals and groups as decision makers has been in the area of what has come to be called *risky shift*. A number of studies have produced evidence that in a face-to-face group discussion individuals will make decisions with a higher implicit risk element than when they are alone (11, 20). Risky shift has been demonstrated with regard to stock market investment decisions, for instance (21). On the other hand, under certain circumstances there may be a movement to greater caution and conservatism in the group context. The crucial factor appears to be the type of decision-making norm that comes into evidence during the group discussion. Individuals tend to shift toward such a perceived norm; the resulting change may well be in the direction of greater risk, but this is not always the case.

The state of knowledge regarding the risky shift phenomenon is by no means as complete as might be desired. Serious questions have been raised about the adequacy of at least some of the research in this area (4, 36). The most that can be said at this point is that there is a distinct possibility in any given instance of group decision making, that the outcome will have a higher degree of risk attached to it than many of the participants would have been willing to take on their own. Whether or not such risk taking is desirable from the point of view of goal attainment is another question. In any event it seems important that managers should be aware of this potential influence on decision-making processes.

Differences Between Groups. Despite the findings reported in the previous section, there seems little doubt that a number of firms will frequently resort to group decision making in a face-to-face context. They may do so because implementation is an important consideration, or for other reasons. Given the fact, in any event, that decisions are to be made on a group basis, how best might the group be constituted? This too has been the subject of considerable research.

A frequent topic of investigation has been the relative merits of brainstorming, where the group members produce ideas as they come to mind without any criticism, versus the more usual intermixing of idea production and criticism. The best available evidence seems to indicate some superiority for brainstorming, where creative solutions are needed (5). More specifically, if all that is desired are a few reasonably good ideas, as implied by the satisficing concept, then brainstorming is not worth the additional effort to initiate it. But if additional good ideas might well yield sizable benefits in the final decision, they can be obtained at little extra cost through brainstorming, whereas the typical critical group decision procedures are unlikely to yield them.

Other evidence points up one of the factors that may contribute to the superiority of "alone" versus "face-to-face group" decision making. The effectiveness of three types of brainstorming groups was compared (16). In the first type none of the members was considered to be an expert in the brainstorming technique; in the second one perceived expert was present; in the third all were presented as experts. Actually there were no experts present at all. Yet the mere perception that an expert was present had an inhibitory effect on creativity. This was most pronounced in the "all expert" groups. The group members clearly felt threatened by the expert presence and did not divulge their ideas. Once again this study confirms the very fragile nature of the creative process in the face of environmental threat.

Studies have also been carried out relating personality characteristics of group members to group decision-making effectiveness. It has been found for instance that when personality tests are administered, and then groups are constituted so as to contain members who are either very much alike or very different, the diverse groups produce more and better solutions. More viewpoints and perspectives are brought to bear (32). Also certain kinds of people do better in the brainstorming context (5). These are people with highly developed social skills who are outgoing, self-assured, somewhat dominant and aggressive, and enthusiastic. In many respects they are probably the more creative members. Although there is little evidence of the practice being used to any significant extent at present, the research being conducted in this area suggests that in the future many companies may well structure decision-making groups so as to contain that mix of members most likely to yield the best decisions. Research and development decisions appear particularly amenable to this approach. Consulting teams represent another likely area of application.

Differences Between Individuals. One factor clearly related to decision-making effectiveness is intelligence. People differ considerably in this regard, and there is ample evidence that in higher-level positions, where complex decisions must be made, the incumbents tend to be individuals of relatively high general intelligence (42). In one study of 39 officers of large corporations all were found to score in the top 26 percent of the population on an intelligence measure. On the other hand, it is important to recognize that where the problems are not particularly complex, decision making may not require very high levels of intelligence; those who are average may do as well as those who approach the genius category. Furthermore, creativity and intelligence are only weakly related, and personal values may distort the decision making of even the most brilliant individual. All in all the evidence appears to indicate that whether or not high intelligence is beneficial depends not only on the type of decision to be made, but on other characteristics of the individual as well.

Individuals also differ in the knowledge they bring to decisions. Table 6-9 contains a comparison of effectiveness scores obtained by students with different majors playing a top management game. The scores were based on the relative profitability, extent of cash planning, and inventory control resulting from the decisions made by each team (19). There were 11 teams containing all accounting majors, 11 teams whose members all had the same majors other than accounting (actually four of marketing majors and seven from general business), and 11 with mixed majors none of whom had accounting specialization. The three types of teams were so established that no intelligence differences existed between them. Yet it is evident that those with more knowledge of accounting outperformed those

Table 6-9 Mean Scores on a Management Game for Different Types of Teams

		Type of Team	
		Nonaccounting Majors	
Period of Play	All Accounting Majors	Same Major	Different Majors
1	76	70	62
2	75	69	61
3	67	63	75
4	75	62	60
5	77	65	68
6	79	63	63
All combined	75	65	65

Source: F. E. Dalton and J. B. Miner, "The Role of Accounting Training in Top Management Decision Making," *The Accounting Review*, Vol. 45 (1970), 137.

with little knowledge on 11 of the 12 comparisons for the six periods of play. Accounting knowledge is evidently a major asset in making the decisions required by this particular business game. It seems apparent that having the particular type of knowledge or information required is an equally important consideration in many other business decision situations. Without such knowledge it is hard to imagine how business decisions can be truly effective. Yet there is good reason to believe many managers are sadly deficient in this regard (27).

Finally—and this is relevant to the discussion of the risky shift phenomenon—there is definite evidence that people differ in their generalized tendencies to take individual risks (67). High risk takers who are in jobs with a minimal amount of risk tend to be relatively dissatisfied. High risk takers consider promotion very important and are less concerned about steady employment. If they become unemployed, they are more willing to accept completely new types of employment and as a result find new jobs more quickly. It is apparent that differences in risk-taking propensity can have a major influence on personal decisions; it is likely that organizational decisions are influenced in a similar manner. In this connection it is interesting to note that the tendency to take risks is greater among younger managers (65).

Taking the findings considered in this section as a whole, there is strong support for the view that clear differences in decision-making skills and propensities exist between individuals themselves, as well as between groups and individuals.

Questions

1. Show how a research design might be used to determine whether management by objectives is an effective means of reducing turnover among lower-level managers.
2. What is the relationship between values and decision making? Give examples. Does a heavy involvement of values in the decision process argue for or against economic man theory? administrative man?
3. How might one organize the decision-making process for a group of research managers to get both the best idea for a new product and agreement on actually manufacturing the product?
4. Given the characteristics of creative people and the conditions for the emergence of creative accomplishments, what problems should a company anticipate as costs against the benefits derived from creativity?
5. What special problems are associated with the following decision-making techniques?
    a. Decision trees
    b. Return on investment
    c. Linear programming
    d. PERT
    e. Systems analysis

References

1. Anderson, L. R., and F. E. Fiedler. "The Effect of Participatory and Supervisory Leadership on Group Creativity." *Journal of Applied Psychology*, Vol. 48 (1964), 227–236.
2. Barnard, C. I. *The Functions of the Executive*. Cambridge, Mass.: Harvard University Press, 1938.
3. Barron, F. *Creative Person and Creative Process*. New York: Holt, Rinehart and Winston, 1969.
4. Belovicz, M. W., and F. E. Finch. "A Critical Analysis of the Risky Shift Phenomenon." *Organizational Behavior and Human Performance*, Vol. 6 (1971), 150–168.
5. Bouchard, T. J. "Personality, Problem-Solving Procedure, and Performance in Small Groups." *Journal of Applied Psychology Monograph*, Vol. 53 (1969), No. 1, Part 2, 1–29.
6. Bower, J. L. "Descriptive Decision Theory from the Administrative Viewpoint." In R. A. Bauer and K. J. Gergen (eds.), *The Study of Policy Formation*. New York: Free Press, 1968, pp. 103–148.

7. Brown, R. V. "Do Managers Find Decision Theory Useful?" *Harvard Business Review*, Vol. 48 (1970), No. 3, 78–89.
8. Bruner, J. S., and C. C. Goodman. "Value and Need as Organizing Factors in Perception." *Journal of Abnormal and Social Psychology*, Vol. 42 (1947), 33–44.
9. *Business Week*. "Airlines Take the Marginal Route," April 20, 1963.
10. Campbell, J. P. "Individual versus Group Problem Solving in an Industrial Sample." *Journal of Applied Psychology*, Vol. 52 (1968), 205–210.
11. Cartwright, D., and A. Zander. *Group Dynamics*. New York: Harper & Row, 1968.
12. Churchman, C. W. "Managerial Acceptance of Scientific Recommendations." *California Management Review*, Vol. 7 (1964), No. 1, 31–38.
13. Clarkson, G. P. E. "A Model of Trust Investment Behavior." In R. M. Cyert and J. G. March, *A Behavioral Theory of the Firm*. Englewood Cliffs, N.J.: Prentice-Hall, 1963, pp. 253–267.
14. Cleland, D. I., and W. R. King. *Systems Analysis and Project Management*. New York: McGraw-Hill, 1968.
15. Cleland, D. I., and W. R. King. *Systems, Organizations, Analysis, Management: A Book of Readings*. New York: McGraw-Hill, 1969.
16. Collaros, P. A., and L. R. Anderson. "Effect of Perceived Expertness upon Creativity of Members of Brainstorming Groups." *Journal of Applied Psychology*, Vol. 53 (1969), 159–163.
17. Cummings, L. "Organizational Climates for Creativity." *Academy of Management Journal*, Vol. 8 (1965), 220–227.
18. Cyert, R. M., and J. G. March. *A Behavioral Theory of the Firm*. Englewood Cliffs, N.J.: Prentice-Hall, 1963.
19. Dalton, F. E., and J. B. Miner. "The Role of Accounting Training in Top Management Decision Making." *The Accounting Review*, Vol. 45 (1970), 134–139.
20. Davis, J. H. *Group Performance*. Reading, Mass.: Addison-Wesley, 1969.
21. Deets, M. K., and G. C. Hoyt. "Variance Preferences and Variance Shifts in Group Investment Decisions." *Organizational Behavior and Human Performance*, Vol. 5 (1970), 378–386.
22. Dunnette, M. D., J. P. Campbell, and K. Jaastad. "The Effect of Group Participation on Brainstorming Effectiveness for Two Industrial Samples." *Journal of Applied Psychology*, Vol. 47 (1963), 30–37.
23. Edwards, A. L. *Experimental Design in Psychological Research*. New York: Holt, Rinehart and Winston, 1969.
24. Edwards, W. "The Theory of Decision Making." *Psychological Bulletin*, Vol. 51 (1954), 380–417.
25. Emory, C. W., and P. Niland. *Making Management Decisions*. Boston: Houghton Mifflin, 1968.

26. Ferber, R. C. "The Role of the Subconscious in Executive Decision-Making." *Management Science*, Vol. 13 (1967), B519–526.
27. Gannon, M. J., and J. P. Noon. "Management's Critical Deficiency." *Business Horizons*, Vol. 14 (1971), No. 1, 49–56.
28. Gordon, G., and E. V. Morse. "Creative Potential and Organizational Structure." In P. P. LeBreton and W. G. Scott (eds.), *Organization Structure and Behavior. Proceedings of the 1968 Annual Meeting*. Academy of Management, 1969, pp. 37–49.
29. Guth, W. D., and R. Tagiuri. "Personal Values and Corporate Strategy." *Harvard Business Review*, Vol. 43 (1965), No. 5, 123–132.
30. Hill, J. W., A. R. Bass, and H. Rosen. "The Prediction of Complex Organizational Behavior: A Comparison of Decision Theory with More Traditional Techniques." *Organizational Behavior and Human Performance*, Vol. 5 (1970), 449–462.
31. Hinton, B. L. "Environmental Frustration and Creative Problem Solving." *Journal of Applied Psychology*, Vol. 52 (1968), 211–217.
32. Hoffman, L. R., and N. R. F. Maier. "Quality and Acceptance of Problem Solutions by Members of Homogeneous and Heterogeneous Groups." *Journal of Abnormal and Social Psychology*, Vol. 62 (1961), 401–407.
33. Kerlinger, F. N. *Foundations of Behavioral Research*. New York: Holt, Rinehart and Winston, 1964.
34. Korman, A. K. "Organizational Achievement, Aggression and Creativity: Some Suggestions Toward an Integrated Theory." *Organizational Behavior and Human Performance*, Vol. 6 (1971), 593–613.
35. Luce, R. D., and H. Raiffa. *Games and Decisions*. New York: Wiley, 1957.
36. Mackenzie, K. D. "An Analysis of Risky Shift Experiments." *Organizational Behavior and Human Performance*, Vol. 6 (1971), 283–303.
37. Maier, N. R. F. *Problem Solving and Creativity in Individuals and Groups*. Belmont, Calif.: Brooks/Cole, 1970.
38. Maier, N. R. F., and L. R. Hoffman. "Using Trained Developmental Discussion Leaders to Improve Further the Quality of Group Decisions." *Journal of Applied Psychology*, Vol. 44 (1960), 247–251.
39. Maier, N. R. F., and L. R. Hoffman. "Quality of First and Second Solutions in Group Problem Solving." *Journal of Applied Psychology*, Vol. 44 (1960), 278–283.
40. Maier, N. R. F., and J. A. Thurber. "Innovative Problem-Solving by Outsiders: A Study of Individuals and Groups." *Personnel Psychology*, Vol. 22 (1969), 237–249.
41. Malcolm, D. G. "On the Need for Improvement in Implementation of O.R." *Management Science*, Vol. 11 (1965).
42. Miner, J. B. *Intelligence in the United States*. New York: Springer, 1957.

43. Miner, J. B. *Personnel and Industrial Relations: A Managerial Approach.* New York: Macmillan, 1969.
44. Parnes, S. J. "Effects of Extended Effort in Creative Problem Solving." *Journal of Educational Psychology,* Vol. 52 (1961), 117–122.
45. Parnes, S. J., and A. Meadow. "Evaluation of Persistence of Effects Produced by a Creative Problem-Solving Course." *Psychological Reports,* Vol. 7 (1960), 357–361.
46. Pelz, D. C., and F. M. Andrews. *Scientists in Organizations.* New York: Wiley, 1966.
47. Pollay, R. W. "The Structure of Executive Decisions and Decision Times." *Administrative Science Quarterly,* Vol. 15 (1970), 459–471.
48. Richards, M. D., and P. S. Greenlaw. *Management Decision Making.* Homewood, Ill. : Irwin, 1966.
49. Rotter, G. S., and S. M. Portugal. "Group and Individual Effects in Problem Solving." *Journal of Applied Psychology,* Vol. 53 (1969), 338–341.
50. Rowe, A. J. "Computer Simulation—A Solution Technique for Management Problems." *Proceedings—Fall Joint Computer Conference,* Vol. 27, Part 1 (1965), 259–267.
51. Schoderbek, P. P. "A Study of the Applications of PERT." *Academy of Management Journal,* Vol. 8 (1965), 199–210.
52. Scott, W. A. *Values and Organizations.* Chicago: Rand McNally, 1965.
53. Simon, H. A. *Administrative Behavior.* New York: Free Press, 1957.
54. Simon, H. A. *Models of Man.* New York: Wiley, 1957.
55. Simon, H. A. "Theories of Decision Making in Economics and Behavioral Science." *American Economic Review,* Vol. 49 (1959), 253–283.
56. Soelberg, P. "Unprogrammed Decision Making." In M. P. Hottenstein and R. W. Millman (eds.), *Research Toward the Development of Management Thought. Proceedings of the 1966 Annual Meeting.* Academy of Management, 1967, pp. 3–16.
57. Steiner, G. A. *The Creative Organization.* Chicago: University of Chicago Press, 1965.
58. Steiner, G. A. *Top Management Planning.* New York: Macmillan, 1969.
59. Taylor, C. W. *Creativity: Progress and Potential.* New York: McGraw-Hill, 1964.
60. Taylor, D. W. "Decision Making and Problem Solving." In J. G. March (ed.), *Handbook of Organizations.* Chicago: Rand McNally, 1965, pp. 48–86.
61. Torrance, E. P. "The Minnesota Studies of Creative Behavior: National and International Extensions." *Journal of Creative Behavior,* Vol. 1 (1967), 137–154.
62. Udy, S. H. "Administrative Rationality, Social Setting, and Organizational Development." In W. W. Cooper, H. J. Leavitt, and M. W. Shelly (eds.), *New Perspectives in Organization Research.* New York: Wiley, 1964, pp. 173–192.

63. Van de Ven, A., and A. L. Delbecq. "Nominal Versus Interacting Group Processes for Committee Decision-Making Effectiveness." *Academy of Management Journal*, Vol. 14 (1971), 203–212.
64. Varney, G. H., and G. F. Carvalho. "PERT in the Personnel Department." *Personnel*, Vol. 45 (1968), No. 1, 48–53.
65. Vroom, V. H., and B. Pahl. "Relationship Between Age and Risk Taking Among Managers." *Journal of Applied Psychology*, Vol. 55 (1971), 399–405.
66. Webster, E. C. *Decision Making in the Employment Interview*. Montreal: Industrial Relations Centre, McGill University, 1964.
67. Williams, L. K. "Some Correlates of Risk Taking." *Personnel Psychology*, Vol. 18 (1965), 297–310.
68. Zeckhauser, R., and E. Schaefer. "Public Policy and Normative Economic Theory." In R. A. Bauer and K. J. Gergen (eds.), *The Study of Policy Formation*. New York: Free Press, 1968, pp. 27–101.

Part II
Planning: The Establishment of Role Prescriptions

B
Organization Planning

7 Organization Structure: Vertical Aspects

I. Hierarchic Position, Delegation, and Decentralization
 1. Differences Associated with Organizational Level
    a. Decision-Making Autonomy and Scope
    b. Satisfaction and Motivation
    c. Formal and Informal Status
 2. Delegation
 3. Centralization and Decentralization
    a. Historical Trends
    b. Existing Forms
    c. Influences of Technology and Environment
    d. Centralization vs. Decentralization

II. The Number of Hierarchic Levels and Span of Control
 1. Tall and Flat Organizations
    a. Studies in Organizations
    b. Laboratory Studies
 2. Span of Control
    a. Spans in Existing Organizations
    b. Small Group Research

III. The Role of the Board of Directors
 1. Board Composition
 2. Nature and Extent of Activities
 3. Vertical Relationships at the Top

Policy planning deals with one type of role prescription in organizations; organization planning deals with role prescriptions of a somewhat different kind. In the case of organization planning the concern is with those role prescriptions or expectations that attach to individual positions. Policy and organization plans both guide work performance, but whereas policies tend to apply over broad sectors if not the whole company, organization plans are position specific.

When the role prescriptions associated with management positions are viewed together, either in sets or for the total organization, a structure or organizational design emerges. This structure establishes the decision-making powers and jurisdictions of various managers, the sanctions the managers can bring to bear in implementing decisions, and the relationships between managers in different positions. Inherent in the organization structure, then, is the expectation that managers in different positions will behave in different ways and that these sets of role behaviors will be combined so as to contribute as much as possible to goal attainment.

Organization structures may be viewed in two dimensions. There is first the vertical, also referred to as the hierarchic, or scalar, aspect. Here the concern is with the level at which certain decisions are made and certain role behaviors occur. Also related to the vertical aspect of structure is the length of the chain of command or, put somewhat differently, the number of levels in the managerial hierarchy. This latter consideration is directly tied to the number of people reporting to managers at various levels, the so-called span of control or span of management.

The horizontal, or lateral, aspect of structure, on the other hand, deals with relationships that flow across the organization—departmentation and division of labor, line and staff, and other structural procedures related to decision-making differentials between sectors of the organization, the role of interdepartmental committees and teams. In this horizontal aspect the emphasis tends to be somewhat less on differences in authority and more on who does what. Yet there are horizontal as well as vertical differences in authority, just as there are vertical divisions of labor.

This chapter is concerned with vertical aspects of organizational structure; the chapter following with horizontal aspects. The third and final chapter on organization planning takes up the matter of organizational change in relation to technology, the existing value structure, and patterns of growth. It is more concerned with the internal constraints imposed by the organization structure existing at a given point in time than are this and the following chapter.

Hierarchic Position, Delegation, and Decentralization

One of the major issues that has concerned organization planners over the years has been the allocation of decision-making and -implementing authority along the vertical hierarchy of management positions. There are some strong arguments favoring having decisions made at as low a level as possible, but there are also advantages associated with making them at the top. This section will consider these varying arguments and the research evidence bearing on them.

Differences Associated with Organizational Level

Considerable research has been conducted with the objective of finding out what differences do exist between individuals holding positions at different points in the managerial hierarchy. This evidence, although not directly concerned with the hierarchic level at which certain types of decisions *should* be made to maximize goal attainment, does provide a context for viewing the problem of centralization-decentralization. It reveals a great deal about the kinds of role prescriptions, formal and informal, that typically are built into positions at various levels.

Decision-Making Autonomy and Scope. In Chapter 2 marked differences in the proportion of time devoted to various management functions by managers at different levels were noted. The Minnesota research, for instance, indicated an increase in the number of individuals who were primarily planners, generalists, and evaluators at each higher level (30). The proportion who were essentially supervisors, on the other hand, showed a sharp decrease. These findings appear to be typical.

Other studies provide further evidence on the differences in scope and type of decision making between various levels. A comparison was made between executives and nonexecutives within five profit-making and five governmental organizations (17). Perceptions regarding their organizations were obtained from members using a comprehensive questionnaire. The executives appeared to have much fewer restrictions on their decision-making powers, to deal with a greater range of problems, to have fewer procedural restrictions, to be less impersonal in relationships with others, and to place more emphasis on merit-based hiring and promotion (the evaluation process).

A second study dealt only with managers (5). A questionnaire specifying certain types of decisions was administered to 190 managers in eight companies. The managers described aspects of the decision-making process in their companies. At each successively higher level of management a greater degree of autonomy from superiors was found. Top-level managers were more likely to make the final choice and to exert strong influence on decisions. On the other hand those at the top relied heavily on subordinates to bring problems to their attention and make recommendations. Decisions were most frequently *initiated* at the middle management level.

The research evidence consistently indicates a close association between hierarchic level and the degree of autonomy as well as the scope of decision making in administrative organizations. As a result one might expect higher levels of job satisfaction toward the top of these organizations.

Satisfaction and Motivation. In general the evidence supports the hypothesis of increasing satisfaction at each higher level (39). The motives of managers toward the top of the hierarchy are more likely to be fulfilled presumably because of the greater freedom to do what they wish and the greater breadth of the positions, which permits finding some aspects of the work that are enjoyable.

As indicated in Figure 7-1 this finding is not restricted to the United States. A survey of managers in 14 countries rather consistently indicated that motives are more likely to be fulfilled at higher than at lower levels (16). This is particularly true of such motives as self-actualization, or self-realization, autonomy, and esteem. Of the countries studied only Denmark does not show a clear superiority for the higher-level managers; in Japan the relationship is particularly striking.

Similar studies have been carried out within the military and, again, the finding of greater satisfaction at higher levels emerges, but a comparison of military officers and business executives reveals that at all levels the officers are less satisfied than their business counterparts (40). This finding has been extended to other types of governmental work as well (37, 44). Also there is evidence that within government, satisfaction is greater for managers in field work, where there is considerable self-defining of role prescriptions, than in central office locations.

Research indicates that not only are certain motives more likely to be fulfilled at higher levels but certain types of motives are more likely to be found there as well. Table 7-1 presents data obtained with a measure of various motives at all managerial levels below the store manager in a large

Figure 7-1 Fulfillment of Motives at Higher and Lower Managerial Levels

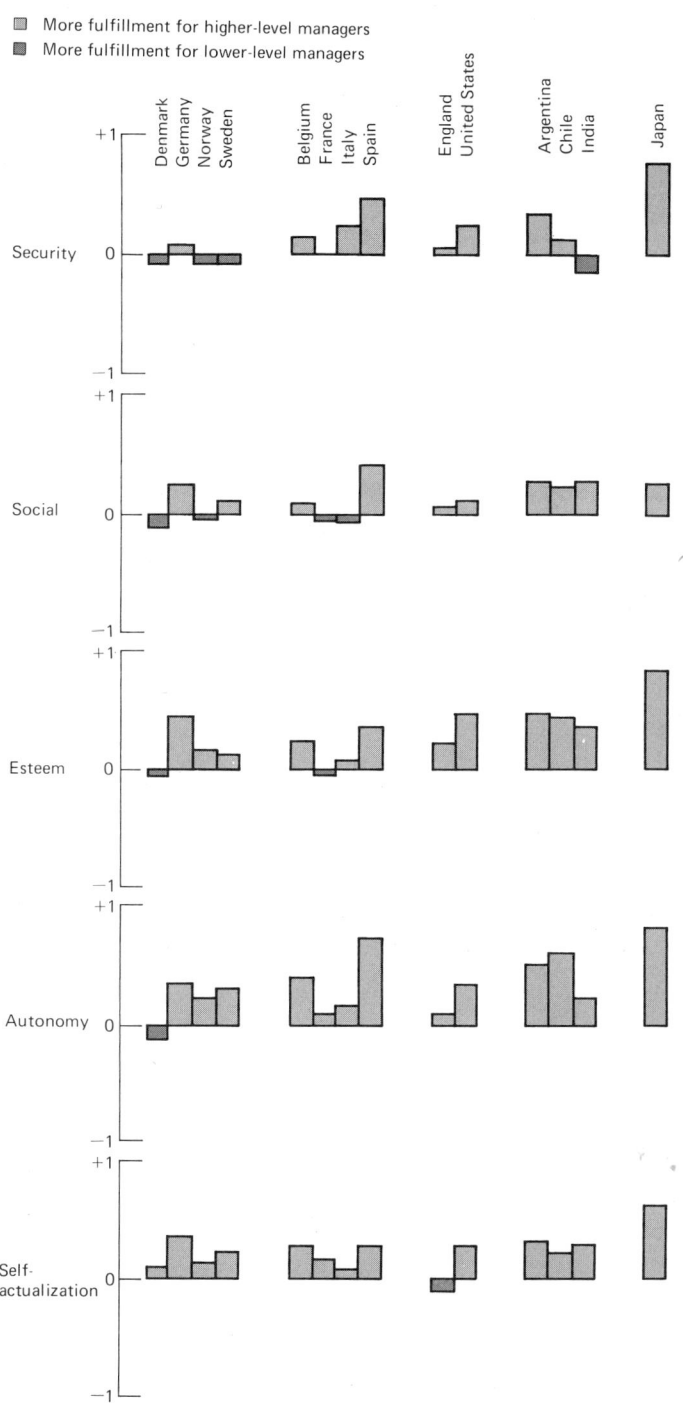

Source: M. Haire, E. E. Ghiselli, and L. W. Porter, *Managerial Thinking: An International Study* (New York: Wiley, 1966), p. 128.

Planning: The Establishment of Role Prescriptions

department store (35). Competitive and power motivation decrease consistently with each successive lower level. The desire to perform routine administrative duties is marked at the department supervisor level, but the other two managerial levels do not differ. The masculine role motivation measure rises from the lowest to middle level, but then declines at the next highest level. These findings, especially those for competitive and power motivation, appear to be typical for large administrative organizations. Furthermore, there is reason to believe that motives precede promotion and contribute to movement into higher-level positions (35).

Table 7-1 Differences in Mean Motivation Scores at Various Organizational Levels in a Department Store

		Motivational Measures			
Job Level	N	Overall Index of Managerial Motivation	Competitive Motivation	Desire to Behave in Masculine Role	Power Motivation	Desire to Perform Routine Administration
Department Supervisor	20	6.60	—.15	.40	.80	1.40
Assistant Department Supervisor	17	4.76	—.41	1.06	.29	.65
Selling Supervisor	33	3.03	—.79	.21	—.15	.70

Source: J. B. Miner, *Studies in Management Education* (New York: Springer, 1965), pp. 74, 76.

Formal and Informal Status. The studies reviewed to this point have dealt with formally designated status in administrative organizations. We have considered differences associated with the hierarchy of positions within the management of such organizations. This hierarchy represents part of the reward structure of these organizations in that the prospect of promotion to a higher-level position is one of the role sanctions that can be brought to bear in influencing role behavior and one of the rewards that can be offered. There is abundant evidence that placing individuals in such formal positions of leadership makes it possible for them to exert greater influence on the behavior of others (18).

Yet it would be a mistake to assume that such formal, hierarchic status is the only basis for exercising power and exerting influence in organizations. As indicated in Chapter 2 influence patterns do not mesh with the managerial hierarchy nearly as closely in professional organizations as they do in administrative ones. Furthermore, there is reason to believe that even in many administrative organizations reward structures are not well synchronized with value structures (36). As Barnard noted a number of years ago informal structures tend to develop alongside the formal, based on differing values and considerations (3). Within formal organizational levels there may be wide differences in recognized status which are in no sense a part of the formal role prescriptions.

This point is brought out clearly in a study conducted among managers at the lowest level of supervision in one state government agency and two business organizations (2). In response to standard questions only a small proportion of the supervisors accepted the view that people at the same organizational level really had the same status. Furthermore, data were obtained which indicated that in all three organizations greater task complexity was associated with greater perceived status. It is interesting to note that the supervisors were reluctant to discuss this value structure related to task complexity in any detail with the researchers. It is right and proper to talk about differences in formal status openly; it is quite another matter to be equally open in discussing factors associated with informal status structures which are not officially supposed to exist.

Delegation

In spite of the fact that the freedom and scope of decision making appear to be greater at higher levels of management, classical management theory has tended to favor delegation, whereby decisions are moved downward to the lowest level possible. This is not meant to imply that all decisions should be made by the first level of management, however. Delegation assumes that there will be differences in the information available at different levels and in the competence of managers. It also assumes that certain kinds of decisions and tasks should not be passed down to lower levels (46). Thus much of the policy-planning process is viewed as appropriately remaining at the top of the organization. Furthermore, although the delegation concept states that managers should permit their subordinate managers to make their own decisions whenever possible and should allow them to implement these decisions, it also states that the subordinate manager is responsible and accountable for the results of his action. This means that the managers who do the delegating must follow up on the decisions of their subordinates and evaluate the results. Delegation does not in any sense mean complete freedom to act as one pleases without concern for consequences.

The purposes served by delegation are many. Without resort to some delegation most companies of any size would face such a mass of decisions at the top that effective operation would be practically impossible. The press of day-to-day decisions would almost certainly preclude realistic planning. Delegation has the apparent value that it can save time in communicating up and then back down the managerial hierarchy and permit reasonably rapid decisions at whatever level the needed information first becomes available. In addition, the man who is actually on the scene may well be in a position to make better decisions than a top executive far removed at corporate headquarters. To these advantages might be added the fact that implementation is more likely if it occurs close to the decision point and that experience in making decisions is valuable in developing managers to assume higher-level responsibilities.

Given these positive considerations, the reasonable and appropriate use of delegation down the vertical chain of managerial levels appears to have many advantages for all but the very smallest companies. Yet the findings from several studies conducted to determine the effectiveness of formal delegation do raise a note of caution (31, 32).

In simulation studies carried out both with practicing managers and with college students it has been found that although some subordinates will go well beyond the freedom delegated to them, others will not use the freedom that is given. Thus, formal delegation may be less important to the final outcome than the individual tendencies of managers to make their own decisions or defer to superiors. Clearly many managers are unwilling to take the risk of making decisions and being held accountable. They claim that their freedom of action is restricted when in fact it is merely that they do not want to accept responsibility for their own decisions. It seems apparent from this research that if delegation is to prove effective, managers must be found or developed who can accept delegation and make decisions in accordance with the requirements of this particular type of role prescription.

Centralization and Decentralization

Where delegation is at a minimum, decision making will be highly centralized. To the extent delegation is extended far down the managerial chain on a larger number of issues decentralization will prevail. The term *decentralization* may also be applied to those situations where decision making moves to lower levels, but without the follow-up, control, and responsibility for results implied by the concept of delegation.

As it is most widely used today, however, decentralization means an organization structure analogous to that implied by the profit center concept discussed in Chapter 3. This is the divisionalized structure which has emerged in so much of American industry since World War II.

Historical Trends. Prior to the 1920s the predominant mode of organization was by functions. The firm was segmented into major units such as manufacturing, marketing, and finance. The individual in charge of each of these units reported to the president. Typically such companies had one or only a few related product lines. Although such functionally segmented organization structures can exist with considerable decentralization, research indicates that the more functional units there are the greater the probability of centralized decision making at the top (34). This is true even when organizations of the same size are compared.

Shortly after World War I a number of firms began to develop decentralized, divisionalized structures along the lines set forth in Figure 7–2. Among

Figure 7–2 Decentralization with Divisionalization by Product Lines

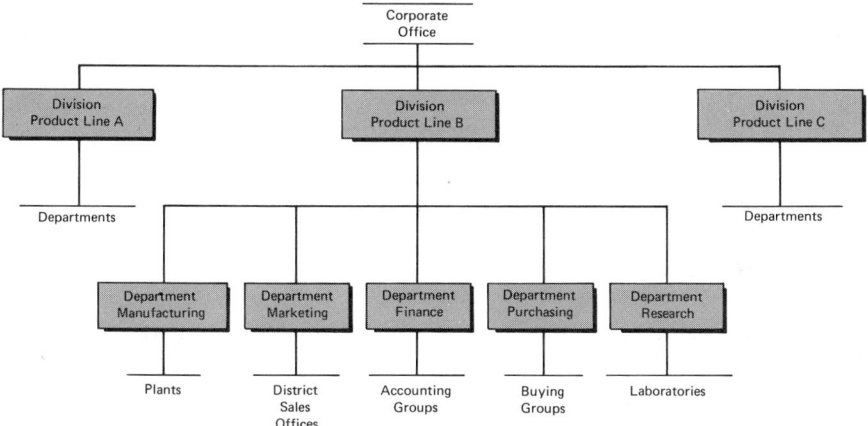

the first to do so were duPont, General Motors, Standard Oil of New Jersey, and Sears, Roebuck (8). Each seems to have moved in this direction independently in response to its own special circumstances. Other companies making similar changes in this early period were United States Rubber, B. F. Goodrich, Union Carbide, Westinghouse Electric, and the A. and P. grocery chain. The impetus for change in all cases appears to have been the development of a strategy of diversification into new markets.

Primarily this meant new product lines, but overseas expansion was often involved as well. The diversification of product lines frequently resulted in crises of overproduction; the resort to a decentralized structure occurred as a means of getting to new markets and coping with the problems of increasing size.

Although the depression of the 1930s and World War II delayed the spread of the new decentralized form, widespread adoption occurred in the late 1940s and the 1950s. More recently some writers have claimed that a shift back toward centralization was imminent, and in fact under way (13). However, the available evidence indicates that at least through the 1960s no such reversal occurred. Overall, it appears that the number of firms using the decentralized form, either on a product line basis or less frequently on a geographic basis, is steadily increasing (4, 20). Decentralization with functional units has become less attractive because of the difficulties associated with establishing meaningful profit centers for the functional divisions.

Existing Forms. The type of decentralization under consideration involves a corporate office which carries out strategic planning, appraises the work of the divisions primarily in terms of profit center performance, and allocates resources (monetary, material, and human) to the divisions. Thus a number of activities do remain centralized in the corporate office. Among these are setting corporate objectives, strategic planning, determination of basic policies, finance, accounting systems, basic research, consummation of mergers and acquisitions, approval of capital expenditures above certain limits, executive compensation, executive selection, setting guidelines for collective bargaining settlements with unions, and many aspects of public relations (20). In addition to the various staff executives handling these activities the corporate office also includes the president and/or chairman of the board, and in a number of instances various executive vice-presidents or group vice-presidents who have specific responsibilities for groups of divisions.

Division managers are delegated responsibility for decisions on such matters as the performance of their component functional departments, pricing, design and quality of products, product development, and marketing. Typically they operate within a broad framework established by corporate policy and have considerable autonomy. While decision making at the corporate level is often a group process, it tends to become more individualized at the division level (8). The division manager alone is responsible for the day-to-day operation and profit performance of his unit. If he fails to meet acceptable standards, someone else will take his place.

As contrasted with centralized forms, those with decentralized divisions do appear to move many decisions downward. Delegation from the very top to the next level usually does occur. But it is also true that in most cases decentralization occurs only in positions that are well up in the managerial hierarchy (56). Below the division manager level renewed centralization is characteristic. Thus, while decentralization with divisionalization tends to equalize the decision-making powers of corporate management and division managers to a considerable degree, it has little impact on the great bulk of the organization. For this reason it is probably best considered a special variant of centralization applicable to large and complex organizations; the term *decentralization* applied to such structures is correct only in a very limited sense.

That this organizational form has achieved its widest application in the more complex companies is evident from Table 7–2. The four industries

Table 7–2 Relationship Between Decentralized Structure and Other Factors

Industry	Index of Decentralization*	Index of Diversification*	Percent Foreign Investment	Percent Research Employees
Transportation	.36	.73	35	34
Chemicals	.58	.75	28	22
Electrical	.64	.67	24	47
Rubber	1.00	.70	41	16
Food	1.18	.93	13	3
Machinery	1.19	.81	22	13
Paper	1.30	.89	17	2
Primary and Fabricated Metals	1.55	.81	20	6

* Low scores indicate presence of characteristic.
Source: L. E. Fouraker and J. M. Stopford, "Organizational Structure and the Multinational Strategy," *Administrative Science Quarterly*, Vol. 13 (1968), 62.

where there is the most widespread use of decentralized divisions are also the ones with the greatest diversity of products, the greatest investment in foreign operations, and the largest amount of research and development activity (14). What appears to have happened is that as they grew more complex, many companies in these industries have split up into a number of smaller partial companies held together and coordinated by a single corporate umbrella.

Influences of Technology and Environment. An increasing body of research evidence, accumulated in recent years, relates the degree of centralization or decentralization in organizations to aspects of the task performed or technology used, and to aspects of the external environment in which a company operates (23). In this research, decentralization has been taken to mean a much more complete delegation of decision making than that implied by the divisionalized forms considered in the preceding section.

Several studies indicate that where the work is of a relatively routine nature with a high degree of uniformity, there is likely to be considerable centralization of decision making (15, 17). Where the work is less routine and where many individuals with professional specialization and training are involved, decentralization is characteristic and many decisions are delegated to lower levels and to the professionals.

A widely cited research program conducted by Woodward in England relates the degree of centralization to more specific types of production technologies (58). Centralization was found to be most pronounced where production was on a large-batch or mass-production basis. This included the usual assembly line operation. With simpler technologies involving unit production or small batches, or with more complex technologies of a continuous process nature such as those used in the chemical industry, a greater degree of decentralization was characteristic.

Subsequent studies in England have failed to yield results comparable to those obtained by Woodward. In this later research the nature of the production technology has not proved particularly important in relation to centralization (19). On the other hand, the Woodward research was conducted with relatively small organizations, the great majority having fewer than 500 employees. Here it seems reasonable to expect that the nature of the technology would have its greatest impact on structure, since the whole company is very close to the production process. In larger organizations of the type considered in the more recent studies this "technological imperative" appears to be diluted by other considerations.

Among these other considerations, aspects of the external environment loom large. Centralization appears to be particularly pronounced in organizations that are highly dependent on other organizations or groups in their environment for survival and continued operation (24, 43). These environmental factors are represented by a corporate headquarters, labor unions, suppliers, industrial users of products, and the like. To the extent a company is at the mercy, so to speak, of such environmental forces—a powerful corporate headquarters or a single major purchaser—it tends to resort to a highly centralized structure. Where it is less dependent on such stable outside factors, where the environment is less predictable and more in flux, a company is likely to be more decentralized.

Centralization vs. Decentralization. It seems improbable from what has been said thus far that a single solution to the centralization-decentralization problem will be most appropriate under all conditions of technology and environmental variation. The evidence tends to support this conclusion (42, 58). The degree to which centralization of decision making contributes to goal attainments is clearly contingent on other factors.

Studies of effective and ineffective organizations make it clear that some centralization, particularly of strategic planning and decisions, is highly desirable in all organizations (42). A very high degree of centralization seems particularly appropriate in relatively small administrative organizations with considerable routine work, using an assembly line type of technology, having a dependent relation to the environment, and operating under stable circumstances. To the extent organizations with many of these features become large and complex in terms of product lines and markets, resort to a decentralized, divisionalized form of organization seems almost essential. But, as previously noted, this is typically only a special variant of centralization and represents a very limited decentralization at best.

On the other hand, in professional organizations a much more pronounced decentralization seems to be required, at least insofar as day-to-day operating decisions are concerned. Lawyers, accountants, and consultants must make their own decisions regarding advice to clients with reference to the particular circumstances existing at a point in time. Attempts to centralize such decisions often result in a considerable loss of professional staff. Furthermore, the requisite knowledge and information is typically available at the level of the practicing professional. A similar degree of decentralization appears appropriate when a company is operating in an unpredictable environment, which is constantly changing and characterized by high risk. Here the organization needs to be rapidly responsive to new cues wherever they may arise. Too highly centralized a decision structure can easily result in inappropriate and outdated responses, or in no response at all. Yet even under those conditions which make decentralization most desirable, the practice should not be carried to the point where the top levels of management become relatively powerless. There is ample research evidence that when that occurs organizations become much less effective (49).

The Number of Hierarchic Levels and Span of Control

The association between the number of levels of management in an organization and the number of individuals reporting to a manager at the next higher level is clearly very close. If one structures an organization of any size so that on the average each manager has very few people as subordinates, the resulting shape will be tall and narrow. If the average span of control for each manager is sharply increased, given the same-size organization, the managerial pyramid will flatten and the number of levels in the hierarchy will be less.

In this section the two aspects of structure will be considered separately, since the available research tends to stress one or the other. Yet almost without exception the two factors are so intimately interwoven that in interpreting a study it is impossible to separate the effects of one from the effects of the other. This characteristic confounding of the vertical span and the span of control variables should be kept in mind as the research is considered.

Tall and Flat Organizations

As companies grow larger they tend to increase the number of hierarchic levels; the positive relationship between size in terms of number of employees and levels is pronounced (19). In many of the larger corporations, for instance, a level of management has appeared between the vice-presidents who are in charge of divisions or functional units and the president. The titles executive vice-president and group vice-president are often used to apply to managers who supervise a number of product line division managers. These same titles may be used on occasion with managers who have a grouping of functional units under them—personnel, public relations, legal, research and development, and so on. However, in such cases it is more typical to use the title vice-president for administration (20).

Studies in Organizations. This tendency to increase the number of levels has occurred in the face of strong arguments favoring a relatively flat structure emerging out of the Sears, Roebuck experience in carrying out its shift to the decentralized form (8, 59). The essence of these arguments was that the flat organization with wide spans of control produces less control from the top, greater individual initiative and thus more satisfied as well as more effective managers.

The available research evidence often fails to support the proponents of flat structures, although it does not universally favor tall structures either (39). A comprehensive survey of over 1,500 managers in many companies throughout the United States revealed that for the group as a whole those in flat structures were no more satisfied than those in tall (38). However, in smaller companies (under 5,000 employees) there was a tendency for the flat structure to be associated with greater job satisfaction; in the larger companies this relationship was reversed—job satisfaction was greater in the tall structure. A companion survey conducted among managers in 13 countries produced much the same pattern of results (41). A survey of physiologists working in relatively small, nonuniversity research laboratories generally found little evidence that the number of levels has much relation to satisfaction and performance, although what positive findings there were tended to favor a tall structure in the larger organizations (33).

Evidence from the Woodward study of English firms, most of them relatively small, indicates a close relationship between the type of technology and the number of levels of management (58). The small-batch and unit-production firms usually had three levels and if they did they were most likely to be successful; more or fewer levels were likely to be associated with below-average success. In the large-batch and mass-production firms the typical and desirable number of levels rose to four. In the continuous process firms the average was six, and firms with many fewer or more levels in the hierarchy were usually the less successful. At least in these latter organizations a relatively tall structure was desirable, although even here the number of levels could be carried too far.

Laboratory Studies. Given the uncertainties arising from the studies in organizations, several researchers have recently turned to the laboratory situation for a solution. In these studies business simulation problems have been employed with different types of structures.

The first such study conducted by Jones used three structures as indicated in Figure 7–3 (25). No clear relation was found between the number of levels and profitability or number of errors. The data indicate that the three-level structure was the fastest, the two-level next, and the four-level slowest. Satisfaction was greatest in the two-level structure; there was no difference between those of three and four levels. The study suffers

Planning: The Establishment of Role Prescriptions

Figure 7–3 Organization Structures Used in Laboratory Studies

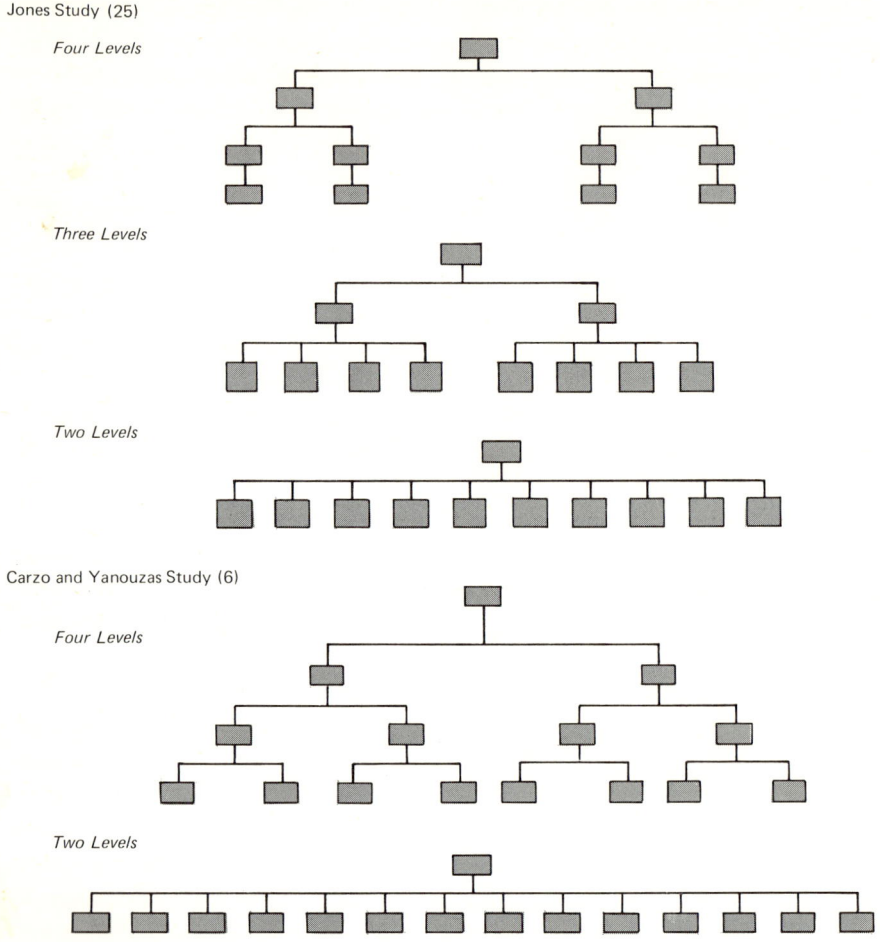

because the measures were often sufficiently unstable to preclude meaningful results.

A later study comparing four- and two-level structures only (Figure 7–3) and thus dealing with more extreme variations yielded considerably more support for the tall structure (6, 7). In this instance the time needed to learn to operate most effectively within a given type of structure was taken into account. Since such learning typically does occur in ongoing organizations, this study appears to provide a better simulation of the usual corporate situation. The tall structure produced greater profits and rate of return on sales revenue than the flat, although time to reach decisions did not differ. The findings are explained by the fact that the greater number of levels permitted more frequent evaluation of decisions and the fact that the narrower span of control introduced a more orderly decision process.

Overall, the data on tall and flat organizations seem to suggest that there may be advantages associated with the taller structures, especially in larger companies and under certain conditions of technology. Yet it is probably premature to conclude with any certainty what the contingent conditions are in this case. In any event the early conclusions derived from the Sears, Roebuck experience do not seem to be generalizable. Flat structures are not always the best.

Span of Control

From the conclusions emerging from the research on hierarchic levels one might anticipate that more often than not narrow spans of control, with few subordinates reporting to each superior, would prove advantageous in administrative organizations. This is in fact the position taken by many of the early writers. Fayol felt that above the first level, spans should usually be fewer than 6 (12). However, where the work was routine he recommended a span of 20 or 30 production workers reporting to each foreman. R. C. Davis made a similar distinction between higher-level and first-level spans using the terms *executive span* and *operative span* to describe them (10). He felt that the executive span could vary from 3 to 9 depending on such factors as a company's growth rate and the nature of the work. Where the work is maximally interacting he showed that the marginal increase in the complexity of a superior's job resulting from adding a subordinate is greatest beyond spans of 5. Like Fayol he recommended increasing the operative span to as many as 30.

The proponents of narrow executive spans have not gone unchallenged. Particular emphasis has been placed on the cost savings that can accrue when spans are increased and the number of hierarchic levels consequently reduced (48, 51). Perhaps even more frequent is the charge originating with the Sears, Roebuck experience that narrow spans result in excessive control on the part of superiors and a stifling of initiative among subordinates (59). Wider spans are viewed as desirable because a superior cannot possibly make all decisions for so many subordinates, and thus decentralization becomes inevitable.

Recent research, however, has made it clear that there need not be a close relation between span of control and degree of centralization or control over decisions (57). It is true that to the extent the work is highly routine and standardized, narrow spans of control go with centralization. But when the work becomes less routine, as in most professional organizations, this relationship breaks down—a narrow span of control may or may not mean centralized decision making and a wide span may or may not mean decentralization.

Spans in Existing Organizations. Considerable research has been done merely collecting information on spans in various organizations, particularly those at the top level involving individuals reporting to the chief executive. One such study based on 100 large companies revealed top-level spans ranging from 1 to 24; in only about a quarter of the firms did the span go as low as 6 (9). Other studies have generally found a somewhat smaller average span, but there is no question that there is tremendous variation from company to company (22).

Efforts to account for these variations in spans have begun to yield meaningful results. It is clear that certain factors are consistently associated with the size of the span of control (47). Both executive and operative spans tend to become larger in larger organizations. Executive spans at the very highest level appear to increase with technological complexity, being largest in continuous process industries; at the middle management level this same technology effect does not appear to be present. Technology has a definite relation to the operative span. The number of workers reporting to a foreman tends to reach its maximum in the middle range of technological complexity where large-batch and mass-production procedures predominate (see Table 7–4).

Other findings on factors related to the size of the span of control derive from a study carried out with 67 sales and marketing executives (52). Among these top-level managers the span tended to be greater, 9 or more, when they had assistants helping them, when their subordinates were supervised in certain aspects of their work by others, when the subordinates were spread out over a number of locations, when the subordinates did essentially the same kind of work, and when subordinates had considerable experience, amounting to 10 years or more. These results are given in detail in Table 7–3.

The crucial question, however, is not what factors may contribute to existing structures, but how are existing structures related to goal attain-

Table 7-3 Span of Control as Related to Other Factors (N = 67)

Factors	Span of Control		
	Fewer than 6 %	6, 7, or 8 %	9 or more %
Having personal assistants			
With assistants	4	31	65
No assistants	46	20	34
Subordinates supervised in part by others			
Supervision from others	0	10	90
No other supervision	37	26	37
Subordinates' dispersion			
Same office	48	28	24
Different office, same city	56	25	19
Not in the same city	0	19	81
Similarity of subordinates' functions			
Similar functions	13	17	70
Different functions	46	30	24
Subordinates' average experience in job			
Under 5 years	57	14	29
5 to 10 years	37	30	33
10 or more years	12	23	65

Source: J. G. Udell, "An Empirical Test of Hypotheses Relating to Span of Control," *Administrative Science Quarterly*, Vol. 12 (1967), 426, 433.

ment? On this point the evidence is more sparse. Once again the Woodward study, although tending to concentrate on smaller companies, is among the most significant (58). Unfortunately the detailed data reported deal only with operative spans, although the span of the chief executive is said to follow a similar pattern. The findings are given in Table 7-4. Within each type of technology the successful firms have "average" spans; the less successful, spans that are either too low or too high for their particular technological system.

A second study found that within the plastics industry success was associated with major differences in span of control—narrow spans in production, somewhat larger spans in sales, and very wide spans in research (28). Similar spans in all three functions were characteristic of the less successful companies. However, these firms operated in a constantly changing, risk-laden environment. In the more stable environment of the container industry successful firms had essentially equal spans in the three functional areas. From this and the Woodward research it is clear that span of control is related to success in a complex manner, but that the relationship is highly contingent on technological and environmental conditions.

Table 7–4 *Average Span of Control of First-Line Supervisors Analyzed by Type of Technology and Success Level*

Production System	Span of Control					
	Up to 20	21 to 40	41 to 60	61 to 80	Over 80	Total
Unit and Small Batch						
All firms	7	12	4	0	1	24
Above-average success		5				5
Below-average success	2		3			5
Large Batch and Mass						
All firms	1	7	13	6	4	31
Above-average success			5			5
Below-average success	1	2		1	2	6
Continuous Process						
All firms	18	7				25
Above-average success	6					6
Below-average success	1	3				4

Source: J. Woodward, *Industrial Organization: Theory and Practice* (London: Oxford University Press, 1965), p. 69.

Small Group Research. Several recent discussions of the span of control concept have pointed to the particular relevance of research in group dynamics, and in particular to those studies which utilize group size as one of the major variables (11, 22). These studies have typically been conducted in a laboratory setting and utilize groups that have not worked together before. Thus the groups are devoid of both an organizational context and a history. Yet it is appropriate to view a manager and the subordinates reporting to him as a group. This group feature of the organizational hierarchy has been stressed in particular by Likert in developing his linking pin concept (29). In this view the hierarchy consists of a series of overlapping groups as in Figure 7–4. Each manager is both in charge of his own group and a member of the next higher group. He thus forms a linking pin between the two groups. Implicit in this is the idea that managing involves frequent face-to-face meetings with all subordinates present at once, rather than a series of one-to-one interactions between the manager and each separate subordinate at different points in time.

Given such a group aspect of the span of control concept, then, what can studies dealing with small groups of various sizes tell us that might be of

Figure 7-4 Likert's Concept of Overlapping Groups and the Linking Pin Function

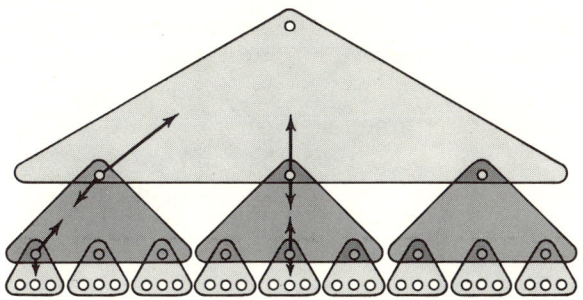

(The arrows indicate the linking pin function)

Source: From R. Likert, *New Patterns of Management* (New York: McGraw-Hill, 1961) p. 113. Used with permission of McGraw-Hill Book Company.

value in deciding how large a particular span should be? The combined evidence from a variety of studies suggests a number of conclusions (22). As groups become larger they tend to split into cliques and factions. Thus the leadership and coordination requirements of the manager's job become much more difficult. Members of larger groups are likely to become dissatisfied, and each individual participates less in the affairs of the group. It is harder and takes longer to reach a consensus when many people are involved. In general a more formal and structured pattern of leadership tends to emerge in larger groups, and members prefer this.

On the other hand, larger groups can make more resources available for decision making, especially if considerable heterogeneity exists. Beyond this value of increased size in certain types of decision making, there is insufficient evidence to be certain about the effects of size on individual performance (50). Evidence is available, however, indicating that very small groups of up to four members suffer from a general inhibition of discussion and disagreement. Thus ideas often do not get an adequate hearing (21).

Taking all of the evidence together, certain generalizations regarding span of control seem warranted:

1. The optimal span for most situations is in the range of 5 to 10.
2. The larger spans, within this range, say, 8 through 10, are most appropriate at higher levels in an organization where the greater resources for diverse decision making that can result are most likely to be needed.

3. The size of the operative span is appropriately influenced by both the type of technology and the costs associated with the smaller spans. Spans below 10 may not be economically feasible because of the number of foremen required in spite of other potential advantages.
4. In establishing a span of control for a specific situation, factors such as the desirability of group solidarity, the need for job satisfaction, the amount of control required, the nature of the work, the stability of the environment, and the extent of assistance to the manager must be taken into account.

The Role of the Board of Directors

The discussion to this point has scanned the management hierarchy from top to bottom, being particularly concerned with upward or downward shifts in decision making and with factors related to the length of the vertical chain. In this section the spotlight focuses on a more limited vertical segment, the one at the very top. We will be concerned first with the composition and nature of what in the business world is typically called the board of directors; in other contexts such terms as *regents*, *trustees*, or simply *board members* may be used. Then the discussion will deal with relationships between this board, its chairman, and the top corporate officers.

Board Composition

The state laws governing the creation of a corporation characteristically require a board of directors with at least three members. These directors represent the stockholders and may be held legally liable for their actions vis à vis the company on whose board they serve.

Although board size tends to vary considerably from company to company, a survey of 100 major corporations yielded an average figure of 13.0 for 1969 (4). Ten years earlier these same firms had an average of 12.4 directors. The increase is accounted for by the normal tendency for companies to add board members as they themselves grow. In general, boards in insurance and in banking, particularly, run considerably larger. Banks tend to add board members from the business community as they grow. Yet the evidence that is available on the subject indicates no relationship between a bank's board size and its profitability (1). As might be anticipated from the discussion in the previous sections of the tendency toward subgroup formation in groups of any size, the typical board contains a number of committees within itself.

Board members may be officers of the company or they may come from other sources. In most cases they do have other employment and in many instances will be serving on the boards of other corporations as well. Whether or not one views the proportion of directors from inside the firm as increasing or decreasing depends on the particular sample of companies studied, the times compared, and the definition of an inside director (Are former officers who have since retired but remain on the board to be considered as insiders?) The most recent data indicate that over the 1959–1969 period the proportion of actual officers has moved from 45 percent to 40 percent in large corporations (4). Thus there appears to be some current trend toward the use of outsiders, or at least those who are not currently serving as company officers.

Table 7–5 gives data on the sources of directors for 35 of the 50 largest U.S. manufacturing firms in 1967. It is clear that the proportion of officer directors in these firms is somewhat above that for large corporations

Table 7–5 Percent of Directors from Various Sources in 35 Major Manufacturers

Background	Percent of Directors
Officer Directors	46.0
Former Officers	12.1
Industrialists	13.2
Banks	8.4
Investment Firms	7.8
Education	2.8
Utilities	2.6
Law	2.0
Merchandising	1.3
Insurance	.9
Government	.7
Railroads	.6
Foundations	.4
Publishing	.4
Other Sectors	.7

Source: S. C. Vance, *The Corporate Director—A Critical Evaluation* (Homewood, Ill.: Dow Jones-Irwin, 1968), p. 33. Reproduced with permission.

generally; so too is the average number of directors per firm—15.4 (55). It is also evident, however, that the business world provides the major proportion of its own directors. The numbers from education, government, and the foundations are quite small. Business knowledge and experience, rather than representation of a special interest group, appears to be the primary criterion (27).

The empirical question as to whether predominantly inside or predominantly outside boards are desirable has been answered. From integration theory one would assume that the basically inside board, where the majority of members were likely to be consonant with the value system and certainly the reward system of the company, would prove superior. Such does appear to be the case (53). The more successful companies in the aircraft, automobile, chemical, electrical equipment, farm equipment. meatpacking, nonferrous metals, paper, rubber, steel, and tobacco industries have boards of directors which are largely made up of company officers. Of the industries studied only petroleum did not show this trend. These data, however, do not definitely establish cause and effect. It is possible that consistently effective managements have established their right to place a number of valued members on the board of directors. Or it may well be that an inside board is simply more likely to be successful. On this point we cannot be entirely certain as yet.

Although a few large corporations do utilize full-time directors, this is not a common practice. In the past the tendency has been to compensate directors at a rather low level on the assumption that they would be deriving the major part of their income from other sources. In recent years, however, compensation levels have risen drastically (20). Practices vary but payment tends to be in some combination of meeting fees, committee fees, and retainers. Many firms pay all three to outside directors, with as many as 12 board meetings a year and perhaps a number of committee meetings in addition.

Nature and Extent of Activities

The extent of board influence on corporate decisions varies considerably. There are, without question, boards that have practically no influence at all; they exist only for legal reasons (55). On the other hand, the more typical pattern currently appears to be for the board to exert a strong advisory influence, and in certain areas considerable control. And there are boards that do in fact exercise broad powers over almost all areas of company decision making.

The primary areas where boards exert influence are in the determination of broad objectives, the approval of top-level policies, approval of organization structures, appointment of corporate officers, top management compensation, approval of budgets, approval of planned commitments, approval of outside auditors and lawyers, and approval of items that require stockholder action (26). Boards are responsible for declaring dividends and in many cases become actively involved in mergers and acquisitions. In general the role prescriptions for board members call for advice in important areas of operation and for evaluation of decisions, proposals, and actions initiated by operating management. Thus the ideal board member tends to be an individual who is broadly knowledgeable across a sizable sector of business activity. It is not surprising that increasingly boards of directors contain people who have obtained graduate degrees (54).

Vertical Relationships at the Top

The relative status of the chairman of the board and the president, if both positions exist, is a matter that may be thoroughly confusing to anyone who is not intimately familiar with the affairs of a particular company. There are a number of variants. In some cases the chairman of the board merely presides over board meetings acting as would any committee chairman; he has no further formal duties in the company. At the other extreme is the case where the chairman is in fact the chief executive, has the top level of status, and exerts strong influence in all areas including operating, matters.

It is possible that the position title chairman of the board may not exist, and the president perform the necessary duties. Or the same person may hold both positions. Sometimes a separation of role prescriptions along functional lines occurs—usually with the chairman handling finance, legal, public relations, stockholder relations, and long-range planning (26). The president then is in charge primarily of the operating functions, such as marketing and production.

It is not possible to say that any one pattern is best, just as one cannot establish with certainty whether the board of directors or the operating executives should exert the greatest influence. The needed evidence in these areas simply is not available. However, evidence from role theory does

Planning: The Establishment of Role Prescriptions

indicate that to the extent role conflict and ambiguity exist as between the chairman of the board, the president, the board of directors, and company officers the consequences will be distinctly negative (45). The great diversity of status relationships currently in existence suggests that power conflicts are frequent at the top and that considerable potential for role conflict and role ambiguity exists.

On the other hand, there is some evidence indicating that improvements have occurred in this regard at least in large corporations (4). In 1969 out of 100 companies surveyed 53 used the title chief executive officer—34 appended it to the chairman of the board position and 19 to the president. There was negligible use of the chief executive officer title to designate the highest status position in 1959. Similarly 54 percent of the companies now clearly specify the board of directors as the ultimate authority. The degree of ambiguity at the top seems to be declining.

In this chapter the discussion has concentrated on vertical aspects of structure while tending to brush aside such questions regarding horizontal aspects as might arise, as in the treatment of decentralized divisions and span of control. In the next chapter the horizontal dimension of structure will be added, so that a complete picture may be obtained.

Questions

1. What factors might account for the finding that boards of directors having a membership consisting primarily of managers from inside the company rather than outsiders are more likely to be found in more successful companies? Can you explain why the number of outside directors appears to be increasing, nevertheless?
2. What exactly is meant by delegation? Is it the same as decentralization? Why would a manager want to resort to delegation?
3. How do early formulations regarding the span of control compare with existing practice and the research evidence on the most effective spans? What relevance does small group research have for the span of control question?
4. What relationships exist between degree of centralization, company size, type of technology, and environmental pressures?
5. What would appear to be the consequences of using a flat organization structure with a large span of control? Why might such a structure prove more effective in a firm such as Sears, Roebuck than in other types of companies?

References

1. Baker, H. K. "An Analysis of Selected Factors Relating to the Size and Relative Profitability of National Banks in the State of Maryland." Unpublished paper. College Park: University of Maryland, 1970.
2. Balk, W. L. "Status Perceptions of Management Peers." *Academy of Management Journal*, Vol. 12 (1969), 431–437.
3. Barnard, C. I. *The Functions of the Executive.* Cambridge, Mass.: Harvard University Press, 1938.
4. Battalia, Lotz, and Associates. *A Decade of Change in Top Management Organization and Executive Job Titles.* New York: The Firm, 1969.
5. Blankenship, V., and R. E. Miles. "Organizational Structure and Managerial Decision Behavior." *Administrative Science Quarterly*, Vol. 13 (1968), 106–120.
6. Carzo, R., and J. N. Yanouzas. "Effects of Flat and Tall Organization Structure." *Administrative Science Quarterly*, Vol. 14 (1969), 178–191.
7. Carzo, R., and J. N. Yanouzas. "Justification for the Carzo-Yanouzas Experiment on Flat and Tall Structures." *Administrative Science Quarterly*, Vol. 15 (1970), 235–240.
8. Chandler, A. D. *Strategy and Structure.* Cambridge, Mass.: The M.I.T. Press, 1962.
9. Dale, E. *Planning and Developing the Company Organization Structure.* AMA Research Report No. 20. New York: American Management Association, 1952.
10. Davis, R. C. *The Fundamentals of Top Management.* New York: Harper, 1951.
11. Delbecq, A. L. "The World Within the Span of Control." *Business Horizons*, Vol. 11 (1968), No. 4, 47–56.
12. Fayol, H. *General and Industrial Management.* London: Pitman, 1949.
13. Fisch, G. G. *Organization for Profit.* New York: McGraw-Hill, 1964.
14. Fouraker, L. E., and J. M. Stopford. "Organizational Structure and Multinational Strategy." *Administrative Science Quarterly*, Vol. 13 (1968), 47–64.
15. Hage, J., and M. Aiken. "Routine Technology, Social Structure, and Organizational Goals." *Administrative Science Quarterly*, Vol. 14 (1969), 366–376.
16. Haire, M., E. E. Ghiselli, and L. W. Porter. *Managerial Thinking: An International Study.* New York: Wiley, 1966.
17. Hall, R. H. "Intraorganizational Structural Variation: Application of the Bureaucratic Model." *Administrative Science Quarterly*, Vol. 7 (1962), 295–308.

18. Hare, A. P. *Handbook of Small Group Research*. New York: Free Press, 1962.
19. Hickson, D. J., D. S. Pugh, and D. C. Pheysey. "Operations Technology and Organization Structure: An Empirical Reappraisal." *Administrative Science Quarterly*, Vol. 14 (1969), 378–397.
20. Holden, P. E., C. A. Pederson, and G. E. Germane. *Top Management*. New York: McGraw-Hill, 1968.
21. Holloman, C. R., and H. W. Hendrick. "Problem Solving in Different Sized Groups." *Personnel Psychology*, Vol. 24 (1971), 489–500.
22. House, R. J., and J. B. Miner. "Merging Management and Behavioral Theory: The Interaction Between Span of Control and Group Size." *Administrative Science Quarterly*, Vol. 14 (1969), 451–464.
23. Hunt, R. G. "Technology and Organization." *Academy of Management Journal*, Vol. 13 (1970), 235–252.
24. Inkson, J. H. K., D. S. Pugh, and D. J. Hickson. "Organizational Context and Structure: An Abbreviated Replication." *Administrative Science Quarterly*, Vol. 15 (1970), 318–329.
25. Jones, H. R. "A Study of Organization Performance for Experimental Structures of Two, Three and Four Levels." *Academy of Management Journal*, Vol. 12 (1969), 351–365.
26. Koontz, H. *The Board of Directors and Effective Management*. New York: McGraw-Hill, 1967.
27. Koontz, H. "The Corporate Board and Special Interests." *Business Horizons*, Vol. 14 (1971), No. 5, 75–82.
28. Lawrence, P. R., and J. W. Lorsch. *Organization and Environment: Managing Differentiation and Integration*. Boston: Graduate School of Business, Harvard University, 1967.
29. Likert, R. *New Patterns of Management*. New York: McGraw-Hill, 1961.
30. Mahoney, T. A., T. H. Jerdee, and S. J. Carroll. "The Job(s) of Management." *Industrial Relations*, Vol. 4 (1965), 97–110.
31. Maier, N. R. F. "The Subordinate's Role in the Delegation Process." *Personnel Psychology*, Vol. 21 (1968), 179–191.
32. Maier, N. R. F., and J. A. Thurber. "Problems in Delegation." *Personnel Psychology*, Vol. 22 (1969), 131–139.
33. Meltzer, L., and J. Salter. "Organizational Structure and the Performance and Job Satisfaction of Physiologists." *American Sociological Review*, Vol. 27 (1962), 351–362.
34. Meyer, M. W. "Two Authority Structures of Bureaucratic Organization." *Administrative Science Quarterly*, Vol. 13 (1968), 211–228.
35. Miner, J. B. *Studies in Management Education*. New York: Springer, 1965.
36. Miner, J. B. "Bridging the Gulf in Organizational Performance." *Harvard Business Review*, Vol. 46 (1968), No. 4, 102–110.

37. Paine, F. T., S. J. Carroll, and B. A. Leete. "Need Satisfaction of Managerial Level Personnel in a Government Agency." *Journal of Applied Psychology*, Vol. 50 (1966), 247–249.
38. Porter, L. W., and E. E. Lawler. "The Effects of Tall versus Flat Organization Structures on Managerial Job Satisfaction." *Personnel Psychology*, Vol. 17 (1964), 135–148.
39. Porter, L. W., and E. E. Lawler. "Properties of Organization Structure in Relation to Job Attitudes and Job Behavior." *Psychological Bulletin*, Vol. 64 (1965), 23–51.
40. Porter, L. W., and V. F. Mitchell. "Comparative Study of Need Satisfactions in Military and Business Hierarchies." *Journal of Applied Psychology*, Vol. 51 (1967), 139–144.
41. Porter, L. W., and J. Siegel. "Relationships of Tall and Flat Organization Structures to the Satisfactions of Foreign Managers." *Personnel Psychology*, Vol. 18 (1965), 379–392.
42. Price, J. L. *Organizational Effectiveness*. Homewood, Ill.: Irwin, 1968.
43. Pugh, D. S., D. J. Hickson, C. R. Hinings, and C. Turner. "The Context of Organization Structures." *Administrative Science Quarterly*, Vol. 14 (1969), 91–114.
44. Rhinehart, J. B., R. P. Barrell, A. S. DeWolfe, J. E. Griffin, and F. E. Spaner. "Comparative Study of Need Satisfactions in Governmental and Business Hierarchies." *Journal of Applied Psychology*, Vol. 53 (1969), 230–235.
45. Rizzo, J. R., R. J. House, and S. I. Lirtzman. "Role Conflict and Ambiguity in Complex Organizations." *Administrative Science Quarterly*, Vol. 15 (1970), 150–163.
46. Sherman, H. *It All Depends—A Pragmatic Approach to Organization*. University, Ala.: University of Alabama Press, 1967.
47. Starbuck, W. H. "Mathematics and Organization Theory." In J. G. March (ed.), *Handbook of Organizations*. Chicago: Rand McNally, 1965, pp. 335–386.
48. Stieglitz, H. "Optimizing Span of Control." *Management Record*, Vol. 24 (1962), No. 9, 25–29.
49. Tannenbaum, A. S. *Control in Organizations*. New York: McGraw-Hill, 1968.
50. Thomas, E. J., and C. F. Fink. "Effects of Group Size." *Psychological Bulletin*, Vol. 60 (1963), 371–384.
51. Thompson, R. E. "Span of Control: Conceptions and Misconceptions." *Business Horizons*, Vol. 7 (1964), No. 2, 49–58.
52. Udell, J. G. "An Empirical Test of Hypotheses Relating to Span of Control." *Administrative Science Quarterly*, Vol. 12 (1967), 420–439.
53. Vance, S. C. *Boards of Directors: Structure and Performance*. Eugene: University of Oregon Press, 1964.

54. Vance, S. C. "Higher Education for the Executive Elite." *California Management Review*, Vol. 8 (1966), No. 4, 21–30.
55. Vance, S. C. *The Corporate Director—A Critical Evaluation*. Homewood, Ill.: Dow Jones-Irwin, 1968.
56. Whisler, T. L. "Measuring Centralization of Control in Business Organizations." In W. W. Cooper, H. J. Leavitt, and M. W. Shelly (eds.), *New Perspectives in Organization Research*. New York: Wiley, 1964, pp. 314–333.
57. Whisler, T. L., H. Meyer, B. H. Baum, and P. F. Sorensen. "Centralization of Organizational Control: An Empirical Study of Its Meaning and Measurement." *Journal of Business*, Vol. 40 (1967), 10–26.
58. Woodward, J. *Industrial Organization: Theory and Practice*. London: Oxford University Press, 1965.
59. Worthy, J. "Organization Structures and Employee Morale." *American Sociological Review*, Vol. 15 (1950), 169–179.

8 Organization Structure: Horizontal Aspects

I. Division of Labor and Job Enlargement
1. Job Analysis
2. Evidence on Job Enlargement
   a. The Bell System Studies
   b. Managerial and Professional Job Enlargement
3. Division of Labor vs. Job Enlargement

II. Departmentation
1. Bases of Departmentation
   a. Comparative Merits
   b. Multinational Structures
2. Size of Departments

III. The Line-Staff Structure
1. The Nature of Staff Roles
   a. General Staff
   b. Professional and Specialist Staff Units
2. Line-Staff Differences and Decision Making

IV. Project Management and Related Forms
1. Product Management
2. Project Management
   a. Role Prescriptions of Project Managers
   b. Effectiveness of the Structure
3. Matrix Structure

V. Committees
1. Types of Committees
2. Conditions for Success

235

Discussion of the horizontal, or lateral, aspects of organization structure should begin with consideration of the individual jobs themselves. In Chapter 1, one of the defining characteristics of an organization was said to be a division of labor. This raises the question of how broad in scope jobs should be. Should they be highly specialized or should the role prescriptions cover a wide variety of duties and tasks? Which alternative is most likely to contribute to the attainment of organizational goals?

In addition to division of labor the horizontal aspect of organization structure encompasses a number of types of job groupings. Departmentation is concerned with the number of separate units and the bases on which grouping occurs—by product, by function performed, by geographical area, or whatever. Line and staff groupings are even more comprehensive in that all departments are placed in one or the other of these two categories. There are also units, frequently of a temporary nature, which flow across the organization. Among these are project teams and committees. The matrix structure, which is being used increasingly, is a series of such horizontal project teams superimposed on an existing hierarchic structure.

All these groupings of role prescriptions—into jobs, departments, projects, and committees—will be considered in this chapter.

Division of Labor and Job Enlargement

Division of labor refers to the extent to which the tasks to be performed in an organization are subdivided and assigned to different individuals. Modern industrial technology has tended to utilize machinery and equipment that requires considerable specialization of work. The consequence has been a routinization of jobs, particularly at lower levels. The division of labor has often been extreme, although the overall result has been a major contribution to productivity. Studies of manufacturing organizations indicate that increased division of labor often does make for increased output (44). Presumably this is so because the dexterity of workmen is increased and time is saved which otherwise would be lost in moving from one set of tasks to another.

Job Analysis

Historically job analysis is closely tied to the work of Frederick Taylor. In the context of scientific management it characteristically meant a narrowing down of the tasks included in a job and the trimming off of non-repetitive activities such as planning. Thus job analysis became identified with highly routinized division of labor.

In its current applications, however, job analysis does not necessarily produce this kind of *job simplification*. There is no particular reason why it cannot result in what has been called *job enrichment*, the inclusion of certain role prescriptions previously assigned to superiors, or in *job enlargment*, the inclusion of role prescriptions previously assigned to others at roughly the same level. Thus a job analysis can serve to shrink the scope of the work, but it can also expand it, both vertically and horizontally. In any event it is the process by which tasks are subdivided and assigned to individuals, the means to achieving a particular division of labor.

The task of job analysis, like organization planning, is merely to specify the particular set of role prescriptions attached to a given job. It yields a statement of what the incumbent *should* do (39). Usually, very detailed job descriptions are established only for positions below the managerial level. However, some firms extend their job analysis program well up the managerial hierarchy, with the result that a considerable overlap with organization planning occurs.

Job analysis information is derived from a number of sources. Among these are observation of the job occupant, interviewing the occupant, a written description prepared by the occupant, existing job descriptions, examination of work tools and materials, and actually performing the job. Which of these are most appropriate in a particular situation will depend on the nature of the job. The outcome often is a lengthy statement indicating job title, salary grade, title of immediate superior, duties, qualifications of an educational nature and in terms of job knowledge, physical requirements, responsibilities, working conditions—both physical and social—and promotional paths. Inherent in these statements for jobs that are part of the same operation is the degree of division of labor.

Evidence on Job Enlargement

With strong prodding from both the human relations and behavioral humanist schools of management thought a number of companies have introduced rather extensive job enlargement programs (40). In most of these cases the job enlargement has actually included both horizontal and vertical aspects. Thus a machine operator's job might be extended horizontally to include both setup and inspection operations, but at the same time

237

the operator might be given discretion with regard to certain matters such as repairs and scheduling which were previously under the control of his superior. In a number of instances job enlargement has involved breaking up assembly lines so that each worker performed a wider range of tasks and actually produced a meaningful unit of production, if not a total product.

There has been a considerable amount of research dealing with the effects produced by a shift to jobs of greater scope. On an overall basis the evidence derived from this research can only be described as conflicting (15, 22, 28, 33). In one study, for instance, in which a machine-tending job was considerably enlarged there was evidence of an associated increase in satisfaction with the use of skills and abilities, but of a decrease in satisfaction with respect from superiors (1). In another case, merely changing the job, without enlargement, had much the same impact as job enlargement (6). There are a number of studies providing positive support for job enlargement in that improvements in productivity, quality, job satisfaction, and/or turnover rates have been obtained. But there are other instances where there has been no change at all, or even negative consequences. The most consistent improvements have been in the quality of work (as a result of combining the inspection process into the job) and in aspects of job satisfaction.

The Bell System Studies. One of the most comprehensive programs of job enlargement has been carried out within A.T. & T. and other parts of the Bell System (17). The initial impetus for the program came from a rapid rise in turnover rates which were becoming increasingly costly because of lost training expenses and hiring costs. To date some 18 studies within the Bell System have been reported on, which contrast groups experiencing job enlargement with similar control groups whose jobs were not changed. These groups are described in Table 8–1. The studies in the Treasury Department and in Commercial were the most successful. Those in the Comptroller's Department showed the next largest gain. In Traffic, Plant, and Engineering the improvements were modest. Among the large urban group of installers in California there was no change at all. Some idea of the extent and type of changes produced by job enlargement in one of the more successful studies is provided by the data of Table 8–2. Although the program as a whole appears to be one of the most effective reported in the literature to date, improvement still has not been universal. Problems have been most pronounced among blue-collar workers.

Organization Structure: Horizontal Aspects

Table 8–1 Bell System Job Enlargement Studies

Department	Job	Location	Number with Enlarged Jobs
Treasury	Shareholder correspondent	New York City	28
Commercial	Service representative	Toronto	50
		Montreal	75
		Chicago	40
		Illinois—Suburban	25
		Illinois—Suburban	25
		Northern Massachusetts	70
		Rhode Island	60
		Maryland	65
Traffic	Toll operator	Saginaw, Michigan	250
		New York City	350
Plant	Installer	California—Large Urban	45
		Chicago	30
	Frame cross-connection	New York City	40
Comptroller's	Service order reentry clerk	Los Angeles	30
	Service order transcription clerk	Atlanta	20
	Key puncher	Minnesota	13
Engineering	Equipment engineer	Detroit	30

Source: R. N. Ford, *Motivation Through the Work Itself* (New York: American Management Association, Inc., 1969), pp. 48–49. Reprinted by permission of the publisher.

Table 8–2 Saving over an 18-Month Period from Enlarging Shareholder Correspondent Job

1. 27 percent drop, turnover, nonsupervisory specialists	$245,000
2. Investigation and file clerks—salaries, annual (force reduced from 46 to 24 clerks, three management jobs eliminated)	135,000
3. Correspondents' group—salaries (five management, four verifier jobs eliminated)	76,000
4. Stock transfer group—salaries eliminated	40,000
5. Merger of employee stock—pension unit and dividend reconciliation unit—salaries eliminated	100,000
6. Improved productivity (not priced)	
7. Improved service indexes (not priced)	
8. Improved tone of exit interviews (not priced)	
9. Personnel section, job rearrangements (not priced)	
10. Offset—half salary, six employees working on job enlargement program part-time	(38,000)
	$558,000

Source: R. N. Ford, *Motivation Through the Work Itself* (New York: American Management Association, Inc., 1969), p. 44. Reprinted by permission of the publisher.

Managerial and Professional Job Enlargement. Most of the research on job enlargement has been conducted with employees below the management level, much of it with blue-collar workers. However, such evidence as there is bearing on higher level positions is favorable. The Bell System study of equipment engineers was moderately successful. In another study foremen were given broader responsibility for all aspects of product manufacture rather than for a single narrow function such as calibrate and test (11). Although there was no improvement in absenteeism, turnover, and the like, there were significant increases in quality and decreases in costs.

The most comprehensive data derive from a study of research and development scientists and supervisors working in 11 different laboratories (41). A consistent finding was that those who spent all of their time in technical work were less productive than those who spent three quarters of their time in technical work and one quarter in administrative duties. The broader job seemed to help. Similarly, scientists who worked in a number of specialized areas tended to outperform those with a single area of specialization, and those who performed a number of functions (basic research, applied research, development, technical services, etc.) did better than those with only a few. Yet it was also true that these scientific jobs could become too diverse; a man could engage in multiple functions to the point where he was spread so thin that his performance suffered. It would appear that job enlargement can be carried to the point where the advantages of division of labor are lost.

Division of Labor vs. Job Enlargement

The evidence from studies of scientific personnel suggests that job enlargement can be carried too far. Other evidence points to the same conclusion. Studies have repeatedly indicated that role overload, where a man is required to do more than he possibly can in the time available, can have serious negative consequences. Clearly job enlargement carried to the extreme can result in role overload. The result, according to a number of studies, may well be a buildup of serum cholesterol, which is closely associated with coronary disease (47).

One study measured serum cholesterol levels of tax accountants (20). During the first two months of the year the levels remained steady and low; then there was a sharp acceleration up to the income tax deadline of

April 15, followed by a drop back to the level of earlier months. When role overload becomes marked, job dissatisfaction increases, the serum cholesterol level increases, and the probability of coronary disease increases (47).

This suggests that there is an optimum degree of job enlargement; also that division of labor may be fine up to a point where the work becomes boring and motivation to perform is lost. Some division is essential merely because there are limits on the skills, abilities, and extent of knowledge that one individual can possibly possess. On the other hand, too much division of labor can create major motivational and emotional problems, just as too much enlargement can.

Motivation, however, is an individual matter. What is excessive role overload for one person may be just right for another; what is too much routinization and specialization for one may also be optimum for another (48). In one study of factory workers in a large plant a negative relationship was found between job scope and satisfaction (51). The broader the job, the less the satisfaction. And there was no relationship between the degree of job enlargement and individual effectiveness. Results such as these suggest that there are people who do not want bigger jobs, and who respond negatively to job enlargement. For these people the optimum point is a rather specialized and routinized job—a considerable division of labor. Anything beyond this is too much; it introduces the stress of role overload. For other people a rather large job is ideal. This appears to be the reason for the conflicting results obtained in studies of job enlargement programs. Whether job enlargement is successful depends very much on the job to begin with, the extent of change, and the particular personalities of the individuals involved.

Can we say anything about the nature of these individual differences? The answer appears to be Yes. In general, studies of managerial, professional, and white-collar employees indicate that rather broad jobs are appropriate for them. Most such employees respond favorably to job enlargement well beyond what is currently typical. But among blue-collar workers the results are more mixed, as illustrated in the Bell System studies. It appears that workers in rural areas and small towns who are committed to middle-class values of upward mobility and accomplishment, as well as others who desire autonomy and an opportunity for personal development, tend to respond favorably to larger jobs (25, 28). Urban blue-collar workers who are largely alienated from society, on the other hand, may well view job enlargement merely as an imposition and respond negatively to it.

To these conclusions should be added certain findings related to industry characteristics (46). It appears that division of labor tends to be more pronounced in those industries where the product is very hard—primary metals and fabricated metals—than where it is soft—petroleum refining and tobacco manufacture. Furthermore, there are industries, often where the product is hard, where there is vast capital investment in mass-production equipment and where only fractions of jobs are left to human beings after machinery has taken over most of the work. Here extensive division of labor becomes almost inevitable, and employees should be selected accordingly. In many other instances division of labor can be relaxed considerably with positive results. However, the decision to enlarge jobs should be taken with full understanding that it may well involve considerable initial cost—for revised selection procedures, for retraining, and for duplication of facilities and equipment.

Departmentation

When division of labor is carried out on an organization-wide basis with groupings of employees, the term *departmentation* is applied to the process. All levels of the managerial hierarchy may use the same bases for departmentation, or the bases may be changed from one level to another. In general, when the subject of departmentation is considered, the greatest concern is with the type of grouping used at the upper levels. Thus the decentralized divisions considered in Chapter 7 are most frequently organized on a product-line basis, but below the top level there is no clear preference for one basis over another. Some decentralized firms continue on downward with smaller groupings of products; others shift to other bases.

Bases of Departmentation

In departmentation by *product* or *service* all the activities necessary to produce and market a given product or provide a particular service are placed under a single manager. For the highest level this arrangement may be schematized as follows:

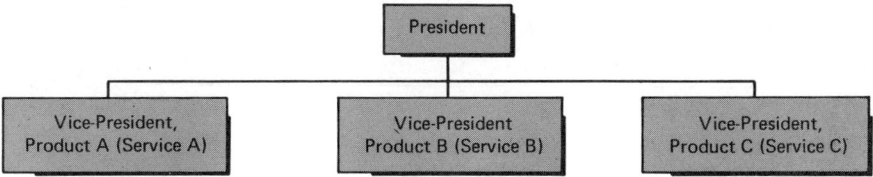

The widest divergence from this product grouping, and from the other major bases as well, occurs when departmentation is carried out by *functional area*. Here all products are acted upon or influenced by all departments; specialized technical skills are paramount. At the top level one most frequently finds such titles as vice-president—industrial relations, finance, manufacturing, marketing, purchasing, research and development, personnel, production, sales, public relations, corporate development, and administration, as well as that of treasurer (3). Schematically this type of organization looks as follows:

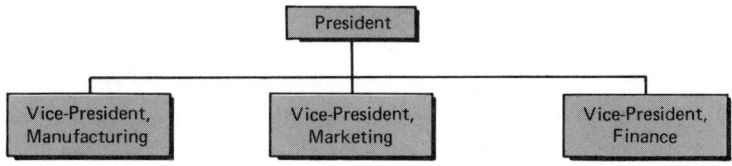

Departmentation by *geographical location* is particularly likely to appear at the highest level when the company operates internationally. Service organizations such as management consulting and accounting firms typically have offices located in major cities. Marketing activities often are organized by regions, districts, stores, territories, and the like. At the top level geographical departmentation might appear as follows:

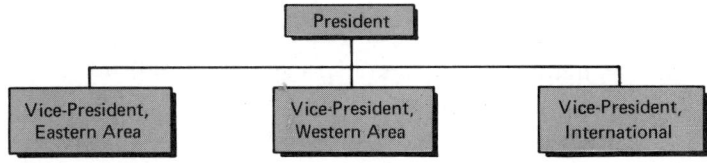

The fourth major basis for departmentation is *customer* type or *clientele*. This approach is strongly market oriented. Groupings are based on divisions such as government—business, men—women—children, and shippers—passengers. The approach may be schematized as follows:

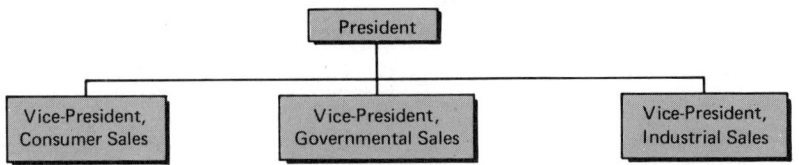

Other bases usually are not used at upper levels in the organization but may well appear further down. Within manufacturing, grouping frequently occurs by *process* or *equipment*. This approach is closely allied to the functional, since individuals are grouped by specialized technological skills. Another alternative may be simple numbers, where 100 people, all of whom do essentially the same thing, are arbitrarily placed in five groups of 20. Labor gangs are often constituted in this manner.

Comparative Merits. In view of the sizable significance that attaches to decisions on the bases for departmentation, particularly at the highest level, one would hope that considerable research evidence might be available and that this evidence would clearly point the way to the particular basis that should be emphasized in a given situation. In actual fact, evidence of this kind has begun to accumulate only in the late 1960s and as yet has had little impact on practical organization planning. Thus, companies tend to shift back and forth from one structure to another as particular considerations are given top priority. A sizable amount of reorganization is carried out in many companies—much of it probably unnecessary— which occurs largely because no one is sure which approach is best (9). In particular, companies tend to fluctuate between a functional and a product emphasis.

In recent years some evidence has appeared bearing on this function-product dilemma. There is now good reason to believe that in relatively small and simple organizations with few products the functional form is preferable (7, 44). As the company becomes more complex in terms of products, and in number and types of specialists, this advantage disappears and a product basis for departmentation at the top, and perhaps further down as well, becomes the most effective. The product- or service-based organization appears to be particularly responsive to changing technologies and product markets (26, 57). It yields better results where innovative decision making is required and shifts in the outside environment may occur suddenly and unpredictably. The functional approach is best in situations requiring stable performance of routine tasks. What evidence is available suggests that the geographical and customer bases operate in a manner comparable to product departmentation.

The functional approach tends to provide a context that is favorable to the exercise of influence by professionals and specialists. Under ideal conditions it provides for a dual emphasis on professional competence and customer service. But as an organization becomes larger and more complex, difficulties arise in coordination and maintaining a common value structure; integration suffers (34). The consequence appears to be insufficient attention to customers and clients; their needs get lost in the conflicts among groups with diverse values. A shift to product groupings splits up the professional and specialist interest groups and assigns these individuals to different product departments. As a result the influence of professionals declines, and customer or client considerations become paramount (15, 32). It seems clear that an organizational form that does not permit sufficient attention to consumer requirements is unlikely to contribute effectively to organizational goal attainment.

Multinational Structures. The use of geographical departmentation becomes increasingly important at upper levels as a company moves into the international sphere. Different cultures introduce different external constraints and facilitators. An organizational form that will be responsive to these cultural differences often is needed. The essential requirement appears to be a type of decentralized, geographical divisionalization with some control maintained, for purposes of coordination, at the corporate headquarters level (30).

The initial structural approach usually is the international-headquarters company. In this pattern a vice-president for international operations is added to the existing product-line or functional vice-presidents, and a separate subsidiary company is formed for international affairs. This company undertakes all functions carried out abroad, and its departmentation is based on the countries or geographical areas in which the company operates (29). As a company moves to true multinational status, it typically utilizes geographical departmentation increasingly at the top level. Eventually geographical factors may become completely dominant, and a true world company emerges. In this form United States operations are but one among many, rather than being coequal or dominant over all international efforts. At most, there may be divisions for the eastern and western United States, as well as Europe, Latin America, the Near East, and the Far East (29). This resort to geographical area as the paramount basis has been characteristic in the international sphere. Whether it is in fact the best approach is as yet an unanswered question (50).

Size of Departments

A number of studies have been conducted that relate the size of subunits within an organization to various indexes of effectiveness (43). The evidence is clear that below the managerial level job satisfaction is greater in smaller departments. In small departments absenteeism tends to be low, turnover is low, and labor disputes are less frequent. Thus the available data appear to support the view that splitting an organization up into many small departments will make a positive contribution to the maintenance goal.

As to productivity, however, the picture is less clear. There have been a sufficient number of studies favoring smaller units to indicate that such units may well have greater productivity, but this is not a universal outcome. It is rare, on the other hand, to find the larger departments more productive (43). Thus, taking all considerations into account, the evidence argues strongly for an approach to departmentation that produces relatively small units.

The Line-Staff Structure

In many organizations there are definite, formalized differences in decision-making authority of a horizontal nature. The most common structure incorporating this differential is the line-staff form. The role prescriptions of line managers call for a greater influence on decisions than do those of staff managers.

The line-staff structure is most prevalent in manufacturing industry. In this context personnel, purchasing, accounting, legal and quality control are almost universally considered staff departments, while sales and production are considered line (15). Research and development tends to be a staff unit and finance a line unit.

It is important to recognize that the line-staff structure is not characteristic of all organizations. Efforts to identify horizontal differentials of this kind where they do not exist on a formal basis can lead to considerable confusion and ambiguity. Thus in professional organizations decisions are characteristically made by the professionals such as lawyers in a law firm, accountants in an accounting firm, and consultants in a management consulting firm. These individuals would almost always be located in staff units in an administrative organization. Yet within a firm where they hold partner status they function as line managers. Those members of professional firms who do not serve clients directly, but rather handle financial, personnel, and marketing matters from so-called administrative positions function as staff. In a sense, in professional organizations the line-staff relationship is reversed. But it seems more meaningful to view these organizations as not incorporating the line-staff structure at all.

Even within administrative organizations the line-staff form is far from universal. Within manufacturing organizations, Woodward found line-staff most fully developed in firms with large-batch or mass-production technologies (59). In unit production companies the requisite technical know-how tended to be incorporated in the line managers, and there often were few if any recognizable staff units. With continuous process technology the line-staff differential often became blurred so that those who might otherwise have been considered staff managers came to exercise more influence than the staff designation would warrant. Thus, in pure form the line-staff structure appears to be used most frequently in mass-production, administrative organizations. The fact that it is not used in all instances, however, does not imply a lack of importance; nor does it imply that the structure cannot be effective.

The Nature of Staff Roles

The discussion to this point has dealt primarily with professional or specialized staff units in administrative organizations. It is important to distinguish such units from a general staff, which often performs under very different role prescriptions.

General Staff. Typically a so-called general staff is part of the office of the executive it serves. Thus assistants to the president or other managers fall in this category. These "assistants to" are essentially extensions of the manager they report to. They do whatever he does not have time or the capability to do. There is a limited delegation involved in their work, but it falls short of full delegation to the next lower level. For this reason there has been some feeling that "assistant to" positions should be reduced or

Planning: The Establishment of Role Prescriptions

eliminated. There are those who consider them merely a crutch. For lack of adequate evidence it seems best at present to consider this still an open question. Certainly positions of this kind can provide a valuable training ground.

A more extensive application of the general staff concept occurs in many companies with the decentralized division structure. Within the corporate headquarters and reporting to the chief executive there are often vice-presidents of such functional areas as finance, manufacturing, personnel, marketing, and the like. These individuals are not expected to make decisions in their speciality areas with reference to day-to-day operations in the divisions. That is entirely within the jurisdiction of the division managers. These general staff specialists, are, however, deeply involved in broad policy formulation and planning for the company as a whole. They often exert considerable influence on these decisions, but as staff they are not expected to make the decisions.

Professional and Specialist Staff Units. Within the line-staff structure the term *staff* applies to professional and specialist staff units rather than to general staff. In many cases these staff units are of considerable size and have a number of levels of hierarchy within them. Their role prescriptions call for activities in one or more of five areas (52):

Advice
Control
Administrative services
Specialized programs
Troubleshooting

Traditionally the staff role has been considered primarily advisory: to provide specialized information and advice to the line as a basis for decision making by line managers. Depending on the knowledge and nature of the individuals involved, this advice may exert considerable influence or very little. A line manager with a background primarily in engineering may well have little basis for questioning the advice given by lawyers, physicians, psychologists, and similar professionals. Thus their influence can be great.

Staff units may also conduct evaluations of other organizational units comparing actual performance against expectations and reporting exceptions to higher management. Quality control units provide an example of this type of activity. In the case of the control function the staff role calls for a considerable influence on decisions at least within the limits established by existing policies. Where the same unit is expected to advise and control at the same time, the disparate influence patterns inherent in the two roles can easily lead to role conflict with all its constituent problems.

In the service role a staff unit may merely provide services to the organization which could as well be done within the line, except that the use of a single unit permits economies of scale that would not otherwise be possible. A typing pool is an example. But the services provided may also be of a highly professional nature such as drawing up legal contracts, conducting physical examinations, and carrying out psychological evaluations. Usually the service role, like the advisory, involves little formal influence over decisions, although in both cases informal role prescriptions may give much greater power to the staff manager.

The two final types of staff role prescriptions—those related to specialized programs and troubleshooting—deal with short-term efforts which are assigned to staff units because of specialized know-how. Examples would be the conduct of a public relations campaign in a community where the climate of public opinion was hurting the firm, or an evaluation of managerial practices in a division that had experienced a steady decline in profits. These two types of activities are as likely to be built into general staff positions as into staff positions of the professional and specialized nature.

Line-Staff Differences and Decision Making

In recent years a number of writers have come to view the line-staff structure as obsolete, contending that decision-making and authority differentials between the two groups have actually disappeared and that the structure often exists in name only (16, 36). This hypothesis may be tested with reference to those studies comparing managers in line and staff units.

In one such study almost 2,000 managers completed a questionnaire designed to indicate the extent to which various motives are satisfied at work (42). Those whose positions were of a staff nature were then contrasted with the line managers. Differences were minimal at the vice-presidential level, but below that line managers were consistently more satisfied than staff. Although of a lesser degree, these horizontal differences parallel those of a vertical nature noted in Chapter 7. This and evidence from other studies consistently support the view that staff managers are

Planning: The Establishment of Role Prescriptions

less satisfied, feel they have to adjust more to the desires of others, and exhibit different patterns of behavior than line managers (43). Not surprisingly they tend to be less authoritarian (23).

More direct evidence bearing on the question of decision-making influence derives from two studies of personnel managers in staff units. In one of these studies 25 personnel managers were rated on a 6-point scale of decision-making authority (18). The ratings were made by the personnel manager, his superior, and another manager at the same level. The average ratings for different personnel decision areas are given in Table 8–3. It is clear that these staff managers typically do not exert anything approaching complete and unilateral influence on decisions in their areas of expertise. Assuming that a score of at least 3.50 would be needed to indicate a primary influence by the personnel manager in a decision

Table 8–3 *Personnel Managers' Authority in Different Aspects of Personnel Management*

Decision Area	Authority Rating
Selected Individual Questions	
Use of psychological tests	4.70
Determining collective bargaining strategy	4.13
Use of reference checks	4.10
Making job evaluations	3.78
Adopting discharge procedures	3.63
Grouping jobs for pay grades	3.28
Final approval in hiring	3.04
Approving pay and rank cuts	3.02
Selecting employees for training	2.88
Physical examinations	2.78
Approving transfers	2.53
Granting extra time off	2.31
Establishing output standards	1.90
Adopting training programs	1.88
Type of wage incentive plan	1.67
Determining area or equipment unsafe	1.66
Hiring requisitions for new positions	1.37
Determining profit-bonus ratios	1.28
Maximum collective bargaining concessions	1.21
Groups of Questions for Subfunctions	
Hiring	3.17
Promotion, demotion, and transfer	2.99
Collective bargaining	2.84
Training and development	2.47
Wage and salary administration	2.28

Source: W. French and D. Henning, "The Authority-Influence Role of the Functional Specialist in Management," *Academy of Management Journal,* Vol. 9 (1966), 198, 199.

area, it becomes clear that only a limited number of such areas exist. In most areas line influence is the greater. Even the personnel managers themselves rarely viewed themselves as having the predominant influence.

A second study dealt with the decision making of 71 personnel managers as viewed by themselves and line managers (4). There was considerable agreement. Both groups perceived the personnel managers as primarily engaged in gathering and providing information, and spending very little time in exercising any authority over the personnel actions of line managers. Both saw the role of the personnel managers as essentially staff advisory with line managers actually making the decisions.

Taking the evidence as a whole there can be little doubt that line-staff has not become obsolete and that it remains a viable organization form in many companies. Horizontal differences related to influence in decision making have consistently emerged from the research. Other differences have been noted as well. Thus, in one study effort expenditure levels were found to be a much more important consideration in line performance than for staff managers (35). On the other hand, it is apparent that the line-staff structure operates with varying degrees of effectiveness in different organizations, and that there are many situations where it is totally inappropriate.

Project Management and Related Forms

The major competition for the traditional line-staff form has come from a group of closely related structures having titles such as project management, program management, systems organization, product management, brand management, and matrix organization. All of these have in common that they provide for a horizontal grouping together of a number of functions which might otherwise be labeled as either line or staff. Thus in this type of organizational structure the line-staff decision-making differential *is* effectively eliminated. Furthermore, this type of structure has much more in common with product- or service-based forms than those of a pure functional nature. It seems most suitable, therefore, in larger firms where there are multiple products, varied specialists, changing technologies, major uncertainties in the market, and a need for innovation (57). In the following discussion the three principle variants of this general approach will be considered under the headings Product Management, Project Management, and Matrix Structure.

Product Management

Of the three forms to be considered product management appears to have the earliest origin (21). It was used at Proctor and Gamble during the late 1920s and seems to have been developed in response to the same problems of multiproduct complexity that spawned the decentralized divisions of such firms as duPont and General Motors.

Although the use of the form varies considerably from company to company, product management typically places major stress on marketing. A unit is created to handle a single product. This is a continuing effort as long as the product is on the market. The role prescriptions include responsibility for such matters as product quality, packaging, advertising, promotion, pricing, market research, distribution, market planning, budgets, and sales. The product manager is expected to take the product from its inception, guide it through the organization to a market, and then maintain it in the marketplace.

A major problem in the use of product management, and a major factor differentiating its use in different companies, is the degree to which influence on decisions is exercised by the product manager and his unit. In some instances the product management structure provides only for communication and advice centered on the product. The product manager is a coordinator and integrator; he makes very few decisions. In other instances he does make decisions in certain areas such as advertising and sales, or perhaps in all aspects of marketing, but has much less decision-making authority in other areas related to his product. Or the product manager may exercise discretion within set limits established by departments such as legal, accounting, manufacturing, personnel, and marketing. As companies grow larger and more complex, and product changes occur more frequently, the influence of the product manager appears to increase (13). Although the product management unit itself remains small in terms of individuals permanently assigned, the impact on the work of other units tends to expand.

Project Management

Although some firms apply the term *product management* to horizontal structures which focus more heavily on research and manufacturing considerations, the term *project management* is more common in these areas.

In addition, project management has several other characteristics (8, 53, 54, 58). The organizational units are formed on a temporary basis—for the purpose of producing a weapons system, building a bridge, or developing a new product. There is a definitive objective, and when this is accomplished the particular unit disbands. The size of the project unit varies. In aerospace and construction all individuals needed to complete the project typically are assigned directly to it, being phased in and out as the work progresses and their skills are needed. They often do not have membership in any other unit while working on the project. In other industries the actual project unit tends to be small, operating in a manner analogous to product management. Additional resources are drawn from outside the project unit.

Under project management there is a strong emphasis on direct horizontal relations between specialists; communication rarely goes up a scalar chain and then back down. In such industries as aerospace and construction and in certain professional areas such as management consulting the project unit operates very much as a team. These teams may not even be limited to members of a single organization. It is not uncommon for consulting engagement teams to contain both consultants and representatives of the client company. Members of the armed services are frequently included in the project units of defense contractors.

Role Prescriptions of Project Managers. Although research on the activities of project managers is limited, one such study has been conducted (10). Three managers, who directed projects where most of their personnel were from departments outside their immediate jurisdiction, and who thus had to coordinate the activities of many others, were studied. They spent almost all of their time communicating in a face-to-face manner with members of such departments as engineering and sales. Controlling was their major managerial function, with planning a somewhat distant second. Most of the time they dealt directly with only one other person. The picture that emerges is that of a generalist integrator, not a technical specialist.

The actual authority over decisions exerted by project managers varies from almost complete control of matters relevant to the project to mere persuasion. In general the form adopted in aerospace and construction yields greater influence to the project manager (53). Yet a certain amount of role ambiguity seems to be built into the project manager position. On many issues it is not entirely clear what he is supposed to do. A study of

26 project managers in six companies compared responses among those holding the position and the other managers with whom they worked (24). Results are given in Table 8–4. It is clear that although there was considerable agreement regarding who would make a number of decisions

Table 8–4 Agreement on Crucial Project Decisions

Decisions	Percent Agreement
Initiate work in support areas	87
Assign priority of work in support areas	89
Relax performance requirements	76
Authorize total overtime budget	80
Authorize subcontractors to exceed cost, schedule, or scope	74
Contract change in schedule, cost, or scope	72
Make or buy	80
Hire additional people	91
Exceed personnel ceilings when a crash effort is indicated	70
Cancel subcontract and bring work in-house	70
Select subcontractors	63
Authorize exceeding of company funds allocated to project	87
Determine content of original proposal	87
Decide initial price of proposal	87
Average	80

Source: R. A. Goodman, "Ambiguous Authority Definition in Project Management," *Academy of Management Journal,* Vol. 10 (1967), 401.

there were still many points on which there was uncertainty, such as selecting subcontractors. Role prescriptions in the project management structure may lack the specificity of line-staff. Often this situation tends to cause problems. Does this mean project structures are less effective?

Effectiveness of the Structure. The available evidence suggests that project structures do have both positive and negative aspects. There is reason to believe that flexibility and responsiveness to innovative ideas are greater in temporary groups of the kind utilized in project management (56). Thus, where resistance to change constitutes an important potential problem and original solutions are often needed to cope with a varying environment, the project structure appears to produce better task performance. Status differences tend to be diminished, and attention is focused on the specific task.

On the other hand, this major strength of the form is also the source of its greatest weaknesses. A questionnaire was administered to groups of engineers working in a line-staff structure and in the project structure (45). Both groups were employed in aerospace. When comparisons were made, it became evident that the project form does create some very special problems for those working in it. There is considerable fear that the termination of a project will bring discharge rather than reassignment to a new project. Role ambiguity is a source of frustration. The fact of varying status as between different projects, the frequent up-and-down assignment pattern, creates considerable worry about career progress. Organizational loyalty is at a minimum, and personal development is given insufficient attention. Furthermore—and this is surprising in view of the concern for innovation—project members appear to be frustrated frequently by excessive close supervision and multiple controls. Clearly flexibility is achieved at a cost. In spite of the considerable popularity of project management at the present time, its use outside the circumstances for which it is especially suited—for example, where flexibility and innovation are particularly needed—does not seem desirable.

Matrix Structure

When project management is superimposed on a stable hierarchic structure, usually of a functional nature, the term *matrix structure* is used. Here the individuals working on a project have a continuing dual assignment: to the project and to their base department. This is a major departure from the usual line-staff structure as Figure 8–1 indicates.

As might be anticipated, matrix structure introduces a serious possibility of role conflict. It is at variance with Fayol's principle of unity of command, and has certain features in common with the functional management scheme of Frederick Taylor, which Fayol decried (14). Under the Taylor approach, however, an individual could have many superiors directing different aspects of his work; under matrix structure there are but two.

If role prescriptions are clearly defined and the decision-making authority of the project manager differentiated from that of the functional managers so that each individual knows who will decide regarding specific matters, matrix structure can be effective. Its greatest drawback is that it tends to foster a lack of jurisdictional clarity (19). Role conflict can easily emerge, and efforts to avoid this may only produce role ambiguity. There is good

Planning: The Establishment of Role Prescriptions

Figure 8–1   *Matrix Structure*

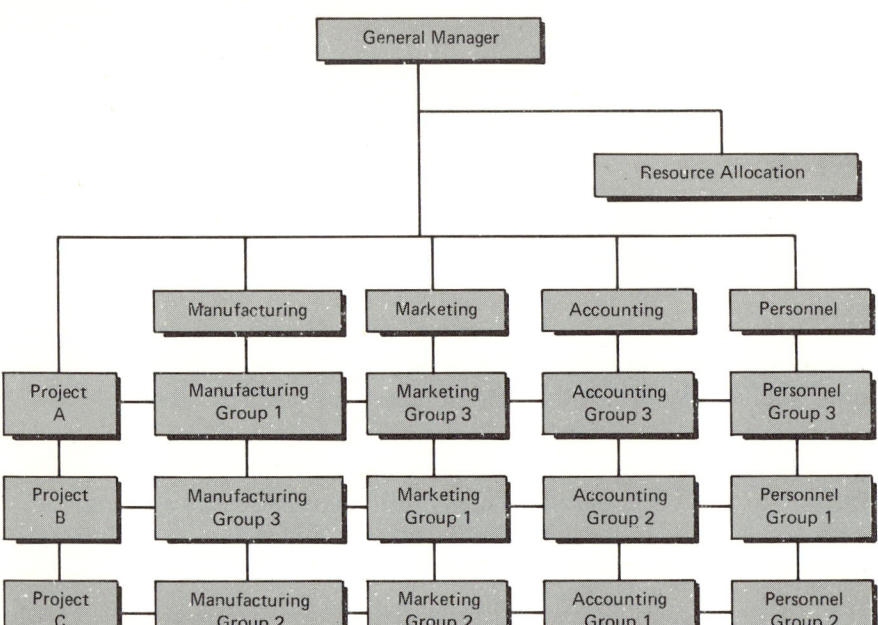

reason to believe that these negative consequences are most likely to occur when the project and functional managers fail to openly discuss any differences between them (34).

Committees

Committee organization has much in common with the matrix structure. Committees are superimposed on an existing line-staff or perhaps some other type of organizational form. They are usually constituted of individuals from diverse functional areas and specialities. They may have a limited duration and a specific task or objective to accomplish, although these conditions do not exist for all committees. Characteristically the same potential problems of role conflict and role ambiguity exist as in the matrix structure. Classical writers have often raised serious questions regarding the extensive use of committees because of this violation of unity of command, because of the cost in salaries of management time spent in meetings, and on other grounds (31).

Types of Committees

Committee organization appears to be most characteristic of the larger companies (55). There is also reason to believe that in these companies the number of standing committees, with continuing existence and stable membership, is declining somewhat, whereas ad hoc committees which exist to perform a specific task in a limited time period are being used more frequently (27).

As noted in Chapter 7, committees are frequently formed within the board of directors. Almost all large companies have an executive committee, whose membership usually consists of the inside board members. These executive committees are almost without exception a major force within the corporation (27). Other standing committees that are reasonably common are planning, research, finance and control, marketing, production, labor and personnel, and public relations (55).

Committees exist for a variety of purposes. In some cases the major role is to exchange information and opinions; communication is the primary objective, and not infrequently maintenance goals are the major ones served. Committees may also exist to recommend actions and advise. This is particularly true of ad hoc committees that are formed to develop recommendations in specific areas. In some cases the committee is constituted merely for the purpose of generating a variety of ideas and obtaining new and original solutions to important problems. There are also committees that exist for the most part to assist in the training and development of members. An example is the type of junior board of directors employed in multiple management, where a group of individuals from middle management make recommendations directly to the regular board in various areas, primarily for purposes of learning and development (38). Finally, there are the more powerful committees, of which the executive or general management committee is the best example, which actually make decisions and institute policies.

There is some tendency to have the members of a given committee drawn from a common organizational level and thus to make the committee a direct horizontal slice across the company. The bases for selection can vary considerably. Perhaps most common is a decision at a higher level that certain individuals, because of their positions, known areas of competence, or personalities, should be members. In other cases existing members of a committee may select new members. Or there may be some type of election process, although this is probably more characteristic

Planning: The Establishment of Role Prescriptions

outside the business world. Closely related is the use of a committee on committees which serves entirely for the purpose of establishing committee memberships. In a few cases membership is on a voluntary basis.

Conditions for Success

Certain conditions contributing to committee success have already been indicated in other connections. Committees are groups, and what was said in Chapter 6 regarding group decision making is relevant. A sense of participation which facilitates implementation may be generated by committee action. If committee members produce their ideas independently, the quality of decisions tends to be higher. Under brainstorming conditions creativity is fostered. Heterogeneous groups also tend to be better at creative problem solving, but not routine work. In addition, the evidence considered in Chapter 7 in connection with the discussion of span of control seems to favor groups ranging in size from 5 to 10. In business generally the average size of committees appears to be about 8, although managers tend to prefer a number close to 5 (55). The available evidence suggests that a membership approximating 5 is the most desirable (15).

Studies conducted using simulations indicate that although a strong emphasis on committees in decision making and policy formulation can prove to be a major asset, the potential advantages may be lost if individual members are not fully conversant with the committee structure and feel uncomfortable within it (2). Where managers were previously trained in group processes and interaction skills, committee organization proved highly effective. Where such training was lacking, the committee form was entirely unsatisfactory.

An analysis of the group dynamics literature and of specific experiences with existing committees indicates certain other conditions for effective committee operation (12):

1. A clearly defined committee task should exist.
2. Members should be selected so as to have some definite relationship to task accomplishment.
3. Superiors and subordinates should not serve on the same committee, but the fact that a manager holds a position at a given level should not in and of itself be a basis for inclusion.
4. Committees must have time to evolve interpersonal relationships before they can move on effectively to problem solutions.

5. To function most effectively committees require the support of those groups or individuals to whom the results of their deliberations are to be submitted.
6. Committees with a task to perform should be clearly differentiated from those whose major role is to develop the managerial competence of members.

Although the general topic of leadership will concern us in later chapters, it is important to note the role of the committee chairman here. It appears that committees are most effective when the chairman exerts considerable influence and does not attempt to share his role with others (5). A certain amount of "take-charge" attitude seems required, along with a focusing on task considerations. Generally chairmen perceived as fulfilling role expectations, structuring activities, and exercising control are viewed as more skillful (49). There is ample evidence that effectively chairing a committee is a demanding task requiring considerable training and ability (37).

This concludes the consideration of basic aspects of organizational structure. Although the approaches to establishing managerial role prescriptions noted are diverse, new organizational forms are constantly emerging and the future may well see drastic departures from what has been described here. In fact, change is one of the most characteristic features of organization planning. It is this matter of change and the problems associated with it that will be of concern in the next chapter.

Questions

1. It might be argued that project management is only a modern version of the widespread use of committees. To what extent does this appear to be the case? Are the disadvantages associated with the two forms the same?
2. "Line-staff is dead." Why would anyone say this? What is the evidence?
3. What is meant by the following?
    a. General staff
    b. Matrix structure
    c. Job enrichment
    d. International-headquarters company
    e. Job simplification

4. In what sense are job analysis and departmentation conceptually similar? To what extent do the findings regarding the effects of job size parallel those for department size?
5. What basis for departmentation would you expect to be favored by professionals and specialists? What problems can arise when departmentation of this kind is utilized?

References

1. Alderfer, C. P. "Job Enlargement and the Organizational Context." *Personnel Psychology*, Vol. 22 (1969), 418–426.
2. Bass, B. M. "Production Organization Exercise: An Application of Experimental Techniques to Business Games." In W. W. Cooper, H. J. Leavitt, and M. W. Shelly (eds.), *New Perspectives in Organization Research*. New York: Wiley, 1964, pp. 97–114.
3. Battalia, Lotz, and Associates. *A Decade of Change in Top Management Organization and Executive Job Titles.* New York: The Firm, 1969.
4. Belasco, J. A., and J. A. Alutto. "Line Staff Conflicts: Some Empirical Insights." *Academy of Management Journal*, Vol. 12, (1969), 469–477.
5. Berkowitz, L. "Sharing Leadership in Small Decision-Making Groups." *Journal of Abnormal and Social Psychology*, Vol. 48 (1953), 231–238.
6. Bishop, R. C., and J. W. Hill. "Effects of Job Enlargement and Job Changes on Contiguous but Nonmanipulated Jobs as a Function of Workers' Status." *Journal of Applied Psychology*, Vol. 55 (1971), 175–181.
7. Chandler, A. D. *Strategy and Structure.* Cambridge, Mass.: The M.I.T. Press, 1962.
8. Cleland, D. I., and W. R. King. *Systems Analysis and Project Management.* New York: McGraw-Hill, 1968.
9. Daniel, D. R. "Reorganizing for Results." *Harvard Business Review*, Vol. 44 (1966), No. 4, 96–104.
10. Davis, K. "The Role of Project Management in Scientific Manufacturing." *IRE Transactions on Engineering Management*, Vol. 9 (1962).
11. Davis, L. E. "The Design of Jobs." *Industrial Relations*, Vol. 6 (1966), 21–45.
12. Drought, N. E. "The Operations Committee: An Experience in Group Dynamics." *Personnel Psychology*, Vol. 20 (1967), 153–163.
13. Egloff, W. F. "Product Management: Status of the Art—1969." In W. G. Scott and P. P. LeBreton (eds.), *Managing Complex Organizations. Academy of Management Proceedings*, 1970, pp. 95–110.
14. Fayol, H. *General and Industrial Management.* London: Pitman, 1949.

15. Filley, A. C., and R. J. House. *Managerial Process and Organizational Behavior*. Glenview, Ill.: Scott, Foresman, 1969.
16. Fisch, G. G. *Organization for Profit*. New York: McGraw-Hill, 1964.
17. Ford, R. N. *Motivation Through the Work Itself*. New York: American Management Association, 1969.
18. French, W., and D. Henning. "The Authority-Influence Role of the Functional Specialist in Management." *Academy of Management Journal*, Vol. 9 (1966), 187–203.
19. Friedlander, F. "The Relationship of Task and Human Conditions to Effective Organizational Structure." In B. M. Bass, R. Cooper, and J. A. Haas, *Managing for Accomplishment*. Lexington, Mass.: Heath, 1970, pp. 111–138.
20. Friedman, M., R. H. Rosenman, and V. Carroll. "Changes in the Serum Cholesterol and Blood Clotting Time of Men Subject to Cyclic Variation of Occupational Stress." *Circulation*, Vol. 17 (1957), 852–861.
21. Fulmer, R. M. "Product Management: Panacea or Pandora's Box." *California Management Review*, Vol. 7 (1965), No. 4.
22. Golembiewski, R. T. *Men, Management, and Morality*. New York: McGraw-Hill, 1965.
23. Golembiewski, R. T. "Personality and Organization Structure: Staff Models and Behavioral Patterns." *Academy of Management Journal*, Vol. 9 (1966), 217–232.
24. Goodman, R. A. "Ambiguous Authority Definitions in Project Management. *Academy of Management Journal*, Vol. 10 (1967), 395–407.
25. Hackman, J. R., and E. E. Lawler. "Employee Reactions to Job Characteristics." *Journal of Applied Psychology Monographs*, Vol. 55 (1971), No. 3, 259–286.
26. Harvey, E. "Technology and the Structure of Organizations." *American Sociological Review*, Vol. 33 (1968), 247–259.
27. Holden, P. E., C. A. Pederson, and G. E. Germane. *Top Management*. New York: McGraw-Hill, 1968.
28. Hulin, C. L., and M. R. Blood. "Job Enlargement, Individual Differences, and Worker Responses." *Psychological Bulletin*, Vol. 69 (1968), 41–55.
29. Kolde, E. J. *International Business Enterprise*. Englewood Cliffs, N.J.: Prentice-Hall, 1968.
30. Kolde, E. J., and R. E. Hill. "Conceptual and Normative Aspects of International Management." *Academy of Management Journal*, Vol. 10 (1967), 119–128.
31. Koontz, H., and C. O'Donnell. *Principles of Management: An Analysis of Managerial Functions*. New York: McGraw-Hill, 1968.
32. Kover, A. J. "Reorganizing in an Advertising Agency: A Case Study of a Decrease in Integration." *Human Organization*, Vol. 22 (1963), 252–259.

33. Lawler, E. E. "Job Design and Employee Motivation." *Personnel Psychology*, Vol. 22 (1969), 426–435.
34. Lawrence, P. R., and J. W. Lorsch. *Organization and Environment: Managing Differentiation and Integration.* Boston: Graduate School of Business, Harvard University, 1967.
35. Lifter, M. L., A. R. Bass, and H. Nussbaum. "Effort Expenditure and Job Performance of Line and Staff Personnel." *Organizational Behavior and Human Performance*, Vol. 6 (1971), 501–515.
36. Logan, H. H. "Line and Staff: An Obsolete Concept?" *Personnel*, Vol. 43 (1966), No. 1, 26–33.
37. Maier, N. R. F. *Problem-Solving Discussions and Conferences.* New York: McGraw-Hill, 1963.
38. McCormick, C. *Multiple Management.* New York: Harper, 1938.
39. Miner, J. B. *Personnel and Industrial Relations: A Managerial Approach.* New York: Macmillan, 1969.
40. Myers, M. S. *Every Employee a Manager: More Meaningful Work Through Job Enrichment.* New York: McGraw-Hill, 1970.
41. Pelz, D. C., and F. M. Andrews. *Scientists in Organizations.* New York: Wiley, 1966.
42. Porter, L. W. "Job Attitudes in Management: III. Perceived Deficiencies in Need Fulfillment as a Function of Line versus Staff Types of Job." *Journal of Applied Psychology*, Vol. 47 (1963), 267–275.
43. Porter, L. W., and E. E. Lawler. "Properties of Organization Structure in Relation to Job Attitudes and Job Behavior." *Psychological Bulletin*, Vol. 64 (1965), 23–51.
44. Price, J. L. *Organizational Effectiveness.* Homewood, Ill.: Irwin, 1968.
45. Reeser, C. "Some Potential Human Problems of the Project Form of Organization." *Academy of Management Journal*, Vol. 12 (1969), 459–467.
46. Rushing, W. A. "Hardness of Material as Related to Division of Labor in Manufacturing Industries." *Administrative Science Quarterly*, Vol. 13 (1968), 229–245.
47. Sales, S. M. "Organizational Role as a Risk Factor in Coronary Disease." *Administrative Science Quarterly*, Vol. 14 (1969), 325–336.
48. Sales, S. M. "Some Effects of Role Overload and Role Underload." *Organizational Behavior and Human Performance*, Vol. 5 (1970), 592–608.
49. Schlesinger, L., J. M. Jackson, and J. Butman. "Leader-Member Interaction in Management Committees." *Journal of Abnormal and Social Psychology*, Vol. 61 (1960), 360–364.
50. Schollhammer, H. "Organization Structures of Multinational Corporations." *Academy of Management Journal*, Vol. 14 (1971), 345–365.
51. Sexton, W. P. "Organizational and Individual Needs: A Conflict?" *Personnel Journal*, Vol. 46 (1967), 337–343.

52. Sherman, H. *It All Depends—A Pragmatic Approach to Organization.* University: University of Alabama Press, 1967.
53. Steiner, G. A., and W. G. Ryan. *Industrial Project Management.* New York: Macmillan, 1968.
54. Stewart, J. M. "The Promise of Project Management." In R. Mann (ed.), *The Arts of Top Management.* New York: McGraw-Hill, 1971, pp. 326–338.
55. Tillman, P. "Committees on Trial." *Harvard Business Review*, Vol. 38 (1960), No. 3, 6–12, 162–172.
56. Torrance, E. P. "Some Consequences of Power Differences on Decision Making in Permanent and Temporary Threeman Groups." In A. P. Hare, E. F. Borgatta, and R. Bales (eds.), *Small Groups: Studies in Social Interaction.* New York: Knopf, 1955, pp. 600–609.
57. Walker, A. H., and J. W. Lorsch. "Organizational Choice: Product vs. Function." *Harvard Business Review*, Vol. 46 (1968), No. 6, 129–138.
58. Wilemon, D. L., and J. P. Cicero. "The Project Manager—Anomalies and Ambiguities." *Academy of Management Journal*, Vol. 13 (1970), 269–282.
59. Woodward, J. *Industrial Organization: Theory and Practice.* London: Oxford University Press, 1965.

9 Organizational Growth and Change

I. Resistance to and Facilitation of Change
  1. Factors Blocking Effective Change
     a. Individual and Group Factors
     b. Organizational Factors
  2. Facilitators of Change

II. Direct Change Through the Hierarchy
  1. The Role of Top Management
  2. The Role of Organization Planning Units
  3. The Role of Management Consultants

III. Organization Development and Other Participative Procedures
  1. Participation in Restructuring Work
     a. Peer Group Procedures
     b. Systematic Feedback and Group Discussion
  2. Sensitivity or T-Group Training
  3. Organization Development

IV. The Impact of Technological Change
  1. The Effects of Computers on Vertical Aspects of Structure
  2. The Effects of Computers on Horizontal Aspects of Structure

V. The Impact of Growth
  1. Growth and Aspects of Structure
  2. Mergers and Acquisitions

Changes in organization structure may come about in one of two ways. They may be introduced in a deliberate effort to develop an ordering of role prescriptions that will yield a higher level of goal achievement. Reorganizations of this kind may be undertaken at any time, whenever a superior form is thought to exist or the available human resources are such that another organizational structure seems to offer the prospect of better utilization. Much organization planning is directed toward carrying out planned changes of this kind.

The other type of structural change occurs largely in response to shifts in the nature, environment, or technology of the organization. Among these factors, which almost force organizational change, two have been studied extensively. The first is the advent of automation and the introduction of computers into many spheres of company operations. The second is the fact of corporate growth, either through internal expansion or through acquisition and merger. Considerable research has been aimed at determining what structures are most likely to appear in response to technological advance and corporate growth.

The complex interactions among people, value structures, technology, size and organization structure are the concern of this chapter.

Resistance to and Facilitation of Change

In Chapter 5, in connection with the discussion of policy acceptance, it was noted that new policies frequently meet resistances which may cause a failure or distortion of implementation. The resistance may even be sufficiently strong to block the decision to adopt a policy at all. The same phenomenon may occur when changes in organizational structure are contemplated. Knowing what type of organizational form is most appropriate to a given situation is not enough. It is at least as important to know how to achieve the change effectively.

Factors Blocking Effective Change

Early writings on the subject used the term *resistance to change* in a manner that implied an irrational and often blind opposition to what, on any other grounds, must be viewed as a desirable innovation (10). Anyone who attempted to block a proposed change for whatever reason was labeled a resister. More recent work in the field, however, has moved well beyond this kind of gross simplification and has begun to identify the characteristics of individuals, groups, and organizations that tend consistently to block, retard, or distort change efforts.

Individual and Group Factors. A major factor in resistance to change is that new organization structures almost invariably bring with them a redistribution of power and influence on decisions. Groups and individuals who are negatively affected by a reorganization, in the sense that their impact on decisions is reduced, typically are opposed to the change (19). When self-assured and successful individuals are faced with the prospect of a change that is viewed as threatening, this opposition tends to become overt (71). The objective may be to block the change entirely, but not infrequently it is merely to get something out of the change, to strike as good a bargain as possible. In the sense of fostering self-interest this type of resistance is entirely rational. It may not, however, contribute to organizational goal achievement.

Research also indicates that there are certain types of individuals who are particularly likely to resist change, quite apart from other considerations. These are people who rely heavily on their own personal experience in making decisions, who assume that prior conditions will continue to prevail, who take the position that there is always one best way of doing things (55), and who have little general propensity to take risks (48). They tend to be more anxious and worried about their work. In addition, they tend to be less well educated and less intelligent; and females are represented with a disproportionately high frequency (65). The impression is that those who have the most to lose by change are most likely to resist it. But the loss may not be merely a material one, or even a matter of decision-making authority. Resistance may stem from a threat to basic assumptions, personal values, sources of security, and to friendship relationships.

Certainly the social characteristics of a work group have a relation to resistance to change. This has been established clearly as a result of studies carried out in England subsequent to a change in the technology used in coal mining operations (63, 64). Where the response to the new mining methods was a restructuring so that existing work groups were broken apart and individualized effort prevailed, the consequence was a high absenteeism rate and low productivity. Where the work groups remained intact absenteeism was much less, productivity high, and costs were lower.

It appears that the inevitable anxiety produced by the nature of the work was reduced by the presence of strong group ties (57). When these group ties were removed and a new and strange technology added as well, anxiety became manifest and effectiveness declined.

There is evidence from other sources that where group members feel a strong sense of belonging, evince a desire to remain in the group, and perceive their group as superior to others, resistance to change is likely to be considerable (65). This is particularly true if the manager in charge of the group is himself predisposed to resist change and tends to be somewhat dogmatic.

Organizational Factors. In addition to the individual and group sources of resistance, there are others which stem from the existing structuring of role prescriptions in the organization and from the value structure. A study of 20 English firms, primarily in the rapidly changing electronics industry, revealed that there are certain companies, referred to as *mechanistic*, which by their very nature tend to be resistant to change (15). Mechanistic firms were characterized by:

1. Considerable division of labor along lines of functional specialties.
2. An emphasis in the role prescriptions for positions on means to organizational goal attainment rather than on the goals themselves.
3. The use of hierarchy to tie diverse jobs together and relate them to organizational goals.
4. Precise definitions of role requirements with little role ambiguity and role conflict.
5. A strong emphasis on hierarchy with considerable centralization of decision making, vertical communication, and information at the top.
6. Stress on loyalty to the company and acceptance of existing status designations.
7. Close ties to the employing organization and its values rather than to outside reference groups such as a profession.

Much of what is described is consistent with the effective structuring of role prescriptions in administrative organizations. However, the strong commitment to existing forms, which in and of itself is a strength, also serves as a constraint against adopting alternatives. Decisions to change are unlikely merely because the organization has attained considerable unity in support of a structure which typically has achieved a measure of success at some point in time. Furthermore, role sanctions tend to be firmly lined up behind existing role prescriptions. Forces for change have been systematically eliminated.

However, organizational resistance need not be based on the existing formal structure. It may also be inherent in a value structure and the informal role prescriptions that go with it. Where the value structure emphasizes one set of behaviors and a proposed change would result in a diametrically opposed set of behaviors being defined as good and indicative of effective performance, resistance can be expected to be widespread and intense (44). Thus if the existing structure permits overstaffing, and if low work motivation and effort are valued, a change to a structure where smaller organization units do the same work, and high work motivation might consequently be valued, would almost inevitably face massive resistance. Probably much of what has been considered irrational resistance to change stems from this source. Where a fully integrated value structure has been attained, managers may support it because it is their organization's value structure. To outsiders this may appear irrational; to insiders it is a necessary condition for achieving the advantages of integration (43).

Facilitators of Change

To the extent the various factors considered as blocks to change are eliminated or reversed, reorganizations may be carried out more easily. Thus, many of the factors which facilitate change need little elaboration. However, there are several new considerations that emerge when the discussion turns from resistance and constraints to facilitation and implementation. As these are considered it is important to keep in mind that change per se is not necessarily good; it does not always contribute to better goal attainment, and can even have detrimental effects. This caution is necessary because many change-supporting factors are of a kind which on other grounds, such as their relation to science and democracy, are highly valued in our society at the present time.

Support for change is most likely to come from individuals who are interested in personal growth, desirous of new experiences, risk takers, open to alternative courses of action, and who are less conventional (55). As managers they tend to be generalists who rely on their subordinates for specialized expertise. However, on occasion strong support for change may come from individuals who have many of the characteristics of resisters.

In these cases the new form tends to be grasped as the answer to all problems; it is not really evaluated at all. If the old structure is not working, it is quickly rejected in favor of the first new alternative in order to stave off the threat of continuing ambiguity and uncertainty.

This suggests that changes occur most frequently under conditions of some degree of crisis or at least where there are strong pressures for improvement. The evidence supports this conclusion (4, 19). Often there is a picture of declining profits. Departments or divisions of a company that reorganize are often under strong pressure from corporate headquarters to show improvements. Tension is high. Usually, in addition, there is some powerful individual or group pressing for change. The nature of these latter forces and the various strategies that may be employed are considered in subsequent sections of this chapter.

In contrast to the mechanistic firms in the English electronics industry study, those that found it easy to reorganize to meet changing environmental demands—those termed *organic*—have the following characteristics (15):

1. A close and direct relationship between individual role prescriptions and organizational goals.
2. Continual redefining of role prescriptions through discussions with others.
3. Rejection of the "it's not my responsibility" response as an excuse for failures.
4. The substitution of a broad sense of commitment to organizational goals in place of the inducements-contribution contract as a basis for work effort.
5. The presence of information and knowledge at various points in the organization network as appropriate to the task.
6. Stress on horizontal as opposed to vertical communication, and consultation rather than command; hierarchy is minimized.
7. Strong commitment to task rather than maintenance goals, coupled with a status system which is often related to relevant outside reference groups.

It is apparent that organic firms have much in common with those utilizing project management and matrix structures considered in Chapter 8. The very nature of these structures commits them to change; they are in fact constituted of temporary systems. Thus the project form, once adopted, in and of itself facilitates change. Project members know that change is inevitable even though they may not like it. There is thus a preconditioning to accept an ongoing process of restructuring roles. The role prescriptions call for revised prescriptions at frequent intervals.

Often the value structure emphasizes a readiness for change. People who facilitate change are considered good and effective; people who resist are poor performers. Such a value structure coupled with the project management form may produce excessive instability for some purposes. In management consulting, however, it has proved highly effective (45).

Direct Change Through the Hierarchy

The characteristic method of change in organizations has been through the use of the management hierarchy. Decisions regarding the new structure are made at the top level and then communicated to lower levels, often through the medium of organization charts and position descriptions. Appointments are made to new positions, and those whose positions are abolished are shifted to some other assignment. Implementation occurs because organization members view it as legitimate, or within its rights, for management to do these things.

Sometimes such changes are made solely with a view to establishing a desired structure of role relationships; they are made initially without consideration of the people available to fill jobs. Sometimes the people available for higher-level positions are considered first and a structure then formulated to maximize their effectiveness. Most commonly, both factors —ideal structures and people characteristics—are taken into account to a degree. The hierarchic approach typically gives little direct attention to value structures and to the personal values, attitudes, and motives of many of those affected. To the extent value structures are changed this occurs because new individuals are moved into higher-level positions, and these individuals have new conceptions of what is desirable behavior in management jobs. If a major reassignment process does not accompany structural change, the probability of a shift in the value structure is minimal and the likelihood of initial resistance pronounced.

Direct hierarchic change by its very nature requires strong support from top management; this is where the impetus for action comes from. In some instances the only major agent of change is the chief executive or some other individual at a high level. In other instances the agent of change is associated with an internal organization planning unit or with a management consulting firm employed to carry out a reorganization. In the latter two instances the hierarchy is employed as the major *means* to change in that inputs regarding the new structure are decided upon and introduced at the top, and then communicated downward.

The Role of Top Management

When the hierarchic approach is used, it is essential that top management give the change strong and consistent support. If this is not done, and in the absence of any other impetus, change simply will not occur (26). Decentralization plans have often failed even using the hierarchic approach to achieve increased delegation, because in the final analysis top executives did not delegate themselves nor take steps to get their subordinates to do so. Difficulties may also occur if the change is viewed as a personal power grab by a single executive and thus more in the interest of an individual than of the organization as a whole. Clear and unambiguous support from the top with decisions made where they are expected to be made can help to minimize this problem.

A sufficient number of instances where changes initiated by top management have in fact contributed to task accomplishment have now been recorded so that there seems little doubt that the approach can work (15, 32, 46). Changes may be blocked or distorted and there is always the possibility that the particular change may contribute little even if fully implemented, but such failures are certainly not inevitable. On the other hand, there is a strong possibility that if changes instituted in this manner are viewed as arbitrary and the reasons behind them are not fully understood, organizational maintenance may suffer considerably (46).

Data on the consequences of one change introduced via the management hierarchy are given in Figure 9–1. In this instance the major structural changes were made at Plant Y which was the focus of the study. They were a marked decentralization of decision-making authority down to the plant manager, which left him free to exercise his very considerable leadership skills, and the introduction of a number of meetings and committees within the plant, which served to foster horizontal interaction (32, 50). During the three-year period following change, Plant Y moved from the least to the most efficient plant in the company.

Figure 9-1 Changes in Direct Labor Costs for Six Plants of the Same Company, 1953 and 1956 (In percent above 100% of labor standards)

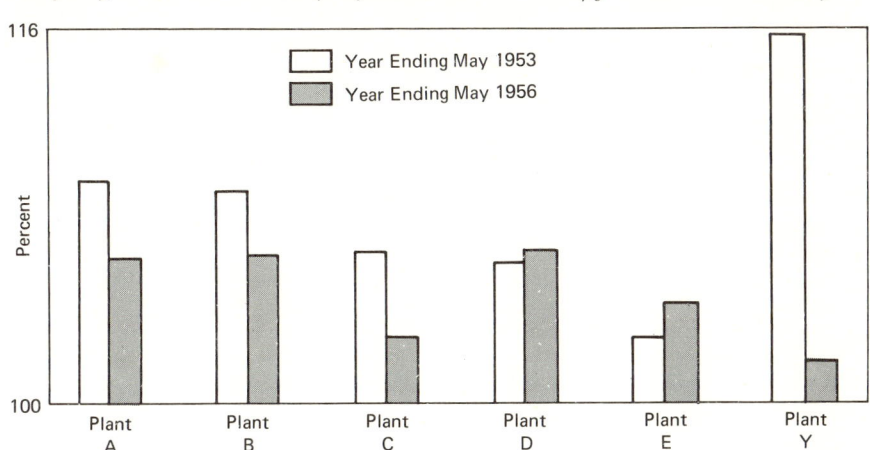

Source: R. H. Guest, *Organizational Change: The Effect of Successful Leadership* (Homewood, Ill.: Irwin-Dorsey, 1962), p. 99. Reproduced with permission.

The Role of Organization Planning Units

In many firms organization planning groups exist as separate entities reporting directly to the chairman of the board or president; in other cases they are placed within a functional department, usually personnel or industrial relations (3, 31).

The nature of the activities carried out by these units is indicated in Table 9-1. These are all groups operating to achieve change through the hierarchic structure (29). If an importance rating (given by organization unit managers) of 80 or above is accepted as indicative of a major activity, it becomes clear that these units are involved primarily in accumulating information and working with line managers to reach decisions on organization structures. Activities having to do with training and attitude change throughout the organization as a whole, as well as the actual staffing of the positions created, are relatively insignificant. The strong tie between these units and the vertical hierarchy is evident from Table 9-1. They achieve changes by working with and through this hierarchy. It is not surprising that they tend to stress vertical differences in decision-making authority in developing their recommendations.

273

Planning: The Establishment of Role Prescriptions

Table 9-1 Importance Ratings for Certain Activities Carried Out by Organization Planning Units Using a Hierarchic Approach

Activity	Importance Rating
Organization studies and audits	98
Planning future of the organization structure or environment with management	92
Analysis of grouping of activities into departments	92
Teach organization analysis to line executives	88
Stimulate line executives to perform their own organization analyses	87
Resolve organization conflicts	85
Organization, Procedures, and Policy Manuals and Directories	83
Review and approve all proposed organization changes	81
Defining the organization problem to be studied with line management	80
Expediting the organization changes approved by management	71
Analysis of objectives of units of the firm	70
Training in group goal setting	61
Changing the organization's work climate	59
Training for better group or team development	56
Training in better interpersonal relations	56
Executive replacement and development policies	55
Changing of personnel at times of organization changes	51
Changing individual attitudes and opinions on how to work with people	45

Source: W. F. Glueck, "Applied Organization Analysis," *Academy of Management Journal*, Vol. 10 (1967), 226.

The Role of Management Consultants

In a number of respects the activities of those management consulting firms that attempt to achieve change through the hierarchy are very similar to those of the organization planning units just described. The use of consultants has the added advantage, however, that these outsiders can take the brunt of internal resistance. Thus when they leave at the completion of a change effort, there is likely to be considerably less residual enmity within the organization (although the consultant may never be invited back) (59).

As with internal units using direct change through the hierarchy, management consultants have employed the method successfully. In one study a consulting team recommended and helped to introduce major changes which were concentrated primarily in the branch offices of a large insurance company (49). The assistant manager position was changed from that of supersalesman—operating largely in a staff, "assistant to" relationship to the branch manager—to that of a true first line supervisor reporting to the branch manager. Thus, in effect, a level of management was added at the bottom of the organization, above the agents. The consultants were brought in by the senior vice-president of sales management and after diagnostic studies, made their recommendations to top management. The recommendations were accepted at that level and lower managers were notified of what changes were to be made and how. The management consultants assisted initially at the branch level in actually implementing the recommendations.

It is apparent that major changes in role prescriptions and role behavior did occur in the branch offices, although the new patterns of behavior were not identical to plans in all respects. Also comparisons of pre- and post-change data indicate that in all probability the structural change did contribute to profits. Policy lapses decreased, expenses decreased, and after some delay there was an overall improvement in net new premiums. The available evidence suggests that hierarchically imposed changes initiated by management consultants as agents can prove effective, although there may be specific instances when this is not the case.

Organization Development and Other Participative Procedures

In contrast to direct change through the hierarchy are those change procedures which start with a broad attempt to alter the values, attitudes, and beliefs of a significant number of organization members. Once the value structure has been revised it is assumed that structural modifications will follow (30). Although value change efforts are typically carried on at the top management level so that subsequent structural changes will not be blocked there, they are not limited to the upper reaches of the hierarchy. Similar efforts are made throughout management, and sometimes below the managerial level as well. Thus the hierarchy is not used to introduce the new organizational structure; the structure arises out of the organization as a whole, as a consequence of a highly integrated value structure produced by the value change procedures. The approach assumes that resistance to change can be anticipated if values are not modified first, and thus any sizable disparity between the value structure and the final organizational form is prevented.

Planning: The Establishment of Role Prescriptions

Although this does not appear to be a necessary consequence of the approach, these change procedures have almost without exception been used to foster a value structure which emphasizes power equalization and democracy (37). Thus the organizational forms that result often include considerable decentralization to the lower levels, large spans of control, flat managerial hierarchies, job enlargement, linking pin or overlapping group structures, and project or matrix approaches. Role prescriptions are largely self-established. Hierarchy is not used directly to facilitate changes primarily because to do so would be inconsistent with the power equalization goal.

A picture of the differences between the organization development and participative approaches and the direct use of hierarchy may be obtained by comparing Table 9–2 with Table 9–1 (data in parentheses). Table 9–2

Table 9–2 *Importance Ratings for Certain Activities Carried Out by Organization Planning Units Using an Organization Development Approach*

Activity	Importance Rating	*
Training for better group or team development	99	(56)
Training in better interpersonal relations	99	(56)
Analysis of objectives of units of the firm	97	(70)
Defining the organization problem to be studied with line management	96	(80)
Expediting the organization changes approved by management	96	(71)
Teach organization analysis to line executives	96	(88)
Executive replacement and development policies	95	(55)
Changing individual attitudes and opinions on how to work with people	94	(45)
Training in group goal setting	93	(61)
Stimulate line executives to perform their own organization analyses	92	(87)
Planning future of the organization structure or environment with management	91	(92)
Organization studies and audits	88	(98)
Changing of personnel at times of organization changes	85	(51)
Changing the organization's work climate	85	(59)
Analysis of grouping of activities into departments	82	(92)
Resolve organization conflicts	82	(85)
Organization, Procedures, and Policy Manuals and Directories	64	(83)
Review and approve all proposed organization changes	52	(81)

* Ratings by managers of units using a hierarchic approach in parentheses.
Source: W. F. Glueck, "Applied Organization Analysis," *Academy of Management Journal*, Vol. 10 (1967), 232.

contains the importance ratings given by managers of organization planning units using an organization development approach, to the same 18 activities rated by the managers of units using a hierarchic approach (29). Under the organization development concept, organization planning expands to include many activities which are relatively unimportant when the hierarchy is employed. Of the 11 activities with importance ratings in the 90s in Table 9–2 only four are in the 80s in Table 9–1 and five are below 70. The organization development groups are less concerned with line management interaction and much more concerned with training and changing individuals. In actual fact training has become the method of choice when value-based approaches to organizational change are utilized.

Participation in Restructuring Work

A rather large number of participative change procedures have been developed since the late 1940s. Most of these had their origins in work done either at the University of Michigan or at Massachusetts Institute of Technology. In general, since they attack the value structure directly as a prerequisite to other changes, they may be used in policy planning as an aid to implementation (see Chapter 4), as well as for the purpose of revising organization structures. Typically when a broad power-equalization effort is involved eventual changes in both policies and organizational form are anticipated.

Peer Group Procedures. Some of the earliest studies involving participative approaches dealt with group discussions and decisions by individuals at the same organizational level. Through these discussions group pressures are brought to bear so that there is widespread agreement based on common values and beliefs. The outcome is a decision by the group, made independently of hierarchic influence, on how the work is to be structured. The group accepts the need for change and does something to achieve it, at least in the ideal case.

This approach has produced some very striking results. In one instance the peer group procedure was used to achieve a major change in individual role prescriptions among production workers in a garment factory (18). The result was a sizable increase in productivity and a decrease in turnover. However, other studies have not yielded equally positive findings (27). There is a limit to the amount of true reorganization that may be achieved by peer groups in the same work unit (35). One group may well run up against the conflicting values of another. Furthermore, there is no guarantee that unanimity will emerge or that if it does, the resulting structure will make a contribution to organizational goal achievement. It may foster objectives of the particular peer group at the expense of the company. Generally, this approach seems most effective when the company or unit faces a major crisis and the peer group is thoroughly convinced of a need for change (35).

Systematic Feedback and Group Discussion. A related procedure incorporates more explicit recognition of the realities of the existing managerial hierarchy (41). Initially a comprehensive attitude survey is conducted. The results of this survey are then fed back to the organization starting at the top on a group basis with the focus being primarily on data relevant for the particular group. Thus the first group might be the president and the vice-presidents reporting to him, the second a specific vice-president and his department heads, and so on down through the organization. Discussions focus on survey data and seek to rectify problems uncovered. Solutions are developed at the level at which the problem exists and are then reported back up the hierarchy. The overlapping group discussion aspect tends to foster an integrated value structure; the attitude data provide a problem-oriented focus. Actual changes frequently originate at lower levels with higher levels merely approving or disapproving them.

Systematic feedback of this kind appears to be most effective in bringing about changes to correct specific, but usually somewhat isolated, problems. A change instituted in one sector of an organization may not be reflected in other sectors (35). Thus broad-scale reorganizations are unlikely to result. A shift from a functional organization to a decentralized, divisionalized structure based on product lines, for instance, is as unlikely to arise from systematic feedback as from peer group procedures.

Sensitivity or T-Group Training

In Chapter 1, in connection with the discussion of role conflict, brief reference was made to laboratory training. This approach, of which sensitivity or T-group sessions are the major component, is primarily identified with the behavioral humanist school of management thought. It seeks to teach managers to express feelings freely, to collaborate on a democratic basis, to provide freedom for individual decision making to their subordinates, and to be authentic in their relations with others (8). Thus it is strongly oriented toward power equalization and seeks to change values accordingly.

Although the formats and procedures used by different trainers vary considerably, Figure 9-2 presents a reasonably typical schedule for a one-week laboratory or for the first week of the more common, two-week laboratory (58). The general sessions are devoted to lectures or demonstrations. The exercises are group affairs and may involve role playing, simulations, or group observation.

The T-groups of from 10 to 15 managers usually have a trainer present, although he does not perform an active leadership role other than to indicate that the group is to learn about group processes from its own experience. The emphasis is very much on the "here and now" rather than organizational problems. Initially members are often frustrated and embarrassed. They want someone to tell them what to do, to structure the situation. Gradually the discussion turns to the group and its members. The participants expose their feelings about themselves and each other. Such matters as the effects of authority, the motives of others, competition for power, and the need to be understood are considered. In many cases the group members eventually become quite close.

For this approach to have any meaningful impact in bringing about organizational change a large number of managers must be exposed to it. Some firms such as Aluminum Company of Canada (70) and TRW Systems (20) have established extensive internal programs for this purpose. Although some use may be made of outside laboratories where people from a variety of organizations are combined in the T-groups, these companies concentrate primarily on internal groupings—a diagonal slice with managers from different levels in different departments, the managerial hierarchy of a single department, or line and staff managers from two departments that must work together.

A considerable amount of research has been done aimed at determining whether the T-group approach does actually change people. The answer appears to be a clear Yes (14, 16). Thus, potentially at least it can alter value structures on a broad basis and pave the way for widespread reorganization. Managers appear to become more sensitive, more open in their communication, more flexible, and more understanding of others.

The problem is whether the individual changes and the new values result in a value structure which is integrated with organizational task and

Figure 9-2 *Typical Schedule for Laboratory Training (First Week)*

	Sunday	Monday	Tuesday	Wednesday	Thursday	Friday
9:00–11:00		T-group	T-group	T-group	T-group	T-group
11:00–11:30		Coffee break	Coffee break	Coffee break	Coffee break	Coffee break
11:30–12:30		General session	General session	General session	General session	General session
12:30–1:30		Lunch	Lunch	Lunch	Lunch	Lunch
1:30–3:30		T-group	T-group	Exercise	Exercise	Exercise
3:30–6:00	Opening session	Free time	Free time	Free time	Free time	Free time
6:00–7:30	Dinner	Dinner	Dinner	Dinner	Dinner	Dinner
7:30–9:30	T-group	T-group	Tape-listening exercise	Free time	Exercise or training film	Free time

Source: E. H. Schein and W. G. Bennis, *Personal and Organization Change Through Group Methods: The Laboratory Approach* (New York: Wiley, 1965), p. 14.

maintenance goals. Does the T-group approach contribute role behaviors that are really useful for a company? It may, or it may be irrelevant to a firm's goals, or it may actually be harmful. On this very crucial point there is little data.

However, there is some reason to believe that sensitivity or T-group training in the form described here may contribute a great deal more to individual than organizational development (5, 53). The destruction of the hierarchic authority structure in the T-group with a view to promoting change in individual members, coupled with the stress on values such as democracy and group participation, may well result in antiauthoritarian attitudes and thus a real reduction in managerial contributions at times when more directive leadership is required. Under this view the T-group experience is actually harmful to managers. Alternatively it may simply miss the point because it does not concern itself with real problems of existing organizations, thus minimizing transfer of learning back to the work environment. As has been suggested T-grouping may yield better husbands and fathers, but not better managers (70).

Organization Development

Organization development has arisen in response to the need for a value-based change procedure which is oriented toward solving the real problems of existing organizations. Although, as with sensitivity training, there are marked differences between various organization development efforts, certain features are characteristic. Typically the focus is on groups within a given organization made up of people that work together; this change effort eventually becomes organization-wide (6). The outcome is a series of planned alterations in existing policies and structures instituted to increase the organization's effectiveness in achieving its goals.

Although features of the T-group usually remain in the organization development effort, the groups also attempt to diagnose problems within the company. Relevant information is collected and discussed by the group prior to planning (28). Frequently this information is obtained via interviews conducted within the company by an organization development specialist or consultant. Like the other participative procedures, organization development has consistently emphasized power equalization (1, 2, 9). Thus the changes that result tend to be of a kind that are consistent with these values—job enlargement, decentralization, and so forth. Often

Planning: The Establishment of Role Prescriptions

participative goal setting in the management-by-objectives model is a component of the total effort.

When used on a large-scale basis this approach tends to extend over a number of years. In many cases organization members move through a series of phases. A list of these phases as employed in the so-called Grid approach to organization development follows (11):

Phase 1. Participants study the theory of managerial effectiveness underlying the approach and engage in T-group activities.
Phase 2. The behavior dynamics of existing organizational teams are studied.
Phase 3. The experience of phase 2 is extended to include the interworkings of organizational units which must cooperate and achieve coordination of effort.
Phase 4. Top management develops an ideal strategic corporate model for the firm with the assistance of other groups.
Phase 5. Implementation tactics are developed to move the company to the ideal strategic corporate model.
Phase 6. Changes are measured from before phase 1 to after phase 5 in order to stabilize and evaluate achievements and plan for the future.

Although truly comprehensive organization development efforts of this type have not yet been evaluated on a scientific basis, research has been conducted related to some smaller-scale approaches. In one such study a number of changes were identified (47). Problem-solving competence increased, there was a shift to participative values, communication improved, power equalization increased, interpersonal and group skills and attitudes improved, and management goals became clearer. On the other hand, a caution is raised by a second study which suggests that T-groups made up of managers who will work together may have the effect of creating *too much* trust in others (22). Everyone is confident each man will do his share on his own, controls are relaxed, and in the end the group does not organize effectively to do its work; the managers in a sense know each other too well. It would seem likely that this potential defect could be minimized if organization development efforts were to place somewhat less emphasis on participative values and power equalization. In any event organization development does appear to be by far the most sophisticated value-based change procedure devised to date.

The Impact of Technological Change

Although much change in organization structures is initiated simply out of a desire to establish a set of role prescriptions that will operate more effectively in a given situation, changes also occur as an adjustment to the introduction of new technology. In preceding chapters the relationships between manufacturing processes and organizational forms have been noted on numerous occasions. An even larger amount of research has been conducted in recent years to establish what changes appear to follow when computers are introduced, primarily in the office environment.

The Effects of Computers on Vertical Aspects of Structure

It has been argued that one outgrowth of the introduction of computers on any sizable scale is likely to be a shift toward more centralized decision making (60). In a very general sense this expectation appears to have been confirmed. The more comprehensive studies involving a number of companies have typically noted a tendency for at least some types of decisions to move upward in the hierarchy and for a greater amount of control to be exercised from the top down over the role behaviors of those at lower levels (39, 40, 56, 66, 68, 69).

A primary factor in this increased centralization is the availability of information at higher levels which the computer makes possible. Where computers are used merely to perform routine computational tasks rather than to provide information for decision making, little centralization occurs (56, 66). Furthermore, centralization following the introduction of computers does not appear to operate as a technological imperative. Higher-level management can use the computer to obtain data for decision making that would not otherwise be available; as a result it may choose to make many decisions, and in fact typically does so. But this same information may be made available at lower levels as well. There are instances in which top management simply does not have the time to make all the decisions it now is in a position to make with its new fund of information (21). Thus certain types of decisions may actually be decentralized as a result of computerization.

In a study of state employment offices, for instance, some tendency toward greater decentralization of decisions on hiring new employees was found in association with greater degrees of computerization (36). The introduction of computers typically leads to the centralization of matters related to data processing and logistics (21). It tends to have a major impact on manufacturing. But the same degree of centralization does not usually appear in the marketing component (56). The best evidence currently available suggests that at least in the long term, computers move decisions to those individuals who are most qualified to make them, while upgrading the quality of these decisions by providing more and more valid data. In many cases this means centralization, but not of all types of decisions.

Another commonly observed vertical change has been in the number of positions at various hierarchic levels. Almost invariably routine clerical positions are replaced by the computer (13). If a reduction in personnel occurs at the managerial level, it is much less pronounced (23, 33, 39, 69). The pattern represented in Table 9–3 is characteristic—line units shrink, data processing units expand, but in both instances there is a shift toward a higher proportion of managers.

At the same time there is often a decrease in the span of control (69),

Table 9–3 *Manpower Requirements* Before *and* After *the Introduction of a Computer in a Shoe Company*

Groups Studied	Before the Computer		After the Computer		Net Change	
	No.	%	No.	%	No.	%
Line Departments						
Managerial	36	19	32	27	− 4	−11
Clerical	150	81	88	73	−62	−47
Total	186	100	120	100	−66	−36
Data Processing Departments						
Managerial	10	22	24	26	+14	+140
Clerical	36	78	67	74	+31	+ 86
Total	46	100	91	100	+45	+98
All Affected Segment						
Managerial	46	20	56	27	+10	+22
Clerical	186	80	155	73	−31	−17
Total	232	100	211	100	−21	− 9

Source: H. C. Lee, "Human Resources Administration: In the Computer Age," in W. J. Wasmuth, R. H. Simonds, R. L. Hilgert, and H. C. Lee, *Human Resources Administration: Problems of Growth and Change* (Boston: Houghton Mifflin, 1970), p. 367.

at least at the lower levels of the organization. Prior discussions would indicate that such decreases in span should yield an increase in levels of hierarchy. But this assumes a constant work force. When computers come in, the work force is reduced in the affected units unless considerable overall company growth occurs. As a result the decreased span of control at lower levels tends to occur with practically no overall change in the number of levels. If anything, the structure may become flatter (69).

The Effects of Computers on Horizontal Aspects of Structure

Additional consequences of a shift to computers appear in the horizontal aspects of structure. From the increase in standardization of role prescriptions and control which computers make possible it might be assumed that an increased division of labor would occur. Actually, as Table 9-4 indicates, most jobs had not changed at all in this respect. These data derive from studies conducted in 23 life insurance companies (69). However, when changes do occur they are likely to be in the direction of increased division of labor within the clerical component. Yet this is not true of all types of

Table 9-4 Computer Impact on Clerical and Managerial Jobs in Insurance Companies

Groups Studied	Job Diminished (Percent)	Job Enlarged (Percent)	Job Unchanged (Percent)
New Business			
Managerial	14	28	58
Clerical	24	24	52
Policy Service			
Managerial	0	25	75
Clerical	14	31	55
Accounting			
Managerial	4	40	56
Clerical	39	24	37
Actuarial			
Managerial	0	36	64
Clerical	26	15	59
All Groups Studied			
Managerial	4	35	61
Clerical	31	22	47

Source: T. L. Whisler, *The Impact of Computers on Organizations* (New York: Praeger, 1970), pp. 131-132.

clerical work—job enlargment is typical in policy service units, for instance. And at the managerial level there is a consistent pattern of job expansion, rather than diminution, with the introduction of computers.

In the area of departmentation computers tend to foster a functional emphasis. Data processing and other units in decentralized divisions tend to be collapsed into a single, higher-level corporate unit (69). Thus the advent of computer use on an extended basis appears to offer the prospect of moving many firms back toward a more centralized, functional structure and away from geographical departmentation in particular, but perhaps also away from product line departmentation as well.

Consistent with this pattern is the increased decision-making authority which tends to accrue to staff units, especially those closely allied to data processing (56, 68). Yet this shift in the horizontal power balance is not usually reflected in formal structural changes. At the present time it is much more a function of revised value structures and informal role prescriptions (56). It remains to be seen whether it will eventually be reflected in new horizontal forms.

Many of these structural effects associated with technological change may represent transitory states in the advance of computerization. The predicted decrease in the role of middle management, for instance, has not occurred, but it may appear at some later date (38). On the other hand, it does seem clear that in its present state of development computer technology often yields structural effects that differ sharply from those that organization development and the other participative procedures seek to achieve.

The Impact of Growth

Growth, like technological change, appears to require adaptation in organizational structure. As a firm grows in terms of such factors as assets, sales, profits, number of employees, number of stockholders, and value added, structural adjustments tend to occur. Furthermore, as with the introduction of computers, these adjustments follow certain patterns and thus exhibit a degree of consistency; this in spite of the fact that conscious organization planning by top management is by no means a universal concomitant (42). Nor do those firms that carry out purposeful reorganizations to adjust to growth necessarily achieve a better result than those whose adjustment occurs on a less formal basis.

Within the United States, industry growth has generally been looked upon with favor. Growth is widely recognized as an operative goal (24). If greater size may be considered as a consequence of growth, which appears to be a reasonable assumption in most cases, there is evidence linking growth to the attainment of other goals as well. At least in administrative organizations size does appear to be associated with increased effectiveness in achieving goals, especially those of a task nature (54). On the other hand this relationship does not hold for professional organizations; in fact the reverse has often been found, smaller professional organizations being the more effective.

Studies that focus specifically on maintenance considerations using measures of job satisfaction and work attitudes yield an interesting pattern. At the managerial level there is clear evidence that the larger companies elicit more positive reactions. Managers in large firms see their work as more challenging and interesting, as requiring more imagination, and they report greater motive satisfaction than do managers in smaller companies (52). Yet where the measures of job satisfaction have concentrated on employees below the managerial level just the reverse appears to be true— those in smaller firms are more satisfied (7).

Growth and Aspects of Structure

The findings regarding the goal-related consequences of growth lead to the conclusion that typically managers will seek to expand the scope of their enterprises. What changes in structure can be anticipated as a result? Do these changes represent meaningful adaptations to the pressures introduced by growth?

One of the first changes produced by growth appears to be a greater differentiation of work, more division of labor (7, 12). The result is an increase in the number of managerial levels and in the size of the span of control, both executive and operative (7, 42, 61). Furthermore, as companies grow they institute more committees (42).

Considerable research has been carried out dealing with the growth of staff personnel relative to line. The conclusion seems to be that in the early phases, when firms have employees numbering in the hundreds, there is a point at which staff growth is rather rapid, especially among "assistant to," general staff personnel. Later on true staff departments tend to emerge, but there are no necessary relationships beyond this early period. As the company grows further, staff personnel show no clear tendency to increase or decrease in proportion to line (25, 67).

An equally common topic of research has been the ratio of administrative personnel (usually defined to include managers, professionals, and clerical workers) to direct production workers. Two major forces appear to be at work here. The previously noted tendency for growth to yield greater degrees of differentiation creates a need for administrative coordination and control. Thus there is pressure for expansion of the administrative component. At the same time larger size produces the possibility of economies of scale; administrative efforts can be spread over more employees and thus the proportion of administrative workers held to a minimum (12). When these two factors are arrayed against each other, the matter of economies of scale appears to be dominant. The proportion of administrative personnel does tend to be smaller in large firms of the same type (51, 62). As firms grow, their administrative expansion is somewhat less pronounced than the growth of the company as a whole.

It seems clear from what has been reported above that the natural responses to growth do appear to be goal related in many instances. The major organizational problems that may emerge are too great a division of labor, an excessive emphasis on general staff when full-blown staff departments might be more appropriate, and a resort to extended spans of control beyond the levels that research suggests are optimal.

Mergers and Acquisitions

The effects of growth on structure noted in the preceding section have been identified in part through longitudinal studies, in part through comparisons of different-sized organizations of the same kind. In both instances the analyses have dealt almost exclusively with internally generated growth. Although occasional instances of external growth via merger and acquisition have been included in some of the research, separate analyses have not been carried out to identify the specific consequences of this particular type of expansion. In fact no systematic studies appear to have been conducted to determine how external growth changes organizations. The literature on the subject of acquisitions has been much more concerned with financial and legal considerations than with organizational consequences (34).

About all that can be said with any certainty at the present time is that the cost reduction programs which typically follow acquisitions and mergers tend to result in a sizable decrease in work force, which is usually concentrated in the administrative component. Thus external as well as internal growth permits economies of scale and a proportionate reduction in administration. In addition those firms which have grown by multi-industry acquisitions, the so-called conglomerates, have almost without exception resorted to some version of the decentralized form, divisionalized on the basis of product lines. In many cases they have developed highly innovative structures of this general type (17).

Questions

1. Distinguish among sensitivity training, organization development, and organization planning. To what extent and in what ways is each likely to be related to the achievement of company task and maintenance goals?
2. What is currently known about the impact of the introduction of computers on organization structure? How do these changes relate to those advocated by adherents of participative procedures and power equalization?
3. As chief executive of a company you recognize the need to drastically revise the organization's structure to adequately accommodate continuing growth. What sources of resistance might you anticipate? How would you deal with them?
4. Which of the following seem most closely related to the *mechanistic* form? Which to the *organic*?
    a. Functional departmentation
    b. Participative management
    c. Project management
    d. Role ambiguity
    e. A cosmopolitan orientation to outside reference groups
    f. Professional organizations
5. How would you account for the finding that managers seem more satisfied in larger firms and workers in smaller firms? Does what we know about the effects of growth on organization structure help to explain the satisfaction findings?

References

1. Argyris, C. *Intervention Theory and Method.* Reading, Mass.: Addison-Wesley, 1970.
2. Argyris, C. *Management and Organizational Development.* New York: McGraw-Hill, 1971.

3. Bailey, J. K. "Organization Planning: Whose Responsibility?" *Academy of Management Journal*, Vol. 7 (1964), 95–108.
4. Barnes, L. B. "Organizational Change and Field Experiment Methods." In V. H. Vroom (ed.), *Methods of Organizational Research*. Pittsburgh: University of Pittsburgh Press, 1967, pp. 57–111.
5. Bass, B. M. "The Anarchist Movement and the T-Group: Some Possible Lessons for Organizational Development." *Journal of Applied Behavioral Science*, Vol. 3 (1967), 211–217.
6. Beckhard, R. *Organization Development: Strategies and Models*. Reading, Mass.: Addison-Wesley, 1969.
7. Beer, M. "Organizational Size and Job Satisfaction." *Academy of Management Journal*, Vol. 7 (1964), 34–44.
8. Bennis, W. G. *Changing Organizations*. New York: McGraw-Hill, 1966.
9. Bennis, W. G. *Organization Development: Its Nature, Origins, and Prospects*. Reading, Mass.: Addison-Wesley, 1969.
10. Bennis, W. G., K. D. Benne, and R. Chin. *The Planning of Change*. New York: Holt, Rinehart and Winston, 1969.
11. Blake, R. R., and J. S. Mouton. *Building a Dynamic Corporation Through Grid Organization Development*. Reading, Mass.: Addison-Wesley, 1969.
12. Blau, P. M. "A Formal Theory of Differentiation in Organizations." *American Sociological Review*, Vol. 35 (1970), 201–218.
13. Brink, V. Z. *Computers and Management: The Executive Viewpoint*. Englewood Cliffs, N.J.: Prentice-Hall, 1971.
14. Buchanan, P. C. "Laboratory Training and Organization Development." *Administrative Science Quarterly*, Vol. 14 (1969), 466–480.
15. Burns, T., and G. M. Stalker. *The Management of Innovation*. London: Tavistock Publications, 1961.
16. Campbell, J. P., and M. D. Dunnette. "Effectiveness of T-Group Experiences in Managerial Training and Development." *Psychological Bulletin*, Vol. 70 (1968), 73–104.
17. Carroll, D. T. "Conglomerates Revisited." *Business Horizons*, Vol. 13 (1970), No. 4, 42–44.
18. Coch, L., and J. R. P. French. "Overcoming Resistance to Change." *Human Relations*, Vol. 1 (1948), 512–533.
19. Dalton, G. W., L. B. Barnes, and A. Zaleznik. *The Distribution of Authority in Formal Organizations*. Boston: Graduate School of Business, Harvard University, 1968.
20. Davis, S. A. "An Organic Problem-Solving Method of Organizational Change." *Journal of Applied Behavioral Science*, Vol. 3 (1967), 3–21.
21. Dearden, J. "Computers and Profit Centers." In C. A. Myers (ed.), *The Impact of Computers on Management*. Cambridge, Mass.: The M.I.T. Press, 1967, pp. 174–203.

22. Deep, S. D., B. M. Bass, and J. A. Vaughan. "Some Effects on Business Gaming of Previous Quasi-T Group Affiliations." *Journal of Applied Psychology*, Vol. 51 (1967), 426–431.
23. Delehanty, G. E. "Computers and Organization Structure in Life-Insurance Firms: The External and Internal Economic Environment." In C. A. Myers (ed.), *The Impact of Computers on Management*. Cambridge, Mass.: The M.I.T. Press, 1967, pp. 61–106.
24. England, G. W. "Organizational Goals and Expected Behavior of American Managers." *Academy of Management Journal*, Vol. 10 (1967), 107–117.
25. Filley, A. C. "Decisions and Research in Staff Utilization." *Academy of Management Journal*, Vol. 6 (1963), 220–231.
26. Fisch, G. G. *Organization for Profit*. New York: McGraw-Hill, 1964.
27. French, J. R. P., J. Israel, and D. Äs. "An Experiment in Participation in a Norwegian Factory." *Human Relations*, Vol. 13 (1960), No. 1, 3–20.
28. French, W. "Organization Development–Objectives, Assumptions, and Strategies." *California Management Review*, Vol. 12 (1969), No. 2, 23–34.
29. Glueck, W. F. "Applied Organization Analysis." *Academy of Management Journal*, Vol. 10 (1967), 223–234.
30. Glueck, W. F. "Organization Change in Business and Government." *Academy of Management Journal*, Vol. 12 (1969), 439–449.
31. Glueck, W. F. *Organization Planning and Development*. New York: American Management Association, 1971.
32. Guest, R. H. *Organizational Change: The Effect of Successful Leadership*. Homewood, Ill.: Irwin-Dorsey, 1962.
33. Hill, W. A. "The Impact of EDP Systems on Office Employees: Some Empirical Conclusions." *Academy of Management Journal*, Vol. 9 (1966), 9–19.
34. Hilton, P. *Planning Corporate Growth and Diversification*. New York: McGraw-Hill, 1970.
35. Katz, D., and R. L. Kahn. *The Social Psychology of Organizations*. New York: Wiley, 1966.
36. Klatzky, S. R. "Automation, Size, and the Locus of Decision Making: The Cascade Effect." *Journal of Business*, Vol. 43 (1970), 141–151.
37. Leavitt, H. J. "Applied Organizational Change in Industry: Structural, Technological, and Humanistic Approaches." In J. G. March (ed.), *Handbook of Organizations*. Chicago: Rand McNally, 1965, pp. 1144–1170.
38. Leavitt, H. J., and T. L. Whisler. "Management in the 1980's." *Harvard Business Review*, Vol. 36 (1958), No. 6, 41–48.
39. Lee, H. C. "Human Resources Administration: In the Computer Age." In W. J. Wasmuth, R. H. Simonds, R. L. Hilgert, and H. C. Lee, *Human Resources Administration: Problems of Growth and Change*. Boston: Houghton Mifflin, 1970, pp. 323–426.

40. Lipstreu, O., and K. A. Reed. "A New Look at the Organizational Implications of Automation." *Academy of Management Journal*, Vol. 8 (1965), 24–31.
41. Mann, F. C. "Studying and Creating Change: A Means to Understanding Social Organization." In C. M. Arensberg, S. Barkin, W. E. Chalmers, H. L. Wilensky, J. C. Worthy, and B. D. Dennis (eds.), *Research in Industrial Human Relations*. New York: Harper, 1957, pp. 146–167.
42. McNulty, J. E. "Organizational Change in Growing Enterprises." *Administrative Science Quarterly*, Vol. 7 (1962), 1–21.
43. Miner, J. B. "Bridging the Gulf in Organizational Performance." *Harvard Business Review*, Vol. 46 (1968), No. 4, 102–110.
44. Miner, J. B. *Management Theory*. New York: Macmillan, 1971.
45. Miner, J. B. "Personality Tests as Predictors of Consulting Success." *Personnel Psychology*, Vol. 24 (1971), 191–204.
46. Morse, N., and E. Reimer. "The Experimental Change of a Major Organizational Variable." *Journal of Abnormal and Social Psychology*, Vol. 52 (1956), 120–129.
47. Nath, R. "Dynamics of Organizational Change: Some Effects of a Change Program on the Client System." In P. P. LeBreton and W. G. Scott (eds.), *Organization Structure and Behavior*. Academy of Management Proceedings, 1969, pp. 51–66.
48. Nedd, A. N. B. "The Simultaneous Effect of Several Variables on Attitudes Toward Change." *Administrative Science Quarterly*, Vol. 16 (1971), 258–269.
49. O'Connell, J. J. *Managing Organizational Innovation*. Homewood, Ill.: Irwin, 1968.
50. Perrow, C. *Organizational Analysis: A Sociological View*. Belmont, Calif.: Wadsworth, 1970.
51. Pondy, L. R. "Effects of Size, Complexity, and Ownership on Administrative Integrity." *Administrative Science Quarterly*, Vol. 14 (1969), 47–60.
52. Porter, L. W. "Where Is the Organization Man?" *Harvard Business Review*, Vol. 41 (1963), No. 6, 53–61.
53. Powell, R. M., and J. E. Stinson. "The Worth of Laboratory Training." *Business Horizons*, Vol. 14 (1971), No. 4, 87–95.
54. Price, J. L. *Organizational Effectiveness*. Homewood, Ill.: Irwin, 1968.
55. Pym, D. "Effective Managerial Performance in Organizational Change." *Journal of Management Studies*, Vol. 3 (1966).
56. Reif, W. E. *Computer Technology and Management Organization*. Iowa City: Bureau of Business and Economic Research, University of Iowa, 1968.
57. Schachter, S. *The Psychology of Affiliation*. Stanford, Calif.: Stanford University Press, 1959.

58. Schein, E. H., and W. G. Bennis, *Personal and Organizational Change Through Group Methods: The Laboratory Approach.* New York: Wiley, 1965.
59. Sherman, H. *It All Depends—A Pragmatic Approach to Organization.* University: University of Alabama Press, 1967.
60. Simon, H. A. *The Shape of Automation for Men and Management.* New York: Harper & Row, 1965.
61. Starbuck, W. H. "Organizational Growth and Development." In J. G. March (ed.), *Handbook of Organizations.* Chicago: Rand McNally, 1965, pp. 451–533.
62. Tosi, H., and H. Patt. "Administrative Ratios and Organizational Size." *Academy of Management Journal*, Vol. 10 (1967), 161–168.
63. Trist, E. L., and K. W. Bamforth. "Some Social and Psychological Consequences of the Long-wall Method of Coal-getting." *Human Relations*, Vol. 4 (1951), 3–38.
64. Trist, E. L., G. W. Higgin, H. Murray, and A. B. Pollock. *Organizational Choice.* London: Tavistock Publications, 1963.
65. Trumbo, D. A. "Individual and Group Correlates of Attitudes Toward Work-related Change." *Journal of Applied Psychology*, Vol. 45 (1961), 338–344.
66. Vergin, R. "Computer Induced Organization Changes." *MSU Business Topics*, Vol. 15 (1967), No. 3, 61–68.
67. Wasmuth, W. J. "Human Resources Administration: Dilemmas of Growth." In W. J. Wasmuth, R. H. Simonds, R. L. Hilgert, and H. C. Lee (eds.), *Human Resources Administration: Problems of Growth and Change.* Boston: Houghton Mifflin, 1970, pp. 1–103.
68. Whisler, T. L. "The Impact of Information Technology on Organizational Control." In C. A. Myers (ed.), *The Impact of Computers on Management.* Cambridge, Mass.: The M.I.T. Press, 1967, pp. 16–60.
69. Whisler, T. L. *The Impact of Computers on Organizations.* New York: Praeger, 1970.
70. Winn, A. "Social Change in Industry: From Insight to Implementation." *Journal of Applied Behavioral Science*, Vol. 2 (1966), 170–183.
71. Woodward, J. *Industrial Organization: Theory and Practice.* London: Oxford University Press, 1965.

Part III
Directing: An Input-Improving Mediator

10 Authority and Motivation

I. Authority, Power, and Influence
1. Theories of Formal Authority
   a. Classical Theory
   b. The Views of Max Weber
2. Acceptance Theories of Authority
   a. Relevant Research
   b. Formal vs. Acceptance Theories
3. Bases of Power and Authority
   a. Classification Systems
   b. Relationships with Performance and Satisfaction
   c. Using and Not Using Power

II. Process Theories of Motivation
1. The Law of Effect and Economic Motivation
   a. Restriction of Output
   b. Research on Pay Incentives
2. Expectancy Theories
3. Equity Theory

III. Content Theories of Motivation
1. Theory of Achievement Motivation
   a. Achievement Motivation and Success
   b. Goal Difficulty
2. Role Motivation Theory
3. Need Hierarchy and Self-actualization
4. Two-factor Theory
   a. The Conflicting Evidence
   b. Important Motives for Management

The management function considered here under the title *directing* has been designated in different ways by various writers. Essentially the same meaning is inherent in such terms as activating, motivating, leading, command, securing essential efforts, and supervising.

Whatever its designation, the directing function basically involves influencing or inducing subordinates to role behavior that matches role prescriptions as closely as possible. It focuses on the *motivation* of work and attempts to obtain a *maximal* contribution to organizational goals. It is because of this latter feature that directing is described as an input-*improving* mediator, rather than as input-sustaining or controlling. In its most important application, directing is concerned with motivation to achieve the highest levels of performance possible. This does not deny that on occasion directing may be aimed at achieving coordination or control which by their very nature, result in much lower levels of contribution to task or maintenance goals on the part of organization members.

A knowledge of human motivation and the processes that activate human behavior in the work context is basic to understanding the directing function. Equally important is the existing knowledge related to how one individual may exercise authority or power, or exert influence, on another. It is these two fundamental concepts—authority and motivation—and the research bearing on them that will be of concern in this chapter. Data on methods of directing effectively, to maximize goal attainment, are considered later in Part III.

Authority, Power, and Influence

The terms *authority*, *power*, and *influence* are used with a great variety of meanings in the management literature. Disagreements and conflicting definitions occur frequently (12). For this reason the definitions employed here should be viewed as generally consistent with common usage, but certainly not possessed of universal acceptance.

Of the three terms, *influence* is the broadest in coverage. It refers to any behavior on the part of one individual which alters the behavior, attitudes, feelings, and so on, of another. Thus advertising is as much an influence process as is a directive from a management superior. One person may influence another by virtue of control over sanctions, by persuasion, by playing upon attitudes held toward him, by exercising control over significant aspects of the other person's environment, or as a consequence of an exchange agreement which provides for influence as one part of the bargain (10). Influence may be attempted by whatever means and, in some instances, still fail of success.

Power implies the potential to exert influence. A person may have the power to influence another even though he never in fact attempts to do so. Generally this power stems from obvious control over sanctions (30). A policeman typically can bring strong negative sanctions to bear; a manager may utilize positive sanctions such as pay increases and promotions, as well as negative ones. To the extent this potential for exerting influence is recognized, power exists.

Authority is the most controversial concept of the three. It is clearly narrower in meaning in that it represents only institutionalized power. The term *authority* refers to power that is inherent in the role prescriptions for a position within an organization. It is common practice to speak of authority as having the support of legitimacy. It is power that is viewed as right and proper by organization members.

It is at this point, however, that the authority concept runs into difficulty. Who legitimizes power and thus gives it the status of authority? Who designates the areas in which a manager may legitimately exercise power, that is, exert his authority? One view is that authority derives from higher levels; this is normally referred to as the theory of formal authority. This theory says that legitimacy is present when a manager's superiors will consistently support him in a particular type of influence attempt (63). In other words, because a man in a given position has support from above he is said to possess authority. Acceptance theories, on the other hand, put the greatest emphasis on legitimization from below, by subordinates. According to this view, authority is conferred by those below a given manager. To the extent this legitimization upward fails to occur, real authority is lacking.

There is a controversy here which has much in common with that between economic man theory and administrative man theory. The discussion which follows is concerned with the specific nature of formal and acceptance theories of authority, and with the conflict between them.

Theories of Formal Authority

As in many areas, the views of classical management theorists and those of Max Weber, the forerunner of the structuralist school, on the nature of authority have much in common, in spite of their independent development. Both are theories of formal authority which stress hierarchy and legitimization from the top.

Classical Theory. The classical position holds that the authority inherent in a managerial position is achieved by delegation from higher levels. The chief executive delegates to his subordinates, they to theirs, and so on down the line. Each manager thus has a specific set of authority rights delegated to him and built into the role prescriptions of his position. These rights specify the things he should have the power to get his subordinates to do, the role behavior he can legitimately expect from them.

This much of the theory is rather consistently accepted among classical writers. There is some inconsistency, however, as regards the specific source of the *chief executives'* authority (34). Different writers have attributed it to the institution of private property, the Constitution, public opinion, the national will, the nature of man, and to God. Whatever the source it is seen as providing a basis for the right to command and expect obedience. It gives a manager the right to be completely authoritarian, although he may not exercise this right fully (68).

Closely allied to authority in classical theory is the concept of responsibility. Responsibility is the obligation to perform, to do or have done that which a superior requires. Authority is delegatable; responsibility is not. Thus the theory holds that even when a manager delegates the authority to get something done to a subordinate manager, he still remains fully responsible for the results. He cannot divest himself of that obligation, even though the subordinate also assumes responsibility when authority is delegated. One of the major classical management principles states that the authority delegated should correspond to the responsibility (16).

Irrespective of the specific source to which the ultimate authority is attributed, the classical theory of authority (and responsibility) is basically a statement of what the situation should be if goal attainment is to be maximized. It establishes role prescriptions for managerial jobs.

The Views of Max Weber. Weber's views on authority have this same prescriptive character: if an effective administrative organization is to exist, authority should be of a certain kind. In developing this theme he contrasts three types of authority: rational-legal, traditional, and charismatic (72).

According to Weber, *rational-legal* authority is the preferred form for most organizations of the type existing today. It has its source in the enactment of law. This type of authority rests not in individuals, but in positions and the rules and regulations that surround them. Thus a manager who leaves a position cannot take his authority with him. In this sense the authority is functionally specific. There is a hierarchy of positions, and clear definitions of the authority associated with each should be established by a rational and legal process, which confers legitimacy.

Weber contrasts this type of authority with two others. The first is *traditional* authority, which has its source in the sacredness of the social order. This authority is inherited and follows long-established precedent. Feudal systems are an example of this type of authority; obedience and loyalty are achieved because the dignity of the lord is hallowed by tradition. Here authority is diffuse and far-ranging rather than tied to specific legal enactments associated with a given position.

This same diffuseness appears in *charismatic* authority, which has its source in the affectual and personal devotion of subordinates. Often supernatural or divine qualities are attributed to the man in authority, whose power derives from his relationships with those who follow him. The personalities of both the "great man" and those who respond to his directives are part of the authority process. There is in this instance a considerable overlap with acceptance theory, an overlap which is not present in the rational-legal and traditional types of authority.

Acceptance Theories

Acceptance theories view authority as being present when a directive is legitimized by virtue of its acceptance from below. Authority exists when subordinates are willing to be directed. Major proponents of this definition of authority were first, Chester Barnard (6, 20), and somewhat later, Herbert Simon (64).

Under the acceptance view, organization members make what amounts to a contractual agreement when they enter employment. They agree to work and to accept authority in return for rewards such as pay. This implicit contract involving contributions and inducements does not, however, extend to acceptance of all directives, whatever their nature. There is in fact a *zone of indifference* within which employees will permit authority to be exercised. Beyond this zone, acceptance does not occur, and thus

Directing: An Input-Improving Mediator

authority does not exist. The zone may be extended if role sanctions are changed, with a new inducements-contributions balance as a result.

Relevant Research. Acceptance theories define authority in terms of what subordinates do and do not do, in terms of role behavior and its limits. They hypothesize that actual behavior may not conform to formally defined patterns; that the structure of authority established by delegation down the hierarchy is not necessarily indicative of the way "things really work" (and thus by implication they are saying that this is not an *authority* structure at all). It becomes important, therefore, to determine whether authority patterns that do not coincide with the formal hierarchic structure can be identified in organizations. The discussion in Chapter 7 of formal and informal status suggests that this is possible, and thus provides some support for the acceptance view. Other research provides additional confirmation.

In one study data were collected on authority patterns in two Air Force wings (67). Wing executives were asked to score each other in terms of "who has the most to say about how the wing gets its work done and meets requirements." As is clear from Table 10–1 the two wings did not yield the same results even though their formal authority structures were identical. In Wing A both the director of matériel and the maintenance control officer had much less influence than in Wing B. Yet in both wings the directors of operations, matériel, and personnel were exercising con-

Table 10–1 Power Hierarchies in Two Air Force Wings

Wing Executive	Power Score	
	Wing A	Wing B
Director of Operations	29	31
Director of Matériel	16	27
Deputy Wing Commander	22	16
Director of Personnel	13	10
Maintenance Control Officer	1	11
Commander, Squadron A	6	2
Commander, Squadron B	5	2
Commander, Squadron C	5	2
Executive Officer	3	0
Wing Intelligence Officer	1	0

Source: J. D. Thompson, "Authority and Power in Identical Organizations," *American Journal of Sociology*, Vol. 62 (1956), 294.

siderable authority over the squadron commanders, a pattern that was totally inconsistent with expectations from the formal structure.

Other studies have established similar deviations from the formally delegated authority pattern among prison inmates, secretaries, and attendants in mental hospitals (43). It is clear that in many instances theories of formal authority do not provide an adequate description of actual authority relationships, informal role prescriptions, and existing role behavior.

Furthermore, the idea that certain areas of behavior are legitimate areas of managerial influence (within the zone of indifference and thus acceptable under the inducement-contributions contract), whereas others are not, has also received considerable support. Studies comparing the areas of managerial authority as perceived by different groups have established that there is a great deal of agreement (13, 59). These studies have utilized students, Air Force personnel, labor leaders, and police chiefs, as well as a variety of management samples from both government and business. The zone of indifference for managerial influence has been defined most broadly by managers of supermarkets and by police chiefs; labor leaders establish the narrowest zone. But it is still true that even the labor leaders are in essential agreement with the other groups on what is legitimate in terms of managerial authority. Table 10-2 provides data on those matters which have consistently been placed within the zone of indifference, that is, considered highly legitimate, and those placed outside it and thus considered much less legitimate by the groups studied. It is evident that there is a strong feeling of legitimacy for influencing the work environment and directing job performance, but not for personal and family matters.

Formal vs. Acceptance Theories. The research evidence appears to provide strong support for the acceptance view; hypotheses generated from the theory have been consistently confirmed. Does this mean that the theories of formal authority are invalid? Or is it possible, as at least one writer has suggested, that the two views are not really in basic conflict (28)?

As with the economic man and administrative man theories of decision making discussed in Chapter 6, it appears that formal and acceptance theories of authority are concerned with somewhat different aspects of the same problem. Theories of formal authority deal with the authority managers *should* possess. They are normative in nature and relate to role prescriptions. They specify what kinds of formal role prescriptions should be built into management positions. Because role behavior tends toward

Directing: An Input-Improving Mediator

Table 10–2 Items on Which There Is Agreement on High and Low Legitimacy of Managerial Authority

Item	Mean Legitimacy Score
High Legitimacy	
The amount of time he spends talking to his wife and children on the telephone while at work	78
The tidiness of his office	77
His working hours	77
The kind of temperament he exhibits on the job	76
How much importance he attaches to getting along with other people	69
The amount of time he spends doing job-related reading while at work	67
How he divides his working day among his various duties	66
Low Legitimacy	
The church he attends	−95
Where he maintains charge accounts for personal shopping	−94
Where he spends his vacation	−94
Where he sends his children to school	−93
What political party he belongs to	−93
The kind of woman he marries	−90
The kind of car he drives	−90
Whether he owns his own house or not	−88
Whether his wife works or not	−88
The kind of house or apartment he lives in	−85
How much he entertains	−83

Source: K. Davis, "Attitudes Toward the Legitimacy of Management Efforts to Influence Employees," *Academy of Management Journal,* Vol. 11 (1968), 157.

but rarely matches role prescriptions one would not expect the formal approach to yield perfect predictions of actual behavior.

On the other hand, acceptance theory *is* concerned with role behavior, with the actual authority patterns that are accepted and that do motivate job behavior. It is a descriptive theory. As such it is strongly supported by existing research and appears to have considerable validity. But this does not invalidate the tenets of formal authority theory, since they speak to a quite different matter—the matter of how managerial role prescriptions *should* be constituted to maximize organizational goal attainment.

Bases of Power and Authority

In recent years the most important contributions to our understanding of power and authority have come from a sizable body of research that had its roots in Weber's classification of rational-legal, traditional, and charismatic authority. This research attempts to distinguish the various bases upon which authority is accepted and power attributed, and to study these bases. It is concerned with questions such as: Why are people motivated to role behavior by directives or communications from others? What types of power contribute the most toward organizational goals? Why do managers sometimes fail to use the power they have?

Classification Systems. One of the first studies dealing with the bases of authority classified the statements of respondents in a police department, a welfare office, and an elementary school into four categories (53). These were authority of legitimacy (laws, rules, policies), of position, of competence (professional and technical experience), and of person. Legitimacy and position were reported rather consistently as important bases in all three organizations. Other major findings were that authority of person was stressed particularly in the police department and authority of competence in the elementary school.

A second study, conducted in a professional organization, utilized a somewhat more comprehensive data-gathering procedure and identified eleven types of reasons one individual would seek a decision from another on various work-related matters (17). In the list below the various bases are noted in order of frequency of mention, from most to least frequent.

1. Responsibility and function (the person with authority is responsible for the particular matter).
2. Formal authority (the person with authority is in a position to make decisions generally).
3. Control of resources (the person with authority controls money, information, etc.).
4. Collegial (a group of peers has the right to be consulted).
5. Manipulation (the person with authority can get the decision made in the manner desired).
6. Default or avoidance (the person with authority is available and will deal with the problem).
7. Bureaucratic rules (the rules specify the person to consult).
8. Traditional rules (custom, tradition, or seniority specify the person to consult).
9. Equity (the person with authority is a fair decision maker).
10. Friendship (the person with authority is personally liked).

11. Expertise (the person with authority has superior knowledge of the subject).

In both of these studies acceptance of the role prescriptions of formal authority structures is clearly evident. But other bases of authority also emerge—competence and person in the first study; collegial, manipulation, default, equity, friendship, expertise, and in certain of its aspects control of resources in the second. This type of research is important because it moves beyond the somewhat artificial formal-acceptance controversy.

Several other classification systems, which were developed originally without reference to any specific study, have subsequently provided a basis for research investigations. The most widely used of these is a system developed by French and Raven (18):

Reward (the person with authority can give something that is desired).
Coercive (the person with authority can administer punishments).
Legitimate (the person with authority is right in exercising power according to the values of the person influenced).
Referent (the person with authority is one on whom the person influenced wishes to model his own behavior).
Expert (the person with authority has expert status and thus is likely to be correct and accurate).

Two additional bases probably should be added to this list in the light of the available evidence. The first of these has been called *internalization* and refers to the instance where an individual accepts a directive merely because its content is congruent with his own personal values (31). The second, called *positive transference* in psychoanalytic theory, has also been termed legitimation by a general deference to authority (56). Here attitudes learned originally in the early parental environment are transferred uncritically to the later hierarchic work environment. The superior replaces the parent, but early tendencies to obedience remain. Both internalization and transference may have strong nonrational and unconscious elements from the viewpoint of the individual. It is probably for this reason that they do not emerge clearly in lists of the bases of authority derived from research using self-report procedures. It is not easy, or perhaps not even possible, to say that such factors may operate to determine one's behavior.

Relationships with Performance and Satisfaction. There have been relatively few studies relating the effectiveness of a work group to the extent to which the manager in charge of the group utilized various power bases, but what research has been done has produced important results. In one instance 40 production groups in two plants of a company manufacturing home appliances were studied (65). A measure of the five bases noted by French and Raven was obtained from ratings of their foremen made by the members of each group.

These results indicated that the use of reward power was associated with good cost performance but low average earnings per worker (productivity). The same two-sided effect was found for coercive power, which was positively related to the number of suggestions submitted and negatively related to cost performance. Legitimate power showed no relation to performance, but referent power was consistently associated with favorable outcomes (lower absenteeism, better cost performance, higher quality, and more suggestions). Expert power shows a similarly positive picture being found in conjunction with few accidents, low absenteeism, good cost performance, and high quality.

Another study conducted in sales offices produced similar results (5). Where referent and expert power predominated, performance was high and the salesmen were satisfied with their office manager. Where reward power was high, performance tended to be poor and there was marked dissatisfaction. Coercive and legitimate bases of power were associated with dissatisfaction, but unrelated to performance effectiveness. The same results insofar as satisfaction-dissatisfaction are concerned were also obtained when faculty members in 12 liberal arts colleges described the bases of power of their academic deans (4).

These studies consistently support the use of nonformal sources of the referent and expert type over the formal bases of authority. Yet as Table 10–3 indicates, legitimacy tends to be the predominant basis in administrative organizations. In professional organizations, represented by liberal arts colleges, expert power is ranked highest as might be expected. On the other hand, the coercive basis which stresses punishment is considered least important in all three studies. In general the rankings of Table 10–3 show a very high degree of consistency.

Using and Not Using Power. Another group of studies utilizing both measures within organizations and laboratory simulations has been concerned with the conditions under which managers will attempt to actually exercise power (22, 32, 33). The results consistently indicate that inexperienced managers and those who lack self-confidence are much more

Directing: An Input-Improving Mediator

Table 10–3 *Ranking of Importance for Various Bases of Power in Three Organizational Contexts*

Bases of Power	Importance Rank		
	Production Workers (61)	Salesmen (5)	College Faculty (4)
Reward	3	4	4
Coercive	5	5	5
Legitimate	1	1	2
Referent	4	3	3
Expert	2	2	1

likely to refer the problems of subordinates to others rather than dealing with the problems themselves. Thus they often fail to use the full range of powers at their disposal and resort to what amounts to "buckpassing." A similar tendency to actually utilize power less was also found where the manager's span of control was larger.

These studies yield additional evidence on tendencies to utilize different bases of power when faced with different types of problems. When problems of attitude and cooperation appear, managers more frequently resort to coercive power. When the problems relate to ineptness and low productivity, expert power is likely to be used. Thus the relationships between the various bases of power and performance appear not to operate in a single direction only. Performance can influence the type of power used. In all likelihood the power base selected can also influence performance.

Process Theories of Motivation

Ideally it would be possible to consider different types of motivation at work in direct relationship to various bases of power and authority as well as to other types of influence. Unfortunately the existing theories of motivation do not approach the subject in this manner, and the major research investigations are arrayed primarily around these theories.

There are a large number of these theories bearing on motivation as related to work which are currently viable. Some are in conflict with one another; more frequently the theories deal with different aspects of the total motivational process. The objective here is first to provide some understanding of these different viewpoints and second to attempt on the basis of available research to find a meaningful and valid path through the forest of theory.

Existing theories appear to fall rather clearly into two categories (9). Certain theories deal predominantly with the *process* of how behavior is energized. They are concerned with general concepts and broad classes of variables applying to motivation at work, and typically have given little attention to specific motives as such. It is interesting to note, however, that all the major process theories have given pay a central position. *Content* theories, on the other hand, tend to focus on a specific motive or set of motives. Basic processes are not ignored, but they are considered only as they relate to the operation of particular motives for achievement, security, power, self-realization, and the like. These content theories focus much less sharply on money and pay than the process theories; some ignore monetary incentives completely.

The Law of Effect and Economic Motivation

The law of effect had its origins in psychological experimentation with animals and was originally stated in relation to the learning process. Since its formulation by Edward Thorndike in the early 1900s (24), however, it has been implicit in much of business practice. As applied in managing organizations, the law of effect states that *behavior which seems to lead to reward tends to be repeated, while behavior which seems not to lead to reward or seems to lead to punishment tends not to be repeated.* When joined with the philosophy of hedonism as incorporated in the theories of Adam Smith, the law of effect has produced a view of man as essentially economic. Thus, he is highly responsive to the perceived probability of being rewarded with more money or punished with less (58).

The writings of Frederick Taylor implicitly assume such a concept of motivation, although Taylor did not view money as the only possible sanction available to management. He did, however, exercise strong influence in the development of a variety of piece rate payment plans to reward role behavior that closely approximated role prescriptions, thus resulting in high productivity. Since Taylor's time a great variety of plans have been developed by industrial engineers and compensation specialists predicated on the assumption that if sufficient financial reward is offered for high productivity, high productivity will be maintained by the underlying motivational processes.

Restriction of Output. Unfortunately for this view, evidence developed rather rapidly that these financial incentive plans may not consistently yield the high levels of productivity the theory would predict. In fact this finding was one of the major weapons used by proponents of the human relations viewpoint in attacking scientific management.

It has become evident that for a variety of reasons many people will not exert maximum effort to produce under financial incentives. Rather, they tend to approximate some standard established by a peer group, a standard that is usually well below the capabilities of most of them. Typically strong group pressures are brought to bear to enforce this limitation or restriction of output (73). When faced with a conflict between group pressures and the incentive value of money, not all individuals will go along with the group, however. Some people clearly are very strongly motivated by financial considerations. In one study among college students, for example, these individuals were found to come from somewhat materialistic, well-to-do, disciplined families which emphasized religion, had many close friends, and participated actively in the community (50).

Research on Pay Incentives. In spite of the clear demonstration from the research on restriction of output that motives other than those of an economic nature are important, it does not follow that the economic theory is completely wrong. It is clear that some people do act as the law of effect combined with economic rewards would suggest. It is possible that there are enough such people that financial incentives really do have a significant, even if not maximum motivational effect. Perhaps there are other considerations that might contribute to a similar result.

On balance the evidence indicates that the installation of incentive pay plans usually does have a somewhat positive impact on output (49) and that tying monetary rewards to performance does yield greater motivational effort (36, 60). Yet the theoretical formulations considered to this point are insufficient in a number of respects. The law of effect does not give adequate attention to the anticipation of rewards, economic considerations are only part of the total picture, and there are marked motivational differences between individuals.

Expectancy Theories

Several different versions of expectancy theory have appeared in the past few years, each successive version incorporating more variables and achieving greater specificity, as well as complexity (23, 35, 55, 70). These theories have in common the view that people have certain built-in *expectancies* regarding the outcomes or consequences that are likely to follow from their role behavior and that they prefer certain outcomes over others. Thus an individual may expect that certain kinds of behavior will earn him a raise and he may want a raise very much. As a consequence he will be motivated to the behavior involved. Formulations of this kind tend to be more precise than those based on the law of effect, but they are not necessarily at variance with it.

Expectancy theories typically incorporate the concept of *instrumentality*; that is, an outcome may be preferred because it is instrumental to the achievement of other outcomes. Thus the desire for a raise may exist not so much for its own sake as because the raise is viewed as a means to higher status, or wider recognition, or some other second-level outcome.

Early formulations of expectancy theory did not consider the individual's performance goals, as reflected in the management by objectives approach, for example (38). People may have varying expectancies not only regarding the consequences of their role behavior, but regarding the likelihood that they will be able to achieve established goals or standards. This type of expectancy, too, may influence motivation.

A schematic presentation of these various components of expectancy theories is given in Figure 10–1. This model establishes motivation as a

Figure 10–1 *A Schematic Representation of a Hybrid Expectancy Model of Work Motivation Outlining the Determinants of the Direction, Amplitude, and Persistence of Individual Effort*

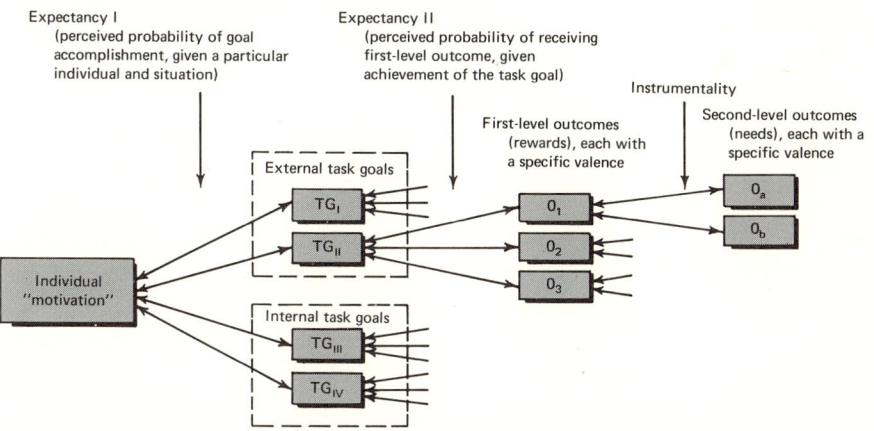

Source: From J. P. Campbell, M. D. Dunnette, E. E. Lawler, and K. W. Weick, *Managerial Behavior, Performance and Effectiveness* (New York: McGraw-Hill, 1970), p. 347. Copyright 1970 by McGraw-Hill Book Company. Used with permission of McGraw-Hill Book Company.

function of expectancies, goals (whether established by others in the organization or by the individual himself), outcomes, valences (preference level), and instrumentality (9). It should be evident that as given this is entirely a process formulation. It says nothing about the specific preferred outcomes and expectancies of human beings and thus about the content of motivation.

When various content factors such as pay and achievement are incorporated, the theory becomes testable. Results of such studies to date have been encouraging (19, 23, 55, 74). Although not all derivations from expectancy theory have been confirmed, it is becoming increasingly clear that variables of the kind indicated in Figure 10-1 are important keys to understanding motivation at work. On the other hand, the exact nature of the relationships among these factors remains uncertain (9).

Equity Theory

Equity theory extends the formulations based on the law of effect and economic motivation in a direction that appears to be somewhat different from expectancy theory. It posits that people are concerned with maximizing not only the amount of payment but the fairness of the payment as well. The theory is concerned with comparisons among inputs and outcomes (1, 2). The primary concern is with the relation between an individual's own input/outcome ratio and that of a person or persons with whom he compares himself. This comparison is shown as follows:

$$\frac{\text{Inputs}}{\text{Outcomes}} \text{ for the individual} \quad \text{compared with} \quad \frac{\text{Inputs}}{\text{Outcomes}} \text{ for others}$$

Inputs are whatever the individual perceives as an investment in the job (effort, education, time)—the contributions. Outcomes are those things that are viewed as returns on this investment (money, recognition, working conditions)—the inducements broadly construed. When the comparison process yields an imbalance (inequity), tension is produced in the individual. This tension provides the basis for motivation. The individual does something to reduce the tension and restore balance: he strives for what he perceives as equity and fairness.

The theory is potentially applicable to a variety of input-outcome relationships, but in fact has been used almost entirely in studying various role behaviors as they relate to compensation. In this context the theory would predict, for example, that when people feel overpaid for a given job they will increase the quantity of work produced if on straight hourly pay, but will increase quality (at the expense of quantity) when on piece rate. In the latter case increased quantity, with the resulting increase in pay, would only make them feel overpaid.

Equity theory has generated a sizable amount of research. In general this research tends to support the theory, as applied both to overpayment and to underpayment (9, 21). On the other hand, the equity concept appears to be somewhat lacking in specificity regarding the underlying motivational processes (69) and the particular methods an individual will use in reducing tension and restoring balance. There are major differences in this latter regard between individuals. Thus in one study underpaid proofreaders responded to the inequity by speeding through the job, making many careless errors (14). In addition there are some data indicating that at least part of the findings from equity research can be explained within the broader framework of expectancy theory (15). It seems likely that equity theory as related to compensation may prove most useful in understanding short-term and thus more transitory work behaviors (36).

Most studies related to equity theory have been concerned with the compensation outcome and with role behavior inputs. However, there are some findings related to turnover (66). A comparison of relatively high and low turnover shops of the Boeing Company revealed much greater felt inequity in the shops experiencing the greatest number of separations. Inequity was most pronounced with regard to the outcomes of supervision, leadman, working conditions, intrinsic aspects of the job, and social aspects of the job. Pay, security, and advancement were studied as well, but low and high turnover groups did not differ in their sense of inequity in these areas. These findings suggest that equity theory might well yield more fruitful results if it were applied more broadly outside the compensation field.

Content Theories of Motivation

The content theories concentrate on various individual *motives* which are considered important in relation to job performance and satisfaction, although in some instances these theories contain certain process elements. The specific types of motives identified in content theories could be incorporated in process theories, especially those of an expectancy nature. Many of the motives can be considered as second-level outcomes having varying preference levels or valences. Content theories typically focus on hierarchies of motives either implicitly or explicitly.

Theory of Achievement Motivation

Achievement motivation theory has its origins in clinical psychology and personality theory. However, applications of the theory have been primarily in the economic sphere. Although the achievement motive has received the greatest attention and has given the theory its name, two other motives are also considered—the need for power and for affiliation.

High achievement motivation is characteristic of those who spend considerable time thinking about doing better work, advancing their careers, or accomplishing important things. Such people are said to enjoy situations in which they take personal responsibility for finding solutions to problems, to set moderate achievement goals and to work hard only when the chances of success are in the middle range, to desire specific feedback on how well they are doing, and to exhibit considerable initiative in searching their environments for opportunities to try new things (40).

If an individual is largely concerned with influencing people, winning arguments, changing others' behavior, he has a strong power motive. Such people tend to seek out positions where they can exercise power over others; they do not hesitate to use it when placed in these positions. In contrast, the affiliation motive is concerned with warm, friendly relationships with other people. Those with a strong affiliation need like companionship and helping others; they are drawn to jobs which permit close social interaction and the development of friendships.

Insofar as business success is concerned these three motives are ranged in a definite hierarchy (40). The achievement motive is considered most important, power comes next, and affiliation may in fact have negative consequences. Individuals are viewed as differing considerably in the strength of these motives, that is, in their readiness to produce a particular type of behavior given a situation which might arouse it (3). Aroused motivation of the kind that can become manifest in behavior is a function of the strength of the basic motive, the expectancy of attaining a goal, and the incentive value the individual perceives the goal to have (valence). Individuals who are high (or low) on one of the three motives need not exhibit any particular level of strength on the others.

Achievement Motivation and Success. The basic proposition that achievement motivation is a major ingredient in economic success has received considerable support (40). The motive appears to be important in the economic development of societies as well as in the success of individual managers. Table 10-4 provides data on the relationship between economic growth, as reflected in increased electrical output, and cultural achievement motivation levels, as determined by an analysis of the readers used to teach children in the early school grades. It is clear from the table that the

Table 10-4 *Rate of Growth in Electrical Output (1952-58) and National Achievement Motivation Levels in 1950 for Various Countries*

Achievement Motivation Level	Growth Rate	
	Above Expectation	Below Expectation
High	Turkey	Argentina
	India	Lebanon
	Australia	France
	Israel	Union of So. Africa
	Spain	Ireland
	Pakistan	Tunisia
	Greece	Syria
	Canada	
	Bulgaria	
	U.S.A.	
	West Germany	
	U.S.S.R.	
	Portugal	
Low	Iraq	New Zealand
	Austria	Uruguay
	United Kingdom	Hungary
	Mexico	Norway
	Poland	Sweden
		Finland
		Netherlands
		Italy
		Japan
		Switzerland
		Chile
		Denmark
		Algeria
		Belgium

Source: From *The Achieving Society* by D. C. McClelland, © 1961 by Litton Educational Publishing, Inc. Reprinted by permission of Van Nostrand Reinhold Company.

achievement-oriented societies are particularly likely to have unexpectedly high economic growth rates.

Other evidence indicates that individuals with strong achievement motivation are more frequently attracted to the business world than to government and the professions (41). They particularly like entrepreneurial occupations and tend to do well in them, as well as in managerial positions in challenging and developing industries.

Goal Difficulty. One aspect of achievement motivation theory, however, has not been consistently supported by research. This is the view that goals of intermediate difficult produce the greatest effort and hard work; that hard goals do not, because the chances of achieving them are less, and thus the probability of experiencing the satisfaction of accomplishment is less. This is directly antithetical to the statement in Chapter 4 that very difficult goals yield better performance. A sizable amount of research supports the Chapter 4 statement (37, 51).

A key to a solution to the discrepancy between achievement motivation theory and most research evidence appears to be the concept of *goal acceptance*. If a very difficult goal is accepted as one's own, it will yield high levels of motivation and continual striving for accomplishment. But many goals established by managers for their subordinates may never actually be viewed as meaningful and realistic by those who are to accomplish them. If these goals are very difficult they may well not be accepted, and in such situations motivation can be expected to peak in the middle range. The task for management is to get people to fully incorporate difficult goals.

Role Motivation Theory

Role motivation theory posits certain generalized role requirements characterizing managerial jobs in large, administrative organizations. It assumes further that motives matching these requirements will contribute to managerial success (in both value and reward terms). These motives should be toward the top of an individual's preference or valence hierarchy if he is to be a successful manager (45). The motives so specified are:

1. Positive attitude toward those holding positions of authority (especially superiors).

2. Desire to engage in competitive endeavor (especially with peers).
3. Desire to behave in accordance with the requirements of the masculine role.
4. Desire to exercise power over others (especially subordinates).
5. Desire to assume a differentiated role relative to others in the work situation, to stand out.
6. Desire to accept routine administrative responsibilities.

The available evidence indicates that certain of these motives are consistently associated with success in large administrative organizations (45). In addition they have been shown to precede and condition success. This is true of positive attitudes toward authority, competitive motivation, and power motivation. The other three motives have been related to success less frequently, but all have yielded meaningful results in at least one study. On the other hand, studies carried out in professional organizations have produced little evidence for the importance of any of these motives (46, 47).

Research indicates that motives of this kind are important, not only in relation to success within the managerial hierarchy, but in the choice of a managerial career. Data on this point are given in Table 10–5 for students at

Table 10–5 Managerial Motivation Scores for Business Students with Managerial and Nonmanagerial Career Goals

Group Studied	N	Motivation Score
Graduate Students		
Managerial goals	41	7.71
Nonmanagerial goals	65	.94
Undergraduate Students		
Managerial goals	33	2.27
Nonmanagerial goals	75	−.20

Source: J. B. Miner and N. R. Smith, "Managerial Talent Among Undergraduate and Graduate Business Students," *Personnel and Guidance Journal*, Vol. 47 (American Personnel and Guidance Association, 1969), 997–999.

the University of Oregon. Among graduate students those with managerial goals scored much higher on a measure of the six motives incorporated in role-motivation theory. At the undergraduate level this differentiation in terms of relevant motivation is much less pronounced (48), although a significant difference in score in the predicted direction is still present. Overall, it is apparent that those who aspire to be managers in business organizations do exhibit disproportionate amounts of the hypothesized motivation. The motives included in the theory are high on their preference hierarchies.

Need Hierarchy and Self-actualization

A considerably different content theory has been set forth by Maslow (39) and popularized by McGregor (42). This theory posits a hierarchy of motives as follows:

Physiological: Hunger, thirst, sex, activity, and the like—the basic needs of the organism.
Safety: Freedom from bodily harm, protection against danger—the need for a predictable, stable, and secure environment.
Social: Friendship, affection, love, belongingness—something very much akin to the affiliation motive.
Ego: Needs relating to self-esteem, on the one hand, such as self-respect, self-confidence, autonomy, achievement, and competence; on the other hand, needs relating to reputation such as status, recognition, attention, and prestige.
Self-actualization: Growth, development, achieving one's full potential, creativity, self-fulfillment—essentially an existential concept.

This classification system is not so important in itself as the way in which the various types of motives are said to relate to each other. An individual's actual behavior can be expected to reflect the lowest category of motives which are not fulfilled or satisfied. Thus people can be expected to start out by satisfying their physiological and then safety motives. Once this is accomplished these motives lose their force and the higher-level motives guide behavior. In general in our society physiological and safety motive satisfaction occurs quickly. This is less true of social, ego, and self-actualization motives, especially the latter. To the extent the higher motives move toward satisfaction, one can expect to find a more fully motivated individual. Thus it is important from a managerial viewpoint to stress these motives and to attempt to satisfy them. Satisfying lower-level motives will accomplish little, since they are already satiated.

One criticism of this type of formulation is that it leaves no room for differences between individuals (71). The postulating of a single hierarchy of motives for all people appears as a major oversimplification. The idea of an individual, motive-preference hierarchy which is learned as a function of different individual experiences, rather than of a set hierarchy for all mankind, has been proposed as more consistent with the facts (44, 58). Under this view self-actualization might be a dominant motive for one person and thus determine a large part of his behavior, but another individual working under essentially the same circumstances might well be guided primarily by social, safety, or even physiological motives much of the time. Should this be the case—that motive hierarchies do differ depending on particular individual learning experiences—one would not expect to find much research support for the Maslow-McGregor theory.

One line of research has utilized the techniques of factor analysis with items designed to measure the various motives. Studies designed to test the theory have been carried out with both managers and factory workers. They have generally failed to yield groupings of items which match the categories of the Maslow typology (52, 57). Thus the research appears to raise a serious question regarding the inherent, basic nature of the particular motives considered, insofar as "people in general" are concerned. It is possible, however, that these studies have not used appropriate items to measure the motives of the theory.

On the other hand, those studies that tend to *support* the theory utilize essentially these same items (54). They indicate that managers at successively higher levels do experience greater satisfaction of self-actualization and ego motives and that in general the higher-level motives are less satisfied among managers than those lower in the motive hierarchy. The theory would predict these findings. But it is also true that the studies indicate social motives are *not* less satisfied than safety motives, and neither of these two motives exhibits a tendency to greater satisfaction at successively higher managerial levels.

Other research has failed to establish any relationship between the extent to which higher-level motives are satisfied, or the opportunity to satisfy them, and the overall force of work motivation (7). Another study aimed at determining whether an increase in the satisfaction of one type of motive serves to strengthen motives at a higher level also produced no evidence in support of the theory (25). Furthermore, there was no evidence that managers who became more successful and attained better salaries changed their motive strengths any differently than the less successful. Overall, research to date has provided little support for the concept of a fixed motive hierarchy which changes in a preestablished scalar fashion as a function of satisfaction patterns.

Two-factor Theory

Two-factor theory was developed primarily by Herzberg as a result of his studies of job attitudes (26, 27). In several respects it is similar to the need hierarchy approach. There are two classes of motives which roughly approximate the lower- and higher-level categories of the Maslow system:

> Extrinsic or hygiene factors: Company policy and administration, the technical aspect of supervision, the interpersonal relations aspect of supervision, interpersonal relations with peers, interpersonal relations with subordinates, working conditions, pay increases, and under certain circumstances factors in one's personal life, accoutrements of status and job security.
> Intrinsic (job content) factors or motivators: Achievement, recognition of achievement, being given responsibility, advancement, the work itself, and under certain circumstances the possibility of growth.

Extrinsic factors are viewed as primarily related to job dissatisfaction. The most management can accomplish from them is the minimization of dissatisfaction. Intrinsic factors, on the other hand, can contribute to real satisfaction in work. Much of the recent emphasis on job enlargement (see Chapter 8) has been generated out of a desire to build intrinsic motivators into jobs. There is in this development a very clear implication, which is reinforced by Herzberg's writings, that motivators are not only the source of job satisfaction but of effective role *behavior* as well. Thus two-factor theory may be viewed as a general theory of work motivation.

The Conflicting Evidence. The hypothesis that factors extrinsic to the job and those intrinsic to it have completely different motivational effects, that separate classes of incentives contribute to negative and positive consequences, has generated a great deal of research—and a great deal of controversy. It has become increasingly apparent that support for two factor theory is most likely to be obtained when the critical incident method originally used by Herzberg in developing the theory is invoked (8). Finding results which confirm the theory is closely tied to the particular way in which Herzberg classified incidents (61).

Evidence obtained using other research approaches generally fails to confirm the theory (29). It seems apparent that extrinsic factors often are a source of satisfaction and intrinsic factors a source of dissatisfaction. A given factor can cause job satisfaction for one person and dissatisfaction for another. As with the research on need hierarchy theory, that on two-factor theory contradicts the concept of a fixed preference hierarchy characteristic of all mankind. In one study only 44 percent of the 85 managers studied gave responses consistent with predictions from two-factor theory (62). The remainder clearly utilized some other motive preference hierarchy.

Yet it is also true that taken alone the extrinsic-intrinsic approach to classifying incentives has proved useful. The differentiation is an important one. In one study a selected cross section of employed adults in the Los Angeles area was asked to rank six job factors in terms of their importance to them (11). The results are given in Table 10–6. A factor was classified

Table 10–6 Percentage of People in Various Occupations Indicating a Job Factor as of Considerable Importance to Them

		Intrinsic Job Factors			Extrinsic Job Factors		
Occupation	N	Interesting Work	Self-expression	Satisfying Work	Pay	Job Security	Good Co-workers
Professional and Managerial	217	68	64	68	59	16	25
Clerical and Sales	183	62	48	46	66	31	46
Skilled	98	61	51	46	70	33	40
Semiskilled and Unskilled	135	50	35	39	74	49	52

Source: R. Centers and D. E. Bugental, "Intrinsic and Extrinsic Job Motivations Among Different Segments of the Working Population," Journal of Applied Psychology, Vol. 50 (1966), 195. Copyright 1966 by the American Psychological Association. Reproduced by permission.

as important for a person if it appeared in one of the top three ranks. From the table it is apparent that the extrinsic-intrinsic classification system consistently differentiates factors which relate to occupational level in very different ways.

Important Motives for Management. Whatever the deficiencies of two-factor theory, research stimulated by it does confirm the findings obtained in relation to other content theories that intrinsic motives such as achievement, recognition, and self-actualization are important in managerial work, and in many other higher-level occupations as well. In fact the consistency with which the various content theories emphasize certain motives is striking. Again and again the significance of having certain motives at a high preference level, or high in valence, or dominant over other motives is stressed by the research. These motives which appear to "make a

Directing: An Input-Improving Mediator

difference" in higher-level occupations are achievement, power, competition, self-esteem, recognition, and self-actualization. Furthermore, the research consistently indicates that although a number of these motives may be easily and readily aroused in some individuals, there are others whose behavior is rarely if ever guided by this type of motivation. *Individual variation, rather than a fixed preference hierarchy, seems to best explain the motivational processes underlying human behavior.*

The next chapter will take up the core of the directing function—how authority, power, and influence may be exercised to motivate role behavior so as to bring it in as close alignment as possible with existing role prescriptions.

Questions

1. In what sense is it possible that formal and acceptance theories of authority are both true? How do concepts such as the zone of indifference, legitimacy, and charisma relate to these theories?
2. What major problems limit the usefulness of the following motivation theories?
    a. Need hierarchy and self-actualization
    b. The law of effect and economic motivation
    c. Theory of achievement motivation
    d. Two-factor theory
3. How do you account for the fact that theories of motivation have been advanced in such abundance and that pay has had such a central position in many of them? Which theories de-emphasize pay in explaining motivation at work? Which ignore it?
4. List as many bases or sources of power and authority as you can think of. For each indicate whether you feel compliance on this basis would be expected to be a largely rational process.
5. What theory of motivation or combination of theories would you find most useful in understanding the behavior of your subordinates if you were a supervisor? Why?

References

1. Adams, J. S. "Toward an Understanding of Inequity." *Journal of Abnormal and Social Psychology*, Vol. 67 (1963), 422–436.
2. Adams, J. S. "Inequity in Social Exchange." In L. Berkowitz (ed.), *Advances in Experimental Social Psychology*. Vol. 2. New York: Academic Press, 1965, pp. 267–299.

3. Atkinson, J. W. *An Introduction to Motivation.* Princeton, N.J.: Van Nostrand, 1964.
4. Bachman, J. G. "Faculty Satisfaction and the Dean's Influence: An Organizational Study of Twelve Liberal Arts Colleges." *Journal of Applied Psychology*, Vol. 52 (1968), 55–61.
5. Bachman, J. G., C. G. Smith, and J. A. Slesinger. "Control, Performance, and Satisfaction: An Analysis of Structural and Individual Effects." *Journal of Personality and Social Psychology*, Vol. 4 (1966), 127–136.
6. Barnard, C. I. *The Functions of the Executive.* Cambridge, Mass.: Harvard University Press, 1938.
7. Beer, M. *Leadership, Employee Needs and Motivation.* Columbus: Bureau of Business Research, Ohio State University, 1966.
8. Bockman, V. M. "The Herzberg Controversy." *Personnel Psychology*, Vol. 24 (1971), 155–189.
9. Campbell, J. P., M. D. Dunnette, E. E. Lawler, and K. E. Weick. *Managerial Behavior, Performance, and Effectiveness.* New York: McGraw-Hill, 1970.
10. Cartwright, D., and A. Zander (eds.). *Group Dynamics: Research and Theory.* New York: Harper & Row, 1968.
11. Centers, R., and D. E. Bugental. "Intrinsic and Extrinsic Job Motivations Among Different Segments of the Working Population." *Journal of Applied Psychology*, Vol. 50 (1966), 193–197.
12. Dalton, G. W., L. B. Barnes, and A. Zaleznik. *The Distribution of Authority in Formal Organizations.* Cambridge, Mass.: Division of Research, Harvard Business School, 1968.
13. Davis, K. "Attitudes Toward the Legitimacy of Management Efforts to Influence Employees." *Academy of Management Journal*, Vol. 11 (1968), 153–162.
14. Evan, W. M., and R. G. Simmons. "Organizational Effects of Inequitable Rewards: Two Experiments in Status Inconsistency." *Administrative Science Quarterly*, Vol. 14 (1969), 224–237.
15. Evans, M. G., and L. Molinari. "Equity, Piece-Rate Overpayment, and Job Security: Some Effects on Performance." *Journal of Applied Psychology*, Vol. 54 (1970), 105–114.
16. Fayol, H. *General and Industrial Management.* London: Pitman, 1949.
17. Filley, A. C., and A. J. Grimes. "The Bases of Power in Decision Processes." In R. W. Millman and M. P. Hottenstein (eds.), *Promising Research Directions. Academy of Management Proceedings*, 1968, pp. 133–160.
18. French, J. R. P., and B. Raven. "The Bases of Social Power." In D. Cartwright (ed.), *Studies in Social Power.* Ann Arbor: Research Center for Group Dynamics, University of Michigan, 1959, pp. 150–167.
19. Galbraith, J., and L. L. Cummings. "An Empirical Investigation of the

Motivational Determinants of Task Performance: Interactive Effects Between Instrumentality-Valence and Motivation-Ability." *Organizational Behavior and Human Performance*, Vol. 2 (1967), 237–257.
20. Gazell, J. A. "Authority-Flow Theory and the Impact of Chester Barnard." *California Management Review*, Vol. 13 (1970), No. 1, 68–74.
21. Goodman, P. S., and A. Friedman. "An Examination of Adams' Theory of Inequity." *Administrative Science Quarterly*, Vol. 16 (1971), 271–288.
22. Goodstadt, B., and D. Kipnis. "Situational Influences on the Use of Power." *Journal of Applied Psychology*, Vol. 54 (1970), 201–207.
23. Graen, G. "Instrumentality Theory of Work Motivation: Some Experimental Results and Suggested Modifications." *Journal of Applied Psychology Monograph*, Vol. 53 (1969), No. 2, Part 2, 1–25.
24. Haire, M. *Psychology in Management.* New York: McGraw-Hill, 1964.
25. Hall, D. T., and K. E. Nougaim. "An Examination of Maslow's Need Hierarchy in an Organizational Setting." *Organizational Behavior and Human Performance*, Vol. 3 (1968), 12–35.
26. Herzberg, F. *Work and the Nature of Man.* Cleveland: World, 1966.
27. Herzberg, F., B. Mausner, B. B. Snyderman. *The Motivation to Work.* New York: Wiley, 1959.
28. Hopkins, T. K. "Bureaucratic Authority: The Convergence of Weber and Barnard." In A. Etzioni (ed.), *Complex Organizations: A Sociological Reader.* New York: Holt, Rinehart and Winston, 1961, pp. 82–98.
29. House, R. J., and L. A. Wigdor. "Herzberg's Dual-Factor Theory of Job Satisfaction and Motivation: A Review of the Evidence and a Criticism." *Personnel Psychology*, Vol. 20 (1967), 369–389.
30. Katz, D., and R. L. Kahn. *The Social Psychology of Organizations.* New York: Wiley, 1966.
31. Kelman, H. C. "Compliance, Identification, and Internalization: Three Processes of Attitude Change." *Journal of Conflict Resolution*, Vol. 2 (1958), 51–60.
32. Kipnis, D., and J. Cosentino. "Use of Leadership Powers in Industry." *Journal of Applied Psychology*, Vol. 53 (1969), 460–466.
33. Kipnis, D., and W. P. Lane. "Self-confidence and Leadership." *Journal of Applied Psychology*, Vol. 46 (1962), 291–295.
34. Koontz, H., and C. O'Donnell. *Principles of Management: An Analysis of Managerial Functions.* New York: McGraw-Hill, 1968.
35. Lawler, E. E. "Job Attitudes and Employee Motivation: Theory, Research, and Practice." *Personnel Psychology*, Vol. 23 (1970), 223–237.
36. Lawler, E. E. *Pay and Organizational Effectiveness: A Psychological View.* New York: McGraw-Hill, 1971.
37. Locke, E. A. "Toward a Theory of Task Motivation and Incentives." *Organizational Behavior and Human Performance*, Vol. 3 (1968), 157–189.

38. Locke, E. A. "Job Satisfaction and Job Performance: A Theoretical Analysis." *Organizational Behavior and Human Performance*, Vol. 5 (1970), 484–500.
39. Maslow, A. H. "A Dynamic Theory of Human Motivation." *Psychological Review*, Vol. 50 (1943), 370–396.
40. McClelland, D. C. *The Achieving Society*. Princeton, N.J.: Van Nostrand, 1961.
41. McClelland, D. C. "The Role of Achievement Orientation in the Transfer of Technology." In W. H. Gruber and D. G. Marquis (eds.), *Factors in the Transfer of Technology*. Cambridge, Mass.: The M.I.T. Press, 1969, pp. 61–81.
42. McGregor, D. *The Human Side of Enterprise*. New York: McGraw-Hill, 1960.
43. Mechanic, D. "Sources of Power of Lower Participants in Complex Organizations." In W. W. Cooper, H. J. Leavitt, and M. W. Shelly (eds.), *New Perspectives in Organization Research*. New York: Wiley, 1964, pp. 136–149.
44. Miner, J. B. *The Management of Ineffective Performance*. New York: McGraw-Hill, 1963.
45. Miner, J. B. *Studies in Management Education*. New York: Springer, 1965.
46. Miner, J. B. "Personality Tests as Predictors of Consulting Success." *Personnel Psychology*, Vol. 24 (1971), 191–204.
47. Miner, J. B. "Changes in Student Attitudes Toward Bureaucratic Role Prescriptions During the 1960s." *Administrative Science Quarterly*, Vol. 16 (1971), 351–364.
48. Miner, J. B., and N. R. Smith. "Managerial Talent Among Undergraduate and Graduate Business Students." *Personnel and Guidance Journal*, Vol. 47 (1969), 995–1000.
49. Opsahl, R. L., and M. D. Dunnette. "The Role of Financial Compensation in Industrial Motivation." *Psychological Bulletin*, Vol. 66 (1966), 94–118.
50. Paine, F. T., D. R. Deutsch, and R. A. Smith. "Relationship Between Family Backgrounds and Work Values." *Journal of Applied Psychology*, Vol. 51 (1967), 320–323.
51. Patchen, M. *Participation, Achievement and Involvement on the Job*. Englewood Cliffs, N.J.: Prentice-Hall, 1970.
52. Payne, R. "Factor Analysis of a Maslow-Type Need Satisfaction Questionnaire." *Personnel Psychology*, Vol. 23 (1970), 251–268.
53. Peabody, R. L. "Perceptions of Organizational Authority: A Comparative Analysis." *Administrative Science Quarterly*, Vol. 6 (1962), 463–482.
54. Porter, L. W. *Organizational Patterns of Managerial Job Attitudes*. New York: American Foundation for Management Research, 1964.
55. Porter, L. W., and E. E. Lawler. *Managerial Attitudes and Performance*. Homewood, Ill.: Irwin, 1968.

56. Presthus, R. V. "Authority in Organizations." *Public Administration Review*, Vol. 20 (1960), No. 2, 86–91.
57. Roberts, K. H., G. A. Walter, and R. E. Miles. "A Factor-Analytic Study of Job Satisfaction Items Designed to Measure Maslow Need Categories." *Personnel Psychology*. Vol. 24 (1971), 205–220.
58. Schein, E. H. *Organizational Psychology*. Englewood Cliffs, N. J.: Prentice-Hall, 1965.
59. Schein, E. H., and G. L. Lippitt. "Supervisory Attitudes Toward the Legitimacy of Influencing Subordinates." *Journal of Applied Behavioral Science*, Vol. 2 (1966), 199–209.
60. Schneider, B., and L. K. Olson. "Effort as a Correlate of Organizational Reward System and Individual Values." *Personnel Psychology*, Vol. 23 (1970), 313–326.
61. Schneider, J., and E. A. Locke. "A Critique of Herzberg's Incident Classification System and a Suggested Revision." *Organizational Behavior and Human Performance*, Vol. 6 (1971), 441–457.
62. Schwab, D. P., and H. G. Heneman. "Aggregate and Individual Predictability of the Two-factor Theory of Job Satisfaction." *Personnel Psychology*, Vol. 23, (1970), 55–66.
63. Scott, W. R., S. M. Dornbusch, B. C. Busching, and J. D. Laing. "Organizational Evaluation and Authority." *Administrative Science Quarterly*, Vol. 12 (1967), 93–117.
64. Simon, H. A. *Administrative Behavior*. New York: Free Press, 1957.
65. Student, K. R. "Supervisory Influence and Work-Group Performance." *Journal of Applied Psychology*, Vol. 52 (1968), 188–194.
66. Telly, C. S., W. L. French, and W. G. Scott. "The Relationship of Inequity to Turnover Among Hourly Workers." *Administrative Science Quarterly*, Vol. 16 (1971), 164–172.
67. Thompson, J. D. "Authority and Power in Identical Organizations." *American Journal of Sociology*, Vol. 62 (1956), 290–298.
68. Thompson, V. A. *Modern Organization*. New York: Knopf, 1961.
69. Valenzi, E. R., and I. R. Andrews. "Effect of Hourly Overpay and Underpay Inequity When Tested with a New Induction Procedure." *Journal of Applied Psychology*, Vol. 55 (1971), 22–27.
70. Vroom, V. H. *Work and Motivation*. New York: Wiley, 1964.
71. Vroom, V. H. *Motivation in Management*. New York: American Foundation for Management Research, 1965.
72. Weber, M. *The Theory of Social and Economic Organization*, ed. T. Parsons. New York: Free Press, 1947.
73. Whyte, W. F. *Money and Motivation*. New York: Harper, 1955.
74. Wofford, J. C. "The Motivational Bases of Job Satisfaction and Job Performance." *Personnel Psychology*, Vol. 24 (1971), 501–518.

11 Leadership and Supervision

I. Does Leadership Make Any Difference?
1. The Effect of Performance on Leadership
2. Leadership Rotation Studies

II. Characteristics of Successful Managers
1. Multicompany Comparisons
   a. The University of Minnesota Studies
   b. The Ghiselli Research
   c. Characteristics Most Likely to Relate to Success
2. Organizational Differences
3. Success as an Entrepreneur
4. Fiedler's Contingency Approach
   a. Theoretical Formulations
   b. The Nature of the Evidence

III. Role Behaviors of Successful Managers
1. Considerate and Structuring Leadership Styles
   a. Consideration for Subordinates
   b. Initiating Structure for Subordinates
   c. Close Supervision
2. Autocratic, Democratic (Participative), and Laissez-Faire Styles
   a. Participative Management
   b. Effects of Autocratic and Democratic Styles
   c. Laissez-Faire as a Leadership Style
3. Achievement, Power, and Affiliation Styles
4. Organizational Character and Managerial Behavior

In administrative organizations the usual practice is for managers to be appointed by other managers at higher levels. Acceptance of the new manager's authority follows the actual appointment, in certain areas and in varying degrees.

This is the usual pattern, although it is by no means universal. Leadership also may be *emergent*. Emergent leadership appears frequently in professional organizations, but it is far from unknown in the administrative context as well (24). The emergent leader arises from the group; often he is elected. He achieves a certain degree of acceptance of his authority as a prior condition for leadership. Power bases of the referent and expert types are likely to play a major role in his acceptance. In general, group decisions related to emergent leadership are strongly influenced by the existing value structure.

In many instances the distinction between appointed, or imposed, leadership and emergent leadership has little meaning; this is true if the individual appointed is already in many respects emergent, or if at some point subsequent to appointment he achieves a set of relationships which guarantee emergent status. For all practical purposes imposed and emergent leadership become one and the same. But it also is true that the two types of leadership may exist side by side in different individuals. An appointed leader may fail to fulfill group expectations, may lack acceptance, or may behave in ways inconsistent with the existing value structure. In such instances another leader may emerge from the group. Thus, informal and formal leadership will both exist—perhaps with each person carrying out different aspects of the leadership function, perhaps with almost all power in the hands of the emergent, informal leader.

In the discussions which follow, the major concern is with the characteristics and behavior styles of formally appointed leaders in relationship to various indexes of effectiveness and success—what makes a good leader. In addition some of the studies bear on emergent leadership. There is very little known, however, about effective informal leadership in the context of existing formal leadership. This is one of the major voids in research related to the directing function.

Does Leadership Make Any Difference?

It is generally assumed that managers vary in their capacity to influence subordinates to role behavior which matches role prescriptions. Managerial reward systems frequently are established with this assumption in mind.

When a unit is highly productive, it is viewed as appropriate to reward the manager in charge in the belief that his behavior must have contributed to the group result.

Observation of production units, sales districts, and the like tends to support this assumption. Groups clearly differ in a number of performance-related respects—quantity of output, quality, turnover, absenteeism, cooperation. And one frequently notes sizable differences between managers of more and less effective groups. It is easy to conclude that the differences between managers *cause* the differences in group performance. On the face of it leadership does seem to make a very sizable difference.

Yet there are certain findings reported in Chapter 10 which raise a note of caution. Using the critical incident method, Herzberg found that supervision was generally reported to be a dissatisfier and operated as a hygiene factor. Variations in perceived supervisory behavior could serve to minimize negative motivational consequences, but did not operate as true motivators (22). The implication is that supervision is unlikely to be a major factor producing differences in performance. This conclusion might be discounted on several grounds, but certain other findings discussed in the preceding chapter suggest a similar conclusion. It was noted, for instance, that problems of attitude and cooperation in subordinates typically elicit the use of coercive power by superiors; problems of ineptness and low productivity elicit expert power (17). Thus role behavior of subordinates can cause managers to act in certain ways. These findings suggest that the association between managerial actions and group performance levels so frequently observed is not entirely a consequence of managers behaving differently and thus causing their units to do well or poorly. At least part of the relationship may well exist because more or less effective units *cause* their managers to behave differently.

In view of these research findings and the frequent observation that workers are in many cases so rigidly controlled by company policies, job requirements, aspects of technology, and union rules that first-level supervision can have little impact (33), it seems best to take another look at the question of whether leadership does in fact make a difference. What does the research evidence show when viewed in a more comprehensive manner?

The Effect of Performance on Leadership

Research clearly indicates that the level of an individual's performance can have considerable impact on his behavior and relationships in an

Directing: An Input-Improving Mediator

organization. In one instance measures of the performance effectiveness of 151 research engineers in an electronics firm were related to various organizational factors, two and a half years subsequent to the time the performance data were obtained (8). The evidence indicated that effective performance contributed not only to a higher salary but to greater involvement in one's work, greater influence in the organization, and a greater diversity of role behaviors. It seems likely that if performing well can have these effects on an individual's own behavior, having a highly effective work unit might have a similar impact on a manager.

Laboratory research generally supports this conclusion. In such studies the level of performance is artificially established as either high or low, and subsequent effects on the behavior of an appointed leader are observed. Findings are that poor performers tend to elicit very close supervision with frequent directions and checking; the ideas of the subordinate are ignored, and he is held closely to prescribed procedures; he is viewed as irresponsible and treated with a minimum of kindness and consideration (43).

In another such study leaders of high and low past performance groups were rated by their subordinates on a number of aspects of their behavior using a 7-point scale (9). Table 11-1 contains the average ratings where significant differences appeared between high and low past performance groups. It appears that the leaders of high performance groups were more

Table 11-1 Leader Behavior as a Function of Past Performance

	Mean Amount of Behavior Characteristic	
Behavior Characteristic	Past Performance High	Past Performance Low
Sensitive to needs and feelings of workers	5.1	4.2
Gives recognition for a job well done	4.2	2.9
Has trust and confidence in his men	5.1	4.2
Punitive or critical of group's performance	1.8	3.6
Exerts unreasonable pressure for better performance	2.8	3.5
Maintains high performance standards	5.1	3.9
Stresses a feeling of pride in the group	4.6	3.1
Allows members freedom and autonomy in their work	4.8	4.1
Encourages speaking out and listens with respect	5.5	4.9
Communicates clearly and effectively	4.8	4.1
Emphasizes that people work together as a team	4.0	3.3

Source: G. F. Farris and F. G. Lim, "Effects of Performance on Leadership, Cohesiveness, Influence, Satisfaction, and Subsequent Performance," *Journal of Applied Psychology,* Vol. 53 (1969), 493. Copyright 1969 by the American Psychological Association. Reproduced by permission.

supportive, emphasized performance goals more, and facilitated interaction more.

From these data it seems certain that performance can influence leadership behavior and that at least part of the commonly observed relationship between various leader behaviors and group performance levels may be accounted for on this basis. In addition there is good reason to believe that leader behavior and/or the type of person who emerges into leadership may be determined by such factors as the degree to which the task to be accomplished is clear and unambiguous, as well as by the degree of stress in the situation (35). Since both of these factors can influence performance outcomes as well, there is basis for concluding that observed leader-performance relationships may be caused by the concomitant influence of additional factors on both leader behavior and subordinate performance. *At this point there remains the serious question of whether leadership does make a difference at all.*

Leadership Rotation Studies

The ideal research design for studying the nature of the causal relationships between leader behavior and performance involves rotating managers and observing changes in unit performance. If a manager of a high-producing group is put in charge of a low-producing group and the new group improves drastically, this would be the kind of evidence needed to demonstrate that leadership does make a difference.

One such study was conducted with 22 clerical groups in the home office of an insurance company (10). Midway through an extended cost reduction effort, supervisors were rotated so that those who had been in charge of groups where costs had been held down were reassigned to groups which had not reduced costs, and vice versa. Cost levels followed the supervisors, rather than staying with the work groups. Thus in this instance leadership definitely appears to have made a difference.

Another somewhat more complex study was carried out with production groups on the assembly lines of a furniture factory (65). Here the reassignments were made based on certain characteristics of the foremen known to be related to productivity differences among the groups. In this instance the results did not support the leadership-as-cause hypothesis nearly as strongly as in the insurance company study. In fact the impact of group performance levels on leadership seemed to be greater than leader impact on performance. Yet both types of causal sequences were in evidence to some degree.

Taken as a whole these studies and others considered in subsequent sections of this chapter indicate that leadership may make a difference, but that it rarely achieves the degree of impact that simple observation of leader behavior and group performance at a point in time might suggest. Leaders of effective groups behave as they do at least in part because of various situational factors, and among the most important of these is the effectiveness of their groups. In some instances situational factors may so dominate the scene that managers have practically no discretion and operate only as figureheads (7). Controls instituted by higher management, existing policies, regulated technology, and union restrictions, among other factors, may leave no room for a manager to influence motivational levels in his group. This appears most likely in certain types of manufacturing contexts.

On the other hand, there are many instances where leadership differences are reflected in group performance, where managers can motivate. The clerical component of the insurance company appears to fit this description. Supervisors accomplish this motivational impact in a number of ways (40). They may assign tasks or structure jobs to fit existing subordinate interests and motives. They may provide recognition, status, and rewards. They may contribute to the establishing of performance goals and to acceptance of them. They may provide assistance, support, and instruction to aid in attaining these goals. All of these things require a degree of discretion. When the role prescriptions for a given managerial job do not provide for such discretion and consequently when the incumbent manager does not make any important decisions regarding his subordinates, the leader behavior of that manager does *not* make any difference.

Characteristics of Successful Managers

One of the major directions taken by those who have studied leadership and supervision involves relating various characteristics of managers to indexes of success. Initially, at least, this approach was inspired by the "great man" concept. It represented an attempt to determine those characteristics which contribute to successful leadership irrespective of the organization and the "walk of life."

Studies in this vein typically involve measures of intelligence, attitudes, personality, and biographical factors, which are then related to such value and reward indexes as performance ratings, managerial level, promotion rate, compensation, and rate of compensation change. The question to be answered is, Do individuals who give evidence of success have certain characteristics which differentiate them from less successful managers?

Multicompany Comparisons

Research aimed at identifying characteristics associated with managerial success consistently across a number of organizations, even organizations of the same type, has not been nearly as rewarding as the "great man" concept would imply. A study of graduates of the Stanford University School of Business revealed few characteristics that were predictive of level of success five years later, even though a number of psychological measures were used (21). Such findings as did emerge tended to be specific to certain graduating classes and types of companies. Similarly a comprehensive study of administrators in four school districts gives little reason for optimism that a particular type of person can be identified who will consistently succeed in the educational field (50).

The University of Minnesota Studies. A few multicompany studies have produced somewhat more positive results. Among these, research carried out with a sample of 468 managers from 13 Minnesota companies ranging in size from 100 to 4,000 employees is particularly significant (45, 46, 57). Success was defined in terms of an effectiveness rating by managers at a higher level.

Table 11–2 provides data on those measures related to success. The more valued managers had occupational interests which were at a higher level and more business related; they were more intelligent, better educated, and more dominant (stronger power motivation); they had been involved in more activities and organizations. Further analyses of the interest blank responses indicated a preference for activities involving independent, intense thought and some risk, enjoyment in relationships with people, especially in a leadership role, and a dislike of close, detailed work.

These findings emerged with some consistency across the various companies, but there were nevertheless many exceptions. Not all successful managers, by any means, had the characteristics identified, nor were the

Directing: An Input-Improving Mediator

Table 11–2 *Factors Associated with Managerial Success in University of Minnesota Studies*

Measure	Score Level Among Successful Managers
Vocational Interest Blank	
Dentist	Low
Veterinarian	Low
Printer	Low
Carpenter	Low
Vocational agricultural teacher	Low
Farmer	Low
Sales manager	High
Purchasing agent	High
President, manufacturing firm	High
Occupational level	High
Intelligence Test	High
Personality Test	
Dominance	High
Educational level	High
Wife's educational level	High
Years wife worked after marriage	Low
Number of sports and hobbies	High
Number of offices in organizations	High
Number of high school organizations	None or high

Source: T. A. Mahoney, T. H. Jerdee, and A. N. Nash, "Predicting Managerial Effectiveness," *Personnel Psychology*, Vol. 13 (1960), 158.

relationships found in all companies. Even in this relatively successful study the evidence for generalizable managerial traits was far from conclusive.

The Ghiselli Research. Another major study utilizing 306 managers employed by 90 different companies was carried out by Edwin Ghiselli at the University of California (16). There were too few individuals from any one firm to determine the consistency with which the results held across organization. However, a number of characteristics did show a significant relationship both to ratings of performance effectiveness made by superiors and to level in the organizational hierarchy for the group as a whole. For the latter purpose the managers were compared with samples of line supervisors and line workers, also drawn from a wide assortment of companies. The characteristics were measured using a short self-description form requiring choices between pairs of adjectives.

The most pronounced relationships with success were found for supervisory ability, achievement motivation, intelligence, self-actualizing motivation, self-assurance, and decisiveness. Somewhat less important were a low level of security motivation, a lack of affinity with the working class, and high initiative. It is quite possible that some of these characteristics may have been consequences of success rather than causes. However, a number clearly did antedate the managerial accomplishments. Although this study is clearly one of the most successful multicompany analyses to date, the small number of managers from each firm preclude the type of firm-to-firm comparisons that would ideally be possible.

Characteristics Most Likely to Relate to Success. Given the failure to identify leadership characteristics which strongly and consistently relate to success in a variety of organizations, it seems appropriate to recast the question and ask whether there are certain characteristics which are more likely to relate to success in particular types of organizations. Viewed in this light the University of Minnesota and Ghiselli researches do identify characteristics that have a reasonably high likelihood of relating to managerial success in administrative organizations within the business sector.

Research already reviewed dealing with motivation leads to the identification of a number of characteristics which have some likelihood of relating to success in administrative organizations—achievement motivation, power motivation, competitive motivation, high self-esteem, a desire for recognition, self-actualizing motivation, and a positive attitude to authority figures. An example of the support that exists for two of these motives comes from a multicompany study carried out with 52 managers employed by various firms in the Boston area (6). Measures of six motives were obtained—achievement, affiliation, power, autonomy, aggression, deference. The managers were then divided into two groups on the basis of salary progression relative to their age group. In the case of both achievement and power motivation a concentration of high scorers in the successful group was found. The other four motives were unrelated to success.

General intelligence also has emerged rather frequently in association with managerial success (15). Managers who achieve promotion into the higher-level positions often are found to be more intelligent; so too are those who perform more effectively at a given level.

In terms of interests, studies have revealed a pattern of relationships with success which does appear with some consistency (49, 56). For example, successful managers are likely to exhibit considerable interest in persuasive, verbal, and literary pursuits; they are more interested in the business world generally and are more drawn to business occupations; they

Directing: An Input-Improving Mediator

like supervising others and tend to reject scientific work and activities associated with occupations below the managerial level.

Several additional personality characteristics and background factors may be added to the list of characteristics likely to relate to managerial success in administrative organizations within the business sector (4). These include dispositions toward hard work, being active, and taking risks; traits such as confidence, a tendency to independence, and low anxiety; and a background of effectiveness and success. This latter frequently means not only a history of good health, but scholastic and extracurricular leadership in high school and college, as well as participation and leadership in a variety of other types of organizations.

It should be emphasized that the characteristics noted relate only to success in administrative organizations and that few studies have been done outside the business world. Furthermore none of the findings have emerged with anything like universal consistency.

Organizational Differences

If one restricts the analysis to individual organizations or even components of organizations, the degree to which characteristics associated with success can be identified precisely increases sharply. In almost every organization there are characteristics which are highly valued and rewarded. As indicated in the preceding section certain of these characteristics appear frequently, but others are specific to a particular organization. Thus, in an overall sense, what makes for success in one organization is not the same as in another; organizations tend to have their own unique characters.

Table 11-3 contains data on characteristics that are strongly associated with success in two business firms. Company A is a small, marketing-oriented organization; Company B a large financial firm (51). Valued characteristics are defined in relation to performance ratings by superiors; these are the characteristics of men who are rated high. Rewarded characteristics are defined in relation to promotion into higher levels of management; these are the characteristics that typify the men at the top. It seems clear that the type of person who achieves success by either definition in one of these firms, would not be particularly likely to do so in the other. Marked differences of this kind between companies are more the rule than the exception.

Studies conducted among managers at Sears, Roebuck have consistently identified certain characteristics as associated with success in that firm (2). These include high intelligence, high activity level, social leadership, masculinity, self-confidence, tolerance of others, values which stress power and the political rather than the aesthetic, and strong persuasive interests. While studies in other companies have often identified certain background or biographical factors as related to success, these factors do not appear to be similarly related at Sears, Roebuck (41).

Table 11-3 Valued and Rewarded Characteristics in Two Companies

	Company A	Company B
Valued Characteristics	Emotional control Desire to be with people Low interest in hard work Desire to be at the center of things	Youth Nonconformity Self-confidence Interest in hard work (especially problem solving)
Rewarded Characteristics	Age Independence Desire to avoid people Low self-confidence Low interest in hard work Low assertiveness Emotional control Anxiety	Age Anxiety Desire to avoid people Independence Intelligence

Source: J. B. Miner, "Bridging the Gulf in Organizational Performance," *Harvard Business Review*, Vol. 46 (1968), No. 4, 108.

On the other hand, a variety of biographical factors were consistently found related to managerial success within the Standard Oil Company of New Jersey (4). There was evidence of a continuing life-pattern of accomplishment and leadership extending from high school through college and into the period of employment. The more successful managers were also more intelligent and exhibited better managerial judgment, but the personality characteristics emphasized at Sears, Roebuck were not particularly significant at Standard Oil of New Jersey. Comparison of the data from these two large corporations indicates once again that success in one company may well mean a very different person and a very different pattern of role behaviors than in another.

Directing: An Input-Improving Mediator

Success as an Entrepreneur

Most analyses designed to reveal characteristics associated with managerial success have focused on relatively large corporate organizations, and very little has been done in relation to professional organizations, but there is a growing body of research on the entrepreneur who starts his own firm. One such study was mentioned in Chapter 4, where it was noted that strong achievement motivation characterized men who headed up the more successful of a group of technically based small companies in the Boston area (77). Other studies have confirmed that the achievement motive is closely related to entrepreneurial success (25, 29, 47).

In addition to studies focused on achievement motivation, the most comprehensive investigation of factors related to success as an entrepreneur has been conducted by a group of researchers at Michigan State University (5). They studied the founders of 110 small firms engaged primarily in the manufacture of hard goods and located in the state of Michigan. The findings indicate that the successful entrepreneur experiences a good deal of tension in dealing with authority figures. Accordingly he tries to avoid them. Founding his own firm is viewed as a specific instance of this avoidance process. The entrepreneur escapes from the large corporation with its authority figures and levels of hierarchy above him, and becomes "his own boss." Inherent in this is a strong desire for independence—a need to be autonomous and free and to avoid leaning on others for assistance, encouragement, and support. This tendency has been noted in other studies (25, 38). In addition to this avoidance reaction to authority the Michigan State University researchers also noted that upward social mobility was not a strong motive in the entrepreneurs studied and that they were typically dominated by middle-class values.

There is good reason to believe that successful entrepreneurs, like successful managers in larger administrative organizations, are not all of one type (68). At least two varieties have been identified, associated with particular kinds of firms. Firms may be grouped as either rigid or adaptive in terms of whether they have maintained the same or changed customer and product mixes, whether they have changed production methods, whether they have dispersed production facilities and markets, and whether they have concrete plans for change.

The more rigid firms tend to have a craftsman entrepreneur at their head. Such a person exhibits some narrowness of education and training, low social awareness and involvement, a limited or circumscribed time orientation, and feels a lack of competency in dealing with the social environment. In contrast, the opportunistic entrepreneurs who frequently head the more adaptive firms react to a much broader range of culture. They exhibit breadth in education and training, high social awareness and involvement, an orientation to the future, and feel confident of their ability to deal with the social environment.

There is also some evidence to suggest the existence of a third type, in addition to the craftsman and opportunistic—an inventor-entrepreneur. These men have taken out a large number of patents. They are oriented neither toward turning out the best product nor toward building a large business; rather, the firm is viewed as a means to allow the entrepreneur to invent and produce various products as he sees fit. Thus it becomes a vehicle for his creativity.

Fiedler's Contingency Approach

A very extensive program of research has almost from its inception been predicated on the assumption that characteristics of managers that strongly and consistently relate to success in the same manner and irrespective of the situation are unlikely to be found. This is the research carried out by Fred Fiedler, originally at the University of Illinois and more recently at the University of Washington.

Fiedler has focused on a single aspect of the manager which was viewed in his earlier writings as essentially a personality trait (11). More recently he has tended to emphasize leadership styles and leader behaviors associated with his measure. Although this latter emphasis might argue for a discussion of the Fiedler research in the context of the following section of this chapter, which is concerned with the effects of various managerial behaviors, the actual measure employed by Fiedler is in fact very similar to the measure of motives, interests, and personality characteristics considered in the present section. The findings from this research form an effective bridge into the literature dealing explicitly with leader behavior.

Theoretical Formulations. The aspect of the managerial personality that forms the basis of the theory is best described in terms of a dimension extending from a strong task orientation at one extreme to a strong human relations or interpersonal relations orientation at the other (20). In terms

Directing: An Input-Improving Mediator

of the organization, managers are viewed as emphasizing either task or maintenance goals. This basic orientation is established on the basis of a brief questionnaire.

Whether a task or maintenance orientation is most appropriate is viewed as contingent upon the nature of the situation (12). The eight situations considered are given in Table 11-4. Three factors are used to define these situations: (1) Leader-member relations are said to be good or poor based on the indicated feelings of the leader regarding his acceptance by his subordinate group. (2) Task structure is said to be high or weak depending on the degree to which the work to be done and the goal to be achieved are clear and unambiguous. (3) The position power of the leader is said to be strong or weak in terms of the amount of reward, coercive and legitimate power possessed. The theory predicts that the task-oriented manager will be most successful where the situation is very favorable for leadership or very unfavorable. In other situations a manager who gives more attention to maintenance considerations is more likely to succeed. In most studies success has been defined objectively in terms of the measured output of the group. However, there is evidence that comparable results are obtained when performance ratings of leaders made by superiors are used (23).

Table 11-4 Classification of Group Task Situations and Predicted Relationship Between Group Performance and Task or Maintenance Orientation of the Leader in Each

Situation	Leader-Member Relations	Task Structure	Position Power	Leader Orientation Producing Success
1	Good	High	Strong	Task
2	Good	High	Weak	Task
3	Good	Weak	Strong	Task
4	Good	Weak	Weak	Maintenance
5	Poor	High	Strong	Maintenance
6	Poor	High	Weak	Maintenance
7	Poor	Weak	Strong	Maintenance
8	Poor	Weak	Weak	Task

Source: F. E. Fiedler, *A Theory of Leadership Effectiveness* (New York: McGraw-Hill, 1967), p. 34.

The Nature of the Evidence. A number of studies have been carried out to test Fiedler's contingency theory. Taken as a whole this research cannot be said to consistently support the theory in its present form (18, 19, 52). It appears that the task-maintenance orientation characteristic is an important factor in managerial success, and that there are situations where one or the other orientation is of particular significance. The evidence in support of leader-member relations, task structure, and position power as the critical factors defining these situations, however, is far from convincing. Only task structure has emerged as an important situational determinant with some consistency; highly task-oriented managers tend to succeed when the work is lacking in structure (4). It appears likely that other situational factors, not incorporated in the Fiedler model, are also important sources of contingency. Furthermore, in line with the preceding discussion of the effects of performance on leadership, there is good reason to believe that group performance and other situational factors can have a sizable impact influencing the task-maintenance orientation of a manager (55).

To date the evidence related to Fiedler's theory as well as that from other sources appears most consistent with the view that group effectiveness will be most pronounced when the manager possesses characteristics and exhibits role behaviors which are closely integrated with the existing value and reward systems of the particular organization. If task-oriented behavior is valued and rewarded it should yield a productive group of subordinates; the same holds true for maintenance-oriented leadership. If neither one is valued or rewarded, neither will have an influence on output. This is not to deny the possibility that other situational factors such as the amount of structure in the work and the nature of the technology may also be important to a degree.

Role Behaviors of Successful Managers

A second major research approach has concentrated on the *behaviors* of managers, usually as described by their subordinates. These behaviors often have been classified into categories not unlike the task- and maintenance-oriented characteristics which are central to Fiedler's contingency theory. Furthermore a sizable proportion of the research on role behaviors has followed the practice, noted in connection with the contingency approach of using the actual output or behavior of the group supervised to define managerial success, rather than using ratings, compensation, and promotions. Such output measures are most easily obtained when the manager is at the first or lowest level and, in fact, much of the research to be considered does focus on the foreman, or his equivalent in nonmanufacturing departments.

Directing: An Input-Improving Mediator

Considerate and Structuring Leadership Styles

Two aspects of managerial behavior that have been studied frequently in conjunction with each other are most commonly referred to as *consideration* and *initiating structure*. These names were developed by researchers connected with the Bureau of Business Research at Ohio State University who undertook an extensive study of leadership styles beginning in 1945 (71).

Consideration refers to behavior which indicates friendship, mutual trust, respect, and interpersonal warmth between supervisor and subordinate. *Initiating structure* refers to behavior that organizes and defines subordinate activities and relationships; and establishes clear patterns of work organization, channels of communication, and ways of getting work done. Statements descriptive of these two dimensions of leader behavior are given in Table 11–5. The statements have been rated by judges as to the extent the behaviors indicated would reflect consideration and initiating structure (44). The statements noted as indicative of consideration are those rated high on that scale and irrelevant to initiating structure; those noted as indicative of initiating structure are the ones high on that scale, but irrelevant to consideration. Typically the two aspects of managerial role behavior have been treated as separate dimensions, each varying from high to low, rather than as two ends of a single continuum.

Not all of the research bearing on these two leadership styles has utilized the Ohio State terminology and measures. There have been other entirely independent studies that have used behavior categories of a similar nature (3). Many of these studies have been carried out by members of the Institute for Social Research at the University of Michigan. Concepts similar to consideration are providing support, employee orientation, human relations skill, providing direct need satisfaction, and group maintenance skill. Concepts similar to initiating structure are work facilitation, production orientation, enabling goal achievement, differentiation of supervisory role, and utilization of technical skills. In its emphasis on management process (organizing, planning, coordinating, controlling) initiating structure has much in common with classical management theory (13).

Consideration for Subordinates. The most comprehensive attempt to determine relationships between managerial consideration, as described by subordinates, and employee satisfaction and performance utilized data on 1,225 managers in 27 organizations (70). In a very general sense the

Table 11–5 Descriptive Statements Indicative of Consideration and Initiating Structure at the Second Level of Management

	Ratings by Judges*	
Statement	Consideration Scale	Initiating Structure Scale
Consideration		
He does personal favors for the foreman under him.	1.88	4.91
He helps his foremen with their personal problems.	1.45	4.61
He stands up for his foreman even though it makes him unpopular.	1.88	4.24
He tries to keep the foremen under him in good standing with higher authority.	1.55	4.42
He stresses the importance of high morale among those under him.	1.39	4.55
He backs up his foremen in their actions.	1.97	4.27
He is friendly and can be easily approached.	1.52	4.61
Initiating Structure		
He encourages overtime work.	4.48	1.52
He criticizes poor work.	4.76	1.94
He asks for sacrifices from his foremen for the entire department.	4.64	1.58
He sees to it that people under him are working to their limits.	4.30	1.24
He stresses being ahead of competing work groups.	4.55	1.36
He decides in detail what shall be done and how it shall be done.	4.85	1.12
He emphasizes meeting of deadlines.	4.09	1.18
He emphasizes the quantity of work.	4.85	1.55

*On a scale from 1.0 (always characteristic) through 4.0 (irrelevant) to 7.0 (never characteristic).
Source: A. Lowin, W. J. Hrapchak, and M. J. Kavanagh, "Consideration and Initiating Structure: An Experimental Investigation of Leadership Traits," *Administrative Science Quarterly*, Vol. 14 (1969), 239–240.

results indicate that where consideration is high there is likely to be more subordinate satisfaction, especially satisfaction with the degree of freedom of action and decision making at work. This finding did not occur consistently in all organizations or within certain industries. It did emerge in all four of the metals companies studied, but appeared in only three of the six aircraft companies. A number of the organizations did not reveal any relationship between consideration and satisfaction at all. Yet relationships with satisfaction were far more prevalent than with performance effectiveness. Even in the metals industry, where consideration seems to make the most difference, only two of the four companies tended to have more considerate leaders in charge of more productive subordinates.

Reviews dealing with numerous studies point to much the same conclusions (13, 34); so do other comprehensive studies (30). Considerate behavior is particularly likely to be found in association with high levels of satisfaction among subordinates. It may be found in conjunction with high productivity as well. But in both cases there are a number of instances where no relation has been found, and there are data which tend to show that high consideration can be associated with dissatisfaction and/or low productivity. An extensive investigation of the relationship between consideration as a leadership style and subordinate *work motivation* produced no evidence that considerate supervision had a positive impact on motivation in the company studied (1).

An initial study produced clear evidence that high grievance rates among unionized employees go with low consideration, but beyond a certain level consideration did not further relate to grievances (14). The same was true for turnover. When consideration was low, separation rates were high, but only to a point; after that the two were unrelated. A second study produced much the same results (67). Yet a third study utilizing a conceptually similar index of organizational maintenance yielded quite different findings (28). Once again it seems clear that whether supervisory consideration has positive consequences depends in large part on the organization in which it occurs.

Research conducted independent of an organizational context, in the laboratory setting (44) or using computer simulation (31), has consistently indicated that supervisory consideration has positive consequences for productivity, quality of work, profits, and satisfaction. Furthermore, there is reason to believe from such studies that consideration *causes* the positive outcomes. Yet when this relationship is inserted into a specific organization, it may disappear completely, or only a segment may survive —usually that involving job satisfaction.

Initiating Structure for Subordinates. As with consideration, initiating structure has frequently been found in association with positive outcomes, but not with the degree of consistency needed to establish a standing guide for managers (4, 13, 21). In the comprehensive study of 27 organizations initiating structure appeared most frequently in conjunction with high satisfaction with the company and loyalty to it (70). It rarely had any relation to measures of actual productive output. The major conclusions from this study were that (a) leadership styles serve primarily to increase the capacity of a company to cope with emergencies and survive in the long run (organizational maintenance), and (b) *the researcher who wishes to speak with assurance in regard to his hypothesis should not study more than one organization.* Organizational variation is the rule, rather than the exception. Thus, while the study of the 27 organizations tended to find initiating structure positively related to organizational maintenance, when any relationship was found at all, another study of a single manufacturing plant indicated just the reverse (14).

Research to date bearing on the *causal* impact of initiating structure on productivity, work quality, and job satisfaction has failed to reveal a relationship (44). As previously indicated students responded to considerate supervision in a laboratory setting with better performance and greater satisfaction. But meaningful differences were not found when initiating structure was manipulated so that student groups were exposed to high and low amounts of this style of leadership. This finding, in conjunction with the data considered earlier in this chapter, suggests that when initiating structure is found in association with certain outcomes, the usually expected sequence may be reversed: the outcome may *cause* the leadership style.

Close Supervision. A leadership style which appears to have something in common with both the consideration and initiating structure dimensions is the closeness of supervision (3). Close supervision is indicated by such things as checking on subordinates often, frequent instructions about the work, and little discretion placed in the hands of subordinates to perform in their own way. Typically, close supervision has been viewed as an aspect of both low consideration and high initiating structure.

Much of the early research on leadership style served to stress the negative consequences of close supervision (32). Studies conducted in an insurance company and a tractor manufacturing plant indicated that close supervision is usually found in conjunction with low productivity. Yet subsequent research in a company manufacturing plastic materials produced just the opposite result, in that close supervision had positive consequences (58). The supervisor who exhibited this type of behavior was not viewed as pressuring his men to increase production or reduce waste, but rather as being the kind of person who works closely with his subordinates as a part of "the team that works together."

As with consideration and initiating structure, apparently close supervision may or may not yield positive consequences depending on the par-

Directing: An Input-Improving Mediator

ticular organization being considered. It may also be a consequence of poor performance (43).

Autocratic, Democratic (Participative), and Laissez-Faire Styles

There has been a widespread tendency to view considerate supervision as essentially synonymous with a democratic or participative approach and structuring supervision as autocratic. This interpretation is partially reinforced by findings which link the participative style with high consideration and low initiating structure (44). However, there is other evidence indicating that autocracy does not necessarily imply a lack of consideration (69).

The data of Table 11–6 bear on the relationships involved. Managers of clerical employees in two companies completed questionnaires to obtain measures of their attitudes regarding consideration, human relations orientation, and initiating structure. The human relations orientation score provided an alternative measure of the considerate approach (69). One of the companies was shown to be characterized by widespread use of a democratic-participative approach; the other by an autocratic approach. The data of Table 11–6 suggest a slight tendency to greater consideration in the democratic company. However, the differences between the two firms are not sufficient to warrant interpretation; for all practical purposes the companies are identical in this regard. On the other hand, the autocratic company is clearly much higher on initiating structure.

In view of findings such as these it seems most appropriate to consider the research on autocratic and democratic supervision (the two have typically been studied together) independently from the research on con-

Table 11–6 *Consideration, Human Relations Orientation, and Initiating Structure in Democratic and Autocratic Firms*

Leadership Style	Manager Attitude Score	
	Democratic Firm ($N = 28$)	Autocratic Firm ($N = 58$)
Consideration	54.5	52.6
Human Relations Orientation	29.4	27.8
Initiating Structure	50.1	56.4

Source: E. S. Stanton, "Company Policies and Supervisors' Attitudes Toward Supervision," *Journal of Applied Psychology*, Vol. 44 (1960), 24. Copyright 1960 by the American Psychological Association. Reproduced by permission.

sideration and initiating structure, while still recognizing that on occasion some overlapping of these supervisory role behaviors may exist. Such research as there is on the laissez-faire style has typically been done in conjunction with studies of autocratic and democratic approaches. Thus the three are grouped together here.

Participative Management. The participative approach has already been discussed in several different contexts. In Chapter 3 participative management was noted as one of the major thrusts of the behavioral humanist school. Among the writers of that school Douglas McGregor (48) has entitled it *Theory Y* management (contrasting it with his more autocratic *Theory X* approach), and Rensis Likert (36) has labeled it *System 4* management (contrasting it with increasing degrees of autocracy down to *System 1*).

In connection with the discussion of policy planning in Part II(A) the approach was considered on several occasions. Among the major points made were that participation in decision making often tends to foster organizational maintenance; that its relationship with productivity is much less clear-cut; that it may facilitate acceptance and implementation of policies, budgets, and the like, especially in the personnel area; that it can provide a fertile climate for creative effort; and that it can improve the decision-making process by bringing the knowledge and capabilities of more than one person to bear. In Chapter 9 the use of participative techniques in introducing organizational change was discussed with emphasis on some of the advantages and disadvantages of power equalization.

Actually not a single major firm in the United States has applied the participative approach in its totality on a truly large scale, although a number of companies have utilized aspects of the approach or introduced it in certain locations (41). The more comprehensive corporate applications have tended to appear in firms with a high proportion of professional employees. Participative management in some form is common in professional organizations.

Much of the evidence on the use of the participative style is favorable, especially the evidence derived from studies relating the degree to which a manager exhibits participative behavior to measures of group productivity, loyalty, job satisfaction, and so on, taken at the same point in time (42, 76). There is often an observed correlation. Thus in a study relating the degree of participation in six divisions of a West Coast firm to measures of profitability and satisfaction strong relationships were found (64). Similarly within the Tennessee Valley Authority the degree of participation in eight divisions was highly associated with identification with the organization and with acceptance of changes (59).

Other findings suggest that a variety of factors may condition the effectiveness of participation. For instance, at the Detroit Edison Company the positive relationship between participation and employee attitudes emerged only when the managers involved had the capacity to exert influence and exercise power up the line in the organization (61). Within the research and development component of another company managerial influence had no such effect (27). In the United Parcel Service the relation of participation to satisfaction and performance of the groups supervised was definitely positive only when the individuals in the group were very independent and/or low on authoritarianism (75). Yet a comparable study in a consumer finance company produced sizable relationships between the degree of participation and positive outcomes (attitude toward the job and profitability) quite independent of subordinate independence and authoritarianism (74).

In spite of all the favorable findings serious questions have been raised regarding the participation approach (60, 72). The change in value structure required to implement participation on a large scale can be costly both to the organization and society. Many managers must be retrained to the participative leadership style; many others will find change difficult and end by seeking other employment. Among these latter may be individuals with considerable talent in aspects of the management process other than directing, such as planning, coordinating, and controlling. It has also been noted that individuals whose opinions are rejected by the group can become alienated both from the group and the organization; that participation may yield a sense of closeness and belonging in a group that is mobilized behind objectives not in the best interest of the organization, that individual and group goals, not organizational, may be served; and that participative decision making is a slow process which may not be adequately responsive to rapid changes in an organization's environment. To these can be added the finding that, on occasion, participation may not in fact yield power equalization at all—especially when the leader is much more expert than other group members (54).

These are important points, but the really crucial question is whether participation works, whether the use of this more democratic leadership style does result in increased contributions to task and maintenance goals. Does the use of participation *cause* more positive outcomes?

Effects of Autocratic and Democratic Styles. A number of studies involve the introduction of a democratic leadership style with extensive subordinate participation in decision making. The results are measured by contrasting subsequent job satisfaction or productivity, either with similar measures obtained earlier from the same groups and/or with measures obtained at the same time from groups supervised in an autocratic manner.

The results of such studies indicate with some consistency that a democratic approach tends to increase job satisfaction and other indexes of organizational maintenance, while a more autocratic approach frequently has the reverse effect (13). There are some exceptions to both of these conclusions (and more frequently to the latter). On the other hand, there is no basis for concluding that a democratic leadership style is preferable to the autocratic insofar as task accomplishment is concerned (13, 66). Several studies appear to indicate that greater productivity occurs under participative conditions. But in most of these instances, it seems clear that the major factor in the increased output was not so much the democratic supervision as the fact that the participation groups set production goals, whereas the comparison groups did not (39). Goal setting under autocratic leadership conditions would be expected to have a similar motivating effect.

The results obtained in one of the best-known and most comprehensive experimental studies are given in Table 11-7. The index of productivity is a measure of cost reduction (53). It is evident that under democratic supervision both clerical divisions increased productivity, but the other two divisions placed under strong autocratic supervision did also; in fact, they increased to an extent that made them clearly superior to those where participative management was installed. The individual satisfactions of those in the democratic groups increased considerably, however, whereas under autocracy satisfaction declined.

Given findings of this kind from experimental research, where causal relationships can be examined, the fact that democratic leadership has in a number of instances been observed in conjunction with high productivity is probably best explained in accordance with the discussion at the beginning of this chapter. Much of what has been observed appears to be a consequence of a tendency for managers in charge of highly effective groups to respond with a democratic, participative style of leadership. They respect the competence of their subordinates. This does not deny that in certain organizations participative management may yield a whole range of positive outcomes including increased productivity.

Table 11-7 Comparison of Divisions with Democratic and Autocratic Supervision on Clerical Productivity for the Year Preceding Introduction of the Leadership Styles with the Year Following Introduction

	Index of Productivity		
Group Studied	Mean for Initial Year	Mean Under Leadership Style	Difference %
Democratic Supervision			
Divison A	46.3 %	55.2 %	+ 8.9
Division B	51.0	62.0	+11.0
Average	48.6	58.6	+10.0
Autocratic Supervision			
Division C	50.2	63.2	+13.0
Division D	46.8	62.0	+15.2
Average	48.5	62.6	+14.1

Source: N. C. Morse and E. Reimer, "The Experimental Change of a Major Organizational Variable," *Journal of Abnormal and Social Psychology,* Vol. 52 (1956), 127. Copyright 1956 by the American Psychological Association. Reproduced by permission.

Laissez-Faire as a Leadership Style. The laissez-faire style is what its name implies. The manager gives complete freedom for group or individual decision. He does not participate in discussions other than to provide information if asked and he makes no effort to see that decisions are in fact made or work performed. In a sense the manager abdicates and turns over position power and control to his subordinates. He does little, if anything, to motivate role behavior toward role prescriptions.

Early research contrasting laissez-faire with autocratic and democratic approaches indicated that it yields less concentration on work and poorer quality work than the other two, and a general satisfaction level below the democratic style, but still somewhat above the autocratic (78). Where laissez-faire has been considered at all it has consistently been found ineffective insofar as contributions to task goals are concerned. Organizations that fail to utilize sanctions, in the manner of laissez-faire, tend to be less effective (63). Organizations with control concentrated at the bottom and no compensating influence exerted at higher levels or with very little control anywhere in the system tend to be less effective (73). Under such conditions group and individual goals often take precedence over organizational goals with the result that the organization is in a very real sense plundered. A study of scientists in research laboratories indicated that at very high levels of freedom to do what one pleased, in the manner of laissez-faire, performance effectiveness declined (62).

Achievement, Power, and Affiliation Styles

As already noted the major focus of research dealing with leader behavior has been on concepts such as consideration, initiating structure, participative management, and autocracy, with somewhat less emphasis on close supervision and laissez-faire. In addition, several applications of achievement motivation theory have also been made in this field (37).

In one study an extended simulation was used to assess the relative impacts of leadership styles which stressed achievement, power, and affiliation, and which served to arouse these motives within the respective groups. The results indicated a much lower level of satisfaction under the power style than under the two other styles. Productivity and profit within the simulation were highest for the achievement style and lowest for the affiliation style, but the power style produced only slightly better performance than affiliation. Innovation was most pronounced under achievement leadership, intermediate under affiliation, and low under power. But the power style did yield a high level of product quality.

Although studies dealing with these styles as they actually operate in existing organizations are limited, both in number and comprehensiveness, the results are promising. Research to date seems to support the positive results obtained with the achievement style in the laboratory setting. On the other hand it appears that the achievement style is not the most effective in all organizations and under all conditions (37).

Organizational Character and Managerial Behavior

It is evident that research aimed at identifying role behavior of successful managers has produced mixed results, just as has that focusing on managerial characteristics. The one consistent finding is that organizations vary considerably with respect to what type of leadership style is effective.

This is consistent with the conclusions reached in connection with the discussion of integration theory in Chapter 1. Organizations tend to value and reward managers who behave in certain ways. The behaviors which are valued and rewarded in a given organization will vary depending on a number of factors including the particular problems in its environment which the organization currently faces and has faced in the past.

When a manager consistently behaves in a way that fits the existing value and/or reward structure, perhaps with consideration in a company where this type of behavior is viewed positively, his authority is legitimized. This legitimization may come from below him or above him or from both directions. In any event his leadership style now makes a difference. He will get support from managers at higher levels or from his subordinates or from both. To the extent that there is integration around this value structure (both among subordinates and superiors) and that reward structures are placed behind it, the manager's behavior (the use of consideration) will lead to positive outcomes.

On the other hand, the same resort to consideration in another organization with equally integrated but diametrically opposed value and reward structures would yield quite different results. Here the same manager would be considered poor, be promoted rarely, and be paid relatively little. His behavior would be deprecated and legitimization of his authority would be minimal. What he said and did really would not matter. For all practical purposes the effects would be the equivalent of a laissez-faire style, irrespective of the style actually employed. As a result the manager's behavior would be unlikely to contribute to positive outcomes. A completely laissez-faire style by its very nature cannot be goal relevant in an organization.

Furthermore, there is a high probability under these circumstances that informal leadership of an emergent nature will appear. Such leadership may not be legitimized from above, but it can be assumed by its very nature to have legitimization from the subordinate group, and thus to fit this component of the value structure. Accordingly the informal leader's style has a potential for impact. Where a formally appointed manager behaves in ways that yield negative evaluations and few rewards in the organization, and where an informal leader emerges, the behavior of the informal leader is most likely to be predictive. The result may be high productivity or low, depending not so much on the manager holding the leadership position as on the man who actually leads. It is not surprising, therefore, that a number of studies which have focused on the behaviors of individuals in management positions have failed to find meaningful relationships with measures related to task and maintenance goals in certain organizations.

In concluding this chapter it should be noted that the interpretation of the leadership research presented here, which utilizes integration theory as its conceptual framework, is not, in fact, the only one which has been proposed. Other writers have offered interpretations based on such approaches as expectancy theory of motivation (26) and on formulations which have considerable conceptual similarity to Fiedler's contingency theory (79). Although a treatment of these theories is beyond the scope of this book, it does seem that in focusing on subordinate motivation and work relationships as they do, rather than on organizational factors, these approaches may prove, at least in part, to be supplemental rather than antithetical to those derived from integration theory.

Questions

1. "The researcher who wishes to speak with assurance in regard to his hypothesis should not study more than one organization." What does this statement mean in the context of leadership research? How does it relate to Fiedler's contingency theory?
2. How do participative and laissez-faire leadership differ? What is the evidence on the relative effectiveness of each?
3. Describe how you would carry out a study to determine whether differences in leadership style actually do influence employee performance in a particular company. What factors might lead the management of the company to refuse you permission to conduct such a study?
4. What do we know about the relation of the following to managerial success?
   a. Intelligence
   b. Affiliation motivation
   c. Agricultural interests
   d. Achievement motivation
   e. Tendency to avoid risks
5. What is the significance of integration theory for an understanding of the results of the leadership research?

References

1. Beer, M. *Leadership, Employee Needs and Motivation.* Columbus: Bureau of Business Research, Ohio State University, 1966.
2. Bentz, V. J. "The Sears Experience in the Investigation, Description and Prediction of Executive Behavior." In F. R. Wickert and D. E. McFarland

(eds.), *Measuring Executive Effectiveness*. New York: Appleton-Century-Crofts, 1967, pp. 147–205.
3. Bowers, D. G., and S. E. Seashore. "Predicting Organizational Effectiveness with a Four-Factor Theory of Leadership." *Administrative Science Quarterly*, Vol. 11 (1966), 238–263.
4. Campbell, J. P., M. D. Dunnette, E. E. Lawler, and K. E. Weick. *Managerial Behavior, Performance and Effectiveness*. New York: McGraw-Hill, 1970.
5. Collins, O. F., D. G. Moore, and D. B. Unwalla. *The Enterprising Man*. East Lansing: Bureau of Business and Economic Research, Michigan State University, 1964.
6. Cummin, P. C. "TAT Correlates of Executive Performance." *Journal of Applied Psychology*, Vol. 51 (1967), 78–81.
7. Dubin, R., and others. *Leadership and Productivity*. San Francisco: Chandler, 1965.
8. Farris, G. F. "Organizational Factors and Individual Performance: A Longitudinal Study." *Journal of Applied Psychology*, Vol. 53 (1969), 87–92.
9. Farris, G. F., and F. G. Lim. "Effects of Performance on Leadership, Cohesiveness, Influence, Satisfaction, and Subsequent Performance." *Journal of Applied Psychology*, Vol. 53 (1969), 490–497.
10. Feldman, H. *Problems in Labor Relations*. New York: Macmillan, 1937.
11. Fiedler, F. E. "The Leader's Psychological Distance and Group Effectiveness." In D. Cartwright and A. Zander (eds.), *Group Dynamics: Research and Theory*. Evanston, Ill.: Row, Peterson, 1960, pp. 586–606.
12. Fiedler, F. E. *A Theory of Leadership Effectiveness*. New York: McGraw-Hill, 1967.
13. Filley, A. C., and R. J. House. *Managerial Process and Organizational Behavior*. Glenview, Ill.: Scott, Foresman, 1969.
14. Fleishman, E. A., and E. F. Harris. "Patterns of Leadership Behavior Related to Employee Grievances and Turnover." *Personnel Psychology*, Vol. 15 (1962), 43–56.
15. Ghiselli, E. E. *The Validity of Occupational Aptitude Tests*. New York: Wiley, 1966.
16. Ghiselli, E. E. *Explorations in Managerial Talent*. Pacific Palisades, Calif.: Goodyear, 1971.
17. Goodstadt, B., and D. Kipnis. "Situational Influences on the Use of Power." *Journal of Applied Psychology*, Vol. 54 (1970), 201–207.
18. Graen, G., K. Alvares, J. B. Orris, and J. A. Martella. "Contingency Model of Leadership Effectiveness: Antecedent and Evidential Results." *Psychological Bulletin*, Vol. 74 (1970), 285–296.
19. Graen, G., J. B. Orris, and K. M. Alvares. "Contingency Model of Leadership Effectiveness: Some Experimental Results." *Journal of Applied Psychology*, Vol. 55 (1971), 196–201.

20. Graham, W. K. "Description of Leader Behavior and Evaluation of Leaders as a Function of LPC." *Personnel Psychology*, Vol. 21 (1968), 457–464.
21. Harrell, T. W. *Follow-up of Management Potential Battery*. Stanford, Calif: Graduate School of Business, Stanford University, 1967.
22. Herzberg, F., B. Mausner, and B. B. Snyderman. *The Motivation to Work*. New York: Wiley, 1959.
23. Hill, W. "The Validation and Extension of Fiedler's Theory of Leadership Effectiveness." *Academy of Management Journal*, Vol. 12 (1969), 33–47.
24. Hollander, E. P. *Leaders, Groups, and Influence*. New York: Oxford University Press, 1964.
25. Hornaday, J. A., and J. Aboud. "Characteristics of Successful Entrepreneurs." *Personnel Psychology*, Vol. 24 (1971), 141–153.
26. House, R. J. "A Path Goal Theory of Leader Effectiveness." *Administrative Science Quarterly*, Vol. 16 (1971), 321–338.
27. House, R. J., A. C. Filley, and D. N. Gujarati. "Leadership Style, Hierarchical Influence and the Satisfaction of Subordinate Role Expectations: A Test of Likert's Influence Proposition." *Journal of Applied Psychology*, Vol. 55 (1971), 422–432.
28. House, R. J., A. C. Filley, and S. Kerr. "Relation of Leader Consideration and Initiating Structure to R and D Subordinates' Satisfactions." *Administrative Science Quarterly*, Vol. 16 (1971), 19–30.
29. Hundal, P. S. "A Study of Entrepreneurial Motivation: Comparison of Fast- and Slow-Progressing Small-Scale Industrial Entrepreneurs in Punjab, India." *Journal of Applied Psychology*, Vol. 55 (1971), 317–323.
30. Indik, B. P. "There is No Pat Answer to the Supervision Question." *Personnel Administration*, Vol. 26 (1963), No. 6, 15–19.
31. Kaczka, E., and R. V. Kirk. "Managerial Climate, Work Groups, and Organizational Performance." *Administrative Science Quarterly*, Vol. 12 (1967), 253–272.
32. Kahn, R. L., and D. Katz. "Leadership Practices in Relation to Productivity and Morale." In D. Cartwright and A. Zander (eds.), *Group Dynamics: Research and Theory*. Evanston, Ill.: Row, Peterson, 1960, 554–570.
33. Katz, D., and R. L. Kahn. *The Social Psychology of Organizations*. New York: Wiley, 1966.
34. Korman, A. K. "Consideration, Initiating Structure and Organizational Criteria—A Review." *Personnel Psychology*, Vol. 19 (1966), 349–361.
35. Korten, D. C. "Situational Determinants of Leadership Structure." *The Journal of Conflict Resolution*, Vol. 6 (1962), 222–235.
36. Likert, R. *The Human Organization: Its Management and Value*. New York: McGraw-Hill, 1967.
37. Litwin, G. H., and R. A. Stringer. *Motivation and Organizational Climate*. Boston: Division of Research, Harvard Business School, 1968.

38. Litzinger, W. D. "The Motel Entrepreneur and the Motel Manager." *Academy of Management Journal*, Vol. 8 (1965), 268–281.
39. Locke, E. A. "Toward a Theory of Task Motivation and Incentives." *Organizational Behavior and Human Performance*, Vol. 3 (1968), 157–189.
40. Locke, E. A. "The Supervisor as Motivator: His Influence on Employee Performance and Satisfaction." In B. M. Bass, R. Cooper, and J. A. Haas, *Managing for Accomplishment*. Lexington, Mass.: Heath, 1970, pp. 57–67.
41. Lopez, F. M. *The Making of a Manager*. New York: American Management Association. 1970.
42. Lowin, A. "Participative Decision Making: A Model, Literature Critique, and Prescription for Research. *Organizational Behavior and Human Performance*, Vol. 3 (1968), 68–106.
43. Lowin, A., and J. R. Craig. "The Influence of Level of Performance on Managerial Style: An Experimental Object-Lesson in the Ambiguity of Correlational Data." *Organizational Behavior and Human Performance*, Vol. 3 (1968), 440–458.
44. Lowin, A., W. J. Hrapchak, and M. J. Kavanagh. "Consideration and Initiating Structure: An Experimental Investigation of Leadership Traits." *Administrative Science Quarterly*, Vol. 14 (1969), 238–253.
45. Mahoney, T. A., T. H. Jerdee, and A. N. Nash. "Predicting Managerial Effectiveness." *Personnel Psychology*, Vol. 13 (1960), 147–163.
46. Mahoney, T. A., T. H. Jerdee, and A. N. Nash. *The Identification of Management Potential*. Dubuque, Iowa: William C. Brown, 1961.
47. McClelland, D. C., and D. G. Winter. *Motivating Economic Achievement*. New York: Free Press, 1969.
48. McGregor, D. *The Human Side of Enterprise*. New York: McGraw-Hill, 1960.
49. Miner, J. B. "The Kuder Preference Record in Management Appraisal." *Personnel Psychology*, Vol. 13 (1960), 187–196.
50. Miner, J. B. *The School Administrator and Organizational Character*. Eugene: Center for Advanced Study of Educational Administration, University of Oregon, 1967.
51. Miner, J. B. "Bridging the Gulf in Organizational Performance." *Harvard Business Review*, Vol. 46 (1968), No. 4, 102–110.
52. Mitchell, T. R., A. Biglan, G. R. Oncken, and F. E. Fiedler. "The Contingency Model: Criticisms and Suggestions." *Academy of Management Journal*, Vol. 13 (1970), 253–267.
53. Morse, N. C., and E. Reimer. "The Experimental Change of a Major Organizational Variable." *Journal of Abnormal and Social Psychology*, Vol. 52 (1956), 120–129.
54. Mulder, M. "Power Equalization Through Participation?" *Administrative Science Quarterly*, Vol. 16 (1971), 31–38.

55. Muller, H. P. "Relationship Between Time-Span of Discretion, Leadership Behavior, and Fiedler's LPC Scores." *Journal of Applied Psychology*, Vol. 54 (1970), 140–144.
56. Nash, A. N. "Vocational Interests of Effective Managers: A Review of the Literature." *Personnel Psychology*, Vol. 18 (1965), 21–37.
57. Nash, A. N. "Development of an SVIB Key for Selecting Managers." *Journal of Applied Psychology*, Vol. 50 (1966), 250–254.
58. Patchen, M. "Supervisory Methods and Group Performance Norms." *Administrative Science Quarterly*, Vol. 7 (1962), 275–293.
59. Patchen, M. *Participation, Achievement, and Involvement on the Job*. Englewood Cliffs, N.J.: Prentice-Hall, 1970.
60. Patten, T. H. *The Foreman: Forgotten Man of Management*. New York: American Management Association, 1968.
61. Pelz, D. C. "Leadership Within a Hierarchical Organization." *The Journal of Social Issues*, Vol. 7 (1951), 49–55.
62. Pelz, D. C., and F. M. Andrews. *Scientists in Organizations*. New York: Wiley, 1966.
63. Price, J. L. *Organizational Effectiveness*. Homewood, Ill.: Irwin, 1968.
64. Roberts, K., R. E. Miles, and L. V. Blankenship. "Organizational Leadership, Satisfaction, and Productivity: A Comparative Analysis." *Academy of Management Journal*, Vol. 11 (1968), 401–414.
65. Rosen, N. A. *Leadership Change and Work-Group Dynamics, An Experiment*. Ithaca, N.Y.: Cornell University Press, 1969.
66. Sales, S. M. "Supervisory Style and Productivity: Review and Theory." *Personnel Psychology*, Vol. 19 (1966), 275–286.
67. Skinner, E. W. "Relationships Between Leadership Behavior Patterns and Organizational-Situational Variables." *Personnel Psychology*, Vol. 22 (1969), 489–494.
68. Smith, N. R. *The Entrepreneur and His Firm: The Relationship Between Type of Man and Type of Company*. East Lansing: Bureau of Business and Economic Research, Michigan State University, 1967.
69. Stanton, E. S. "Company Policies and Supervisors' Attitudes Toward Supervision." *Journal of Applied Psychology*, Vol. 44 (1960), 22–26.
70. Stogdill, R. M. *Managers, Employees, Organizations*. Columbus: Bureau of Business Research, Ohio State University, 1965.
71. Stogdill, R. M., and A. E. Coons. *Leader Behavior: Its Description and Measurement*. Columbus: Bureau of Business Research, Ohio State University, 1957.
72. Strauss, G. "Some Notes on Power-Equalization." In H. J. Leavitt (ed.), *The Social Science of Organizations: Four Perspectives*. Englewood Cliffs, N.J.: Prentice-Hall, 1963, pp. 39–84.
73. Tannenbaum, A. S. *Control in Organizations*. New York: McGraw-Hill, 1968.

74. Tosi, H. "A Reexamination of Personality as a Determinant of the Effects of Participation." *Personnel Psychology*, Vol. 23 (1970), 91–99.
75. Vroom, V. H. *Some Personality Determinants of the Effects of Participation.* Englewood Cliffs, N.J.: Prentice-Hall, 1960.
76. Vroom, V. H. *Work and Motivation.* New York: Wiley, 1964.
77. Wainer, H. A., and I. M. Rubin. "Motivation of Research and Development Entrepreneurs: Determinants of Company Success." *Journal of Applied Psychology*, Vol. 53 (1969), 178–184.
78. White, R., and R. Lippitt. "Leader Behavior and Member Reaction in Three Social Climates." In D. Cartwright and A. Zander (eds.), *Group Dynamics: Research and Theory.* New York: Harper & Row, 1968, pp. 318–335.
79. Yukl, G. "Toward a Behavioral Theory of Leadership." *Organizational Behavior and Human Performance*, Vol. 6 (1971), 414–440.

12 Communication in Organizations

I. Interpersonal and Intragroup Communication
1. Communication Breakdown
   a. Redundancy and Error Reduction
   b. Verification, Feedback, and Two-Way Communication
2. Communication Network Studies
   a. Experimental Results
   b. Implications for Organizations

II. Organizational Communication
1. Formal Communication in the Hierarchy
   a. Distortion in Upward Communication
   b. The Downward Flow
2. Nonformal Communication
   a. Horizontal and Diagonal Flow
   b. The Grapevine
3. The Information Overload Problem
   a. The Nature of Overload
   b. Responses to Overload

III. Management Information Systems (MIS)
1. Definitions and Descriptions
2. Present and Potential Use
   a. Historical Trends
   b. Employee Information Systems
3. Problems with MIS

Communicating, like decision making, permeates all the important components of the management process. Certainly it is an aspect of directing, thus capable of serving as an input-improving mediator, but it also is involved in planning, coordinating, and controlling as well as in the secondary management functions: staffing and representing.

Just as planning and decision making have become closely associated through common usage and the frequent interchangeable use of the terms in theory and research, directing and communicating have developed a similar relationship. Thus it has become traditional to consider communicating within the directing rubric. However, at least one recent book has grouped decision making and communication together and labeled them "linking processes" (27). Although this approach has considerable appeal, much of the literature on communication has developed in close relation to leadership, and thus the present discussion will utilize the more traditional grouping.

As the review of research on management functions in Chapter 2 indicated, communicating is even more an all-encompassing managerial activity than decision making. Further evidence on the pervasive nature of communication is contained in Table 12–1. In this study 232 managers and professionals in a research and development installation reported on their communication activities using a work sampling procedure (31). The analyses dealt separately with nonsupervisory professionals, three

Table 12–1 Major Breakdowns of Time Distribution for Research and Development Personnel. (All data are percent of eight-hour day)

Activities	Non-supervisory	Supervisory Ladder			Technical Ladder		Weighted Average Co.-wide
		First Level	Second Level	Third Level	First Level	Second Level	
Not Communicating (total)	44	26	19	13	43	40	39
Communicating (total)	56	74	81	87	57	60	61
Listening, speaking	30	48	57	62	28	33	35
Writing	16	17	14	13	17	16	16
Reading	10	9	10	12	12	11	10
Oral Communications:							
Unplanned, informal	17	26	26	23	12	14	19
Scheduled meetings	8	14	23	31	10	13	10
Telephone	5	8	8	8	6	6	6
Number of Individuals Covered	59	59	58	19	17	20	232

Source: J. R. Hinrichs, "Communications Activity of Industrial Research Personnel," *Personnel Psychology*, Vol. 17 (1964), 199.

levels of management, and two levels of technical status. The company in which the study was conducted used the so-called *dual ladder* of promotion whereby comparable levels of purely technical positions parallel the managerial hierarchy.

The evidence indicates not only that the majority of work time is devoted to communication, but that in general the proportion of time so used rises with managerial and technical level. This increase is largely a function of the greater amount of time devoted to scheduled meetings and to unplanned, informal discussions at the higher levels.

Interpersonal and Intragroup Communication

Communication often is considered in terms of four levels of analysis: intrapersonal, interpersonal, organizational, and technical (55). The intrapersonal level includes research dealing with neurological and brain processes, communication pathologies, human factors, media technology, verbal learning and conditioning, language, linguistics, semantics, cognition, thinking, problem solving, and personality. These are matters concerned with how the *individual* takes in, processes, and produces communications; they will be given relatively little attention here.

The interpersonal level deals with interactions between individuals and within small groups. There is considerable research from the field of group dynamics that is relevant here, especially that concerned with so-called communication nets. This is the level of analysis that relates most closely to the directing function. In this section particular attention is given to factors which may distort and disrupt interpersonal communication, such as that between superior and subordinate, and to techniques for overcoming these breakdowns.

The two remaining sections of the chapter consider the organizational and technical levels. The former is concerned with the flow of communications through various channels in an organization. It is thus closely related to organization and management theory. The technical level is concerned with the design and operation of management communication and information systems, with heavy reliance on computer applications. This represents a special domain within the organizational context.

Communication Breakdown

The problem of communication breakdown has been a matter of consideration in the management literature for a number of years. Authors have long pointed to the frequency with which intended communications are blocked or distorted and to the consequent negative effects insofar as leadership and supervision are concerned (48, 50).

Documentation of communication breakdown typically has come from studies which compare a sender's statement of intent with a receiver's statement of the meaning communicated. Thus in one instance a department manager recorded giving instructions or communicating his decisions to his subordinates on 165 separate occasions. Yet similar records maintained by the subordinates indicated that in only 84 of these cases was an instruction or decision meaning communicated. In the remaining cases the communication was treated as information or advice with no utilization of authority intended (8). This finding that only approximately 50 percent of the interactions between people result in true mutual perception appears to be typical (58). Furthermore this distortion rate applies to interactions that actually do register on the individuals involved. Many more communications are simply lost, in that participants do not recall them even a few hours later.

In part, of course, communication breakdown is a consequence of language. People may well use words, often of a technical nature, that other people do not understand. Furthermore many words are ambiguous, and there are many aspects of human experience and feeling that are not really effectively conveyed by any words in existing language. Closely related to these factors is the distortion which occurs when people with somewhat different categories of thought attempt to communicate (57). Thus, for the several million discriminable colors most people utilize only about a dozen categories. But painters and interior decorators use many more categories, with the result that a manager may find his office painted and furnished in a manner far different from what he anticipated unless he makes absolutely certain that his wishes have been communicated effectively. Studies comparing boss-subordinate pairs indicate that communication tends to be more effective when both use similar cognitive categories (56).

Distortion may also occur when a communication arouses one of the numerous defense mechanisms people use to ward off and protect themselves against anxiety and other unpleasant emotions (20). These mechanisms are referred to in the psychological literature by such terms as displacement, projection, turning inward, repression, denial, and identification with the aggressor. Certain types of communications appear to elicit these defensive reactions more frequently and thus meet with distortion in a greater proportion of cases (23). In general anything that reflects evaluation or judging of the receiver tends to arouse defensiveness with a resulting disturbance of concentration on what is really being communicated. The same is true of communications that attempt to control, that suggest the use of a manipulative strategm, that reflect a lack of concern for the receiver's welfare, that indicate some superiority in the sender, and that convey a dogmatic certainty of opinion. Even the most casual observation will indicate that a great many things said by people, especially by organizational superiors, have the potential for evoking the first tingle of anxiety and thus mobilizing defensiveness and producing communication failure.

Redundancy and Error Reduction. Two major types of procedures have been used to maintain and restore accuracy of communication: (1) repetition or redundancy and, (2) verification, usually through feedback (24). Of these two, repetition is the simpler. It involves sending the same message again and again utilizing various media and different forms of statement. An example is the inclusion of certain material from the textbook, that a professor wished to emphasize, in his lecture. Here written and oral communication channels are used. Incorporating the material in an examination question may provide for another repetition, in a somewhat different form. The more ways the material is communicated and the more the words used to communicate it are varied from transmission to transmission, the less likelihood that error and distortion will occur. On the other hand, the introduction of redundancy in this manner reduces the amount of information that can be communicated in a given time period.

An example of how redundancy may be used to reduce error is provided by analyses of the language used by control tower operators at an airport in communicating with aircraft in the process of landing and takeoff (21). Although written English appears to be approximately 60 percent redundant, the redundancy of the control tower operators rises to 96 percent when the situational context as well as the words spoken to pilots are taken into account. This is a very high level of repetition; yet it seems appropriate in view of the consequences of error in such a situation.

Verification, Feedback, and Two-Way Communication. A second approach to the communication breakdown problem is to require the receiver to feed back his understanding of a message. This permits verification of whether accurate reception has occurred and correction of errors through subsequent messages. This type of two-way interaction, which gradually narrows down to full and complete understanding, may be contrasted with one-way communication of the kind that occurs when one watches a television program. In the management context one-way communication occurs when there is heavy reliance on memos and announcements and when emotional barriers exist such that a manager does not receive feedback from his subordinates.

Several laboratory experiments have been conducted contrasting one-way with two-way communication (28, 38). From these it appears that two-way communication is less frustrating, much more accurate, and produces greater confidence in the correctness of interpretations. But it is time consuming, as is redundancy, and does not appear necessary when the message becomes familiar and routinized. These results have been confirmed in cross-cultural studies using groups of managers from Belgium, Denmark, India, Italy, Norway, the United Kingdom, and the United States (3). In all the countries two-way communications was viewed as less frustrating and more satisfying. In all instances it also produced greater accuracy while requiring more time (50 percent longer on the average). Further evidence on the degree to which open, two-way communication between superior and subordinate is associated with satisfaction is provided in Table 12–2. Measures of both job satisfaction and openness of two-way communication were obtained by questionnaires from 323 telephone operators in six offices (7).

Communication Network Studies

A rather large body of research has been concerned with the effectiveness and satisfaction-producing qualities of various structures or patterns of communication in groups. These so-called communication network studies are, of course, indirectly concerned with communication breakdown, but they go beyond differences in degree of redundancy and opportunity for feedback to ask whether merely setting up channels of communication among the people in a work group in certain ways will yield positive consequences.

Table 12-2 Relationship Between Degree of Openness of Superior-Subordinate Communication and Subordinate Job Satisfaction

Mean Satisfaction Score*

Satisfaction Measure	Both Completely Open	Both Mostly Open	Both Half-Open Half-Closed	Both Somewhat Closed	Both Mostly Closed
Satisfaction with Company	7.0	7.5	9.0	9.6	9.1
Satisfaction with Job	27.8	29.4	34.9	36.5	36.4
Satisfaction with Performance Appraisal	7.7	9.9	15.0	17.0	17.3
Helping Relationship	3.8	5.1	7.6	8.8	12.0
Satisfaction with Supervisor	12.1	16.6	22.0	23.1	26.9

* Low scores on each measure equal higher satisfaction.
Source: R. J. Burke and D. S. Wilcox, "Effects of Different Patterns and Degrees of Openness in Superior-Subordinate Communication on Subordinate Job Satisfaction," *Academy of Management Journal*, Vol. 12 (1969), 325.

Experimental Results. Research on communication nets has been conducted in laboratory settings. The participants are restricted in their communications, so that they can only communicate with certain other group members. The usual approach involves written communication in a situation where partitions prevent the participants from seeing each other. Some of the more commonly used nets are depicted in Figure 12–1. Groups in each type of net are given the same task to accomplish or problem to solve.

The early and still most general finding from this type of research is that in terms of time, number of errors, number of messages to achieve a solution, and rate of group learning the Wheel is preferable. Performance then declines from the Y to the Chain, and the Circle is least effective (37). It is clear that a crucial factor in the success of a given net is the degree to which it provides a central position where information can be collected, analyzed, and compared. The person in the central position is particularly likely to become the leader of the group, although it appears that other factors such as personal ascendance may also be involved in the emergence of leadership (25). The person in the central position is also more likely to be satisfied with his participation in the group than those at the periphery.

Research conducted since the basic studies in the early 1950s has added a number of qualifications. It appears, for instance, that although the Wheel with its greater centrality has advantages for the performance of

Figure 12–1 Diagrams of Communication Networks

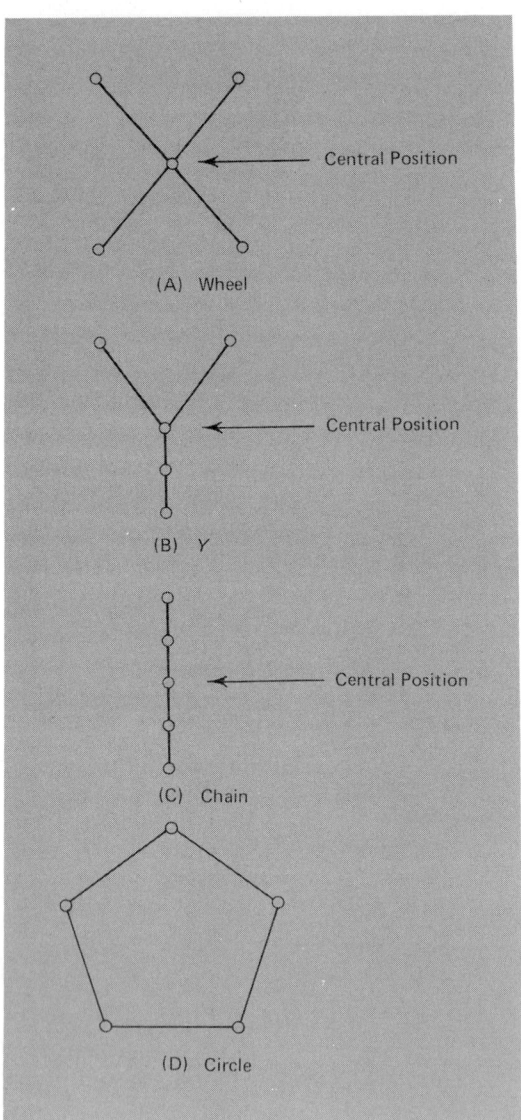

relatively simple tasks, this is not true for complex problem solving requiring the use of logic and deductions (51). In the latter instance the Circle is generally superior. Furthermore, the prior experiences of a group clearly make a difference. Groups shifting from the Wheel to the Circle were able to transfer their earlier structure and did well; groups whose early experience was with the Circle, and who then shifted to the Wheel, were clearly handicapped by their prior experience (10). Thus, in recommending a particular network, one must consider not only the advantages of a given communication structure, but the previous structure of the group.

Finally, there is considerable evidence indicating that communication structure tends to operate as an internal constraint which may be overcome with sufficient effort and the opportunity to develop an efficient organizational pattern over time (6, 26). After being in existence for a considerable period, the Wheel and the Circle tend to develop efficient operating structures that are reflected in negligible performance differences. Thus, although particular communication nets do have an impact on initial performance, once a group solves the problem of how to overcome the constraints imposed and utilize the facilitators available it can do about as well in one net as another. This assumes of course that the context does provide sufficient freedom and there is adequate motivation within the group, so that the preliminary organizing problem is in fact solved. The communication structure affects performance primarily through the relative difficulty it creates for a group in developing an effective work organization to deal with a particular type of task.

Implications for Organizations. It is apparent that under certain circumstances differences in communication networks do yield differences in performance. This early finding led to a widespread hope that studies of this kind would produce a major theory of group, and ultimately, organizational structure (12). To date, after some two decades of research, this simply has not occurred.

Practically no work has been done to generalize the findings of the laboratory studies to ongoing organizations. Since the laboratory research has dealt with small groups, usually five people or fewer, it seems likely that the results obtained are more applicable to work groups within organizations than to total organizations. Certainly the findings seem most relevant for temporary groupings which have a short life or a constantly shifting membership, and which accordingly are faced with the problems of organizing to perform tasks. Committees and project or task teams often are of this type. Long-standing groups and organizations would be expected to have developed methods for overcoming constraints inherent in existing communication networks. The time it will take a newly formed committee to produce effective work would seem to depend on the communication network used and the nature of its task. But to understand the consequences of communication patterns for ongoing organizations as a whole, it is necessary to look to research extending beyond the laboratory setting.

Organizational Communication

Research dealing with communication through organizations, beyond the individual superior-subordinate relationship, has tended to focus on two topics. One is the problem of breakdown in the formal communication system which uses the established organizational structure to provide its channels. The other is the nature of those communication processes that operate outside the formal system and the prescribed channels. In addition, there has been some research bearing on the question of the total amount of communication an organization should have.

Formal Communication in the Hierarchy

According to classical management theory, communication should follow the linkages of the scalar chain of command. Such a procedure tends to foster vertical communication, but to keep horizontal communication flow to a minimum. Strictly interpreted it means that messages intended for another individual at the same level should go up the hierarchy to the point where a common manager exists and then back down to the desired recipient. If a foreman in manufacturing wants to communicate with a salesman, this can be a very cumbersome process—the chief executive may well be the common manager.

To circumvent this problem Fayol (19) proposed that horizontal communication be facilitated through its authorization by the managers at the next higher level. This view was discussed in Chapter 3 and the concepts involved diagrammed in Figure 3–1. Yet even with this added inducement administrative organizations often experience difficulties in the horizontal flow of information. Project management, committees, and the matrix structure represent one type of response to this problem. Without such horizontal structures, formal communication is primarily a vertical matter.

Distortion in Upward Communication. Although the primary mode of upward communication is through the superior-subordinate channel utilizing either written or oral forms, it is important to recognize that there are alternatives which move directly from lower levels to upper. A person toward the bottom of the hierarchy may simply bypass intervening managers and communicate with an upper-level executive. Most formal systems tend to discourage this, but there are exceptions, such as the "open door" policies maintained by some members of top management. In addition companies often institute such upward channels as attitude surveys, suggestion systems, grievance or appeal systems, meetings, and employee counseling programs. In general these are methods of transmitting information from the nonmanagerial level well up into the management hierarchy.

Studies dealing with upward communication in whatever form have consistently found it particularly prone to distortion. Experimental research with small laboratory groups shows a clear tendency for distortion and suppression of information to increase the greater the status differential between the lower-level sender and the higher-level receiver; also there is a tendency for these effects to be most pronounced when the higher-level person has the power to make or withhold promotions (2, 11).

This same type of blocking and distortion has been found when the research is extended into ongoing organizations (1). The more ambitious a subordinate manager is to be promoted and thus move upward in the hierarchy himself, the more likely he is to communicate to his superior in an inaccurate manner (47). This tendency is particularly pronounced when the subordinate manager distrusts his superior, and the communication breakdown is unaffected by whether the superior has previously held the subordinate's job (39). Ambitious managers who report to superiors who have been promoted into their current positions from the same position the subordinate manager now holds distort and withhold information just as much as ambitious managers who do not work for a superior who has has this opportunity to learn about their jobs. As noted previously, where the evaluative context is strong, as it clearly is when a subordinate has a

Directing: An Input-Improving Mediator

strong desire for promotion, there is a high probability of defensiveness and communication breakdown quite independent of other considerations that might be expected to foster more effective communication.

The Downward Flow. The higher the level of an individual's position in the hierarchy the wider his range of job-related communication contacts (60) and the more time spent in communication (31). This is true for both line and staff managers, although staff managers generally tend to have more such contacts than do line managers. The result in most organizations appears to be a large amount of downward information flow characterized by considerable redundancy both in channels used and in terms of repetition within the same channel. Although difficulties in upward communication may limit the effectiveness of feedback in error reduction, one would still expect downward communication to operate relatively effectively.

Data bearing on the effectiveness of downward flow through the hierarchy are given in Table 12–3. In this instance information was given to higher-level managers in production meetings with instructions to pass it down through the chain of command to the assistant foremen as quickly as possible (14). In Section A the information dealt with the opening of a new entrance to the management parking lot and in Section B with a prospective layoff of some production workers. Follow-ups were made 26 hours after the information was first given out. From Table 12–3 it is clear that even downward flowing information may not reach its intended destination, or may do so only after an unexpected delay. On the other hand, really important communications, such as the anticipated layoff,

Table 12–3 Knowledge of Two Events by Organizational Levels

Organizational Level and Title	Section A Parking Information			Section B Layoff Information		
	Number Surveyed	Number Knowing	Percent Knowing	Number Surveyed	Number Knowing	Percent Knowing
1 Section Head	1	1	100	1	1	100
2 Superintendent	3	3	100	3	3	100
3 General Foreman	4	4	100	6	6	100
4 Foreman	13	5	38	17	16	94
5 Assistant Foreman	26	4	15	27	19	70
Total	47	17	36	54	45	83

Source: K. Davis, "Success of Chain-of-Command Oral Communication in a Manufacturing Management Group," *Academy of Management Journal*, Vol. 11 (1968), 383.

appear to have a better record than less important ones. In this instance all of the communication failure regarding the layoff was attributable to a single general foreman.

Nonformal Communication

A large proportion of communication using formal channels is written, although the written form may well be supplemented verbally to insure valid transmission. In contrast, communication outside the formal channels, which does not coincide with formal role prescriptions as established by organization planning, job analysis, and policy statements, tends to be largely verbal (42). Presumably, in the absence of legitimization from above, many individuals prefer not to have a permanent written record of the communication exist, and so resort to the impermanence of the oral form.

Horizontal and Diagonal Flow. Much of the literature dealing with communication assumes that information flow between individuals at the same level or between individuals at different levels but not in the same chain of command is invariably outside the formal system. Yet where committee structures, project teams, or authorization processes are established to facilitate horizontal and diagonal communication there seems little question that components of the formal system are being utilized. Given these exceptions, however, it still remains true that information flow which crosses the organization in any manner may well be transmitted outside formal channels. It may well represent an attempt to contribute to goal attainment, made necessary by the fact that formal role prescriptions have not been established in an entirely satisfactory way (45).

Horizontal communication appears to be particularly prevalent across the lower levels of the management hierarchy (52). At this level horizontal communication among foremen is disproportionately greater than vertical and tends to focus on joint problem solving and coordination of work flow —both clearly goal related.

Further evidence on the high proportion of communication at the lower management levels which occurs outside the regular vertical channels is given in Table 12–4. Approximately two-thirds of the communications reported by the managers of this study were horizontal or diagonal. The managers studied worked for a number of different companies in marketing, production, finance, engineering, and research and development. The data

Directing: An Input-Improving Mediator

Table 12–4 Direction of Communication Flow as a Percent of Total Entries for Each Purpose and for All Communications (Based on Data from 48 Managers)

Direction of Communication	Purpose					All Purposes
	Information	Instruction	Approval	Problem Solving	Scuttlebutt	
Vertical	30	39	42	31	24	33
Horizontal	31	25	22	33	43	30
Diagonal	39	36	36	36	33	37

Source: A. K. Wickesberg, "Communications Networks in the Business Organization Structure," *Academy of Management Journal*, Vol. 11 (1968), 256.

derive from daily logs they maintained (59). Over half of the communications recorded involved receiving or disseminating information. Giving or receiving instructions was next in frequency and problem solving followed. Nonbusiness-related communications (scuttlebutt) and giving or receiving approvals were relatively infrequent. Overall, the data from this study reinforce the view that much horizontal and diagonal communication occurs with the intended objective of carrying out work efficiently and contributing to task and maintenance goals.

As previously noted, however, formal communication systems tend to facilitate vertical flow, frequently at the expense of horizontal. Information transmission across an organization often fails to reach an appropriate source. In one study four different pieces of information were planted with salesmen. This information was of a kind that would be extremely important to a particular manager who was in a diagonal relationship to them (1). In only one of the four instances did the information ever reach the manager; in the other three instances communication quickly became blocked. As data derived from studies of the grapevine indicate, nonformal communication may also be seriously distorted and in error. The frequency and goal-related nature of such communications say nothing about how well informal channels work.

The Grapevine. Studies of the grapevine indicate that considerable informal, unofficial communication is very likely to occur in any organization. This communication may well contribute to task and maintenance goals. However, it seems clear that a company that relied primarily on the grapevine for information transmission would be in serious trouble. The existence of a formal system which is the predominate mode of communication appears essential (46).

Systematic research dealing with the grapevine has yielded several consistent findings (13, 54). It appears that only about 10 percent of the people in an organization are active transmitters of information in the grapevine. The majority of people tend to receive information, but not pass it on. For any given item there will be a sizable number of people who do not receive it at all and these people tend to increase disproportionately as one moves down the hierarchy. Generally, staff groups receive more items of grapevine information than line. There appear to be some groups in most organizations which almost never receive such information; they are almost entirely isolated from the informal system.

In addition to the uncertainties of transmission and reception which appear to plague all communication systems but which are particularly acute in the grapevine, there are major problems of distortion and error. Instances where the grapevine has maintained considerable validity over an extended time period have been reported (9). But in most organizations this appears unlikely, except where some feedback process is operative. In this instance rumors are repeatedly checked against a source where correct information is available and those that are in error are either corrected or blocked. In one study of the operation of the grapevine in six companies, 30 separate items were studied. Of these, 16 turned out to be groundless, 9 were accurate, and 5 had an element of accuracy but some distortion as well (29). The rumors dealt with such matters as personnel transfers, procedural changes, promotions, possible company relocation, possible departmental relocation, employee share in the profit-sharing plan, company reorganization, no replacement of a retiree, retirement of a manager, pay raises, and union disaffiliation from the international. They were consistently work related, and when they were correct they predicted events an average of 44 days in advance. Unfortunately, they were often wrong.

The Information Overload Problem

Although the *direction* of communication flow has received more attention in the literature, the *amount* of communication is also an important aspect of organizational communication systems. Does the system transmit a large number of messages or very few? From what has been said about the efficacy of redundancy and verification in preventing communication breakdowns one would anticipate that a large amount of communication might prove desirable in an organization. There is evidence to support

Directing: An Input-Improving Mediator

this view (46). It seems evident that a number of organizations would become more effective in achieving their goals were they to increase communications.

The Nature of Overload. In spite of the distinct advantages associated with more information transmission and more communication generally, there are limits on what an organization's communication system or certain of its components can handle. Full and free information flow to everyone is an appealing ideal, but the result can be so much communication that the system fails to function effectively (35). Under such circumstances individuals may be flooded with information they do not need to do their work, to the point where they cannot concentrate on the information they do need. Furthermore, sorting and selecting from among the myriad messages may be so time consuming that there is little opportunity to do anything else.

Typically in organizations this kind of flooding or overloading occurs at certain points in a communication system. When channels prove to be very reliable, when there is rarely any omission or distortion, they tend to be used more. Thus a particular transmitter in the grapevine may be asked to receive and pass on more and more items. A suggestion system that is viewed as an important source of changes and that pays for ideas put into effect may attract an increasing number of suggestions. As a result of this spiraling usage, such channels may become overloaded, thus losing their reliability, accuracy, and value. One of the problems in utilizing redundancy and verification to minimize communication breakdown is that these techniques contribute sizably to overload. They achieve their intended objective up to a point, but beyond this they may become a source of distortion in their own right (24).

Overload is particularly likely to become a problem toward the top of the managerial hierarchy. As indicated in Table 12-1, the amount of time spent communicating tends to increase at each higher managerial level. At some point overload sets in. Almost without exception chief executives are faced with the overload problem and must develop some method of coping with it (5). There do appear to be differences between individuals in their ability to process information effectively (49). Thus what would be overload for one manager may well not be for another. In all likelihood many individuals who move into top-level positions have exhibited considerable information-processing skill. Yet at some point a chief executive, no matter how great his skill, will face the information overload problem.

Responses to Overload. All responses to overload involve a reduction in the amount of information received. The basic question is not whether to reduce communication or attempt to handle all of it, but how the reduction shall be carried out. Certain methods of coping with overload are clearly maladaptive and minimally effective (35). Among these is simply omitting information when the press of communication becomes too acute, and also distorting data in the rush to process as much as possible. Certain types of queuing or delaying mechanisms and filtering procedures are also maladaptive if they fail to take into account the content and relevance of the information. To work through one's in-basket in the order in which messages appear, leaving many items completely unseen for days, or to deal with every fifth message, irrespective of the content, may serve to get communications back under control, but the loss in effectiveness is sizable. The crucial requirement is that what is really important be somehow sorted out, processed, and acted upon.

One approach is to substitute multiple individuals for the one. This is what is involved in delegation and decentralization. Information appropriate to different problems is transmitted to those individuals who are expected to make decisions in each area, rather than having all information flood to a single chief executive.

Another approach is to establish a mechanism for queuing and filtering communications so that what is really important and requires immediate action gets through to the decision maker immediately; other messages may be delayed to a degree appropriate to their content and urgency, but still be transmitted; still others may be essentially irrelevant and be blocked off from their intended source entirely, as a means to eliminating overload. The most common mechanism for achieving this type of relevant queuing and filtering is the creation of a general staff. The White House staffs established by numerous presidents represent an example. A number of individuals, rather than one, receive the information and sort and distill it so as to bring it within the capabilities of a single person.

An alternative is to simply omit messages transmitted in certain channels, but to select those channels which will be utilized on the basis of meaningful criteria. Thus executives may come to utilize data and recommendations made by one subordinate, but not another. Studies indicate that decision makers do in fact become very proficient in identifying such information sources that continually provide accurate information (44).

On the other hand, it is not necessarily true that information quality will dominate over matters of accessibility and ease of use in the selection of channels. Analyses of data provided by research scientists and engineers indicate that the frequency with which a channel is used is much more closely associated with accessibility than with technical quality (22). It is also influenced by the perceived norms or values within an organization regarding information sharing (15). Thus it appears to be extremely important, if channel selection is to be used to cope with overload, that steps be taken to correct for differences in the extent to which channels are physically and psychologically accessible. It may be easiest to consult one's immediate subordinates, but the best answers may emerge only from a somewhat more difficult and time-consuming search of the relevant literature.

All of these methods for dealing with overload have their drawbacks as well as their advantages. It is not possible to say one is better than the others. It is common to use all of them in conjunction with one another. As the discussion which follows indicates, the advent of the computer and the development of management information systems based upon it have not only intensified the information overload problem but offered an additional means for coping with it as well.

Management Information Systems (MIS)

At the beginning of this chapter four levels of analyses related to communication were distinguished: the intrapersonal, interpersonal, organizational, and technical. Management information systems are at the technical level. They represent a part of a company's formal communication system.

Definitions and Descriptions

In discussions of management information systems the terms *data*, *information*, and *intelligence* often are used. *Data* represent facts cataloged according to some scheme for retrieval. *Information* represents data marshaled to satisfy a requirement and understand a situation; it is problem related. *Intelligence* results from the analysis of organized information and provides a decision maker with a preferred course of action among alternatives (33).

These distinctions may be related to a hierarchy of management information-decision systems (16):

Clerical systems
Information systems
Decision systems
Interactive systems
Programmed systems

Clerical systems are at the lowest level and also are the most frequent. Data are stored and processed in a computerized system rather than in a manual file system. Such systems often are used to handle payrolls, customer billing, dividend calculations, and the like. This is the type of computer use for routine tasks and computations, which was noted in Chapter 9 as having no impact in the direction of more centralized decision making.

In contrast to the clerical systems, those dealing with information do provide inputs to managerial decision making. They organize, compress, and select data so that they become meaningful information, available at an appropriate time for dealing with a problem. Although such management information systems now typically utilize computers to process data, this is not an essential requirement for the existence of an information system. In rather small companies, in particular, a manual approach may be more appropriate than a computerized one.

At the decision system level there is a concern with assisting the decision process itself in addition to providing relevant information. One now becomes concerned with intelligence. This is the point at which communication and decision making come together. Various decision-making tools of the kind discussed in Chapter 6—such as marginal analysis, statistical decision theory, and linear programming—are integrated into or superimposed on the information system. At this level, management science and operations research become so closely tied to computer science and information systems management that the fields are virtually indistinguishable.

The two remaining levels, interactive and programmed systems, are essentially extensions of the decision system level. In an interactive system the manager and the information system are coupled in a problem-solving network. The manager utilizes a remote console to obtain the specific information he needs from the computer; he may even simulate various courses of action on the computer and observe the results. In such a

Directing: An Input-Improving Mediator

system it may be possible to utilize data which are very recent and up-to-date; the manager asks questions of the computer which are answered in terms of the current situation using a so-called real-time system. The programmed level moves one step further and removes the manager from the system completely. In this instance decision making is turned over entirely to the information-decision system (although, of course, implementation cannot be). This level is currently a matter of research investigation rather than practical application.

Examples of complex management information systems are given in Figures 12–2 and 12–3. These are not actually operational systems, but rather illustrations of what is possible. Figure 12–2 presents a total information-decision system for a company (30). Data are collected from a great many sources both within and outside the firm. They are processed through various systems (business record, management-information, information-decision, operating) to yield operating results. Such a system would transmit whatever information is needed to managers at all levels. The information would be current, correct, and there would be a capability for obtaining supplementary information on inquiry. Instructions for the implementation of decisions would flow automatically to the point of action, and deviations from standard would be immediately flagged according to the exception principle. The use of operations research techniques and of outside data banks containing environmental information would be integral to the system.

The system presented in Figure 12–3 includes communication system components above and beyond the MIS, many of which have been considered in prior sections of this chapter. It also details a number of separate information systems that the manager may call upon and utilize. These separate systems are connected to a common data base, which is in turn connected with a number of outside data banks. The result is a complex and wide-ranging communication system with access to a tremendous amount of information. Such systems will achieve widespread usage during the present decade, according to at least one knowledgeable writer (53).

Present and Potential Use

In defining and describing management information systems only minimal attention has been given to the extent of actual use. In this area changes are so frequent that the past rapidly blends into the future. It is

Figure 12–2 Schematic of Plan for Information Flows in a Management Information System for a Major Oil Company

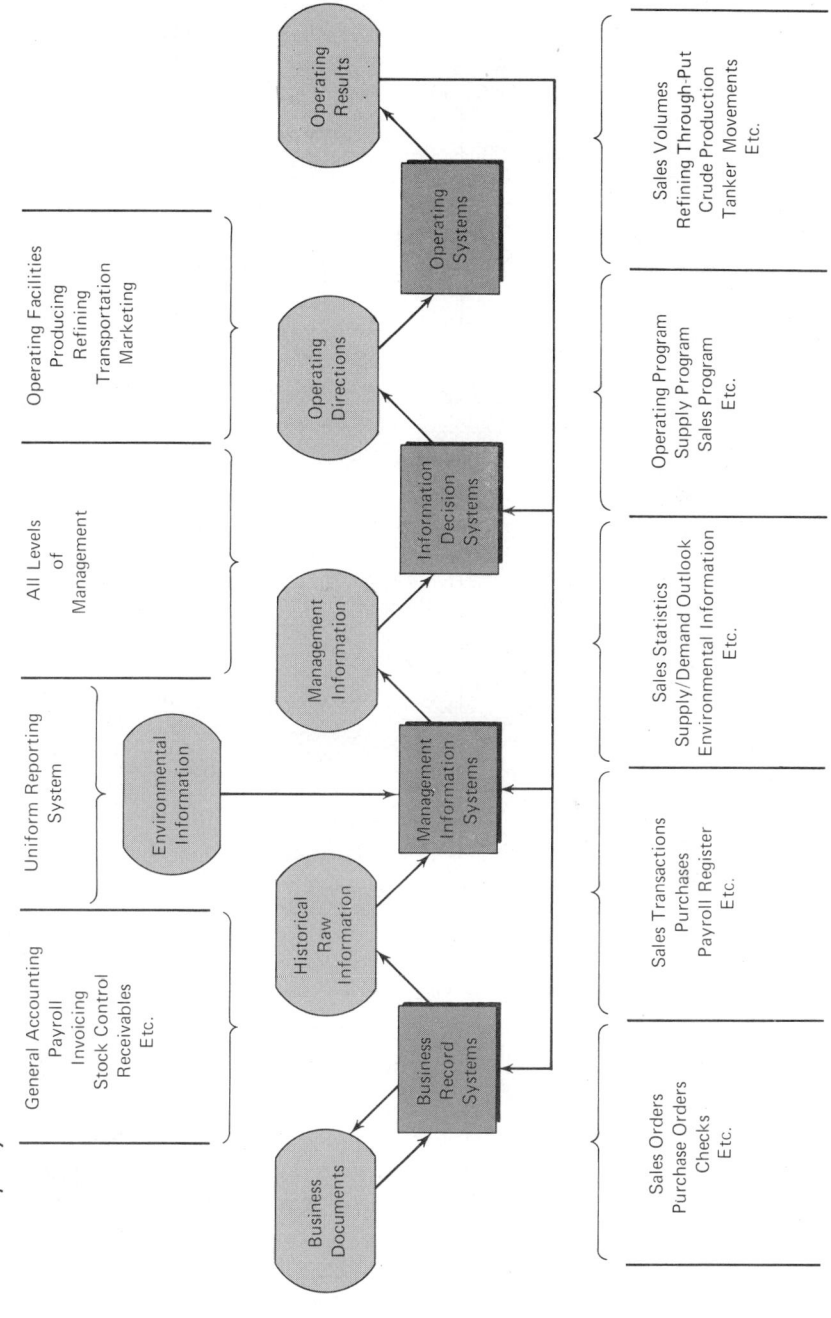

Source: C. Heyel, *Computers, Office Machines, and the New Information Technology* (New York: Macmillan 1969), p. 177.

Directing: An Input-Improving Mediator

Figure 12–3 The Manager in the Context of a Management Information System

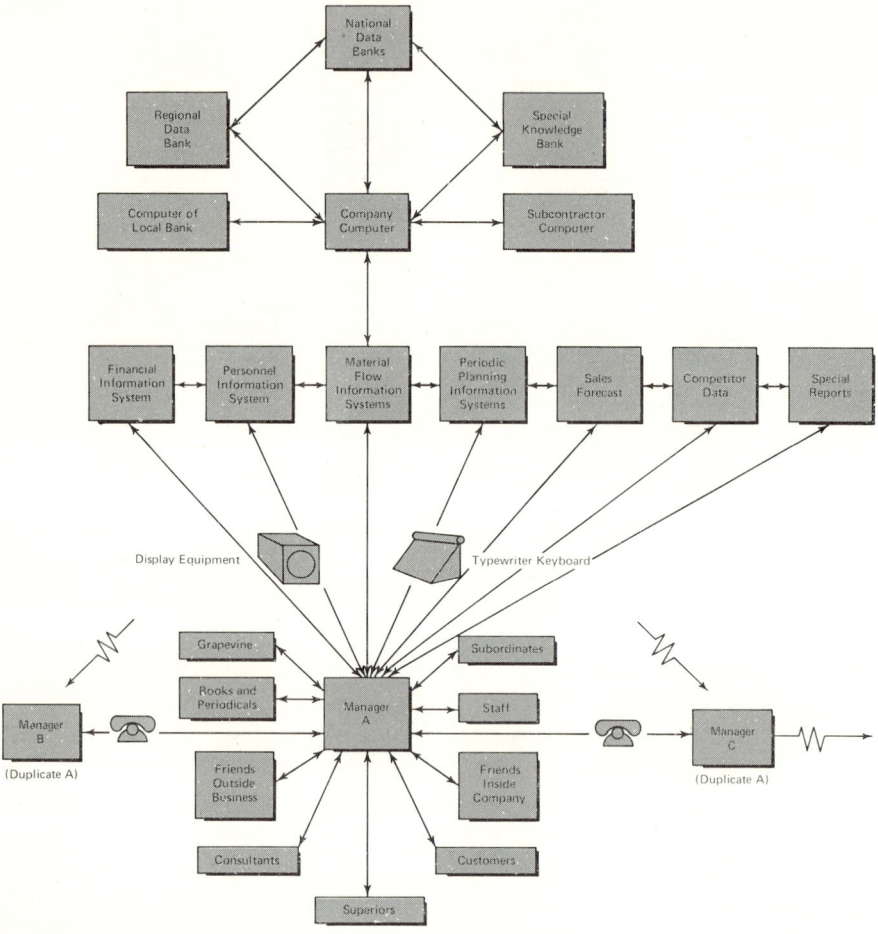

Source: G. A. Steiner, *Top Management Planning* (New York: Macmillan, 1969), p. 508.

also clear that technological capabilities are increasingly outstripping actual applications (41). Most of what is described in the preceding section is now technically feasible, but there are as yet few if any actual applications of the more advanced systems. For instance, in spite of its great potential use in planning, MIS use is much more extensive for purposes of control (34).

Historical Trends. When computers first began to achieve extensive usage in the business world during the 1950s, their major application was in the accounting area, primarily in connection with clerical systems. At least in the larger corporations this phase of development now appears to be virtually complete (41). Applications in connection with material resources followed quickly upon those in the financial area—inventory control, production scheduling, product distribution. In general these information systems communicate only partway up the management hierarchy. They are not a basis for top-management decision making.

Although much computer use is still in connection with accounting, production, and marketing activities, and many of the systems have very little if any information component, there is an increasing movement into higher-level systems (32, 53). The result has been a greater concern with MIS on the part of top management decision makers. There is every reason to believe this trend will continue. If this is so, management information systems consisting of computers connected with input sources at a variety of locations are likely to become the major channel of upward communication from the bottom to the top of the management hierarchy. It is significant that with MIS upward communication does not move step by step up the hierarchy, but rather flows directly from the bottom to the top bypassing intervening levels.

Evidence on the extent and value of overall planning for a full range of computer applications derives from a study of 36 large corporations in this country and Europe (40, 41). The companies were divided into the 18 more and 18 less successful. There were 14 that had not carried out any planning for higher-level computer uses; 12 of these were in the less successful category. On the other hand, among the 22 with such plans 16 were successful. There appears to be a clear relationship between planning to move into information and decision systems on an extensive basis in the future and successful operation. Yet, the rate of actual implementation has been far slower than predicted during the past ten years, and the present implementation rate remains quite slow.

Employee Information Systems. In the early period of computer use, when clerical systems were being installed to handle financial and material resource problems, very little attention was given to human resource applications. A number of firms did develop computerized payroll systems, but this is as much an application in the financial area as in personnel. Data from a recent survey of the use of employee information systems in 408 companies with over 500 employees, many of them much larger, are given in Table 12–5 (43). Areas of application reported by 10 percent

Directing: An Input-Improving Mediator

Table 12–5 Computer Applications for Purposes of Employee Information in 408 Companies

Area of Application	Payroll Related	Percent of Companies
Payroll	X	89
Pensions	X	48
Insurance	X	48
Wage and Salary Records	X	38
Employment and Staffing Records		34
Seniority		33
Profit Sharing	X	22
Separations		22
Wage and Salary Surveys	X	22
Transfers		20
Statistical Studies		20
Absenteeism		18
Promotions		17
Turnover		15
Skills Inventory		15
Wage and Salary Structure	X	14
Workmen's Compensation	X	13
Layoff		13
Sales to Employees	X	12
Credit Union	X	12
Turnover Studies		11
Separation Studies		11
Job Evaluation		10

Source: E. J. Morrison, *Developing Computer-Based Employee Information Systems*. AMA Research Study No. 99 (New York: American Management Association, Inc., 1969), p. 14. Reprinted by permission of the publisher.

or more of the companies are noted. The strong emphasis on payroll and payroll-related application is still in evidence; so too is the stress on record keeping at the level of a clerical system. These same trends have been found in another survey which included smaller organizations (5). It is clear from both surveys that employee information systems are much more prevalent in the larger companies, although a few exist in companies with fewer than 100 employees.

The survey of 408 companies provides further data bearing on the movement toward higher level systems (43). A sizable number of companies report plans for developing information systems dealing with manpower forecasts, turnover studies, manning studies, statistical studies, selection, and other areas which are more closely related to decision processes. Yet not a single company reports a completely integrated employee information system in existence. Furthermore there is little evidence that total systems encompassing human, material, and financial resources are on the immediate horizon. Generally it appears that plans for developing higher level applications are being made in other areas with very little concern for the inclusion of human resource factors.

Problems with MIS

It is important to evaluate management information systems in terms of their effectiveness, just as one would any other communication channel. Are there problems of error, omission, and distortion? Is overload a matter for concern?

The most general answer appears to be that anything that can go wrong in other communication systems can appear in MIS. Potentially at least computer-based systems can be freed of most of the communication problems considered in this chapter, but they often are not. Furthermore, because of the technological aspect and the aura which has come to surround the computer, there is a major risk that redundancy and verification will not be utilized sufficiently, that confidence in the MIS channel will be too great, with the result that errors will go undetected.

There is ample evidence that information derived from a computer is not necessarily correct. Machine breakdown, incorrect programming, and garbled data can be a problem. Many errors have their origins in personal resistance to the introduction of a management information system and to the changes involved. This resistance can extend to outright sabotage (17). Errors may also occur because of failure to update data inputs to the system and to include all information that is in fact needed (50).

One of the most frequently noted sources of difficulty is a failure of coordination between those who design management information systems and the managers who use them (32, 36, 41, 43). Again and again, systems yield quantities of information that is rarely needed while failing to provide much of what is needed. This can contribute to a considerable information overload. There is a tendency to distribute information much more widely than necessary merely because it is so easily available from the computer (53). Furthermore, there is a tendency to utilize real-time systems with continued updating extensively once they are initiated, with the result that managers can be flooded with data (34).

Management information systems need not incorporate these problems. Data may be utilized with primary concern for a manager's specific

Directing: An Input-Improving Mediator

information needs. Sampling, queuing, filtering, selection, delay, and the like can be carried out via computer. In fact the computer is an ideal mechanism for data compression (18). There is every reason to believe, therefore, that management information systems of the future will cope with problems such as that of overload with increasing effectiveness. They certainly offer the promise of an extremely effective communication channel, although it appears unlikely that MIS communication will ever fully replace the other channels discussed earlier in this chapter.

Questions

1. What do we know about the operation of the grapevine as a communication system? How might some of the problems characteristic of grapevine communications be overcome?
2. Why are management information systems particularly prone to information overload? How might the various techniques for coping with information overload be applied to such systems?
3. Describe three instances of communication breakdown taken from your own experience. How might each have been avoided? What communication procedures are involved in these approaches to avoiding breakdown?
4. What special problems in communication are likely to arise when messages must go upward, either vertically or diagonally? How would you expect a company which operated strictly in accordance with Fayol's principles of management to fare in terms of these communications problems? Explain with reference to specific principles.
5. What is meant by the following?
    a. Interactive MIS
    b. Defense mechanisms
    c. Redundancy
    d. Two-way communication
    e. Employee information systems

References

1. Albaum, G. "Horizontal Information Flow: An Exploratory Study." *Academy of Management Journal*, Vol. 7 (1964), 21–33.
2. Barnlund, D. C., and C. Harland. "Propinquity and Prestige as Determinants of Communication Networks." *Sociometry*, Vol. 26 (1963), 467–479.

3. Barrett, G. V., and R. H. Franke. "Communication Preference and Performance: A Cross-Cultural Comparison." *Proceedings, 77th Annual Convention*. American Psychological Association, 1969, 597–598.
4. Bavelas, A. "Communication and Organization." In G. P. Schultz and T. L. Whisler (eds.), *Management Organization and the Computer*. New York: Free Press, 1960, pp. 119–130.
5. Bureau of National Affairs, Inc. *Personnel Policies Forum: The Personnel Department*. Washington, D.C.: BNA, Inc., 1970.
6. Burgess, R. L. "An Experimental and Mathematical Analysis of Group Behavior Within Restricted Networks." *Journal of Experimental Social Psychology*, Vol. 4 (1968), 338–349.
7. Burke, R. J., and D. S. Wilcox. "Effects of Different Patterns and Degrees of Openness in Superior-Subordinate Communication on Subordinate Job Satisfaction." *Academy of Management Journal*, Vol. 12 (1969), 319–326.
8. Burns, T. "The Directions of Activity and Communication in a Departmental Executive Group." *Human Relations*, Vol. 7 (1954), 73–97.
9. Caplow, T. "Rumors in War." *Social Forces*, Vol. 25 (1946–1947), 298–302.
10. Cohen, A. M. "Changing Small-Group Communication Networks." *Administrative Science Quarterly*, Vol. 6 (1962), 443–462.
11. Cohen, A. R. "Upward Communication in Experimentally Created Hierarchies." *Human Relations*, Vol. 11 (1958), 41–53.
12. Davis, J. H. *Group Performance*. Reading, Mass.: Addison-Wesley, 1969.
13. Davis, K. "Management Communication and the Grapevine." *Harvard Business Review*, Vol. 31 (1953), No. 5, 43–49.
14. Davis, K. "Success of Chain-of-Command Oral Communication in a Manufacturing Management Group." *Academy of Management Journal*, Vol. 11 (1968), 379–387.
15. Dewhirst, H. D. "Influence of Perceived Information-Sharing Norms on Communication Channel Utilization." *Academy of Management Journal*, Vol. 14 (1971), 305–315.
16. Dickson, G. W. "Management Information-Decision Systems." *Business Horizons*, Vol. 11 (1968), No. 6, 17–26.
17. Dickson, G. W., and J. K. Simmons. "The Behavioral Side of MIS." *Business Horizons*, Vol. 13 (1970), No. 4, 59–71.
18. Emery, J. C. *Organizational Planning and Control Systems*. New York: Macmillan, 1969.
19. Fayol, H. *General and Industrial Management*. London: Pitman, 1949.
20. Freud, A. *The Ego and the Mechanisms of Defense*. New York: International Universities Press, 1946.
21. Frick, F. C., and W. H. Sumby. "Control Tower Language." *The Journal of the Acoustical Society of America*, Vol. 24 (1952), 595–596.

22. Gerstberger, P. G., and T. J. Allen. "Criteria Used by Research and Development Engineers in the Selection of an Information Source." *Journal of Applied Psychology*, Vol. 52 (1968), 272–279.
23. Gibb, J. R. "Defensive Communications." *ETC: A Review of General Semantics*, Vol. 22 (1965), 221–229.
24. Guetzkow, H. "Communications in Organizations." In J. G. March (ed.), *Handbook of Organizations*. Chicago: Rand McNally, 1965, pp. 534–573.
25. Guetzkow, H. "Differentiation of Roles in Task-oriented Groups." In D. Cartwright and A. Zander (eds.), *Group Dynamics: Research and Theory*. New York: Harper & Row, 1968, pp. 512–526.
26. Guetzkow, H., and H. A. Simon. "The Impact of Certain Communication Nets Upon Organization and Performance in Task-oriented Groups." *Management Science*, Vol. 1 (1955), 233–250.
27. Haimann, T., and W. G. Scott, *Management in the Modern Organization*. New York: Houghton Mifflin, 1970.
28. Haney, W. V. "A Comparative Study of Unilateral and Bilateral Communication." *Academy of Management Journal*, Vol. 7 (1964), 128–136.
29. Hershey, R. "The Grapevine . . . Here to Stay But Not Beyond Control." *Personnel*, Vol. 43 (1966), No. 1, 62–66.
30. Heyel, C. *Computers, Office Machines, and the New Information Technology*. New York: Macmillan, 1969.
31. Hinrichs, J. R. "Communications Activity of Industrial Research Personnel." *Personnel Psychology*, Vol. 17 (1964), 193–204.
32. Holden, P. E., C. A. Pederson, and G. E. Germane. *Top Management*. New York: McGraw-Hill, 1968.
33. Johnson, R. L., and I. H. Derman. "How Intelligent Is Your MIS?" *Business Horizons*, Vol. 13 (1970), No. 1, 55–62.
34. Kast, F. E., and J. E. Rosenzweig. *Organization and Management: A Systems Approach*. New York: McGraw-Hill, 1970.
35. Katz, D., and R. L. Kahn. *The Social Psychology of Organizations*. New York: Wiley, 1966.
36. King, W. R., and D. I. Cleland. "Manager-Analyst Teamwork in MIS." *Business Horizons*, Vol. 14 (1971), No. 2, 59–68.
37. Leavitt, H. J. "Some Effects of Certain Communication Patterns on Group Performance." *Journal of Abnormal and Social Psychology*, Vol. 46 (1951), 38–50.
38. Leavitt, H. J., and R. A. H. Mueller, "Some Effects of Feedback on Communication." *Human Relations*, Vol. 4 (1951), 401–410.
39. Maier, N. R. F., L. R. Hoffman, and W. H. Read. "Superior-Subordinate Communication: The Relative Effectiveness of Managers Who Held Their Subordinates' Positions." *Personnel Psychology*, Vol. 16 (1963), 1–11.

40. McFarlan, F. W. "Problems in Planning the Information System." *Harvard Business Review*, Vol. 49 (1971), No. 2, 75–89.
41. McKinsey and Company, Inc. *Unlocking the Computer's Profit Potential.* New York: McKinsey, 1968.
42. Melcher, A. J., and R. Beller. "Toward a Theory of Organization Communication: Considerations in Channel Selection." *Academy of Management Journal*, Vol. 10 (1967), 39–52.
43. Morrison, E. J. *Developing Computer-Based Employee Information Systems.* New York: American Management Association, 1969.
44. Naylor, J. C. "Accuracy and Variability of Information Sources as Determiners of Performance and Source Preference of Decision Makers." *Journal of Applied Psychology*, Vol. 48 (1964), 43–49.
45. Paine, F. T. "Why Don't They Cooperate." *Personnel Administration*, Vol. 29 (1966), No. 3, 15–21.
46. Price, J. L. *Organizational Effectiveness: An Inventory of Propositions.* Homewood, Ill.: Irwin, 1968.
47. Read, W. H. "Upward Communication in Industrial Hierarchies." *Human Relations*, Vol. 15 (1962), 3–15.
48. Rogers, C. R., and F. J. Roethlisberger. "Barriers and Gateways to Communication." *Harvard Business Review*, Vol. 30 (1952), No. 4, 46–52.
49. Schroeder, H. M., M. J. Driver, and S. Streufert. *Human Information Processing.* New York: Holt, Rinehart and Winston, 1967.
50. Scott, W. G. *Organization Theory: A Behavioral Analysis for Management.* Homewood, Ill.: Irwin, 1967.
51. Shaw, M. "Communication Networks." In L. Berkowitz (ed.), *Advances in Experimental Social Psychology*. Vol. I. New York: Academic Press, 1964, pp. 111–147.
52. Simpson, R. L. "Vertical and Horizontal Communication in Formal Organizations." *Administrative Science Quarterly*, Vol. 4 (1959), 188–196.
53. Steiner, G. A. *Top Management Planning.* New York: Macmillan, 1969.
54. Sutton, H., and L. W. Porter. "A Study of the Grapevine in a Governmental Organization." *Personnel Psychology*, Vol. 21 (1968), 223–230.
55. Thayer, L. *Communication and Communication Systems.* Homewood, Ill.: Irwin, 1968.
56. Triandis, H. C. "Cognitive Similarity and Interpersonal Communication in Industry." *Journal of Applied Psychology*, Vol. 43 (1959), 321–326.
57. Triandis, H. C. "Getting Through to Your Boss—A Research Report on Cognitive Similarity, Communication and Interpersonal Attraction." *Personnel Administration*, Vol. 24 (1961), No. 3, 11–17.
58. Weinshall, T. D. "The Reciprocal Perception of Communication." In R. Dubin (ed.), *Human Relations in Administration*. Englewood Cliffs, N.J.: Prentice-Hall, 1968, pp. 339–342.

59. Wickesberg, A. K. "Communications Network in the Business Organization Structure." *Academy of Management Journal,* Vol. 11 (1968), 253–262.
60. Zajonc, R. B., and D. M. Wolfe. *Cognitive Consequences of a Person's Position in a Formal Organization.* Ann Arbor: Institute for Social Research, University of Michigan, 1963.

Part IV
Coordinating and Controlling: Sustaining and Restoring Input Potential Levels

13 Managing Internal Conflict

I. The Coordination Function Defined

II. Conditions for Conflict
1. Joint Decision-Making Situations
   a. Degree of Autonomy
   b. The Balance of Power and Authority
2. Differences in Objectives and Values
   a. Intergroup Competition
   b. Role Conflict Situations
   c. Status Incongruence
3. Differences in Perceptions
4. Loose-Lying Power
   a. Role Ambiguity
   b. Uncertainty at Organizational Boundaries
5. Aggressive and Conflict-Prone Personalities
6. Role Dissatisfaction
   a. The Absenteeism Response
   b. The Separation Response

III. The Prevention of Conflict
1. Clear and Accepted Role Prescriptions
2. Hierarchic Coordination
3. Structural Integration
4. Superordinate Goals and Cohesive Groups
5. Confrontation Approaches
6. Providing Valid Information
7. Appeal Procedures and Organizational Due Process
8. Bargaining

IV. Labor-Management Conflict
1. The Potential for Conflict
2. Conflict Prevention Procedures
   a. Appeal Systems
   b. Collective Bargaining

The discussion to this point has focused on the input-improving or maximizing aspects of the management process. Policy planning, organization planning, and directing all are of this nature, as are a number of components of the staffing function to be considered in Part V. These input-improving mediators have been the subject of a sizable amount of study and research, much of which has been noted in preceding chapters.

The input-sustaining and input-restoring mediators to which we now turn have not been analyzed nearly as extensively. For this reason the discussion here in Part IV is much briefer than in the parts dealing with the planning and directing functions. It is not that coordinating and controlling are less important aspects of the management process, but rather that less is known about them, particularly as applied to human resources. In the case of coordination, furthermore, by far the largest body of knowledge has developed in the area of labor-management conflict. This is an extremely important matter for many managers, but it is also a highly specialized area with major contributions coming from the law, economics, psychology, and sociology. It is not possible to deal with the labor relations field in depth within a general discussion of the management process such as this volume attempts to provide.

In the case of the input-restoring function controlling, there is a real paucity of knowledge relating to the management of human resources, in proportion to what is known regarding the management of monetary and material resources. This situation is epitomized by the fact that the position title, Controller, is almost universally associated with accounting or financial occupations. Potentially at least, such a person might be concerned with the control function as applied to all types of resources—monetary, human, and material. Since such topics as financial control, production control, inventory control, and the like are basic components of the fields of accounting and production management, the sizable amounts of knowledge which have been developed in these areas are considered here only as they relate directly to human resource management.

The Coordination Function Defined

As noted in Chapter 2, coordination was stressed as an important management function by a number of the early classical writers. In these writings coordination is viewed as the process of managing conflict so as to prevent it from becoming rampant and disrupting task accomplishment. This emphasis on the close association between coordination and conflict appears repeatedly, in the writings of Fayol (19), of Mary Parker Follett (20, 54), and of others.

The conflict may be between various functional groups in an organization, such as between staff and line or between marketing and production; much of the writing on the subject of coordination ties it closely to division of labor (35). But there also may be conflict between subordinate and superior, between the individual and the organization, or between two managers who are at the same level. Wherever large numbers of people are working together there are an almost infinite variety of relationships between individuals and groups. Any one of these relationships is a potential source of conflict. Should coordination fail to occur and conflict become overt, as in the case of strikes, slowdowns, fighting, and the like, organizational goal attainment suffers. There is an indirect impact on task accomplishment because energies are devoted to the conflict rather than to productive effort. Even such low levels of conflict as are evidenced by "disliking" and "difficulty in getting along with" are often associated with reduced productivity (17). There is also a direct effect on organizational maintenance owing to low morale, heightened dissatisfaction, and increased turnover. In the extreme case the organization in its current form simply dissolves in the dissension among its members. Given these considerations it is difficult to accept the view that conflict in and of itself can operate as a positive force within an organization (31).

Conflict has its origins in differences in objectives, interests, efforts, approach, timing, attitudes, and so forth. Much of it is consciously recognized by the participants and intentionally produced. But there are also unintentional conflicts, as where a manager responsible for production scheduling becomes so immersed in the immediate problems of his job and the existing time pressures that he fails to obtain adequate information on sales from the marketing department. The consequence may be that a sizable excess of goods are produced. In cases such as this there is no intention to subvert the goals of the enterprise, but conflicting efforts among various groups are nevertheless in evidence.

Coordinating protects against any diminution of the potential inherent in inputs that might be created by conflicts, however produced. It is a preventive function concerned with heading off conflict and misunderstanding. It is in this sense that it is an input-sustaining mediator. To the extent coordination is successful, conflict that might increase the gap between role prescriptions and role behavior beyond what already exists is prevented, and integration of effort behind corporate goals is fostered.

It should be understood that coordinating is not the only management function related to internal conflict. When prevention fails and conflict becomes overt, there is a need to restore a more peaceable state, where task and maintenance goals can be achieved. This is a matter of control, or conflict *reduction*, which is treated in Chapter 14. In this chapter the focus is on the various conditions which tend to produce conflict and on the coordinating procedures used to handle it.

Conditions for Conflict

Theories of conflict focus on four different concepts (9). There are first the *parties* involved, second the *field* within which conflict may occur, third the *dynamics* of the situation—what the parties do—and fourth the *management* and control of conflict. A discussion of management process is concerned primarily with concepts in the fourth category. However, it is almost impossible to manage conflict and to carry out the coordination function without some understanding of how conflicts may arise. Managers need to know what type of field conditions yield a high probability that open conflict may occur. When is it important to have preventive procedures readily available or already in operation?

The various conditions likely to result in conflict that are considered here are in no sense mutually exclusive. They interrelate and overlap in a number of respects. Furthermore, the discussion does not exhaust all possibilities that have been proposed, or even all the conditions identified by research. The listing does, however, serve to emphasize what appear to be the most important conditions operating in business organizations.

Joint Decision-Making Situations

One potential source of conflict that has been recognized for some time is a feeling on the part of individuals or groups that there is a mutual dependence or interdependence, a need for joint decision making with other individuals or groups, if organizational goals are to be achieved (35, 39). In fact these situations may generate conflict even if the dependence is not clearly perceived. Such situations of a joint decision-making nature arise when two units both use a common service unit, such as a typing pool, or when one production unit has as its input the output of a preceding unit, or when subunits are financed out of a common budget. The conflict often revolves around matters of resource allocation and scheduling.

Degree of Autonomy. There is evidence from a variety of sources that where two groups can operate independently of each other, as for instance two sales districts in different parts of the country selling unrelated products, conflict is unlikely. As this separateness decreases the probability of conflict increases (66). The interdependence of sales and production has been noted as frequently a potential source of conflict. If an individual or group can operate with considerable freedom from the rest of the organization as a whole, as partners in some law firms do in dealing with clients, the potentiality for conflict with *any* other part of the organization is low. In a study of 400 manufacturing foremen in 12 plants of a single company, for example, the amount of conflict reported increased steadily as the decision-making autonomy of the foreman decreased (32).

A major factor contributing to conflict in joint decision-making situations seems to be the way in which the decision-making process is approached. A common tactic under such circumstances is for one or both parties to overstate needs or the urgency of problems. Thus a crisis situation is portrayed, where in fact it does not exist, in order to get the best of the decision. The results of one study dealing with the consequences of such overstatement are given in Figure 13–1. The analysis was based on data obtained from 310 managers in a single company (15). It is clear that as the amount of overstatement in joint decision making increases the probability of annoyance increases sharply. Out of the angry emotionality that may well be involved can come a complete breakdown of the decision-making process and open conflict.

The Balance of Power and Authority. One factor that appears to be especially important in determining the conflict potential of a particular joint decision situation is the balance of power represented. Where one group is dominant over the other and its viewpoint consistently prevails, conflict is very likely (66). The less influential group tends to utilize a variety of tactics to win greater power. The frequent consequence of such situations is illustrated by a comparison of turnover data derived from

Figure 13-1 The Probability of High Annoyance Given Various Levels of Overstatement

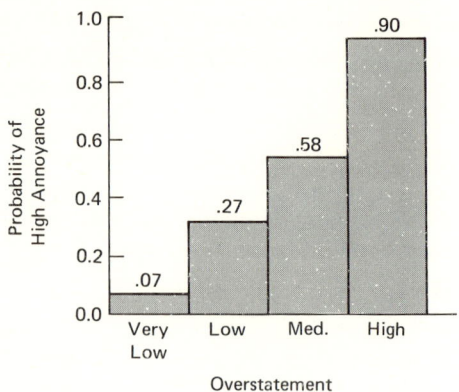

Source: J. M. Dutton, "Analysis of Interdepartmental Decision-Making," in R. W. Millman and M. P. Hottenstein (eds.), *Promising Research Directions, Proceedings of the 27th Annual Meeting* (Academy of Management, 1969), p. 94.

plants where the usual dominance of line over staff groups prevailed, with similar data from a rather unusual firm where staff units actually had greater power than the line organization (13). In the line-dominated situation, staff separations were nearly three times as great as those for the line over a period of four successive years. In the staff-dominated company there was practically no turnover of staff personnel, but line turnover ran consistently at approximately 60 percent a year. Although not all of these differentials in separation rates are attributable to power differentials in joint decision making, this does appear to be a major factor.

Under certain circumstances a power imbalance may not operate to produce conflict. The conflict potential of a situation appears to be drastically reduced when the differentials are widely legitimized and accepted. In one instance joint decision making was found to progress with minimal friction under a generally accepted prestige hierarchy running from research at the top to production at the bottom (53). The power differentials did not contribute to conflict because they were viewed as appropriate by those involved.

In another instance, where this type of legitimization was lacking, conflict became overt. In this case an industrial engineering unit was responsible for an invention which appeared to permit a major product improvement. Normally such inventions would have originated in the research group. The research people felt that industrial engineering was intruding on their domain; the industrial engineers felt that research was trying to take away the credit for their invention. The conflict became sufficiently acute that the two groups stopped talking to each other completely, joint decision making ceased, and the effectiveness of the organization was reduced markedly.

Differences in Objectives and Values

A second potential source of conflict, which is often in evidence in the joint decision context, involves conflicting or competing objectives and values. Where a group or individual wants or stands for one thing, and directly antithetical desires or values exist in the situation as well, the need for coordinating mechanisms is likely to be acute. In such cases self-coordination is rarely sufficient (40). Some externally devised coordination procedure is required to keep conflict from becoming overt.

Intergroup Competition. Within ongoing industrial organizations the most common focus of research has been on departmental units with frequently conflicting interests, such as sales and manufacturing (68), or the various divisions, such as commercial, plant, and traffic of a telephone company (67). These studies consistently have indicated that higher levels of competition between units are associated with more numerous signs of incipient conflict.

However, some of the major insights into the dynamics of intergroup competition derive from laboratory studies using specially contrived groups. Such studies suggest that where the first condition, joint decision making, and the second, competition, exist together the resulting conflict is likely to have a negative impact on productivity (42). This negative impact does not emerge, however, if the intergroup competition occurs under conditions of reasonably autonomous functioning.

Another line of research emerged initially from studies conducted with rival groups at a boys' camp (56). Subsequent studies in other contexts, in particular with groups of managers engaged in management development programs, have produced confirmatory results (7). This research yields a highly consistent picture of what happens under conditions of intergroup competition. Within the competing groups:

1. Members tend to compete with each other less, to become more loyal to their group, and to conform to group norms more. There is a marked pulling together.

2. A greater degree of formality and structure emerges coupled with a more pronounced emphasis on task accomplishment.
3. More autocratic patterns of leadership appear and are tolerated by the group. The particular needs and desires of individuals are given less attention.

At the same time the introduction of intergroup competition yields certain patterns in the relationships *between* groups:

1. Members of each group come to view the members of the other as enemies, and hostility increases.
2. Interaction and communication between the groups decreases.
3. Perceptual distortions emerge which serve to magnify the positive features of one's own group and denigrate the opposition. Thus stereotypes replace reality-based views.

The potential for open conflict in such cases of uncoordinated intergroup competition is clear. Furthermore the winning group, should clear-cut victory occur, tends to retain its cohesiveness while maintaining its stereotypes and beliefs. Task accomplishment becomes less important, but the tendency to overevaluation of the group continues. The losing group, on the other hand, often tends to look for a scapegoat. If this fails, the group may disintegrate with considerable internal dissension emerging. Typically the former leader is replaced. It is apparent that if competition between related units of a company is permitted to go to a win-lose resolution, both groups may well emerge less prepared to contribute effectively to organizational goals.

Much of what has been said regarding competition between groups applies to individuals as well. The need for procedures to prevent the debilitating effects of conflict is equally pronounced. One instance where competing individual objectives may have particularly negative consequences has already been noted in Chapter 6. There it was indicated that heterogeneous groups serve to make diverse resources available for decision making and problem solving, and these are often more effective. Yet at the same time the resulting diversity of values and objectives within such groups produces considerable potentiality for conflict. It is a measure of the coordinating skill of the manager in charge of such a group whether he can elicit the full problem-solving potential, while keeping the conflict potential in the background.

Role Conflict Situations. Role conflict occurs when an individual identifies with two or more groups having different and conflicting objectives and values. The intergroup conflict extends to the level of the specific individual with the result that he receives antithetical sets of role prescriptions and experiences uncertainty about which set to follow. In a very real sense he is at war with himself. Much the same situation can occur if a person legitimizes the authority of multiple superiors who stress different and conflicting role prescriptions.

Further insight into the nature of role conflict is provided by the data of Table 13-1. The statements are placed in order in terms of their closeness of association with role conflict based on a factor analysis of replies from 199 managers in a single company (47). In essence many of the managers are pulled apart by competing forces. The result often is increased dissatisfaction and anxiety, and a reduced contribution to task accomplishment.

One of the most frequently noted instances of role conflict occurs with foremen who receive competing role prescriptions from the management group, of which they are the lowest level members, and from their work groups, of which they are the highest. Although some foremen are able to cope with such situations without experiencing internal conflict, many are not. A particularly high level of role conflict appears to result when programs to employ the culturally disadvantaged are introduced into business organizations for the first time.

Table 13-1 *Questionnaire Responses Closely Related to Role Conflict*

Item	Extent of Relation (factor loading)
I have to do things that should be done differently.	.60
I work under incompatible policies and guidelines.	.60
I have to work under vague directives or orders.	.59
I receive an assignment without the manpower to complete it.	.56
I receive incompatible requests from two or more people.	.56
I have to break a rule or policy in order to carry out an assignment.	.54
I receive an assignment without adequate resources and materials to execute it.	.52
I work on unnecessary things.	.52
I work with two or more groups who operate quite differently.	.43
Lack of policies and guidelines to help me.	.43
I do things that are apt to be accepted by one person and not accepted by others.	.41

Source: J. R. Rizzo, R. J. House, and S. I. Lirtzman, "Role Conflict and Ambiguity in Complex Organizations," *Administrative Science Quarterly*, Vol. 15 (1970), 156.

In one study conflicting role prescriptions and value positions were found to be bombarding the foremen from all sides (48). Some managers at higher levels emphasized humanitarian values, helping the underprivileged, and providing an environment of understanding and tolerance; others stressed the enforcement of rules on an equal basis for all. A special training program for the foremen conducted by a professor of clinical psychology at a nearby university focused on the problems of the new employees, providing information on their disadvantaged backgrounds and the need for understanding if the problems were to be solved. Long-term employees in the various work groups indicated considerable resentment of any "preferential treatment" given the new hires. Many of the foremen themselves held values related to maintaining standards and the company image which were firmly rooted in their organizational identifications and cultural backgrounds. It is little wonder that with all of these conflicting forces operating many of the foremen were unable to cope with the program effectively and that it had only limited success.

Another frequent source of role conflict emerges from those situations where an individual identifies both with a professional or specialty group and with his employing organization. Thus, among scientists the professional code emphasizes making new knowledge available to the whole scientific community to advance understanding, while business organizations often tend to stress greater secrecy so that inventions can be turned to economic advantage.

This same type of conflict has been noted recently among personnel managers (46). There are strong organizational pressures on these managers to follow the dictates of the line-staff concept and thus primarily to provide advice while leaving decision making largely to others. At the same time the rising professionalization of the field serves to foster independent decision making in areas of expertise. There is evidence that some personnel managers may be resolving this conflict by resorting to independent action more frequently while continuing to espouse the values of line-staff. For others there appear to be no satisfactory resolutions.

Status Incongruence. A closely related phenomenon which produces results in terms of anxiety, dissatisfaction, decreased productivity, and conflict potential very similar to those resulting from role conflict is that of status incongruence (28, 29). Status incongruence occurs when a person is high on one index of status, but low on another. A very low-paid chief executive or a person who is continually given high performance ratings

Table 13-2 Status Factors, Status Congruence, and Total Status in a Hypothetical Group

	Age		Education		Job Grade		Status Congruence		Status	
	Years	Rank	Years	Rank	Grade[a]	Rank	Index[b]	Rank	Index[b]	Rank
Jones	57	1	14	1	12	1	0	1.0	3	1
Smith	49	2	10	3	10	2	2	2.5[c]	7	2
Green	31	3	12	2	3	4	4	4.0	9	3
Black	26	4	6	4	6	3	2	2.5[c]	11	4

[a] Low grade means low job.
[b] Low score means high congruence or status.
[c] When ranking tie values it is conventional to give them the average of the ranks they would have occupied if not tied. Since these values would have been 2 and 3, respectively, their average rank is 2.5.
Source: Table extracted from article, "Status Congruence: An Important Organization Function," by J. G. Hunt. Reprinted by permission from the January–February 1969 issue of *Personnel Administration*. Copyright 1969, Society for Personnel Administration, 485–87 National Press Building, 14th and F Streets, N.W., Washington, D.C. 20004. Vol. 32, No. 1, 22.

but no raises are examples. The status incongruence concept is closely related to integration theory as discussed in Chapter 1.

Status incongruence occurs when two different groups award differential status or when the same group awards unequal status on different dimensions. Thus in the case of Green in Table 13-2 the educational system has awarded a higher rank than has the current employing organization. Black's job grade ranking departs to a somewhat lesser extent from his status based on age. Table 13-2 provides an example of how overall indexes of status and of status incongruence may be computed.

Differences in Perceptions

The potential for conflict is likely to be high where groups or individuals perceive and interpret the same phenomena differently. Such situations are closely tied to differences in objectives and values, and to competition. They also are frequently related to the existence of barriers to communication flow (67).

A number of studies have been conducted in which laboratory groups have been set in competition with each other on various problem-solving tasks. One finding of these studies is that groups consistently evaluate their own solutions as better and their groups as more effective than others (3, 6). When members of several groups that have been developing competitive solutions to the same problem review these solutions afterward, each member tends to rate his own product higher: the same solution is rated high by those who created it and lower by those who did not. This result closely parallels the N.I.H. (not invented here) factor long noted in research and development laboratories (13). N.I.H. refers to the frequent tendency for scientists to view ideas developed outside the organization as inferior, research conducted in other departments as inferior to that in one's own, and others as less competent and creative researchers than oneself. In short, if things are "not invented here" they are viewed as unlikely to be of much value.

Similar distortions, with the same potential for arousing controversy, as well as producing errors in task accomplishment, have been noted when different occupational groups are compared. An early study involved judgments regarding a single case by 23 executives of a single company (14). The results are presented in Table 13-3. The sales executives tended to view the basic problem as of a sales nature. The production executives stressed organizational clarification. The accounting executives, all of whom were involved in analyzing aspects of *product* profitability, emphasized sales aspects. Within the miscellaneous category all three public and employee relations executives noted human relation problems. Apparently the same problem elicits very different decision recommendations depending on the individual's functional identification. Such disparate perceptions carry tremendous conflict potential involving as they do implications for resource allocation and power relationships within an organization.

Studies of lower-level supervision have produced evidence of a similar kind of selective perception associated with functional areas among first-level supervision (33). The tendency is to distort one's own activity in a favorable manner. Comparisons of the views of corporate executives in

Table 13-3 Number of Executives from Various Departments Who Mentioned Sales, Clarifying Organization, and Human Relations as Most Important Problems in the Same Case

		Most Important Problem		
Department	N	Sales	Clarifying Organization	Human Relations
Sales	6	5	1	0
Production	5	1	4	0
Accounting	5	3	0	0
Miscellaneous	8	1	3	3

Source: D. C. Dearborn and H. A. Simon, "Selective Perception: A Note on Departmental Identifications of Executives," *Sociometry,* Vol. 21 (1958), 142.

several conglomerate firms with those of executives within the subsidiary divisions indicate the same tendency to selective perception and over-evaluation of one's own group (37). In all these cases the differences in perception appear to provide a potential source of conflict.

Loose-Lying Power

In some organizations institutionalized systems of authority having the support of legitimization from above and below are lacking or, to say the least, inadequate. The result is a tendency to loose-lying power, where the control of sanctions is not clearly tied to specific positions and in the hands of specified individuals. This type of situation often fosters conflict. Since power is in a real sense "up for grabs," various groups and individuals seek to gain it. Competition ensues, often over extended periods and without moving any closer to a legitimized system of authority.

This source of conflict is particularly prevalent in professional organizations. Loose-lying power has plagued universities for many years in the form of conflicts between administrations and faculties, either individually or collectively (1, 11). More recently students have sought to gain control over sanctions as well. In the latter instance a combination of power motivation coupled with a dislike of bureaucratic authority (either in others or for oneself) appears to have produced much more open conflict than existed previously (44). Yet the arena of loose-lying power within which administrators and faculties have been jousting for so long has certainly provided a fertile ground for dissension.

Role Ambiguity. Closely related to the concept of loose-lying power, and in fact overlapping with it in most instances, is role ambiguity. Role ambiguity exists when individuals have no clear picture of what they are supposed to do, when the role prescriptions are vague and uncertain. There is ample evidence that situations of this kind generally have high conflict potential, although the underlying fact of loose-lying power appears to be the crucial determinant.

A number of specific situations involving role ambiguity have been found to yield a high probability of conflict (66). Difficulty in assigning credit or blame between two groups, because it is unclear who did or was supposed to do various things, provides one such instance. Often means to objectives and criteria for the evaluation of performance are so lacking in specificity that it is not possible to establish where an error was made. Arguments and mutual recriminations shortly come to dominate the scene. Similarly, conflict may arise out of mutual desires to avoid or claim jurisdiction over certain tasks in the face of uncertainty and ambiguity. Typically groups seek to avoid responsibility for tasks requiring time and personnel; they seek to claim jurisdiction over tasks that increase their power (67).

Uncertainty at Organizational Boundaries. Several writers have noted the high potentiality for conflict existing at the boundaries of organizations, where members are in frequent interaction with members of other organizations (63, 70). Relationships with customers, clients, suppliers, governmental representatives, and the like tend to have a high degree of uncertainty and unpredictability in them. Such people are not under the direct control of the organization. Accordingly precise rules and role prescriptions often do not prove very effective in dealing with them. The result has been considerable ambiguity in the role prescriptions for boundary jobs, an ambiguity which is matched by the uncertainty surrounding the actions of those on the other side of the interface. This ambiguity has in turn bred conflict, extending both backward into the organization and forward to the representatives of related organizations.

One of the most intensive analyses of this particular source of conflict has involved the purchasing function (59, 60). Purchasing agents usually are given much freedom to establish their own role prescriptions in order that they may be maximally responsive to changing conditions in the marketplace. Often the result has been considerable ambiguity as regards power differentials vis-à-vis other related units of the company. Purchasing agents have developed a variety of tactics calculated to corral this loose-lying power. In the process the potential for conflict with internal units such as engineering and production scheduling has become marked. Purchasing typically wants considerable discretion in deciding what to buy, in what quantity, and when; other units may well desire to exert considerable influence on these same decisions.

Aggressive and Conflict-Prone Personalities

There is ample evidence that certain people are more likely to express aggression openly than others. These individuals have a predisposition to aggression such that they are particularly responsive to threatening or frustrating aspects of their environments, and particularly likely to respond with anger (4). In addition, there are certain individuals such as the creative people discussed in Chapter 6, who exhibit nonconformity, independence, and the like so frequently that they often tend to trigger aggression in others, even if they themselves are not particularly aggressive. Given a sufficient accumulation of such aggressive and conflict-prone personalities in any one situation, the probability that conflict will become open is considerable.

This proclivity becomes even more pronounced where aggression is embedded in group action. For many people the major deterrents to aggression are a fear of punishment and a sense of guilt. In a group or crowd context a process of *sharing the guilt* may occur such that an individual does not anticipate punishment either from others or from his own conscience (21). He tends to believe that if others feel that aggressive behavior is all right, it must be all right for him too. A gradual escalation occurs with each person serving to reduce the other's guilt. Furthermore, there are feelings that so many people could not possibly all be guilty, that punishment for such a large number of people would be unthinkable, and that one can always get lost in the crowd. It is clear that the group context can easily serve to nurture the predisposition to conflict inherent in individual personalities.

Studies conducted to identify characteristics of aggressive people have yielded further evidence regarding the potentiality for conflict (66, 69). People who have tendencies to authoritarianism and dogmatism are particularly conflict-prone. So too are individuals with low self-esteem, and those with a predisposition to distrust and suspicion. These characteristics all contribute to what in clinical psychology and psychiatry is known as a *paranoid* character structure.

Role Dissatisfaction

A final source of conflict is intense dissatisfaction with one's role as defined by the organization and its members (66). Dissatisfied employees are particularly likely to be involved in conflicts. This factor certainly may be related to personality structure; yet it is also true that dissatisfaction may exist quite independently of an aggressive or conflict-prone personality. The major manifestations of conflict produced by dissatisfaction are failure or refusal to work, either temporarily or permanently—thus resulting in absenteeism and separation. There is no evidence to indicate that poor work performance is equally likely to result from dissatisfaction, although in some few cases this may be the case. The findings, where dissatisfaction and poor performance are found together, appear to indicate that the dissatisfaction is a consequence of the performance, rather than the reverse (10, 36).

The Absenteeism Response. A considerable amount of research has been done relating absence rates to job attitudes (45). This research indicates a clear association between extended absenteeism and dissatisfaction toward such factors as immediate supervision, one's co-workers, and the typical working conditions. However, this finding does not extend to such things as the company compensation structure, the company as a place to work, and other organization-based factors. It appears, therefore, that being absent from work is a response to aspects of the immediate work situation more than to any conflict inherent in the individual-organization relationship. High absenteeism thus can be viewed as a conflict response which is tied primarily to problems in the immediate work environment, although it is true that larger organizations tend to have a higher rate of lost time than smaller ones (30).

A specific example of the relationships between absenteeism and such factors as satisfaction with working conditions and the bosses' fairness is provided by a study of 148 female production employees in two companies (23). The data are given in Table 13–4. In both instances those with more absences have more negative attitudes.

The Separation Response. Unlike absenteeism, turnover appears to correlate frequently with overall satisfaction measures dealing with organizational factors, as well as with measures focused on the immediate work context (45). Workers who leave tend to be dissatisfied with management practices, working conditions, compensation, the fairness of company policies, the amount of required overtime, immediate supervision, co-workers, and the nature of the work. They are often concerned about excessive role ambiguity (38) and experience extensive inequity (62). Thus the breadth of their complaints is much greater than for those who are merely absent frequently. This is not surprising in view of the more drastic nature of their response. On the other hand, it is not necessarily true that very dissatisfied workers will leave. This depends in large part on the

Table 13-4 Relationships Between Absenteeism and Measures of Dissatisfaction Among Female Production Workers

Working days missed during the past year	Compared to other companies in this area, working conditions here (heat, light, ventilation, and so on) are:		
	Very good or good	Fair, bad, or very bad	
0–5	36 %	64 %	100 %
6 or more	17 %	83 %	100 %
	Do you think your boss is fair?		
	Always or most of the time	Sometimes, seldom, or never	
0–5	77 %	23 %	100 %
6 or more	56 %	44 %	100 %

Source: Adapted from A. Gerstenfeld, "Employee Absenteeism: New Insights," *Business Horizons*, Vol. 12 (1969), No. 5, 55.

nature of the labor market and the availability of other work. Where other jobs are not available the individual may well stay while remaining dissatisfied; in such a situation conflict is likely to manifest itself in other ways.

The Prevention of Conflict

With some understanding of how conflict is produced it is now possible to turn to the actual management of conflict, that is, the procedures used in carrying out the coordination function. In the early writings Fayol gave special attention to such techniques as periodic conferences of department heads to resolve differences, and the use of liaison managers, usually from a general staff, who integrated the work of various groups (19). These approaches are important. But the variety of procedures now available to achieve coordination has grown considerably beyond what Fayol discussed. As indicated at the beginning of this chapter the consequences of open conflict tend to be negative for an organization and thus conflict prevention by managers is desirable. A problem arises, however, because conflict is frequently a by-product of other factors that contribute to goal accomplishment. Examples of such factors that tend to have positive consequences for organizations, while carrying with them considerable potential for conflict, are competition among peers, creativity and originality, the use of diverse resources in decision making and problem solving, organizational change and growth. There is no reason to interpret this relationship as indicating a positive value of conflict itself as some writers have done. Rather what appears to be the case is that conflict frequently is found in association with other things that are organizationally desirable.

The real managerial challenge in this situation is to find some method of preventing the conflict from becoming debilitating, while retaining the full positive potential of competition, creativity, or change. It is not very difficult to manage conflict by holding to the status quo, tradition, and the solutions of the past; it is quite another thing to manage it while fostering creative ideas and widespread change. The greatest risk in using any of the prevention techniques considered here is that the solution may work too well. Conflict may be prevented, but at the expense of eliminating the very things that were originally desired, and that were the reason for permitting conflict to become a possibility in the first place. It is crucial not to "throw the baby out with the bath."

Clear and Accepted Role Prescriptions

One method for dealing with problems created by role conflict and ambiguity, joint decision making, intergroup competition, and the like is to establish clear role prescriptions in the beginning before conflict situations develop and emotions are aroused. The idea is to gain acceptance of policies, organization structures, job descriptions—in short, a comprehensive set of role prescriptions which define the jurisdictions of groups and individuals—on a rational, goal-related basis. Later, if conflict becomes imminent, these role prescriptions can be appealed to as a basis for resolution. Since they have previously been accepted as legitimate by all parties, they are more likely to act as an effective buffer.

Clear and definite role prescriptions can serve to make groups and individuals more autonomous and to reduce the need for joint decision making. If it is established, for instance, that decisions regarding the use of psychological tests are to be made by personnel representatives rather than line management, then there is no need for joint decisions in this area. Under such conditions, where there is considerable autonomy, competition between groups—personnel and manufacturing, for example—would not be expected to have a negative impact on productivity (42). Also the existence of a clear statement regarding who is to make decisions in a particular area serves to ward off the conflict potential inherent in loose-lying power.

An example of how the introduction of clear policies which are accepted as equitable can contribute to conflict prevention is provided by a study of turnover rates and dissatisfaction among female clerical employees in a large manufacturing company's corporate office (27). For some time turnover had remained at about 30 percent a year. An attitude survey indicated considerable dissatisfaction especially with regard to the inconsistent administration of payment procedures. Subsequently wage and salary administration policies were revised to make them more constant across departments, as well as to formalize procedures for giving raises. A specific policy on transfers and promotions was instituted, and revised job descriptions were developed. In short, clearer role prescriptions were introduced which were of a kind the employees could support. As anticipated, satisfaction levels rose considerably, especially with regard to pay and promotions; turnover dropped to 18 percent in the first ensuing year and 12 percent the second.

Hierarchic Coordination

Probably the most frequently used approach in conflict prevention is the application of legitimized hierarchic authority. Like clear and accepted role prescriptions this approach carries with it a major risk that desirable flexibility may be supressed, but applied with appropriate discretion it has considerable value. Within classical management theory it is the preferred approach to coordination (26).

Hierarchic coordination may take a variety of forms. Frequently it involves a decision by an immediate superior on what role behaviors a given person should perform. Thus, if two subordinates are in disagreement on an appropriate course of action, a decision on the matter is obtained from their common superior. Provided the authority of this individual is adequately legitimized, his decision is accepted and actual conflict is prevented. A recent study of managerial decision making at the very highest levels of major corporations indicated that this approach to managing conflict is used frequently in dealing with the differing views of vice-presidents (58). The power of the chief executive was observed repeatedly to be the final arbiter.

Hierarchic authority may also be used to bring sanctions to bear against any manifestation of conflict. Those who engage in conflict, or give any indication that they might, are restricted by the prospect of limitations on salary progress or promotional opportunity, or even of dismissal. Those who avoid any manifestation of conflict are rewarded. Hierarchic procedures of this kind are frequently used with aggressive and conflict-prone personalities. In an extension of this approach, steps are taken to keep from hiring people of this kind in the first place. Personnel selection procedures, in particular the interview, are used to keep those who might be expected to become "troublemakers" from being employed at all.

Structural Integration

A variety of structural arrangements have been introduced into organizations to mediate potential conflicts between groups with differing objectives and values. Fayol's discussion of the use of liaison personnel attached to a general staff, who maintain continuing contact among departments that must engage in joint decision making, has already been noted. Other examples are product managers, project managers, production expediters, and interdepartmental committees and teams. Integrators, whether individual or group, operate primarily to prevent conflict between units that are in a horizontal relationship to each other, but some vertical peacemaking may be involved as well.

Evidence on the relationship between the effectiveness of integrative components of this kind and company success is provided by a study of six firms in the plastics industry (34). An index of the degree of integration actually achieved by the company was developed and then compared with such measures as profit change over the preceding five years, change in sales volume for the preceding five years, and the number of new products developed in the preceding five years taken as a percent of current sales. From Table 13–5 it is apparent that these effectiveness measures are closely associated with integration. The company ranked highest on degree of integration has an average rank of 2.0 on the three performance indexes; the one ranked lowest an average of 5.0.

In their efforts to prevent conflict from having deleterious effects, integrators may function in different ways. One approach is to interpose an integrating unit between units which must engage in joint decision making. Thus in one instance a sales order liaison department was placed between all sales and manufacturing units. All communications between sales and manufacturing had to pass through this integrator group (61). Matters relating to production capacity, sales requirements, delivery schedules,

Table 13-5 *Relationship Between Effectiveness of Integration and Performance for Six Plastics Firms*

	Rank Order			
Company	Change in Profits over 5 years	Change in Sales Volume over 5 years	New Products Developed in Last 5 Years as % of Sales	Degree of Integration
High A	2	3	1	1
High B	1	1	3	2
Medium A	3	2	4	3
Medium B	6	4	2	4
Low A	4	6	6	5
Low B	5	5	5	6

Source: P. R. Lawrence and J. W. Lorsch, *Organization and Environment: Managing Differentiation and Integration* (Boston: Graduate School of Business Administration, Harvard University, 1967), p. 40.

and pricing were worked out through the sales order liaison department without any direct contact between the primary parties.

The use of interdepartmental committees to achieve coordination between units involved in joint decision making has produced mixed results. There is a great tendency for members to continue to represent their own interests and thus fail to collaborate in any meaningful sense (72). If the reward structure can be shifted so that increased pay and promotion are attached to the successful accomplishment of the coordination task, rather than to individual achievement, the likelihood of success is much greater. Rewarding individual members of a coordinating committee for getting the most possible for their own group is not consistent with effective committee operation and coordination.

Superordinate Goals and Cohesive Groups

When two or more groups face the prospect of continued conflict, it is sometimes possible to find a purpose toward which all those involved can strive, thus pulling the groups together. Such a purpose represents a goal above and beyond the objectives of the competing groups—a superordinate goal. When this type of goal can be introduced or mobilized in a given situation, it can serve as a very effective conflict-prevention device (55). A crisis situation which affects all groups equally and which all must band together to conquer is of this nature. It has often been observed that one method of dealing with widespread internal conflict and dissatisfaction in a country is to provide a common enemy, perhaps to the extent of provoking a war. On the other hand, the superordinate goal concept is also involved when a disagreement between departments is resolved by appealing to the goals of the company as a whole, and their rational pursuit (58).

A question remains whether fostering the cohesiveness, the closeness of internal ties, within work groups in and of itself is desirable for an organization in terms of conflict prevention and productivity. The answer appears to be that it may be, but only where the groups are in turn integrated into the organization through commitment to superordinate goals. If a group is cohesive but has negative attitudes toward the company and its representatives, the close ties within the group make it easier for group leaders to mobilize opposition (52). The result may be restriction of output or other evidence of conflict between the group and the organization of which it is a part. Here cohesion has negative implications. On the other hand, cohesion appears to be quite effective in keeping individuals from leaving a company in response to conflict (12).

Confrontation Approaches

An approach to coordination which has achieved considerable impact in recent years involves the use of a neutral third party who engineers the relationship between potentially or actually conflicting parties so as to bring about an open and frank discussion of the sources of disagreement. This approach has its origin in sensitivity or T-group training and is closely allied to organization development as well (see Chapter 9). It may be used with either individuals (65) or groups (7).

The key ingredient is that a confrontation is arranged in which the parties openly discuss their differences. This approach contrasts with those of smoothing over differences and pretending they do not exist, or of a forced resolution on orders from higher authority. The third party mediator attempts to assist the other parties in learning to understand each others' points of view and eventually to come to trust each other enough to engage in effective joint problem solving. Every effort is made to bring differing objectives, values, and perceptions out into the open where they can be dealt with and to neutralize aggressive personalities.

In group applications it is common to obtain answers to the following three questions from all those involved:

1. How do we see ourselves in relation to the relevant other?
2. How does the relevant other see us?
3. How do we see the relevant other?

The answers to these questions are then exchanged between groups and form the basis for the confrontation discussion. Such an approach clearly reveals differences in values, attitudes, perceptions, and information. There is evidence that it does bring about changes in attitudes of a kind which might be expected to prevent conflict (25).

Further evidence on the potential value of confrontation is given in Table 13–6. These data should be related to the performance measures given in Table 13–5 for the same six firms. The confrontation score was developed based on questionnaire responses obtained from managers within the companies (34). It is apparent that the firms, such as High A and High B, with the better performance records were more likely to utilize open confrontation to deal with conflict. In this particular study, however, confrontations were not necessarily carried out in the presence of a neutral third party.

Table 13–6 Extent to Which Confrontation Was Used in Six Plastics Firms with Differing Performance Levels

Company	Confrontation Score
High A	13.0
High B	13.1
Medium A	12.4
Medium B	12.0
Low A	11.7
Low B	11.8

Source: P. R. Lawrence and J. W. Lorsch, *Organization and Environment: Managing Differentiation and Integration* (Boston: Graduate School of Business Administration, Harvard University, 1967), p. 77.

Providing Valid Information

Although open information exchange is unlikely to prevent conflict in and of itself, it can make a sizable contribution in that direction. Distortion and blocking of communication flows may easily lead to differences in perceptions, role dissatisfaction, and difficulties in joint decision-making situations. Open communication channels help to eradicate these sources of conflict and thus tend to be associated with more cooperative behavior (16).

Several studies which demonstrate the value of various kinds of management information systems as an aid to coordination under joint decision-making conditions have been conducted (22). To date MIS has proved most useful in dealing with certain sequential scheduling situations. The requisite information is developed so that delays can be minimized and resources utilized as fully as possible. To the extent the management information system can actually take over the decision process in such situations, joint decision making is reduced and a major potential source of conflict is eliminated. This feature of MIS is only beginning to be appreciated. It may well be that the conflict prevention aspects of information systems will prove to be one of their most valuable contributions in the future.

Appeal Procedures and Organizational Due Process

Appeal procedures, which constitute what amount to organizational legal systems, are designed to provide an equitable adjudication of differences in accordance with previously established guidelines. The extent to which these procedures actually approximate the due process of law varies considerably. At one extreme is the use of an open door policy by high level managers. Any employee can come in, thus bypassing lower level managers who may be responsible for his complaint, and air his dissatisfactions. He appeals to top management to arbitrate the disagreement or to change the conditions that disturb him. The approach tends to be informal, there are few formal "laws" to guide decisions, and the top executive is rarely in a position to be completely impartial. Furthermore, the bypassed superior may well make things difficult for the subordinate who appeals. The open door approach therefore often fails to contribute much to conflict prevention (57).

Other more formal approaches, however, can prove very effective. These come much closer to approximating the due process of law. Formal grievance procedures negotiated under a union-management contract are of this kind, but there are many appeal systems in existence which operate independent of union participation. If appeal procedures are to achieve real due process, judgment must ultimately be rendered by an outside, impartial arbitrator, should agreement fail within the organization. Systems with and without union involvement may include this kind of arbitration, although it is much more common under grievance systems negotiated with a union (51).

Examples of some typical appeal systems are given in Figure 13–2. The appeal process starts at the lowest level. If the dispute is not settled to the satisfaction of all parties at that level, it moves up to the next level. This process is repeated as necessary until a final judgment is made at the highest level. In Figure 13–2 this is the president. It could also be an outside arbitrator. The variant involving the personnel department at some level is much more common than the all-line system, especially in the medium and larger firms where formal appeal systems are most frequently found (51).

Appeal systems of this kind are widely used to prevent conflict in many types of organizations ranging from the Catholic Church to government. However, they are rarely used to deal with disagreements at the managerial level. In certain respects this is surprising, and probably unfortunate. In a study conducted in two research laboratories, one governmental and the other industrial, the number of individuals reporting having experienced disputes with higher-level managers increased steadily from the professional to the first-line supervisory to the second-line supervisory levels (18).

Figure 13–2 Steps in Formal Appeal Systems

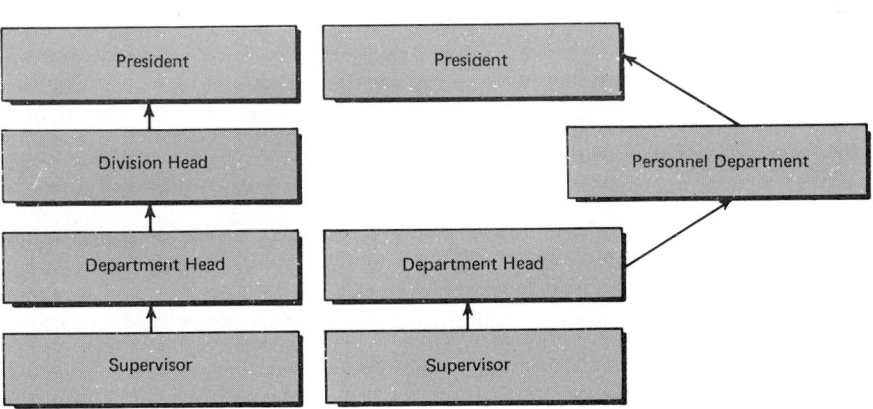

Such findings suggest that the need for appeal procedures may be greatest above the level of the rank-and-file employee. Yet it is at the lower levels that these procedures are most widely used. In many companies the negotiated grievance system involving the union is the only one that exists.

Bargaining

A final approach to coordination involves bargaining or negotiating a solution so that differences in objectives are reconciled short of open conflict. In Chapter 2 negotiating was described as in many respects closely allied to representing. This is the type of negotiating that bank loan officers, for instance, undertake. But there is also negotiating within an organization, which is carried out to achieve coordination among groups and individuals. Here negotiation melds into the total coordination function.

Three polar types of bargaining relationships have been identified, although most actual bargaining situations involve elements of more than one type (69). There is first *distributive* bargaining, which occurs when differences in objectives and values are clearly in evidence. The orientations of the parties yield what game theorists refer to as a fixed-sum game, in that one person's gain is the other person's loss; a win-lose situation exists. Bargaining operates to distribute that which is available among the parties in a peaceable manner. If bargaining fails or deadlocks, one can assume that open conflict will occur. There is in fact a good chance that bargaining will not achieve the conflict prevention objective when a pure distributive relationship exists.

Integrative bargaining involves joint problem solving. It occurs where there are common or complementary interests, often in the form of superordinate goals. Integrative potential exists when the nature of a disagreement permits solutions which benefit both parties, or at least where one party's gains do not represent equal losses for the other party. Since conflict within an organization occurs in a context of common task and maintenance goals, there always is integrative potential in such situations. But in many cases this potential is not realized because perceptions and orientations operate to produce a distributive situation.

A third type of bargaining relationship, which in many cases is more properly defined as an *aspect* of bargaining, is *attitudinal structuring*. Here the attitudes of the parties are altered during the course of the bargaining interactions. Ideally, if conflict prevention is to be the result, there should be a shift toward greater friendliness, more trust and respect, and a reduction in competitiveness. In contrast to the joint decision-making characteristic of distributive and integrative bargaining, attitudinal structuring is a social and emotional process. Attitudes and relationships change so as to facilitate conflict prevention in much the same manner as with confrontation approaches.

A major shortcoming of the bargaining approach to conflict prevention is the pronounced tendency to move to distributive relationships when opposing groups are involved. There is a strong proclivity for bargaining representatives to hold fast to previously established group positions out of loyalty and responsiveness to group pressures (5). Where groups plan strategies in advance, and then bargain through group representatives, bargaining is most likely to fail. This, of course, is the nature of the situation in most union-management relationships. Where two *individuals* bargain to work out their differences or where the group interaction is limited to studying issues rather than planning strategies, bargaining is a much more effective conflict prevention approach (2). There also is evidence that where the bargaining representative is the type of person who is particularly prone to risk taking, there is a greater tendency to hold fast rather than yield (57). Thus two high risk takers can easily deadlock, with the result that the bargaining approach fails.

Labor–Management Conflict

As indicated at the beginning of this chapter, there is no intention of considering the labor relations field in any depth here. Yet so much of the work dealing with conditions for conflict and with conflict prevention has been conducted in this sphere that a separate discussion seems warranted. However, such topics as labor law, union organization, and contract terms, which are typically covered in detail in any treatment of the personnel and industrial relations field as a whole, are not of concern.

The Potential for Conflict

All of the conditions for conflict that have been mentioned may exist in a particular labor-management relationship, and a number of them always do. Joint decision making is invariably present, often with the type of unlegitimized imbalance of power that seems to maximize the chances of conflict. First, there is the type of generalized joint decision making

Coordinating and Controlling: Sustaining and Restoring Input Potential Levels

on the issues that management and the union undertake at the time of contract negotiation. Second, there is the continuous joint decision making that occurs between union stewards representing work groups and representatives of management on a day-to-day basis in the work place.

The degree of conflict potential inherent in the latter situation appears to vary considerably from one kind of group to another. Four types of industrial work groups have been identified, each characterized by differing propensities insofar as conflict is concerned (49). These groups and the differences between them in terms of grievance activity, spontaneous outbursts, internal unity, union participation, and management's evaluation are noted in Figure 13-3. The erratic and strategic groups emerge as

Figure 13-3 Conflict-Related Differences Between Four Types of Industrial Work Groups

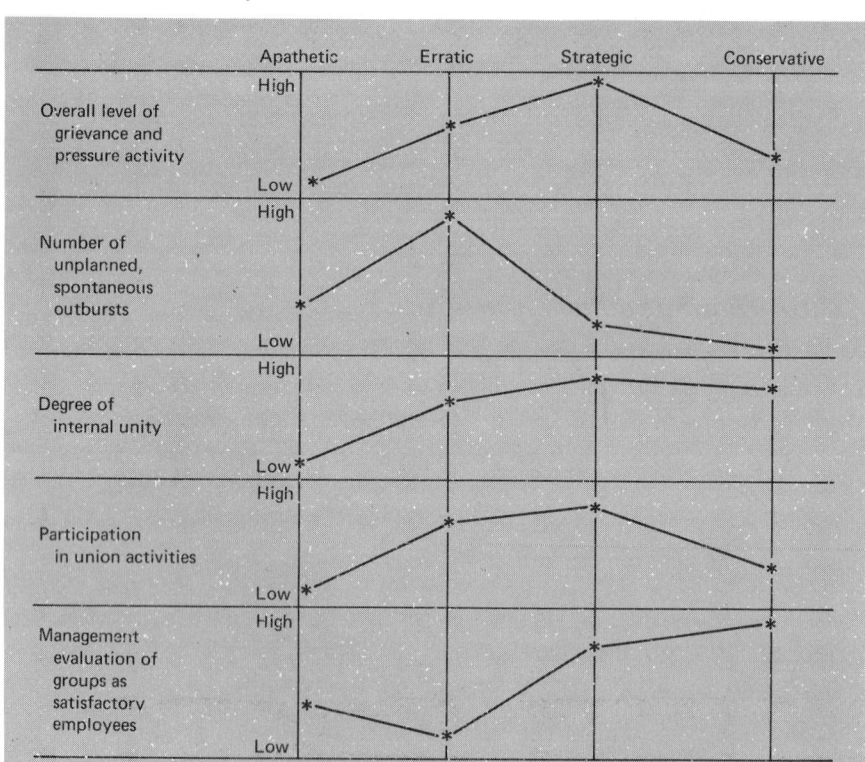

Source: L. R. Sayles, *Behavior of Industrial Work Groups—Prediction and Control* (New York: Wiley, 1958), p. 39.

considerably more conflict-prone than the apathetic and conservative, although the specific manifestations tend to differ. Underlying each of the four types of groups appear to be differing technologies and conditions of work. These job differences in turn produce differences in the extent and kind of joint decision making with management.

Differences in objectives and values between management and union have been widely recognized and documented, especially through analysis of cases which have been appealed all the way to the arbitration level (24). These differences are often paralleled by sharp differences in perceptions. Table 13-7 gives an indication of how union stewards and officers tend to depart from managers in their reactions to certain words used frequently in the industrial relations context. It is apparent that the union leaders respond much more favorably to all the words (50). In a sense these words appear to *mean* different things to union and management. Such differences can easily provoke conflict behavior. When a union officer mentions a strike he is talking about something "good," but a middle manager hears something very "bad."

Loose-lying power with its potential for role ambiguity may or may not be a significant source of labor-management conflict depending on the situation. The same holds true for aggressive and conflict-prone personalities. There is some evidence that union leadership positions may attract individuals who are conflict-prone (8). In one study, groups of union and management trainees were contrasted in terms of their performance on a number of personality measures. Although not more aggressive in an overall sense, the union trainees did reveal a long-standing propensity to

Table 13-7 Words Which Consistently Elicit Differences in Favorableness Ranking Between Union Leaders and Managers

	Favorableness Ranking			
Words	Shop Stewards ($N=45$)	Union Officers ($N=41$)	Foremen ($N=73$)	Middle Managers ($N=28$)
Labor	1.2	1.2	1.7	2.1
Strike	1.6	1.5	4.2	4.9
Solidarity	1.3	1.2	2.6	2.2
Seniority	1.2	1.2	2.7	3.2
Union	1.1	1.2	2.4	2.4
Organizer	1.3	1.3	2.7	2.6
Grievance	1.4	1.4	2.9	3.1

Source: M. M. Schwartz, H. F. Stark, and H. R. Schiffman, "Responses of Union and Management Leaders to Emotionally-Toned Industrial Relations Terms," *Personnel Psychology*, Vol. 23 (1970), 364.

overt conflict with authority figures and a background of nonconformity. The managers did not emerge as being nearly as conflict prone. However, evidence on the personality characteristics of those particular managers who spend most of their time in labor relations activities was not obtained. It may be that they tend to be as conflict prone as the union representatives.

Role dissatisfaction is a common ingredient in labor-management conflict. Historically unions have found employment situations that are characterized by widespread discontent fertile ground for their organizing efforts (64). Once organized such employees often take the lead in pushing their demands on management. They may well vote to reject settlements their leaders support, thus forcing the situation to the point of a strike. Unions typically resist attitude surveys conducted by management among company employees because the surveys might unearth sources of dissatisfaction that management could correct on a unilateral basis, thus taking the initiative away from the union.

Conflict Prevention Procedures

In view of the many factors contributing to labor-management conflict, it is surprising that strikes and other forms of work disruption such as slowdowns, sabotage, and planned absenteeism are not more rampant than they are. What success has been achieved in preventing open conflict is primarily attributable to two procedures: appeal systems and bargaining.

This is not to say that other conflict prevention procedures are not used in the labor-management area, nor is it true that appeal systems and bargaining are necessarily the best approaches. Clear and specific job description and payment systems based on accepted job evaluation procedures can make a sizable contribution. Approaches utilizing superordinate goals, problem solving, and confrontation techniques have been found successful (7). Many companies make extensive use of employee information campaigns and downward channels of communication. Yet for many years the real weight of conflict prevention in the labor-management area has fallen on appeal systems and bargaining.

Appeal Systems. The concept behind the use of grievance procedures negotiated between management and union is that these procedures will replace emotion with rationality and justice. The intent is that precedents established by previous practice, agreements such as those embodied in the contract, and past grievance decisions will override attitudes and feelings to the point where conflict is prevented. A question may be raised as to whether this objective is typically achieved.

Results obtained from a study in which the grievance decisions made in case situations were compared for individuals with varying attitudes toward unions revealed a strong tendency for attitudes to influence the positions taken (71). However, precedents had an effect too. If a strongly pro-management individual was faced with a set of precedents that argued for a pro-union decision, he was likely to follow the precedents rather than his feelings. This tendency was not in evidence among those with pro-union attitudes, who tended to reject precedents that were dissonant with their attitudes. Thus the study indicates that the conflict-prevention value of appeal systems is likely to be greater on the management than on the union side and that although the effects of differences in attitudes and values are partially vitiated, the grievance process is not sufficient to accomplish this objective completely.

These conclusions hold where the grievance process is operating with reasonable efficiency. In actual fact there are many systems that have almost completely broken down, especially in mass-production industries (41). In many cases the number of grievances filed has increased to such proportions that processing becomes impossible. The machinery is overwhelmed, and settlements may take as long as ten years. In some such instances companies have simply bought out the backlog by making payments irrespective of merit. In other instances dispositions have been made en masse, again with little attention to the facts. Where appeal systems have become demoralized in this manner, they no longer possess much conflict-prevention potential. In fact they may well become instruments of conflict and channels for communicating the antagonistic messages.

Collective Bargaining. Under existing law in the United States a company is required to bargain with a union which has been certified as the representative of its employees and to do so in "good faith." Thus bargaining has been given a central position in the prevention of labor-management conflict. It has been so established by public policy, and in fact that policy seeks to foster insofar as possible a degree of equality between the parties such that neither will be able to completely dominate the other.

The major difficulty with the bargaining solution as it has developed since the passage of the Wagner Act in 1935 is that the result in a very high proportion of cases has been distributive bargaining, with all the deficiencies noted previously. Prime among these is the fact that such an approach often fails to achieve its conflict-prevention objective. Yet approaches involving sizable amounts of integrative bargaining and attitudinal structuring have appeared with some frequency in recent years, especially where new problems such as the advent of a more automated technology must be solved (43). In many instances the shift out of the distributive mold has been successful in preventing conflict, but it also appears to place a major strain on the relationships between bargaining representatives and their constituencies. Union leaders in particular face the threat of being voted out of office when they relinquish the distributive approach. There is reason to believe that changes in existing constraints in the form of laws and legal interpretations may be required before bargaining approaches of a more fruitful nature emerge on a large scale.

This chapter has dealt with matters of prevention and input-sustaining mediators, with particular emphasis on conflict. The discussion now moves to problems in the area of control of conflict and of performance in general, where input potential has already been lost and action is needed to restore it.

Questions

1. What are some of the potential sources of conflict when the marketing department of a company must work with the company's research scientists to develop a marketing program for a very complex new product?
2. What is the difference between coordination and control as related to conflict? What would you anticipate happening to an organization where there is an extensive breakdown of such coordination and control procedures?
3. The major approaches to preventing open labor-management conflict have been appeal systems and bargaining. Yet there is no logical reason why other conflict prevention procedures might not prove at least equally effective. How would you envisage these other procedures being used in dealing with labor-management conflict?
4. What differences in the sources of conflict and in the applicable techniques of coordination would you anticipate finding between a small professional organization and a large administrative one?
5. How do role conflict and role ambiguity relate to conflict between individuals and groups in organizations? Describe a specific situation where modification of role prescriptions might serve to prevent conflict. Can you think of any risks for an organization that extensive use of role prescription modification might entail?

References

1. Baldridge, J. V. *Power and Conflict in the University*. New York: Wiley, 1971.
2. Bass, B. M. "Effects on the Subsequent Performance of Negotiators of Studying Issues or Planning Strategies Alone or in Groups." *Psychological Monographs*, Vol. 80 (1966), No. 6, 1–31.
3. Bass, B. M., and G. Dunteman. "Biases in the Evaluation of One's Own Group, Its Allies and Opponents." *Journal of Conflict Resolution*, Vol. 7 (1963), 16–20.
4. Berkowitz, L. *Aggression: A Social Psychological Analysis*. New York: McGraw-Hill, 1962.
5. Blake, R. R., and J. S. Mouton. "Loyalty of Representatives to Ingroup Positions During Intergroup Competition." *Sociometry*, Vol. 24 (1961), 177–183.
6. Blake, R. R., and J. S. Mouton, "Overevaluation of Own Group's Product in Intergroup Competition." *Journal of Abnormal and Social Psychology*, Vol. 64 (1962), 237–238.
7. Blake, R. R., H. A. Shepard, and J. S. Mouton. *Managing Intergroup Conflict in Industry*. Houston, Texas: Gulf, 1964.
8. Bogard, H. M. "Union and Management Trainees—A Comparative Study of Personality and Occupational Choice." *Journal of Applied Psychology*, Vol. 44 (1960), 56–63.
9. Boulding, K. "A Pure Theory of Conflict Applied to Organizations." In G. Fisk (ed.), *The Frontiers of Management Psychology*. New York: Harper & Row, 1964, pp. 41–49.
10. Bowen, D., and J. P. Siegel. "Relationship Between Satisfaction and Performance: The Question of Causality." *Proceedings, 78th Annual Convention, American Psychological Association*, 1970, 583–584.
11. Caplow, T., and R. J. McGee. *The Academic Marketplace*. New York: Basic Books, 1958.
12. Cartwright, D. "The Nature of Group Cohesiveness." In D. Cartwright and A. Zander (eds.), *Group Dynamics: Research and Theory*. New York: Harper & Row, 1968, pp. 91–109.
13. Dalton, M. "Changing Staff-Line Relationships." *Personnel Administration*, Vol. 29 (1966), No. 2, 3–5, 40–48.
14. Dearborn, D. C., and H. A. Simon, "Selective Perception: A Note on the Departmental Identifications of Executives." *Sociometry*, Vol. 21 (1958), 140–144.
15. Dutton, J. M. "Analysis of Interdepartmental Decision-Making." In R. W. Millman and M. P. Hottenstein (eds.), *Promising Research Directions*.

Proceedings of the 27th Annual Meeting. Academy of Management, 1968, pp. 85–100.
16. Emshoff, J. R. Analysis of Behavioral Systems. New York: Macmillan, 1971.
17. Evan, W. M. "Conflict and Performance in R and D Organizations." Industrial Management Review, Vol. 7 (1965), 37–45.
18. Evan, W. M. "Due Process of Law in a Governmental and an Industrial Research Organization." In E. B. Flippo (ed.), Evolving Concepts in Management. Academy of Management Proceedings, 1965, pp. 110–119.
19. Fayol, H. General and Industrial Management. London: Pitman, 1949.
20. Follett, M. P. Freedom and Co-ordination. London: Management Publications Trust, 1949.
21. Freud, S. Group Psychology and the Analysis of the Ego. New York: Bantam Books, 1960.
22. Galbraith, J. R. "Achieving Integration Through Information Systems." In P. P. LeBreton and W. G. Scott (eds.), Organization Structure and Behavior. Academy of Management Proceedings, 1969, pp. 111–120.
23. Gerstenfeld, A. "Employee Absenteeism: New Insights." Business Horizons, Vol. 12 (1969), No. 5, 51–60.
24. Ginzberg, E., and I. E. Berg. Democratic Values and the Rights of Management. New York: Columbia University Press, 1963.
25. Golembiewski, R. T., and A. Blumberg. "The Laboratory Approach to Organization Change: Confrontation Design." Academy of Management Journal, Vol. 11 (1968), 199–210.
26. Gulick, L. "Notes on the Theory of Organization." In L. Gulick and L. Urwick (eds.), Papers on the Science of Administration. New York: The Institute of Public Administration, 1937, pp. 31–37.
27. Hulin, C. L. "Effects of Changes in Job-Satisfaction Levels on Employee Turnover." Journal of Applied Psychology, Vol. 52 (1968), 122–126.
28. Hunt, J. G. "Status Congruence in Organizations: Effects and Suggested Research." In R. W. Millman and M. P. Hottenstein (eds.), Promising Research Directions. Academy of Management Proceedings, 1968, pp. 178–184.
29. Hunt, J. G. "Status Congruence: An Important Organization Function." Personnel Administration, Vol. 32 (1969), No. 1, 19–24.
30. Ingham, G. K. Size of Industrial Organization and Worker Behavior. Cambridge, Eng.: Cambridge University Press, 1970.
31. Kelly, J. "Make Conflict Work for You." Harvard Business Review, Vol. 28 (1970), No. 4, 103–113.
32. Klein, S. M., and J. R. Maher. "Decision-Making Autonomy and Perceived Conflict Among First-Level Management." Personnel Psychology, Vol. 23 (1970), 481–492.
33. Korman, A. K. "Selective Perception Among First-Line Supervisors." Personnel Administration, Vol. 26 (1963), No. 5, 31–36.

34. Lawrence, P. R., and J. W. Lorsch. *Organization and Environment: Managing Differentiation and Integration.* Boston: Graduate School of Business Administration, Harvard University, 1967.
35. Litterer, J. A. *The Analysis of Organizations.* New York: Wiley, 1965.
36. Locke, E. A. "Job Satisfaction and Job Performance: A Theoretical Analysis." *Organizational Behavior and Human Performance*, Vol. 5 (1970), 484–500.
37. Lorsch, J. W. "Organizing for Diversification." In P. P. Le Breton and W. G. Scott (eds.), *Organization Structure and Behavior. Academy of Management Proceedings*, 1969, *pp.* 87–100.
38. Lyons, T. F. "Role Clarity, Need for Clarity, Satisfaction, Tension, and Withdrawal." *Organizational Behavior and Human Performance*, Vol. 6 (1971), 99–110.
39. March, J. G., and H. A. Simon. *Organizations.* New York: Wiley, 1958.
40. McFarland, D. E. *Management: Principles and Practices.* New York: Macmillan, 1970.
41. McKersie, R. B. "Avoiding Written Grievances by Problem-Solving: An Outside View." *Personnel Psychology*, Vol. 17 (1964), 367–379.
42. Miller, L. K., and R. L. Hamblin. "Interdependence, Differential Rewarding, and Productivity." *American Sociological Review.* Vol. 28 (1963), 768–777.
43. Miner, J. B. *Personnel and Industrial Relations: A Managerial Approach.* New York: Macmillan, 1969.
44. Miner, J. B. "Changes in Student Attitudes Toward Bureaucratic Role Prescriptions During the 1960s." *Administrative Science Quarterly*, Vol. 16 (1971), 351–364.
45. Miner, J. B., and J. F. Brewer. "The Management of Ineffective Performance." In M. D. Dunnette (ed.), *Handbook of Industrial and Organizational Psychology.* Chicago: Rand McNally, 1973.
46. Ritzer, G., and H. M. Trice. *An Occupation in Conflict: A Study of the Personnel Manager.* Ithaca, N.Y.: New York State School of Industrial and Labor Relations, Cornell University, 1969.
47. Rizzo, J. R., R. J. House, and S. I. Lirtzman. "Role Conflict and Ambiguity in Complex Organizations." *Administrative Science Quarterly*, Vol. 15 (1970), 150–163.
48. Rosen, R. A. H. "Foreman Role Conflict: An Expression of Contradictions in Organizational Goals." *Industrial and Labor Relations Review*, Vol. 23 (1970), 541–552.
49. Sayles, L. R. *Behavior of Industrial Work Groups–Prediction and Control.* New York: Wiley, 1958.
50. Schwartz, M. M., H. F. Stark, and H. R. Schiffman. "Response of Union and Management Leaders to Emotionally-Toned Industrial Relations

Terms." *Personnel Psychology*, Vol. 23 (1970), 361–367.
51. Scott, W. G. *The Management of Conflict: Appeal Systems in Organizations*. Homewood, Ill.: Irwin, 1965.
52. Seashore, S. E. *Group Cohesiveness in the Industrial Work Group*. Ann Arbor: Survey Research Center, University of Michigan, 1954.
53. Seiler, J. A. "Diagnosing Interdepartmental Conflict." *Harvard Business Review*, Vol. 41 (1963), No. 5, 121–132.
54. Sethi, N. K. "Mary Parker Follett: Pioneer in Management Theory." *Academy of Management Journal*, Vol. 5 (1962), 214–221.
55. Sherif, M. *In Common Predicament*. Boston: Houghton Mifflin, 1966.
56. Sherif, M., O. J. Harvey, B. J. White, W. R. Hood, and C. W. Sherif. *Intergroup Conflict and Cooperation: The Robbers Cave Experiment*. Norman: University of Oklahoma Book Exchange, 1961.
57. Shull, F. A., A. L. Delbecq, and L. L. Cummings. *Organizational Decision Making*. New York: McGraw-Hill, 1970.
58. Stagner, R. "Resolving Top-Level Managerial Disagreements." *Business Topics*, Vol. 13 (1965), No. 1, 15–22.
59. Strauss, G. "Tactics of Lateral Relationships: The Purchasing Agent." *Administrative Science Quarterly*, Vol. 7 (1962), 161–186.
60. Strauss, G. "Workflow Frictions, Interfunctional Rivalry, and Professionalism: A Case Study of Purchasing Agents." *Human Organization*, Vol. 23 (1964), No. 2, 137–149.
61. Sykes, A. J. M., and J. Bates. "A Study in Production-Sales Liaison." *Management International*, Vol. 5/6 (1964), 57–67.
62. Telly, C. S., W. L. French, and W. G. Scott. "The Relationship of Inequity to Turnover among Hourly Workers." *Administrative Science Quarterly*, Vol. 16 (1971), 164–172.
63. Thompson, J. D. *Organizations in Action*. New York: McGraw-Hill, 1967.
64. Vogel, A. "Your Clerical Workers Are Ripe for Unionism." *Harvard Business Review*, Vol. 49 (1971), No. 2, 48–54.
65. Walton, R. E. *Interpersonal Peacemaking: Confrontations and Third-Party Consultation*. Reading, Mass.: Addison-Wesley, 1969.
66. Walton, R. E., and J. M. Dutton. "The Management of Interdepartmental Conflict: A Model and Review." *Administrative Science Quarterly*, Vol. 14 (1969), 73–84.
67. Walton, R. E., J. M. Dutton, and T. P. Cafferty. "Organizational Context and Interdepartmental Conflict." *Administrative Science Quarterly*, Vol. 14 (1969), 522–542.
68. Walton, R. E., J. M. Dutton, and H. G. Fitch. "A Study of Conflict in the Process, Structure, and Attitudes of Lateral Relationships." In A. H. Rubenstein and C. J. Haberstroh (eds.), *Some Theories of Organization*. Homewood, Ill.: Irwin, 1966, pp. 444–465.

69. Walton, R. E., and R. B. McKersie. *A Behavioral Theory of Labor Negotiations*. New York: McGraw-Hill, 1965.
70. Wrenn, D. A. "Interface and Interorganizational Coordination." *Academy of Management Journal*, Vol. 10 (1967), 69–81.
71. Zand, D. E., and W. E. Steckman. "Resolving Industrial Conflict—An Experimental Study of the Effects of Attitudes and Precedent." In G. G. Somers (ed.), *Proceedings of the Twenty-First Annual Winter Meeting, Industrial Relations Research Association*, 1969, pp. 348–359.
72. Zander, A., and D. Wolfe. "Administrative Rewards and Coordination Among Committee Members." *Administrative Science Quarterly*, Vol. 9 (1964), 50–69.

14 Control Procedures and Human Resource Utilization

I. The Control Model
 1. Types of Measures
 2. Types of Standards
 3. Types of Corrective Actions

II. Performance Control
 1. Performance Analysis
 2. Corrective Procedures
 3. An Example
    a. Case Description
    b. Analysis

III. The Auditing Approach
 1. Nonfinancial Measures
 2. External Management Audits
    a. Investor Data
    b. Audits of Management Quality
 3. Responses to Audit

IV. Accounting, Human Resources, and Behavior
 1. Human Assets and Company Value
    a. Significance of Human Asset Measurement
    b. Methods of Evaluation
 2. Human Assets and Managerial Performance
 3. Responses to Accounting Control Systems
    a. Types of Responses
    b. Sources of Problems
    c. Effective Control

Management control is closely tied to planning at one end of the process and often to direction at the other. It appears to subsume many aspects of the management functions of evaluating and investigating as they have been described by some writers (see Chapter 2). It invariably requires some form of communication and frequently there is a decision-making requirement. It may operate to erase the effects of conflict or eliminate the conflict itself where coordination has failed in its input-sustaining intent.

These multiple relationships with other aspects of managerial work have created a situation where the term *control* is used with a great variety of meanings. In fact the word has achieved such a high level of ambiguity in the management literature that anyone writing on the subject at the present time is almost forced to define it for his purposes before proceeding. For this reason our discussion starts with a treatment of the control model—what it is and what it is not—thus providing a definition for the present purposes. Against this backdrop, later sections of the chapter deal with specific types of control procedures as they relate to organizational utilization of human resources.

The Control Model

Probably the greatest confusion associated with the use of the word *control* arises because it has frequently been used as synonymous with *directing*. In this sense it refers to the use of influence, of power or authority however legitimized. Thus one major program of research has been concerned with the study of control defined as "any process in which a person or group of persons or organization of persons determines, that is, intentionally affects, the behavior of another person, group or organization" (47). This is *not* the sense in which control is used in this volume, although it is true that directing *may* be involved at some point as one feature of the total control process.

The control model as it is used here is outlined in Figure 14-1. Control involves a comparison against some previously established standard and then taking appropriate corrective action when an unacceptable deviation occurs. This corrective action may involve the exercise of authority and thus directing, but this need not be the case. For instance, the appropriate corrective action may be to revise the existing standards so as to make them more realistic in view of existing employee capabilities.

The model of Figure 14–1 describes an open-loop control system, which is the most common type where human resources are involved. Such a control procedure does not operate automatically to correct deviations as they are identified. Rather a decision-making or diagnostic step intervenes. This process of deciding what is wrong in order to select an *appropriate* corrective action may extend over a considerable period of time. It often does, for instance, when physicians carry out a series of diagnostic tests to identify a disease and prescribe a treatment appropriate to the specific nature of the disorder. A fully closed control system operates without this human diagnostic step. The existence of a given deviation triggers a corrective action which feeds back on performance and corrects it automatically, much in the manner of a thermostat's action in maintaining a set temperature. Computer-based control systems, as they are used in manufacturing for example, are typically of the closed-loop variety.

It is the nature of control procedures that they introduce corrective action only when an unacceptable deviation occurs. They are input-*restoring* mediators. Thus performance may fluctuate widely within the acceptable zone without corrective action being mobilized. A manager may spend a large amount of money or very little; no corrective action will be taken as long as he stays within his budget. But should he commit himself to sums in excess of his budget, corrective action is introduced—if possible, to get expenditures back inside the budget, certainly to adjust payments so that the same situation does not occur again. The corrective action may be as simple as a revised budget, or as drastic as the replacement of the manager.

The literature of control contains a number of discussions of what is variously called precontrol (26) or forward-looking control (27). This concept does not appear in the model of Figure 14–1 and is inconsistent with the definition of control used here. Precontrol is basically preventive

Figure 14–1   Model of Control Process

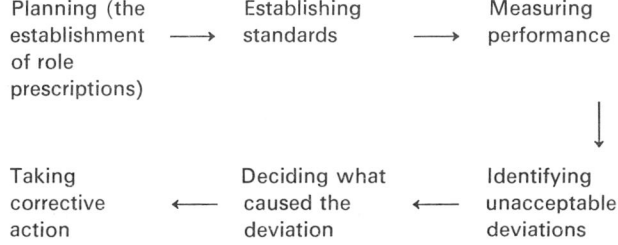

and input-sustaining in nature. Thus the actions a manager might take to prevent expenditures beyond his budget (when faced with the prospect that such expenditures might otherwise occur at some point in the future) would fit the definition of precontrol. Actions of this kind are not intended to restore performance to an acceptable level and thus control a deviation from standard that has already occurred. They seek rather to prevent the deviation and to sustain performance. In the context of the theoretical model of the management process set forth in Chapter 2, therefore, they are more closely allied to coordination than to control. This is not to say that preventing potential deviations before they occur is necessarily less important than after-the-fact correction. Experience does indicate, however, that precontrol is rarely so effective that corrective actions need never be mobilized.

Types of Measures

The number of measures that may be introduced into the control process appears to be almost boundless. In the past there has been a tendency to view control largely in financial terms and thus to stress financial measures. Increasingly, however, the control concept has broadened to include a much more diverse array of control measures (35). Thus physical measures such as facilities utilization and the productivity of facilities have been added to the more traditional profit ratios in developing indexes of overall company performance (16). Injury rates have been used by plant managers for control purposes (20). In the following sections of this chapter a number of other control measures related to human performance are considered.

The increase in the use of nonfinancial controls has occurred in a context of rapidly expanding numbers of controls of all kinds. While 25 years ago only half of a sample of large corporations were found to use budgetary controls of any kind, such controls were universal in a recent study of a comparable group of companies (22). In addition to budgets other commonly noted financial measures were profit and loss performance and return on investment.

This burgeoning of control measures carries with it a number of risks. Control is of positive value insofar as goal attainment is concerned only as long as it pays for itself. It is quite possible to overcontrol to the point where the cost of the control system exceeds the gain in performance that is realized. There are often sizable costs associated with developing measures, reporting systems, corrective procedures, and the like. But there are other economic consequences as well. Complex control procedures may operate to produce resentment and thus contribute to conflict. They may also lead to a variety of attempts to circumvent the controls with negative consequences for performance (43). These responses are not inevitable results of the control process, but they may occur and they appear more likely to occur when a great variety of measures are viewed as restricting the individual at every turn.

There is also some tendency to favor objective, numerical control measures such as those providing data in dollar terms or in number of units produced. Unfortunately, however, some of the most significant factors for organizational goal attainment are not easily measurable in objective terms. To measure only that which is easy to measure with a high sense of certainty can misdirect the organizational effort. Under such circumstances the control system may do more harm than good. The alternative tends to be the use of more subjective measures, such as supervisory performance ratings, simply because they provide the only method of getting at certain crucial factors such as organizational value structures.

Types of Standards

The types of standards beyond which corrective action should be taken vary considerably, depending in large part on the particular nature of the measure. Unidirectional controls are most common, but bidirectional types are also used, and in areas such as manufacturing one may find multidirectional systems which respond to many variables and provide a number of alternate actions (19). Budgeting entries are typically unidirectional as are quality controls which reject products that exceed a certain tolerance standard. In both cases, however, bidirectional standards can be introduced. Corrective action may be introduced for spending too little as well as too much, on the grounds that performance standards are below an acceptable level. The quality of a product may be too high; it costs more to obtain such quality than can ever be recovered in the marketplace. Inventory controls tend to be bidirectional with standards set so as to identify both insufficient and excess inventory.

Another somewhat more flexible approach to standard-setting utilizes variance controls (31). Under most control systems corrective action is introduced every time a deviation from standard that is unacceptable occurs. In variance control, statistical sampling techniques are used and corrective action is called for only when the *total pattern* of performance deviates more than the anticipated amount. The usual approach is to establish a normal expected amount of variation around average (mean) performance. Should performance consistently exceed these normal limits the indication is that some new factor has been introduced into the situation. When one can say with some certainty that such a new factor has been introduced and that the old expected distribution of performance levels no longer describes the situation, then an unacceptable deviation from standard has occurred, and corrective action is required. The new factor might be an inexperienced worker or a broken part or practically anything else, depending on what is being measured.

There is in the variance control approach an element of self-established standard-setting of the kind which occurs in many applications of management by objectives. Past performance establishes the normal range of variation that is acceptable. Furthermore, the approach accepts the fact that some mistakes and failures will inevitably occur, and that corrective action may not be needed in every such instance. As a result of these factors the use of variance controls can be expected to produce less resistance and resentment than most other control procedures (31).

Types of Corrective Actions

The type of corrective action taken to restore acceptable performance will depend on the factor measured and on the decisions made on the causes and appropriate methods of correcting deviations. It has been found, for instance, that quality control can be maintained through a continuing manipulation of monetary rewards and punishments to reinforce control standards (1). Probably the most common type of corrective action involves the use of authority in some way to motivate a change in behavior. In such cases the directing function becomes an integral part of control. The possibility that corrective action may involve a redefinition of measures or an adjustment of standards has already been noted. A variety of other corrective procedures applicable to human performance failures having different patterns of causation are considered in the next section.

An example of corrective action, and the decision-making processes that go into selecting an appropriate action, is provided by the strike situation.

This is a situation involving the control of conflict. Conflict has become open to the point where productivity is drastically impaired, if it has not ceased entirely. In some instances the survival of the organization is severely threatened. Some type of corrective action is needed to restore productivity levels and eliminate the open conflict. This is clearly a control situation where an unacceptable deviation from standard has occurred. Coordination and prevention have failed.

The usual corrective approach in such a situation is continued bargaining, which now occurs under the constraints of lost revenues to the company and lost wages to the employees. But there is an alternative approach. The company may decide to continue operating in spite of the strike. Such an approach may serve as a corrective action in that productivity is restored; it may also force the end of the strike if it becomes evident that only the employees are suffering. On the other hand, attempts to operate during a strike may fail while intensifying the conflict and putting the company in an even worse bargaining position. Clearly the choice of a corrective action in such circumstances requires a careful evaluation of alternatives. The findings from an extensive analysis of such decisions in 45 companies yields lists of those conditions which appear to favor the choice of continued operation as a corrective action in response to a strike and those which would seem to argue against such a decision (23). These data are given in Table 14-1.

Performance Control

One of the most widespread applications of control occurs in the area of individual performance. Organizations and their managers typically establish certain minimum acceptable levels which serve to define ineffective performance. Below these levels the deviation is considered excessive, and some action is taken to correct the situation. This action may be firing, or there may be an attempt to determine what is wrong and take appropriate corrective action. Job performance is usually measured using such factors as quantity of output, quality of output, absenteeism, impact on the performance of others, contribution to conflict, and dishonest behavior. Whenever an individual falls below the standards established by the organization or by his immediate superior on one or more such factors, corrective action is called for.

Table 14-1 *Considerations Influencing the Decision to Operate During a Strike*

Conditions Under Which Operation Is Feasible

1. The union is poorly led, has organizational and internal (political) instability, has limited financial resources, and has limited support from other unions.
2. The company has strong public and political support.
3. The production process is primarily machine-paced and managerial personnel are trained in its use.
4. There are strong competitive or public service reasons for maintaining continuous operations.
5. The company has a good inventory position or has other products or product lines that will support a long, hard-fought conflict.
6. The company enjoys progressive leadership and a good public image—particularly in the local community.
7. The company has a sound legal position.

Conditions Under Which Operation Is Not Feasible

1. The union is mature and well led, is financially sound, has strong internal organization, and is supported by other unions.
2. The company has a limited amount of public or political support. (This is particularly important as it relates to the local community.)
3. The firm's production operations and processes are worker-paced (that is, they require a large amount of labor for continuing operation).
4. Competitive and structural forces are not strongly pressing for (or are not in dire need of products that would result from) continuous operation.
5. The company's financial and leadership resources are limited. The former is important in the short run; the latter becomes critical if a strike does not end quickly.
6. The legality of the company's actions is questionable.

Source: J. G. Hutchinson, *Management Under Strike Conditions* (New York: Holt, Rinehart and Winston, 1966), pp. 123–124.

Performance Analysis

In the case of performance control an open-loop system exists; corrective action is not mobilized automatically, but rather requires that there be a preceding step devoted to deciding what caused the deviation. Thus, if appropriate solutions are to be applied, there must be some process of decision making by a manager. This diagnostic step is called *performance analysis*.

The potential causes of ineffective performance are many and diverse. The ideal approach in attempting to determine what factors have combined to make a particular individual fail on the job is to consider a list of all possible alternatives, comparing each against what is known about the person (33, 34, 46). In terms of what is known, does it seem likely that a specific cause is operative in the particular instance? Such a list of possible causes would include the following:

    Intellectual aspects of the individual
        Deficiency in some ability required by the job
        Insufficient job knowledge
        Defects of judgment or memory
    Emotional aspects of the individual
        Continuing disruptive emotions (aggression for instance)
        Emotional illness
    Motivational aspects of the individual
        Dominant motives inappropriate to the job
        Low personal work standards
        Generalized lack of work motivation
    Physical aspects of the individual
        Deficiency in some physical skill required by the job
        Inappropriate physical characteristics
        Physical illness or handicap
    Aspects of the individual's family relationships
        Family crises
        Lack of family support
        Predominance of family over work demands
    Aspects of the individual's work group relationships
        Ineffective leadership
        Inappropriate managerial standards
        Inadequacies in relations with work group members
    Organizational actions
        Placement error
        Organizational overpermissiveness or neglect
        Utilization of excessive span of control
        Inappropriate organizational standards
        Deficient coordination and excessive conflict
    Aspects of society and its value systems
        Conflicts between organizational and individual values
        Application of society's legal sanctions
    Aspects of the work situation and the environment
        Detrimental conditions of work
        Excessive danger

Negative factors associated with geographical location
Negative factors associated with the economy

It is rare to find only one such cause operating in a given instance of ineffective performance. Almost always a number of factors combine to produce the problem. In any given case the average number of factors appears to be about four (32). The most frequent contributor is some kind of organizational action; this occurs in some 80 to 90 percent of all cases. About three-quarters of the cases with organizational causes involve placement errors. Usually the individual is placed in a job which is inappropriate on an intellectual, emotional, or motivational basis; or in an inappropriate work group. After organizational actions the most frequent causes are emotional and motivational factors, each appearing in from 60 to 70 percent of all cases. Other types of causes are identified considerably less frequently than the three primary ones—organizational, emotional, and motivational. Aspects of the individual's family relationships and of society's value systems are least common, but such factors can have a predominant influence when they do appear.

Corrective Procedures

Once a set of operative causes has been identified through performance analysis the next step in the control process is to determine which factors can and which cannot be changed, as well as whether a particular change would be sufficient to correct the performance deviation entirely. Thus a strategy for corrective action is developed. In this instance, as in all applications of control procedures, one must take into account the costs of corrective action and the probability of their success. If the costs are greater than any possible benefits, or the probability that the corrective strategy chosen will achieve its end is low, then it may well be that termination of employment is the most appropriate solution.

A variety of corrective actions are available for use in performance control. Which are appropriate will depend on the specific causes identified. The list that follows provides some idea of the range of alternatives (34).

Job redesign and changed role prescriptions
Promotion, transfer or demotion
Management development and training
Changes in supervision
Changes in compensation

Personnel policy modification
Threats and disciplinary action
Counseling and psychotherapy
Medical treatment
Alcoholics Anonymous

These procedures are considered in detail in books concerned with personnel management. Some have been discussed already in preceding chapters of the present volume; others are considered in Chapter 15, which deals with staffing or executive personnel management.

An Example

The following case history* provides an example of how performance control can work in practice. In this instance the corrective action decided upon to control performance was replacement and demotion. This solution was in fact successful, and an acceptable level of performance was restored.

Case Description. The most important thing in Wayne Tindall's early life was basketball. He was a star in high school and went on to a small college which was known outside the state primarily for its ability to develop top-ranking teams in this sport. There he did well enough to attract the attention of one of the professional clubs, and after graduation and a brief period of military service, he received an offer which was sufficiently attractive to start him on a career in pro basketball. Although never a really outstanding player, he managed to hold on for a number of years and in the process made a comfortable living. In fact he was well into his thirties before he began to think seriously about what life might be like after his playing days were over. He and his wife had operated a fishing camp during the summer months ever since their college days, and both had always assumed, almost without thinking, that this would be their vocation after basketball ceased to provide an income. When, however, it came to the point where he could expect to play for only one or two more seasons at best, the need for somewhat more realistic planning forced Wayne to the conclusion that the fishing camp was no long-term solution. It had never been a particularly profitable venture, and there was little likelihood that it ever would be.

His thinking had progressed about this far when he got into a conversa-

* From J. B. Miner, *The Management of Ineffective Performance*, pp. 315–323, New York: McGraw-Hill Book Company, 1963. Reprinted by permission.

tion with a businessman who was staying at the camp. This man urged him to try selling, pointing out that it was a field which required no special previous training. By the time they got through talking, Wayne had agreed to get in touch with the man at the end of the next season and to apply for a job with his company. The man was sure there would be a sales position available—and as it turned out, he was right.

It was company practice to break new men in by having them work under very close supervision at first. Then, as they learned, it was expected that they would require less and less direction until finally they could handle a territory almost entirely on their own. Something like three years was characteristically required before a man was considered competent to work under minimal supervision. Wayne almost from the beginning was expected to complete his training in record time—perhaps as little as two years. He was older than many of the others and had a background of experience as an athlete. This kind of background was widely respected in the company. Furthermore, he gave every indication of being a topnotch salesman. He learned quickly, worked hard, and people liked him. He was one of those individuals who never see anything but the best in others and act accordingly. After a ten-minute conversation, people usually considered him a close and loyal friend. The progress reports sent in by his supervisor contained many glowing statements and emphasized his skill in handling people. There were several notations that he appeared to have considerable potential for supervisory work.

Largely because of these reports, Wayne had a very brief career as a salesman. Eight months after he started, he was pulled off the job and sent back to the home office to work in the advertising department. In part, this decision was based on a wish to provide him with a broader background of experience than was possible in sales work alone. The company tried to give men who showed some promise of rising into the ranks of management as much opportunity to gain diverse training as possible. But it was also true that the advertising department badly needed another man. Had that not been the case, Wayne would have remained in selling for a much longer period of time.

To an ex-basketball player who liked to spend his vacations out in the woods hunting and fishing, the world of advertising was something less than appealing. He stayed with it only because his job represented a road back to sales work, which he had enjoyed very much during his limited period of exposure. As it turned out, it was a rather long road. He spent over three years in the advertising department, devoting most of the time to seemingly interminable discussions with agency people. When he left, however, it was with a promotion and a solid record of accomplishment behind him. He was generally considered to have an unusually promising future in the company, although he himself had never indicated agreement with this opinion, nor did he appear terribly interested in achieving managerial success.

The new job placed him in charge of marketing a special line of products, which the company sold through a completely separate sales force assigned only to this work. The country as a whole was divided into two segments. Wayne was sales manager for the Western area. It was a big jump for a man with no supervisory, and very little sales, experience. Management recognized this, but there was widespread confidence in the ex-basketball player. He would do all right.

It was impossible to evaluate Wayne's work adequately until about a year had passed. The sales figures are the crucial measure, and it takes a while for the impact of a new manager to show up in the figures. When sufficient time had passed for his leadership to be felt, however, the results, at least as indicated by the sales criterion, were not as good as had been expected. In fact, the Western area had slipped behind the Eastern in terms of percentage gain for the first time in many years.

The trouble seemed to be partly in his handling of salesmen. Whenever a man got in any trouble for whatever reason, Wayne was there to defend him. At times he came to the defense of his men unnecessarily, so eager was he to appear as their representative rather than their master. He would on occasion go to fantastic lengths to do a favor for one of the salesmen or to help out when one was in a jam. As might have been expected under these circumstances, he rarely pushed a man for more work or offered any criticism. Often when he knew that something had to be done, he would do it himself rather than ask someone else to do the job. There were innumerable times when he made special trips hundreds of miles out of his way to see complaining customers. Normally the salesman in the territory would have been notified of the complaint and told to handle it and see that there were no more of the same. Although they liked and respected Wayne for his honesty and sincerity, many of the salesmen, especially the green ones, obviously had some feeling that they should be receiving more constructive coaching which might help them to see what mistakes they had made and how they could improve. Their sales manager seemed to find it so hard to talk about the work at all that no one really knew where he stood.

This same reticence was not apparent in his dealings with people at higher levels. He usually checked on any proposed action that was not strictly routine, to get assurance from his supervisors that it was within policy. On such occasions he frequently revealed a surprising failure to understand the situation facing him. He would raise a number of questions which indicated either that he lacked information regarding sales procedures or that he had not taken the time to think his problem through. It was hard to tell which. In any event, he was obviously not considering many factors which he should have taken into account in making his decisions. There were at least two occasions when he revealed that he did not know policy regarding acceptable charges on a salesman's expense account. In another instance he allowed a territory to remain unserviced for an excessive period of time because of a misunderstanding regarding company policy in this respect. The list could be extended almost indefinitely.

In addition, Wayne had not yet been able to organize his work well enough so that he could plan against future eventualities. He moved from one crisis to another trying to do a great amount of work normally handled by the salesmen, trying to follow orders and policy to the letter, trying to keep up with his own work load. It was a difficult existence. At times there was some hope that he might break through and get on top of the situation. In recent months, however, this hope had become rather dim. Yet he maintained his air of outward calm, of sincerity and friendliness. He was without question trying to do the best job he could.

When these problems were discussed with him, Wayne exhibited the almost excessive deference which always characterized his relations with his superiors. He agreed entirely with the criticisms. He should set higher standards for his men and follow up to see that his orders were carried out. He should think things through before seeking help at higher levels. He should devote more thought to organizing his own work and should let the salesmen do theirs. He should exhibit greater confidence in himself. One could not help feeling, although the man agreed with every comment made, that there was little likelihood of his behavior actually changing very much. If only he could argue a point, could give some indication that he cared about proving himself right. Without a strong wish to show that he could do the job and win out over adversity, he was not likely to change.

Time proved this prognosis to be correct. After three years the Western area had definitely established its inferiority to the Eastern. Sales were down and the sales force was disorganized and inadequately trained. Wayne had not changed at all, in spite of repeated efforts to help him.

There was no alternative but to put him back in a sales position, a move which represented a sizable demotion. He appeared somewhat bitter when told of the change, but agreed it was the only thing to do. He should have done a better job as a sales manager. He should have forced himself to follow the advice of his superiors more closely.

Analysis. Wayne Tindall was not sufficiently well informed regarding his company's sales programs and policies to perform his job in an entirely satisfactory manner. Among other things he lacked knowledge of policies dealing with expense accounts and staffing procedures, areas in which, as a sales manager, he could hardly afford to make many mistakes. Although some of his difficulties in the intellectual sphere appear to reflect poor judgment, probably due to the intrusion of emotional reactions when he attempted to think through certain types of problems, he clearly did not possess sufficient job knowledge. This deficiency does not account for all aspects of his failure, but it was a major factor.

It is always possible in such instances that the man may lack the mental competence to learn the many aspects of his job in a reasonable period of time. Verbal or other special abilities may be insufficient. Wayne, however, was a college graduate, and he had manifested a capacity to learn very rapidly while in his original assignment as a salesman. His work in the advertising job had been entirely satisfactory. Although the intellectual demands of the sales-manager position were probably greater than anything he had faced before, it still seems almost certain that factors other than intelligence were largely responsible for his lack of knowledge.

The most likely explanation is that he did not have sufficient training. Normally salesmen in the company were expected to work under close supervision for approximately three years before being considered fully qualified. Wayne took over major managerial responsibility after only eight months. The position in advertising could not have taught him much that he would need out in the field, and unfortunately it removed him from the selling end of the business for three very important years. Opportunities to learn what he should have known as a sales manager were without question severely restricted by the nature of his previous placements.

The deficiencies in judgment may have been nothing more than additional instances of inadequate information. More probably, they may have reflected the impact of emotion on thinking. In any event there is considerable evidence indicating that emotional factors were strategic. Although before his promotion Wayne had been a relatively cool and collected person, this pattern disappeared, except as a surface façade, once he moved into the managerial position. Outwardly he remained the same calm, friendly person. But a closer look indicates that a drastic change in fact occurred. Eventually he reached a point where he could not bring himself to discuss the work at all with his subordinates; the situation was too disturbing to him. As a result, new salesmen received very little individual coaching with respect to their performance, and the men did not really know whether they were doing satisfactory work or not. The constant checking with higher management almost certainly reflects a desire for reassurance against a pervasive fear of error. Anxiety is also evident in Wayne's attempts to do his own work and most of his subordinates' work as well.

But the most striking indication of emotional factors is the tendency to blame himself for everything that went wrong. The discussions with his superiors were full of self-condemnation. Everything was his fault. He could not seem to do anything to correct the many problem situations, but he did not question any of the judgments that were made regarding him and his performance. If anything, he embellished upon the criticisms of others. The picture suggests a man overcome with guilt, a man who at times evidently wanted to fail in the performance of his job in order to escape an intolerable situation.

It is this guilt which seems to be behind much of Wayne's behavior as a sales manager. Although there must have been times when his emotion overwhelmed him, and thus made effective performance impossible, the more typical pattern appears to involve a continuing effort to escape from these disturbing experiences, an effort which was not integrated with job demands. This was his basic motive in the work situation. At times it almost appears to have been his only motive. His tendency to rise to the defense of his men even when such a reaction was totally unwarranted is understandable in this context. He seemed to view himself continually as one of the salesmen rather than as their manager. Apparently, by escaping into the role of a subordinate he hoped to avoid the guilt that the managerial role provoked. In fact, he seemed to be constantly afraid that the salesmen would condemn him as a manager. He did almost nothing that he thought might anger them. He would not criticize or reprimand. He continually did things himself, rather than tell his subordinates to do them. This tendency to take over and perform the work himself in order to avoid giving orders was most pronounced when the task was unpleasant or difficult. The result was that much of Wayne's own managerial work was left undone. The tasks taken over from the salesmen were not effectively performed either; a man cannot do everything himself.

Toward the end this wish to escape the experience of guilt and anxiety appears to have evolved to the point where Wayne really wanted to fail and be removed from the job. This type of negative motivation usually operates at the unconscious level, since the individual would not want to view himself as a quitter or as too weak to withstand a little anxiety. Yet the desire to get out of a situation which is terribly disturbing takes precedence over nearly everything else. It is not as bad to fail on the job as it is to continue in it, especially if the person is completely unaware that a wish to fail is instrumental in his ineffective performance. Although it is not certain from the evidence available that Wayne's behavior was guided by this kind of motivation, there is every reason to believe that it was. On the surface he appeared to be trying to do a good job, yet he did not approach his work in a way that would seem to offer much chance of success. In spite of continual advice and guidance from those at higher levels, he maintained the same pattern of behavior inflexibly throughout the three years. He agreed with all criticisms, but he did nothing about them and gave the impression that he never would.

Physical, family, and group factors do not seem to be strategic. Wayne had been an athlete for many years and was presumably in good physical condition. There is no indication that he had any family problems. Throughout his career with the company he had been very popular; everyone seemed to like him. In fact, it was this ability to get along with others that originally led to his being suggested as a supervisor. Eventually some of his men became somewhat disenchanted with him because of his failure to provide adequate guidance. This, however, was a result of other factors and did not serve as a cause of failure.

The company seems to have contributed in two ways, both of which have already been touched on briefly. For one thing, Wayne was promoted without adequate training. Although existing plans and policies called for approximately three years of instruction followed by several years of independent work as a salesman before a man moved up to managerial responsibility, Wayne had only eight months of directly relevant experience. Other factors operated to deprive him of an adequate opportunity to learn what he needed to know. He was older than most beginning salesmen, he had been a professional athlete, and his initial performance on the job was very impressive. These circumstances contributed to the company's conclusion that an exception to the usual policies regarding training should be made in his case. Presumably, the shortage of personnel in advertising was also influential. In any event, he did not get the training a manager was normally expected to have and which he needed to perform effectively.

There was a placement error in addition to this. Although adequate preparation would presumably have eliminated Wayne's intellectual difficulties, the emotional and motivational problems would have remained. The fact that a person makes friends easily and appears to get along well with nearly everyone provides no basis for concluding that he will necessarily prove successful as a manager. The jump from the advertising position to that of area sales manager was a sizable one. It appears that factors such as Wayne's popularity and his experience as a basketball player contributed in no small way to the decision to make the move. Unfortunately, a much more important predictor of future performance was overlooked: Wayne never did give any indication that he was really interested in achieving success as a manager.

The major stimulus which set off his guilt seems to have been the managerial situation. Wayne was not obsessed with guilt until he became a manager, and it was only then that he became ineffective. Previously he had been outstanding in nonsupervisory work. It is difficult to say exactly what the unacceptable impulses aroused by the managerial situation may have been. Presumably such factors figured strongly in his motivational hierarchy. Strongly held cultural values would then have led him to believe that he was bad and worthy of severe punishment. Unfortunately we do not have the kind of information that would permit an exact reconstruction of the processes involved, but the fact of guilt and its impact on performance are clearly evident.

This analysis provides a rather long list of strategic factors; intellectual, emotional, motivational, organizational, cultural, and situational determinants were all involved. The intellectual aspect could presumably have been rectified by more extended training. It would appear, however, that Wayne could not learn as long as he continued to face the emotional pressures of his managerial job. There were too many other problems constantly demanding attention to permit him to stop and acquire the knowledge he needed. This means that it would have been necessary to relieve him of managerial responsibilities for a period of time, perhaps a year, so that he could devote his efforts entirely to making up for past deficiencies in training.

Such an approach would, however, have supplied only a partial solution. The personality problems associated with emotional, motivational, and cultural factors and stimulated by the managerial situation would still remain. These alone would have been sufficient to guarantee continued failure. Since something had to be done immediately, in view of the continuing decline in sales throughout the Western area, a change in the situation seems to be the only short-term solution available. Wayne apparently wanted to escape from the environmental context which had provoked so much guilt and anxiety. A transfer to some type of work other than the managerial would seem to have provided the most appropriate method of satisfying his desires and thus solving the company's problem. It is unfortunate, in fact, that this move was delayed as long as it was. Not only was a great deal of business lost as a result of the three-year wait, but Wayne's successor was faced with the problem of revitalizing a poorly trained and sadly demoralized sales force. In addition, higher marketing management had to devote a tremendous amount of time to the problems existing in the Western area and to the personal difficulties of the area's manager.

The best long-term solution is probably also the one actually employed. Any change in Wayne's emotional patterns, motives, or values would have taken a long time, if it could have been accomplished at all. Yet the change had to be made immediately because of the declining product sales. Thus some type of transfer was imperative. But if this transfer resulted in an appropriate placement, and the demotion to a sales position would seem to provide such a solution, then all reasons and motives for personality change would probably disappear. Wayne's guilt would be reduced, his negative motivation minimized, and his performance improved. There would be no incentive for him to seek professional help or for his superior to attempt to change his behavior. This would presumably mean that he would spend much of his life in actual selling rather than in managing, but a topflight salesman can contribute much more to a company than a completely ineffective manager.

The Auditing Approach

Much control represents an ongoing process with information on the relationships between performance and standards collected continuously. An alternative is for control to operate through the medium of an intensive audit, which utilizes data for an extended time period, but actually is carried out within a limited time span. Such audits may be one-time affairs, as in the case of many troubleshooting efforts. Or they may be of a periodic nature, initiated at regular intervals to assess an organization, or one of its units, to determine the match between expectations and performance on a variety of measures (4).

The concept of auditing is frequently associated with financial investigation and measurement, and in fact much auditing is of this kind. But even among the accounting firms there are some that extend their auditing procedures beyond financial indexes to a variety of other measures. As the concept is used here, auditing means much more than the financial approach. Auditing is an investigative, analytical, comparative process applied to any type of variable that might be considered important to success. Such audits have frequently been applied to personnel and industrial relations units and their functions, for instance, with only occasional reference to dollar-based measures (50).

Nonfinancial Measures

Audit measures are often focused on results. Although these results may be expressed in financial terms, they may also deal with such considerations as injury rates, absenteeism, turnover, grievances, selection ratios, transfer rates, units produced, overtime worked, and many other factors. A great variety of such measures have been developed in the human resources area (42).

A second approach attempts to achieve control at the level of procedures. It is assumed that if rules are followed and standardized practices implemented, effective results will be achieved. Thus the audit focuses on identifying significant departures from established procedure. Such an approach may include an audit of policies, as well, in terms of their clarity, comprehensiveness, soundness, and the like.

A source of data for audits is the product of the normal written communication process—records, reports, computer print-outs, and so forth. These often are supplemented by interviews with certain key individuals. In the human resources area it also has been common practice to incorporate attitude surveys of various kinds into the auditing process. Employees may be asked questions which provide an overall index of attitudes toward the company. If dissatisfaction is prevalent in a particular unit, corrective action is called for. On the other hand a variety of specific factors may be singled out for evaluation by employees. A recent study indicates that equity of rewards and adequacy of performance evaluation procedures are particularly important considerations in audits (39). When employee reactions in these areas are negative, rated organizational effectiveness is likely to be low.

External Management Audits

Individuals conducting audits may vary considerably in their independence of the unit evaluated (25). At one extreme are those cases where a group of managers carry out a self-audit. There may also be an auditing unit within the organization which conducts control analyses in many sectors of the organization. The Civil Service Commission provides such a service in the United States government. In contrast to these internal audits are those of an external nature. External audits may be conducted because they are legally required (in the case of financial data), because their results are desired for control purposes by a company's management, or because the data are needed by some outside group (such as investors).

Investor Data. Historically external audits to provide data for lenders, investors, or those interested in acquisitions have focused on financial considerations. Thus, lenders of short-term funds are concerned with such ratios as current assets to current liabilities, inventories to sales, and net working capital to sales; lenders of longer-term funds compare sales to fixed investment and long-term debt to net worth (16). Investors emphasize additional ratios: net earnings per share to book value per share, book value per share over the most recent five years to book value at the beginning of this period, total dividends per share over the five years to total net earnings per share over the same time span, increase in earnings per share over the five years to amount of earnings per share not paid out in dividends for the same period (25). Financial analysts have frequently supplemented these figures with less quantitative impressions derived from interviews with top executives, key customers, and perhaps research scientists capable of evaluating technological factors in the industry.

If the ratios obtained deviate from preestablished standards or the interview comments concentrate in certain categories, the firm is considered a poor risk. Lenders or investors are advised to stay away and unless the firm can take appropriate action to correct the deficiencies they often remain away.

The strong financial emphasis of such audits had not always proved adequate to the task (8). Factors such as the nature of product lines and their relationship to competitive position, research capabilities, and management competence and potential usually are downplayed. There is clearly a need for the inclusion of measures directly related to material and human resources, as well as to financial resources, if external audits are to effectively guide decisions on investments and acquisitions.

Audits of Management Quality. In response to the recognized need for more comprehensive measurement, a variety of management audit procedures have been developed which attempt to take the quality of a company's management into account, as well as other factors (17). Among these probably the oldest and most widely known is the approach developed by the American Institute of Management. This started as a tool of financial analysis and is still heavily weighted in that direction. However, data in the human and material resource areas are also obtained, and executive evaluation is considered to be the most important single appraisal category (30). Information is obtained by means of a standardized questionnaire, through interviews with members of the organization and of its various publics, and from published statistics. A point system for scoring the organization is used. The ten categories considered are:

Economic function
Corporate structure
Health of earnings
Service to stock owners
Research and development
Directorate effectiveness
Fiscal policies
Production efficiency
Sales vigor
Executive effectiveness

Several writers have envisaged the possibility of constructing a certified management audit based on the functions and principles of classical management theory (18, 27). Such a procedure is considered to be the crucial step required to move the field of management from the status of an art to that of a profession. Yet the more widely held view appears to be that a great deal needs to be learned about effective organizations before a single audit procedure could be developed which would prove fully adequate. Premature standardization can inhibit research at the time when it is most urgently needed. Furthermore, the success of existing approaches such as that of the American Institute of Management has not been sufficient to warrant optimism regarding the creation of a truly effective overall company audit procedure in the near future (8).

Responses to Audit

The assumption behind the use of internal audit procedures and some external audits is that the result of the application of the control procedures will be improved performance. In part this is expected to occur as a consequence of the introduction of corrective actions. But there is also the prospect that the fact of audit per se, or even the anticipation of audit, may influence performance.

A series of studies has been conducted to test the latter hypothesis in a laboratory setting (12). The evidence indicates that if an audit is to influence performance, it must be perceived as having the power to go beneath the surface to get at what really happens. Give this, different types of people responded differently to the audit-type situation. Men currently employed in industry tended to respond positively in terms of performance levels, but students without prior experience with audits responded negatively. Excessive auditing, however, yielded negative results even among the industrial personnel. The differences between students and those employed in industry noted in this study would appear to be related to the general finding that students tend to respond somewhat less rationally than practicing managers in business simulations of this type (36).

Evidence from other sources indicates that there are often basic disagreements between parties on what are the major factors being measured in an audit, and that when there is a lack of agreement on the objectives involved audits tend to be viewed as ineffective (38). This appears to indicate that whether audits are well or poorly done may have a lot to do with the motivational consequences. If people are unclear regarding what is being measured, appropriate performance goals are unlikely to result and performance is unlikely to improve; it may well decline as a consequence of the ambiguity.

Research in this area is far from sufficient. Yet the implications of what has been done so far are that auditing has a very unstable relationship to job behavior. Behavioral responses can be anticipated, but they may be of a negative nature. If so, more controls may follow and hence more negative influences on motivation—unless appropriate corrective action reverses the process. We are just beginning to learn what influences some time-honored business practices really have on organization members.

Accounting, Human Resources, and Behavior

There has been an increasing trend in the past few years to consider human resources and their effective utilization in relation to accounting systems. One aspect of this development has been to study accounting measures, budgets, and the like in terms of the motives and responses they elicit. This task closely parallels the work on responses to audits.

A second approach has involved incorporating measures of human resources into accounting systems on the assumption that the quality of the work force is an important asset which varies considerably from firm to firm. This kind of *human asset accounting* has been considered both in determining the total value of the company as it might be established in an overall audit carried out by financial analysts, and in developing measures of the performance effectiveness of individual managers.

Human Assets and Company Value

The basic position of those who advocate human asset accounting is that current measures such as return on investment seriously distort the true value of a company. This situation is depicted in Figure 14–2. It is evident from the figure that a sizable proportion of a firm's assets are currently unmeasured; physical and financial resources are measured, human resources are not (41). Human assets are understood to include those internal to the firm as well as external ones. The latter encompasses much that is usually designated by the term *goodwill*.

Significance of Human Asset Measurement. Companies consistently spend large sums of money acquiring and developing long-term human capabilities. In most accounting systems these outlays are treated as operating expenses, thus assuming the benefits occur only in the short

Figure 14–2 The Nature of Human Assets

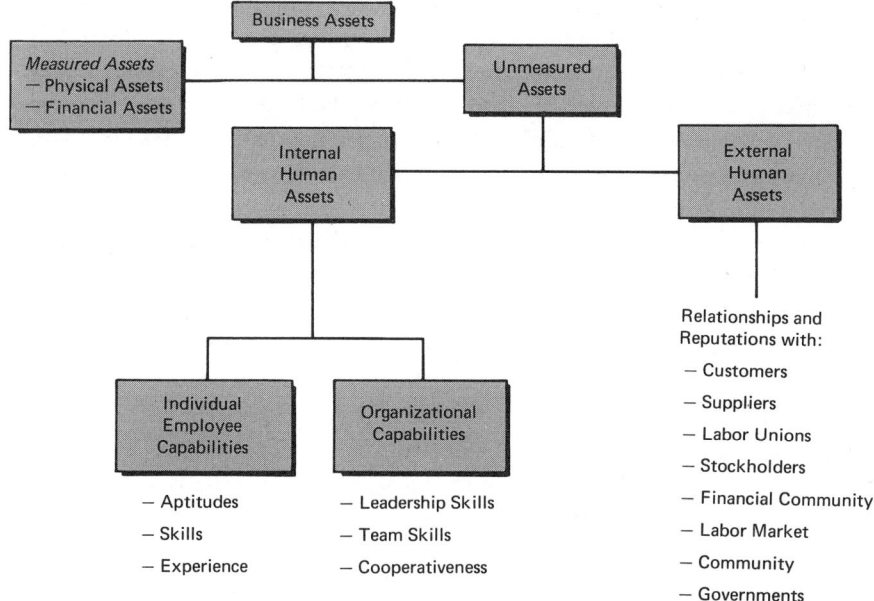

Source: W. C. Pyle, "Human Resource Accounting," *Financial Analysts Journal*, Vol. 26 (1970), No. 5, 8.

term (40). Human resources are not reflected in the capital budget. This means that if a company is investing more heavily in recruiting and training employees than these capabilities are being consumed, the usual accounting procedures overstate expenses and understate profits. Similarly, if the company's managerial practices are such that it loses or reduces the input potential of existing employees while failing to create an equal capability in other ways, thus in effect liquidating some human assets, conventional accounting serves to understate operating expenses and overstate profit. The latter case would be comparable to a company's selling off a portion of its business without fully incorporating the transaction in its financial reports.

From the point of view of those concerned with evaluating a company for purposes of investment or acquisition this failure to incorporate human assets in accounting statements can yield major problems in reaching correct decisions of a go—no go nature. There is evidence to indicate that long-term profits are related to expenditures for the acquisition, training, and retention of human resources and that the ratio of human asset investment to total assets is a useful guide to decision making (7). This is particularly true of professional organizations and others providing primarily services—consulting firms, market research firms, advertising agencies, and the like.

For purposes of external audit it is much easier to fully evaluate a company if data are available to indicate where funds are going in terms of various employee groups and customer relationships. Are these investment decisions as regards people appropriate? External control is also concerned with major shifts in the overall value of a firm's human assets during a given period and with the extent to which investments made in human assets in prior years are now being returned in terms of lower costs. It is possible that a company may be overinvesting in human assets beyond the point where it can effectively use the capabilities it has developed. Perhaps expenditures for goodwill or job satisfaction could be reduced appreciably with no significant effect on overall company performance. All these questions regarding aspects of total company value require that data on human assets be developed. Such measures appear to be important in predicting the future value of a company as well (28).

Methods of Evaluation. A variety of approaches to the problem of measuring human assets have been proposed (37). Of these the easiest to implement appears to be one which utilizes human resource costs such as hiring costs, training costs, and the like, as a basis for valuation (41). Such a system has been tried out with some evidence of success. An alternative to actual costing would be the use of replacement costs.

The second major category of measures stresses existing economic value. This requires an estimate of the contribution of human resources to the total economic value of the company. One such approach requires that future earnings be forecast, discounted to establish present value, and allocated to human resources in terms of their relative contribution. Another approach assumes that earnings in excess of the average in an industry may be considered as goodwill and allocated to human resources in terms of the ratio of human resources to total assets. In this instance human resources are viewed as adding value to a firm only when its performance exceeds the industry average, an assumption which has been seriously questioned (37). The value of human assets might also be established by a bidding process among the divisions, subsidiaries, project teams, or other structural groupings of a given company. A man with specialized and scarce skills, needed widely in the firm, would achieve a high present value; a man easily replaced from the outside labor market a very low one. Thus economic value would be established by the market mechanism.

The most ambitious economic value approach involves periodic measures of such factors as level of intelligence, quality of leadership, level of training, capacity for coordination, and motivation to contribute to the organization (28). If relationships can be established between these human aspects and earnings, then dollar values may be assigned to various amounts of each. Should a firm be in the process of expending its human assets more rapidly than they are being replaced this will be revealed in reduction in intelligence levels, leadership quality, motivation, and so forth. Accordingly the total value of human assets would show a decline. In many respects this approach is the most attractive, but it is also the most difficult to implement. The coalescing of psychological and accounting measurement procedures which is required presents some formidable obstacles.

Human Assets and Managerial Performance

One concomitant of the advent of decentralized divisionalized structures in American industry has been the use of profit centers within a company to evaluate divisions and division managers (25). Thus units within a company become a basis for developing accounting data, and the profitability of each is calculated as if it were a separate and distinct company. Transactions between units are given dollar values on the basis of transfer prices which are frequently established to reflect conditions in existing markets outside the firm. Wherever a profit center has been established the manager in charge of it may be evaluated in terms of its earnings performance. If this performance falls below a preestablished standard, corrective action is instituted. Not infrequently correction takes the form of the action applied to Wayne Tindall—the manager is replaced.

Accounting control systems of this kind are widespread. In fact there is reason to believe that decentralization would have been much less palatable to many chief executives had it not been possibile to utilize accounting data for purposes of maintaining responsibility (6). In all probability the major factor which has prevented decentralization from being carried on down to the lower levels of management in most companies is that the profit center concept and responsibility accounting are difficult to apply there.

From the point of view of an effective control system the profit center concept as currently applied often suffers from some major shortcomings

(9). When transactions between units are involved, and this appears to be almost inevitable, transfer prices must be developed. This calls for joint decision making in a context of competition between units. The conflict potential in such situations is tremendous, and this potential is frequently realized to a sizable degree. Furthermore, evaluating managers in terms of such measures as profit and loss, or return on investment, provides no information that might be used in deciding what caused an unacceptable deviation from standard. All too often the only corrective action considered is the removal of the manager, without adequate diagnostic analyses devoted to establishing causes and selecting appropriate corrective actions.

A final criticism of the profit-center approach relates to the matter of human assets (28). To the extent an accounting system for evaluating managers fails to include the human resource dimension it may well induce managers to give little attention to such matters or even to liquidate human assets in order to show greater profits in the short term. By stressing measures in the financial and material areas an accounting system tends to distort managerial behavior in the direction of these measures.

Some progress has been made in overcoming this difficulty with regard to measuring human assets. The R. G. Barry Company, a manufacturer of footwear and textile products, has instituted a human resource accounting system based on outlay costs which may be applied at the level of the individual manager (49). A model for such a system is given in Figure 14–3. Developments of this kind, plus an increasing understanding of the need for open-loop control systems when dealing with human performance, suggest that accounting systems will prove much more effective as a means of evaluating individual managerial performance in the future.

Responses to Accounting Control Systems

At a number of points in this volume, data have been presented which might suggest that accounting control systems do not always elicit responses from the people exposed to them that are congruent with the achievement of organizational task and maintenance goals. In Chapter 5, in connection with the discussion of budgeting as a component of policy planning, it was noted that budgets are often established on a political basis with biased estimates and strong pressures playing a considerable and inappropriate role. In Chapter 12 evidence regarding the tendency to respond to evaluation and control in communications with defensiveness and distortion was

Figure 14-3 Model of an Outlay Cost Measurement System

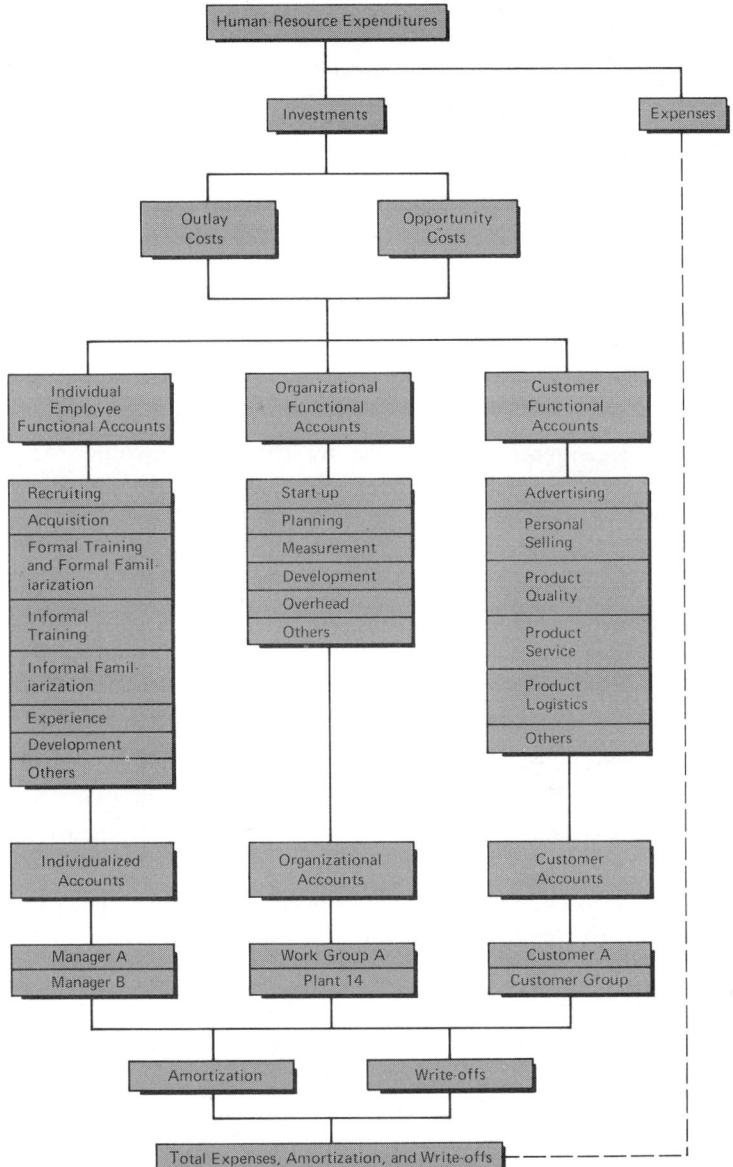

Source: R. L. Woodruff and R. G. Whitman, "The Behavioral Aspects of Accounting Data for Performance Evaluation at the R. G. Barry Corporation (With Special Reference to Human-Resource Accounting)," in T. J. Burns (ed.), *The Behavioral Aspects of Accounting Data for Performance Evaluation* (Columbus: College of Administrative Science, Ohio State University, 1970), p. 15.

considered. In the present chapter the finding that audits do not have a consistently positive impact points up a similar question. Do accounting control systems provide overall net benefits to the firms that use them, or might not organizational goals be achieved more fully if such systems were banished?

Types of Responses. There is ample evidence from a variety of sources that accounting controls can produce unanticipated and undesired responses. An early study considered reactions to manufacturing budgets among foremen (2). Numerous instances of conflict, dissatisfaction, tension, and frustration were noted. In another study which focused at higher managerial levels a host of devices calculated to circumvent budgets were unearthed (13). Among these was the practice of having conspirators charge expenditures to the budgets of other departments in order to free money for purposes not considered appropriate by those responsible for budget approvals. Other examples have been given of wasted time, production jams, increased maintenance costs, false data reports, low morale, impaired recruitment, conflict, higher costs, and decreased quality, all of which could be attributed to aspects of the control system (24). Data have been presented indicating that the introduction of tight cost controls may have positive effects on productivity and costs at the expense of long-term goal attainment (29).

Although these reports have tended to focus on negative consequences rather than positive, and thus do not provide a balanced picture of the total range of responses to control systems, it is evident that accounting control as practiced is not always an unmixed blessing. It apparently does yield considerable resentment in many cases with the result that either the control procedures are neutralized or negative results accrue in addition to those of a positive nature which were intended.

Sources of Problems. There is some evidence which taken as a whole suggests that the major source of many of the problems noted in accounting control systems may reside in the attitudes and beliefs of those who devise and administer them. Table 14–2 sets forth some of the assumptions which seem to underlie management accounting practice (10). This model has been tested using a standardized interview form. The answers provided by the controllers and accountants studied indicated that in fact assumptions of this kind were inherent in their control systems (11). The strong evaluative emphasis in the assumptions would be expected to arouse some

Table 14–2 Behavioral Assumptions of an Accounting Model of the Firm

I. Assumptions with Respect to Organization Goals
   A. The principal objective of business activity is profit maximization.
   B. This principal objective can be segmented into sub-goals to be distributed throughout the organization.
   C. Goals are additive—what is good for the parts of the business is also good for the whole.
II. Assumptions with Respect to the Behavior of Participants
   A. Organizational participants are motivated primarily by economic forces.
   B. Work is essentially an unpleasant task which people will avoid whenever possible.
   C. Human beings are ordinarily inefficient and wasteful.
III. Assumptions with Respect to the Behavior of Management
   A. The role of the business manager is to maximize the profits of the firm.
   B. In order to perform this role, management must control the tendencies of employees to be lazy, wasteful, and inefficient.
   C. The essence of management control is authority. The ultimate authority of management stems from its ability to affect the economic reward structure.
   D. There must be a balance between the authority a person has and his responsibility for performance.
IV. Assumptions with Respect to the Role of Managerial Accounting
   A. The primary function of management accounting is to aid management in the process of profit maximization.
   B. The accounting system is a "goal allocation" device which permits management to select its operating objectives and to divide and distribute them throughout the firm, i.e. assign responsibilities for performance.
   C. The accounting system is a control device which permits management to identify and correct undesirable performance.
   D. There is sufficient certainty, rationality, and knowledge within the system to permit an accurate comparison of responsibility for performance and the ultimate benefits and costs of that performance.
   E. The accounting system is "neutral" in its evaluations—personal bias is eliminated by the objectivity of the system.

Source: E. H. Caplan, "Behavioral Assumptions of Management Accounting," *Accounting Review*, Vol. 41 (1966), 497.

defensiveness. But even more significant is the view of employees as lazy, wasteful, and inefficient (II. B, II. C, and III. B). Although not considered in this study, many accounting control systems also assume dishonesty in that no one person is permitted to handle a transaction from beginning to end (25). All these views of employees may be entirely correct insofar as certain individuals are concerned, but the control systems are applied to everyone. That many respond with righteous anger and resentment is not too surprising.

This problem appears to be compounded by another factor. A study of those responsible for the controllership function in 25 medium-sized firms revealed a consistent tendency for controllers to overstate their authority relative to the perceptions of others (21). In a variety of areas such as internal control, budgeting, and accounting reports there was considerable disagreement among controllers, their superiors, and other managers at the same level as the controllers. The general trend of this disagreement was for the controllers to view their authority as considerable, the superiors to view it as less, and managerial peers to view it as much less. What this amounts to is that the controllers lacked the support of legitimization for many of their decisions. They tried to wield influence that others did not consider their right. Again a capacity for resentment and conflict seems to permeate the control situation. If those who devise and operate accounting control systems appear to hold others in low regard, even to be attacking them, and at the same time are viewed as frequently overextending their authority beyond any conceivable right, it is not surprising that control systems often have negative side effects.

Yet the evidence does not indicate that such controls invariably produce a punitive and repressive management system—quite the contrary. In a study of 31 managers from several different firms a measure of budget pressure experienced was related to subordinate perceptions of leadership style (14). It was found that those managers who experienced the most pressure from all sources, and particularly from their superiors, were rated high on initiating structure, as might be expected. They tended to pass some of the pressure on down. But they were also rated high on consideration. In this instance at least budget pressure did not go along with the kind of leadership behavior most likely to induce negative consequences such as anger and dissatisfaction. Rather the managers under pressure appeared to be acting in a way calculated to win the support of legitimization for the budgetary controls.

Effective Control. Results such as this suggest that accounting control systems need not yield sizable negative consequences. Thus the answer to the earlier question regarding overall net benefits would appear to be that effective control is possible and that a positive contribution to goal achievement can result. The basic requirements appear to be that the control system be clearly understood, that it be viewed as equitable, and that the authority utilized be legitimized (29, 44).

The most widely recommended method of obtaining these conditions is participative management. If those to be subjected to the controls participate in developing the system, the measures, and the standards, they will be more likely to understand them, to consider them fair, and to comply with actions taken for control purposes (5). It has also been suggested that the accountants involved function primarily as consultants to line management and that deviations from standard be reported directly to the manager responsible for the deviation rather than to a budget director (3).

On the other hand, as in other applications of the participative approach (see Chapter 11), research evidence on its use in the area of accounting control is not uniformly positive (15, 45). Furthermore, engineers and others simply may have no interest in becoming extensively involved in accounting measurement; they may well resist participation in the decision making even though given every opportunity to do so (48).

Actually there seems no necessary reason why participative approaches should provide the only means of developing and operating a fully legitimized accounting control system. Provided the system is generally understood, an effort is made to win acceptance, actions are not taken in the name of the system which go beyond the degree of acceptance obtained, and an open-loop concept is utilized which seeks to determine the causes of deviation, there is every reason to believe that effective accounting control can be achieved in many companies without extensive resort to participation. Whether or not this is true would appear to depend on the value structure of the organization. In some firms any attempt to initiate such a control system without extensive participation would deprive it of acceptance and legitimized authority from the start; in other firms just the reverse might be expected to be the case.

Questions

1. Describe the specific steps involved in performance analysis and performance control. Take an instance of performance failure either in school or at work with which you are familiar and show how these steps might be applied.
2. What is meant by the following?
   a. Variance controls
   b. Precontrol
   c. Open-loop control system
   d. Bidirectional control
3. What problems would you anticipate might arise if an accounting firm were

to introduce a complex budgeting and accounting control system into a company that had previously utilized few financial controls? How might these problems be minimized?
4. What are some of the various approaches to measuring human assets? What appear to be the advantages and disadvantages of each?
5. The auditing concept is often thought of as primarily a monetary matter. What other kinds of audits are there? What purposes do they serve?

References

1. Adam, E. E., and W. E. Scott. "The Application of Behavioral Conditioning Procedures to the Problems of Quality Control." *Academy of Management Journal*, Vol. 14 (1971), 175–193.
2. Argyris, C. "Human Problems with Budgets." *Harvard Business Review*, Vol. 31 (1953), No. 1, 97–110.
3. Argyris, C. *Intervention Theory and Method: A Behavioral Science View*. Reading, Mass.: Addison-Wesley, 1970.
4. Barkdull, C. W. "Periodic Operations Audit: A Management Tool." *Michigan Business Review*, Vol. 18 (1966), No. 4, 19–25.
5. Becker, S. W., and D. Green. "Budgeting and Employee Behavior." *Journal of Business*, Vol. 35 (1962), 392–402.
6. Benston, G. J. "The Role of the Firm's Accounting System for Motivation." *Accounting Review*, Vol. 38 (1963), 347–354.
7. Brummet, R. L., E. G. Flamholtz, and W. C. Pyle. "Human Resource Measurement—A Challenge for Accountants." *Accounting Review*, Vol. 43 (1968), 217–224.
8. Buchele, R. B. "How to Evaluate a Firm." *California Management Review*, Vol. 5 (1962), No. 1, 5–17.
9. Burns, T. J. *The Behavioral Aspects of Accounting Data for Performance Evaluation*. Columbus: College of Administrative Science, Ohio State University, 1970.
10. Caplan, E. H. "Behavioral Assumptions of Management Accounting." *Accounting Review*, Vol. 41 (1966), 496–509.
11. Caplan, E. H. "Behavioral Assumptions of Management Accounting—Report of a Field Study." *Accounting Review*, Vol. 43 (1968), 342–362.
12. Churchill, N. C., and W. W. Cooper. "Effects of Auditing Records: Individual Task Accomplishment and Organization Objectives." In W. W. Cooper, H. J. Leavitt, and M. W. Shelly (eds.), *New Perpsectives in Organization Research*. New York: Wiley, 1964, pp. 250–275.

13. Dalton, M. *Men Who Manage.* New York: Wiley, 1959.
14. DeCoster, D. T. and J. P. Fertakis. "Budget-Induced Pressure and Its Relationship to Supervisory Behavior." *Journal of Accounting Research,* Vol. 6 (1968), 237–246.
15. Dunbar, R. L. M. "Budgeting for Control." *Administrative Science Quarterly,* Vol. 16 (1971), 88–96.
16. Gold, B., and R. M. Kraus. "Integrating Physical and Financial Measures for Managerial Controls." *Academy of Management Journal,* Vol. 7 (1964), 109–127.
17. Greenwood, W. T. "The Management Audit in the Business School Curriculum." In D. E. McFarland (ed.), *Proceedings of the Annual Meeting, 1962.* Academy of Management, 1963, pp. 172–175.
18. Greenwood, W. T. *Management and Organizational Behavior Theories: An Interdisciplinary Approach.* Cincinnati: South-Western, 1965.
19. Gutenberg, A. W. "A Perspective on Management Control Theory." In E. B. Flippo (ed.), *Evolving Concepts in Management. Academy of Management Proceedings,* 1965, pp. 82–92.
20. Haberstroh, C. J. "Control as an Organization Process." *Management Science,* Vol. 6 (1960), No. 2, 165–171.
21. Henning, D. A., and R. L. Moseley. "Authority Role of a Functional Manager: The Controller." *Administrative Science Quarterly,* Vol. 15 (1970), 482–489.
22. Holden, P. E., C. A. Pederson, and G. E. Germane. *Top Management.* New York: McGraw-Hill, 1968.
23. Hutchinson, J. G. *Management Under Strike Conditions.* New York: Holt, Rinehart and Winston, 1966.
24. Jasinski, F. J. "Use and Misuse of Efficiency Controls." *Harvard Business Review,* Vol. 34 (1956), No. 4, 105–112.
25. Jerome, W. T. *Executive Control—The Catalyst.* New York: Wiley, 1961.
26. Kast, F. E., and J. E. Rosenzweig. *Organization and Management: A Systems Approach.* New York: McGraw-Hill, 1970.
27. Koontz, H., and C. O'Donnell. *Principles of Management: An Analysis of Managerial Functions.* New York: McGraw-Hill, 1968.
28. Likert, R. *The Human Organization: Its Management and Value.* New York: McGraw-Hill, 1967.
29. Likert, R., and S. E. Seashore. "Making Cost Control Work." *Harvard Business Review,* Vol. 41 (1963), No. 6, 96–108.
30. Martindell, J. "The Management Audit." In D. E. McFarland (ed.), *Proceedings of the Annual Meeting, 1962.* Academy of Management, 1963, pp. 164–171.
31. Miles, R. E., and R. C. Vergin. "Behavioral Properties of Variance Controls." *California Management Review,* Vol. 8 (1966), No. 3, 57–65.

32. Miner, J. B. *The Management of Ineffective Performance.* New York: McGraw-Hill, 1963.
33. Miner, J. B. *Introduction to Industrial Clinical Psychology.* New York: McGraw-Hill, 1966.
34. Miner, J. B., and J. F. Brewer. "The Management of Ineffective Performance." In M. Dunnette (ed.), *Handbook of Industrial and Organizational Psychology.* Chicago: Rand McNally, 1973.
35. Mockler, R. J. "The Corporate Control Job: Breaking the Mold." *Business Horizons,* Vol. 13 (1970), No. 6, 73–77.
36. Moskowitz, H. "Managers as Partners in Business Decision Research." *Academy of Management Journal,* Vol. 14 (1971), 317–325.
37. Paine, F. T. "Human Resource Accounting—The Current State of the Question." *Federal Accountant,* Vol. 19 (1970), No. 2, 57–67.
38. Paine, F. T. "Organizational Assessment Dimensions as Related to the Overall Effectiveness of Assessment Teams." In M. W. Frey (ed.), *Management Research and Practice. Proceedings of the Seventh Annual Conference.* Eastern Academy of Management, 1970, pp. 114–123.
39. Paine, F. T., and M. J. Gannon. "An Analysis of Organizational Effectiveness." Unpublished paper. University of Maryland, 1971.
40. Pyle, W. C. "Monitoring Human Resources—On Line." *Michigan Business Review,* Vol. 22 (1970), No. 4, 19–32.
41. Pyle, W. C. "Human Resource Accounting." *Financial Analysts Journal,* Vol. 26 (1970), No. 5, 1–10.
42. Rabe, W. F. "Yardsticks for Measuring Personnel Department Effectiveness." *Personnel,* Vol. 44 (1967), No. 1, 56–62.
43. Ridgway, V. F. "Dysfunctional Consequences of Performance Measurements." *Administrative Science Quarterly,* Vol. 1 (1956), 240–247.
44. Schwan, C. C. "The Behavioral Aspects of Accounting Data for Performance Evaluation at Industrial Nucleonics." In T. J. Burns (ed.), *The Behavioral Aspects of Accounting Data for Performance Evaluation.* Columbus: College of Administrative Science, Ohio State University, 1970, pp. 79–110.
45. Stedry, A. C. *Budget Control and Cost Behavior.* Englewood Cliffs, N.J.: Prentice-Hall, 1960.
46. Steinmetz, L. L. *Managing the Marginal and Unsatisfactory Performer.* Reading, Mass.: Addison-Wesley, 1969.
47. Tannenbaum, A. S. *Control in Organizations.* New York: McGraw-Hill, 1968.
48. Wallace, M. E. "Behavioral Considerations in Budgeting." *Management Accounting,* Vol. 47 (1966), No. 12, 3–8.
49. Woodruff, R. L., and R. G. Whitman. "The Behavioral Aspects of Accounting Data for Performance Evaluation at the R. G. Barry Corporation (with Special Reference to Human Resource Accounting)." In T. J. Burns (ed.),

The Behavioral Aspects of Accounting Data for Performance Evaluation. Columbus: College of Administrative Science, Ohio State University, 1970, pp. 1–34.
50. Yoder, D. *Personnel Management and Industrial Relations.* Englewood Cliffs, N.J.: Prentice-Hall, 1970.

Part V
Secondary Management Functions

15 Staffing: Executive Personnel Management

I. Management Recruiting
  1. The Role of Manpower Planning
  2. College Recruiting
  3. Direct Search and the Experienced Man

II. Management Selection
  1. Interviews
  2. Application Blanks and Biographical Data
  3. Reference and Background Checks
  4. Testing
  5. Psychological Evaluations
  6. Assessment Centers

III. Management Development
  1. Management Games and Simulations
  2. The University Approach
  3. Motivational and Attitude Change
  4. Transfer and Promotion

IV. Executive Compensation
  1. Compensation and Motivation
     a. Performance Relationships
     b. Secrecy
  2. Elements of the Compensation Package
     a. Salary and Its Determinants
     b. Bonuses
     c. Stock Payments
     d. Deferred Compensation

V. Management Appraisal
  1. The Scope of Appraisal
  2. Appraising Congruence with the Value Structure
  3. Appraising the Role Behavior— Role Prescription Match

The analysis of research on managerial behavior in Chapter 2 provided only limited support for inclusion of staffing and representing as important management functions. In contrast with planning, directing, coordinating, and controlling, these two appear to be important only under certain circumstances—in particular kinds of companies or in specific types of jobs. Clearly staffing is a major function for any manager working in the personnel area, and representing is equally important for managers concerned with public relations.

For the present purposes staffing is defined as executive personnel management. Thus the discussion focuses on what is done to fill management positions with individuals whose behavior matches role prescriptions as closely as possible. The personnel process as applied to positions below the managerial level is typically considered in detail in books dealing with the personnel and industrial relations field as a whole. The major components of executive personnel management, and those with which the ensuing discussion is concerned, are outlined in Figure 15–1.

Management recruiting and selection are input processes in that they are devoted to getting people into the organization and into specific positions. Management development and compensation are mediators. Primarily they are input-improving mediators in that they seek to make role behavior as effective as possible. However, as noted previously, management development efforts can be used to prevent or reduce conflict, and thus for purposes of sustaining or restoring input potential levels. Similarly some compensation programs focus on providing equality and preventing discord, while many more strive to motivate outstanding performance (8). Management appraisal is an output process in that it seeks to establish the degree of match between role behavior and role prescriptions. Chapter 14 dealt in some detail with the use of accounting data in the context of the control model for this purpose.

This division of the staffing function into its three components—input, mediating, and output processes—is important in developing personnel strategies for specific occupational groups and organizational units (36). In many instances it is possible to stress one, or at most two, of the three,

Figure 15–1 *The Management Staffing Function*

Input Processes	Mediating Processes	Output Processes
Management recruiting	Management development	Management appraisal
Management selection	Executive compensation	

investing heavily there, while playing down the others. There is often a trade-off such that major investments in all three areas are superfluous. Thus, when dealing with professionals, who are already highly educated and dedicated to their work, a strategy emphasizing input processes, with extensive recruiting and selection of only the very best, usually precludes the need for similar investment in mediator and output processes. Similarly an organization which utilizes an up or out policy for managerial or professional personnel should put its major stress on the output process of performance evaluation. It is essential that the individuals who are retained and promoted be those who in fact can contribute role behaviors of the kind needed to accomplish organizational goals. In this case there is a kind of delayed selection process which is invoked some time after hiring. Accordingly initial selection is less crucial, and extensive investments in certain mediator processes such as training and development are not warranted because many individuals will not be retained long enough to yield a return on the investment.

Management Recruiting

The first step in staffing is obtaining an adequate pool of candidates who desire employment. There is a close association between the size of this applicant pool and the effectiveness of selection. If there are three positions to be filled and only three candidates can be located, the most effective selection techniques in the world will not be of much help. On the other hand, if the recruiting effort produces 100 candidates, all at least minimally qualified and eager for employment, the same selection procedures can skim off the best with almost an absolute certainty that the three positions will be filled with highly effective performers.

A variety of techniques are used to build up candidate pools of appropriate sizes. A listing of these sources is given in Table 15-1. For purposes of management recruiting the first two sources have proved most important in recent years—colleges and universities in relation to developing a group of management trainees and potential future managers for promotion from within; executive recruiting firms in relation to filling existing management positions from the outside (32). These two sources receive more detailed consideration later in this section. But first it is necessary to establish a basis for management recruiting in the manpower-planning process.

Table 15–1 *Possible Recruiting Sources*

Colleges, universities, and other educational institutions
Employment agencies, executive recruiting firms, and executive consulting firms
Advertising—newspapers, radio, television, magazines, technical journals, direct mail
Field recruiting at locations known to have high concentrations of the desired candidates
Technical and professional society meetings and placement offices
Referrals by present employees
Walk-ins and write-ins
Unions
Posting, nomination and identification internally to obtain candidates already employed in other jobs (recruiting from within)

The Role of Manpower Planning

It is widely recognized that recruiting efforts should have their origins in detailed planning, preferably of a long-term nature (23, 24). These planning activities serve to establish role prescriptions for those who will do the actual recruiting. Working backward from planned expansions and contractions, and market forecasts, attempts are made to establish what skills will be needed when and where. Such plans dealing with what the company will be doing in the future provide a basis for projecting managerial requirements both in terms of numbers and specializations.

Converting these data into recruiting plans requires certain assumptions regarding the number of leads needed to generate a particular number of hires. How much recruiting needs to be done to fill the anticipated openings at a given point in time? Also, how many candidates can a given recruiter produce a year? What are the relative costs of various sources in proportion to their anticipated return? What are the time lags associated with various sources? How long will it take an average college graduate before he is ready for his first management position, his second, and so on? All of these factors have to be worked out using past company experience as a major guide (23). Only after such premises have been established can a recruiting plan be developed which will predict how much recruiting will be needed, when, using what sources, and focusing on what particular kinds of candidates.

Ideally such a plan will yield a steady inflow of individuals with managerial capabilities such that future needs are in fact continually met without expensive crash efforts and without excessive overstaffing costs (24). This assumes a planning process which stretches many years into the future. Yet it is apparent that a large number of companies are operating in a much shorter term and are markedly responsive to unanticipated economic fluctuations. A survey of 35 companies that normally hire sizable numbers of college graduates indicates that in November 1969 they planned to hire just under 15,000 individuals from 1970 classes. They actually hired 29 percent less. At the master's degree level the cutback from plan was 9 percent (18). Data clearly indicate that under the impact of the economic downturn a large number of companies suddenly shifted from a plan calling for increased college recruiting in 1970 to a marked reduction. Furthermore, many companies responded to the immediate economic situation by deciding against recruiting visits to campuses that characteristically had been visited in previous years. This appears to reflect sudden budget cuts in the recruiting area (6). Clearly the ideal relationship between manpower planning and recruiting often gives way before shorter-run exigencies.

College Recruiting

In an overwhelming majority of companies positions in the management hierarchy are typically filled by promotions from within, and the primary original source of these candidates, especially in large companies, is college recruiting (8). Recruiting on college campuses is costly in comparison with many other sources. A company representative has to travel to the campus; then active candidates have to be brought to a company facility for further evaluation and to learn about the company they might join. College recruiting is also of reasonably recent vintage. Although some firms have been engaged in it for many years, the majority started during the manpower shortages of the early 1950s (32). A number of factors suggest that changes now under way in our society and in the labor market may well produce a drastic reduction in college recruiting, with potential employees forced to seek out employers rather than the reverse. The supply of qualified college graduates may well be outstripping the demand. There can be little doubt that most companies would prefer such a change. Recruiting on the campus has been a mixed blessing considering costs, yields, salary competition, and high turnover rates among new college graduates.

Some of the difficulties associated with college recruiting are brought out by certain research studies. In one instance various characteristics of students interviewed by company representatives at the University of Minnesota were related to indexes dealing with the number of company visits and jobs offered (10, 11). The most pronounced finding was that those who were consistently rated more handsome were particularly likely to fare well. Yet the available research indicates that handsome people have no particular proclivity for subsequent managerial success. Clearly with the brief time available for campus interviews the company recruiters were resorting to one of the few criteria they could use to separate one person from another. But this criterion was not helping the companies to get any better managers than would have been achieved by drawing straws.

Another study was concerned with the tendency of some college seniors to back out of a job acceptance between the time of initial commitment and the time they are scheduled to start work (26). A survey of 19 companies doing considerable recruiting on college campuses indicated a range of back outs from less than 1 percent to over 16 percent. Although for most of the companies the problem was not of significant proportions, 7 of the 19 had rates over 3 percent. Further study revealed that the use of three telephone calls emphasizing positive aspects of the company in the period between acceptance and employment drastically reduced back outs. Data for the two companies which had consistently had back-out rates in the vicinity of 10 percent are given in Table 15–2. Those who did and did not

***Table 15–2** Back-out Frequencies in Two Companies With and Without Telephone Follow-up*

Group	Did Not Back Out	Did Back Out	Percent Backing Out
Company A			
Telephone calls	91	2	2.2
No telephone calls	83	10	10.8
Company B			
Telephone calls	100	3	2.9
No telephone calls	92	11	10.7

Source: J. M. Ivancevich and J. H. Donnelly, "Job Offer Acceptance Behavior and Reinforcement," *Journal of Applied Psychology*, Vol. 55 (1971), 121. Copyright 1971 by the American Psychological Association. Reproduced by permission.

receive the phone calls were chosen strictly by chance. It is clear that the back-out problem can be reduced, but only at the cost of considerable time and money. Again the college recruiting source emerges as far from ideal for many companies.

Staffing: Executive Personnel Management

Direct Search and the Experienced Man

A frequent alternative to college recruiting has been a search for individuals already employed, often in competing firms, who might be recruited directly into management positions. The oldest such source is the employment agency. Employment agencies, however, attract individuals who are looking for work and the agency's compensation depends on finding a position for these individuals. This means that an agency may not have a company's best interests in mind, and that it may tend to foist off something less than the highest levels of talent on companies lacking adequate selection procedures. Most companies respond favorably to the employment agency source at lower levels, but look on it with decreasing favor as the level of the position rises.

A much more recent, but similar entry on the recruiting scene is the executive consulting firm. These organizations are in fact engaged primarily in vocational guidance, although they try to make placements in the field selected. They have burgeoned in periods of business recession when many companies reduce their managerial force and executives at all levels are often looking for new opportunities. Such firms have also been very active in finding new careers for former clergymen (16).

The major direct search source, however, is the executive recruiting firm which is employed by a company, rather than by the candidate, and which attempts to locate individuals already employed elsewhere who might qualify for an opening. Firms of this kind charge anywhere from 15 to 30 percent of the selected manager's first year compensation, depending on the prestige of the search organization (32). They often make extensive investigations aimed at identifying candidates for high-level positions. Typically the search is at least initially anonymous in that potential candidates are not told the name of the firm until an initial screening interview has been conducted. With multiple contacts throughout the business world these executive recruiting organizations can be a highly effective source, especially if they do considerable work for a particular client and come to have an extensive understanding of the organization's needs.

Management Selection

Research on individual motives and other characteristics that might be stressed in selecting people for management positions has been reviewed in Chapters 10 and 11. It is apparent that there are wide differences between companies insofar as the characteristics of effective managers are concerned. In this section the discussion will focus less on the *kind* of people who should be selected and more on the *procedures* that are used in managerial selection. Among these are interviews, application blanks, biographical inventories, references, background investigations, physical examinations, psychological testing, psychological evaluations, and assessment centers. All of these procedures may be used, either for selection among outside candidates for management trainee and management positions or for selection among internal candidates for promotion, although certain approaches tend to be preferred for one purpose or the other.

Interviews

As currently used the interview is a two-edged tool. It is a means to both recruiting and selection. This kind of flexibility is lacking in most other selection procedures and accordingly the interview has achieved considerable popularity and very widespread application. The almost universal pattern in selecting individuals for managerial positions is for the candidate to be exposed to a series of interviews with members of the personnel group and with the managers with whom he would work. He may spend time with as many as eight or ten people. Judgments derived from these interviews tend to be the main factor in the decision whether or not to make an offer. For the great majority of companies the interview is the key aspect of the management selection process (8).

The research evidence is clear in indicating that interviews *can* prove quite effective in identifying those who will, and will not, achieve subsequent success on the job (38, 50). It is equally clear that in many cases they do not come close to actually demonstrating this potential. There are a host of factors associated with this failure in practice. Again and again it has been found that interviewers do not agree, and no one really knows who is right. There is good reason to believe that some people consistently conduct better interviews and make better predictions than others, but in many companies the better interviewers either are not known or their recommendations are given little weight. Often interviewers jump to conclusions on minimal evidence or place great emphasis on factors that actually make no difference insofar as subsequent performance is concerned. Some characteristics are very difficult, if not impossible, to identify clearly in the interview situation: creativity, loyalty, dependability, and honesty, for instance. Yet interviewers frequently do make guesses about these matters, even in the absence of adequate information. They are very likely to be wrong.

A number of approaches have been identified which can serve to decrease these deficiencies and make the interview an effective selection procedure (9). These approaches are in use in some firms. One approach is to structure the questions asked so that the same things are investigated by all interviewers and for all candidates. Interviews have also been found more effective where data are recorded on an ongoing basis as the interview progresses, where interviewers have been extensively trained, and where they receive feedback on how well their predictions agree with those of other interviewers and with actual performance once a man is on the job so they can learn from their mistakes. Employment quotas should not be established in such a way as to put interviewers under pressure to make favorable judgments which are really not warranted.

Application Blanks and Biographical Data

Use of resumés, application blanks, and the more comprehensive biographical inventories is as widespread as the interview. In addition an increasing although still small number of companies are conducting studies aimed at determining which particular response categories, and consequently what types of characteristics and past experiences, are associated with more effective or less effective job performance (8).

An example of the type of result that may emerge from such analysis is given in Table 15–3. The study attempted to differentiate between those who succeed and fail in a major consulting firm. The firm has an up or out policy, under which if an individual is not elected a partner within eight or nine years of his initial employment he is asked to leave (40). Thus, in Table 15–3 those who achieve election (go up) are contrasted with those who do not (go out). It is clear that the individual who held a commission in the armed forces, who had previous experience as a manager in business, who graduated from the Harvard Business School, who served in the Navy or Marines, and who did his undergraduate work somewhere other than at a state university represents the best type of prospect for success in this particular organization.

Secondary Management Functions

Table 15–3 *Relationship Between Certain Biographical Factors and Election to Partnership in a Consulting Firm*

Biographical Factor	N	Percent Up (Elected)	Percent Out (Separated)
Held a commission in the armed forces			
Yes	104	39	61
No	75	16	84
Previously achieved the management level, if in business			
Yes	70	39	61
No	70	19	81
Graduate of Harvard Business School, if any graduate degree			
Yes	74	41	59
No	66	18	82
Served in the Navy or Marines, if any service			
Yes	67	42	58
No	77	26	74
Undergraduate degree from a state university			
Yes	36	16	84
No	143	33	67

Reference and Background Checks

Reference data may be obtained from friends, neighbors, and the like, in which case it is generally concerned with character and reputation only, or from previous employers, in which case it is concerned with work experience and behavior. It may be obtained through letters, telephone conversations, or in some cases, especially at the higher managerial levels and in positions where security is an important issue, through personal interviews and field investigations.

Such research as has been done on the value of references as predictors of subsequent performance has concentrated almost entirely on the written form. Yet there is reason to believe the telephone approach is used considerably more often (43). Furthermore, employers appear to actually contact only something less than half of the previous employers noted by the applicant, and often even these contacts occur subsequent to a decision to hire. Generally previous immediate supervisors are most likely to be contacted. Questions asked stress such things as whether the previous employer would rehire, overall evaluations, reasons for leaving previous employment, length of the employment period, and absenteeism record. It is difficult to determine how much weight is given to reference data, but it appears to be somewhat less than the interview and about equal to the application blank.

Much of the research conducted on written references certainly would not warrant placing a great deal of faith in this approach, although a recent study indicates that under certain conditions more favorable results can be obtained (41). The study found that greater accuracy is achieved if the evaluations are obtained from immediate supervisors who had the candidate as a subordinate for a considerable time and when he worked in a job very similar to the one he is being considered for. Furthermore, references obtained from supervisors of the same sex, race, or country of origin as the candidate tend to show an upward bias which makes them less useful as predictors. These findings derive from research on people below the managerial level and accordingly must be used with caution. Yet it does seem likely from what is known to date that prior supervisors are the best source of references, that they are most useful when they know the person well and understand the kind of work he will be doing, and that to the extent the supervisor has no reason to be biased the references will be more valid. In addition it seems evident that to the extent the potential employer seeks out the reference source, and obtains the data in a personal, two-way communication context, distortion and evasion will be less. As many firms have learned, printed forms and impersonal procedures yield few useful results.

Testing

In addition to the physical examination, tests used in industry cover a broad spectrum of characteristics: mental abilities, psychomotor abilities, interests, personality, specific job skills, and knowledge. Insofar as management positions are concerned tests are more likely to be used at the lower levels than at the upper and more frequently given to outside candidates than to those already employed by the company (8). To the extent a person has a proven record of managerial performance and/or is already well-known to the organization, test data are less likely to be needed.

A number of factors have combined in recent years to produce a considerable advance in the usefulness of tests as predictors of subsequent success (48). It is increasingly clear that the best results are obtained when

Secondary Management Functions

a number of different test measures are combined, and when the pattern of measures that will in fact predict success is determined separately for distinct occupational and organizational groups. The advent of high-speed computers has made the complex statistical analyses required by these approaches entirely feasible. Furthermore, in earlier years the testing of mental abilities and knowledge progressed much more rapidly than the testing of motives and personality, but this no longer appears to be the case. Very effective personality measures are now being developed.

Evidence on these points is given in Table 15-4. The data presented derive from the same management consulting organization that provided the data of Table 15-3. It is apparent that the personality tests used consistently permit the selection of a high proportion of individuals who will be successful consultants (39). These results are obtained in very different ways, however, for the United States consultants and those overseas. In fact the characteristics making for success in one environment are almost the exact opposite of those making for success in the other, even though all the consultants work for the same firm. It was also found that the degree of

Table 15-4 *Relationship Between Personality Test Composite Scores and Overall Success in Management Consulting*

		Personality Test Score	
Group	N	Percent Above Average Score	Percent Below Average Score
U.S. Consultants			
Successful	25	76	24
Less successful	33	27	73
European Consultants			
Successful	16	75	25
Less successful	18	22	78
Factors Contributing to Personality Test Composite Scores			
U.S. Consultants			
Low work motivation (7 measures)			
High social motivation (4 measures)			
Low self-confidence (3 measures)			
Independence (1 measure)			
Emotional stability (1 measure)			
High power motivation (2 measures)			
Low peer group motivation (1 measure)			
European Consultants			
High work motivation (6 measures)			
Low social motivation (2 measures)			
Dependence (1 measure)			
High competitive motivation (2 measures)			

predictive accuracy obtained requires combining a number of measures of a number of different characteristics—for the U.S. consultants a total of 19 measures, for the European consultants 11 measures.

Psychological Evaluations

Psychological evaluations typically involve some combination of testing, intensive interviewing, and reference checks—the weighting among these factors differs considerably from one psychologist to another. Usually the evaluations are made by an outside psychological consulting firm and the end product is a written personality description and recommendation. Psychological evaluations are most widely used at the managerial level and some firms obtain them even on candidates for top management positions. Candidates evaluated may be from the outside, but the approach is also used when considering individuals for promotion from within.

Evidence on the extent to which psychological evaluations are used and their effectiveness in selecting among candidates for hiring or promotion is not extensive. It would appear that when companies do use this approach they are likely to place considerable reliance on it and to apply it widely within the organization. Research on effectiveness has provided mixed results, but with some quite favorable findings insofar as management selection is concerned; within the management consulting firm where the previously noted studies of other selection procedures were conducted the results were not favorable (37). Five studies were conducted using different groups of consultants. In no case did the psychologists' hiring recommendation have any relation to subsequent performance levels. There was evidence, however, that different psychologists recommended hiring markedly different proportions of the candidates they evaluated—all the way from 69 percent for one psychologist down to 25 percent for another.

Results such as these suggest that the future will see a movement away from the art of psychological evaluation to multiple-measure testing of the kind described in the previous section, with biographical data also incorporated in the analyses, and to the assessment center approach. At least this would seem likely insofar as the selection problem is concerned. On the other hand, psychological evaluations are likely to remain useful as sources of information on the causes of ineffective performance in the performance control context and as an aid in counseling. This is in fact their traditional usage in clinical psychology from which the approach was exported to the business world.

Assessment Centers

The assessment center approach also seeks to focus a variety of measures and types of data on the selection decision; in fact the diversity is greater than with any other procedure. The usual plan is to bring a small group of individuals, generally around 12, to a central location where they take tests covering a variety of areas and participate in a number of exercises and simulations over a two- or three-day period. The exercises include group discussions focused on various topics, simulated in-basket situations, business games, and presentations, role playing, and case analysis; some are of a group nature, some individual. There are also intensive interviews. In addition to the scores obtained from the tests and exercises, ratings are made on a variety of characteristics such as self-confidence, administrative ability, and the like by trained assessors (psychologists or line managers from the company) who observe as the various tasks are performed.

Evidence from a number of studies in different companies indicates that the results of this approach are valuable in predicting later managerial success (7). The technique is costly and for this reason is more frequently used with candidates for promotion who are already employed than with outside applicants. It appears to predict potential for management positions above the first level better than for jobs such as foreman. To date it has been employed mostly by the larger corporations; few candidates for top management positions have been exposed to it. Research indicates that the various components of the assessments—the tests, the exercises, and the ratings—all make important contributions to the final results (49). As the discussion in Chapter 11 would suggest, the kinds of measures that are effective in one company often are not of equal value in another. Thus, while mental ability measures proved very useful at A.T. & T. and personality tests much less so, just the reverse has been found at I.B.M. It seems apparent that individual firms must conduct their own research to determine which of the many measures obtained should be stressed in making selection and promotion decisions in that company.

Management Development

One major type of management development effort, T-group or sensitivity training, has already been considered at some length in Chapter 9 in relation to organization development and change. The confrontation approaches to conflict prevention discussed in Chapter 13 are closely allied, although the development aspect is not quite as clearly in evidence. This section considers a number of other methods that have been devised to improve the performance of managers. These efforts may be oriented toward present job performance or they may be future oriented in that they attempt to prepare a manager for some anticipated higher-level assignment.

Management Games and Simulations

Simulations present the individual with an artificial representation of the job situation and require him to perform within that context. Ideally he receives feedback of some kind on how well he is doing and thus is able to adjust his responses—he learns to do the things that make for success and not to do the things that make for failure. Many of the simulation exercises utilized in assessment centers, such as the in-basket measure, can be reconstituted for purposes of learning. The major additional requirement is that some provision be made to feed back results. Case study and role playing exercises represent other simulation approaches.

In the context of the management job, simulations rather consistently focus on problem solving or decision making, although the degree of approximation to reality built in tends to vary considerably. The most realistic procedure developed to date appears to be the management game. This utilizes a dynamic model of a business situation with the players, usually grouped into teams, making operating and policy decisions much as managers would in real life. The mathematical relationships built into the model provide a basis for processing decisions and feeding back performance reports. There are a number of these decision-report cycles and consequently time may be compressed so that decisions normally made over many years of operations can be experienced in a single day.

A great variety of management games are now available, all developed since the late 1950s; most now utilize a computer for computations (14). The top management games deal with total company operations in a context of competing firms and often changing economic forces. But there are other games which focus on functional areas within the business, or even on particular jobs. Specific games have often been developed to reflect the unique conditions in a given industry.

Although there is considerable evidence indicating that other types of simulations can have positive effects, data on the impact of management games is surprisingly sparse (8). One study, however, has yielded results indicating that learning is facilitated. In this case groups were taught using a relatively simple management game, a more complex game, and the case method only (44). Comparison of the three groups on a measure of learning indicated that those with game experience improved more than those without it. But there was no effect attributable to the level of game complexity. What evidence is available suggests that the experience of actually practicing in the managerial role and finding out what happens as a result of making decisions is of value in acquiring new knowledge. On the other hand, training directors generally tend to describe management games as most effective in developing problem-solving skills (13). It seems likely that the two (problem solving and knowledge) are closely associated in this instance.

The University Approach

Most of the programs given by universities for practicing managers also stress content learning, the acquisition of knowledge, and problem-solving skills. Cases and other simulations are widely used, although lectures with discussion probably predominate. Since the primary objective of these programs is to provide a broadening experience, the content tends to be quite varied. However, participants express a strong preference for topics such as business policy, human relations or administrative practices, and social responsibility (2). It seems clear that they want to learn things related to top management decision making; in large part that is what they do learn.

A recent survey identified programs of two weeks' duration or longer (up to 16 weeks) in 42 United States universities (46). In addition several of the larger companies have created their own executive development centers offering programs very similar to those in the universities. Participants tend to be middle- or sometimes upper-level managers in the age range of 35 to 55. Often attendance at a program is closely related to promotion to higher levels of responsibility. It is rare for any single company to send more than one or two persons to a particular university program at the same time.

Although programs of this kind stress intellectual learning and knowledge, there is evidence that at least in some cases a side effect occurs which influences values and motives. A number of university programs have been instituted which teach liberal arts subject matter—humanities, physical and social sciences. Again the idea is to achieve a broadening of knowledge and understanding. Studies of these programs clearly indicate that they serve to reduce the value placed on economic pursuits and the desire to stress the practical and pragmatic (22). Whether changes of this type make for more effective executives is an open question; it is entirely possible that the reduction in economic values would have a negative effect in some companies.

Motivational and Attitude Change

What is at best a side effect of simulations and university programs becomes the central objective of many other management development efforts. The value-changing aspects of the T-group or sensitivity training approach have already been noted. A major objective is to foster democratic, participative values and thus power equalization. This same goal is also sought by a number of other efforts, usually offered internally within a firm, which may be loosely classified as human relations training programs.

That these programs often do achieve their objectives has now been clearly established. In one study the degree of influence on decisions exerted by managers, adjusters, and clerical personnel in an insurance company was measured before and after the managers were exposed to a human relations program (4). The findings indicated that as a result of the course the managers came to exert less influence, the adjusters changed very little, and the clerical workers had more influence. Thus a shift toward greater power equalization did occur, apparently because the managers came to desire it.

The sensitivity and human relations approaches are closely associated with two content theories of motivation—need hierarchy and the two-factor view (see Chapter 10). The object of the programs is to change managers so that they will foster ego needs, self-actualization, and intrinsic motivation in their subordinates. As might be anticipated management development programs have also been formulated with a view to fostering the motives emphasized by other content theories of motivation as well. Data related to achievement motivation theory are given in Table 15-5. The study was conducted with managers in India and utilized measures both of achievement motivation and of the degree to which the individual was active in stimulating business growth and in new economic ventures (33). Achievement motivation was increased by the training. In addition those

Table 15–5 Percentages of Managers With and Without Achievement Motivation Training Classified as Active in Business Development During 2-year Periods

Group	N	Before Course 1962–64	After Course 1964–66
Training—In Charge of Business	46	26 %	67 %
Training—Not in Charge of Business	30	3 %	30 %
No Training	73	22 %	25 %

Source: D. C. McClelland and D. G. Winter, *Motivating Economic Achievement* (New York: Free Press, 1969), pp. 213, 253.

who underwent training were subsequently much more active in an economic sense than those who did not, particularly if they had the opportunity for increased activity offered by being in charge of a business.

Similar results have been obtained in relation to role-motivation theory (34). Training efforts have consistently increased the type of motivation implicit in the theory—positive attitudes toward authority, competitive motivation, power motivation, and so forth. In addition sharp differences in subsequent promotion rates and performance evaluations have been found between those who did and those who did not have the course.

The results obtained with various management development programs related to content motivation theories often have been favorable. But this is not a universal finding. In some instances motives fostered may be directly antithetical to the value structure of the organization. As a result individuals may be viewed as less effective after training, not more. Dysfunctional consequences of this kind have been reported sufficiently often to make this a realistic consideration in planning any program (25). Furthermore, such learning as occurs even in knowledge-oriented efforts may well not be put to use on the job. The individual must view what he has learned as a path to the attainment of some job-related goal and he must believe he has the freedom to use his new knowledge, if full application is to occur (12).

Transfer and Promotion

The most popular of all approaches to management development appears to be job rotation, which often is combined with on-the-job coaching by immediate superiors (5). This approach is widely used with management trainees just recruited from college who spend several months in each of a number of nonmanagement assignments. Within the ranks of management itself rotation may involve lateral transfer or promotion, but the placements are of longer duration. As with many management development efforts the major objective is broadening. Thus positions are not always filled with the man who can be expected to meet the immediate role prescriptions most closely; an additional consideration is long-term contribution to the company and the full development of potential. Sometimes rotation serves the purpose of permitting evaluation of an individual's performance and potential by a number of different superiors.

Not infrequently the use of transfers and promotions for development involves a change of location. Changes of this kind occur most commonly simply because a vacancy must be filled, but development is also a consideration in many instances. The geographic transfer approach is used most often with middle-level managers in marketing or general management and in companies with a large number of operations of varying size located in different parts of the country (21). Thus a manager may be given experience in small, medium, and large plants in that succession. Staff managers and those in companies with few installations or many of approximately the same size make geographic transfers less often. Where the plants are very similar, anyway, rotation within a single location appears to be preferred.

Broadening is the major consideration in developmental transfers, but managers are also shifted in order to prepare them to take over a specific position at a subsequent date. In these cases the individual may be made a direct line assistant to the man he will replace or utilized in a general staff capacity as an "assistant to." In some cases "acting" appointments are used for the same purpose. As with job rotation for broadening, this understudy approach has never been effectively evaluated in terms of the effects on the individual and the organization. There is reason to believe, however, that coaching may well be minimal (8).

Executive Compensation

The level of a manager's pay is related in part to recruiting and retention considerations. It costs a certain amount to induce a person to join a particular company and one must then pay at some specific level to keep him from moving on to another firm. These compensation rates are largely,

Secondary Management Functions

although certainly not exclusively, determined by conditions in the labor market outside the company. But simply inducing an individual to make his performance contributions to one organization rather than another is not the only role that pay plays. Particularly at the managerial level it is intended that money should induce certain types and levels of performance, not just any performance. This places executive compensation squarely in the context of motivation theory. In order to fully understand this input-improving aspect of pay it is essential to consider it in this wider motivational context.

Compensation and Motivation

Viewed in the context of expectancy theory, pay operates as a first-level outcome which is instrumental to the satisfaction of certain second level outcomes or needs (see Figure 10-1). Research indicates a definite tendency for pay to be considered a means to satisfying some motives, and not others (29). It is most closely related to such motives as status, esteem, recognition, and security. To a somewhat lesser degree it relates to autonomy and independence motivation. But pay is rarely instrumental for social and self-actualizing motives. This means that for managers who want status or security more than almost anything else, pay has a high potential for motivating their job behavior; for managers who are particularly concerned with social interaction or personal growth, it is much less likely to make a difference.

Given the existence of a motivational hierarchy in which pay-related motives have a high valence, or are dominant, certain other factors must be present for pay to motivate good job performance.

1. There must be an expectation that good performance will actually yield high pay; pay must be tied to performance, at least in the mind of the individual.
2. There must also be an expectation that it is possible through one's own efforts to achieve those goals which serve to define good performance.

It is the first of these expectations that is most closely related to the way executive compensation programs are designed and administered, and that creates the biggest problem in using pay as an input-improving mediator, even with those individuals who have the kind of motivational hierarchies that make them particularly responsive to the pay incentive.

Performance Relationships. There is ample evidence that in many organizations pay is not tied to performance at all; the outstanding managers are paid no more and do not get larger raises than the less effective (29). In many other organizations performance level is much less important as a determinant of compensation than other considerations. Yet there is evidence that given any basis in reality for believing that their performance determines their pay, managers will hold this expectation (27). Within three divisions of a state government, where performance level had no relation to pay, managers indicated that they did not expect good performance would be rewarded in financial terms. But in four business firms, where there was at least a minimal relationship between performance and compensation, the managers seemed if anything to exaggerate the extent to which merit was viewed as an important factor in pay.

If managers want so much to believe that pay is tied to performance, why does such a relationship fail to exist in so many organizations? One factor of course is that an emphasis may be placed on staying with the organization, on length of service, at the expense of merit. Certain other factors which tend to dilute the motivational potential of pay have been identified in a laboratory study utilizing a simulation of the decision processes involved in determining raises for subordinates (3). It was found that individuals with strong social and religious values, who themselves were somewhat less intelligent and successful, and who viewed service to others as a major life goal, were particularly likely to recommend large raises quite independent of whether the man was a good performer or not. It seems apparent from this study that such factors as sympathy, a desire to help others, and a wish not to make anyone angry may easily intrude into compensation decisions and move them away from a strong dependence on merit.

Secrecy. Although the lack of any relationship between performance and pay appears to be the major factor leading to an expectation that good performance will not be rewarded, and thus to a failure to realize the motivational potential inherent in compensation, secrecy about the money various individuals are receiving also contributes. If an outstanding manager does not know that the raise he receives is considerably larger than that received by most other managers, much of the motivational impact is lost.

The objective of a secrecy policy is to prevent friction and dissatisfaction. The assumption is that if people do not know what others make they will not be jealous and feelings of inequity will be minimized. This makes considerable sense where in fact a compensation program is characterized by inequity and a lack of performance ties. But it is not true that a lack of public information on pay necessarily prevents comparisons. Such comparisons are made and the available evidence indicates that under conditions of secrecy they are typically wrong (28). There is a consistent tendency to overestimate the pay of subordinates and of other managers at the same level, while underestimating what superiors make. This perceptual compression of pay differentiation is a source of dissatisfaction in and of itself. Thus secrecy does not solve the inequity problem, although it may reduce it when the inequities are in fact of major proportions.

Even more important, however, is the effect of these distortions on expectations that good performance will be rewarded. If an effective manager sees his own pay as closer to that of his peers and subordinates than it is, he can hardly believe that his efforts have been very worthwhile. It may well be that he will so misperceive the situation that what is in fact a sizable monetary reward for good performance is viewed instead as so small relative to what others receive that it constitutes negative criticism. Furthermore, the tendency to underestimate the pay of superiors makes promotion less attractive and thus discourages striving for that goal.

All in all it seems clear that secrecy policies serve to shackle the motivational potential of compensation, at least in the presence of a true tie between performance level and monetary reward. Yet secrecy is particularly common at the management level, just where compensation is most frequently intended as an input-improving mediator (29).

Elements of the Compensation Package

Top-level executive compensation has become an increasingly complex mélange with an almost infinite number of possible components. In part the complexity stems from a desire to achieve a positive motivational impact; in part it is a consequence of the fact that tax considerations become of considerable significance at this level, both for the individual and for the company. Among the possible components of an executive compensation package are base salary, bonuses, profit sharing, stock purchases, stock options, pensions, insurance, deferred compensation, and employment contracts.

There has been a tendency in recent years to formulate different compensation packages for different managers. It is now almost universal to utilize different combinations at the three managerial levels: first-line, middle, and top. But in addition other factors, such as the different compensation needs of different age groups, are sometimes taken into account (19). In some cases, especially at the very top levels, a certain amount of individual choice of package components occurs. This is particularly true if an individual is hired-in at a high level and can negotiate his own employment terms.

Trends in top-level compensation over time have been analyzed using data for the five highest paid individuals in 50 large corporations (30). Between 1940 and 1963 these executives' total compensation after taxes approximately doubled. All of this growth occurred in the decade 1945–1955; there has been little change since that time. Most of the growth has been in the form of contingent compensation (bonuses, stock options, etc.) rather than salary, to the point where salary now accounts for only about half of the total package. In terms of *real* after tax income, taking inflationary effects into account, top-level executives appear to be no better off today than they were in 1940. By almost any standards the companies studied have grown much more rapidly than their executives' compensation. Furthermore, many other occupational groups have experienced more rapid compensation growth than the top executives. This is true of physicians, lawyers, dentists, and particularly of manufacturing production workers.

Salary and Its Determinants. A number of factors have been identified as determinants of managerial salaries—many of them having little if any relation to performance effectiveness (20). As might be anticipated managerial level is most important, but years of experience (especially in management work) is a close second. However, among those who reach the division manager level this seniority factor is less important in accounting for salary differentials, and the size of the organization as measured by sales volume and number of employees is much more important. Such factors as the number of employees supervised, the skill level of subordinates, and the average pay of subordinates are significant factors irrespective of managerial level.

Secondary Management Functions

At the very highest levels there are differences associated with the particular industry, with the functional area of work, with level, and with company size, although it is apparent that salaries have not kept pace with growth in many instances (42). Data on typical functional area differentials are given in Table 15-6. These differentials, like that between chief executives and their highest-paid subordinates, which tends to run at about 30 percent, have remained remarkably stable over the years. Yet Table 15-6 does suggest some tendency to increase rewards to executives concerned with financial and human resources more rapidly than to those concerned with material resources.

Bonuses. At least at the higher levels base salary has not been viewed as the primary motivating or input-improving aspect of the compensation package. This role has fallen primarily to the bonus, and to a lesser degree to certain other components. However, when bonuses are paid out over a number of years, rather than in the year in which they are earned, they would appear to lose some of their value in motivating performance.

In general, executive bonuses are closely related to profits. They are high when the company is doing well and low or nonexistent if it is doing poorly. To some degree bonuses are scaled according to level with the highest proportion of base salary going to the chief executive (40 percent is a common figure) and smaller proportions to those at successively lower levels (1). The argument here is that the higher the position the greater the opportunity to make decisions that directly influence profits and thus the greater the return on incentive compensation.

Although initially most bonus plans do operate in close parallel with performance measures, there is a persistent tendency to erosion over time

Table 15-6 Compensation of Top Executives in Various Functional Areas

Position	Mid-1969	Mid-1959
Executive Vice-President	$73,500	$68,000
Top Marketing Executive	55,000	52,500
Top Manufacturing Executive	49,000	48,000
Top Financial Executive	58,000	51,500
Top Engineering Executive	40,000	37,000
Top Industrial Relations Executive	34,000	28,000
Top Purchasing Executive	27,500	24,500

Source: A. Patton, "Executive Compensation Inequities," *Business Horizons*, Vol. 13 (1970), No. 1, 75.

(15). The group covered tends to expand, and may in the end include many individuals who have little direct influence on profits. Thus payments often drop to a level where they have little meaning. Furthermore, a pattern sets in such that practically everyone is rewarded and level and seniority gain dominance over performance. These departures from the original motivational intent are not universal, but they are common. There is reason to believe, however, that the management by objectives approach which ties bonus levels to the achievement of specific goals can be an effective antidote (1).

Stock Payments. Firms may pay a part of the executive bonus in company stock. It also is not uncommon to offer managers stock purchase opportunities, often at somewhat below market value. The most significant stock payment procedure, however, is the stock option plan. The company offers to sell a given number of shares to a preestablished set of executives at a stated price. The executives can complete the purchase any time within a specified time period at that price. If the stock increases in value there is an incentive to buy because the executive now has an opportunity to make the purchase at below market value. If no such increase occurs, he does not purchase and loses nothing.

The idea is to encourage executives to contribute to company profits and thus raise stock values. In addition, any gains realized on the difference between the cost of the stock and what it is ultimately sold for are subject to tax at a lower rate than salary compensation would be. These tax advantages have been increasingly restricted by various laws and Internal Revenue Service rulings to the point where many executives are no longer able to meet the conditions for obtaining them (47). Yet companies continue to utilize stock options widely. There is a serious question whether in doing so they have contributed much to the cash compensation of managers in the past few years (42).

Deferred Compensation. In one sense stock options are a type of deferred compensation. It rarely happens that the stock increases in value immediately after the option is granted; that typically takes some time and maximal gains may require several years. Furthermore, the stock must then be held without sale for several more years to obtain a tax advantage. Bonuses also may have a similar time span to realization. It is not uncommon to pay a bonus earned in one year in five yearly installments.

In addition to such short-term deferral arrangements, there are a variety of plans which withhold part of the compensation until retirement. This compensation is paid after the executive leaves the company, at a time when his total income can be expected to be much less and thus when the applicable tax rate is lower. Payment may be in stock and/or cash. Long-term deferrals of this kind as well as those of a shorter nature usually require continued employment for realization. Thus a major objective is to keep the executive from moving to another firm. Generally deferral of income until after retirement is not attractive to younger managers whose primary need is for cash to meet expenses; later on in the 50s, however, it tends to be viewed much more favorably (19).

There is considerable disagreement as to the merits of the deferred compensation approach, and long-term deferral in particular. It has been argued that it is effective in motivating performance and that it is important to recruiting and retention (45). On the other hand, the motivational impact has been questioned, since rewards are separated from performance by a matter of years. It is also argued that the retention value is limited to the less effective; that good managers will be able to move anyway, since their new employers will be willing to buy out any unpaid deferred compensation (29). Research which would shed some light on these disagreements is currently completely nonexistent.

Management Appraisal

The evaluation of managerial performance is basic to all other aspects of the staffing function. Its impact on recruiting occurs because separation and promotion decisions are based on performance considerations, and thus the openings that need to be filled are a function of the appraisal process. Selection is ideally carried out to yield more of the kind of managers whose performance is judged effective. Management development is at least in part carried out to overcome deficiencies, either current or potential, which management appraisal identifies. Compensation must be closely tied to performance levels if it is to achieve an adequate motivational impact.

It is not at all uncommon to use different evaluation procedures for these different purposes. Thus the accounting approach stressing profit center performance as discussed in Chapter 14 may be used for purposes of executive compensation and in particular to establish bonus levels. It is unlikely to be used as a basis for making decisions regarding management development; some other procedure, perhaps incorporating elements of the assessment center approach, would be used instead.

The Scope of Appraisal

Profit performance, assessment center evaluations, and performance against goals established in a management by objectives program are all used in connection with the appraisal of management personnel. The most common approach, however, utilizes some type of rating procedure. Almost without exception these ratings are made by one or more superiors. Subordinates characteristically prefer to have their work evaluated in this manner (31).

It appears that as companies have shifted away from formal evaluation systems for employees below the managerial level, often under union pressure, they have steadily increased their use with managers (35). Only at the very top executive levels are such programs a rarity. Approximately 80 percent of U.S. companies that are large enough to warrant it have some type of formal management appraisal system. Recently systems related to management development, and involving some type of feedback to the individual regarding the level of his performance, have appeared in increasing numbers. Many of these development-oriented procedures have severe limitations insofar as decisions regarding promotion, selection, and compensation are concerned. Thus the trend to increasing use of multiple appraisal systems for different purposes.

Appraising Congruence with the Value Structure

A common approach in management appraisal is to obtain an overall rating of effectiveness, either by ranking a group of managers or by using some type of scale ranging from high to low or good to bad. Often the ratings of several superiors are combined into a composite either by averaging or as a result of discussions which yield group ratings. Although overall effectiveness is the major concern in this approach, specific aspects of the job may be recognized to some extent by obtaining additional ratings on a few gross categories of behavior, usually loosely defined. A management potential or future effectiveness rating is also included in some instances.

Secondary Management Functions

Typically all of these ratings are closely related; a person who is high on one is likely to be high on the others. All of the measures appear to be tapping a general tendency to be considered good or bad, or be valued or not valued in the particular organization.

Figure 15-2 provides an example of such a global approach to evaluation. This particular form was developed to obtain measures of the per-

Figure 15-2   *Evaluation Form Used to Obtain Estimates of the Overall Value Placed on the Performance of Management Consultants*

1. Problem Solving
   Effectiveness in diagnosing and proposing solutions to client problems
   Clearly outstanding   _____
   Approaches outstanding   _____
   Well above standard   _____
   Somewhat above standard   _____
   Clearly meets the standard   _____
   Barely up to standard   _____
   Clearly below standard   _____
   Entirely unsatisfactory   _____

2. Client Relations
   Effectiveness in obtaining client action and confidence
   Clearly outstanding   _____
   Approaches outstanding   _____
   Somewhat above standard   _____
   Well above standard   _____
   Clearly meets the standard   _____
   Barely up to standard   _____
   Clearly below standard   _____
   Entirely unsatisfactory   _____

3. Work Output
   Effectiveness in getting work done and in meeting deadlines
   Clearly outstanding   _____
   Approaches outstanding   _____
   Well above standard   _____
   Somewhat above standard   _____
   Clearly meets the standard   _____
   Barely up to standard   _____
   Clearly below standard   _____
   Entirely unsatisfactory   _____

4. Firm Relations
   Effectiveness in working with people in the Firm
   Clearly outstanding   _____
   Approaches outstanding   _____
   Well above standard   _____
   Somewhat above standard   _____
   Clearly meets the standard   _____
   Barely up to standard   _____
   Clearly below standard   _____
   Entirely unsatisfactory   _____

5. Overall Evaluation
   General effectiveness, taking into account the four previous factors and any other factors you consider important in associate peformance
   Clearly outstanding   _____
   Approaches outstanding   _____
   Well above standard   _____
   Somewhat above standard   _____
   Clearly meets the standard   _____
   Barely up to standard   _____
   Clearly below standard   _____
   Entirely unsatisfactory   _____

6. Advancement Potential
   Prospects for developing into an effective management group member (assuming continued employment)
   Clearly outstanding   _____
   Approaches outstanding   _____
   Well above average   _____
   Somewhat above average   _____
   About average   _____
   Somewhat below average   _____
   Well below average   _____
   None   _____

formance effectiveness of management consultants so that specific psychological test measures which would predict success could be identified (39). In this instance the ratings of either two or three superiors were averaged to obtain the evaluation of each individual. Questions 1 through 4 were combined to yield a second overall effectiveness measure. This composite turned out to yield results very similar to those obtained with questions 5 (overall evaluation) and 6 (advancement potential).

Approaches such as that used in Figure 15–2 do not really say much about what it is that leads an individual to be considered good or poor. The ratings are heavily influenced by informal role prescriptions and thus by the value structure of the organization as a whole. Specific aspects of behavior in a particular position tend to be much less important. This approach to appraisal essentially indicates the extent to which a person's behavior fits those concepts of good and bad that exist in his organization at a point in time. For this reason it is highly desirable to obtain ratings which represent a consensus of a number of individuals.

Appraising the Role Behavior—Role Prescription Match

A second approach focuses on formal role expectations and requires a rater who has had an opportunity to observe the manager being evaluated very closely as he performs his job. In this case there may only be one such person, and to include others with less detailed knowledge in the rating process only serves to distort the results. Since the ratings are closely tied to formal role prescriptions, different rating scales must be developed for each type of managerial position, each focusing on those particular behaviors that are considered important in the specific type of work. The emphasis is strongly on job behavior, in relation to what is expected. In most cases it is necessary to have some kind of job analysis data available as a basis for constructing the rating scales.

Figure 15–3 provides an example of one such scale developed for the position of department manager in the J. C. Penney Company stores (17). Nine different scales of this kind were constructed from job analysis information:

1. Supervision of sales associates
2. Handling customer complaints and making adjustments

Secondary Management Functions

Figure 15–3 Department Manager Job Behavior Rating Scale for the Dimension: Assessing Sales Trends and Acting to Maintain Merchandising Position

— Could be expected, after noting that shipment of 60 turtleneck sweaters sold out in 2 days, to take quick action to order 500 more and to give them space and display emphasis to ensure they all sold without a markdown.

Could be expected to note competitors' featuring a particular fashion item, shop a sample of competitors, and select and order a line so that his department would have the right "fashion look." —

— Could be expected to re-evaluate his estimates on boys' jackets and secure quick approval on additional purchase to ensure higher volume on the item in his department.

Could be expected to reorder checkouts promptly and to give full information to Buying Office on results obtained. —

— Could be expected to be aware quickly of a best-seller but to buy only a token quantity at the outset with result that it might take several reorders before he built up sufficient quantity.

Could be expected to reorder an item only after its demand becomes obvious through frequent requests from customers and sales associates. —

— Could be expected to delay reordering in order "to be sure" even after 70% of an initial large volume purchase sold out in two weeks' time.

Could be expected to fail to determine the rate of dress shirt sales at Christmas time and come close to running out of them by early December. —

— Could be expected to develop a seriously overstocked position in his department by arbitrarily doubling the suggested coverage of merchandise without any factual basis and without authorization.

Source: M. D. Dunnette, "Managerial Effectiveness: Its Definition and Measurement," *Studies in Personnel Psychology*, Vol. 2 (1970), No 2, 14.

3. Meeting day-to-day deadlines
4. Merchandise ordering
5. Developing and planning special promotions
6. Assessing sales trends and acting to maintain merchandising position
7. Using company systems and following through on administrative operations
8. Communicating relevant information to associates and to higher management
9. Diagnosing and alleviating special department problems.

It is apparent that an approach such as this which is strongly rooted in formally specified job behaviors is likely to yield somewhat different results than the global ratings of the value structure approach. Yet both are important. Ideally both would be included in a comprehensive management appraisal program.

In the next, and final, chapter the discussion shifts from internal human resource considerations to the matter of dealing with external environmental forces. How do companies adapt to and attempt to mold the world around them? What environmental forces are of paramount significance at the present time?

Questions

1. What management development techniques have been used to change motives, attitudes, and values? How successful do these techniques appear to be in contributing to the attainment of company goals?
2. What differences exist between appraisal procedures aimed at determining the closeness of role behavior to role prescriptions and those concerned with determining congruence with the value structure?
3. Discuss the relationships among manpower planning, management recruiting, and management selection. How does each influence the others?
4. How do the following elements of the compensation package tend to rate in terms of their potential for influencing performance?
   a. Bonuses
   b. Salary (publicly stated)
   c. Stock options
   d. Deferred compensation
   e. Salary (secret)

5. The management consulting firm referred to in the text utilized interviews, application blanks, testing, and psychological evaluations as the primary elements in its selection process. Which of these would you recommend continuing to use? Why?

References

1. Allaway, R. H. "Incentives and Bonuses: Their Role in Compensating Executives." In R. F. Moore (ed.), *Compensating Executive Worth*. New York: American Management Association, 1968, pp. 106–125.
2. Andrews, K. R. *The Effectiveness of University Management Development Programs*. Boston: Graduate School of Business Administration, Harvard University, 1966.
3. Bass, B. M. "Ability, Values, and Concepts of Equitable Salary Increases in Exercise Compensation." *Journal of Applied Psychology*. Vol. 52 (1968), 299–303.
4. Baum, B. H., P. F. Sorensen, and W. S. Place. "The Effect of Managerial Training on Organizational Control: An Experimental Study." *Organizational Behavior and Human Performance*, Vol. 5 (1970), 170–182.
5. Bureau of National Affairs. "Executive Development." *Personnel Policies Forum*, Survey No. 81 (1967), 1–19.
6. Bureau of National Affairs. "ASPA–BNA Survey: The Economy and the Personnel Department." *Bulletin to Management*, No. 1111–Part 2 (1971), 1–2.
7. Byham, W. C. "Assessment Centers for Spotting Future Managers." *Harvard Business Review*, Vol. 48 (1970), No. 4, 150–167.
8. Campbell, J. P., M. D. Dunnette, E. E. Lawler, and K. E. Weick. *Managerial Behavior, Performance, and Effectiveness*. New York: McGraw-Hill, 1970.
9. Carlson, R. E., P. W. Thayer, E. C. Mayfield, and D. A. Peterson. "Improvements in the Selection Interview." *Personnel Journal*, Vol. 50 (1971), 268–275, 317.
10. Carroll, S. J. "Relationship of Various College Graduate Characteristics to Recruiting Decisions." *Journal of Applied Psychology*, Vol. 50 (1966), 421–423.
11. Carroll, S. J. "Beauty, Bias, and Business." *Personnel Administration*, Vol. 32 (1969), No. 2, 21–25.
12. Carroll, S. J., and A. N. Nash. "Some Personal and Situational Correlates of Reactions to Management Development Training." *Academy of Management Journal*, Vol. 13 (1970), 187–196.
13. Carroll, S. J., F. T. Paine, and J. M. Ivancevich. "The Relative Effectiveness

of Training Methods—Expert Opinion and Research." *Personnel Psychology*, Vol. 25 (1972).
14. Craft, C. J. "Management Games." In R. L. Craig and L. R. Bittel (eds.), *Training and Development Handbook*. New York: McGraw-Hill, 1967, pp. 267–284.
15. Crystal, G. S. "What's Ahead in Executive Compensation." In R. F. Moore (ed.), *Compensating Executive Worth*. New York: American Management Association, 1968, pp. 15–34.
16. Dauw, D. C., and A. J. Fredian. "Executive Career Guidance." *Personnel Administration*. Vol. 34 (1971), No. 2, 26–30.
17. Dunnette, M. D. "Managerial Effectiveness: Its Definition and Measurement." *Studies in Personnel Psychology*, Vol. 2 (1970), No. 2, 6–20.
18. Endicott, F. S. *Trends in Employment of College and University Graduates in Business and Industry*. Berea, Ohio: American Society for Personnel Administration, 1971.
19. Foote, G. H. "Compensation and the Executive Career Cycle." In R. Mann (ed.), *The Arts of Top Management: A McKinsey Anthology*. New York: McGraw-Hill, 1971, pp. 169–177.
20. Foster, K. E. "Accounting for Management Pay Differentials." *Industrial Relations*, Vol. 9 (1969), 80–87.
21. Glueck, W. F. "Management Development and Geographical Transfers." *Journal of Management Studies*, Vol. 6 (1969), 243–251.
22. Gruenfeld, L. W. "Management Development Effect on Changes in Values." *Training and Development Journal*, Vol. 20 (1966), No. 6, 18–26.
23. Hawk, R. H. *The Recruitment Function*. New York: American Management Association, 1967.
24. Hinrichs, J. R. *High-Talent Personnel: Managing a Critical Resource*. New York: American Management Association, 1966.
25. House, R. J. "Leadership Training: Some Dysfunctional Consequences." *Administrative Science Quarterly*, Vol. 12 (1968), 556–571.
26. Ivancevich, J. M., and J. H. Donnelly. "Job Offer Acceptance Behavior and Reinforcement." *Journal of Applied Psychology*, Vol. 55 (1971), 119–122.
27. Lawler, E. E. "Managers' Attitudes Toward How Their Pay Is and Should Be Determined." *Journal of Applied Psychology*, Vol. 50 (1966), 273–279.
28. Lawler, E. E. "The Mythology of Management Compensation." *California Management Review*, Vol. 9 (1966), No. 1, 11–22.
29. Lawler, E. E. *Pay and Organizational Effectiveness: A Psychological View*. New York: McGraw-Hill, 1971.
30. Lewellen, W. G. *Executive Compensation in Large Industrial Organizations*. New York: National Bureau of Economic Research, 1968.
31. Lopez, F. M. *Evaluating Employee Performance*. Chicago: Public Personnel Association, 1968.

32. Lopez, F. M. *The Making of a Manager: Guidelines to His Selection and Promotion.* New York: American Management Association, 1970.
33. McClelland, D. C., and D. G. Winter. *Motivating Economic Achievement.* New York: Free Press, 1969.
34. Miner, J. B. *Studies in Management Education.* New York: Springer, 1965.
35. Miner, J. B. "Management Appraisal: A Capsule Review and Current References." *Business Horizons,* Vol. 11 (1968), No. 5, 83–96.
36. Miner, J. B. "An Input-Output Model for Personnel Strategies." *Business Horizons,* Vol. 12 (1969), No. 3, 71–78.
37. Miner, J. B. "Psychological Evaluations as Predictors of Consulting Success." *Personnel Psychology,* Vol. 23 (1970), 393–405.
38. Miner, J. B. "Executive and Personnel Interviews as Predictors of Consulting Success." *Personnel Psychology,* Vol. 23 (1970), 521–538.
39. Miner, J. B. "Personality Tests as Predictors of Consulting Success." *Personnel Psychology,* Vol. 24 (1971), 191–204.
40. Miner, J. B. "Success in Management Consulting and the Concept of Eliteness Motivation." *Academy of Management Journal,* Vol. 14 (1971), 367–378.
41. Nash, A. N., and S. J. Carroll. "A Hard Look at the Reference Check." *Business Horizons,* Vol. 13 (1970), No. 5, 43–50.
42. Patton, A. "Executive Compensation Inequities." *Business Horizons,* Vol. 13 (1970), No. 1, 73–84.
43. Pyron, H. C. "The Use and Misuse of Previous Employer References in Hiring." *Management of Personnel Quarterly,* Vol. 9 (1970), No. 2, 15–22.
44. Raia, A. P. "A Study of the Educational Value of Management Games." *Journal of Business,* Vol. 39 (1966), 339–352.
45. Stayton, J. P., and J. L. Lesher. "Recent Developments in Deferred Compensation." *Business Horizons,* Vol. 12 (1969), No. 2, 73–80.
46. West, J. P., and D. R. Sheriff, *Executive Development Programs in Universities.* New York: National Industrial Conference Board, 1969.
47. Wettling, R. E. "An Up-to-Date Look at Stock Options and Their Use." In R. F. Moore (ed.), *Compensating Executive Worth.* New York: American Management Association, 1968, pp. 126–145.
48. Wittreich, W. J., and J. B. Miner. "People: The Most Mismanaged Asset." *Business Horizons,* Vol. 14 (1971), No. 2, 69–77.
49. Wollowick, H. B., and W. J. McNamara. "Relationship of the Components of an Assessment Center to Management Success." *Journal of Applied Psychology,* Vol. 53 (1969), 348–352.
50. Wright, O. R. "Summary of Research on the Selection Interview Since 1964." *Personnel Psychology,* Vol. 22 (1969), 391–413.

16 Representing: Dealing with the External Environment

I. Public Relations and the Corporate Image
  1. The Scope of Public Relations
  2. The Sources of a Corporate Image

II. Social Responsibility and Business Ethics
  1. Pressures for Humanism
  2. Social Responsibility vs. Profitability
     a. Conflicting Values
     b. Responses to Pressures
  3. Ethics, Morality, and the Law

III. Helping the Culturally Disadvantaged
  1. The Law and Employment Discrimination
     a. The Impact of Governmental Action
     b. The Process of Discrimination
  2. Training the Hard-Core Unemployed
     a. Problems in Employment
     b. Suggested Solutions
  3. Black Economic Development
     a. Types of Corporate Support
     b. Pros and Cons

IV. International Management in Varying Cultural Contexts
  1. Dimensions of External Forces
  2. Cultural Variations
     a. Motives, Attitudes, and Values
     b. Education
  3. Dealing with Cultural Contexts

Chapter 1 began with a discussion of the interactions between an organization and its environment. The concept of organizational goals was introduced and a distinction was made between goals of an official and operative nature. These goals, especially those of an official nature, often serve to constrain the activities of an organization. Other factors in the environment, and in the societal environment in particular, may have a similar restrictive effect. While the external environment does limit certain decisions and courses of action, it also facilitates others.

Organizations respond to these forces in the world around them in various ways. They may attempt to alter the nature of the forces, or the balance among them, or to forestall or promote the emergence of new forces. They may respond to existing circumstances in such a way as to comply with external pressures, and they may go to considerable pains in making their compliance known to the society as a whole. All of these organizational actions and responses are included in the management function of representing. Thus this final chapter returns in greater detail to those topics with which this book began.

In many of its aspects, representing is synonymous with public relations. Yet it would require an unusually broad definition of the public relations field to contain all that representing connotes. Certainly public relations departments as they currently exist in corporations do not often have such a broad role. The company's response to a government antitrust action, efforts to recruit in the vicinity of a new company location, and a special advertising campaign to promote a new product are all instances where representing is likely to be carried out by managers other than those in the public relations area. Similarly responses to societal pressures in such areas as responsibilities to consumers, pollution control, and assistance to the disadvantaged have not typically come from the public relations department (34). In fact it has been proposed that companies should establish separate social affairs departments to deal with these matters. A few companies have actually moved in this direction.

The discussion which follows attempts to define more specifically what the role of public relations has been in carrying out the representing function. It then concerns itself with the whole matter of ethics in the business world and the responsibility of managers to the larger society. Special attention is given to societal pressures related to minority groups and the disadvantaged. Finally the focus shifts to the international scene and the variations in cultural forces to which business firms are exposed in different parts of the world.

Public Relations and the Corporate Image

Representing is involved in both words and actions. Of these two, public relations managers have been concerned primarily with the former, with representing the company through the written and spoken word. Furthermore, public relations managers have been more concerned with techniques and methods of representation than with content. The public relations field provides expertise in how verbally to represent an organization to its publics; what is to be represented, what message is conveyed, may be influenced by public relations managers, but the actual decisions that are reported to the public are characteristically made at higher levels.

The Scope of Public Relations

In representing a company to its publics, public relations is likely to become involved in many aspects of company functioning (49). It is intended to win people to causes and products, to attract people to the company as a place of employment, and to encourage favorable responses from the financial community. Most of what public relations managers do is for the purpose of creating goodwill in the external environment. This goodwill can pay off in sales, in effective employees, in ease of financing, in favorable tax consideration, in a positive legal milieu, and in many other ways.

Government relations are a major consideration. Many large firms maintain staffs in Washington, D.C. for this purpose. These staffs are often involved in lobbying and efforts of other kinds to influence the legislative process, but they also gather information, interpret government actions to management, and support sales to the government. Similar processes often are carried out at the various state capitals where actions having particular significance for a company may occur.

Public relations departments may be organized under a vice-president who reports directly to the chief executive. In other instances they report at a lower level. It is not uncommon to combine the personnel function with public relations in a single all-encompassing "relations" department. Some companies rely primarily on outside consultants and public relations agencies rather than on an internal staff. Generally philanthropic efforts, intended to generate goodwill also, are handled through a separate foundation in large business organizations.

Since a sizable portion of the public relations program tends to be focused on press relations, press clippings are widely used to justify corporate expenditures in this area (49). But public relations personnel may also draft speeches for company executives, put out publications for stockholders and others, encourage employee participation in community affairs, conduct public tours of company installations, arrange public meetings involving the firm's executives, and do an almost infinite variety of other things. There are a great many ways in which a company may represent itself to one public or another.

The Sources of a Corporate Image

The corporate image is the total of all impressions of a company in the consciousness of the various publics—customers, suppliers, stockholders, bankers, potential investors, competitors, government officials, and the general public. These impressions are created by products, services, business dealings, community relations, labor relations, securities investments, the appearance of properties, and a host of other considerations. To some degree this image becomes focused on the various symbols such as corporate names, emblems, and trademarks employed by a corporation, but this is not all of the image (33). Such simple things as the tone of a voice on a telephone, the upkeep of a building, the ease of opening a package, the nature of the billing process, and the way in which letters are typed are also important.

There is ample evidence that a favorable corporate image can make a positive contribution to sales and earnings (33). However, it is not so clear that this image may be manipulated at will by a company. Such efforts not only may fail, but they may create a false sense of security in management (16). Often a company's management is the first, and only, group convinced by such a public relations effort.

Clearly outside factors, quite independent of the company's control, may have a major impact on the image which emerges. Ralph Nader's charges regarding unsafe products have had such an influence on the image of General Motors. Peace activists have affected the image of Dow Chemical as a consequence of its production of napalm for the Vietnam War. Congressional hearings have influenced the image of several pharmaceutical firms. Widely publicized boycotts of California table grapes growers have resulted from the image of racial discrimination emerging from labor organizing attempts. Research findings of a link between cigarettes and cancer have damaged the image of tobacco companies. These are but a few examples of image effects which have occurred quite independent of public relations efforts.

If one is to determine what the image of a given firm really is, the various publics must be questioned. When this is done the picture that emerges often is quite different from that held by the company's management (33). In general, management views the image as more favorable than it really is. It is also true that many companies are almost totally lacking in a corporate image of any meaningful kind, or the existing image is markedly out of date. It is under such circumstances that public relations efforts can be most valuable. When, as a result of mergers and acquisitions, a company has drastically changed its character or a new corporate entity has in fact emerged image building can serve an extremely useful purpose for all concerned.

It is not uncommon for companies to pick an image which is considered as a potential source of goodwill and mount a massive public relations campaign behind it. Thus a firm may portray itself as innovative, growing, a good neighbor, well managed, and so on. This is effective as long as other, less well-controlled messages emanating from the company say the same thing. But a firm cannot control all messages to its environment. Thus a public relations campaign may run afoul of reality and the composite image produced may be so muddied that no clear picture is obtained at all. It seems best then for a company to attempt to build an image around its real and established strengths. Such representing is not only useful to the company, but makes known to society the major areas in which the organization can contribute.

Social Responsibility and Business Ethics

A prominent theme in the business literature deals with pressures from society on business organizations and management to be socially responsible—to not only obey the law, but the dictates of morality as well. For the moment the discussion will focus on those laws and conceptions of morality that are endemic to the United States; later the legal and moral systems of other countries will be considered as well.

In general, these pressures have taken three forms (11). First, there are the pressures for humanism and equalitarian treatment of employees. Second, there are the pressures for social responsibility with the objective of funneling profits into use for the social good rather than stockholder and managerial reward. Third, there are the pressures for better ethics, stricter personal morality, and observance of legal strictures. These three are not totally independent; they do overlap, but it is still possible to treat them separately.

Pressures for Humanism

Some of the strongest pressures on business management may be traced back to the human relations school of management thought. Similar pressures are exerted by the members of the more recently formed behavioral humanist school. The essence of this viewpoint is that management should become more democratic and less authoritarian, more humane and less pragmatic, more equalitarian and less hierarchic. In some formulations this type of value pressure is related to religious belief and the Judaeo-Christian ethic (19). In other instances it is more closely associated with the democratic political values of American society (51). In either case the message to management with its strong emphasis on power equalization and participation is much the same.

A recent statement of this position from the behavioral humanist viewpoint provides a rather comprehensive catalog of what is negatively and positively valued in this approach and thus of what management should become (55).

Negatively Valued	Positively Valued
A view of man as essentially bad	A view of man as basically good
Avoidance or negative evaluation of individuals	Confirming individuals as human beings
A view of individuals as fixed	A view of individuals as being in process
Resisting and fearing individual differences	Accepting and utilizing individual differences
Utilizing an individual primarily with reference to his job description	Viewing an individual as a whole person
Walling-off the expression of feeling	Making possible both appropriate expression and effective use of feeling
Maskmanship and game-playing	Authentic behavior
The use of status for maintaining power and personal prestige	The use of status for organizationally relevant purposes
Distrusting people	Trusting people
Avoiding facing others with relevant data	Making appropriate confrontation
Avoidance of risk taking	Willingness to risk
A view of process work as being unproductive effort	Seeing process work as essential to effective task accomplishment
A primary emphasis on competition	A much greater emphasis on collaboration

Inherent in this value system is the idea that management should drastically revise its beliefs, attitudes, and behavior in relation to those at lower levels. Because managers have been brought up in this society and have in many instances been exposed to extensive religious training as well, these appeals to democratic values have a profound power. Most managers find it very difficult if not impossible to reject the appeals of humanism and participative democracy. At the same time they may have considerable difficulty in reconciling such values with the realities of the business world and the sometimes antithetical values of a capitalistic economic system. The results of the humanistic pressures have often been feelings of personal conflict and uncertainty, but there have been some instances of adaptation and change as well. At this point in time it is not possible to say what the long-term response to these particular value pressures will be.

Social Responsibility vs. Profitability

A second and often closely related set of value pressures has to do with the use of management's resources and efforts for social ends. In its most fully developed form this view holds that management should not work for profits and for stockholder interests, but for the welfare of society directly. However, the extent to which the social responsibility ethic comes in direct and full conflict with the capitalistic ethic varies considerably from one formulation to another.

In an earlier period this value system was espoused primarily by university administrators and religious leaders who appear to have been at least in part interested in providing a rationale for corporate gifts in support of their organizations. More recently the circle of support has widened considerably as has the range of problems, causes, and activities to which companies are urged to devote energies and resources (26). Included are the education of children, policing the streets, cleaning up polluted air and water, helping the disadvantaged to earn a living, rebuilding slums, and even contributing to the more efficient operation of city governments.

Conflicting Values. The basic conflict here is between those who believe the primary goal of business organizations should be the social welfare and those who believe it should be profitable operation. In general the latter feel that society is in fact served indirectly by their approach because a capitalistic system emphasizing profits and return on stockholder investments is the best way of guaranteeing an effective economic system and an abundance of goods and services.

It should be understood that the value conflict revolves around the consistent primacy of one goal or the other when decisions must be made which involve a choice between them. A commitment to profitability does not necessarily always mean a lack of social responsibility. In fact social responsibility may be good business in a profitability sense when it contributes to goodwill, minimizes the number of governmental constraints, or motivates employees in ways related to profit. Yet there are a number of individuals who feel that capitalism has in essence lost any moral legitimacy it ever had and that the profit ethic is no longer appropriate to our time (4, 44). There has been considerable urging that business organizations move out of the economic sphere into other areas, many of them currently primarily within the domain of government (58).

Given these strong pressures to espouse social responsibility at the expense of capitalism, the profit ethic, and a commitment to economic endeavor alone, it is instructive to ask what business executives themselves believe. What are their values? One type of finding is reflected in Table 16–1. In this instance a survey of both chief executives and chief financial officers revealed a consistent commitment to stockholders and relatively less commitment to society as a whole. The same pattern emerged irrespective of company size (32). These data suggest that the profit ethic remains overriding.

Yet a second study indicates that management's acceptance of profitability is not totally at the expense of social responsibility. A questionnaire study

Table 16–1 Average Ranking of Various Groups in Terms of Responsibilities to Them by Chief Executives and Chief Financial Officers

	Average Rank	
Group	Chief Executives	Chief Financial Officers
Stockholders	1.28	1.20
Employees	2.20	2.16
Customers	2.22	2.55
Creditors	2.92	2.75
Society	3.78	3.91

Source: A. W. Lorig, "Where Do Corporate Responsibilities Really Lie?" *Business Horizons*, Vol. 10 (1967), No. 2, 53.

of almost 250 executives found that nearly all considered the involvement of business in urban affairs a permanent thing (37). There is a widespread feeling that social responsibility value pressures are real, continuing, and important. These business leaders do see a number of risks associated with responding to these pressures. These are noted in Table 16-2. However, the same table indicates that not getting involved at all is one of the greatest risks. The risk of stockholder disapproval was hardly mentioned at all in this study.

Clearly management is torn in dealing with these pressures. There is a feeling that the profit ethic should be served and that it represents a valid contribution to society. At the same time social responsibility is not ignored, although it is not primary. Managers seem to feel that such values must be taken into account in running an organization, just as any strong values in the larger society must be considered. These values produce very real constraints. Furthermore, managers are part of the society, they are influenced by its values, and as individuals they cannot ignore their own feelings in such matters.

Responses to Pressures. It is not possible to cite any one response to social responsibility value pressures as typical of the whole business community. In general it appears that those companies most subject to government

Table 16-2 *Risks Associated with Company Involvement in Urban Affairs Cited by 247 Executives*

Type of Risk	Percent Citing
Excessive cost. Trying to do too much for too many too fast	95
Trying to go it alone	90
Not getting involved at all	85
Token or "showcase" activity	80
Agonizing retrenchment if economic slowdown	80
Scattering of efforts among too many projects	75
Lack of expertise in many subject areas	70
Overpromising beyond corporate resources	70
Disillusionment, waste from government red tape	70
Arousing unfulfilled expectations	65
Inability to withdraw gracefully when others fail	65
Overreacting to strong pressure groups	60
Conflict of interest, real or imaginary	55
Political controversy for which unprepared	50
Heavy unanticipated losses from promising projects	50

Source: J. W. McGuire and J. B. Parrish, "Status Report on a Profound Revolution," *California Management Review,* Vol. 13 (1971), No. 4, 82.

regulation, such as the utilities, have engaged in the most widespread social welfare efforts presumably at least in part as a means of thwarting prospective legislative constraints. It is clear that a variety of other companies also have responded to pressures for social involvement with increased activity of this kind. Organizations must adapt to the cultural environments in which they operate or change the environment; otherwise there is a high probability that they will not survive. In the case of social responsibility pressures the major response has been to change the organization and adapt to the environment. This adaption process is as much an aspect of the representing function as the typical public relations effort.

One method of adapting is *co-optation*. In this instance individuals from the outside environment who are associated with the sources of pressure are brought inside the organization to participate in its decision-making processes. Thus a company might appoint a leader of an environmental preservation group or an influential person in the black community to its board of directors. Another approach is for managers to go outside the company and devote a certain proportion of their time to activities within social action groups. Both of these forms of interaction with the sources of external pressures appear to make for a more effectively functioning organization (46).

There are firms which have restricted their efforts in the social arena to those instances where at least some immediate profit could be realized. Such situations have often involved a contractual arrangement with the federal government. In other cases the profit potential of the endeavors has been at best very long range in the form of future goodwill. A number of senior executives do appear to be willing to put profit in the background relative to social responsibility at least in some of their decisions (58). Whether it is "good" that they should do this depends on one's value position. Many would argue that such socially oriented decisions represent an unwarranted diversion from official goals.

The field of pollution control is one in which many business firms have felt the greatest pressures and have exhibited the greatest concern (41). The response has been varied. The major problems in adapting to pressures appear to be cost and a lack of technological know-how. Where these problems are minimal, adaptation has been rapid; in other cases it has been slow. There is a widespread feeling that if some companies in an industry are to assume substantial costs in this area, all should be required to do so, thus maintaining competitive relationships. This implies government regulation rather than individual company response. Yet the problem of foreign competitors without pollution control requirements remains. There is also considerable interest in government incentives such as accelerated depreciation or a tax credit on the capital investment in pollution-abatement equipment. Clearly the cost problems associated with pollution control represent a serious threat to the survival of some firms.

Ethics, Morality, and the Law

Societal mores, many of them codified into law, establish what amounts to a minimum level of responsible or moral behavior for managers; deviation can elicit strong negative sanctions. In addition there is typically a somewhat higher level of morality established by the particular industry (36). Certain rules, although often amorphous and lacking in precise specification, do exist to guide behavior in particular situations that are of special significance in an industry. Among the pressures emanating from society and the industry are those relating to conflict of interest, misrepresentation of products and services, just pricing, fair interest rates, planned limitations on product life, safe operation and use, truthful advertising, and fair competition (57). As with social responsibility pressures the primary mode in dealing with pressures of an ethical or legal nature is adaptation. When new laws are passed and new moral conceptions emerge managers may try to change them, or they may ignore them, but most frequently they behave in accordance with them.

A comprehensive analysis of business ethics derives from a series of questionnaire and interview studies utilizing over 1,700 individuals in all (3). In general the study indicated a great deal of concern about ethical matters, especially as related to personnel considerations such as firing, layoffs, and the like. There was a frequently expressed desire to eliminate such things as price discrimination, unfair pricing, price collusion, bribes, and excessive gifts or favors. Clearly most of the businessmen viewed themselves as ethical, but they were aware that many unethical practices exist. The evidence seemed to indicate that the business world is far from being as unethical as many people outside it, especially students, believe. The author concluded that any manager with a well-defined personal code could act ethically if he wished without suffering in his career as a result and that in fact many managers did fit this description.

A number of differences were noted between various groups (3). Older managers emerged as more ethical than younger ones, in part at least

Secondary Management Functions

because they had achieved a degree of financial security. As noted in Table 16–3 certain occupations and industries are considered more ethical than others. There is a pronounced feeling that purchasing and sales are characterized by questionable ethics. A negative trend in the nominations is also in evidence for the garment, construction, and advertising industries. In general it appears that where competition is extremely intense ethics may suffer.

Table 16–3 Occupations and Industries Nominated as Ethical and Unethical

	Number Who Say It Is	
Occupation ($N = 75$)	Ethical	Unethical
Accounting	11	2
Engineering and Research	6	0
Purchasing	2	16
Selling	0	28
Others	9	1
Industries ($N = 72$)		
Banking, Investment, Insurance	8	2
Transportation, Public Utilities	1	1
General Manufacturing	8	10
General Marketing	2	3
Advertising, Media, Publishing	0	4
Construction	0	5
Garment	0	10
Others	8	10

Source: From *An Honest Profit* by Raymond Baumhart, S.J. (New York: Holt, Rinehart and Winston, 1968) pp. 97, 116. Copyright © 1968 by Raymond Baumhart, S.J. Reprinted by permission of Holt, Rinehart and Winston, Inc.

There is a widespread view that the professionalization of management would contribute to an improved ethical climate. Professions typically develop codes of ethics which are incorporated into professional training and which form the basis for judgments of professional conduct. It is interesting to note that accounting and engineering—the two professions noted in Table 16–3—are judged as most ethical. To date, however, little real movement toward professionalization of management as a whole has occurred. In view of the crucial role of entrepreneurship in the American economic value system, it seems unlikely that any rapid shift toward a fully developed profession of management will occur.

Helping the Culturally Disadvantaged

Starting in the early 1960s, and with increasing momentum since then, the business world has devoted its energies and resources to helping the culturally disadvantaged, particularly blacks and residents of inner-city ghettos. Much of what has been done is clearly more consistent with a social responsibility ethic than with short-term profit considerations. This is particularly true of efforts by individual managers working with social action groups as community volunteers.

The evidence is clear that altruism is a major factor in such community work, that more of it is being done all the time, and that increasingly company policies are supportive of these efforts (14). Managers in large companies and particularly the service industries are somewhat more likely to be involved than those from smaller firms and manufacturing. In spite of this widespread individual activity, however, it seems likely that other types of efforts by the business community having to do with the *employment* of the disadvantaged actually have achieved more to date. In part this is because executives' skills have often been underutilized in social action organizations and their efforts misdirected (14); in part it is simply because the greatest potential for impact is in the employment sphere.

Although the values of individual managers and their desire to help have been a factor in the upsurge of assistance to the culturally disadvantaged, other considerations are clearly involved as well. There have been strong direct pressures on companies from their environments. The commerce-crushing threat of riot and curfew in slum areas has been a real and meaningful force ever since the riots in the Watts area of Los Angeles in 1965 (8). Much of what has been done has been motivated by a desire to maintain a viable economic system against the threat of anarchy. At least equally important has been the impact of direct governmental action backed up by legal and economic sanctions.

The Law and Employment Discrimination

The expressed intent of governmental action has been to reduce, if not end employment discrimination against minority groups. Such discrimination may occur at the point of the hiring decision, in upgrading and promotion, or in separations and layoffs. Although action is directed at minority group members rather than the culturally disadvantaged per se, the end result has been a major concern with the culturally disadvantaged on the part of many firms. Among blacks, for instance, there simply are not enough educated, skilled individuals with good employment records and no criminal convictions to meet the government's demands for increased hiring. Thus companies have often been forced into a personnel strategy of training the underqualified rather than selecting the most highly qualified.

The Impact of Governmental Action. Under the Civil Rights Act of 1964 companies are required to file a statement indicating employment of minority group members—Negro, Oriental, American Indian, and Spanish American—at various occupational levels. The data that have been accumulated clearly indicate an underrepresentation of minority group members in higher-level, white-collar jobs (24). A great variety of governmental pressures have been brought to bear to correct this situation as well as to eliminate disproportions in unemployment figures.

In part these pressures derive from the enforcement provisions of the federal law. Companies can be forced to end discriminatory practices. In addition certain state governments have become very active in this area. In Massachusetts, for instance, the state agency involved has initiated complaints against a number of companies and has worked very closely with certain minority group organizations (10). The most effective pressure device, however, appears to be the threat of lost government contracts if there is inadequate employment of minority group members. This approach has even spread to the private sector itself. Certain firms such as Nieman-Marcus of Dallas, The Dayton Company of Minneapolis, and Levi-Strauss of San Francisco require their purchasing department to check out suppliers regarding minority employment patterns before placing orders (59).

An example of the extent to which companies have adapted under contract compliance pressure is provided by the Plans for Progress program which operated until 1969 (31). In 1961 President Kennedy issued an executive order indicating that there should be no discrimination in employment by government contractors and that contracts would be canceled if a company was found in violation. Subsequently complaints were received regarding the Lockheed Aircraft plant in Marietta, Georgia. The company then proceeded to develop a " Plan for Progress " in order not to be in violation of the executive order. This plan called for integration of facilities, placement of minority personnel in jobs for which they were qualified, equal training and advancement opportunities, and active recruiting of minority group members. The plan was filed with the government, and progress was actively monitored.

Other companies soon developed similar plans under the threat of losing contracts. These plans were carried out to a sufficient extent that real changes in employment patterns occurred. The data of Table 16–4 indicate that in these particular companies there was a marked increase in nonwhites in higher level occupations, while lower-level employment remained at least stable.

The Process of Discrimination. The process of discrimination within an organization operates to place minority group members at low levels in the value and reward structures simply because of their minority status. Thus where discrimination is an accomplished fact one can expect to find such individuals described as poor performers or troublemakers, placed in low-level positions, and paid small salaries. It is apparent that such conditions do exist in a number of companies.

A recent study has vividly portrayed the many difficulties that blacks and Mexicans face in achieving promotion (45). Even where promotion has become more widespread, as it clearly has in recent years, there is some doubt about whether many of the professional and managerial positions established for minority group members are of central and lasting significance to the organization. Often the positions are in public or personnel

Table 16–4 *Percentage Increases in Nonwhite Employment in 91 Plans for Progress Companies Between May 1961 and December 1963*

	Percentage Increase	
Occupational Group	All Employees	Nonwhite Employees
Officials and Supervisors	12	47
Professionals and Administrative	23	37
Sales	9	53
Technicians	17	32
Office and Clerical	9	16
Craftsmen	11	13
Operatives	12	16
Service	8	5
Laborers	3	3

Source: H. Lockwood, "Progress in Plans for Progress for Negro Managers," in The Executive Study Conference, *The Selection and Training of Negroes for Managerial Positions* (Princeton, N.J.: Educational Testing Service, 1965), p. 7.

Secondary Management Functions

relations and involve a specialization in problems of blacks and the disadvantaged. There is little opportunity for further development and promotion to greater responsibilities (48).

Research indicates that certain kinds of people are much more likely to place considerable emphasis on nonability factors such as race in reaching promotion decisions than are other people (47). Such managers tend to place a high value on friendly and cooperative social interaction. When they feel pressured by others to discriminate and when they feel unclear as to whether company personnel policies would forbid discrimination, these managers are most likely to refuse to promote a minority group member of high ability. What emerges from this study is a clear picture of discrimination in promotion as a consequence of conformity pressures, in a context of unclear company policy, influencing managers who are particularly responsive to such pressures. These results argue for the existence of clear and widely circulated policies against discrimination if a company is to adapt successfully to societal and governmental pressures in this area. They also argue for placing promotion decisions in the hands of task-oriented managers who have less concern with social interaction considerations and who are less responsive to pressures to conform.

Training the Hard-Core Unemployed

A second pressure from society on business organizations has called for the training of the severely culturally disadvantaged, the so-called hard-core unemployed, and their subsequent employment. Here direct government constraints are less than in the case of employment discrimination, and not all those affected are minority group members.

The government has provided some positive financial incentives in this area as a facilitating force (9). The company programs vary considerably in their support arrangements as indicated in Table 16–5. In addition the government has fostered and supported a number of training programs of an institutional nature. The graduates of these training centers have not benefited as much, however, and it now seems clear that the in-company training is more effective (20, 30). Yet it is also apparent that industry tends to view this internal training of the hard-core as detrimental to both short- and long-term profits (28). Most of the training that occurs is clearly a product of the social responsibility ethic.

Table 16–5 A Cross Section of Programs for the Disadvantaged

1. Western Electric
   Newark, New Jersey

   Light electronics manufacturing facilities located in the low-income Newark Central Ward. Facilities are designed to train workers on the job for eventual transfer to the company's Kearny, New Jersey, plant. As of December 1968, 191 persons were employed at the Newark plant and 90 persons had successfully transferred. The program is privately financed.

2. IBM
   Brooklyn, New York

   Light electronics manufacturing facility providing on-the-job training in light electronics assembly. No special transfer arrangements are included in the program. As of December 1968 approximately 195 persons were employed, and an employment level of 450 is forecast.

3. Westinghouse
   East Pittsburgh, Pennsylvania

   Four-week vestibule training program followed by on-the-job training in specific skills. This program is supported by federal funds under the Department of Labor's MA-3 program and has a training capacity of about 25 at any one time.

4. The Equitable Life Assurance Society of the United States
   New York, New York

   A series of programs begun in 1962 for high school dropouts. Training emphasizes development of clerical skills and remedial education.

5. Cooperative Steel Industry Education Program

   A joint labor-management training program involving ten major companies in the steel industry. It provides incumbent employees with remedial education to facilitate their upgrading. The program is supported by federal funds through the US Department of Labor.

6. Woodland Job Training Center
   Cleveland, Ohio

   Cooperative training arrangement between the Cleveland Board of Education and participating employers. This program provides basic education and vocational training concurrently with on-the-job training. Trainees are eventually transferred from the training facility in the Hough ghetto to regular production facilities. The program financed by public and private funds, including an MA–3 contract.

Source: P. B. Doeringer, *Programs to Employ the Disadvantaged* (Englewood Cliffs, N.J.: Prentice-Hall, 1969) pp. 3–4.

Problems in Employment. The degree of cultural disadvantage experienced by participants in these training programs differs considerably. Some programs are in fact concerned with upgrading those who have already conquered the hurdle of continued employment. A basic description of the average hard-core unemployed would, however, read as follows:

1. Unemployed and has been for 18 months.
2. Never received any skill training.
3. Parents were unskilled.
4. Lives with one and one half families.
5. Needs eyeglasses and dental work.
6. Has seen a doctor only once in his life.
7. Has no transportation.
8. Has a sixth grade education and only a fourth grade mathematics background.
9. Is usually a minority group member (1).

As might be anticipated with any group who have not learned the work-related aspects of the culture, the training and employment of these individuals have been fraught with problems. Turnover has typically been very high (29, 39). There are also many complaints of lateness, absenteeism, and unsatisfactory work. Problems are frequently ascribed to such factors as a lack of basic education and skills training, inability to manage personal affairs, lack of knowledge of the requirements of the work situation, inability to defer satisfactions, suppressed hostility toward whites, and low motivation. Through efforts such as the National Alliance of Businessmen a great many jobs have been found in the private sector, but a very high proportion of these placements have subsequently failed.

A brief discussion in Chapter 13 indicated how foremen who supervise newly hired, culturally disadvantaged employees are often faced with major role conflicts. Everybody seems to be saying different things, some appearing to follow a social responsibility ethic and some a profit ethic. This same role conflict and ambiguity extends to the individual himself. In a very real sense the hard-core unemployed who are absorbed into the world of work become the focus of all the uncertainty that exists regarding what role business organizations themselves should play in this area. This very fact can well account for many of the problems that have developed.

In one study considerable conflict between proponents of social responsibility and those of profitability was found in a top management group, with the result that the overall reaction to the training program was ambiguous and uncertain at this level (38). Under these circumstances the attitudes of foremen and fellow workers toward the hard-core trainees became less favorable over the period of training. The ambivalence characterizing the environment in which they found themselves was clearly a source of role conflict and ambiguity for the trainees.

The results of another study of 314 managers in a large corporation reveal major conflicts in values between those at the top and those further down (18). Data are given in Figure 16-1. Again one would expect a climate of uncertainty with lower-level supervision vacillating between the dictates of top management and its own beliefs. It is not surprising that high turnover rates have accompanied many training programs.

Suggested Solutions. A number of approaches in training the hard-core unemployed have been suggested, at least part of these backed up by research. In general these approaches have focused more on the deficiencies of the trainees than on the deficiencies, particularly the conflicting role prescriptions, of the environments in which they work. Thus one study found that reorganizing jobs to make them more specialized and routine seemed to contribute to improved performance (27). Special training, not just in job skills, but also in such things as grooming and hygiene, money management, the use of public transportation facilities, and getting along with others has been found useful (25). So too has the institution of a "buddy" system where a fellow worker is designated to help the disadvantaged employee when he runs into difficulties (42).

The most strikingly favorable results have been obtained, however, when a consistently supportive work climate could be obtained (17, 25). This may involve some downward revision of standards, at least temporarily; it certainly involves acceptance of some strange and unanticipated behavior. Most important, it involves the creation of a social environment that consistently conveys an impression of wanting to help, belief in eventual success, and personal acceptance. Where the immediate environment is characterized by conflicting value positions (social responsibility and profitability), such consistency of support is not possible and role conflict and ambiguity will inevitably prevail. This means that some companies simply are not in a position currently to do an effective job of training the hard-core unemployed. Under such conditions, companies would do better to deal with societal pressures in this area in some other way. Perhaps, for instance, the representing function could be carried out more effectively by making cash contributions to outside organizations working in this area.

Secondary Management Functions

Figure 16–1 Management Support for Special Hiring and Lowering Employment Qualifications at Various Levels in a Large Company

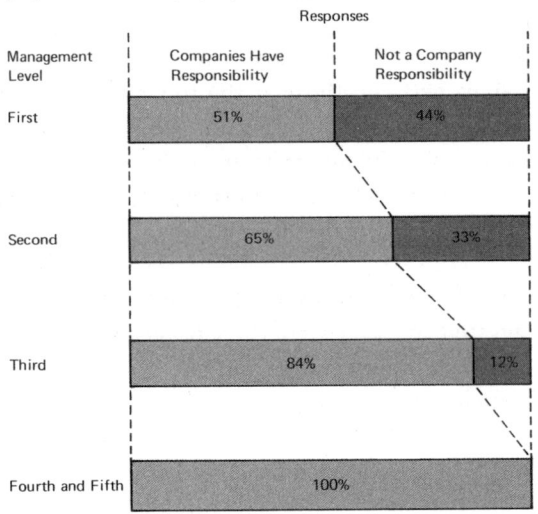

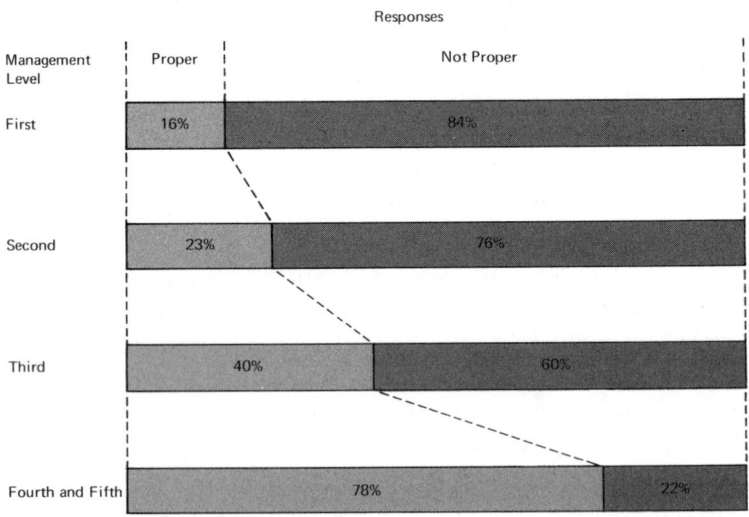

Source: J. R. Goeke and C. S. Weymar, "Barriers to Hiring the Blacks," *Harvard Business Review*, Vol. 47 (1969), No. 5, 146, 149.

Black Economic Development

A third response to pressures for social responsibility in the area of the culturally disadvantaged has been the encouragement of black economic development or black capitalism in order to increase the number of black enterprises which in turn will provide employment to the disadvantaged in inner-city ghettos. Unlike increased employment of minority group members in existing establishments, this response has little current relation to legal enactments and governmental pressures; it is essentially a voluntary response to the values of society. Because it is most consistent with the concept of a capitalistic economic system, it appears to be the preferred response in the business community generally (6).

Types of Corporate Support. Faced with difficulties in obtaining adequate financial, material, and human resources, black enterprise has not fared well to date. The great majority of such enterprises are small, family-operated retail and service operations. If anything there has been a decline in black-owned firms of any significant size in the past several decades; this is clearly true of the number of banks (21). Given these statistics the possibility that the ghetto economy will resurrect itself in the manner of an underdeveloped country seems remote indeed. What appears to be needed is some form of assistance from the government and from the surrounding private enterprise economy to remove the disincentives that have stifled entrepreneurship and self-development (8). This is the argument that has brought a number of long-established companies into the field of black economic development.

A growing number of companies have become so involved (6, 54). One pattern involves establishing operations in a ghetto area with the long-term intention of divestiture. Another approach gives the company no ownership position; that is in the hands of members of the black community. However, management, marketing, and technical know-how are provided. A number of companies have guaranteed protected markets for black manufacturing enterprises. There are programs for special credit terms on the part of the financial community and for special assistance on the part of management consulting firms.

These efforts are currently of limited scope. Their overall impact on the 163 isolated ghettos in the United States has certainly not been substantial (8). Furthermore, at least for the current short term, companies have rarely achieved any meaningful return on these investments; many have taken sizable losses. Yet there has been a considerable amount of learning as to what will and will not work, as well as some truly effective responses to societal pressures.

Pros and Cons. The view that black economic development is the best long-term solution to society's problems is by no means universal. There have been some strong arguments that this approach cannot possibly succeed and that in view of the realities of the situation the perpetuation of this viewpoint approximates a hoax (5). It is apparent that our knowledge of how to found and operate a successful ghetto enterprise is still sadly inadequate. However, the major barriers noted are in the availability of entrepreneurial and managerial talent and in the availability of capital. Where are the people with the experience and desire to run such businesses? Where is the money to get them established?

The most convincing reply to date has come from those who argue for the institution of incentives to make it worth while to do business in the ghetto (8). People will found businesses if the prospects of gain are sizable. Capital will flow in if the investment can be made attractive. In this view reliance on the social responsibility ethic can never be entirely adequate. The government must provide tax incentives, loan guarantees, and the like to create a business climate in the ghetto similar to that induced by the low taxes and high potential returns on investments which characterized the period of rapid business growth in the rest of the country. Existing disincentives must be replaced by strong government-induced facilitating forces. It is too early to say whether this will be done, and much too early to say whether it will succeed.

International Management in Varying Cultural Contexts

The discussion of representing to this point has implicitly assumed a relatively homogeneous external environment to deal with—that which exists in the United States. However, this is too limited a perspective to encompass the international management field which is concerned both with the operation of U.S.-based firms in other parts of the world and with companies based in other countries. External environments differ tremendously in different societies and countries. Without delving at length into the

Dimensions of External Forces

One statement of the various kinds of external constraints and influences that condition managerial decisions and that must therefore be dealt with in one way or another is given in Table 16–6. This outline has been developed for the purpose of actually scoring a society in terms of its favorableness for business development (12, 13). However, it is also useful as a simple listing of the dimensions on which societies vary, insofar as these dimensions are of significance for the functioning of business organizations.

Many of the dimensions noted in Table 16–6 may be viewed as either constraints and facilitators on resource availability or as direct forces in the external environment. Thus View Toward Achievement ($C_{2.5}$) may serve to influence the motivational level of the people available to a company to act as managers, but it may also serve to determine whether a society supports or stifles a company that achieves, that is, is successful financially.

The discussion which follows is most concerned with characteristics in the sociological and to some degree educational categories. How do societies differ in attitudes, values, and preparation for work? This question is central to the problem of cultural variation. Another question relates to the actual process of representing. How do companies cope with these cultural

Table 16–6 *External Managerial Constraints*

I. *Educational Characteristics*

$C_{1.1}$ Literacy Level: The percentage of the total population who can read and write, and the average years of schooling of adults.

$C_{1.2}$ Higher Education: The percentage of the total population with post high school education, plus the quality of such education. Numbers and quality of colleges and universities in the country. The types of persons obtaining higher education.

$C_{1.3}$ Specialized Technical Training: Types and quality of technical training, including apprenticeship programs, engineering training, technical institutes, company training programs, vocational high school training, and similar. The type, quantity, and quality of persons taking such training.

$C_{1.4}$ Attitude Toward Education: The general cultural attitude toward extensive education, in terms of its presumed desirability.

$C_{1.5}$ Educational Match with Requirements: Whether or not the type of training available in a culture fits the needs of productive enterprises on all levels of skill and achievement.

Secondary Management Functions

Table 16–6 *(Continued)*

II. *Sociological Characteristics*

$C_{2.1}$ View Toward Managers as an Elite Group: The general social attitude toward managers of all sorts.

$C_{2.2}$ View Toward Scientific Method: The general social attitude toward the use of rational, predictive techniques in solving various types of social, business, technical, and economic problems.

$C_{2.3}$ View Toward Wealth: Whether or not the acquisition of wealth is considered socially desirable.

$C_{2.4}$ View Toward Rational Risk Taking: Whether or not taking of various types of personal, corporate, or national risks is considered acceptable, as well as the general view toward specific types of economic and productive risks.

$C_{2.5}$ View Toward Achievement: The general attitude toward personal achievement in the culture.

$C_{2.6}$ Class Flexibility: The possibilities of social class mobility, both upward and downward, in the culture, and the means by which it can be achieved.

III. *Political and Legal Characteristics*

$C_{3.1}$ Relevant Legal Rules of the Game: Quality, efficiency, and effectiveness of the legal structure in terms of general business law, labor law, tax law, and general law relevant to business. Degree of enforcement, reliability, etc.

$C_{3.2}$ Defense Policy: Impact of defense policy on productive enterprise in terms of trading with potential enemies, purchasing policies, strategic industry development, labor competition, and similar factors.

$C_{3.3}$ Foreign Policy: Impact of policy on productive enterprise in terms of trading restrictions, quotas, tariffs, customs, unions, etc.

$C_{3.4}$ Political Stability: Influence on productive enterprises of revolutions, changes in regime, stability or instability over protracted periods, etc.

$C_{3.5}$ Political Organization: Type of organization in constitutional terms, degree of centralization or decentralization, pressure groups and their effectiveness, political parties and their philosophies, etc.

$C_{3.6}$ Flexibility of Law and Legal Changes: Degree to which relevant barriers to efficient management can be changed, certainty of legal actions, etc.

IV. *Economic Characteristics*

$C_{4.1}$ General Economic Framework: Including such factors as the overall economic organization of the society (i.e., capitalistic, Marxist, mixed), property rights, and similar factors.

$C_{4.2}$ Central Banking System: The organization and operations of the central banking system, including the controls over commercial banks, the effectiveness of legal policies regarding price stability, commercial bank reserves, discounting, credit controls, and similar factors.

$C_{4.3}$ Economic Stability: The vulnerability of the economy to economic fluctuations of depression and boom, price stability, and overall economic growth stability.

$C_{4.4}$ Fiscal Policy: General policies concerning government expenditures, their timing, and their impact; the general level of deficit, surplus, or balance; total share of government expenditures in gross national product.

Table 16–6 (Continued)

$C_{4.5}$ Organization of Capital Markets: The existence of such markets as stock and bond exchanges, their honesty, effectiveness, and total impact; the size and role of commercial banking, including loan policies and availability of credit to businessmen; the existence of other capital sources, such as savings and loan associations, government-sponsored credit agencies, insurance company loan activities, etc.

$C_{4.6}$ Factor Endowment: Relative supply of capital and land (agricultural and raw materials) per capita; skills and ability of the work force.

$C_{4.7}$ Market Size: Total effective purchasing power within the country, plus relevant export markets.

$C_{4.8}$ Social Overhead Capital: Availability and quality of power, supplies, water, communications systems, transportation, public warehousing, physical transfer facilities.

$C_{4.9}$ Interorganizational Cooperation: Degree to which various firms, government agencies, unions, and other relevant organizations cooperate with each other to achieve desired mutual goals.

Source: R. N. Farmer and B. M. Richman, "A Model for Research in Comparative Management," *California Management Review,* Vol. 7 (1964), No. 2, 39.

differences? The major response appears to be adaptation in one form or another, but there are attempts to influence and change the external forces as well.

Cultural Variations

Research of a cross-cultural nature is mostly of relatively recent origin and most commonly involves comparisons between two countries (40). There are only a limited number of multi country studies which utilize standardized measures of factors important to the functioning of business organizations. Yet it is this type of study which can contribute the most to an understanding of cultural variations.

Motives, Attitudes, and Values. In Chapter 10, in connection with the discussion of achievement motivation theory, the marked variations in the strength of achievement motivation from country to country were noted (35). Table 10–4 describes 39 countries in terms of their achievement motive level in 1950. The data indicate that this motive is closely related to subsequent economic growth. Thus companies operating in countries

Secondary Management Functions

where a strong desire to achieve is widespread are more likely to be successful than those operating where this motive rarely has a high valence.

A second major cross-cultural study also has been noted previously and is similarly tied to a particular content theory of motivation–need hierarchy theory. This study applied a number of motivational and attitudinal measures to groups of managers in 14 countries (22). Some of the findings are noted in Figure 7–1. Although marked similarities were noted among managers irrespective of country, there were some clear cultural variations. The countries tend to group into clusters within which there is great similarity—Nordic-European (Norway, Denmark, Germany, and Sweden); Latin-European (France, Spain, Italy, and Belgium); Anglo-American (Great Britain and the United States); Developing countries (Argentina, Chile, and India); and Japan as clearly distinct. Subsequent research places Australia in the Anglo-American grouping as well (7).

In general the Nordic-European managers and to a somewhat lesser degree those from the Developing countries placed a greater value on directing and the active use of authority (22). Another major difference appeared in the area of motive satisfaction. Dissatisfaction was much more pronounced in the Developing countries and at a relatively low level in the Nordic-European countries. These differences emerged consistently irrespective of the particular motive measured. Japanese culture appears to provide considerable motive satisfaction also, particularly in the case of self-actualization. These differences in values and motivation would seem to place sizable constraints on the way the management process should be carried out in various countries.

This conclusion is supported by another study which obtained information on the traits managers considered important for success and the preferred managerial styles in Belgium, Denmark, Greece, India, Norway, Spain, Switzerland, and Great Britain (50). Sizable variations in valued traits and leadership styles were found from one country to another. For instance, being supervised in a coercive manner was strongly preferred in Switzerland, but not at all in Norway. Having essentially passive and disinterested subordinates received a favorable response in Greece and India, but not in Great Britain.

The research noted so far has used groups of managers from many different companies. An alternative is to study individuals working for the same company all over the world. This has been done using salesmen, technical personnel, and service personnel who were natives of the countries in which they worked (53). One might expect greater uniformity across countries than was found in the multicompany studies because of the single employer. Yet the degree of diversity that emerges is essentially the same. Furthermore, similar groupings appear—Anglo-American, French, Northern Europe, Southern Latin America, Northern Latin America. Once again Japan is separate and distinct, although several other countries share this separate status in this more comprehensive study involving 25 countries. Interestingly, achievement is particularly valued within the Anglo-American cluster and security much less. Conversely, in both South American groupings individual achievement is de-emphasized.

Education. A second factor that has been found to vary markedly from country to country, and also to have considerable significance for business organizations, is education. Clearly business flourishes where a large proportion of the population meet the various indexes of educational accomplishment—literacy, school attendance, university graduation, and the like (23). Furthermore the extent to which this education is relevant for business organizations, dealing with science and technology, for instance, rather than the arts and humanities, appear to be an important consideration.

Although the availability of intellectually capable human resources appears to be a major factor in the significant role that education plays, there is reason to believe it is not entirely independent of the various motives, attitudes, and values just considered (2). Research indicates that the educational attainment level of a given country is related to such things as attitudes toward management practices and motive satisfactions. On the other hand, it is not clear to what extent education creates the attitudes. It seems just as likely that the reverse may be true with motivational factors serving to foster educational attainment. This proverbial chicken and egg problem is an important one for developing countries.

An extensive survey of the attitudes of chief executives throughout the world serves to point up the extent to which university education is viewed as important (43). As indicated in Table 16-7 executives in all parts of the world consider higher education very important, primarily for intellectual rather than social reasons, and as something to be enjoyed by the many rather than the few. There is some tendency to stress the advantages of university education more in Latin America and Asia, where economic development has been less pronounced to date. Also it appears from the last question that there is a more pronounced split between the university and business communities in the United States than elsewhere, and a minimal split in the Asian countries.

Secondary Management Functions

Table 16-7 Attitudes of Chief Executives Toward Management Education

	Mean Score*				
Question	United States ($N = 26$)	Western Europe ($N = 35$)	Latin America ($N = 37$)	Commonwealth Countries ($N = 23$)	Asia ($N = 51$)
A university education is a prerequisite for those seeking positions of business leadership.	2.4	3.0	2.1	3.3	2.6
The subject matter and intellectual training of university education are an excellent preparation for later success in business.	2.3	2.2	1.6	2.5	2.0
Social contacts made at the university level are highly important in the later business career.	4.7	4.2	2.9	3.8	2.7
University education should be limited to a relatively small group who will fill major leadership positions in society.	6.6	5.7	5.4	6.0	5.0
University professors believe that the business sector is important and valuable in making the society economically strong.	4.3	3.1	3.2	3.5	2.1

* The smaller the mean score, the greater the agreement with the statement, i.e., 1 = strongly agree and 7 = strongly disagree.
Source: R. B. Peterson, "Chief Executives' Attitudes: A Cross-Cultural Analysis," *Industrial Relations*, Vol. 10 (1971), 199.

Dealing with Cultural Contexts

Given the widespread cultural differences that do in fact exist, what response should an American firm with extensive international operations make? The most frequently expressed opinion, as noted in Chapter 8, has favored decentralization with decisions made in the culture where they apply, as often as possible by managers who are nationals of that country.

This strategy is clearly one of adaptation to cultural constraints. But what if the country has few educated people, low levels of achievement motivation, and values which are antithetical to business development, to take the most extreme case? In short what if adaptation automatically condemns a company to mediocrity in terms of attaining its goals as defined either operatively or officially by the culture of origin?

Under such circumstances a strong case can be made for a resort to more centralized control in a corporate headquarters located outside the culture and for the use of expatriate managers rather than nationals. The idea under such circumstances would be either to change certain aspects of the culture or to adapt only in the sense of a very minimal compliance. This would create the company as a differentiated cultural island in the sea of the surrounding culture. This strategy carries with it a sizable risk of failure in that the existing constraints may prove too resistant and counterforces may overwhelm the operation. Where full adaptation can only guarantee failure, this risk would seem to be worth taking.

There is one constraint, however, that may serve to limit the use of managers exported from the headquarters country. This has to do with the supply of individuals who will serve in this way and who can do so effectively. There is ample evidence that the supply of capable international managers is severely constricted (56). Many managers do not want an international career, others have strong negative attitudes toward certain foreign cultures, and still others lack the flexibility to work in other parts of the world. The phenomenon of culture shock, whereby people moving into a new culture simply are not able to function effectively when surrounded by a new language, new customs, and a strange people, is a reality with which many companies have had to deal. Many managers and their families have been returned to the United States because of emotional problems thus created. On the other hand, some recent research shows that special cultural training given before leaving for a foreign assignment can help to alleviate this problem (15).

Overall, it would appear that representing should follow the adaptation route where the surrounding culture offers the prospect that task and maintenance goals can achieve reasonable levels of attainment through this strategy. But a complete commitment to adaptation irrespective of the culture can only be an invitation to disaster. There are cases where organizational goals can only be achieved when there is some friction at the organization-society interface and where this friction results in changes in the external environment.

Questions

1. To what extent is public relations synonymous with the representing function?. Explain with reference to the different components of public relations practice and to the areas in which representing occurs.
2. Some argue that management should devote its efforts primarily to profits; some that the welfare of society should be management's major concern. What are the arguments pro and con here? What do you believe? Why?
3. What are the various ways in which multinational companies may deal with cultural differences? Select one highly industrialized and one underdeveloped country and indicate what different approaches in carrying out managerial functions might be appropriate to each.
4. What are the pros and cons of black economic development or black capitalism? Would it seem logical to approach this matter in the same way as the economic development of the underdeveloped countries?
5. You have been asked as an outside consultant to advise on the introduction of a manufacturing training program for the hard-core unemployed. What problems do you foresee? How would you recommend dealing with them?

References

1. Adelberg, M. "Industrial Training of the Hardcore Unemployed." *Personnel*, Vol. 46 (1969), No. 6, 22–28.
2. Ajiferuke, M., and J. Boddewyn. "Socioeconomic Indicators in Comparative Management." *Administrative Science Quarterly*, Vol. 15 (1970), 453–458.
3. Baumhart, R. *An Honest Profit: What Businessmen Say About Ethics in Business.* New York: Holt, Rinehart and Winston, 1968.
4. Bell, D., and I. Kristol. *Capitalism Today.* New York: Basic Books, 1971.
5. Booms, B. H., and J. E. Ward. "The Cons of Black Capitalism." *Business Horizons*, Vol. 12 (1969), No. 5, 17–26.
6. Brower, M., and D. Little. "White Help for Black Business." *Harvard Business Review*, Vol. 48 (1970), No. 3, 4–16, 163–164.
7. Clark, A. W., and S. McCabe. "Leadership Beliefs of Australian Managers." *Journal of Applied Psychology*, Vol. 54 (1970), 1–6.
8. Cross, T. L. *Black Capitalism: Strategy for Business in the Ghetto.* New York: Atheneum, 1969.
9. Doeringer, P. B. *Programs to Employ the Disadvantaged.* Englewood Cliffs, N.J.: Prentice-Hall, 1969.
10. Doeringer, P. B., and M. J. Piore. "Equal Employment Opportunity in Boston." *Industrial Relations*, Vol. 9 (1970), 324–339.

11. Elbing, A. O. "The Value Issue of Business: The Responsibility of the Businessman." *Academy of Management Journal*, Vol. 13 (1970), 79–89.
12. Farmer, R. N., and B. M. Richman. "A Model for Research in Comparative Management." *California Management Review*, Vol. 7 (1964), No. 2, 55–68.
13. Farmer, R. N., and B. M. Richman. *Comparative Management and Economic Progress*. Homewood, Ill.: Irwin, 1965.
14. Fenn, D. H. "Executives as Community Volunteers." *Harvard Business Review*, Vol. 49 (1971), No. 2, 4–16, 156–157.
15. Fiedler, F. E., T. Mitchell, and H. C. Triandis. "The Culture Assimilator: An Approach to Cross-Cultural Training." *Journal of Applied Psychology*, Vol. 55 (1971), 95–102.
16. Finn, D. "The Price of Corporate Vanity." *Harvard Business Review*, Vol. 39 (1961), No. 4, 135–143.
17. Friedlander, F., and S. Greenberg. "Work Climate as Related to the Performance and Retention of Hard-Core Unemployed Workers." *Proceedings, 77th Annual Convention, American Psychological Association*, 1969, 607–608.
18. Goeke, J. R., and C. S. Weymar. "Barriers to Hiring the Blacks." *Harvard Business Review*, Vol. 47 (1969), No. 5, 144–152.
19. Golembiewski, R. T. *Men, Management and Morality: Toward a New Organizational Ethic*. New York: McGraw-Hill, 1965.
20. Greenberg, D. H. "Employing the Training-Program Enrollee: An Analysis of Employer Personnel Records." *Industrial and Labor Relations Review*, Vol. 24 (1971), 554–571.
21. Haddad, W. F., and G. D. Pugh. *Black Economic Development*. Englewood Cliffs, N.J.: Prentice-Hall, 1969.
22. Haire, M., E. E. Ghiselli, and L. W. Porter. *Managerial Thinking: An International Study*. New York: Wiley, 1966.
23. Harbison, F., and C. A. Myers. *Education, Manpower, and Economic Growth*. New York: McGraw-Hill, 1964.
24. Harris, P. "Minority Groups in the Executive Suite." In R. W. Millman and M. P. Hottenstein (eds.), *Promising Research Directions. Academy of Management Proceedings*, 1968, pp. 164–168.
25. Hearns, J. P. "New Approaches to Meet Post-Hiring Difficulties of Disadvantaged Workers." In G. G. Somers (ed.), *Proceedings of the Twenty-First Annual Winter Meeting*. Industrial Relations Research Association, 1969, pp. 207–216.
26. Henderson, H. "Should Business Tackle Society's Problems?" *Harvard Business Review*, Vol. 46 (1968), No. 4, 77–85.
27. Holley, W. H. "Effect of Modifying Job Design to Employ the Hard-Core Jobless." *Personnel Journal*, Vol. 50 (1971), 288–292.

28. Iacobelli, J. L. "A Survey of Employer Attitudes Toward Training the Disadvantaged." *Monthly Labor Review*, Vol. 93 (1970), No. 6, 51–55.
29. Janger, A. R., and R. G. Schaeffer. *Managing Programs to Employ the Disadvantaged*. Personnel Policy Study No. 219. New York: National Industrial Conference Board, 1970.
30. Levitan, S. A., and G. L. Mangum. *Federal Training and Work Programs in the Sixties*. Ann Arbor: Institute of Labor and Industrial Relations, University of Michigan, 1969.
31. Lockwood, H. "Progress in Plans for Progress for Negro Managers." In The Executive Study Conference, *The Selection and Training of Negroes for Managerial Positions*. Princeton, N.J.: Educational Testing Service, 1965, 1–22.
32. Lorig, A. W. "Where Do Corporate Responsibilities Really Lie?" *Business Horizons*, Vol. 10 (1967), No. 2, 51–54.
33. Marquis, H. M. *The Changing Corporate Image*. New York: American Management Association, 1970.
34. Mazis, M., and R. Green. "Implementing Social Responsibility." *MSU Business Topics*, Vol. 19 (1971), No. 1, 68–76.
35. McClelland, D. C. *The Achieving Society*. Princeton, N.J.: Van Nostrand, 1961.
36. McGuire, J. W. "The Social Responsibility of the Corporation." In E. B. Flippo (ed.), *Evolving Concepts in Management. Proceedings of the 24th Annual Meeting*. Academy of Management, 1965, pp. 21–28.
37. McGuire, J. W., and J. B. Parrish. "Status Report on a Profound Revolution." *California Management Review*, Vol. 13 (1971), No. 4, 79–86.
38. Morgan, B. S., M. R. Blonsky, and H. Rosen. "Employee Attitudes Toward a Hard-Core Hiring Program." *Journal of Applied Psychology*, Vol. 54 (1970), 473–478.
39. Myers, C. A. *The Role of the Private Sector in Manpower Development*. Baltimore: Johns Hopkins Press, 1971.
40. Nath, R. "A Methodological Review of Cross-Cultural Management Research." *International Social Science Journal*, Vol. 20 (1968), 35–62.
41. National Industrial Conference Board. "Pollution Abatement in Industry: Policies and Practices." *Conference Board Record*, Vol. 3 (December, 1966), 35–38.
42. Pagano, J. "Union-Management Adaptation to Needs of Disadvantaged New Employees." In G. G. Somers (ed.), *Proceedings of the Twenty-First Annual Meeting*. Industrial Relations Research Association, 1969, pp. 228–235.
43. Peterson, R. B. "Chief Executives' Attitudes: A Cross-Cultural Analysis." *Industrial Relations*, Vol. 10 (1971), 194–210.
44. Petit, T. A. *The Moral Crisis in Management*. New York: McGraw-Hill, 1967.

45. Powell, R. M. *Race, Religion, and the Promotion of the American Executive.* Columbus: College of Administrative Science, Ohio State University, 1969.
46. Price, J. L. *Organizational Effectiveness: An Inventory of Propositions.* Homewood, Ill.: Irwin, 1968.
47. Quinn, R. P. "Differences Between Those Who Do and Do Not Use Nonability Factors in Decisions to Hire or Promote Managers." In B. M. Bass, R. Cooper, and J. A. Haas (eds.), *Managing for Accomplishment.* Lexington, Mass.: Heath, 1970, pp. 26–42.
48. Rambo, L. M. "So You've Hired a Black American." *Personnel Administration*, Vol. 33 (1970), No. 2, 4–7, 21–23.
49. Roalman, A. R. *Profitable Public Relations.* Homewood, Ill.: Dow Jones-Irwin, 1968.
50. Ryterband, E. C., and G. V. Barrett. "Managers' Values and Their Relationship to the Management of Tasks: A Cross-Cultural Comparison." In B. M. Bass, R. Cooper, and J. A. Haas (eds.), *Managing for Accomplishment.* Lexington, Mass.: Heath, 1970, pp. 226–260.
51. Schmidt, W. H. *Organizational Frontiers and Human Values.* Belmont, Calif.: Wadsworth, 1970.
52. Schollhammer, H. "The Comparative Management Theory Jungle." *Academy of Management Journal*, Vol. 12 (1969), 81–97.
53. Sirota, D., and J. M. Greenwood. "Understand Your Overseas Work Force." *Harvard Business Review*, Vol. 49 (1971), No. 1, 53–60.
54. Skala, M. "Inner-City Enterprises: Current Experience." In W. F. Haddad and G. D. Pugh (eds.), *Black Economic Development.* Englewood Cliffs, N.J.: Prentice-Hall, 1969, pp. 151–171.
55. Tannenbaum, R., and S. A. Davis. "Values, Man and Organizations." *Industrial Management Review*, Vol. 10 (1969), No. 2, 69–80.
56. Vansina, L. S., and T. Taillieu. "Comparative Study of the Characteristics of Flemish Graduates Planning Their Careers in National or International Organizations." In B. M. Bass, R. Cooper, and J. A. Haas (eds.), *Managing for Accomplishment.* Lexington, Mass.: Heath, 1970, pp. 262–285.
57. Walton, C. C. *Ethos and the Executive: Values in Managerial Decision Making.* Englewood Cliffs, N.J.: Prentice-Hall, 1969.
58. Walton, C. C. *Business and Social Progress: Views of Two Generations of Executives.* New York: Praeger, 1970.
59. Zimpel, L., and D. Panger. *Business and the Hardcore Unemployed.* New York: Fell, 1970.

Conclusion

In the process of writing a book such as this, one inevitably reviews a sizable literature—statements of theory, research reports, descriptions of practice. Several strong impressions regarding the nature of the management field have emerged from the writer's extended immersion in the literature. These have to do, first, with the usefulness of theoretical frameworks; second, with the role and distribution of research efforts; and third, with the direction in which practice appears to be moving.

Usefulness of Theories

The concept of the management process viewed as including planning (both policy and organizational), directing, coordinating, controlling, staffing, and representing provides a framework which appears to be, not only extremely useful, but sufficiently comprehensive to include all major facets of managerial work. It has the support of considerable behavioral science research while at the same time having its origin in the writings of the early

Conclusion

classical management scholars. Thus the concept provides an effective bridge between the two main strains of management thought. Practically all textbooks with the word *management* in their titles have been organized around a framework provided by some version of the management process. Extended exposure to the literature leaves the conviction that this strong commitment to the management process approach represents a valuable carry-over from the past. Viewing the management field in terms of the functions managers perform seems clearly to have borne considerable fruit, and gives every promise of continuing to do so in the future.

The same cannot be said for the other cornerstone of classical theory—the principles of management. The principles traceable to Fayol (3) and Taylor (10, 11), even with the extensive expansion and revision of writers such as R. C. Davis (2) and Koontz and O'Donnell (7), simply are no longer relevant to much of what is going on in the management field. They have served their purpose and with only a few exceptions now appear to be primarily of historical interest. Large segments of both the research literature and current practice have developed from completely different origins and have to be forced or distorted to make them fit the old management principles framework (4, 5). On this point the writer has been compelled to revise his previous views as a result of the experience of writing this book. It would seem much more fruitful to forget these vestiges of the past and move to new theoretical frameworks which can generate their own ideas for research and guidelines for practice. In actual fact this is what appears to be happening.

Three such frameworks have had a major impact on the present volume. Systems theory provides an extremely useful conceptual approach; other textbook writers in the management field seem to view it as equally valuable (6, 12). Overall, it is clear that systems theory already has firmly established itself as a major contributor to management thought. It has generated research and has had a considerable impact on practice. Although somewhat less widely accepted currently in its relation to the management field, role theory appears destined to exert at least as much influence as systems theory. It has proved useful as a basis for conceptualizing many topic areas, and the amount of management research based on role theory formulations is increasing steadily. Integration theory, by contrast, is clearly more limited in scope. It appears valuable primarily as an adjunct to systems and role theories in certain areas, such as motivation. To date it has not achieved the same level of acceptance and utilization as the other two theories. Yet what use has been made of it suggests an extremely promising future.

Conclusion

Distribution of Research

In the past few years there has been a tremendous upsurge of research in the field of management. The theoretical underpinnings of this research are extremely varied, and there are, in fact, many studies designed and carried out with little reference to major theories of any kind. Often they are simply tests of first-order hypotheses generated by a need to solve practical problems. The strong applied, pragmatic bent of much of the research suggests that contributions to the practice of management in the near future at least are more likely to be in the modification and development of certain already existing approaches, rather than in major breakthroughs to new knowledge. Yet the very fact that research has finally come to the management field in something approximating the abundance required by its complexity is an extremely encouraging sign. When the writer first considered the possibility of doing a book such as this in the early 1960s, he was dissuaded by the mere fact that there was so little research that was truly indigenous to the management field as to make such an effort pointless.

An additional facet of the research productivity relates to its origins. Studies are appearing not just from behavioral scientists but from people with a considerable range of disciplinary training. All of the major schools of management thought are represented. It does appear that when the divisions which currently characterize the field are finally a thing of the past, the common bond of scientific research and more certain knowledge will be a crucial factor. There are signs that this unifying impact of science is already beginning to occur.

A major problem remaining relates to the distribution of research over the various management functions. There is a distinct lack of scientific study in the policy planning area, although this is somewhat less true in regard to decision-making tools and processes. By contrast research in the organization planning area is generating much significant new knowledge. Directing is probably the most extensively studied of any of the management functions, although there is still much to learn. Coordinating, especially insofar as conditions for conflict are concerned, has been a strong research area recently, but there still are many aspects of the coordination functions that have not yet been studied to any meaningful degree. This is even more true of controlling, which, along with policy planning, emerges as the most underresearched function. Except perhaps in the areas of management recruiting and executive compensation, staffing has been an active research area. Representing shows signs of generating an abundance of research in the future. It is in many respects a new area which only recently has attracted the serious study it deserves.

There appears to be a trend of succession as research moves into an area. Typically the first studies are surveys—of practice, of attitudes, of intentions. In the next phase there is a more serious attempt to relate one factor to another, but causal relationships are assumed rather than empirically established. Finally, as the area becomes a major focus of research, studies are conducted, often using simulations, to establish what causes what.

The Direction of Practice

There has been considerable contention that we are currently in a period in which administrative organizations have outlived their usefulness. At least this is said to be true of administrative organizations in anything like their present form. This "decline of bureaucracy" theme has emanated from the behavioral humanist school in particular (1). If one looks closely at current practice, however, there is little to substantiate this claim.

The literature indicates a marked increase in interest in studying professional organizations. These organizations are increasing both in number and importance in our society. But there is nothing to indicate that this is occurring at the expense of administrative organizations. Research indicates that the administrative structure is an important organizational form, especially in major segments of manufacturing (8). If anything, the introduction of computers appears to be moving us toward centralization rather than a more complete decentralization. Clearly there will be a greater diversity of organizational forms in the future, and this trend is in evidence today. Different tasks and environments will impose different requirements for effective goal accomplishment. But there is no reason to believe that the administrative organization is likely to disappear. Study after study records its continuing strength and even prosperity.

On the other hand, there is reason to believe that in this period of attack on our large bureaucracies, and even considerable disenchantment with them, the problem of finding effective managers may become acute (9). There are going to be many opportunities available in administrative organizations for those who have not only the intellectual capability and training but, perhaps more important, the emotional maturity and requisite motivation to function effectively in a managerial capacity. The greatest challenge now facing the schools of business administration is the need to produce graduates who really *want* to manage the large industrial organizations that await them.

References

1. Bennis, W. *Changing Organizations.* New York: McGraw-Hill, 1966.
2. Davis, R. C. *The Fundamentals of Top Management.* New York: Harper, Row, 1951.
3. Fayol, H. *General and Industrial Management.* London: Pitman, 1949.
4. Filley, A. C., and R. J. House. *Managerial Process and Organizational Behavior.* Chicago: Scott, Foresman, 1969.
5. House, R. J., and J. B. Miner. "Merging Management and Behavioral Theory: The Interaction Between Span of Control and Group Size." *Administrative Science Quarterly*, Vol. 14 (1969), 451–464.
6. Kast, F. E., and J. E. Rosenzweig. *Organization and Management: A Systems Approach.* New York: McGraw-Hill, 1970.
7. Koontz, H., and C. O'Donnell. *Principles of Management: An Analysis of Managerial Functions.* New York: McGraw-Hill, 1968.
8. Lawrence, P. R., and J. W. Lorsch. *Organization and Environment: Managing Differentiation and Integration.* Boston: Division of Research, Harvard Business School, 1967.
9. Miner, J. B. "Changes in Student Attitudes Toward Bureaucratic Role Prescriptions During the 1960s." *Administrative Science Quarterly*, Vol. 16 (1971), 351–364.
10. Taylor, F. W. *Shop Management.* New York: Harper, 1911.
11. Taylor, F. W. *The Principles of Scientific Management*, New York: Harper, 1911.
12. Voich, D., and D. A. Wren. *Principles of Management—Resources and Systems.* New York: Ronald, 1968.

Author Index

Aboud, J., 355
Ackoff, R. L., 135
Adam, E. E., 462
Adams, J. S., 322
Adelberg, M., 232
Aiken, M., 231
Ajiferuke, M., 532
Albaum, G., 384
Alderfer, C. P., 260
Alford, L. P., 105
Allaway, R. H., 500
Allen, T. J., 386
Alutto, J. A., 260
Alvares, K. M., 354
Anderson, B. F., 104
Anderson, J. K., 166
Anderson, L. R., 197, 198
Andrews, F. M., 200, 262, 357
Andrews, I. R., 326
Andrews, K. R., 166, 500
Anshen, M., 165
Ansoff, H. I., 165
Anthony, R. N., 39
Arensberg, C. M., 292
Argyris, C., 39, 289, 462
Äs, D., 291
Atchison, T. J., 5
Atkinson, J. W., 323

Bachman, J. G., 323
Bailey, J. K., 290
Baker, H. K., 231

Baldridge, J. V., 423
Bales, R., 263
Balk, W. L., 231
Bamforth, K. W., 293
Barkdull, C. W., 462
Barkin, S., 292
Barnard, C. I., 39, 69, 197, 231, 323
Barnes, L. B., 290, 323
Barnlund, D. C., 384
Barrell, R. P., 233
Barrett, G. V., 385, 535
Barrett, R. S., 136
Barron, F., 197
Bass, A. R., 199, 262
Bass, B. M., 5, 135, 260, 261, 290, 291, 356, 423, 500, 535
Bates, J., 426
Battalia, Lotz, and Associates, 231, 260
Bauer, R. A., 165, 197, 201
Baum, B. H., 234, 500
Baumhart, 532
Bavelas, A., 385
Becker, S. W., 462
Baumhart, R., 532
Beer, M., 290, 323, 353
Belasco, J. A., 260
Bell, D., 532
Bell, E. C., 165
Bell, G. D., 69
Beller, R., 387
Belovicz, M. W., 197
Bendix, R., 39

543

Author Index

Benne, K. D., 290
Bennis, W. G., 39, 104, 290, 293, 541
Benston, G. J., 462
Bentz, V. J., 353
Berelson, B., 105
Berg, I. E., 424
Berkowitz, L., 260, 387, 423
Berrien, F. K., 41
Biddle, B. J., 39
Bierman, H., 39
Biglan, A., 356
Birnberg, J. G., 167
Bishop, R. C., 260
Bittel, L. R., 501
Blake, R. R., 290, 423
Blankenship, L. V., 231, 357
Blau, P. M., 290
Blonsky, M. R., 534
Blood, M. R., 261
Blumberg, A., 424
Bockman, V. M., 323
Boddewyn, J., 105, 532
Bogard, H. M., 423
Booms, B. H., 532
Borgatta, E. F., 263
Boring, E. G., 105
Bouchard, T. J., 197
Boulding, K., 423
Bowen, D., 423
Bower, J. L., 197
Bowers, D. G., 354
Brewer, J. F., 425, 464
Brink, V. Z., 290
Brooks, E., 69
Brower, M., 532
Brown, C. W., 105
Brown, R. V., 198
Brown, W. B., 40
Brown, Z. M., 5
Brummet, R. L., 462
Bruner, J. S., 198
Bryan, J. F., 136, 137
Buchanan, P. C., 290
Buchele, R. B., 462
Bugental, D. E., 323
Bureau of National Affairs, 385, 500
Burgess, R. L., 385
Burke, R. J., 385
Burns, T., 290, 385
Burns, T. J., 462, 464

Busching, B. C., 326
Business Week, 198
Butler, W. F., 166
Butman, J., 262
Byham, W. C., 500

Cafferty, T. P., 426
Campbell, J. P., 69, 198, 290, 323, 354, 500
Cannon, J. T., 166
Caplan, E. H., 462
Caplow, T., 385, 423
Carey, A., 105
Carlson, R. E., 500
Carlson, S., 69
Carroll, D. T., 290
Carroll, S. J., 70, 136, 137, 232, 233, 500, 502
Carroll, V., 261
Cartwright, D., 136, 198, 323, 354, 355, 358, 386, 423
Carvalho, G. F., 201
Carzo, R., 231
Centers, R., 323
Chalmers, W. E., 292
Chandler, A. D., 231, 260
Chin, R., 290
Christensen, C. R., 166
Church, A. H., 105
Churchill, N. C., 462
Churchman, C. W., 198
Cicero, J. P., 263
Clark, A. W., 532
Clarkson, G. P. E., 198
Cleland, D. I., 198, 260, 386
Coch, L., 290
Cohan, A. B., 40
Cohen, A. M., 385
Cohen, A. R., 385
Collaros, P. A., 198
Collins, O. F., 354
Cook, S. W., 107
Coons, A. E., 357
Cooper, R., 261, 356, 535
Cooper, W. W., 5, 200, 234, 260, 325, 462
Cosentino, J., 324
Craft, C. J., 501
Craig, J. R., 356
Craig, R. L., 501

544

Cross, T. L., 532
Crystal, G. S., 501
Cummin, P. C., 354
Cummings, L. L., 105, 198, 323, 426
Cyert, R. M., 40, 198

Dale, E., 69, 231
Dalkey, N., 166
Dalton, F. E., 198
Dalton, G. W., 290, 323
Dalton, M., 40, 423, 463
Daniel, D. R., 260
Dauw, D. C., 501
Davis, J. H., 198, 385
Davis, K., 260, 323, 385
Davis, L. E., 260
Davis, R. C., 69, 105, 231, 541
Davis, S. A., 290, 535
Dearborn, D. C., 423
Dearden, J., 290
DeCoster, D. T., 463
Deep, S. D., 291
Deets, M. K., 198
Delbecq, A. L., 201, 231, 426
Delehanty, G. E., 291
Dennis, B. D., 292
Derman, I. H., 386
Deutsch, D. R., 325
Deutsch, M., 107
Dewhirst, H. D., 385
DeWolf, A. S., 233
Dickson, G. W., 385
Dickson, W. J., 107
Dill, W. R., 5
Doeringer, P. B., 532
Donnelly, J. H., 5, 136, 501
Dornbusch, S. M., 326
Drebin, A. R., 39
Driver, M. J., 387
Drought, N. E., 260
Dubin, R., 69, 105, 354, 387
Dunbar, R. L. M., 463
Duncan, W. J., 105
Dunnette, M. D., 5, 69, 198, 290, 323, 325, 354, 425, 464, 500, 501
Dunteman, G., 423
Dutton, J. M., 423, 426

Edwards, A. L., 198
Edwards, W., 198

Egloff, W. F., 260
El-Assal, M., 71
Elbing, A. O., 533
Emery, J. C., 136, 385
Emory, C. W., 198
Emshoff, J. R., 424
Endicott, F. S., 501
England, G. W., 40, 291
Etzioni, A., 40, 69, 105, 324
Evan, W. M., 105, 323, 424
Evans, M. G., 323

Farmer, R. N., 533
Farris, G. F., 354
Fayol, H., 69, 105, 166, 231, 260, 323, 385, 424, 541
Feldman, H., 354
Fenn, D. H., 533
Ferber, R. C., 199
Ference, T. P., 5
Fertakis, J. P., 463
Fiedler, F. E., 197, 354, 356, 533
Filipetti, G., 105
Filley, A. C., 105, 136, 166, 261, 291, 323, 354, 355, 541
Finch, F. E., 197
Fink, C. F., 233
Finn, D., 533
Fisch, G. G., 231, 261, 291
Fisk, G., 40, 423
Fitch, H. G., 426
Flamholtz, E. G., 462
Fleishman, E. A., 354
Flippo, E. P., 5, 424, 463, 534
Follett, M. P., 70, 424
Foote, G. H., 501
Ford, R. N., 261
Foster, K. E., 500
Foster, R. N., 166
Fouraker, L. E., 231
Fox, W. M., 5
Franke, R. H., 385
Fredian, A. J., 501
French, J. R. P., 136, 137, 166, 290, 291, 323
French, W. L., 70, 261, 291, 326, 426
Freud, A., 385
Freud, S., 424
Frey, M. W., 137, 464
Frick, F. C., 385

Author Index

Friedlander, F., 70, 261, 533
Friedman, A., 324
Friedman, J., 136
Friedman, M., 261
Friedman, N., 105
Fulmer, R. M., 261
Fusfeld, A. R., 166

Galbraith, J. R., 323, 424
Gannon, M. J., 199, 464
Gazell, J. A., 324
George, C. S., 105
Gergen, K. J., 165, 197, 201
Germane, G. E., 5, 40, 136, 232, 261, 386, 463
Gerstberger, P. G., 386
Gerstenfeld, A., 424
Ghiselli, E. E., 105, 231, 354, 533
Ghorpade, J. V., 5
Gibb, J. R., 386
Gibson, J. L., 5
Gilmore, F. F., 166
Ginsburg, S. W., 166
Ginzberg, E., 166, 424
Glasner, D. M., 136
Glueck, W. F., 291, 501
Goeke, J. R., 533
Gold, B., 463
Golembiewski, R. T., 261, 424, 533
Goode, W. J., 40
Goodman, C. C., 198
Goodman, P. S., 324
Goodman, R. A., 261
Goodstadt, B., 324, 354
Gordon, G., 199
Gordon, P. J., 5, 105, 106
Gordon, T. J., 166
Goronzy, F., 106
Graen, G., 324, 354
Graham, W. K., 355
Graicunas, V. A., 105
Green, D., 462
Green, R., 534
Greenberg, D. H., 533
Greenberg, S., 533
Greenlaw, P. S., 200
Greenwood, J. M., 535
Greenwood, W. T., 70, 463
Griffin, J. E., 233
Grimes, A. J., 323

Gross, B. M., 70, 136
Gruber, W. H., 325
Gruenfeld, L. W., 501
Guest, R. H., 291
Guetzkow, H., 386
Gujarati, D. N., 355
Gulick, L., 105, 424
Gutenberg, A. W., 463
Guth, W. D., 166, 199
Gutman, P. M., 166

Haas, J. A., 70, 261, 356, 535
Haberstroh, C. J., 41, 426, 463
Hackman, J. R., 261
Haddad, W. F., 533, 535
Hage, J., 231
Haimann, T., 386
Haire, M., 231, 324, 533
Hall, D. T., 324
Hall, R. H., 70, 231
Hamblin, R. L., 425
Haney, W. V., 386
Harbison, F., 533
Hare, A. P., 232, 263
Harland, C., 384
Harnett, D. L., 105
Harrell, T. W., 355
Harris, E. F., 354
Harris, P., 533
Hart, D. K., 107
Harvey, E., 261
Harvey, O. J., 426
Hawk, R. H., 501
Hearns, J. P., 533
Heidbreder, E., 105
Hekimian, J. S., 5
Helmer, O., 166
Hemphill, J. K., 70
Henderson, A. M., 107
Henderson, H., 533
Hendrick, H. W., 232
Heneman, H. G., 326
Henning, D. A., 261, 463
Herma, J. L., 166
Hershey, R., 386
Herskovitz, M. J., 40
Herzberg, F., 324, 355
Heyel, C., 386
Hicks, H. G., 106
Hickson, D. J., 232, 233

Author Index

Higdon, H., 166
Higgin, G. W., 293
Hilgert, R. L., 291, 293
Hill, J. W., 199, 260
Hill, R. E., 261
Hill, W. A., 291, 355
Hilton, P., 291
Hinings, C. R., 233
Hinrichs, J. R., 386, 501
Hinton, B. L., 199
Hoffman, L. R., 199, 386
Hogan, J. M., 136
Holden, P. E., 5, 40, 136, 232, 261, 386, 463
Hollander, E. P., 355
Holley, W. H., 533
Holloman, C. R., 232
Hood, W. R., 426
Hopkins, T. K., 324
Hornaday, J. A., 355
Hottenstein, M. P., 166, 200, 323, 423, 424, 533
Hough, L., 106
House, R. J., 5, 40, 41, 105, 106, 136, 137, 166, 232, 233, 261, 324, 354, 355, 425, 501, 541
Hoxie, R. F., 106
Hoyt, G. C., 198
Hrapchak, W. J., 356
Hughes, C. L., 136
Hulin, C. L., 261, 424
Humble, J. W., 136
Hundal, P. S., 355
Hunt, J. G., 424
Hunt, R. G., 232
Hutchinson, J. G., 463
Hyman, H. H., 40

Iacobelli, J. L., 534
Indik, B. P., 41, 355
Ingham, G. K., 424
Inkson, J. H. K., 232
Israel, J., 291
Ivancevich, J. M., 5, 136, 500, 501

Jaastad, K., 198
Jackson, J. M., 262
Jahoda, M., 107
Janger, A. R., 534
Jasinski, F. J., 463

Jerdee, T. H., 70, 232, 356
Jerome, W. T., 463
Johnson, R. A., 40, 70
Johnson, R. L., 386
Jones, H. R., 232

Kaczka, E., 355
Kahn, R. L., 40, 70, 136, 166, 291, 324, 355, 386
Kakar, S., 106
Kast, F. E., 40, 70, 386, 463, 541
Katz, D., 40, 70, 136, 166, 291, 324, 355, 386
Katzell, R. A., 136
Kavanagh, M. J., 356
Kavesh, R. A., 166
Kay, E., 136, 137
Kelly, J., 424
Kelman, H. C., 324
Kendall, L. M., 137
Kerlinger, F. N., 106, 199
Kerr, S., 355
King, W. R., 198, 260, 386
Kipnis, D., 324, 354
Kirk, R. V., 355
Klatzky, S. R., 291
Klein, S. M., 424
Kolde, E. J., 261
Koontz, H., 70, 106, 136, 232, 261, 324, 463, 541
Korman, A. K., 199, 355, 424
Korten, D. C., 355
Kover, A. J., 261
Kraus, R. M., 463
Kristol, I., 532
Krupp, S., 106

Laing, J. D., 326
Lane, W. P., 324
Larsen, I. M., 137
Lawler, E. E., 40, 41, 69, 233, 261, 262, 323–25, 354, 500, 501
Lawrence, P. R., 40, 106, 232, 262, 425, 541
Lazarsfeld, P. E., 166
Learned, E. P., 166
Leavitt, H. J., 5, 106, 135, 200, 234, 260, 291, 325, 357, 386, 462
LeBleu, R. E., 166

Author Index

LeBreton, P. P., 5, 136, 199, 260, 292, 424, 425
Lee, H. C., 291, 293
Leete, B. A., 233
Lesher, J. L., 502
Levitan, S. A., 534
Lewellen, W. G., 501
Lifter, M. L., 262
Likert, R., 106, 232, 355, 463
Lim, F. G., 354
Lippitt, G. L., 326
Lippitt, R., 358
Lipstreu, O., 292
Lirtzman, S. I., 41, 233, 425
Litschert, R. J., 136
Litterer, J. A., 425
Little, D., 532
Litwin, G. H., 355
Litzinger, W. D., 106, 356
Locke, E. A., 136, 137, 324–26, 356, 425
Lockwood, H., 534
Logan, H. H., 262
Logan, J. P., 166
Longenecker, J. G., 70
Lopez, F. M., 356, 501, 502
Lorig, A. W., 534
Lorsch, J. W., 40, 106, 232, 262, 263, 425, 541
Lowin, A., 356
Luce, R. D., 199
Lundberg, C. C., 137
Lyon, H. L., 136
Lyons, T. F., 425

McCabe, S., 532
McClelland, D. C., 137, 325, 356, 502, 534
McCormick, C., 262
McFarlan, F. W., 387
McFarland, D. E., 70, 71, 353, 425, 463
McGee, R. J., 423
McGregor, D., 106, 137, 325, 356
McGuire, J. W., 534
Mackenzie, K. D., 199
McKersie, R. B., 425, 427
McKinsey and Company, 387
McLennan, K., 70
McNamara, W. J., 502
McNutly, J. E., 292

Maher, J. R., 424
Mahoney, T. A., 70, 232, 356
Maier, N. R. F., 199, 232, 262, 386
Malcolm, D. G., 199
Mangum, G. L., 534
Mann, F. C., 292
Mann, R., 165, 263, 500
March, J. G., 40, 106, 198, 200, 233, 291, 293, 386, 425
Marquis, D. G., 325
Marquis, H. M., 534
Marrow, A. J., 166
Martella, J. A., 354
Martindell, J., 463
Maslow, A. H., 325
Mason, R. H., 137
Mason, R. O., 166
Massarik, F., 71
Massie, J. L., 70, 106
Mausner, B., 324, 355
Mayfield, E. C., 500
Mazis, M., 534
Meadow, A., 200
Mechanic, D., 325
Melcher, A. J., 387
Meltzer, L., 232
Meyer, H., 234
Meyer, H. H., 136, 137
Meyer, M. W., 232
Miles, R. E., 5, 231, 326, 357, 463
Miller, E. J., 40
Miller, L. K., 425
Millman, R. W., 71, 166, 200, 323, 423, 424, 533
Mills, D. L., 71
Miner, J. B., 5, 40, 41, 71, 106, 137, 166, 198–200, 232, 262, 292, 325, 356, 425, 464, 502, 541
Mitchell, T. R., 356, 533
Mitchell, V. F., 233
Mockler, R. J., 464
Molinari, L., 323
Mooney, J. D., 106
Moore, D. G., 354
Moore, R. F., 500–502
Morgan, B. S., 534
Morrison, E. J., 387
Morse, E. V., 199
Morse, N. C., 137, 292, 356
Moseley, R. L., 463

548

Moskowitz, H., 464
Mouton, J. S., 290, 423
Mueller, R. A. H., 386
Mulder, M., 356
Muller, H. P., 357
Murdick, R. G., 107
Murray, H., 293
Muse, W. V., 107
Muth, J. F., 166
Myers, C. A., 290, 291, 293, 533, 534
Myers, M., 262

Nash, A. N., 356, 357, 500, 502
Nath, R., 292, 534
National Industrial Conference Board, 166, 534
Naylor, J. C., 387
Nedd, A. N. B., 292
Newman, W. H., 71, 166
Niland, P., 198
Noon, J. P., 199
Nougaim, K. E., 324
Nussbaum, H., 262

O'Connell, J. J., 292
Odiorne, G. S., 137
O'Donnell, C., 70, 106, 136, 261, 324, 463, 541
Olson, L. K., 326
Oncken, G. R., 356
Opsahl, R. L., 325
Orris, J. B., 354

Pagano, J., 534
Pahl, B., 201
Paine, F. T., 233, 325, 387, 464, 500
Panger, D., 535
Parker, G. G. C., 167
Parnes, S. J., 200
Parrish, J. B., 534
Parsons, T., 107
Patchen, M., 325, 357
Patt, H., 293
Patten, T. H., 357
Patton, A., 502
Payne, R., 325
Peabody, R. L., 325
Pederson, C. A., 5, 40, 136, 232, 261, 386, 463
Pelz, D. C., 200, 262, 357

Perrow, C., 41, 292
Peterson, D. A., 500
Peterson, R. B., 534
Petit, T. A., 534
Pheysey, D. C., 232
Pickle, H., 70
Piore, M. J., 532
Place, W. S., 500
Pollay, R. W., 200
Pollock, A. B., 293
Pondy, L. R., 167, 292
Porat, A. M., 70
Porter, L. W., 5, 41, 231, 233, 262, 292, 325, 387, 533
Portugal, S. M., 200
Powell, R. M., 137, 292, 535
Presthus, R. V., 326
Price, J. L., 71, 107, 233, 262, 292, 357, 387, 535
Pugh, D. S., 107, 232, 233
Pugh, G. D., 533, 535
Pyle, W. C., 462, 464
Pym, D., 292
Pyron, H. C., 502

Quinn, R. P., 40, 535

Rabe, W. F., 464
Raía, A. P., 137, 502
Raiffa, H., 199
Rambo, L. M., 535
Raven, B., 323
Read, W. H., 386, 387
Reed, K. A., 292
Reeser, C., 262
Reichard, R. S., 167
Reif, W. E., 292
Reimer, E., 137, 292, 356
Rhinehart, J. B., 233
Rice, A. K., 40
Richards, M. D., 200
Richman, B. M., 533
Ridgway, V. F., 464
Ritzer, G., 425
Rizzo, J. R., 41, 138, 233, 425
Roalman, A. R., 535
Roberts, K. H., 326, 357
Roethlisberger, F. J., 107, 387
Rogers, C. R., 387
Rogers, M. S., 137

Author Index

Roman, D. D., 167
Rosen, H., 199, 534
Rosen, N. A., 357
Rosen, R. A. H., 425
Rosenman, R. H., 261
Rosenstein, E., 167
Rosenthal, R. A., 40
Rosenzweig, J. E., 40, 70, 386, 463, 541
Rotter, G. S., 200
Rowe, A. J., 200
Rubenstein, A. H., 41, 426
Rubin, I. M., 138, 358
Rushing, W. A., 262
Ryan, W. G., 263
Ryterband, E. C., 535

Sales, S. M., 262, 357
Salter, J., 232
Sayles, L. R., 71, 425
Schachter, S., 292
Schaefer, E., 201
Schaefer, T. E., 106
Schaeffer, R. G., 534
Schein, E. H., 41, 293, 326
Schiffman, H. R., 425
Schlacter, J. L., 137
Schlesinger, L., 262
Schmidt, W. H., 535
Schneider, B., 326
Schneider, J., 326
Schoderbek, P. P., 200
Schollhammer, H., 262, 535
Schroeder, H. M., 387
Schultz, G. P., 385
Schwab, D. P., 326
Schwan, C. C., 464
Schwartz, M. M., 425
Scott, J. W., 71
Scott, W. A., 200
Scott, W. E., 462
Scott, W. G., 5, 107, 199, 260, 292, 326, 387, 424–26
Scott, W. R., 326
Seashore, S. E., 41, 354, 426, 463
Segura, E. L., 167
Seiler, J. A., 426
Selltiz, C., 107
Sethi, N. K., 426
Sexton, W. P., 262
Shaw, M., 387

Shelly, M. W., 5, 200, 234, 260, 325, 462
Shepard, H. A., 423
Shepard, J. M., 107
Sherif, C. W., 426
Sherif, M., 426
Sheriff, D. R., 502
Sherman, H., 233, 263, 293
Shetty, Y. K., 71
Shull, F. A., 426
Shure, G. H., 137
Siegel, J., 233
Siegel, J. P., 423
Simmons, J. K., 385
Simmons, R. G., 323
Simon, H. A., 41, 106, 107, 200, 293, 326, 386, 423, 425
Simonds, R. H., 291, 293
Simpson, R. L., 387
Singer, E., 40
Sirota, D., 535
Skala, M., 535
Skeaff, L. J. M., 71
Skinner, E. W., 357
Slesinger, J. A., 323
Sloan, A. P., 107
Smith, C. G., 323
Smith, N. R., 325, 357
Smith, R. A., 325
Snoek, J. D., 40
Snyderman, B. B., 324, 355
Soelberg, P., 200
Somers, G. G., 427, 533, 534
Sord, B. H., 167
Sorensen, P. F., 234, 500
Spaner, F. E., 233
Stagner, R., 137, 426
Stalker, G. M., 290
Stanton, E. S., 357
Starbuck, W. H., 233, 293
Stark, H. F., 425
Stark, S., 167
Stayton, J. P., 502
Steckman, W. E., 427
Stedry, A. C., 464
Steiner, Gary A., 105, 200
Steiner, George A., 137, 167, 200, 263, 387
Steinmetz, L. L., 464
Stemp, I., 167
Stewart, J. M., 165, 263

Stieglitz, H., 137, 233
Stinson, J. E., 292
Stogdill, R. M., 41, 357
Stopford, J. M., 231
Strauss, G., 167, 357, 426
Streufert, S., 387
Stringer, R. A., 355
Strother, G. B., 5, 69
Student, K. R., 326
Sumby, W. H., 385
Summer, C. E., 71
Suojanen, W. W., 41, 71
Surface, J. R., 71
Sutton, H., 387
Sykes, A. J. M., 426

Tagiuri, R., 199
Taillieu, T., 535
Tannenbaum, A. S., 233, 357, 464
Tannenbaum, R., 71, 535
Tassone, J., 137
Taylor, C. W., 200
Taylor, D. W., 200
Taylor, F. W., 107, 541
Telly, C. S., 326, 426
Thayer, L., 387
Thayer, P. W., 500
Thomas, E. J., 39, 233
Thompson, J. D., 41, 107, 326, 426
Thompson, R. E., 233
Thompson, V. A., 326
Thune, S. S., 137
Thurber, J. A., 199, 232
Tilles, S., 167
Tillman, P., 263
Torrance, E. P., 200, 263
Tosi, H. L., 136, 138, 293, 358
Triandis, H. C., 41, 387, 533
Trice, H. M., 425
Trist, E. L., 293
Trumbo, D. A., 293
Turner, C., 233

Udell, J. G., 233
Udy, S. H., 200
Unwalla, D. B., 354
Urwick, L. F., 70, 71, 105, 107, 167, 424

Valenzi, E. R., 326
Vance, S. C., 233, 234

Vancil, R. F., 167
Van de Ven, A., 201
Vann, D. H., 136
Vansina, L. S., 535
Varney, G. H., 201
Vaughan, J. A., 70, 291
Vergin, R. C., 293, 463
Vogel, A., 426
Voich, D., 41, 71, 541
Vollmer, H. M., 71
Vroom, V. H., 138, 201, 290, 326, 358

Wadia, M. S., 107
Wainer, H. A., 138, 358
Walker, A. H., 263
Wallace, M. E., 464
Walter, G. A., 326
Walton, C. C., 535
Walton, R. E., 426, 427
Ward, J. E., 532
Warren, E. K., 71, 138
Wasmuth, W. J., 291, 293
Webber, R. A., 5
Weber, M., 107, 326
Webster, E. C., 201
Weick, K. E., 69, 323, 354, 500
Weinshall, T. D., 387
Welsch, G. A., 167
Weschler, I. R., 71
West, J. P., 502
Wettling, R. E., 502
Weymar, C. S., 533
Wheelwright, S. S., 167
Whisler, T. L., 234, 291, 293, 385
White, B. J., 426
White, R., 358
Whitman, R. G., 464
Whyte, W. F., 41, 326
Wickert, F. R., 353
Wickesberg, A. K., 388
Wigdor, L. A., 324
Wikstrom, W. S., 138
Wilcox, D. S., 385
Wilemon, D. L., 263
Wilensky, H. L., 292
Williams, L. K., 201
Winn, A., 293
Winter, D. G., 137, 356, 502
Wittreich, W. J., 502
Wofford, J. C., 326

Author Index

Wolfe, D. M., 40, 388, 427
Wollowick, H. B., 502
Woodruff, R. L., 464
Woodward, J., 234, 263, 293
Woolf, D. A., 107
Worthy, J. C., 234, 292
Wortman, M. S., 5
Wren, D. A., 41, 71, 427, 541
Wright, O. R., 502

Yanouzas, J. N., 231

Yoder, D., 464
Yuchtman, E., 41
Yukl, G., 358

Zajonc, R. B., 388
Zaleznik, A., 290, 323
Zand, D. E., 427
Zander, A., 136, 198, 323, 354, 355, 358, 386, 423, 427
Zeckhauser, R., 201
Zimpel, L., 535

Subject Index

Absenteeism, 406–407
Academy of Management, 1–2
Academy of Management Journal, 2
Acceptance theories, 301–304
Accounting, human asset, 452–61
Achievement motivation theory, 314–16, 351, 485–86, 527–28
Activating, as a management function, 48–50, 65
Administering, as a management function, 48–50, 65
Administration industrielle et générale, 45
Administrative man concept, 172–73
Administrative organizations, 60–63, 540
Administrative Science Quarterly, 2
Aggressive personalities, 404–405
Air Force officers, studies of, 302–303
Aluminum Company of Canada, 279
American Economic Review, 2
American Institute of Management, 450–51
American Political Science Review, 2
American Radiator Company, 162
American Sociological Review, 1
American Telephone and Telegraph Company, 46, 238–41, 482
Antitrust laws, 16
Appeal procedures, 414–16, 420–21
Application blanks, 477–78
Appraisal, management, 37–38, 67, 470, 494–98

Argyris, Chris, 35, 95, 102
Assessment centers, 482
Atlantic and Pacific grocery chain, 213
Attitude change, 485–86
Auditing, 447–52
Authority, 297–326
Avon Products, 142

Babbage, Charles, 83
Balance of power, 395–97
Bank of America, 186
Banks, management functions in, 56–57
Bargaining, 416–17, 421–22
Barnard, Chester, 46–47, 64–65, 101, 103, 172, 210, 301
Barry, R. G., Company, 456
Behavioral humanists, 95, 102–103, 508–509
Behavioral science and scientists, 1–2, 90–98, 100–104
Bell System studies, 238–41
Bennis, Warren, 94, 95, 102
Berelson, Bernard, 92, 96
Biographical data, 477–78
Black economic development, 523–24
Boards of directors, 226
Boeing Company, 313
Bonuses, 492–93
Brainstorming, 194
Budgeting, 153–57
Bureau of Business Research (Ohio State University), 342

553

Subject Index

Bureaucracies, 60–63, 540
Business ethics, 507–14
Business Horizons, 2
Business policy, 149–58
Business students
  job decisions of, 174
  managerial motivation of, 317–18

California Management Review, 2
Capitalistic ethic, 509–13
Carlson, Sune, 55
Carnegie Institute of Technology (now Carnegie-Mellon University), 91, 103, 172
Case history of performance control, 439–47
Centralization, 212–17, 283–84
Change, organizational, 265–93
Changing Organizations, 94
Civil Rights Act of 1964, 516
Civil Service Commission, U.S., 449
Classical management theory, 83–89, 94–98, 100–104, 300, 538
Cohesiveness, group, 412
Collective bargaining, 421–22
College recruiting, 473–74
Commanding, as a management function, 47, 52t, 65
Committees, 256–59
Communicating, as a management function, 46–57, 65, 359–88
Communication
  breakdown, 362–64
  and coordination, 413–14
  interpersonal and intragroup, 361–68
  networks, 364–68
  in organizations, 359–88
Compensation and motivation, 488–90
Computer(s)
  in management information systems, 377–84
  models of decision-making, 173–75
  and organization structure, 282–86
  simulations, 186
Conflict, 391–427
  conditions for, 394–407
  labor-management, 417–22
  prevention of, 407–17
Conflict-prone personalities, 404–405
Confrontation approaches, 412–13

Consideration, in leadership style, 342–47
Constraints, in organizational model, 15–18, 67–68
Consulting firm, studies of, 477–78, 480–81
Content theories of motivation, 313–22
Continental Air Lines, 181
Contingency theory, 339–41
Control, performance, 435–47
Control groups in research, 179–80
Control model, 430–35
Control procedures, 429–61
Controlling, as a management function, 46–68, 389–465
Cooke, Morris, 85
Co-optation, 512
Coordinating, as a management function, 46–68, 389–465
Corporate image, 506–507
Creativity, 189–92
Critical Path Method (CPM), 188
Cross-cultural studies of managers, 527–31
Culturally disadvantaged, programs for, 515–24
Cyert, Richard, 103

Dale, Ernest, 48t, 49
Dartmouth College, 85
Davis, Ralph Currier, 46–49, 88–89, 95, 101, 221, 538
Dayton Company, The, 516
Decentralization, 212–17
Decision-making
  autonomy, 207–208
  joint, 394–97
  line-staff differences in, 249–51
  as a management function, 48t, 50t, 64, 169–97
  processes, 189–96
  school of management thought, 103
  scientific and managerial, 81–82
  tools for, 178–89
Decision trees, 184
Deductive theory, 79
Deferred compensation, 493–94
Delegation, 211–12
Delphi method of forecasting, 163–64
Departmentation, 242–46

554

Subject Index

Description, in scientific method, 75
Detroit Edison Company, 348
Dickson, William J., 101
Directing, as a management function, 48t, 50t, 55, 57, 65, 68t, 297–388
Discrimination in employment, 515–18
Division of labor, 11, 85, 88, 89, 236–42
Dow Chemical Co., 506
DuPont, E. I., de Nemours and Company, Inc., 89, 147, 213, 252

Economic forecasts, 159–63
Economic man concept, 170–78
Eli Lilly Company, 162
Emerson, Harrington, 85
Employee benefits, 164
Employee information systems, 381–83
Employment agencies, 475
Entrepreneurs, 338–39
Environment, external, 216, 503–541
Equitable Life Assurance Society, 519t
Equity theory, 312–13
Evaluating, as a management function, 48t, 50t, 52, 56–57, 66
Exception, management principle of, 84, 89
Executive compensation, 67, 470, 487–94
Executive opinion, jury of, 160–61
Executive personnel management, 469–502
Expectancy theories, 310–12
Experimental research, 179
Explanation, in scientific method, 75–76

Facilitating factors, in organizational model, 15–18, 67–68
Facilitators of change, 269–71
Fayol, Henri, 45–50, 66, 85–90, 95, 97, 98, 101, 140, 221, 255, 368, 393, 407, 410, 538
Fiedler, Fred, 339–41, 353
Follett, Mary Parker, 47, 49, 66, 88, 393
Forecasting, 140, 159–68
Formulating purpose, as a management function, 47, 50t, 64
Fortune, 51
French, J. R. P., 306–307

Games, management, 195–96, 483–84
Gantt, Henry, 85

General Electric Company, 133, 186
General Mills, 132
General Motors, 87, 89, 213, 252, 506
Ghiselli, Edwin, 334–35
Gilbreth, Frank and Lillian, 85
Goals
 difficulty of, 316
 organizational, 11–18, 32, 141–43
 of science, 36
 superordinate, 411–12
Goodrich, B. F., Company, 213
Government relations, 503
Graicunas, V. A., 89
Grapevine, the, 372–73
Greenwood, William T., 48t
Grid approach, 282
Grievance procedures, 414–16, 420–21
Gross, Bertram M., 48t, 49
Group decisions, 192–96
Growth, organizational, 286–88

Hard-core unemployed, 518–22
Harvard Business Review, 2
Harvard University, 85, 101
Hawthorne studies, 101–102
Heidbreder, Edna, 99
Hemphill, John K., 53
Herzberg, F. B., 320–21, 329
Hierarchy, organizational, 218–26
 and change, 271–75
 and coordination, 409–10
 communication in, 368–71
Honeywell Inc., 132
Hospital, occupations in, 60–61
Hoxie, Robert, 85
Human asset accounting, 452–61
Human Organization, 2
Human relations, 101–102, 485, 508–509
Human resources, 17–26, 452–61
Human Side of Enterprise, The, 94
Humanism, pressures for, 508–509
Humble Oil, 186

Incentive pay, 310
Indian managers, study of, 485–86
Individual differences
 in decision-making, 195
 and job enlargement, 241
Inductive theory, 79
Industrial Dynamics, 186

Subject Index

Influence, 298–99
Information overload, 373–76
Information systems, 376–84
Initiating structure, in leadership style, 342–47
Innovating, as a management function, 48–50, 57, 64
Input-output model of organizations, 18–26, 63–68
Institute for Social Research (University of Michigan), 342
Instrumentality, in expectancy theory, 311
Integration, structural, 410–11
Integration theory, 35–38, 351–53, 538
International Business Machines, 482, 519*t*
International management, 524–31
Interviews, selection, 476–77
Investigating, as a management function, 46–56, 66
Investment decisions, study of, 173–75
Investor data, 449–50

Jevons, W. S., 83
Job
  analysis, 236–37
  enlargement, 236–42
  enrichment, 237
  rotation, 486–87
  satisfaction, 208–10, 306–308
    and communication, 364–65
    and leadership style, 349–51
  simplification, 237
Johnson, Richard A., 19*t*, 48*t*
Jones, H. R., 219
Journal of Applied Psychology, 1
Journal of Business, 2

Kast, Fremont E., 19*t*, 48*t*
Koontz, Harold, 48*t*, 538

Labor-management conflict, 417–22
Laissez-faire leadership style, 350–51
Law of Effect, 309–10
Lawrence, Paul R., 35
Leadership, 327–58
Leading, as a management function, 48*t*, 50*t*, 65
Levi-Strauss, 516

Lewin, Kurt, 103
Life insurance companies, studies of, 13–14, 285
Likert, Rensis, 90, 95, 102, 224–25, 347
Line-staff structure, 246–51
Linear programming, 186–87
Linking pin concept, 224–25
Lockheed Aircraft, 516
Longenecker, Justin G., 48*t*
Lorsch, Jay W., 35

McCallum, Daniel, 83
McGregor, Douglas, 94, 95, 102, 318–19, 347
McKinsey & Company, 147
Management
  appraisal, 37–38, 67, 470, 494–98
  audits, 449–51
  consultants, 274–75
  consulting firm, studies of, 477–78, 480–81
  development, 67, 470, 482–87
  functions, 43–71
  games, 195–96, 483–84
  information systems (MIS), 376–84, 414
  international, 524–31
  by objectives, 130–35
  philosophy, 98–104
  principles of, 73–107, 538
  recruiting, 67, 470–75
  selection, 67, 470, 475–82
  theories, usefulness of, 537–38
  thought, schools of, 100–104
Management and the Worker, 101
Managerial
  behavior, studies of, 51–63
  motivation, 208–10
  performance, measuring, 182, 455–56; see also Management, appraisal
  propositions, inventories of, 91–94
Managers, successful, 332–53
Manpower planning, 472–73
Manufacturing, management functions in, 57
March, James, 91–96, 103
Marginal analysis, 180–81
Maslow, Abraham, 318–20
Massachusetts Institute of Technology, 94, 102, 174, 277

556

Subject Index

Massie, Joseph L., 48t, 49, 89
Material resources, 17–26
Mathematical analyses, 162–63
Matrix structure, 255–56
Mayo, Elton, 101, 103
Mechanistic firms, 268
Mediators, in input-output model, 23–26
    control, 24, 66
    input-improving, 25, 65
    input-sustaining, 26, 65–66
Mergers and acquisitions, 288–89
Metcalfe, Henry, 83
Michigan State University, 338
Miner, J. B., 439n
Minority groups, 515–24
Model
    control, 430–35
    input-output, 9–39, 63–68
Monetary resources, 17–26
Monte Carlo simulation methods, 186
Mooney, James D., 87–88, 95, 97, 101
Motivating, as a management function, 48t, 50t, 65
Motivation
    and compensation, 488–90
    managerial, 208–10
    theories of, 308–26
Motivational change, 485–86

Nader, Ralph, 506
Need hierarchy, 318–19, 485
Negotiating, as a management function, 52–54, 56–57, 68, 416–17
New Jersey Bell Telephone Company, 46
Newman, William H., 48t
Nieman-Marcus, 516

O'Donnell, Cyril, 48t, 538
Ohio State University, 46, 342
Onward Industry, 87
Operations Research, 179
Organic firms, 270
Organization
    development, 275–82
    planning, 203–93
    planning units, 273–74, 276
    structure, 205–63
        changes in, 265–93
        integration in, 410–11
        planning in, 116–20

Organizational Behavior and Human Performance, 2
Organizational boundaries, 404
Organizational character, 351–53
Organizational communication, 368–76
Organizational due process, 414–16
Organizational functions, 44
Organizational goals, 11–18, 32, 141–43
Organizational growth and change, 265–93
Organizational level, 207–211
Organizational model, 9–39, 63–68
Organizational specialization, 89
Organizations, definition of, 11
Organizations, 91
Organizing, as a management function, 46–50, 64
Owen, Robert, 83

Participative
    change procedures, 277–80
    management, 347–50
Payoff matrices, 183
Penney, J. C., Company, 497
Perceptions, differences in, 401–403
Performance
    control, 435–47
    job, 306–308, 489, *see also* Motivation
    and leadership, 329–32, 349–51
Person, Harlow, 85
Personnel management, executive, 67, 469–502
Personnel managers, studies of, 250–51
Philosophy, management, 98–104
Planning
    as a management function, 45–68, 109–293
    effectiveness and importance of, 122–28
    history and growth of, 114–16
    time span of, 120–22
Planning-programming-budgeting system (PPBS), 182–83
Plans, development of, 139–65
Plans for Progress, 516
Policy planning, 111–201
Pollution control, 512–13
Poor, Henry, 83
Postulates, in scientific method, 37

Subject Index

Power
  and authority, 298–308
  centers, 11
  loose-lying, 403–404
Premises, in planning, 158–59
Price, James L., 92–93, 96, 97
Principle of supportive relationships, 90
Principles, 80–81; see also Management, principles of
Principles of Organization, The, 87
Principles of Scientific Management, The, 83
Probability theory, 183–85
Process theories of motivation, 308–13
Proctor & Gamble, 252
Product management, 252
Professional organizations, 59–63
Professions, defining characteristics of, 60
Profit centers, 89
Program evaluation and review technique (PERT), 187–89
Project management, 251–56
Promotion, 486–87
Propositions, managerial, 91–94
Psychological evaluations, 481
Psychologists in business schools, 3
Psychology, 99–100
Public relations, 504–507

Rationality in decision-making, 170–78
Raven, B., 306–307
Recruiting management, 67, 470–75
Reference checks, 478–79
Reiley, Alan C., 87
Representing, as a management function, 49–57, 66–68, 503–41
Research and development personnel, studies of, 360–61
Research Center for Group Dynamics, 102
Research design, 179–80
Research in management, 539–40
Resistance to change, 266–68
Resources, 17–26, 187; see also Human resources
Restriction of output, 310
Return on investment, 181–82
Revlon, Inc., 142

Reward structure of organizations, 36–38, 351–52
Risky shift phenomenon, 193, 196
Roethlisberger, Fritz J., 101
Role
  ambiguity, 30, 403–404
  behavior, 20, 27–31
    appraising, 497–98
    of successful managers, 341–53
  conflict, 29, 399–401
  dissatisfaction, 405–407
  formation, 113–14
  motivation theory, 316–18, 486
  perceptions, 30–31
  phenomena and organization goals, 32
  prescriptions, 12, 27–35, 64, 408–409
    establishment of, 109–293
  sanctions, 31
  theory, 27–34, 538
Rosenzweig, James E., 19t, 48t

Sales forecasting, 159–63
Satisficing, 12, 173–74
Scalar chain of authority, 85, 88, 89
Science
  assumptions of, 76–77
  history of, 98–100
  management, 98–104
  nature of, 74–82
  rules of, 77–78
Scientific management, 83–85, 102
Scientific method, 75–78
Scientific research, 179–80
Scientific theory, 78–81
Sears Roebuck and Company, 213, 218, 221, 337
Secrecy and compensation, 489–90
Securing efforts, as a management function, 47, 50t, 65
Selection, management, 67, 470, 475–82
Self-actualization, 318–19
Sensitivity or T-group training, 29, 103, 278–81, 485
Seven Psychologies, 99
Shop Management, 83
Simon, Herbert, 91–96, 103, 170, 172, 301
Simulations, 173–75, 186, 483–84
Smith, Adam, 83, 309
Social responsibility, corporate, 507–14

Subject Index

Societal environment, 16
Span of control, 89, 218–26, 284–85
Staffing, as a management function, 48–52, 57, 66–68, 469–502
Standard Oil of California, 186
Standard Oil of New Jersey, 213, 337
Stanford University graduates, 333
Statistical decision theory, 183–85
Status incongruence, 400–401
Steel Industry Education Program, 519*t*
Steiner, Gary A., 92, 96
Stock payments, 493
Stogdill, Ralph M., 35
Strategic factors in planning, 144–47
Strategies, corporate, 143–49
Strike situations, 434–36
Structuralist school of management thought, 102
Summer, Charles E., 48*t*
Supervising, as a management function, 52–54, 65
Supervision, 327–358
Survey Research Center (University of Michigan), 124
Symbolizing, in scientific method, 75
System 4 management, 347
Systems analysis, 182–83
Systems theory, 17–26, 538

Taylor, Frederick W., 46, 83–85, 88–90, 95, 97, 98, 101, 102, 236, 255, 309, 538
Technological change, 282–86
Technology, and organization structure, 216
Tennessee Valley Authority, 348
Testing, selection, 479–81
Theorizing, in scientific method, 76
Theory Y management, 347
Thompson, James D., 93–94, 96, 97, 103
Thorndike, Edward, 309
Towne, Henry, 83
Training, laboratory, sensitivity, or T-group, 29, 103, 278–81, 485
Transfer, 486–87
Triandis, Harry C., 19*t*
TRW systems, 279
Turnover, 406–407

Two-factor theory of work motivation, 302–22, 485

Union Carbide, 213
Union relations, 417–22
United Air Lines, 186
United Parcel Service, 348
United States Army, 124
United States Department of Defense, 183
U.S. Rubber Company, 213
Unity of command, 85, 89
University education, attitudes toward, 529–30
University programs for managers, 484–85
University of California, 334
University of Colorado, 177
University of Illinois, 339
University of Michigan, 90, 102, 124, 277, 342
University of Minnesota, 51, 59, 333–35, 473
University of Oregon, 317
University of Pennsylvania, 85
University of Washington, 339
Urwick, Lyndall, 46–47, 49, 66, 88, 95, 97, 101, 140

Value structure of organizations, 35–38, 351–52, 495–98
Value system of science, 74
Values, business, 509
and decisions, 176–78
Voich, Dan, 19*t*, 48*t*

Wagner Act, 421
Warren, E. Kirby, 48*t*
Weber, Max, 90–91, 102, 299–301, 305
Western Electric Company, Inc., 101, 519*t*
Westinghouse Electric Corporation, 213, 519*t*
Woodland Job Training Center, 519*t*
Woodward, Joan, 216, 219, 223, 224, 247
Wren, Daniel A., 19*t*, 48*t*

Zone of indifference, 31, 301–302

559